George G. Kundahl served as the Executive Director of the US Securities and Exchange Commission, a Principal Deputy Assistant Secretary of Defense, and a Major General in the US Army. He is the author of *Confederate Engineer: Training and Campaigning with John Morris Wampler*, *Alexandria Goes to War: Beyond Robert E. Lee* and *The Bravest of the Brave: The Correspondence of Stephen Dodson Ramseur*. He holds a PhD in Political Science from the University of Alabama and has been resident on the French Riviera for more than 15 years.

T0347898

'A vivid and stylish account, full of unexpected detail, that says much about politics and daily life as well as war.'

— Richard Vinen, author of *The Unfree French*

THE
RIVIERA
AT WAR
WORLD WAR II
ON THE CÔTE D'AZUR

GEORGE G. KUNDAHL

BLOOMSBURY ACADEMIC
LONDON • NEW YORK • OXFORD • NEW DELHI • SYDNEY

BLOOMSBURY ACADEMIC
Bloomsbury Publishing Plc
50 Bedford Square, London, WC1B 3DP, UK
1385 Broadway, New York, NY 10018, USA
29 Earlsfort Terrace, Dublin 2, Ireland

BLOOMSBURY, BLOOMSBURY ACADEMIC and the Diana logo
are trademarks of Bloomsbury Publishing Plc

First published in Great Britain by I. B. Tauris & Co. Ltd in 2017
This edition published in Great Britain by Bloomsbury Academic in 2021

A catalogue record for this book is available from the British Library.

A catalog record for this book is available from the Library of Congress.

ISBN: PB: 978-1-3501-8181-6
eBook: 978-1-7867-2200-3
ePDF: 978-1-7867-3200-2

Typeset by Free Range Book Design & Production Limited
Printed and bound in Great Britain

To find out more about our authors and books visit
www.bloomsbury.com and sign up for our newsletters.

To Jean-Louis Panicacci whose knowledge of the Côte d'Azur during World War II—the people and events, living conditions, Resistance, occupation and liberation—is peerless; to Claude Solanet, Bernard Crépin and François Widemann for insight and help throughout this endeavor; and for Joy, whose love, patience and support enabled successful completion

I was seated on the jetty of the little port of Obernon near the hamlet of la Salis to look at Antibes at sunset. I have never seen anything so surprising and so beautiful.

The little city, surrounded by its big walls of war constructed by Monsieur de Vauban, going toward the open sea in the middle of the immense gulf of Nice. The high wave of the open sea broke at its foot, surrounding it in a spray of foam; and we saw above the ramparts the houses climbing one on the other up to two towers raised into the sky like the two horns of an ancient helmet. And the two towers took the shape of the milky whiteness of the Alps on the vast and distant wall of snow which blocked all the horizon.

Between the white foam at the foot of the walls and the white snow at the skyline, the little city bright and standing at the bluish base of the first mountains, offered to the rays of the setting sun a pyramid of houses with red roofs whose facades were also white and so different that they seemed all tints.

And the sky above the Alps was itself a blue nearly white as if the snow had rubbed off on it; some silver clouds floated quite near the pale summits; and from the other side of the gulf, Nice lying at the edge of the water stretched like a white thread between the sea and the mountain. Two great Latin sails pushed by a strong breeze seemed to run on the waves. I watched it filled with wonder.

It was one of those things so soft, so rare, so delightful to see that they enter into you, unforgettable like memories of happiness. We see, we think, we suffer, we are moved, we love it by seeing it. The one who knows to appreciate with the eye, to contemplate things and beings, feels the same keen pleasure, refined and profound, as the man with the delicate and sensitive ear for whom music ravages the soul.

Guy de Maupassant, 'Madame Parisse', 1886

Contents

⁊ᘓᑯᖇ

Foreword

One does not need to travel far on the French Riviera, that famous 120-mile stretch of coastline that meanders north-eastwards from the purple rocks of the Estérel heights in the west to the Italian border at Menton in the east, and the back country between the Mediterranean Sea and the Alpes-Maritimes (Southern Alps), to be reminded of the fact that, between the autumn of 1939 and the summer of 1945, this was a rampageous battle zone. In every town and village along the way, street plaques, memorials and crumbling fortifications bear sad and proud witness to the violent conflicts and hardships that took place here, which impacted on the lives of millions of people around the world.

When George K. Kundahl, a former Major General in the US Army, first came to live on the French Riviera almost two decades ago, he asked local residents – as I and many other postwar expatriates have done – for detailed information about the conditions and events of World War II on the area. To the question: "What actually happened here during World War II?", the answers were not easy to find: there was, it seemed, no single coordinated source of information on the subject. So he decided to create one.

It was the beginning of a task for which the author, with his military and academic background and many years' residence on the Riviera, would prove to be uniquely qualified. He was curious to determine, not only historic and strategic facts, but the human experience: details of everyday existence and survival over the period of more than six years during which the region was invaded and ruled by three totalitarian regimes: Fascist Italy, Nazi Germany, and the German-controlled puppet French government based in Vichy. The resulting book, *The Riviera at War*, is a masterful account of the events of the wartime years for the people of the French Riviera; from the initial preparations for war: fortification and mobilisation; through its periods of occupation, to their culmination in the landings by British, American and Commonwealth forces in North Africa, southern France and Normandy, the ultimate liberation, not only of Corsica and the Riviera, but ultimately the whole of France and the rest of Europe. In completing this comprehensive appraisal, the author has created an historical tour de force, drawing copiously from countless original and newly available sources and personal interviews; in the process, exploring such broader questions as the development of the maquis – the French local civilian resistance – and the menace of international anti-Semitism, and describing the postwar efforts in reconstructing the Riviera from the ravages of war to its modern, prosperous state.

Much of this testimony has been distorted by age, failing memory, mistranslation and propaganda. (General de Gaulle's victory speech in Paris on August 25, 1944 attributed its liberation "wholly and completely" to its people alone, disregarding any contribution made by the landings of Allied forces.) A further source of historical distortion derives from the attempts to conceal the fact that, during the German occupation, but less so the Italian one, the pro-Nazi Vichy government conspired in and supported the transportation of tens of thousands of French Jews to concentration and extermination camps in Germany and Central Europe. In correcting such omissions, Kundahl's incisive account will come to be seen as the definitive work on the subject of World War II in southern France.

The author's personal experience and scrupulous research recall a period in modern French history with special interest for residents in and lovers of the Côte d'Azur. Those of us who have had the good fortune to know this fabled region well, whether as residents or tourists, will be intrigued by this moving history of the period, and to learn of the violent and inhuman deeds enacted here a mere 70 years ago, in locations that we know today as peaceful and familiar landmarks.

Of the three distinct dictatorships that opposed the Allies at this period of the war – Germany, Italy and Japan – few sectors experienced total domination by single totalitarian regimes and it was southeastern France that suffered the years of Italian and German Fascism, and the longest total period of occupation.

Ted Jones, author of *The French Riviera: A Literary Guide for Travellers*

List of Illustrations

Maps

Plates

1 Major General Robert Frederick receiving the town flag of Le Muy, August 16, 1944 (US National Archives and Records Administration).

2 Entrance to the Negresco Hotel after the liberation of Nice (Getty).

3 American infantrymen wade ashore, August 15, 1944 (Getty).

4 Women of the French medical corps landing, August 16, 1944 (Getty).

5 Members of the Resistance chatting with a GI after liberation (Getty).

6 Cannes welcomes the American liberators (Getty).

7 Members of the FFI wearing the Resistance's Cross of Lorraine while fraternizing with GIs (Getty).

8 Monaco is off-limits for GIs (Getty).

9 French women with their heads shaved, punishment for collaborating with the occupiers (Musée de la Résistance Azuréenne, Nice).

10 Hélène Vagliano (second from left) with volunteers at the military canteen in Cannes, February 1940 (Musée de la Résistance Azuréenne, Nice).

11 Sapin addressing residents of Lantosque in the valley of Vésubie, August 19, 1944 (Musée de la Résistance Azuréenne, Nice).

Abbreviations

ABTF	Airborne Task Force
AS	Armée Secrète
BCRA	Bureau Central de Renseignements et d'Actions
CDL	Comité Départemental de Libération
CGT	Confédération Générale du Travail
CLL	Comité Local de Libération
CNM	Comité National Monégasque
FFI	Forces Françaises de l'Intérieur
FSSF	First Special Service Force
FTP	Francs-Tireurs et Partisans
LFC	Légion Française des Combattants
LVFB	Légion des Volontaires Français contre le Bolchévisme
MLN	Mouvement de Libération Nationale
MOI	Main-d'Oeuvre Immigrée
MUR	Mouvements Unis de Résistance
OG	Operational Group
ORA	Organisation de Résistance de l'Armée
OSS	Office of Strategic Services
OVRA	Organization for Surveillance and Repression of Anti-fascism
PCF	Parti Communiste Français
PPF	Parti Populaire Français
RAF	Royal Air Force
SAP	Section d'Atterrissage et de Parachutage
SHAEF	Supreme Headquarters Allied European Forces
SI	Special Intelligence
SNCASO	National Aeronautical Construction Company of the Southwest
SO	Special Operations
SOE	Special Operations Executive
SOL	Service d'Ordre Légionnaire
SPOC	Special Project Operations Center

ABBREVIATIONS

SS   Schutzstaffel
STO   Service du Travail Obligatoire
UGIF   Union Générale des Israélites de France

ഇൗരു

Preface

What happened on the French Riviera during World War II? That was a question I asked when I moved there in 2001. No one had an answer. There were some plaques remembering certain people or events, but they were obscure and not obvious to the passer-by. I eventually obtained insights from individuals I met who had been on the Côte d'Azur during the war, contemporary French newspapers and government documents. But there was no book pulling the whole story together in English.

The mosaic of life in southeastern France from 1939 to 1945 portrays not just political figures and military leaders. There are other dimensions largely overlooked, of residents and refugees merely trying to obtain the food, clothing and shelter necessary to survive, individuals resisting a system that threatened their well-being and that of family members, young men thrust into uniform or commandeered to work in Germany, and communities occupied by foreign troops with the power of life or death.

The situation does not become much clearer when reading the local press during the war. How a French newsman assessed his country's response to the Nazi invasion, responsibility for the defeat, and the value of Maréchal Pétain's leadership were all matters filtered by prejudices formed over many years. Not to be forgotten is the censorship during the fascist occupations that restricted and colored what was published.

France's internal memory provides imperfect help. Contemporary Frenchmen may want to forget a black period in their country's past if, indeed, they truly know what went on in the early 1940s. Some alive during that era have feelings of guilt causing them to forget what happened, obscure their own roles during the Nazi and Italian occupations, or refuse to recall that painful time long ago. Indeed, Marcel Ophuls, writer-director of a groundbreaking film looking at the Nazi period in 1969, *The Sorrow and the Pity*, explained his purpose as showing the discrepancy between testimonies and reality, the distortions of memory, and the peace found by many in forgetting what actually transpired. To exonerate Pétain is construed by many as collaborating with fascists or bringing death to tens of thousands of Jews, and not merely as trying to make the best of a bad situation; at the same time, to admit opposing

Pétain's government may be viewed as disloyal to the nation, contributing to the failure of the Vichy experiment.[1] If one did little personally to help liberate France, perhaps an opportunity was not apparent; at least that can be the rationalization in later life. My own interviews encountered that excuse. There is also a common temptation to gild the lily in old age, exaggerating contributions to winning the war, perhaps to bequeath a heroic legacy to descendants.

What one wants to believe happened in the past, what he or she now says was the case, and what actually occurred may well present three distinctly different scenarios. An interviewee's politics in 1939 were not necessarily those in 1942, 1945 or when looking back after seven decades. It is easy to cast aside views subsequently proved incorrect. These feelings are further complicated by opinions about contemporary politics. The Communist Party is an anachronism in France's political landscape today, but old-timers' recollections about what figures and organizations supported the liberation of France may be colored by personal support for or antagonism to communism since the war.

Too often the story is fashioned by national perspectives elucidated in government records, press accounts, military documents and official reports, along with individual testimony and remembrances in Britain, France and the United States, not to mention historical reconstructions. Films and popular reading may also shape or misshape understanding. Researched in archives and libraries in Washington, DC, Pennsylvania and California, as well as London, Paris and, of course, the south of France, complemented by interviews with more than 30 persons involved, this book synthesizes these disparate perspectives. The final product is much more, for it attempts to relate how men and women speaking a different language, but with the same human instincts and needs as other nationalities, coped with challenges unknown to most twenty-first-century Anglo-Americans.

Prologue

> We are leaving the thick clouds and smoky ceiling, we are plunging through into clear moonlight, first edging the thinning clouds like curdled cream, then breaking forth pure and clear, in a spinning, blueness […] The Mediterranean. At first, unbelievable, the moon on that sea, that azure sea I dreamed about on maps in the sixth grade.[1]

So pictured the poet Sylvia Plath upon first viewing the southeast coast of France in 1956.

Stéphen Liégeard's 1887 guidebook by the same name first gave the coastline from Hyères, France, to Genoa, Italy, including the Riviera, the designation *La Côte d'Azur* or azure coast, as the Mediterranean is a light, purplish shade of blue with the brightness and clarity of the air renowned over many years for attracting artists, travelers, and vacationers. The heavenly image is completed by radiant sunshine, luminous sky, and white sailboats bobbing on the water.

What specifically constitutes the French Riviera is stated less easily. Saint-Tropez to Menton, over 55 miles straight across, is a common definition. Yet, when it suits their purposes, writers, publishers and others apply the term westward to include the coastline all the way to Marseille at the mouth of the River Rhône. In the other direction, geographers may use the designation to reach into Italy on the Ligurian coast beyond San Remo. If Nice is the capital of the French Riviera, a designation with no governmental significance, then San Remo is capital of the Italian Riviera. Military action derivative from the 1944 landing reached as far eastward as San Remo. And, the word 'Provence' is equally oblique today as it refers generally to the region of southeast France across the Rhône that in ancient times was a distinct province. The term 'Midi', otherwise designating 12 o'clock, is applied to Provence and more—all the south of France, in fact—which is thought to bake in the warmth of the noonday sun.

The City of Flowers, Nice was the fourth largest city in France in 1940. The nickname derived from hillsides of greenhouses producing blossoms for establishments to make the essence of perfume in nearby Grasse. Yet Nice's recorded history dates back to Grecian times when the settlement was known as Nikea; the 300-foot-high limestone rock of the Château overlooking the harbor was the site of the Acropolis. Afterwards, the Romans came and built a pleasure city at Cemenelum (today known as Cimiez) on the high ground farther from the sea. What attracted these early settlers and later growth into what is present-day Nice is a series of ridges and valleys running at right angles to the Mediterranean that permits access to the hinterland. Bordered on the west by the River Var, Nice occupies high ground on Fabron, Magnan and Cimiez separated by the Madeleine depression and the Vallon des Fleurs. The Var is the principal river in Alpes-Maritimes with the Tinée its longest tributary. Both waterways were important during the war years.

Crossing the River Paillon (now underground at the coast) separating the newer city from Old Nice, one comes to Mont Boron and Mont Alban farther east. Villefranche-sur-Mer, Cap Ferrat, Beaulieu-sur-Mer, Cap Martin and Monaco and Menton (about which a great deal will be said) dot the coastline up to the Italian frontier. Motoring between Nice and Italy is accomplished along one of three routes parallel to the sea, referred to as the upper, middle and lower corniches. A rail line and autoroute follow the same course today.

Driving 15 miles from Nice to the west, one enters a far smaller, though no less colorful community. With broad stone ramparts, two Italianate towers, and a hodgepodge of tile roofs, Antibes is a daily reminder of civilizations centuries ago. Built upon Greek and Roman ruins, the small city looks out across the Baie des Anges (Bay of Angels) to Nice in the distance and the snow-capped Alps beyond. In turn, it is overseen by a geometric citadel just to the east, Fort Carré (Square), enlarged and strengthened in the seventeenth century by Maréchal Le Prestre de Vauban, Louis XIV's chief military engineer. The deep-water harbor separating town and stronghold is also the product of Vauban's genius. Fort Carré garrisoned Chasseurs Alpins (Alpine light infantry) before France signed armistices with Germany and Italy in June 1940. At the war's outset, the locality's population was 21,000–22,000, swollen somewhat since the national census in 1936.

During the late 1920s and early 1930s, Antibes could boast of Jay and Florence Gould developing tourism along its beach at Juan-les-Pins, and Sara and Gerald Murphy attracting the likes of Pablo Picasso, Cole Porter, Ernest Hemingway, and Zelda and Scott Fitzgerald to their Villa America on Cap d'Antibes. Another distinctive feature of Antibes was one quarter of its residents being of foreign birth. The outsiders were principally Italians providing labor, along with a few Anglo-Americans enjoying the climate, although the annual tourist trade was not up to that of Nice and Cannes. The harbor at Antibes was of limited interest as professional fishing was in decline and the yachting world had not yet discovered Port Vauban. Instead, Antibes was important as a horticultural center. Covered with fields and greenhouses, the Cap and high ground not far from the shore propagated carnations, roses and anemones with few crops for human consumption.

Many tourists become acquainted with the Riviera through an initial visit to Cannes five miles farther west. As an oasis for the rich from across Europe, Cannes has long been different from other resorts on the coast, excepting its present upscale facsimile, Monte Carlo. After the British deserted in early 1940, the appearance of Cannes remained distinctive even if the glitter had lost its luster. High-fashion shops along the rue d'Antibes closed. Luxury automobiles remained in shop windows awaiting buyers absent until the holiday trade reappeared. Only the Gestapo had easy access to the fuel needed to glide through largely deserted streets in sleek, black, *traction avant* (front-wheel drive) Citroëns. The showplace hotels lining the famous waterfront known as the Croisette—the Carlton and Majestic, Martinez and Miramar—were largely empty, bleak reminders of happier times. Would the rich and famous ever return?

The eruption of war in Europe could not have occurred at a worse time for Cannes. Statistically, it was the second largest city in Alpes-Maritimes with a population of 49,000 in the 1936 enumeration and making great strides forward. Royalty from maharajahs to kings and princes visited with regularity, and aristocrats like the Rothschilds were in residence. France's tennis team challenging for the Davis Cup trained here in 1939, the same year that a scheduled air service began with London. The Croisette rivaled Nice's Promenade des Anglais as an ebullient walkway beside the sea. The crowning accomplishment, however, was to be a film festival scheduled to begin in September. Biarritz and Algiers had talked about initiating such an event, as had a relatively unknown spa town named Vichy, but Cannes won the right to host the gala. During the summer a galaxy of stars came to promote the inauguration—Charles Boyer, Gary Cooper, Tyrone Power, George Raft, Norma Shearer and Mae West. The films were on hand, everything was ready for opening night when Germany invaded Poland.

Twenty-five miles southwest past the Estérel heights and down the Golfe de Saint-Tropez from Cannes is the smallest of these Riviera locales that would become noteworthy in the conflict to come. The sleepy port of Saint-Tropez was the first town to be liberated during World War II as the result of a mistake in the Allied invasion of Provence. In the nineteenth century it had prospered commercially by trading fish, cork, wine and wood. Early in the twentieth century, however, Saint-Tropez became known for artists such as Paul Signac, Henri Matisse, and Pierre Bonnard, who perfected pointillism and Fauvism to paint its colorful waterfront.

Birthplace of France's national anthem, Marseille was prized for its port, the largest in France, 100 miles west of Nice. Its retention was important to the succession of powers controlling the Midi during the war—the Third Republic,

Vichy, the Nazis and finally the Allies. A city with origins going back to the Phoenicians, the old quarter was ideally suited for clandestine assignations. A labyrinth of alleys, passageways, and detours facilitated avoidance of surveillance and escape from pursuit. With its strong radical tradition dating back before the French Revolution and a vibrant underground rooted in the harbor area, Marseille was a natural spawning ground for dissidence. A socialist bent, strong labor unions, and sympathy for communism constituted fertile soil for resistance. Refugees, smugglers, fugitives and blackmailers lurked in shadows outside the urban mainstream. After the Allied landings in North Africa, Marseille would become even more important for its traffic with Algiers.

In between these principal municipalities are a string of seaside places of various sizes, such as Saint-Laurent-du-Var, Cagnes, Golfe-Juan, La Bocca, and Hyères, that would also be significant during the war years. The largest was the naval port of Toulon. The adjoining towns of Fréjus and Saint-Raphaël with a combined population of 19,000 were the scene of armed confrontations. Stretching behind the coast from Hyères to Saint-Raphaël is a largely uninhabited, wooded, 50-mile ridgeline of hills called the Massif des Maures with heights ranging from 1,000 to 1,500 feet. Communities north of this elevation would be no less significant during the conflict in the 1940s.

Into this tranquil paradise which for more than a century and a half has been a vacation destination for Europeans from Britain to Russia, a profound change began in 1939 as throughout the rest of the Continent with the outbreak of war. While the Riviera was not the scene of armies clashing on the battlefield, capitulation to Germany nevertheless produced hardships and generated apprehension here just as elsewhere in France. Throughout the dark years the Riviera was no longer a habitat renowned for the rich and famous and, instead, lived through a kaleidoscope of experiences without equivalent elsewhere in Europe.

During World War II, three distinct dictatorships opposed the Allies—Germany, Italy, and Japan. Few areas around the world experienced domination by more than a single totalitarian regime, and southeastern France was one. Not only did inhabitants suffer through Italian Fascism and German Nazism but also under a third hardship at times even more oppressive—the rule of Vichy France. Following a nine-month prelude, the reality of World War II burst onto the Riviera in defending itself against the Italian army in June 1940 and ended with a Franco-German/Italian battle in April 1945, a period longer than any other part of France.

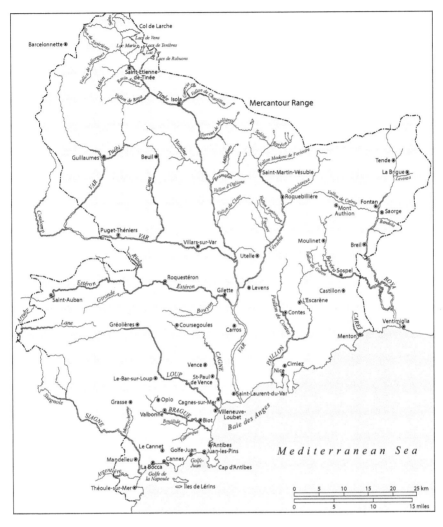

Map 1 Department of Alpes-Maritimes

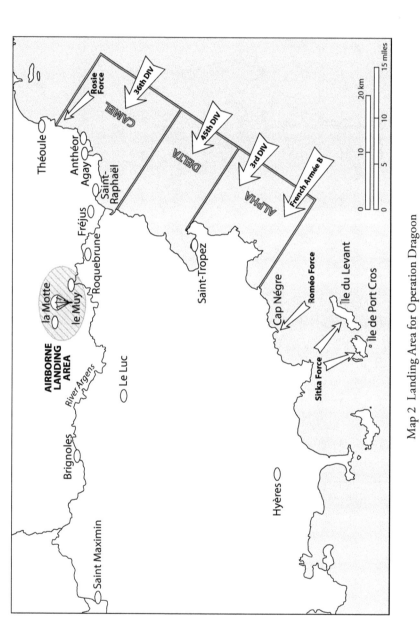

Map 2 Landing Area for Operation Dragoon

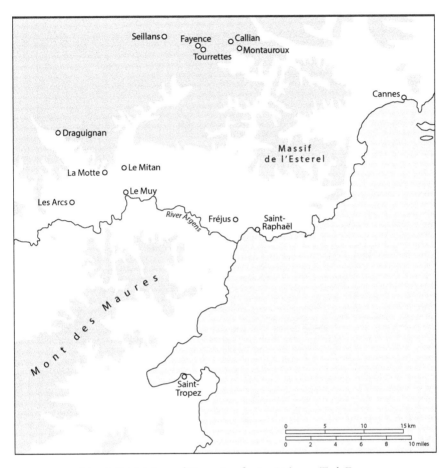

Map 3 Initial Area of Operation for 1st Airborne Task Force

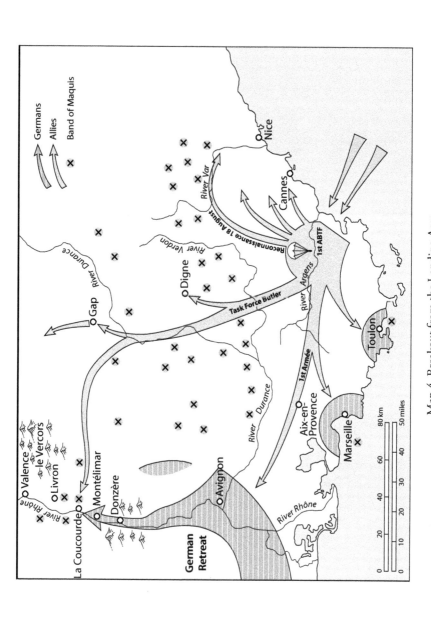

Map 4 Breakout from the Landing Area

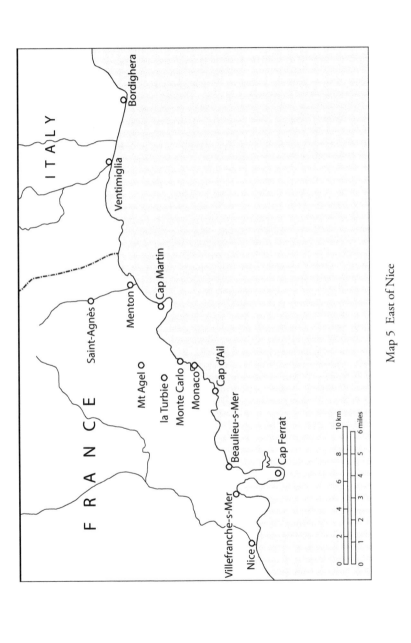

Map 5 East of Nice

1
ℰℴℰℬ

The Phoney War

On September 1, 1939, Germany invaded Poland. In eight days the Polish army was shattered. Great Britain and France formally declared war against Germany on 3 September, launching a general mobilization of Frenchmen. Reservists had already been called up on August 24. Troop trains now took priority over other rail traffic moving across the country. The Allies began mobilizing a force in France that would grow to one-third of the men between the ages of 20 and 45, 5.1 million Frenchmen overall, 2,240,000 combatants assigned to 94 divisions massed along the frontier with Germany alongside ten divisions of British troops.[1] Yet the young men taking up arms did so with less exhilaration than their fathers who marched down avenues past cheering throngs in 1914. Although facing an enemy consisting of a mere covering force of 15 divisions, France and Britain did virtually nothing to take advantage of their vast numerical superiority.[2]

On the Riviera

It was all so sudden, the German invasion and France's reaction. What would be the impact on the South of France? Some inhabitants rushed into the center of Nice to protest against another conflict wasting lives and expending the wealth of a country still exhausted from the war of 1914–18. Others seemed relieved to be finished with the gnawing uncertainty generated by Germany's bellicosity during the late 1930s and began preparations to address the unfinished work of World War I.

Nervous energy was almost tangible. On the Côte d'Azur, requisitions were issued for lodgings and transportation, horses and mules. Educational institutions, such as the school of agriculture in Antibes, and hotels, cinemas, sports facilities, a movie studio, even the airfield on the western edge of Nice, were commandeered for the emergency. The Palm Beach casino at Cannes was turned into a hospital. Apartment buildings received sandbags to pack in front of doors and windows to cushion the shock of bomb blasts and protect against incendiaries. The prefect of Alpes-Maritimes—the chief administrative official of the department—asked residents with second houses in the country to retire to them to reduce the demand for goods and services in built-up areas. Extra trains carried worried vacationers away from the Riviera. In accordance with a pre-agreed plan, mayors prepared to receive refugees evacuated from border communes in the event of an attack by Italy. Juan-les-Pins stored 2,500 mattresses in a casino for use by families driven from their homes.

Without questioning the necessity to do so, people covered the lights of their houses at night with paper attached to the shutters. Street lamps were extinguished. Vehicle accidents increased but that was of small consequence. No one seemed to object to the requirement to obtain *cartes d'identité* at the local police station or to restrictions on venturing outside their neighborhood. The head of historical monuments in the Department of Alpes-Maritimes began moving precious works of art to places of safety; the public health agency started inspecting hospital sanitation. Municipal governments installed and tested air-raid sirens, adding to the citizens' unrest. Was this really an enemy attack or just another practice?

It was natural for older inhabitants who had suffered so deeply in the last war to be apprehensive. Belligerent outbursts on the radio by Adolf Hitler and Benito Mussolini during the summer and autumn were listened to somberly. Distribution of gas masks at *hôtels de ville* (city halls), even though infrequent at first, was nonetheless a chilling reminder of the mustard gas employed against French poilus scarcely two decades earlier. Would chemical weapons now be employed against civilians?

After the tribulations of the Front Populaire, a left-wing coalition which led the country for two years in the mid-1930s, communists were easy to blame for France's quandary. The treachery of the Soviet Union in signing a treaty with Hitler to become partners in the partition of Poland was reason enough to punish France's "Muscovites," as they were called derisively. The militants of the Main-d'Oeuvre Immigrée (MOI), the Movement of Immigrant Workers, largely communist and Jewish, were obvious targets for the authorities. Patriotic Frenchmen decried blatant hawking of the communist press in the streets of Nice. Some 150 posters defending the Nazi–Soviet pact of August 1939 were confiscated from the Niçois Friends of the USSR. A national decree applied a coup de main, dissolving all communist organizations as of September 26. Further measures against their members would soon follow.

There was also reason to be concerned about some residents on the Riviera. The German community in 1939 counted 63 adherents to small political factions. "Front du travail" was under the leadership of a Cannes hairdresser, Friedrich Klein, and an artist in Antibes, Ernst von Maydell. Max Rost, a shopkeeper, led German nationalists in Nice. A far more dangerous figure was Pastor Hans Peters whom the authorities considered "the agent of the Nazi government on the Côte d'Azur." These fascist sympathizers were expelled during the last days before war was formally declared.[3]

Steps were quickly taken as well to confront the legions of foreign refugees in southeastern France and Monaco. An internment facility opened in Antibes at Fort Carré to receive Germanic males, ages 17 to 50, while wives, children, and the elderly were placed on provisional liberty. Two hundred men were rounded up in September, with another 800 the following month. Most were genuine expatriates, but some could be spies or saboteurs. In reality, most fellow travelers of the Third Reich had already left the country.

A German internee, Walter Hasenclever, penned a novel based on his ordeal, *Sans Droits* (*Without Rights*), depicting the horror of confinement. The playwright was living in an artist quarter in Cagnes when on September 3 he saw notices plastered on the walls of public buildings directing German and Austrian nationals to report to Fort Carré. To ignore the order invited arrest and unstated severe repercussions. Released for a brief time, he was returned to custody in October with grave emotional consequences. In December, Hasenclever was transferred along with other detainees to another holding area at Les Milles where he committed suicide with an overdose of barbital.[4]

A decree from Paris on November 18 permitted administrative measures to be taken regarding individuals considered dangerous to national defense or public security. Police in Antibes subsequently raided the Communist Party headquarters on the Place Nationale as well as the homes of militants, seizing tracts and other material. Communist officials who had not broken away from the Third Internationale were to be dismissed in accordance with another law, dated January 20, 1940. This time, a cause célèbre ensued in Alpes-Maritimes.

Henri Pourtalet was a deputy from Cannes-Antibes in the Assemblée nationale. Elected as a Bolshevik, he had seemingly renounced the Communist Party to the relief of many of his constituents. Mobilized with an engineer unit at Avignon during the general call-up, Pourtalet was arrested for distributing communist tracts on the anniversary of the end of World War I. Appearing before a military tribunal on May 1, 1940, he was convicted and sentenced to five years in prison along with a fine of 3,000 francs.

The first general purification of France was underway. Municipal governments were directed to suspend or fire those employees who had not given up communism. The mayor of Cannes complied by dismissing four workers. Twenty-six administrative staff were let go in Grasse, along with the firing or reassigning of 11 elementary school teachers and closing of a primary school on orders from the minister of education. Labor organizations were another target. The prefect decided to abolish 37 unions in Antibes, Cagnes, Cannes, Vallauris and Villefranche that displayed communist sympathies. A roundup netted 82 communist militants who were sent to camps in Chibron and Saint-Maximin in the Department of the Var, two of 200 centers established across

France to confine dissidents. At the same time, clandestine cells of workers formed in the gas company, at the Nice-Saint-Roch train depot, and among municipal day-laborers in Antibes.[5]

At first, military authorities mobilized and stationed between 75,000 and 90,000 soldiers in Alpes-Maritimes organized under XV Corps in a command soon named the Armée des Alpes and led by General René-Henri Olry. It included a wide variety of branches—infantry and artillery, of course, but also pioneers, scouts, Chasseurs Alpins, and even regiments of colonial gunners and riflemen. As time passed, however, and the threat to northern France became more ominous, the best of these units were redeployed to confront it. Left behind was a "waiting army," ill equipped and short of everything, including warm clothing.

An early casualty after the declaration of war was the French economy. This was especially true along the southern coast. To conserve limited financial resources, Great Britain prohibited importing cut flowers, taking away income from Riviera horticulturists. An area which had become heavily reliant on tourism struggled as hotels closed or, as in the case of the Martinez in Cannes, were taken over by the prefecture as lodging for refugees. Ski resorts were prevented from opening due to their proximity to the eastern border. Passenger traffic through the port of Nice fell by 70 percent; cargo shipments dropped by one quarter. Department-store receipts declined, for although quantities of merchandise were abundant during the fall, shoppers held onto their money for the bad days envisioned ahead. Service stations initially experienced a run on fuel, but rationing soon slashed business and revenues. Among the few offsets were increased orders for manufactured matériel and goods required by the ministry of defense.

At the outset, the prefect ordered that basic foodstuffs—wheat, cereal, coffee, rice, salt—not be wholesaled outside the department. The Mediterranean littoral was one of the least-cultivated regions of France, yielding almost no meat, grain, or dairy products. Wine and olive oil were common but the few vegetables were primarily seasonal. Grocers were asked to apply just prices, but relaxed enforcement gradually resulted in higher costs to consumers.

In a groundswell of patriotism, the populace readily entered into the spirit of the mobilization. People voluntarily prepared parcels for soldiers, many containing woolens as the warmth of the Riviera sun waned. According to their consulate, 800 Americans resided on the Côte d'Azur at the war's outset and, consequently, an Anglo-American Ambulance Service was established, as well as a home for French war orphans. Dances, dinners, and sporting events were held to raise money. Each seaside community opened clubs where soldiers obtained pen and paper to write home, play cards, smoke cigarettes, and drink coffee. Soup kitchens served the growing numbers of homeless, plus the wives and children of men inducted into the military, underwritten in Antibes for the most part by the English and Americans. Nice counted 110,000 servicemen passing through its welcome center during a six-month period in 1939–40. Even the Duke and Duchess of Windsor, who lived nearby on Cap d'Antibes, made a point of visiting this rest station in March 1940.[6]

The city of Cannes also established nurseries for the youngsters of women obliged to work in the absence of their husbands. A call went out for old newspapers, used rags, and scrap iron, and families willingly responded. The prefecture soon asked businesses and associations to join in the voluntary campaign to provide support for soldiers and their families. The Aciéries du Nord, a heavy metal foundry at the rail yards west of Cannes, responded by establishing a mutual aid fund to assist fellow workers who had been mobilized. Another firm agreed to fabricate casts for the wounded to come. In addition, those called to the colors were exempted from the country's annual living tax while in uniform.[7]

At first, nighttime restrictions were accepted with good humor. White lines painted on the asphalt in Nice facilitated the circulation of vehicles during blackouts. But after a couple months with no major hostilities on the Franco-German frontier, the threat appeared exaggerated. The mood soon turned to one of resigned indifference. The aerial alert on November 17 seemed to one observer to lack discipline as Niçois considered the whole exercise a big joke. Frenchmen began to refer to the "phoney war." A newspaper philosophized, "Life, indeed, cannot be perpetual bereavement. Life continues."[8]

In the absence of immediate danger, the authorities gradually loosened the reins. November 1 marked the resumption of freedom of movement. A couple of weeks later, intercity football matches kicked off again. By the end of the month, the national railway had doubled the service between Nice and Paris, and Fort Carré was once more available for sporting events. Four cinemas resumed operation in Antibes along with a cabaret that remained open until dawn.[9] First, Antibes, then, Nice permitted cars to display partial lighting at night beginning in December and January, reducing the accident rate. When the Easter tourist season approached, ski stations came back to life. Britain also eased up, relaxing floral restrictions in February to permit the Côte d'Azur to export anemones and ornamental foliage.

Throughout the fall, Prime Minister Edouard Daladier had kept abreast of the extra efforts made in the Southeast to receive and care for refugees. Foreign currency thereby accumulated was not unwelcome. Representatives of Alpes-Maritimes pleaded they could do more if restrictions on transportation were lifted, hotels permitted to receive guests, and crops grown in the region made available to the tourist trade. One result was setting the department outside the official military zone in November, reducing the army's ability to requisition its goods and provisions.

Film stars and other elite began to coalesce at Cannes and on the Cap d'Antibes for the winter season. The Aga Khan visited regularly. There was even talk of restarting the Cannes film festival with Louis Lumière, inventor of an early motion-picture camera in the late nineteenth century, as the featured attraction. "There will always be a fervor for our region," observed one local paper, "where the sky and nature together are sufficient to create an ambiance of quiet and rest."[10]

Regardless of what might appear to civilians to be a make-believe war, teams of Scouts-Skiers patrolled the Italian frontier to observe the strength and movements of a potential enemy. As often happens in wartime, French soldiers encountered their counterparts on the other side. Amicable relations were the norm as remembered by one officer after the conflict: "At a border point in the valley of Castillon, an Italian lieutenant, who was a professor of French in Rome, always waited for me with impatience to discuss Molière and Balzac."[11]

The tension eased somewhat when handfuls of soldiers returned home on leave at Christmas. Yet by the start of 1940, households began feeling the squeeze from higher prices and less availability. Ration cards were sent to municipalities, although not immediately distributed to the populace. Rumors of rationing, however, caused shoppers in Nice to buy quantities of sugar, chicory, and anything else that could be restricted in the near future. Some items, like coffee, peanut oil, rice, and soap, were almost impossible to find.

As winter turned to spring, availability was limited in other ways. On April 1 a whole system of restrictions was instituted. Bakeries were no longer permitted to make rolls or breadcrumbs. A baguette advertised as one kilogram should weigh no more than 700 grams at first, then 500, soon 300.[12] Other controls affected the availability of other basic foods, hopefully to discourage their consumption. Inhabitants were asked to help police enforce these sanctions.

Cannes felt the squeeze on its tourist trade. Restaurateurs were prohibited from serving clientele more than 100 grams of meat at a sitting. Access to the catch of local fishermen thereby assumed importance. Olive oil and butter quickly became uncommon. Soon use of sugar could no longer be placed at diners' discretion. More and more, priority was given to troops in the field and not to hotels and eating places catering to visitors.[13]

As the economy worsened, the labor situation deteriorated. Wage earners lost work when tourism slowed and hotels closed or were preempted for government purposes. Those who retained jobs found employers' expectations raised with no augmentation in salary. The post office began to open on Sunday morning, for example, and was not closed on all holidays. Employees were assigned 48-hour workweeks. Anyone who found these new requirements onerous could leave and would be quickly replaced from a large pool of anxious aspirants.

One way to fit the existing labor pool into a shrinking number of jobs was to purge undesirables. A regional weekly explained:

The formidable force of communist organizations has been imposed through propaganda as well organized as copiously financed, powerful roots in the masses of workers of our country [...] We know that communist tracts have been written, printed, and distributed not only in Paris, but also throughout the country. This proves that the destructive doctrine is not dead, and had only a handful of communists not recanted their errors [...] this handful could do an enormous harm to the country [...] It is necessary at all cost to prevent it [...] It is necessary to win the war! We will win it as we have won that in 1914 because, as in 1914 we have the Right with us, but it is necessary from now on to prepare ourselves to win the Peace [...] Peace for France is to say to Hitler: "Halt the invasions!" [...] But it is also to say to the leaders of the Comintern: "Bolshevism shall not be adopted!"[14]

As phoney-war paralysis set in, it dawned on opinion-makers in southern France that perhaps Germany did not have the means to repeat the atrocities of World War I after all. One piece trumpeted, "Vive la France! Confidence! We are winning." Newspapers in Grasse and Cannes echoed the sentiment. *Le Petit Niçois* went a step farther: "We are winning and Warsaw will ring the bells of the resurrection"; while others proclaimed: "The war continues. We will win!" Another paper was more bombastic: "Each German represents a Hitler [...] Because Hitler is only an imitation product of the race. And it is the entire race that it is necessary to put out of harm's way."[15]

There were other themes worth recalling. The conseil-général of Alpes-Maritimes heralded Italy as a sister Latin country and praised Mussolini for serving the cause of humanity by not participating in the carnage in Poland. The government in Paris looked forward to continuing to live in harmony with its Italian neighbor despite the barbarism exhibited by the Nazis and Bolsheviks. The cataclysmic conclusion to this lull in hostilities, just ahead, would reveal the shallowness of this optimism.

End of the Phoney War

On May 10, 1940 the German army attacked westward, puncturing the illusion that an armed confrontation between fascism and democracy would be avoided. The Reich sent 136 divisions sweeping across the Netherlands, Belgium, Luxembourg, and into France. The French recoiled under the weight of the onslaught. Yet the press on the Riviera initially disseminated a series of glowing reports replete with blind optimism. "The unanimous sentiment, the dominant sentiment, remains the unshakeable confidence in the final victory which will crown two more flags," presumably those of the defenders (May 11); "French tanks have maintained their superiority" (May 14); "The Germans have vainly tried to cross the River Meuse" (May 15); "We triumphed 25 years ago; we will triumph again" (May 18); and "The *Boche* [German in derisive French slang][16] is contained everywhere" (May 21).[17] Rumors spread that America had entered the war; the Russians had bombed Berlin; the Pope had committed suicide; England had been invaded. The truth was that the Nazi blitzkrieg was cutting a swath across Belgium and northern France.

The fighting was far away. What response could be made by patriotic French citizens in the South? Nighttime lighting returned to blackout rules. The mayor of Cagnes made it illegal for women to walk or sit on the beach. Antibes stopped dancing in public.[18] Up and down the shore, casinos shut their doors. It seemed that the only activities the French could freely engage in took place in the dark—like attending the cinema. In reality, the modest steps being taken by Azuréens were of no military importance, but they reassured the populace with a feeling of supporting the war effort.

The conflict brought other changes as well. To be sure not to lose their hard-earned savings, depositors began withdrawing them from banks. Refugees arrived from the north—400 Belgians at Nice, more than 800 homeless French at Antibes, and 200 children evacuated to Cannes from Alsace. At the beginning of June the problem of accommodating people fleeing war and oppression was exacerbated by evacuation of the inhabitants of Menton, Roquebrune-Cap Martin and smaller settlements along the Italian border. This was all according to plan, but nevertheless it strained the resources of the receiving communities to feed and lodge trainloads of displaced persons. Civilian guards were enlisted to protect sensitive sites along the littoral. Key facilities, such as the rail yards at La Bocca, were assigned to the Sureté for safekeeping. Police began to check the identities of faces unknown to them even to the extent of asking for the papers of patrons sitting peacefully at outdoor cafés.

When May became June, the situation north of Paris reached crisis proportions. Belgium surrendered on May 28, adding remnants of its army to the stream of its nationals flowing southward. The first large French city, Lille, fell on the last day of May. German Heinkels and Junkers bombed the port of Marseille on June 1 and 2. On June 10 the government fled from Paris to the Loire Valley. On June 14 the Germans entered Paris. All of France, including its southeastern departments, was at its most vulnerable.

A Knife in the Back

Who first used the knife to symbolize Italian opportunism and treachery? The French attribute it to their ambassador in Rome who, when officially informed of Mussolini's declaration of war, responded, "It is a dagger blow to a man who has already fallen."[19] One author cites Premier Paul Reynaud's cable to President Franklin Delano Roosevelt using the phrase "stab us in the back" to portray the Italian attack.[20] Americans remember Roosevelt employing the same characterization in a radio address to the nation that same day (but six hours later due to the time difference).[21] Or was it William Bullitt, US Ambassador to France, from whom Roosevelt borrowed the phrase in an evening commencement address at the University of Virginia ("The hand that held the dagger has struck it into the back of its neighbor")?[22] By the following day, the French press was employing the term with adjectives such as "bloody" or "wounded" to dramatize further the perfidy to which the country had fallen victim.[23] From the balcony of the Palazzo Venezia de Rome, Mussolini shouted, "We take the field against the plutocratic and reactionary democracies who always have blocked the march and frequently plotted against the existence of the Italian people."[24] Unpublicized was the dictator's declaration to Marshal Pietro Badoglio, "I need a few thousand deaths to be seated at the peace table" (and obtain French territory).[25]

Mussolini's courage was fortified by the assurance of the French ambassador to Rome that his country had no intention of attacking Italy. Orders were given to Italian commanders to remain on the defensive on the Alpine front, taking no initiative; neither troops nor artillery should open fire but engage solely in surveillance. A commentator later observed that "for the first time in history a war had begun with the order not to fire."[26]

For any Frenchman remaining along the Italian border, the Phoney War ended with a bang in Alpes-Maritimes in the early morning hours of June 11. Within hours of the announcement of a state of war, sappers from XV Corps engineers demolished critical military infrastructure according to a preconceived plan of preventive destruction. Bridges, tunnels, viaducts, sections of roadways, even telephone grids were systematically blown up. The roar of explosions cascaded down valleys, echoes ricocheting between rock faces. Boulders hurled high in the air fell pell-mell, often bouncing along the ground to dislodge more stones that rumbled downward into the bottoms. Twisted rails, gaping craters, broken walls, collapsed buildings served as reminders of the man-made tornado. Doors and windows blown out or open in houses and apartments invited pillagers, providing yet another task for the few remaining agents of the police to shutter or secure by other means.

Popular distrust of Italians had grown as Mussolini's diatribes became more vitriolic in the days leading up to his declaration of war. Having heard of civilians aiding insurgents under Generalissimo Francesco Franco during the Spanish Civil War, residents of Alpes-Maritimes envisioned the presence of large numbers of Italians as a fifth column in place to undermine France's resistance to an invasion from the east. Italian nationals living on the Riviera were required to make a declaration of loyalty to France. Long lines of immigrants quickly formed outside local police commissariats. Few of these new inhabitants sided with their country of birth. The daughter of the king of Italy living in Mandelieu, for example, refused to return to the peninsula, and her husband announced his intention to join the military in France or Britain. Extremists known to police were given no choice. French authorities rounded up 250 Italian Fascists and interred them initially at Fort Carré before their transfer to holding areas away from the coast.

The Italian reluctance to penetrate France came to an abrupt end when a French naval squadron bombarded Genoa on June 14, considered a "humiliation" by Mussolini's government. There followed the first air attacks on military targets along the Côte d'Azur—Fort Carré at Antibes and airfields at Cannes-Mandelieu and Fayence. Some 20 shells fell on Cannes just before noon, doing primary damage to private homes. A woman and infant died. At La Bocca the targets were the aeronautical research center, rail yards, and the station where the last elements of the 2nd Division were boarding the cars. No one was injured. No French military personnel lost their lives in any of the air sorties, while a French fighter downed an Italian bomber, killing four of its five crew members.[27]

On June 14 the French government moved farther south to Bordeaux. Three days later, the new head of the French government, Maréchal Philippe Pétain, sued for peace. The fantasy of a miracle to replicate the reversals of 1917–18 was shattered. Many French men and women were stunned, yet civilians cheered Pétain's courage in stopping the slaughter. Foreign nationals were horrified at the prospect of their lot under Nazism. The British consul in Cannes made a final effort on behalf of his countrymen remaining on the Riviera. He arranged for two coal hulks to offload their cargo at Marseille and steam to Cannes to pick up one last group of evacuees.

Two teenage girls with English passports were typical of the last Britons to leave the Côte d'Azur. The sisters had been up until the wee hours of June 17 helping care for refugees who had arrived in Juan-les-Pins by bus, who were carrying animals and bundles of possessions and were provided with straw mats on the floor of the Hôtel Provençal casino. Returning home exhausted, the girls found their own beds occupied by two old peasant women and resigned themselves to sharing a mattress on the sitting-room floor. The youngsters listened to Pétain's midday radio address announcing that France had requested an armistice. Their father, a Czech national, was stunned. "Now, it's all over," he sighed.

An English friend who had a telephone arrived excitedly to report that British nationals who wished to leave France should report to the consulate in two hours. Their British mother insisted that Margaret and Rosemary depart, although she resolved to remain with her husband. The father provided £20 he had been saving, along with some Swiss watches from his shop. Donning Girl

Guide uniforms complete with brassards, and each carrying a suitcase and food for six days, the twosome bade a tearful farewell. Then they began walking toward Cannes, past little groups of refugees huddled together under the palms and children and dogs running about flower beds planted in times of peace.

Bedlam reigned at the diplomatic outpost. In the panic to leave France, Britons abandoned their transportation anywhere, even a Rolls-Royce, Bentley, and MG. Shutting down consular operations while dealing with scores of frantic British nationals generated enormous commotion and confusion. In the early evening the girls were told that the embarkation would not take place until the following morning but to remain close at hand in case of another change in plans. Where could they stay? Using their scant money for a hotel was out of the question. How about the local Anglican church? The organist there offered a sofa in the rectory. The next day, the girls joined 1,000 other Britons, including the likes of Somerset Maugham, on a voyage to safety. Meanwhile, two days later, the Duke and Duchess of Windsor abandoned Château de la Croë on Cap d'Antibes by car for Perpignan on the Spanish frontier.

Passengers were crammed into filthy vessels meant for 38-man crews. Most slept amidst coal dust in the ships' holds. Food and water were severely rationed. The girls were assigned clean-up duty for the two toilets on their ship. Although being escorted by a French submarine, the coal boats were soon hit by a submarine—Italian, they were told. "Remember, you're British" was the admonition to keep a stiff upper lip. Sputtering along, the little convoy finally reached Gibraltar where a converted cruise liner carried the refugees on the final leg to England. Seven passengers died on a passage that took 20 days.[28]

The Two-Week War

In 1940 the Italian frontier in southeastern France ascended through the foothills northward for 25 miles from the sea until reaching the high Alps, where it turned west northwest and then north again. The southernmost fortifications of the Maginot Line closely tracked the border up to the higher elevations, where they were spotted at wider intervals. A dozen formidable works were in Alpes-Maritimes. Generally consisting of a combination of forts, blockhouses, trenches, and tunnels, the Maginot Line featured smaller *fortins* close to the frontier in the more populous area at the coast. Although the Midi had sent their best troops to the German front, the sections of Scouts-Skiers remaining were well armed, trained, and instilled with high morale. They went right up to the border to gather information on Italian deployments and cover intervals between fixed defensive emplacements.

By this time XV Corps totaled 170,000 men. Positioned against them were 400,000 troops of the Italian army, including five battalions of Blackshirts led at least for ceremonial purposes by the heir to the crown, Prince Umberto. France's prime advantage lay in the heavy artillery installed along the Maginot Line during the previous decade. A vivid example of its firepower were shells from long-range artillery on Mont Agel setting fire to the railroad station at Ventimiglia nine miles away in Italy. The French counted 427 barrels of 75-mm, 105-mm, 120-mm, and 155-mm calibers in advance posts and redoubts in addition to the Maginot Line. Along the entire frontier the Italian infantry was supported by 1,000 field pieces and mortars, plus heavy artillery and two armored trains. The Italians also enjoyed local air superiority.[29] But, of course, at the last moment the Italians were cast in the role of aggressors and therefore less reliant on fixed-gun emplacements. France's weakness was the absence of available reserves due to redeployments.

Like the conflict to the north, the Franco-Italian ground war got off to a slow start. For three full days French troops remained on alert while Italian aircraft passed overhead surveying their disposition, but no fighting occurred. On June 13, Scouts-Skiers on reconnaissance learned from their Italian counterparts that they had not yet been authorized to fire into France. The following day scattered attacks erupted up and down the line, resulting in the first death of a French combatant in the Alps. Terrain conceded by the French was retaken before nightfall.

The conflict thereafter evolved into a series of local clashes along the border but no coordinated offensive. The *fortin* on Cap Martin was targeted with the first smoke bombs, obscuring fields of fire and activating its fresh air ventilators. The series of bombardments along the French coast led to the fighter squadron based in the Var pulling back to Perpignan to preserve their aircraft. In the days ahead, however, Italian aviators did little to take advantage of their supremacy. Ironically, when bombers from Italy attacked the old port at Marseille on June 21, most of the casualties were in the adjacent Italian quarter.

An artillery barrage would typically take place to soften a target for assault by the Alpini, but French defenders later recalled that as many as half the shells failed to explode. A rush forward by Italian foot soldiers ensued and, if the attack became too intense, the defenders might withdraw from their redoubt. But, inevitably, the offensive surge stalled and the French reoccupied their positions. Ruses were employed with amusing effectiveness. One stronghold bluffed its aggressors by announcing that their numbers included Senegalese infantrymen renowned for cutting off ears. At another outpost, the vastly outnumbered defenders engaged in the age-old deception of passing back and forth across a point under observation by the enemy to give the impression of far more men than could be mustered. Thus, an onslaught was avoided.

A crisis erupted among French troops preparing to flee on June 18, the anniversary of the Emperor Napoléon's defeat at Waterloo. Once word spread that Maréchal Pétain had asked for an armistice the day before, these soldiers naturally wondered why they should risk their lives now that Paris was occupied and hostilities were about to end. Many, no doubt, were reminded of the endless killing in trenches without tangible results during World War I.

On that same day, Mussolini was meeting with Hitler in Munich. Upon learning that he would obtain only that French territory in his possession when the armistice went into effect, Il Duce gave the order to attack. Until then, military planning had been based solely on a defensive conflict; the Italian army had developed no competence for an offensive. Troops and artillery were positioned to stop a French invasion, not advance to the west. Only 115 of 285 Italian warplanes had succeeded in bombing fixed targets, having negligible impact on the battle of the Alps. Nor were pilots utilized in close air support of ground troops.[30]

June 23 and 24 were the only days of heavy fighting in the Southeast in what could otherwise be described sarcastically as a "gelato war," for it took little more time than required to eat an ice cream cone. A heavy engagement took place in and around Menton, as Mussolini was determined to return the "city of citrons (lemons)" to what he considered its rightful place within Italy. That clash will be examined later. Otherwise, the invaders succeeded in advancing only 1–5 kilometers beyond the frontier, taking 13 French communes and eight hamlets while occupying 840 square kilometers with a total population of more than 28,000 inhabitants, almost 23,000 in Alpes-Maritimes alone.[31] Some acquisitions occurred after the ceasefire at 00:35 on June 25. For the foreseeable future, communities such as Fontan, Sospel, Castellar, and Breil would belong to Italy, as well as the city of Menton. But the aggressors failed to overcome a single fortification manned by French troops. Hence, Frenchmen refused to recognize the Italians as their conquerors.

A downtrodden French army later took pride in this defense, a rare success in an otherwise dismal period in the war. Indeed, the *New York Times* effused, "France, desperately wounded, was never more glorious than in this dark hour of disaster."[32] The determination to stop the Italians reflected not solely antagonism toward their neighbors but also the strategic isolation of the southeastern theater, far from the momentous clashes elsewhere in France. A credible case has been made that the success against Italy was due in large part to the leadership of the commander of the Armée des Alpes—General Olry's flexibility, imagination, initiative, and ability to inspire his men.[33]

If the Armée des Alpes never lost a battle, why did Maréchal Pétain concede Menton and territory along the frontier claimed by the Italians as the former hunting domain of King Victor Emmanuel II of Savoie? French fighters confronted a numerically superior force with little support from their fragile government. Their army's best mountain troops had been transferred to Lorraine to counter the threat of a Nazi advance. Batteries of heavy artillery with adequate range were used sparingly by senior leaders and, other than Mont Agel, the Third Republic had lacked the political will to construct, man, and equip defensive works that could fire into Italy. Counterattacks to retake the western part of Menton were canceled just before the ceasefire went into effect. Moreover, the Mediterranean air assets, which could have contested the Italians or repeatedly bombed Genoa or Savona in retaliation for air attacks on Marseille and Toulon, were repositioned out of danger. Similarly, the naval squadron based at Toulon possessed adequate firepower to challenge the Italian fleet but was held in port with the exception of one hurried sea bombardment of Genoa. In sum, preserving French warplanes and naval vessels in the Mediterranean and diplomatic negotiations being pursued by the new Pétain government were more crucial than retaining territory in a far corner of the country.

Casualties in Alpes-Maritimes during this short conflict amounted to 13 Frenchmen killed, 42 wounded, and 33 taken prisoner, compared with Italian figures of 208 dead, 941 injured, and 131 lost as prisoners.[34] When Mussolini visited Menton on July 1, his generals insisted that the disproportionate losses were due to overwhelming firepower along the formidable Maginot Line.

While mothers, wives, and sweethearts were relieved to learn that their loved ones were out of danger and would soon be returning home, political leaders in the Southeast were nervous about the stated intention of Italian Fascists to reclaim Comté de Nice which had been part of Piémont-Sardinia before 1860. A more sinister threat was appearing on the horizon, however—the influence of the Third Reich throughout France. Stronger initially in the Occupied Zone in the north, the poison of Nazism was about to debilitate the Riviera through its catalytic agent, the national government being seated at a spa town in the Massif Central named Vichy.

2

The Vichy Regime

June 17 and 18, 1940 are days that will long live in the memory of France. At midday on Monday 17, Maréchal Philippe Pétain announced that at the request of the President of the Republic, he had taken leadership of the government of France. Taking on the responsibilities of chief of state in what Charles de Gaulle later characterized as the "shipwreck of old age,"[1] the 84-year-old patriot stepped forward to represent France in dealing with the conquering Germans. Was Pétain simply naïve or increasingly senile in thinking that Hitler would be more considerate of the sole senior military figure remaining from World War I than to just another politician?

Two decades earlier when dispatched to stabilize the front during that war, Pétain had remarked, "They call me only in catastrophes."[2] Now in the hot seat once more, he had concluded it was imperative to stop fighting the Germans. With snow-white hair, clear blue eyes and a calm demeanor, France's greatest living hero from World War I offered to:

> make to France the gift of my person, to mitigate her misfortune. In these painful hours, I think of the poor, destitute refugees walking along our roads. I offer them my compassion and my solicitude. It is with a heavy heart that I tell you today: we must stop fighting. Last night I approached the adversary to ask if he were willing to seek with me, soldier to soldier, after the battle and in good faith, a means of ending the hostilities.[3]

A vast majority of the French were relieved by Pétain's decision to concede to the invaders and remake their national government. At this point in time, Hitler's eventual triumph over Britain seemed certain to almost everyone on the Continent. Nazism represented the wave of the future.

It was two days later before Pétain's request was received by the enemy. In between, on June 18, a 49-year-old unknown promoted to general-officer rank less than three weeks before announced on the radio from London that France had lost a battle but that the war would go on and he, Charles de Gaulle, would lead his country to victory. Few Frenchmen heard the actual broadcast at 10.00 p.m., although millions would claim to have done so. The BBC did not consider the address important enough to make a recording, so de Gaulle repeated a version of his historic remarks before a motion picture camera at the beginning of July following a series of related radio commentaries during the last days of June. Certainly, many French citizens afterwards read de Gaulle's appeal "to all the French" either posted throughout London, pasted on walls across France, or published in an abbreviated version by its regional newspapers. Its importance was that de Gaulle had not surrendered and was in Great Britain trying to make the best of the dire situation by rallying his countrymen to the tricolore.[4]

After some faltering steps, Pétain's government settled into Vichy, a town of 25,000 residents dating back to Roman times with spacious hotels to accommodate convalescents drawn to the baths and now suitable for ministers, administrators, and, before long, a foreign diplomatic corps.[5] On July 10, the Third Republic was abolished by what some commentators referred to as the "harakiri parliament." Pétain was designated head of state, and flags and ceremonies across the country renewed national spirits. Four of the five members of the Assemblée nationale from Alpes-Maritimes, as well as the senator and mayor of Nice, Jean Médecin, voted for a constitutional revision giving full powers to the Maréchal de France.

The rapidity of defeat on the northern fronts in May and June stunned the French nation. Belgian, German, and East European refugees streamed across Paris, their accounts and rumors fueling the fears of Parisians and emptying two-thirds of the city. Some 6 to 10 million refugees, primarily women and children, fled the maelstrom. An endless stream on foot, in addition to animals and vehicles of all descriptions, choked national highways and narrow country lanes leading south, making it impossible for reserve forces to make their way to the fighting.

Many traveled in automobiles "protected" by mattresses roped to their roofs. Boys happily joined the parade shouting that they were going to join the French soldiers. Suddenly, Luftwaffe dive-bombers appeared out of nowhere and swooped down with sirens blaring. People threw themselves to the ground, mothers covering their children. Bullets rained down cutting furrows through the crowds and blocking the roads with demolished conveyances. The destruction of war could be heard in the distance, a bomb destroying the railway line, the explosion of an arsenal, or the whistling of an incendiary. The crush and panic stretched hundreds of miles as nomads wandered as far as the Midi in what became known as *l'exode* (the exodus).[6]

Amidst the frantic flight from Paris were thousands of Polish soldiers who had found refuge there. A secret organization was soon set up in the port of Marseille to send these troops to England and employ them to collect intelligence inside the German occupied zone. A concentration of Poles also assembled in Nice in hopes of escaping through Italy and continuing to their homeland. A native Antibois, Camille Rayon, assisted a Polish network that met in Chatham's bar across from the train station in neighboring Juan-les-Pins, which served as a blind mailbox for clandestine messages. About 300 Polish nationals, military veterans mostly, stayed in a nearby hotel throughout the war. Rayon recruited and sheltered them as well as serving as their liaison with the authorities. His primary task was helping Polish pilots cross Vichy-controlled France and Franco's Spain so they could fly airplanes for Britain, faced with a dire shortage of aviators.[7]

Even after a ceasefire took effect, an estimated 300,000 French refugees remained in the South, unwilling to return home to Alsace-Lorraine, now part of the Reich, or to the prohibited northern industrial zone administered directly by the German High Command. The Armistice divided France, less the three departments annexed by Germany, into Occupied and Non-Occupied Zones. The former encompassed approximately two-thirds of the population and a similar proportion of the land in the north and west and along the Atlantic coast to Spain. The smaller area with 13 million inhabitants was superior only in the production of wine and fruit, and so the supply of food there quickly became a serious problem. The scarce arable land in Alpes-Maritimes grew some wheat and cereals, fruits and vegetables, and lots of flowers for the perfume industry at Grasse. Fishing and raising sheep and cows were other pursuits but not on a scale to feed a population bloated with refugees. Children suffered stunted growth, the death rate from starvation rose among the elderly, and production by workers declined due to sickness.[8] Vichy tried to blame the shortage of foodstuffs on the British naval blockade, but the unwillingness of some prefects to share their local produce with other departments and the extraordinary demands of the Reich for subsistence constituted the real causes. In the *parlance au courant*, France had become the "milk cow" of Germany.

Although at first the southern zone was referred to as the Free Zone, it was still subject to censorship of mail, interception of telegrams and monitoring of telephone conversations. Initially just 300 letters were allowed to cross the demarcation line each day, and only postcards of the pre-printed kind were authorized (ticked off to report "in good health," "tired," "died," etc.). An editor who traveled regularly between Monte Carlo and her publishing house in Paris was summoned to Vichy for not providing extracts of political books before publication, an illustration of restrictions imposed on the press.[9] It followed that newspapers were subject to similar scrutiny. At the turn of the year, the Germans redesignated the "Free Zone" as the "Non-Occupied Zone".

Just as anti-communism had raged in September 1939 when Russia joined Germany in devouring Poland, Anglophobia soon became rampant. Pétain had criticized the British for sending a handful of divisions to France while the French bore the brunt of the German blitzkrieg. The British were further criticized for withholding air support from the campaign on the Continent. On July 3, the Royal Navy attacked the French fleet at Mers-el-Kébir near Oran, Algeria, to keep it out of Nazi hands, killing over 1,300 Gallic sailors. Treachery by their former allies was excoriated by Vichy and many Frenchmen. A corresponding incident but of lesser import occurred on the night of September 2, when a British warplane returning from over Italy offloaded its remaining bombs on the town of Digne in Basses-Alpes[10] above Alpes-Maritimes. Cooperating with the German occupiers appeared less onerous after what was seen as "perfidious Albion" betraying the British–French Entente Cordiale of 1903.

Consequence on the Côte d'Azur

> Our region which has not been conquered nor invaded, will not be occupied, will be demilitarized. During the entire period of the armistice, it will no longer be defended, our troops withdrawing 50 kilometers to a demarcation line which is not close to the border.
>
> We take our share of the misfortune of the country; we have escaped destruction, large-scale evacuations, total occupation: let's thank God and our courageous soldiers for having protected our possessions and ourselves.[11]

Thus Mayor Jean Médecin summarized the situation in Alpes-Maritimes at the beginning of July 1940. The demilitarized zone created by the Italian Armistice extended west of Cannes and Grasse. Consequently, military stocks of XV Corps were relocated to depots in Fayence, Miramas, and Nimes, although nationalists secretly buried certain matériel and camouflaged hidden automatic weapons, cars, trucks, and other stores. Army headquarters moved to Saint-Raphaël from Nice, to Draguignan from Antibes and Cagnes, to Fréjus from Cannes, and to Aix-en-Provence from the casernes in Sospel and Grasse.

Demilitarization of Alpes-Maritimes was in some respects a fiction. To enforce France's obligations, the Italian Armistice Commission installed a control section in Nice to oversee depots, demobilization centers, casernes, and units of the 100,000-man Armée de l'Armistice permitted to the vanquished under the truce with Germany. No more than 8,000 members could be officers. Commission officials came to the Southeast in 1942 to inspect the airports at Nice and Cannes, the aircraft manufacturing and railroad repair yards at La Bocca, and naval workshops at Port Vauban in Antibes. Italian authorities stationed two companies of engineers and a half-brigade of soldiers in five communities along the coast. The Commission also obtained the liberation of Italians interned by Vichy except those sentenced for violations of the law, anarchists, extremists, and veterans of the Spanish Civil War.[12]

A joint delegation from the Italian and German Armistice commissions, headquartered at Torino and Wiesbaden, respectively, set up in the Hôtel Suisse at the east end of the Promenade des Anglais in Nice to control maritime traffic with Corsica and North Africa. Not long thereafter the building also quartered a clandestine section of the Gestapo. German agents circulated on the Côte d'Azur throughout the Vichy period. In accordance with a proviso which prohibited France from sheltering anti-Nazis, Vichy acquiesced to the arrest by French police, accompanied by the Gestapo, of the Ruhr industrialist Fritz Thyssen at Hôtel Montfleury in Cannes in December 1941.[13]

While the vast majority of Frenchmen applauded Pétain for taking France out of the war, the Riviera was an exception. Residents of southeastern France were puzzled by the capitulation as, from their point of view, the war had not been lost. French Chasseurs Alpins, Scouts-Skiers, and defenders of the Maginot Line had repelled the Italian invasion all along the border. Thirty-two Italian divisions failed to overwhelm three French divisions defending the Alpine front. Fewer than 100 officers and men were casualties in the fight against Italy. The suddenness of the armistice announcement was therefore surprising. As recently as May 25, *Le Progrès Provençal de Grasse* and *Le Progrès d'Antibes* had printed strong reassurances, the latter proudly asserting, "All Hitler's calculations will be frustrated [...] Pétain is here. Rejoice. Victory is underway, illuminated by the high-ranking figure of the defender of Verdun, a symbol of energy and the greatest military virtues."[14] Many citizens subscribed to the slogan *vendu pas vaincu* (betrayed not beaten).

However, it was not long before the severity of the outcome was brought home to inhabitants of the Southeast. More than 9,500 of their soldiers did not come back to Alpes-Maritimes from fighting the Boche in the north of France—819 killed, and 8,700 taken prisoner and hauled off to Germany, losses representing almost 2 percent of its population. Another 700 men were killed and 6,000 prisoners lost to the Var.[15]

As common with revolutions, from France in the eighteenth century to Russia in the twentieth, streets and public squares were renamed; in this case, designations for socialists Anatole France and Jean Jaurès, and even philosopher Jean-Jacques Rousseau, were rechristened as symbolic purification. In Nice, rue Alphonse Karr was redesignated in honor of Lieutenant Félix Agnély, a hero of the two wars against Germany, rue Neville Chamberlain became rue Cronstadt, and the name of Marshal Louis Lyautey, an icon of colonial France, replaced that of the immortal Louis Pasteur on a city quai. Pétain's bust appeared in *hôtels de ville* across the Southeast replacing that of Marianne, the feminine embodiment of the République Française dating back to the late eighteenth century. Communities soon followed the lead of Antibes and Grasse in naming a street or square in his honor. Pictures of the head of state appeared in shop windows, and one diarist observed that "everyone bought a calendar with a photo of Maréchal Pétain except the communists." The prevailing slogan became "With the Maréchal or against France."[16]

The right-wing *L'Eclaireur de Nice* quickly published a hagiography deifying Pétain: "Let's follow him. He gives us the example of faith in the future of the country [...] Maréchal Pétain has brought to the people of France a precious comfort: that of confidence that he embodies in his dignity, in his force of spirit, in his patriotism [...] He will help in a brotherly fashion to commune with ourselves, to bandage wounds, to rebuild the ruins, to perpetuate the spirit of France."[17] A weekly newspaper in Grasse ran a first-page article entitled "Maréchal notre père."[18] Other publications along the coast amplified the comparison to Christ by referring to the leader in Vichy as the Great Chief, the Guide, and the Saviour. Among the more subdued characterizations was "first gardener of France" accompanied by a photo of Pétain watering blue, white, and red flowers—blueberries, daisies, and poppies—at his Azuréenne residence.[19]

In an extraordinary session on June 18, the Antibes municipal council sent a telegram supporting the new head of state, and other locales soon followed suit. Local officials worked to remove other reminders of figures now deemed disreputable. The mayor of Cannes removed plaques commemorating Chamberlain and Edouard Daladier, his French counterpart, at Munich in 1938. Municipalities appropriated the properties of prominent figures believed responsible for the downfall, for example, the house in Mandelieu of Pierre Cot, a minister in the Front Populaire.[20]

The new regime in Vichy arbitrarily replaced certain mayors and one-quarter of the council members in Alpes-Maritimes with individuals known to be loyal to the Maréchal. Many of the ousted officials had first been elected in leftist victories in 1935. Mayors Médecin and Jules Grec in Antibes were two notable exceptions due to their stature and amity with Pétain. The arbitrary changes in local leadership were not always willingly accepted, however, Grasse being a notable example.

In the confusion of defeat, population shifts, and civil and economic disorder, the notion of Maréchal Pétain as a leader with powers, albeit restricted, in both the Occupied and Non-Occupied Zones was initially comforting to many. Pétain used the term *Révolution Nationale* to encompass his program to rebuild the "Good France"—a strong centralized state with concentrated capitalism and Catholic moral order. In the wake of military defeat and a defensive xenophobia already flourishing, restoring pride in France demanded a revival of patriotism and traditionalism. Revoked naturalizations stripped 15,000 persons of citizenship, including 6,000 Jews. German demands for heavy reparations followed by requisitions of French goods, services, and manpower required the Révolution Nationale to subject the country to a stringent and centrally controlled war economy. Vichy increasingly ruled by fiat over Pétain's signature, complemented at the local level by appointees whose first loyalty was to the Maréchal. Corporatism envisioned creating units of employers and workers by industry and profession, to include the celebrated peasant, to obliterate the class struggle, and eliminate competition. Utilizing force to uphold public order became necessary when the Parti Communiste Francais (PCF) eventually joined the Resistance and turned to assassinations and other forms of terrorism. The police state that gradually emerged was used to implement Vichy's persecution of Jews long before the Nazis began to apply pressure, for anti-Semitism was at the core of the Révolution Nationale as will be discussed later.

After what conservatives considered the radical and anti-Catholic party of teachers, lawyers, Jews, and Freemasons who ran France in the 1930s, Catholicism experienced a resurgence under Vichy. Churches multiplied the number of prayers said on behalf of France's captives in Germany. "The Day of the Prisoner" collected francs to send to chaplaincies serving this need. Even masses asking for the protection of the Virgin Mary increased in frequency. The Catholic press played on a theme common to the losing country in many conflicts, blaming the defeat on "national sin."[21] Redemption was seen in the Maréchal replacing France's historic motto of "*Liberté, égalité, fraternité*" with his own ethic for the Révolution Nationale, "*travail, famille, patrie*" (work, family, homeland). The practicing faithful occupied important government posts. Education programs returned God to the public schools, and the state offered funding for church schools. Conversely, the Catholic factor also contributed to generating resistance to Vichyism by persons sympathetic to Republican Spain, the Front Populaire, and "*lois laiques*," the secular legacy of the French Revolution.

Pétainism venerated the family, standards of behavior returned to society, and a youth movement instilled patriotic and religious values. The Révolution Nationale taught that a woman's place was in the home. Large families were encouraged; divorce was frowned upon. Female employment took income from a youth or demobilized soldier who needed a job to live. Therefore, women over 50 years of age and wives of civil servants were removed from office. Primary-school teachers felt especially threatened by this policy. It was clearly stated in these prohibitions, however, that widows, spouses of soldiers still not demobilized, and single women would not be prevented from working. In addition, the absence of husbands forced many women to play a new role as head of the house. By the same token, Vichy morality inflicted heavy punishment on the wife of a prisoner of war engaging in adultery.

An ordinance in Cannes prohibited women from promenading along the beach or on city streets in short garb, including bathing suits and culottes. A decree in Nice also made "knee-length, two-piece bathing suits" compulsory for men and women. Police were directed to confront any indiscretion. In the summer of 1942, the Young Christian Workers were led to complain to the mayor of Cannes that attire exhibited by visitors, as well as local inhabitants, was still indecent and disrespectful to the French nation.[22] As general moral laxity was cited as a reason for the country's downfall, the Vichy government also banned public dancing and jazz.

The youth of France were central to realizing Pétain's vision of a renewed nation. Schoolchildren began each day with a hymn still well remembered, "Maréchal, nous voilà":

> Maréchal, we are here,
> Before you, the Savior of France;
> We swear, we your kids,
> To obey and follow in your steps.

Students were in the crowd waiting at the train station upon Pétain's arrival on the Côte d'Azur. Ten pupils from Cannes and Nice were chosen to be received by the Maréchal in Vichy on December 26, 1941. *L'Eclaireur de Nice* organized a contest on the theme "From Jeanne d'Arc to Pétain," pairing Pétain with a saint martyred by the English and thus an icon for his disciples. Some 15,000 children participated in the competition, 3,000 submitting their own portraits of the chief of state.

Of far wider impact were two youth organizations. The foremost was the Chantiers de la Jeunesse, camps inaugurated in the summer of 1940 to remove draft-age, unemployed young men from cities and provide the rudiments of the military training they would have received before the Armistice, including physical exercise and personal hygiene. Hence the Chantiers' motto, *"Toujours Prets"* (Always Ready). By 1941, all males in the Non-Occupied Zone were required to spend eight months in their twenty-first year at an open-air encampment in the countryside. This requirement was not to prepare for renewing the war with Germany but as a means of indoctrination. Days passed attending classes on moral development, social order, and French history, as well as working in the woods. One alumnus recalls making charcoal, an essential ingredient in the fuel propelling many civilian vehicles.[23] When marching in formation or learning the themes of the Révolution Nationale, attendees frequently wore olive-green uniforms and the enormous berets of the Chasseurs Alpins, positioned well down over the left ear.

The second widespread body was the Les Compagnons de France, a voluntary formation for boys aged 15–20, intended to orient them to the new regime. In addition to receiving instruction on social and ethical subjects, agriculture and forestry constituted its principal activities.

Restrictions imposed on the demilitarized area in Alpes-Maritimes required youngsters to go into the Var for instruction until a training site opened in 1942 near Mandelieu. There they took the following oath: "We swear to unite, and to gather all our forces, our faith, our ardor, at the service of the Maréchal, at the service of France."[24] Discipline inculcated in these two programs contributed to almost 1,500 Azuréens enlisting in the Armée de l'Armistice in 1941. Acclimation to outdoor living also made these participants excellent candidates for the Resistance soon to coalesce.

Other young people reacted differently. Inspired by de Gaulle, in 1941 11 pupils in Nice employed a small press to print thousands of copies of tracts and fliers to spread around the city. The Italian Armistice Commission quickly intervened and exposed the amateur enterprise. The tribunal at Aix-en-Provence condemned nine of the activists to one month in prison with fines of 500 francs each. The future mayor of Nice, Jacques Cotta, obtained acquittal for the other two mischievous youth. But, this was just a beginning.[25]

Pétain's Ties with Alpes-Maritimes

Pétain's association with the Midi traced back to 1876–7, his first year at the military academy of Saint-Cyr, France's counterpart to Sandhurst in England and West Point in America. He quickly established a friendship with Alphonse Guide, a senior cadet from Antibes. Apparently due to Guide's influence, upon graduation Pétain chose to wear the uniform of the Chasseurs Alpins stationed on the south coast at the port of Villefranche. Guide introduced Pétain to gambling at Monte Carlo and to high society in nearby Menton where the future Maréchal de France first met his future wife, Nini, then four years old.

Pleasant memories of this tour no doubt influenced Pétain's decision to purchase a domain on the Mediterranean in 1920, at the same time as his long relationship with Nini culminated in marriage. L'Ermitage consisted of a geometric masonry house with two floors above ground, a barn and stable, and small quarters for the caretaker, along with olive trees and a vineyard common to the region. The property was located on the hill of Saint-Véran overlooking the sea just outside the village of Villeneuve-Loubet.[26] When life in Paris during the years between the wars became burdensome for the Maréchal, he would express a desire to retire to his retreat (English for *ermitage*) and raise chickens.

Pétain's other connection with the southeastern corner of France was the Maginot Line. As a renowned militarist, Pétain was called upon three times to inspect construction of this barrier. When doing so in the far south, it was natural for him to yearn for a peaceful life there.

While head of state, Pétain made eight visits to l'Ermitage between 1940 and 1942. Usually accompanied by his personal physician if not always by his spouse, he would climb down from the train at Antibes where a delegation of local civilian and uniformed dignitaries awaited. The Maréchal was then driven to his country home by automobile, sometimes accompanied by Grec, a prominent horticulturist whose friendship with Pétain dated back over 20 years. Once at Villeneuve-Loubet, Pétain was carefully watched over by a security force. As his nation's titular leader he never continued on to Nice. The secretary-general of the prefecture explained that Mussolini's government would consider such an appearance and the ceremonies that followed to be an anti-Italian demonstration hostile to Rome's rightful place as "conqueror."[27]

Important figures like the Bishop of Nice, Monseigneur Paul Rémond, and right-winger Joseph Darnand were occasionally invited to share a meal with Pétain. In the vicinity were the residences of other personalities of note, such as General Maxime Weygand, under police surveillance at Cannes and Grasse in 1942, and Prince Louis of Monaco, along with politicians and elder statesmen who toured the gardens at l'Ermitage while conversing with the Maréchal about affairs of state. The tranquility might be interrupted by dispatches from Vichy brought by airplane landing at Californie in Nice.

The proximity of their governmental leader encouraged nearby residents to pay tribute. On one occasion, a girls' chorus sang "La Marseillaise" outside his coach in the station at Cagnes. On other visits, he inspected local agriculture and conversed with young people. During an annual ceremony in honor of Jeanne d'Arc, Pétain endeared himself by donating 10,000 francs to the community's social program. "I want to say to you how much I am attached to the village of Villeneuve. I thank you for your welcome. I will come back among you every time I have the opportunity."[28]

In January 1943 once again Pétain wanted to spend a few quiet days at his seaside retreat, but by then he was subject to close scrutiny by his German overseers. Villeneuve-Loubet was now in the sector occupied by the Italians, and the Nazis could not be certain that going there was not the first leg of a planned getaway to North Africa. Pétain was consequently denied permission to leave Vichy and, indeed, never saw l'Ermitage again.

Life under the Vichy Regime

Along the coast and across the two zones created by the Germans, many Frenchmen chose the path of least resistance, withdrawing within themselves and focusing attention on obtaining food and retaining or finding jobs in order to survive a period of uncertainty and despair that could continue indefinitely. Pétainism and a wait-and-see attitude seemed the easiest way to cope with the complexities of the situation in the South. The Armistice spared the Côte d'Azur compliance with direct orders issued by the Reich. The demands of the German occupiers only resounded far away to the north and west. This false sense of security in the Non-Occupied Zone was comforting for two years, while at the same time suppressing the urgency to resist controls emanating from Vichy and Berlin.

In recent times Cannes has never been a typical French city, and under Vichy it demonstrated uniqueness while suffering alongside other communities on the Riviera. The municipality lost the confidence of its citizens in the summer of 1941 by augmenting the pay of city employees at a time when many residents were barely surviving at the subsistence level. Furthermore, there was a sense that rationing restrictions were not applicable to these bureaucrats. Reopening the municipal casino again attracted the well-to-do to Cannes, including the "nouveaux riches," opportunists who blatantly displayed gains achieved by lack of scruples at the expense of their neighbors, adding to antagonism among Frenchmen. The Hôtel Grand, a château separated from the Croisette by a magnificent garden, was arguably the beach's plushest hostelry and thus drew a well-heeled clientele. The presence of wealthy Jews fueled the campaign to implement anti-Semitic measures. By arbitrarily replacing the town council, rather than holding an election, the powers at Vichy reinforced the impression that liberté and égalité were now passé.

Hotels along the Riviera lost business, so some blocked off a floor or two during slow months and many closed their doors altogether. Taking a long-term approach to the situation, others like the Carlton and George V in Cannes and the Pacific in Nice sold some guest chambers as apartments. Although the number of vacationers plummeted, the presence of more refugees seeking rooms and Jewish big-spenders and gamblers inflated hotel receipts by 1942–3 to their highest levels ever.[29]

In late 1940, Cannes and other nearby resorts tucked away in the Non-Occupied Zone seemed comfortable hideaways for the rich and famous to wait out the end of the war. At the outset, international figures such as the Aga Khan and the ex-khedive of Egypt initially remained in place before later moving to safer ground outside Europe. The French idol, Jean Gabin, resided on Cap Ferrat until 1941, when 20th Century Fox made an offer that promised to expand his career before a larger movie audience overseas. Colette sold her house at Saint-Tropez. André Gide, thought to be the dean of French letters at that time, lingered in the high ground above Grasse before moving on to Tunisia in 1942.

Other notables were content with their refuge under Vichy control. Georges Rouault spent the occupation in Golfe-Juan, west of Antibes. Pierre Bonnard and Henri Matisse already lived on the Riviera, in Le Cannet and Nice, respectively, and there they stayed. Bonnard was in declining health. Matisse finally abandoned the Hôtel Régina on Cimiez in June 1943 in fear of bombardments by the Allies and moved to Villa Le Rêve outside Vence. He had a reservation to go to Brazil in June 1940 but canceled the trip upon hearing of the collapse of French military forces, writing to his son Pierre that he would feel like a deserter: "If all that has value leaves France, what will be left of France?"[30]

Fashion designers, writers, musicians, and film stars also took refuge on the Côte d'Azur. Jean-Paul Sartre visited Grasse and Saint-Jean-Cap-Ferrat in the summer of 1941, accompanied, of course, by Simone de Beauvoir. Louis Jourdan preferred Cannes as his father managed a hotel there, and Man Ray came to Antibes where Claude Dauphin worked with the Resistance until late 1942. The intelligentsia might well be seen at a little picture gallery in Cannes owned by a young printer, Aimé Maeght, that constituted the nucleus of a collection that grew into the now renowned Fondation Maeght at Saint-Paul-de-Vence. Christian Dior and other couturiers were ensconced on the Riviera as well.[31]

This is not to say that the cinema and performing arts disappeared on the Mediterranean coast under Vichy control. The Victorine studio in Nice, still in use today, operated in combination with production lots in Valbonne and Saint-Laurent-du-Var to film 21 movies between November 1940 and October 1942, including one by Marcel Pagnol who spent some time in Cabris. Jourdan came over from Cannes to make two movies. Films were one way to forget the grim realities of life. Nice alone operated more than 40 cinemas, many exhibiting two films for a single affordable ticket.

Maurice Chevalier recalled that Nice, like Cannes and Monaco, had a high life as well as a low life.[32] Cabarets featured Josephine Baker, Edith Piaf, and Chevalier among other performers well known to Europeans. Songwriters did not hesitate to put daily life to music, composing ditties such as "He lacks tickets, rationed song" and "Vive le rutabaga." Stage plays looked to Molière as well as to contemporary playwrights for inspiration. The well-to-do generously supported galas to benefit a variety of causes ranging from right-wing organizations to the National Aid for the destitute, the Red Cross, prisoners of war in Germany, and war-torn communities far away. A portrait of Marshal Pétain attracted a winning bid of 336,000 francs at a charity auction at the Ruhl in Nice in January 1941; rubies offered by Van Cleef and Arpels brought large sums as well.[33]

Yet, life for the international set was no longer the same in the South of France. Consuelo de Saint-Exupéry, beautiful Salvadoran wife of the author of *The Little Prince* and an aviator of considerable renown, said of Parisian painters and writers marooned in the Midi, "They replaced the wine which was already lacking by often violent discussions on art and politics [...] coffee was the only thing which still retained the image of a future."[34]

Tragedies produced by the brief but destructive war in France and its aftermath revealed the benevolence of the populace. Townsfolk on the Côte d'Azur sought to aid their countrymen in areas devastated by fighting in northern France. Nice adopted Cambrai in the Department of Nord, Cannes paired with Châteauneuf-sur-Loire, and Grasse supported Nesle in the Somme with donations. At the same time, the Riviera itself needed outside assistance to survive. The Red Cross and Catholic and Protestant societies gave considerable help. Swiss Aid and the American Joint Committee were notable for their generosity. Americans contributed large quantities of powdered milk and chocolate, primarily for schoolchildren. In addition, youngsters from the Midi were invited to spend the summer of 1942 in towns throughout Switzerland.

France helped itself, as well. The National Aid and similar charities began serving meals to the needy with the price determined by a recipient's income. From late 1941 through 1942 over 25,000 persons were fed each month in communities along the Mediterranean coast from Cap d'Ail to Théoule. Preference went, of course, to families of prisoners of war, refugees from Menton, and other disadvantaged persons. Where possible, clothes were also distributed. Contributions from casinos in Nice and Cannes underwrote much of this charitable work.

Rationing begun during the Phoney War tightened as the months went by. In September 1940, allocations had been set at 350 grams of bread a day; 50 grams of cheese, 100 grams of fat, and 350 grams of meat per week; and 100 grams of rice, 300 grams of coffee, and 500 grams of sugar per month. In Alpes-Maritimes, with cuisine reflective of its heavy Italian population, even pasta was rationed at 250 grams per month due no doubt to its scarce ingredients of wheat, eggs, and milk. Quantities of all restricted items could vary depending on the consumer's age and occupation. Butter was continually a problem as, according to one resident, bureaucrats in Paris believed that southerners preferred olive oil. In the slang of the day, everyone was looking for BOF—*beurre, oeufs, fromage* (butter, eggs, cheese). Alcohol could not exceed 16 degrees after August 1941, and soon thereafter condensed milk was limited to children less than 18 months old. Bread declined in quality, more bran and coarse rye than wheat flour and frequently stale when purchased.

The passage from 1941 to 1942 was the second in a series of unusually cold winters in France, and inhabitants were authorized only a single kilo of potatoes (or three spuds) per person per month. One concerned father exchanged tobacco tickets with a farmer for milk for his son, only to discover later that it had been diluted. A teenager in Nice at the time summed up the war years by remembering that he was hungry from 1941 through the liberation and beyond.[35]

Only a limited selection of squash, various lettuces, rutabagas (sometimes called swedes), and the like was offered for sale at the Forville market in Cannes. When asked why someone felt under the weather, a cynical reply was "rutabagatism." It was not uncommon for shopkeepers and stall proprietors throughout the region to keep precious staples like sugar and fresh bread for themselves and their high-paying customers. To have a chance of buying what few items were offered for sale, one boy went to the Nice market at 6.00 a.m. to stand in line until his grandmother relieved him in time to go to school. Other youngsters hid in the market area overnight to be first the next morning, even though the vendor might not arrive under 10.00. Reports circulated of thefts of chickens and rabbits, arrests of merchants selling rationed items without coupons, and food sold at inflated prices. A woman reportedly walked with her pigeon on a string to allow it to find nurture before being served at the dinner table. Two francs would buy only a turnip, two carrots, and a quarter of a leek. A liter of olive oil valued at the official price of 11 francs in 1940 brought 18 francs on the black market.

Shoppers from Cannes journeyed to nearby towns where prices were not so high. Niçois often bicycled to Saint-Laurent-du-Var and Cagnes to deal directly with cultivators of fruits and vegetables. City folk grumbled that country cousins who worked the soil were charging exorbitant prices for their crops. As an alternative, the mayor of Cannes asked factories to encourage workers to cultivate plots to grow their own produce. In Nice, the lawns of hotels along the Promenade des Anglais were transformed into gardens.[36]

Admittedly, the southeastern terrain was not well suited to cultivation. A resident of Valbonne had difficulty growing edible plants, for example, because there was only a single fountain in the village to draw water for her kitchen garden.[37] Yet the government's failure to provide foodstuffs was difficult to understand for inhabitants of a department so fervent for the Révolution Nationale. Azuréens had the impression that Vichy did not care as much for them as for those in interior departments less loyal to Pétain.[38] Perhaps the presence in Alpes-Maritimes of so many refugees, considered undesirable elements, accounted for Vichy's coolness.

Ersatz, or *Système D* (Do It Yourself) as it was known to the French, became a necessity to substitute for shortages. Tobacco national contained dried grass and herbs; some pipe smokers used parched grape leaves. Eucalyptus cigarettes were rationed to those over 18 years of age, as even these crude imitations were limited in number and coveted. Hinged wooden soles (and sometimes paper) filled in for shoe leather, and wearing raffia slippers became commonplace indoors. Sweaters made with rough hair scratched the skin, causing the wearer to sweat. Scraps of newspaper crushed into balls and moistened with water burned slowly as fuel. The allocation of one bicycle tire every two years made rubber patches indispensable, but the supply was soon exhausted. So, some riders stuffed papier-mâché into their tires or strung corks along the rim where rubber would normally have been. Light bulbs, too, were in short supply, requiring surrender of an old one to buy a replacement, bringing about a resurgence of candlelight.

People also sought food substitutes or other ways to conserve nutriments. Roasted barley, acorns, and date nuts took the place of real coffee. Youngsters were stationed under oak trees in Nice's Place Garibaldi waiting for acorns to fall.[39] Café national consisted mostly of burned grain. Chestnuts, chick peas, dried apples, and lupine seed were even tried as the basis for hot beverages. Mixing blood with bread provided nourishment. A cookbook entitled *Cuisine for the Present Time* advertised 200 recipes without butter or oil. When hunger became too severe, dogs were killed or released into the wild to conserve food, halving the canine population in Alpes-Maritimes. Yet despite these shortages, starvation in France never reached the extremes of the Soviet Union, Poland, Holland, or Greece.[40]

Transportation also felt the squeeze. *Le Petit Niçois* trumpeted the bicycle as "king" of the road. Their manufacture and sale was a rare growth industry under Vichy, necessitating more places set aside for parking. The riders were not just ordinary folk. Madame Louis Dreyfus, widow of a cereal magnate, and Madame Dupont, mother of Baron de Rothschild, were seen pedaling along, one with a basket holding a Pekinese and the other carrying provisions found in the country. Makeshift bicycle rickshaws began appearing on roadways. Buses and trams attracted additional passengers. The most ingenious means of transport was fueled by *gazogène*—coal, coke, wood, or charcoal mixed with gas to generate power in a wash boiler bolted to the trunk. Ten kilos of combustibles could propel a vehicle 100–150 kilometers, depending upon the speed. A gazogène car required four hours to transit the 50 or so kilometers (roughly 30 miles) from Cannes to Cap Ferrat, for example. After dark, such a trip might be undertaken without benefit of streetlights which the exigencies restricted to limited periods. Motorcycles and commercial vehicles needed petrol, too. Only doctors, clergy, and government employees on official business could expect to obtain fuel for gasoline engines.[41]

Légion Française des Combattants

The most far-reaching reaction to the nation's humiliation was creation of the Légion Française des Combattants (LFC), composed of veterans of the two world wars. On October 1, 1940, Darnand, a decorated hero of both conflicts and deemed a personification of courage, was named head of the branch in Alpes-Maritimes, France's first departmental organization.[42] The Légion's inaugural meeting was six days later. The façade of Nice's Municipal Casino showed only a flag at half-mast, but its interior was brightly adorned with bunting, banners, and tricolore cockades, the national emblem. A huge panel displayed a portrait of the Maréchal with the words "Verdun–Pétain."

More than 7,000 people jammed the hall while another 5,000 listened to loudspeakers outside. The Scouts of France and the Young Christian Workers stood in formation on stage, along with political notables, military leaders, other dignitaries, and men disabled in combat. To enthusiastic applause Darnand exhorted the crowd to empower true patriots in place of the dark-skinned, Jews, and foreigners—the false French who had brought the country to ruin. Adherents to the Légion took the following oath:

> I swear to continue to serve France with honor in peace, as I have served under arms. I swear to consecrate all my strength to the country, to the family, to work. I undertake to provide friendship and mutual aid to my comrades of the two wars, to remain faithful to the memory of those who fell on the field of honor. I freely accept the discipline of the Légion and all who will lead me in pursuit of this ideal.[43]

Similar gatherings took place in the Cimiez district of Nice and at Antibes, Cannes, and Grasse, plus a host of smaller communities. Extending their right arms in a stiff salute akin to Nazi and Italian Fascists, Légionnaires pledged their loyalty to Pétain and Darnand, leading to the characterization of the Légion as "the eyes and ears of the Maréchal." Later in October, a complementary body, Les Amis de la Légion, was formed to allow non-mobilized nationalists, war widows, and others to express support of Vichy France. The first group of wives of the Légion met in Antibes in November. December saw the creation of the Légion's youth auxiliary.

The Révolution Nationale was truly underway with the Légion portraying itself as the incarnation of a reborn France. By February 1941, Alpes-Maritimes could count over 50,000 members of the organization and its auxiliary groups. The strength of the brotherhood in the department's population is shown by the fact that one man in five belonged to the Légion at year's end. The success was due in part to Darnand's strong personality, as well as to promotion by the local press. Not to be overlooked, however, was the inhabitants' ongoing concern with nearby Fascist Italy and Mussolini's stated intention to annex "Comté Nizza." Hitler was said to have promised Nice to Mussolini when they met at the Brenner Pass in October 1940. Indeed, most of the Légion's cadre came from the Chasseurs Alpins, veterans of the defensive struggle in 1940 who stood ready to fight once more against an attempt by Italy to annex Nice.[44]

Thus did Nice acquire the nickname of "the eldest daughter of the Révolution Nationale." Historian Jean-Louis Panicacci cites contemporary estimates of only 15–20 percent devoted Pétainists in the department, plus a larger number moderately behind the Maréchal in 1941-2.[45] Celebrations on May 1, recast under Vichy from labor demonstrations to a celebration of work and union, the festival of Jeanne d'Arc, and Mother's Day all served to demonstrate fealty to the Armistice government. The parade of 50,000 Niçois on May 9, 1941 was noteworthy for the abundance of French tricolores as an expression of the strong local feeling against absorption by Italy. A typical ceremony consisted of a pledge to the flag, a sermon by a Légionnaire, singing "La Marseillaise," and a long procession of patriotic orders. The Cathédrale de Saint-Réparte in Nice played the carillon and sounded the great, deep bourdon reserved for important occasions. Another opportunity for nationalistic exuberance occurred on October 9, when Amiral François Darlan, Pétain's Deputé Premier, came to Nice to be welcomed by formations of Légionnaires that filled Place Masséna and stretched up avenue de la Victoire. "My friends, let me say to you that when I give an account to the Maréchal of the welcome that you have given me, he will not be surprised, because he knows the patriotism of Nice."[46]

With this fervor came witch hunts to ferret out those deemed disloyal—Freemasons, Jews, communists, and even past members of the military who did not acknowledge Pétain's authority, some looking instead to London for leadership. Indeed, after the war the former director of the chief of state's cabinet is reported to have said, "We liked neither one [Jews] nor the other, Freemasons. The Maréchal was obliged to detest them. A Jew, he said, is never responsible for his origins; a Freemason is always responsible for his own choice."[47] Moderation in support of a renewed identity for France lost sway to extremism, and the Révolution Nationale in Nice gravitated toward more admiration of the Teutonic fatherland, certain in the eyes of many to be the victor of the war in Europe.

The Bishop of Nice sought to counter demonizing the Third Republic and castigating divergent elements of the population as traitors. He warned the members of his diocese to beware of dangerous, excessive pronouncements, and preached on the national day of mourning, "Do not listen to the voice outside that seeks to divide us." Indeed, Rémond counseled "Silence, discipline, calm, confidence. Let's add an invincible hope in God."[48] As a veteran of World War I, Rémond's patriotism and long friendship with Pétain led him to support the Maréchal personally at the outset of the new government, but not to endorse hatred and violence.

Other more extreme, right-wing movements followed on the heels of the LFC. In July 1941, the Légion des Volontaires Français contre le Bolchévisme (LVFB) collected 250 men, including 53 from the Côte d'Azur, who marched off to fight the Soviet Union wearing German uniforms. A subsidiary of 600 "friends" of the Volontaires met in Nice in December, demonstrating their support for an organization which soon used Bolshevik as a code word for Jew. The following year, the Volontaires Français morphed into the Légion Tricolore with a mission of rehabilitating France, again with the patina of Nazism. Its first national meeting, held in Nice on August 8, attracted 5,000 attendees.[49]

Darnand was not left behind. His personal relationship with Pétain and the considerable distance between Nice and Vichy allowed him freedom to take action against communists, Freemasons, and Jews far beyond his formal responsibilities. In August 1941, Darnand created a Service d'Ordre Légionnaire (SOL) to attract males too young to have fought in the war but drawn to his ideals. The recruits wore khaki shirts, black berets and ties, and insignia with sword and shield topped with the French *coq*. Kneeling as did chevaliers of yore, the aspirants took an oath to the Maréchal and pledged to protect the Révolution Nationale and fight communism at the swearing-in ceremony in the Arena on Cimiez. At its zenith, 1,674 Azuréens took part in this movement that numbered 30,000 nationwide.[50] Wielding thick batons, their initial function was to keep order at rallies of the LFC. Yet under the guidance of Darnand and Pétain's subsequent deputy, Pierre Laval,[51] who as "head of government" became personally involved the following May, the SOL assumed the role of a private, shadow police force. These radicals soon took action to draw attention to their nationalist cause.

The SOL began with small disruptions, such as breaking the statues of Edward VII in Cannes and Queen Victoria in Nice. Marching through nighttime Nice by torchlight crying "France! France!" garnered public notice. A resort to violence opposed the growing discontent in Alpes-Maritimes, and indeed much of France, with the inability of the Vichy government to deliver on its promises to limit the intrusion of fascism, provide adequate food and jobs, and rebuild the country.

Public demonstrations of dissatisfaction with the authorities because of severe food shortages were by no means uncommon in 1942 Vichy France. In Alpes-Maritimes, women massed at Cannes in January and Cap d'Ail and Beausoleil in July. On Bastille Day, hundreds of young Niçois gathered at Place Masséna chanting "Vive de Gaulle" and anti-Vichy slogans. The display ended in a fist fight with the SOL and members of the pro-Vichy, extreme rightist Parti Populaire Français (PPF),[52] followed by police interrogations.

As for the LFC in Alpes-Maritimes, internal dissension, quarrels with mayors, and promotion of its dynamic leaders to higher posts in other regions caused it to wither, moderates recoiling from its transformation and Darnand's pugnaciousness. By the end of 1942, 40 percent of the enrollment had withdrawn. Anti-Semitism and its dilatory effects contrasted with genuine patriotic ceremonies and aid extended to prisoners of war and their families by the Légion in other parts of France.[53]

The Emergence of Opposition

The longer Pétain's government stayed in power, the more criticism mounted and his image became tarnished. Pétain was not the cause of all the mistakes by his regime, but increasingly its tool. As Vichy governance evolved into an instrument for greater Nazi dominance, the aged Maréchal became more and more the figurehead rather than the originator of its policies.

When France capitulated, strong feelings were triggered for and against fascism, and Nazism was not the only object of these visceral sentiments. In the Southeast, attitudes toward Mussolini and his brand of authoritarianism were foremost in the minds of many inhabitants, particularly those who had recently fled from Italy, along with longer-time residents of Italian ancestry. At the outset, as Pétain and Vichy were in the ascendance, graffiti tended to represent the counterview: "Vive de Gaulle," "Vive l'Angleterre," and "De Gaulle, c'est la liberté," along with numerous scrawls of the letter "V," Winston Churchill's trademark. One Niçois tract screamed in Italian, "The enemy eats your bread, the enemy wants your country, the enemy is Italy, follow De Gaulle"; on the other side, "De Gaulle defeated, Nice to Italy" also appeared.[54]

As the Pétain regime took hold, opposing sentiments quickly surfaced in Antibes. Colonel Thierry, a professor at the *polytechnique*, was thought to be an anti-Pétainist and became an inspiration for others who shared this view. Young men with leftist sentiments began distributing fliers, the first underground newspapers in Antibes. Retired Général de l'Air Gabriel Cochet who had grown up in Cannes was another role model, as his Gaullist information leaflets were disseminated to lycée students in Nice and Cannes, many extolling the success of the Royal Air Force (RAF) in the Battle of Britain.[55]

There were no serious problems with dissent until well into 1941. As domestic life and the economy worsened, however, the Vichy regime relied more and more upon the police to maintain order. When an active resistance began forming in the Non-Occupied Zone, Vichy's responses propelled the fragile government on a downward spiral of repression on behalf of Nazi Germany from which it never recovered. Serving in the community where they lived, officers of the law tended to be sympathetic to their fellow townspeople, but in the many months leading up to liberation, citizens never knew when approached by a policeman whether he was pro- or anti-Vichy and that was frightening for the majority of French men and women seeking simply to blend into the crowd.

Initially under Pétain the media continued to enjoy relative freedom. In Nice, for example, the two leading papers published news from Berlin and London in parallel columns. Censorship of the French press was present but not overbearing. At the same time, the authorities permitted free circulation of Swiss newspapers which recounted a succession of German victories.

As the Wehrmacht became bogged down in Russia, these windows on the outside world closed to perpetuate the myth of Aryan invincibility.[56] Similarly, it was not forbidden to tune into foreign broadcasts in the Non-Occupied Zone immediately following the Armistice. A Nice newspaper ran an article, however, pointing out that some transmissions were pure propaganda. To simple folk just becoming exposed to the wireless, it was natural to consider anything said on a radio to be truthful. The paper recommended that Radio-Liberté and emissions from Stuttgart, specifically, be avoided as the Germans were "past masters in the war of the airwaves."[57] Conversely later during the Occupation, Radio-Vichy was recommended or its German counterpart from the Occupied Zone, Radio-Paris.

In November 1940, Vichy prohibited broadcasting foreign transmissions in public places. By autumn of 1941, tuning into Gaullist programming could lead to a fine of 200 to 10,000 francs plus six days to two years in prison.[58] Nonetheless, "Ici, Londres: Les Français parlent aux Français" (London here: The French speak to the French), the opening of a daily discourse delivered by a countryman, became a staple of patriotic Frenchmen throughout the occupation. A native son of the city, René Cassin, broadcast an "Address to Niçois" on November 30 to assure listeners that de Gaulle was unequivocal on Nice remaining French and not being returned to Italy. As the war progressed, the BBC kept clandestine listeners apprised on the course of battles, the extended combat at Stalingrad lifting Gallic spirits at its outcome. Radio Suisse was another source of truthful information about the war. Later, after the North African landings and its change from pro- to anti-Vichy, Radio Algiers turned into a source of encouragement.

At first the only propaganda in the southern zone was pro-Vichy. When internal expressions of disgruntlement began to appear, they seemed harmless. During raids in the communist sector of Nice in mid-November 1940, police discovered two typewriters and a duplicating machine, 35 stencils for the party's underground newspaper, L'Humanité, 30,000 copies ready for distribution, and 6,000 sheets of paper. A few months later, four youth were apprehended for producing Gaullist material. Next, a Niçois was taken into custody for circulating pamphlets denigrating the premier and his deputy. The formation of the LFC naturally generated handouts in opposition, often in red ink, leading to more arrests.

As usual, young people constituted a hotbed of sedition. Soon after his radio address, a group of youths was reported to have telegraphed de Gaulle to express admiration and volunteer their services when required.[59] Adolescents regularly gathered along Nice's Promenade des Anglais to share stories and experiences, build up courage, and form groups of like-minded friends. One pupil in a Nice college[60] at the time remembered only three Gaullists in the student body and just a single teacher known to oppose the German occupation of France. As people were afraid to speak openly, the youngster discovered other dissidents by tapping Morse code lightly on his school desk. What could boys and girls do to oppose the Vichy government? Distributing handbills was a common expression of opposition. This determined teenager served as lookout for the police while his great aunt, almost blind, marked a "V" with the cross of Lorraine on walls.[61] Another youngster at the time remembered drawing the francisque, an emblem adopted by the Vichy regime that combined a Gallic axe with a marshal's baton, to identify fellow students loyal to Pétain. As discontent grew in 1942, the lights were kept on in cinemas while the news was shown so police could spot viewers, often young scholars, who booed Pétain and other leaders.[62]

In the Var, opposition to the new regime was dominated by Freemasons, socialists, and communists. Christian resistance was notably weak, but there were exceptions. One was a parish priest outside Hyères who, although a captain in the war, refused to join the Légion and instead became head of the underground in his community. Another was the curé of Cavalaire who so aroused the anger of the head of the local Légion branch that he was accused of being chief of the Gaullist party. Some parishioners were no less determined. At the end of 1940, Vichy police dismantled pro-de Gaulle and Anglophile networks in the Var after intercepting a courier for the movement that would become Combat. The messenger and a retailer of radio sets were arrested and sent to Nice where they were mistreated and held for a month. Finally returning home, the courier found that his employment with the national railway had been terminated. In the autumn of 1940, a worker at the maritime arsenal in Toulon organized seven fellow unionists and a Pole to create one of the first intelligence rings which survived until liberation, thanks to taking great care with security. Supported by the British Special Operations Executive (SOE), between 1940 and 1942 the organization recruited 52 agents along the coast as far away as Ventimiglia. Their cover story characterized these men as members of an association of workers who liked gardening. The group became the heart of the non-communist resistance in the department.[63]

These independent expressions of discontent in the South were the beginnings of a struggle of Frenchmen against Frenchmen, encouraging the first overt action against affiliation of Vichy with the Reich. Strike out against those who support Germany by, among other means, marking houses of collaborators with swastikas and vandalizing or destroying overt signs of the occupiers, citizens were told. Ordinary people were forced to take sides, the genesis of civil war. To increasing numbers of his compatriots in the Non-Occupied Zone, "the hero of Verdun" was no longer the savior of France.

The following summer a new reason emerged to generate dissatisfaction with Vichy. Laval announced the *Relève* (relief), which encouraged Frenchmen to volunteer for work in Germany in exchange for the return of prisoners of war.

Posters in France announced, "Germany offers you work." Unemployment and political uncertainty at home, combined with tempting salaries, the promise of vacation time, and a chance to be reunited with friends kept prisoner in Germany made this opportunity attractive to some. In the Var, for example, volunteers came from youth without training or jobs and not from large factories or working-class trades. Some 600 young men departed in a convoy from the Var on August 6, but this was an exceptional turnout for Southeast France. A recruiting office in Cannes sent off another 2,000 workers. Yet, from June to November 1942, a total of only 2,687 Azuréen men departed from the train station in Nice for the Reich.[64]

The response across France was far below expectations, and in September a new dictat from Vichy made men 18–50 years old and single women ages 21–35 eligible for labor at the state's discretion. Later in 1943, the involuntary Service du Travail Obligatoire (STO) produced still more laborers for Germany. From 1941 to 1944, 11,591 workers from Alpes-Maritimes departed, 7,714 of them volunteers, the highest proportion in France. Women constituted 12 percent of this group; foreigners, 23 percent.[65] Overall, 665,000 Frenchmen were working in Germany at the end of 1943, plus over 700,000 prisoners of war. In total, more French citizens were employed in German factories than any other nationality except Russian. When the Wehrmacht was finally pushed out of southern France, more than 40,000 French women were still working in Germany, many doing so to be with husbands captured during the fighting in 1940.[66]

It was not a big step from gathering and publishing war news and expressing opposition to government policies to forming cells of individuals opposed to a repressive regime and the living conditions it imposed. When the Germans and Italians invaded the Non-Occupied Zone in November 1942, all of France could see that Pétain had failed to protect the nation from its fascist oppressors. The domination intrinsic in foreign occupation was soon painfully evident throughout the South of France, as it had been in the Occupied Zone for 30 months. There seemed to many residents of Alpes-Maritimes no good reason to continue supporting Vichy. Pétain had lost his two primary levers against Germany: French colonies were already largely in Allied hands and the fleet scuttled itself at Toulon rather than fall under Nazi control. In addition, the Maréchal had demonstrated that he would not carry out the threat most feared by Berlin—defecting to the Allies. Banding together and organizing to resist by more than just the oppressed elements of Midi society was the next logical step.

Multiple ingredients were simmering for overt opposition to the occupation. Jews and other targets of Nazi genocide had the strongest motivation to strike back. Army officers repulsed by Pétain's ceasefire were already counted among the disgruntled, and the German-mandated dissolution of the Armée de l'Armistice in November 1942 removed any commitment French soldiers still serving might have honored to obey orders from the head of state not to confront the occupying powers. Socialists were primed to retaliate against wounds inflicted as a consequence of the Front Populaire. With notable exceptions, left-wing Catholics could not abide by their Church's support for the Révolution Nationale. Journalists, academics, and intellectuals rebelled against censorship. Housewives and city dwellers especially recoiled against the hunger and deprivation to which virtually everyone was being subjected. Discontent was reinforced by the rage of communists, now freed by severance of the Ribbentrop–Molotov Pact to oppose the Soviet Union's former ally, Nazi Germany. Full discussion of active resistance must wait, however, for the pot to boil over from heat generated by the Italian and German occupations of southeastern France.

3

𝕰𝕏𝕲𝕭

The Italian Occupation

"A glorious day" is how the announcement that the Allies were in North Africa was remembered by Philippe Erlanger, a Jewish French historian taking refuge in Nice and Cannes.[1] The Germans reacted three days later by crossing the Line of Demarcation and entering the former Non-Occupied Zone. As a concession to Mussolini, as well as to conserve his own troops for higher-priority missions, Hitler permitted 150,000 Italian soldiers in seven divisions to occupy seven southeastern departments in entirety, including Alpes-Maritimes and the Var, plus parts of four others and Corsica. By so doing, the Fuhrer was once again disappointing Maréchal Pétain who had asked specifically that Nice not be held by Italian troops.[2] On November 11 the Italians marched into Nice from the east along the three corniches, causing cancellation of the city's annual commemoration of the end of World War I.

General Mario Vercellino, commander of IV Italian Armata, reassured the people of Nice, "With the objective of preventing the soil of France from being a new theater of war, due to the landing of Anglo-American military forces, we are occupying temporarily the demilitarized zone."[3] The government at Vichy gave instructions to avoid incidents and welcome the Italians as "friends." Indeed, Prefect Marcel Ribière instructed his subordinates, "You are not occupied. The Italian troops are not occupation troops, but operation troops. That is the term you will have to use."[4] Leaflets dropped from military aircraft reassured "citizens of the zone Niçoise" but with a warning that "Italy, which is just with all those who are just, is, however, harsh with rebels every time they try to get away."[5] In Rome, Count Galeazzo Ciano, the Minister for Foreign Affairs, noted in his diary, "The march of the Italian-German troops is proceeding in France, and also in Corsica, without encountering the least opposition. The French people are certainly unrecognizable. I thought there would be some gesture of opposition, at least for the honor of the flag." When Ciano informed the French ambassador to Rome of the German–Italian occupation, the envoy is said to have responded, "The Germans are hard masters. You, too, will learn this."[6]

In a single day, Menton was transformed from an advanced base of fascism into its rear area. The commanding general established his headquarters there at the Hôtel Riviera. He assigned the 2nd Division to Nice, the 58th Division to Draguignan in the Var, and the 223rd Division initially to the coast at Cagnes. Subordinate elements were positioned up and down the coast—at Villefranche, Cap d'Antibes, Cannes, La Napoule, Théoule, and smaller towns.

Recollections of the arrival varied widely. Erlanger remembered, "An Italian regiment marched under our eyes with a martial step, bayonet on the barrel. Ah! those rooster feathers that I reproach myself to find stupidly pleasant, as do so many others. They appear as the dove of the Ark." A plume just did not look serious. One onlooker in Cannes recalled that they arrived "with the mandolin." Another eyewitness recounted, "These troops had to arrive by forced march which we could realize by seeing their tired faces and shuffling pace. More than their fatigue, these poorly appearing troops, uniforms dirty, mended, in shabby state, frayed leggings, shoes down at the heels." There was even mounted cavalry. "The horses of good enough size (1.6 meters minimum) were in a low state, dull hair, dirty coats, and bony ribs: they evidently suffered from the fatigue of war." A compatriot noticed, "They arrived with some trucks, they were looking for their cantonment area, they were very dispersed, not orderly."[7]

Joseph Aquilino recalled the first armored columns rumbling into Antibes along the national road. He climbed up on tanks stopped in front of the hospital and began distributing tracts, "Italian soldiers, do not fight your French brothers [...]" The officers were taken by surprise and did not react. No one arrested Aquilino before he ran off.[8]

With a large population of immigrants, Nice was accommodating, at least at first. Italian troops entered the city at 3.00 p.m. One spectator described hundreds of cheering people lining the streets. Another Niçois effused, "It is not even the officers, beautiful boys too well-groomed and elegant, some of whom representing Roman aristocracy, showing their proud faces, who don't inspire the least warlike idea, as much as the immoderate use of strong perfume which seemed to move them away from the cult of Mars."[9]

Some of the incoming soldiers found relatives in Old Nice, producing singing, drinking, and dancing late into the night. Under these circumstances a careful listener could pick up useful intelligence from voluble people. A child living in Cannes at the time remembered that she could not attend school under the Vichy regime, but when the Italians arrived she resumed her education as the daughter of a construction worker from the old country. The soldiers naturally whistled at the pretty women and pinched a behind whenever possible. Looking back, survivors of these times recount that, in contrast, German soldiers behaved properly and never initiated conversations with them. Conversely, the Italian occupiers could be arrogant. Their soldiers might hog the sidewalks, forcing pedestrians into the roadway. A teenager at the time in Toulon recalled Italian sailors boasting that they were the "winners," although he also said he could get away with throwing stones at Italian soldiers, but not at the Germans.[10]

The charm Italian soldiers could display was evident in reminiscences of Sospel during the occupation. The army unit arrived with clicking of boots and stiff-armed salutes, but the locals could not help but notice that the gardens along the national route they had traveled were stripped bare of persimmons and tomatoes. In contrast to the guttural Germanic tongue to follow, these invaders spoke a language not incomprehensible to the inhabitants, and not just those of Italian origin. Their uniforms even bore a slight resemblance to the French. Light infantrymen (*Bersaglieri*) dressed in black with feathers adorning their helmets. Crossing the town, it was not uncommon for them to burst into song. They celebrated mass at the Catholic church and even gave a rendition of "Lili Marlene," not unlike French troops. An unexpected by-product of the occupation was the appearance of young girls from a nearby village across the border, carrying packets of rice in their bodices to trade for Gauloise cigarettes.[11]

To one Italian officer, "The French population welcomed us silently, visibly motivated by a sentiment worse than hatred: contempt. The French were afraid of and detested everything in the German army, while admiring it; they did not fear the Italian army." Its soldiers were disparagingly referred to as "macaronis." He went on to comment that troops entering Antibes, Cannes, and Grasse all found the shops shuttered, few people on the street.[12] In addition, he and his comrades in arms would have noticed hotels and casinos closed, dark and dirty toilets, public gardens transformed into vegetable plots, and, when the populace did reappear, a profusion of bicycles.[13]

Confrontations commenced the following day. Women from the two zones in France, including a delegation from Nice, had organized a march on Vichy for November 11 to demand the return of prisoners and provision of more foodstuffs. As witnessed by one resident of La Trinité outside Nice, "Our husbands were prisoners of war, our only resource was 450 francs per month." Thousands of Niçois backed the pilgrimage by giving money to help pay for the trip. The sudden invasion by the Germans preempted the demonstration. The next day, pedestrians along the boulevard Jean-Jaures in Nice spontaneously erupted into "La Marseillaise" before a group of Italian officers. A group assembling on Place Masséna began chanting "Vive la France! Vive la République! Laval to the firing squad!" At the same hour, women who were communist sympathizers stopped working to symbolize their support.[14]

The populace was united in the belief that the only undefeated French army had been the one which fought the Italians in June 1940, and that the Bersaglieri who now arrived proudly with plumes on their hats would depart with the feathers attached to their behinds. This attitude was expressed in the words of an anti-Italian parody of "La Marseillaise" circulating on the Côte d'Azur: "Allons enfants de l'Italie / Le jour de fuite est arrivé."[15]

Undeterred, Vercellino had renamed a principal boulevard through Nice, "avenue de la Victoire," for his Duce despite the protestations of the mayor. (Ironically, after the war the thoroughfare would be rededicated as avenue Jean-Médecin.) One Niçois recalled overhearing Blackshirts boasting of having rebaptized the Promenade des Anglais "Lungomare [Promenade] Mussolini."[16] The army commander announced his intention to hunt down Freemasons, poorly regarded in Rome. Readying himself for the general's initial visit to his office, Médecin hastily displayed busts of Giuseppe Garibaldi and Maréchal André Masséna, both natives of the city considered their own by Italian nationalists. Reminded of these prominent Masons, the caller never raised the subject.[17]

The Pace of Civilian Life

After increasingly harsh treatment by a Vichy government trying to impress its German masters, the light touch of the Italians was almost a joy. As political and police repression imposed by Vichy was eased, however, hunger became a serious worry for the civilian population. Cessation of imports from France's colonies coincided with collapse of the Non-Occupied Zone. After the Allied landings there, ships from North Africa loaded with olive oil and wheat no longer docked at the port of Nice. Vegetable oil, salted fish, wheat, tomatoes, eggs, peanuts, wines, and other essentials virtually disappeared from store shelves. Fishing was prohibited at Cannes and elsewhere along the coast that December. (Consequently, a resident remembers seafood being especially plentiful in these waters once the occupation ended and fishing resumed.)[18] The quality of bread plummeted as more fiber replaced less grain, producing a foul-smelling concoction that putrefied after a single day. Boiled potatoes took the place of bread as the starch on some school menus. Cake was fabricated from birdseed. Vichy reduced authorized daily rations from 1,700 to 1,500 calories without noticeable effect on demand. Inhabitants who could afford to do so, turned increasingly to the black market, further driving up prices on the open market. Lesser price-gouging occurred in "gray markets," where the premium was half that charged by scalpers.

At first, the Italians themselves provided an alternative. Upon arrival, their army was well provisioned. For a price, like their American brothers-in-arms to follow, Italian soldiers offered residents cigarettes and other scarce and desirable commodities, such as pasta. Grocers of Italian origin profited by dealing with these military wholesalers. When the logistical pipeline from Italy dried up at the outset of 1943, the situation worsened. Bersaglieri turned from small-time businessmen to part-time thieves, stealing cauliflowers, potatoes, and even petroleum from the local economy when they could find it. Larger shipments of watermelons, zucchinis, and corn designated for Alpes-Maritimes also disappeared. In the spring the Toulon train station was found filled with wagonloads of foodstuffs, as well as bicycles, furniture, mattresses, watches, and clothes. The magnitude of these thefts was directly tied to the poverty of the army of occupation.[19]

In May, food rations dropped again, down to 100 grams of bread per day, 120 grams of meat per week, and 310 grams of fat per month. It is hardly surprising, therefore, that in January, February, and March, 82,000 packages were sent by relatives to families in Alpes-Maritimes to ease their hunger. During the first four months of 1943, 366 packages thought to contain nourishment passed through the train station at Antibes but never reached their destinations.[20] With 3,000 inhabitants, Juan-les-Pins was reduced to a single shopkeeper providing vegetables. Consequently, folks along the coast soon took matters into their own hands by going into the interior to help themselves from the fields. They might find leeks, onions, or beans, plus olives, of course. If he were lucky, a city dweller could encounter a peasant who raised pigs, chickens, or rabbits. Indeed, the Nice press estimated that 20,000 cyclists would pedal into the countryside to seek provisions during the summer of 1943.[21] The country folk were not as completely stocked with food as rumored and were known to barter after dark for meat and other scarcities, trading olive oil, fruit, potatoes, and vegetables from their kitchen gardens. The exchange needed to be clandestine as trading was considered illegal black-market activity.[22]

Famine became a serious problem. The mortality rate increased during the winter of 1942–3, especially among the elderly. A municipal soup kitchen opened in the Grand Hôtel in Antibes. The city's mayor asked flower-growers on the surrounding hillsides and Cap d'Antibes to devote their fields to production of victuals on a sliding scale from 30 to 50 percent, increasing with the size of the holding. A call for help from Alpes-Maritimes to other departments surprisingly produced some shipments of food, notably a carload of vegetables from farmers in the Department of Maine and Loire in northwestern France.[23]

Reminiscent of Paris in 1789, the anger of a starving populace flared up in Nice in April. The precursor was an unfulfilled promise of canned goods the previous month, so when a large order of pastries going to the prefecture fell out of a delivery cart spilling sweets onto the ground, the news quickly spread throughout the Old Town. Soon hundreds of women gathered in front of the former palace of the Sardinian kings that served as the prefecture and began chanting, "Milk for our children" and "We want bread, we are hungry." The prefect had the police disperse the crowd, but the next day the square was jammed with far more protestors. A delegation demanded to speak with the head of the department and, when refused, 10,000 women assembled in front of the police headquarters nearby singing "La Marseillaise" with a volume reflecting the intensity of their feelings. A meeting with the prefect resulted in only more promises, followed by additional demonstrations and, finally, the replacement of Ribière with Jean Chaigneau, a competent administrator.[24]

Military restrictions were not entirely unknown during this Italian interlude. From early on, circulation at the water's edge was prohibited between 8.00 p.m. and 7.00 a.m. The explanation was that this area was dangerous for the populace as Allied attacks were possible at any time. In Cannes, boulevard Alexandre III, Cap de la Croisette, Point de la Fourcade, and the underpass at La Bocca were all placed off-limits to civilians. During daylight hours, certain strands were restricted to bathing by soldiers. When the occupiers were ambushed by the Resistance, a curfew was imposed in that particular community. After a coup de main against three Italian officers in Nice in April 1943, the commandant closed theaters and cinemas and levied a fine of 3 million francs on the city, in addition to instituting a curfew. Violence directed against soldiers in Antibes in February, destruction of telephone lines in Saint-Laurent-du-Var, Beausoleil, and Cap d'Ail in March, and aggression against the military in La Trinité in May all led to clampdowns. One inhabitant explained his reluctance to violate the nighttime restrictions because Italian patrols sometimes fired without notice, creating real danger for the curfew-breaker.[25]

The cost of accommodating Italian forces went well beyond a few stolen rutabagas. The Italian Armistice Commission initially imposed an occupation indemnity of 1 billion francs per month. The following June, however, following the example set by the Germans, the demand increased to 1.5 billion on top of ongoing reparations being paid to the Reich. In addition, Henri Michel observed, "The Italians undertook widespread looting. The Italian thesis, expressed by quartermaster general [Raffaello] Operti, was that 'Italy occupied France to defend it and that it then had the right to French resources.'"[26] In the spring the occupiers decided that furniture and other valuables in public buildings should be handed over to the Italian state. In addition, wood, vegetables (23 tons per day), iron, and steel were sent eastward. In May, Italian authorities announced the requisition of automobile repair firms, factories making plaster and cement, and a limited number of bakeries. Several dozen locomotives and thousands of automobiles were seized, along with industrial machinery useful to the Italian war effort. The occupiers even confiscated a thousand mules.[27] The colonel in IV Armata overseeing the plundering declared, "After three years of pillaging you are still richer than we are today."[28]

The Allied landing in North Africa was a first step; replacement of the Vichy regime with fun-loving Italians seemed another half-step toward liberation. Then, the BBC began broadcasting reports, otherwise unheard, of the Battle of Stalingrad and the German defeat at El Alamein. As elsewhere in France, it gradually dawned on the people of the Riviera that Germany would, indeed, lose the war. Of course, no one knew how long fighting would last and who would be alive at the end. Meanwhile, in Vichy Maréchal Pétain began harboring greater fear of the threat to his territory from communism, which would become evident in the Southeast as the Italian occupation matured.[29]

Nizza Nostra

Early targets for the opposing forces of fascism and communism were the soldiers who marched into Alpes-Maritimes and over 80,000 inhabitants of Italian extraction. Officers were thought to be royalist, loyal to the diminutive, aging King Victor Emmanuel III rather than to Mussolini, so the propaganda campaign that followed was not intended for them but for the enlisted men. Médecin summarized his constituents' feelings regarding annexation by Italy: "What causes a lot of people to wish for the victory of the adversaries of the Axis is because they say it is better to live French thanks to the English than to become Italian due to a German victory."[30]

Ezio Garibaldi, descendant of the hero of Italian unification, had a running start on propaganda. As a general in the Fascist Milice (Militia), he had formed battalions named Nizza to agitate in Italy and founded a virulent daily newspaper, *Il Nizzardo*. The first exemplar, printed in Rome in March 1942, called for a "March on Nizza," conjuring up memories of the 1922 rally in the Italian capital that put Mussolini in power. Consequently, the annual fete of Jeanne d'Arc was transformed into an anti-Italian demonstration in Nice. The city covered itself in tricolores with some banners of a fifteenth-century virgin overprinted with the cross of Lorraine. The response from Italian nationalists was a ceremony in Torino to commemorate the 60th anniversary of the death of the patriot and liberator. Celebrants were told that "Garibaldi had great sorrow to see his birthplace [Nice] lost to Italy, but he died full of hope having a vision of justice in the future."[31]

Once Giuseppe Garibaldi's hometown was occupied in November, the next logical step for the radicals was annexation of Contea Nizza. Just after the invasion, Ezio called out, "*Vive l'Italie! Vive Nizza italienne!*" The time to recover the fatherland's lost territories had arrived. A compromise bandied about in 1943 called for detaching Alpes-Maritimes from France and joining it with the Italian Riviera to form an autonomous province called "Ligurie occidentale" (western Liguria).[32] The idea hardly assuaged the fears of patriotic Niçois. Blackshirts and Fascists, including a number of small shopkeepers intent on revenge against someone or other, gathered to plot at Casas d'Italia, Fascist meeting centers for Italians.

The extremism demonstrated by Italian Fascists not only failed to win the allegiance of most of their countrymen residing in *Comté de Nice* (County of Nice), it also outraged members of the French far right. To implement its political philosophy, Italian radicals formed Action Groups encompassing fascists of any nationality. These zealots were soon seen to be at odds with the military occupation's authority, Rome's diplomatic legation, and the Italian police. A harbinger of things to come, Action Groups undertook a purification program to sort out Italians with incorrect political views. But their intellectual and moral basis was weak and the informers so self-serving that the undertaking repulsed Franco-Italians rather than attracting them.[33]

In November, the Action Committee of the Italian People disseminated a tract addressed to newly-arrived officers and soldiers in Menton, Beausoleil, and Antibes: "The defeat of the Axis is from now on certain, inevitable [...] Like us, you want Italy free and independent, you want to save Italy from ultimate ruin [...] Desert, return in arms to your homes, hunt the Germans who ransack them, who make themselves masters of your wives and belongings [...] Live the fight of liberation of the fraternal peoples of France and Italy against the German oppressor."[34] Circulation of propaganda to the military continued well into 1943 with 83 versions of a leaflet *La Parola del Soldato* (The Words of the Soldier).

If Vercellino is to be believed, however, morale was less affected by these flyers than by bad news coming from Russia and Italy.[35] While not won over by these movements, some Italian officers demonstrated sympathy for the Allies confronting totalitarianism. These sources shared information with the French intelligence bureau in London through the local Resistance. On the Côte d'Azur, a high-ranking officer in charge of fortifications for IV Armata passed along precise information on coastal defenses, as well as maps of mines from Marseille to Menton. Another career Italian officer in Southeast France provided plans of German airports which led to the bombing of Orange in the Rhône Valley, destroying 47 warplanes along with petrol storage tanks.[36]

As soon as the Bersaglieri and Alpini mountain troops arrived, the Italian Communist Party had begun circulating handouts in Nice, Saint-Laurent-du-Var, and Beausoleil lauding the Red Army in Russia, calling for Mussolini's death, and advocating overthrow of the German presence in France and Italy. The local party identified an Italian sergeant who adhered to its political orientation and permitted distribution of propaganda to soldiers pleading for, among other measures, "an immediate separate peace for Italy with the United Nations."[37] The Nazi hierarchy took due note of pacifist leanings among Il Duce's troops.

This moment of relative freedom during the overall oppression of 1940–4 was evidenced in a mushrooming underground press. *Le Cri des Travailleurs*, a communist publication, exploded from 4,500 copies in Alpes-Maritimes in

1941 to 12,000 by the end of 1942. *Combat*, the newspaper published by the Resistance organization of the same name, began printing a Nice edition in late 1942.[38] Clandestine religious tracts blossomed as well. *Amitié* was the Catholic successor to *Temps Nouveau*, which had been suppressed. The *Cahiers du Témoignage Chrétien* was the work of a consortium including French Protestants. It might be concluded that here was a rebirth of the old revolutionary spirit of France.[39]

The regional organ of the Communist Party urged the women of Nice to demonstrate en masse with their children on the steps of public buildings, enter hotels and restaurants catering to the Axis, and vandalize warehouses containing food supplies destined to feed hungry mouths in Italy or the Boche.[40] Communist handouts in Alpes-Maritimes at the end of 1942 warned that all fathers, brothers-in-law, and male cousins would be shot, mothers condemned to forced labor, and children up to 17 years of age sent off for supervised education. No imagined horror was too extreme to rouse the proletariat to action.

Again, the opposition countered, this time led by *Le Petit Niçois*, a pro-Vichy daily. On March 13 it ran an article entitled "Do not play with the Milice!" criticizing French citizens who maintained political neutrality by telling themselves that a future communist state would provide everything. Stalingrad had revived public opinion in favor of severe socialism, and the Fascist Milice sought to scare the bourgeoisie with the evils of Soviet communism. Regularly reported by the press, chronicles of the LFC reaffirmed reactionary positions and exalted sacred values. On August 1, for example, with the Riviera sliding from Fascism into Nazism, the Légion addressed the fear that the world was truly upside down, but reminded readers that France was not over there, but here. "Only one country: LA FRANCE!" it cried out.[41]

Resistance and Countervailing Forces

Meanwhile, the laxness in Italian oversight encouraged dissidents in Alpes-Maritimes to take matters into their own hands through open resistance to the invaders. Attacks began on December 18, with an explosion on the railway at Cannes, and continued two days later with the first beating of an Italian Fascist at Villefranche. By far the most prevalent sabotage over the next nine months was directed against the rail system, especially at La Bocca, the principal repair yard along the Côte d'Azur, but targeting, as well, Fascist units, shops, and businessmen, a tanker in Antibes, a yacht requisitioned by the invaders in Cannes, and critical civilian infrastructure.

The foremost authority on the department's wartime experience, Jean-Louis Panicacci, has identified 224 acts of resistance during the Italian occupation,

130 involving weapons. This compares with 435 attacks, 224 armed, in the Var during the same period. In the most spectacular incidents, bombs were thrown into casements of the military messes at Antibes, Cagnes, and Nice in February–March 1943. Communications facilities, restaurants frequented by the military and the Italian Armistice Commission, naval oil storage at Antibes, and individuals or small groups of soldiers were all vulnerable to grenades. Panicacci attributes this surge in violence to Allied military trainers and weapons specialists inserted into the region, delivery of arms and explosives, formation of maquis, and improved organization within the Resistance.[42] Better coordination between *résistants* (resisters) in neighboring communities produced a string of nine attacks on the rail lines across the Riviera in August. But, certainly, the key to the escalating opposition was the permissive environment created by the Italian military command, in contrast with the control exercised earlier from Vichy and predating the firmness of the succeeding occupation. The friendly Bersaglieri were repaid for their gentility with hostility.

Predictably, the reaction to increased activity on the left was a stronger presence on the political right. The LFC, so proudly formed three years earlier to support the hero of Verdun, had fallen into lethargy. The Légionnaires' insignia was no longer common on berets and buttonholes. Five hundred adherents gathered for its anniversary in 1943, whereas ten times that number had participated the previous year and 50,000 the year before. In its place a more virulent body was emerging in Nice headed by Joseph Darnand. On the last day of February in front of giant portraits of Pétain, Laval, and Darnand at the Casino Municipal in Nice, a huge crowd formed to witness the birth of the successor organization, the Milice Française (or French Militia). Referring to the drama underway in Russia, Darnand dwelt on a growing fear by asserting, "At the time when the fate of Europe is being played out in the East, the most serious of the internal dangers threatens even the existence of France— communism." France should not count on foreign arms, he continued. Instead, it should regroup, shoulder to shoulder, for the fight for survival, and the new Milice offers its rank and file to this cause.[43]

Darnand soon turned the local branch of the LFC into a national para-police force of volunteers to fight the Resistance. During the Italian presence, 650 men, younger and more combative than the old soldiers, joined this sinister organization. A youth auxiliary, the Franc-Garde, also came to life. The LVFB, attired in German uniforms, met at the Antipolis cinema in Antibes with the commander of its African branch and a delegation of Italian officers. The firm control of the occupation government over such matters limited the Milice to preparation and dissemination of propaganda and participation in public ceremonies. One such event took place in the Antibes municipal council chambers in July when *Miliciens* decorated meritorious members before city leaders and the local curé. The Milice would assume even greater importance during the German occupation.[44]

In early spring another right-wing body was born. Most Frenchmen are brainwashed by "criminal propaganda" against collaboration, the rationale began. Consequently, it was said, a small group of patriotic, courageous, and disinterested men decided to band together with the objective of encouraging adhesion with the French state as represented by Laval, recalled as prime minister in April 1942, for the fight against hostile misrepresentations. Thus the entity Collaboration undertook to lead the people toward one France and one truth.[45]

A more ominous danger to French dissidents came from the Italian political police, the Organization for Surveillance and Repression of Anti-fascism (OVRA). The Italian counterpart to the Gestapo, the OVRA responded to sabotage with brutality rumored to be as vicious as its Nazi equivalent.[46] Created in 1926, the OVRA had financed and encouraged the fascist-leaning and conspiratorial Cagoule that attempted to overthrow the Third Republic in the 1930s in the Southeast as well as elsewhere in France. OVRA repression was played out against an economic backdrop of constantly shrinking consumer goods and elevated reparations to the two powers now occupying France.[47]

At first, its victims were adversaries of Mussolini taking refuge in Alpes-Maritimes; later, the OVRA targeted the French Resistance. The OVRA used a local Italian national to help eradicate an underground cell in Nice organized by a senator from l'Isère, resulting in 20 arrests. In the early morning hours of April 15, 1943, when the leader drove up to his garage, two "specialists" brought in from Grenoble executed him in three bursts from their sub-machine guns.[48]

Even though Rome prohibited hunting Jews in their occupied zone, Mussolini's enforcers had plenty of other targets—communists, résistants, Freemasons, and persons generally regarded as troublemakers: anyone perceived as constituting a threat. OVRA operatives must have salivated at the prospect of putting their hands on fellow countrymen living in France who succumbed to the enticements of enemies of the Italian state. Working out of Nice, OVRA agents seemed to appear at times all along the coast.

Automobiles, boats, and other means of transportation were commandeered. When the OVRA needed supplies, such as gasoline for its vehicles, the local police turned a blind eye to the theft that followed. Arrests were often arbitrary. Well over 1,300 people were questioned by carabinieri or agents of the OVRA. Of this number, 975 were imprisoned or deported, including Poles, British, Belgians, and Yugoslavs, in addition to Frenchmen and Italians.

As the Italian occupation progressed, torture by the OVRA, carabinieri, and their collaborators became more frequent. Persons arrested in Nice were taken for interrogation to the Italianate Villa Lynwood at 98, avenue de Brancolar in Cimiez. Over the entrance of the subterranean interrogation center was an inscription from Dante's *Inferno*: "Abandon all hope ye who enter." Prisoners were beaten with fists, feet, clubs, and rifles. A common punishment was to force someone to walk endlessly in small circles around a post with ankles manacled. Legs and feet received blows when the victim fell exhausted until being stood up again for more beating. Not only was Villa Lynwood used for this purpose, but torture chambers were also set up in a villa in Antibes, a caserne in Draguignan, and other places along the coast.[49]

Italian against Italian

The first attacks against the Italian army in the Var took place at Fréjus-Saint Raphaël at the beginning of 1943. The instigators were communists in the Francs-Tireurs et Partisans (FTP) who often cooperated with Gaullists in operations against the occupiers and in organizing patriotic demonstrations. The FTP found it was difficult for someone recently arrived from the old country to fire on an Italian soldier. One expatriate rationalized as follows: "They are the representatives of Italian Fascism in France. They are the occupiers. They should understand that they have nothing to do here and although they understand, it is necessary to shoot at them."[50]

In Alpes-Maritimes, Antibes was a particular hotbed of incompatible sentiments. Inhabitants of Italian extraction held conflicting political views. Two Catholic priests were known to be pro-Fascist. A prominent doctor was pro-Mussolini until Italy's declaration of war against France, then he and others began to oppose the dictatorship to the east. Anti-Fascists included 15 Antibois who had returned from fighting in the International Brigades in Spain. Their ranks included communists (some of the Stalinist brand), socialists, and even anarchists.

The longer the Vichy government was in power, the more it did to try to please the regime in Berlin, causing increasing unrest in communities like Antibes. The city participated in May Day demonstrations taking place across the Midi, including three young men from the local cell of the communist underground, Louis Piétri and two comrades.[51] Over several months, Piétri underwent military preparation from a Canadian named George, undoubtedly sent by the British to train the Resistance. Piétri learned to use and maintain weapons like the British Sten sub-machine gun and even the old American Springfield rifle. It was hardly surprising, therefore, that Piétri was eventually arrested along with 30 other Antibois. He remained in jail for two days in August 1942 before being sent to the prison in Grasse. After the Italian invasion in November, the court in Grasse dismissed the case, but Piétri remained under police observation.

Piétri noticed three inspectors following him as he left home on the morning of January 4, 1943. Arriving at the train station, he was suddenly surrounded by Blackshirts and soldiers of the occupation forces. The youth was taken away by the secret police and soon placed in a truck with three other detainees, all in chains. Arriving at Salel caserne in Sospel, the prisoners entered a cell furnished only with canvas field cots. Water running down the walls created what seemed to Piétri to be a humid Siberian cold. Inmates included Britons and Americans, foreign Jews, and others in the country illegally. Carabinieri guarded inside, Italian soldiers outside. Eventually the colonel in charge met with the Antibois and provided military mattresses and blankets from the French army. Questioned individually, they were told they had been taken into custody as "susceptible of causing [sic] public disorder in Antibes" on the recommendation of the mayor, police commissaire, and members of the clergy. Friends from Antibes were permitted to visit, and two carabinieri carried letters back and forth. Other arrivals from Nice, Monaco, Menton, and the Var soon filled the prison.[52]

Four months later, Piétri was transferred to the fort at Embrun, east of Gap in the Hautes-Alpes. There he joined 325 other Italian anti-Fascists, veterans of the International Brigade, and members of the Resistance of whom 248 were Azuréens. Among the detainees were the former mayor of Grasse and future mayors of Grasse and Cannes. As he did repeatedly when Niçois were rounded up and imprisoned, Médecin sent two vans of food for the prisoners from Alpes-Maritimes, and later Chaigneau obtained permission to visit the internment camps to improve moral and comfort. The prisoners soon learned that discipline varied according to the origins of the guards: troops from Sicilia and Napoli were mostly severe; those from northern Italy more flexible; and soldiers from Valle d'Aosta near the border were affable and spoke French.[53] Piétri's confinement was cut short by Mussolini's overthrow and indications that the Italian occupation would soon be preempted by the Nazis. On September 6, 44 prisoners were freed and scattered in different directions, some joining *partigiani* (anti-Fascist partisans) in Italy and others heading for the Vercors where they were hunted by a large force of Milice the following spring. Piétri went to the Var and organized an FTP company near Fayence.

As 1943 progressed, control by Italian authorities tightened when terrorist attacks increasingly targeted the occupiers. On the night of May 7–8 alone, 600 Italian policemen, aided by teams of Blackshirts organized by Ezio Garibaldi, arrested 300 résistants in Nice. Médecin convened an extraordinary session of the city council to express his strong objections:

> The recent police activities practiced by the occupation troops have provoked in our city the most vivid emotions. Numerous Niçois have been arrested and taken to destinations often unknown without [it] having been possible

to know the reasons for these arrests. At the present time, however, gossip has reached us on the fate of these civilian internees whose situation merits all our attention. We have the responsibility to watch over the existence of our co-citizens and the duty to help them materially in these difficult circumstances. Also the first concern of the City has been to take special measures to ease the captivity of Niçois held in internment camps. This material aid is only conceivable by sending to our unfortunate citizens various foodstuffs which they are completely lacking.[54]

When the OVRA finished with them, French captives were transferred for confinement to Sospel; Italians were imprisoned on the Ligurian coast. It was not unknown for Italian communists to break out in a rendition of the "Internationale" while behind bars. One such détenu (prisoner) recalled being assigned the task of convincing militants to join the communist maquis upon release.[55]

It was during this period of intensified police activity that the second-in-command of Polish network Anne, Georges Makowski, committed suicide in his fifth-floor apartment on the rue Verdi, Nice, when he heard the authorities arrive. "While he finished burning his papers, agents of the Gestapo accompanied by carabinieri forced open the door of his apartment. He had always said that he was afraid of talking if he were tortured; at the moment of being seized by the carabinieri, he jumped out the window."[56]

Heightened Unrest

As open warfare in France drew nearer, suspicion abounded. The proprietor of the luxurious Hôtel Réserve on the edge of the Mediterranean at Beaulieu decided to make the best of the absence of guests by digging a large swimming pool. Once the local Italian military commander learned of the project, he suspected the work had something to do with aiding British submarines or landing commandos. The explanation that the owner was preparing for postwar tourism carried no credibility with his interrogator or with the German occupiers who followed, and construction came to a halt.[57] Such was the paranoia in the Axis camp as the Allies racked up victory after victory, first in North Africa and, then, in Sicilia.

Two cases in Cannes are also worthy of note. One concerned Doctor Picaud, nicknamed "the doctor of the poor" and suspected of ties with the Resistance because of his political views. On April 4, 1943, he was taken prisoner in La Bocca, where he had helped the downtrodden, and then tortured at Villa Lynwood. In June, carabinieri in Cannes were undoubtedly delighted to nab Emilio Sereni, leader of the Italian Communist Party, and subject him to sadism in Nice.[58]

Signs of popular unrest with foreign occupation took many forms. At the end of Cap d'Antibes, fuel oil reserves for the Italian navy were ignited in March 1943. Ambushes against isolated soldiers harvested their arms and munitions considered contraband of war. On May 12, a bomb destroyed the Nice headquarters of the ultra-conservative PPF. Two months later an attack on a restaurant in Nice's rue Paganini targeted employees of the Italian consulate who customarily lunched there. These provocations produced counterattacks on the coast and farther away on the Glières plateau where 700 maquisards were killed, in the Vercors in Savoie, and in the Drome where Italian military units conducted offensive operations against the maquis.[59]

One historian tabulated 50 attacks against the railroad in Alpes-Maritimes during the three years ending June 1944. By no means were all successful, nine bombs failing to detonate. Still, under Italian occupation the rail line which transported troops and military matériel between Nice and Cuneo, Italy, was cut 23 times by local partisans. Locomotives were blown up at Nice's Saint-Roch depot in July 1943. That same month the British SOE reported that a cut in the Marseille–Ventimiglia line had interrupted transport of German troops to Italy for four to seven days. Railroad workers themselves were responsible for much of this sabotage.[60]

Public expressions included a demonstration at Place Masséna in Nice on Bastille Day, 1943, when Gaullists sang "La Marseillaise" while displaying the blue-white-and-red flag. Little girls dressed in the tricolore as well. Marching through ranks of police up avenue de la Victoire, the crowd of more than 1,000 Niçois only dispersed at boulevard Victor Hugo in the face of army machine gunners. The more zealous demonstrators shouted "Vive de Gaulle" and "Down with Laval and Hitler," leading to 20 persons being taken to the commissariat for questioning. In the port, small boats proudly flew French colors.[61] Exasperated by disintegrating public order, the Italians forced Médecin to step down as mayor.

There was no longer apprehension of Italians in uniform; only their OVRA agents in mufti generated terror. Perhaps the most brazen display of the growing confidence was the photograph a résistante had taken on the Promenade des Anglais beside British agents who had parachuted into France with Bersaglieri standing in the background. A "Madame Sainson," code-name Delilah, was also known to take tourist-type photos of escaped airmen and once posed in front of Italian soldiers at Nice with the sea in the background.[62] An episode in Cannes provided a different kind of daring. On August 16 at the Cannes-Mandelieu airstrip (today an airport for private planes), a test pilot took off for North Africa in a prototype SO-90 fabricated for the Germans by the French National Aeronautical Construction Company of the Southwest (SNCASO). Hidden aboard were his three sons and three other engineers. The daring defection was organized by the local Resistance. One of its members, Hélène

Vagliano, served as a messenger, circulating by bicycle through the area with a radio in the basket. Her task was to notify the Free French air force not to attack the plane as it flew out over the Mediterranean.[63]

The Burgeoning Allied Threat

The combination of Laval being appointed prime minister and the stationing of Italian troops on French soil strengthened Vichy's resolve to supplant Rome as Berlin's number-one partner in Europe.[64] In September 1942, Laval had authorized several hundred Gestapo agents to infiltrate the Non-Occupied Zone, although in Alpes-Maritimes the Gestapo was already at work. At Cannes, in addition to Villa Montfleury where torture was carried out, the Gestapo had set up operations with the OVRA in the Hôtel Gallia. Each morning during the Italian occupation, worried Cannois looked to its roof to ascertain that the Italian tricolor—green, white, and red, with the emblem of Savoie—was still flying from its staff to be reassured that the Germans had not taken total control of their city.

A number of people fled the growing Nazi threat, many melting into the countryside, some heading to Switzerland where their welcome often depended on wealth, and others risking imprisonment by going to Spain. Spaniards were open in declaring their intention of returning home to fight Franco. Léon Reinach, son of the Hellenist who built Kerylos, the stunning Greek villa at Beaulieu, was among those who chose the perilous road to Spain through the German-occupied Southwest.[65]

The departures were motivated in part by what civilians along the Côte d'Azur observed taking place. Initially, the Italians were content to occupy old French artillery batteries along the coast. Then defensive works began appearing, modest by comparison with the bunkers and blockhouses to follow. Long-range guns positioned at a high point north of old Antibes surveyed the waters from Fort Carré to Villeneuve-Loubet. Strongholds were also established on Cap d'Antibes and Iles de Lérins and at La Napoule, Théole, Saint-Raphaël, Fréjus, Sainte-Maxime, Saint-Tropez, and Cavalaire. The Château de Nice was transformed into one large artillery emplacement. Barbed wire encased the Italian command post on La Croix-de-Gardes, a pine-topped eminence behind Cannes.

Photographs of the coastline were forbidden unless accompanied by an Italian officer. Beginning in August 1943, possession of a weapon or radio capable of communicating with the Allies, or any other action initiated against the military occupation, carried a penalty of death. The attack on a German submarine chaser off Cap d'Ail and the sinking of the French freighter *Général Bonaparte* outside Nice added to the tension.

In the midst of growing anticipation along the coast, the Italian commander received word to requisition the Hôtel Negresco on the Promenade des Anglais, Nice's finest then and now, to accommodate Marshal Gerd von Rundstedt, commander-in-chief of Germany's western front. He arrived aboard an armored train on July 27. After first examining military preparations at Nice and Cannes, the marshal continued on to Menton where he checked the fortifications and watched a live-fire exercise. Two days later von Rundstedt departed after a visit described by an aide as "chilly, formal."[66] A follow-up inspection by General der Infanterie Hans-Gustav von Felber, the German army group commander, took place on August 2. Clearly, the Wehrmacht was sizing up the Mediterranean coastal defenses at a time when their Italian allies were crumbling at home.

When Mussolini was overthrown on July 25, soldiers in the Legnano Division reacted with joy, expressing their anti-fascism with raised fists and shouts of "Bandiera rossa" (The Red Flag). Nice was alive all night as women embraced Italian soldiers, dancing in the streets and granting additional favors. Tracts paraphrased the old adage, "Germany will fight until the last Italian," and asked, "Why not death for Hitler?" Vercellino directed his officers to fire shots in the air to re-establish order. At a conference in Bologne on August 15, the two supreme Axis commands agreed on the progressive redeployment of Italian troops east of the Rhône. The Legnano Division would be the first to return to Italy. The withdrawal into Italy was to be completed by September 9. Only the 223rd and 224th Divisions would remain in Comté de Nice, the area claimed as Italy by the government in Rome, with the River Var as the new demarcation line with German forces. Surprisingly, the Italian navy was allowed to stay in the port of Toulon. The Wehrmacht order of battle then began deploying along the right bank of the Var just across from Nice.[67]

In mid-August the Germans engaged in live-fire exercises into the sea at La Bocca and La Napoule. By the end of the month they were shipping construction materials by rail into southeastern France. The departing Italians thereby gave up all territorial and logistical responsibility.[68] With the concurrence of Vichy, during the early hours of September 3, a Wehrmacht military headquarters was established at Cannes along with a complement of soldiers. For some time a stream of German troops had been passing through Alpes-Maritimes to strengthen Italian defenses along the Ligurian coast. It did not require much imagination for the local populace to foresee a complete occupation by the Reich not far in the future.

The incoming commander of the 19th Army, General der Infanterie Georg von Sodenstern, received orders anticipating dissolution of the Axis.

> I was instructed not to expose the relation to our Italian neighbors to an "unnecessary" strain but to keep a watchful eye on our Ally, and to be

ready to intervene decisively in the event of his notorious offending against obligations stipulated by the treaty of alliance. If it should so happen, immediate disarmament and internment for the time being of the Italian units in question were to be carried through.[69]

It took three weeks before Vercellino would agree to meet von Sodenstern at IV Armata headquarters as divided allegiance to Mussolini appeared to the Wehrmacht leader to be paralyzing the Italian command.

The relatively minor modifications to the beloved Côte d'Azur, the absence of a serious campaign to enforce the STO, unwillingness to engage in rounding up Jews, and the easy-going nature of the Bersaglieri and Alpini, strolling along the streets in their distinctive, outsized black berets, all overshadowed the occasional thefts and other inconveniences experienced during the Italian occupation of the Riviera. There were worse fates than being subjected to rule by modern-day Romans as the populace in the Southeast would soon come to appreciate.

4

𝕏𝕏

The German Occupation

The announcement on September 8, 1943 of the Italians signing an armistice with Allied forces sent occupation troops in Alpes-Maritimes into high spirits. The conflict was over; they could go home to Italy and rejoin their families. French résistants were freed by the OVRA at Hôtel Gallia in Cannes. A Mentonais imprisoned at Imperia was released on condition that he remain "disinterested in political life" and "stay home at night." In some places the revelry carried on well into the wee hours, but the celebration was short-lived. By the next day a more somber mood prevailed as streams of soldiers flowed eastward employing every imaginable means of transportation. Civilians went to the Sospel caserne and found the remaining Italians all too willing for them to carry off abandoned equipment.[1]

The Invasion

The Wehrmacht was poised to react. Employing the 305th Infantry Division stationed in Cannes earlier that month, the Germans occupied the railroad station in Nice that first night. The only real fighting took place at this terminal defended by two Italian officers, four soldiers and four carabinieri against more than 60 assailants. In contrast, at the station in Antibes the next morning a convoy of Mussolini's artillery waited to depart while the Italians argued among themselves. The stationmaster and locomotive engineer stood by impatiently. Suddenly Germans appeared in two armored cars and captured the lot.[2]

German units quickly captured the garrison at Kellermann caserne in Grasse, headquarters of the Italian II Corps, arriving about 11.30 p.m. in vehicles with mounted machine guns. The commanding general was taken prisoner and his soldiers confined. Factories were searched for Italians the following morning. Without spilling any blood, the Germans captured detachments in neighboring communities and took charge of munitions depots. While French inhabitants looked on with curiosity, civilians of Italian extraction expressed grief at the sudden change of command.[3]

At Cannes the Germans also had little difficulty subduing the Italian garrison. The Wehrmacht's presence in the city reduced the chance for Bersaglieri to escape toward the border. Some soldiers tried to flee to the quai Saint Pierre but were halted by bursts of gunfire. Troops posted on Iles de Lérins were also seized. The Italians were assembled in the allées de Liberté where their belts and shoelaces were taken, an indication of the humiliation they would suffer as German prisoners of war. Five patrol boats arrived at the city docks and their Italian crews captured, the Kriegsmarine commandeering the vessels. Members of the Italian Armistice Commission seated at the Hôtels Genève and au Méditerranée were also detained. During a month's time at least 10 Italian officers and 400 soldiers were deported.[4] Thirty other officers and ten troopers avoided the same fate by agreeing to fight alongside the Germans.

The conquerors did not represent the flower of the German army, and the Italians were superior in number and artillery power. Perhaps in the absence of orders from Rome, General Vercellini chose not to organize a defense and conduct an orderly withdrawal. Instead, members of the 224th Division posted at Nice headed for the border, abandoning uniforms and kit as they went. The carabinieri gave away heavy arms and munitions to the gendarmerie at Saint-Étienne-de-Tinée. At Garavan on the border at Menton, gardeners working at villas chose from among abandoned rifles, cartridges, helmets, knapsacks, and even new cleats. Naturally, members of the Resistance also acquired military matériel or destroyed what could not be carried before the new occupation forces recovered the spoils. Twenty mortars and two 75-mm. artillery pieces were spiked at Nice and eight additional cannon at Menton.[5]

In sum, more than 52,000 Italian soldiers were taken prisoner.[6] After the war, the commanding general of the 19th German Army clearly recalled the sense of desolation.

> Everywhere, the appearance of a young German officer or even of a sergeant along with a few soldiers had sufficed to induce whole Italian battalions to deliver up their arms. Readiness to fight on—which meant to continue doing duty in the defensive installations which were not endangered in any sense—was found only in the case of isolated batteries, the men of which quite plainly appeared to base their choice mainly on the hope of more pleasant conditions of life with us [...]
>
> Finally, even the Italian officers did not see properly what they should fight for! In 1940 they had been ready without much thinking to participate light heartedly in a little victorious campaign in Southern France and to bring back home a few morsels of the French Riviera, but they never felt an internal urge to help enduringly to bear that burden which the Germans had

chosen to take upon themselves. I think, therefore, it would not be justified to simply cast any aspersions on the Italian forces because of their behavior in the fall of 1943.

The incorporation of the disarmed Italian soldiers as workmen in the German front as well as in construction detachments in the rear of the front was executed without any friction worth mention. Generally speaking, they remained just a liability.[7]

The prefect of Alpes-Maritimes issued a warning three weeks later informing the population that all Italians in plain clothes belonging to the "occupation" troops were remaining in an illegal status. To shelter or aid them in any way was an act of complicity. The German military command would apply the harshest punishment, including death, to persons found concealing fugitives. That did not prevent residents of Italian origin from establishing an "underground railroad" which enabled one family in Antibes, for example, to provide mufti to fugitive Bersaglieri and lead them under cover of darkness to another guide at Villeneuve-Loubet. In turn, he passed the refugee to other sympathizers until they crossed the border.[8]

It is interesting to note the way the German military command viewed its own occupation as contrasted with how others may have seen it. With troops scattered throughout southeastern France, the 19th Army took pride in mid-1943 in the positive relations established with a resident population which, in turn, exhibited "friendliness and good sense, always keeping up a dignified reserve at the same time." A year later the new commanding general was impressed that his soldiers were "well-disciplined and in good order," after he issued strict orders respecting misuse of civilian property. Again, the relationship with local residents was characterized as "good and correct," an assessment shared by the Army's chief of staff.[9] This attitude, if accurate, may have reflected the civilians' initial innocence and humanity toward the occupiers expressed so well by the Russian Jewish authoress Irène Némirovsky in her 1942 characterization of relations between the two nationalities in rural France.[10]

German army intelligence, the Abwehr, was also present. Detachments of its agents worked out of Nice, Grasse, Toulon, and Hyères. A battalion of special forces in the Brandenburg division set up in Marseille and Toulon and used Armenians, Azerbaijanis, Ukrainians, and the like to infiltrate cells of résistants. The Siecherheitsdienst, the security service apparatus of the Gestapo, posted men in Menton, Gap, and Digne in the Southeast as French gendarmes were considered unreliable. On October 19, for example, German soldiers surrounded Filley caserne of the Nice gendarmerie and apprehended the leaders and men who did not cooperate, plus the female employees. The secretaries and telephone operators were only freed a week later.[11]

The Gestapo established its headquarters in Nice at the old Hôtel Hermitage with an annex for intense interrogations at Villa Trianon on the heights of Cimiez a kilometer away. Only 15 agents initially arrived, but they were reinforced by white Russians and the Action Group of the PPF. Unlike the Gestapo, the Russians were considered especially effective as they could blend into a crowd without being easily recognized. Pro-Nazi organizations, such as the Action Group, Milice, and the Popular Party's social justice auxiliary, totaled about 150 members in Nice and 50 in Cannes. Some inhabitants also helped the new masters of Nice. Barmen, barbers and brothel keepers were used extensively to learn about résistants. A surprising indication of the sentiments of some Niçois was revealed when the commandant sought 40 women to act as informers and received 300 applications. Anonymous letters denouncing residents were other expressions of pro-Nazi attitudes.[12]

Initially under the German occupation, southeastern France was defended by the 715th Infantry Division led by Lieutenant General Otto von Kohlermann. When the Wehrmacht faced a far greater threat in northern France in 1944, the 715th redeployed and its mission was assumed by the 148th Infantry Division commanded by Generalmajor Otto Fretter-Pico. The successor was centered at Grasse and composed of reservists, Austrians and, Poles. Its 8th regiment headquartered at the Hôtel Atlantic in Nice was commanded by Generalmajor Hellmuth Nickelmann. Military engineers, along with Organization Todt, commenced construction on what the Germans called the "Wall of the Mediterranean." Along the border with Italy were troops called "customs agents" who, in fact, were old soldiers or men wounded on the Russian front and no longer fit for arduous duty.

An articulate and learned observer of the new occupying force was the curator of Nice's elegant Musée Masséna, Pierre Nicot de Villemain. His record, written immediately after the war, described the Wehrmacht soldiers as "nearly children or very aged from the last farms of the Landsturm [local militia in the 148th Division]. Uniforms and shoes (boots) worn, magnificent discipline, but very low morale, the men have a sad and worried look." He continued, "In the tramway, the kind of transportation that the Germans use a lot, the soldiers were silent, taciturn, but always stood up to give their seat to the ladies or to old people, helping them to climb in or out." The narrator recounted that he rarely saw a tipsy German soldier.[13]

These troops patronized brothels set up for them in Nice at the Hôtel Métropole and in Cannes at the Hôtel de Paris where hygiene was monitored by military doctors. For this reason and the Wehrmacht's rigor, there were fewer incidents of rape and assault than when the Italians occupied these communities. Consequently, in one way the populace was less anxious about the new occupation troops than previously.[14]

Fortifying the Riviera

Taking photos of the littoral was forbidden in October. Over the subsequent ten months, beaches and plains suitable for amphibious vehicles, landing aircraft, or paratroopers would be seeded with more than 100,000 mines and traps, a density of almost 100 devices per acre. At the top of the list were Nice with 44,722 and Antibes with 11,096 obstacles and explosives.

The Nice Château between the old town and harbor was barely recognizable. Trees were cut down to improve fields of fire, and steps dug up to use the stones for blockhouses. Trenches and tunnels zigzagged here and there. Three horizontal galleries for cannonry faced the sea, the port to the east, and Hôtel Suisse, now headquarters of the Kriegsmarine. On a polygon sat a battery of artillery pieces and machine guns. At other points in the Château were flamethrowers and mortars which would fire on Old Nice and Boulevard Carabacel during the liberation. Two wells ensured a supply of water and a shower. Everywhere else there were mines.[15]

In November, circulation was prohibited on the Promenade des Anglais; denying access to the quai des Etats-Unis came next. Another casualty was Léon Gambetta, a heroic statesman during the Franco-Prussian War, whose statue was pulled off its pedestal to reuse the bronze. The Germans did not think twice about carting off to the smelter a metal church bell or cast bronze effigy but drew the line at military figures whose memorials, regardless of war, were left standing. The most disheartening demolition was the Casino de la Jetée-Promenade in March 1944. Dating from 1891, this elaborate entertainment center was the epitome of the Belle Époque with restaurants, dance salons, and gambling club on a platform of 65,000 square feet hovering over the sea on 250 pylons. Its image was featured on virtually every advertisement for vacationing in Nice. The 4,000 tons of iron in its steel girders were used for antitank barricades erected throughout the region.

Moving westward, the mounds of boulders beside the coastal railroad tracks between Villeneuve-Loubet and Antibes was removed rock by rock and transported elsewhere to construct blockhouses and bunkers for the Mediterranean Wall. In Antibes the Wehrmacht housed its troops in a large villa and abandoned factory in the Croix Rouge district. Anti-aircraft guns were perched high nearby at Les Trois Moulins. Pine trees on the elevation at La Garoupe on Cap d'Antibes fell to the woodman's axe for improved observation, and the semaphore there was blown up shortly before the Allied landing. The wharves at Golfe-Juan were also demolished to facilitate emplacement of explosives.[16]

Reconfiguration of Cannes began in November when civilian access was prohibited to Iles de Lérins. The monks inhabiting the historic monastery on Ile Saint-Honorat were seen crying as they came ashore and sent to a villa in the Californie district. Municipal services were relocated from the *hôtel de ville* to the Hôtel Continental. Palm Beach casino was converted into a bunker, and blockhouses built all along the Croisette. The Citroën showroom on this prominent way closed due to the pillbox constructed immediately in front of it. The lighthouse was destroyed to prevent it from serving as a reference point for enemy attackers by air or sea. Mines lined the jetties. The port was fitted with an anti-submarine net that also obstructed civilian craft. Special provision had to be made for the numerous vessels requisitioned by the Germans to transport sand and cement necessary for construction.

Defensive works completely disfigured a coastline so beloved for its natural beauty and tasteful development. A concrete wall ran along the seaside from Cannes to Mandelieu and blocked streets entering onto the quai des Etats-Unis in Nice. Hundreds of pole mines and concrete tetradrones from Antibes to La Bocca protected against tanks debarking from landing craft. Residents used the common nickname "Rommel's asparagus" to refer to the fraise or pointed stakes cut from trees in the Var and implanted at an angle along the shore.[17]

Boulevard Carnot and its college in Cannes were turned into anti-aircraft batteries and bunkers. The observatory was naturally commandeered. The militarization was not without problems, however. Like many of the old soldiers sent to the South of France, a number of the artillery pieces were antiquated. Obtaining fuel for vehicles became difficult as sources available to the Wehrmacht were the targets of mounting air attacks.[18]

Where there were insufficient laborers or material to construct defenses, the Germans erected credible imitations. Colonel Paul D. Adams commanding a regiment in the US 36th Infantry Division recalled:

> The map of the German fortifications along the coast there clear over to Cannes was such that I wouldn't show it to my battalion commanders [...] I just couldn't believe it. There was just too much of everything on the map and I was right. It turned out that what the Germans had done, while they defended this coast over to and including the town of San Raphaël [...] they had mock defenses set up running clear to Cannes. Most of the antitank guns were nothing in the world but the light poles from Cannes with the top cut off of them and set up so they photographed looking pretty much like an antitank gun. A lot of these works they had were just camouflage, if you want to call it that.[19]

There was a strategic target of utmost importance just west of Cannes. The viaduct of Anthéor was the most vulnerable point on the rail line connecting Marseille and Nice. It was first struck from the air on the night of September 16–17, 1943. Sixty-five feet high at the center of its 450-foot length, only two of the nine brick arches were down at the time of the Allied landing as the structure was rapidly repaired after each bombing. In March 1944 local intelligence reported 50 armed Germans at the viaduct, plus 150–200 French workers and former Italian soldiers guarding and rebuilding the bridge. Consequently, it was extremely difficult for guerrillas to plant explosives, and they called instead for continued aerial attack, yet the interruption to traffic never lasted for long.[20]

To protect the shore from sabotage required evacuation of this sensitive area. The first step on September 20 was to deny foreigners access to the coast. The opera house in Nice was transformed into a city evacuation center and the municipal casino into a warehouse to store clothes and furniture of the displaced. Neighborhoods around train stations, ports, and factories working for the Reich were also off-limits. Persons not indispensable to the life of Nice were encouraged to leave the city in early December, and schools transferred to the suburbs. By the end of January, children 7–14 years of age were evacuated. Henri Matisse and Pierre Bonnard each contributed 25 original lithographs for a sale to benefit youngsters moved from the Riviera. By the time of the Normandy landings, 30,000 inhabitants had been relocated, voluntarily or forcibly. Only special categories of residents were exempted such as pregnant women and mothers of children under five years of age.[21]

It was difficult for all these people to find lodgings elsewhere, and the problem was exacerbated by movers charging exorbitant prices. Once again, the communists rose up in opposition. The Boche want free access to the littoral, they exclaimed, and they also want to empty the cities of patriots. "To leave is to desert." Against all evacuations and deportations, a tract cried out, "organize resistance, go on strike, and undertake an armed fight."[22]

To complete the Mediterranean Wall required more laborers than the Wehrmacht could muster. Men between the ages of 16 and 60 and childless women from 16 to 45 were drafted to help in the work. When the number from his constituency reached 700 a day, Antibes Mayor Jules Grec reacted angrily to dragooning men and women: "As a result, in the country there are no longer workers as there should be, the economic life of the city is paralyzed, an unfavorable food situation will really become critical."[23]

Yet waivers were granted to enterprises important to the Nazi war effort. In Alpes-Maritimes the number of industrial units protected from the involuntary draft of workers reached 62. Employees of the Aciéries du Nord, SNCASO, the postal-telephone-telegraph system, and the railroad were all exempted. So were automotive repair shops, factories making construction material, metal works, electrical enterprises, and forestry concerns. The Chantiers Navals (marine works) at Antibes that built and maintained watercraft for the Kriegsmarine, including construction of wooden patrol boats, was considered vital. Another critical facility in Antibes shipped sausage bombs to an aircraft factory west of Marseille. Informal exemptions were made for workers in the building trades, fishermen, and waiters and waitresses serving German officers, encouraging a sub-rosa industry in fabricating false documents certificating employment in these various capacities. This subterfuge suffered a serious blow in February 1944, however, when 66 alleged "employees" of the aircraft factory were arrested.

By then, however, the demand for skilled workmen in Germany caused the Nazis to requisition 325 specialists (47 percent) from the workforce at the Southwest aviation complex, threatening the continuing viability of that plant and research facility outside Cannes. In total, the department lost 7 percent of its skilled laborers during the German occupation, bringing to 24 percent the proportion of workers taken from the department.[24]

The alternative to being shipped to a German factory under the STO was not always easy. Shifts lasted ten hours three times a week. Working all night with a spade, a man was expected to dig holes three meters deep along the shoreline. Other laborers constructed fortifications and reinforced buildings damaged by Allied bombs. One boy recalled his father being sent to the Camargue to erect cables, pylons, and other devices to prevent landings by gliders. The worst job was walking along train tracks to identify mines placed by the Resistance. It was not unknown for an engine to appear suddenly and crush a lookout on a trestle unable to escape.[25]

"Collabo"

This term of derision derived from the word "collaboration" which entered the popular French vocabulary when Pétain first used it in a radio address after his sole meeting with Hitler in October 1940. "It is in honor and to maintain French unity [...] that I enter today on the road of collaboration [...] This collaboration has to be sincere [...] I have spoken to you up until this day the language of a father, I speak to you today the language of a leader. Follow me [...] It is I alone who history will judge." "Kollaboration" became a new entry in German parlance, as well.[26] Did a Frenchman collaborate if he took a German wounded by an American bomb to the hospital, or was he simply a humanitarian? The derogatory label was more frequently used.

Clear collaboration took many forms. There were *collaboratrice horizontales*, women who slept with Germans. A notorious example from the French Riviera was Florence Gould, a San Francisco divorcée who married the son of an American robber baron and railroad magnate, 18 years her elder. Living on the Cote d'Azur, he developed the elegant Hôtel Provençal in Juan-les-Pins and the Palais de la Méditerranée in Nice. Preferring the Parisien social swirl during the war years, Florence was rumored to have taken a succession of German lovers at her apartment in a trio of block stone buildings at 129 avenue Malakoff.[27]

Frenchmen associated with Germans in myriad capacities. At least 10,000 persons throughout France served as managers of assets confiscated from the Jews. By 1944 Organization Todt and the Wehrmacht employed a half-million laborers. Military units in Alpes-Maritimes alone used 1,800 civilians in administrative tasks.[28] Many of these employees were motivated simply by the need for money to put food on the table.

A case study in Alpes-Maritimes is a man who identifies himself as Louis Martin. He said he joined the Abwehr in late 1943 when he was 18 years old and the Germans had taken control of the Italian corner of France. Martin justified his decision by saying that 50,000 Niçois worked for the Germans to earn money on which to live. He claimed there were 30,000 men across France enrolled in Hitler's army. Why do so? He hated communists, he said. Martin was in Normandy in the summer of 1944 and moved across northern France as the Wehrmacht was pushed back. When the war ended he was in Germany and served five years in prison, first there and then in France.[29]

The most despised collaborators were members of the Milice attired in dark-blue uniforms. The Milice accepted all those seeking to join, being especially attractive to mercenary young thugs and hoodlums, 18–23 years old. The leaders were notables, conservatives, strong Catholics, and even nobility—anti-communists all. The Milice served as a breeding ground for joining the Waffen-SS[30] the following year. Across France the Milice counted 25,000 adherents; in Alpes-Maritimes, the number of Miliciens remained under 700 men. At first, adherents were limited to producing propaganda.[31] After German control became dominant throughout the southern zone, the organization assumed police powers to counter the perceived threat from communists, Jews, and Freemasons.[32] A permanent Milice patrol armed with sub-machine guns protected the rail service at the Nice station, for example. Indeed, one leader of the Resistance reported that the Milice was used to check the reliability of French police.[33] Miliciens knew their locales better than the Germans and could eavesdrop on fellow citizens more easily than the Gestapo. And, they were notorious for never taking prisoners. In sum, their activities might be described as Frenchmen hunting and betraying Frenchmen.

An example of why the Milice was hated more so than the occupiers in many instances concerned a woman from Monaco and her friend who went to Menton, Garavan, and the rural area beyond to look for food. Returning home with their precious acquisitions, they passed by German soldiers who took no notice. But members of the Milice suddenly appeared and confiscated the produce. The women were charged a fine for frequenting the black market.

The Miliciens proceeded to divide the money and booty among themselves in front of their victims.[34] A cinematic caricature was presented by director Louis Malle, *Lacombe, Lucien* (1974), telling the story of a dull young rustic who joined the Milice after being refused admission to the Resistance.

Many years after the war, Camille Rayon admitted that he was more apprehensive of the French citizenry than their German occupiers. This included the Milice. The Germans were usually in uniform, but, dressed in mufti, collaborators could not be identified as such. Rayon said when he recognized old acquaintances on the streets of Antibes where he grew up, he could not be certain of their allegiance. So he would walk right up and announce, "You're dead," meaning that one word passed to the Gestapo would bring immediate death.[35]

In his analysis of collaboration in Alpes-Maritimes, Jean-Louis Panicacci found that membership in the SOL and Milice was essentially an urban phenomenon. More than half the members were from Nice. Most of the remainder came from mid-size cities and towns. He identified three common threads in the membership: they were either Pétainists; monarchists, fascists, right-wingers, and anti-communists; or supporters of a new order determined to fight the black market. Two groups constituting the most extreme collusion with the Nazis were the Waffen-SS, known as the "black order" for its cruel execution of German occupation policies, and Groupe Collaboration. The former was attractive to youth; conversely, 70 percent of Groupe Collaboration were over 45 years old. Laborers tended toward the Waffen-SS and LVFB. These movements demonstrated that manual workers were well represented in French fascism. On the other hand, teachers tended to join the Rassemblement National Populaire and Groupe Collaboration, reflecting their age. Interestingly, the latter was the only organization with a sizeable component of women, attributed to its major activity being planning and holding conferences.[36]

By the end of 1943 the Resistance became bolder, with Allied successes on battlefields across Europe and North Africa bringing closer the day when the Riviera would be liberated. A natural target for attack was the collaborator. Another became the Ost Legions composed of Eastern Europeans forced into military service, especially Armenians. An underground group focusing on these conscripts was the Committee for Free Germany, with a communist cell in the Var headed by a nurse who had served with the International Brigades in Spain before working as a chambermaid in Les Arcs.[37]

Martin confided that a reward eventually reaching 10,000 francs was offered to anyone who shot a collaborator. The bloodletting frequently led to reprisals. Supporters of the German occupation naturally became nervous, desperate, and intent on exacting revenge, which caused the death toll among civilians to climb.

The fratricide began on November 24, when the national secretary of the PPF and adjunct mayor of Nice was shot dead on the steps of Saint-Roch hospital in Nice. Four days later, five Miliciens were killed and four others injured by a grenade explosion at a meeting held by Joseph Darnand and Philippe Henriot, Pétain's Minister of Information and the voice of Radio Vichy. Retaliation came the night after Christmas, when six résistants in prison for the assassination of another member of the PPF were taken away and murdered on prominences overlooking Nice, including the picturesque Observatory Hill. The bodies were discovered along a public road with little cards pinned on their clothing saying "The Anti-terrorist Committee." The person thought to have organized these reprisals, the division inspector of the PPF, died five days later in an "accident" perpetrated by the Resistance near Avignon.

In February 1944 the chief of the Milice was killed in Nice, and in revenge the author of a virulent article castigating the movement was kidnapped from Saint-Jean-Cap-Ferrat. His bullet-riddled body was found the next day. As the Milicien press screamed for more reprisals, its departmental secretary was murdered as well, "cowardly in the shadows" according to right-wing propaganda.

Confrontations became even more newsworthy in March when three members of the FTP-MOI engaged in a shoot-out with police from a building on Nice's rue de France. The résistants were active saboteurs in Antibes and had recently killed an identity-control agent at a roadblock. Over several hours of fighting, two officers and two terrorists died. The lone survivor, blinded and left with one leg, was condemned to death by a Milicien court-martial and executed at the Nice jail by a half-dozen gendarmes. The PPF distributed notices urging the populace to attend the funeral service for one policemen en masse and make monetary contributions to families left destitute by the bullets of "commo-terrorists."[38]

Then, the Milice spearheaded a campaign against Jean Médecin, manhandled and injured by former members of the SOL on June 17. Less than two weeks later, Médecin was picked up by German authorities as a Gaullist and taken with 60 other Niçois to confinement at Fort Hatry in Belfort, just south of the Vosges. The subsequent torture of résistants at the Nice headquarters of the Milice and the PPF earned the new leader of the political party contempt as "the man with the whip."[39]

The violence was not limited to Nice. The Resistance murdered two German collaborators in Antibes on January 31 and March 17. In return, the FTP of Antibes was targeted by fascists during the spring and summer, bringing death to 20 of its members. In late July, six youngsters armed with sub-machine guns killed the mayor of Lantosque, a Légionnaire and member of the PPF, while at home with his wife and son. In another incident, Nazis hung the photogravure of *L'Eclaireur de Nice*, who also secretly worked for *Combat*, in his jail cell. In all, during the German occupation, the Gestapo, aided by the Milice and PPF, was responsible for 1,229 arrests and 184 summary executions in Alpes-Maritimes.[40]

Martyrs were proclaimed by both sides. On May 29, a funeral was held at the Antibes cathedral for six citizens who died three days earlier in an attack on a train crossing the River Var. "Man is no longer only a wolf against man," the curé lamented. "He has made progress in science which serves to massacre entire populations."[41] The ultimate demonstration in Antibes by the faction in power took place on July 4 at a memorial service for Henriot who had finally been murdered in Paris along with his family. A large crowd gathered which included a delegation from the PPF, the president of the Légion d'honneur, and six municipal counselors notorious for collaboration.

Allied Preparatory Bombardment

A plaque at the Sanctuaire Notre-Dame de Laghet, a pilgrim destination located behind Monaco and La Turbie, offers thanks for the lives of the parishioners of Saint-Laurent-du-Var who were spared during 23 air raids beginning on November 14, 1943 and continuing until its liberation. The community was especially vulnerable, situated on the west bank of the River Var beside two bridges, rail and roadway, serving as the main conduits over the water. In 1944 in preparation for the invasion 11 days later, a deluge of bombs fell on Nice and the surrounding area including Saint-Laurent-du-Var. The largest bombardment occurred on August 8, when 50 airplanes flying at 10,000 feet hit spans at both ends of the bridging but did not completely shut off vehicular traffic. The quarter near the town's railway station, however, suffered 65 deaths.[42]

Aerial bombing of communities along the Côte d'Azur had begun at Cannes on the clear night of November 11, 1943. Choosing the anniversary of the fascist invasion of the Non-Occupied Zone may not have been coincidental. At 10.21 p.m. the first in a formation of 20 four-engine RAF Lancasters appeared overhead and dropped flares to mark eight targets. Then, from 1,500 to 4,500 feet overhead, for one hour 35 minutes more aircraft released bombs weighing 250 or 500 pounds each, plus incendiary devices. The railroad repair yard was struck and several storehouses destroyed. The Aciéries du Nord lost only a few roofs, so the interruption in fabricating military matériel for the Reich lasted only three weeks. Other industrial concerns, agricultural facilities, and public buildings were also damaged. Houses collapsed, windows broke, and tiles fell down. Damage to the civilian population was far more severe. Of the 45 deaths, 13 were children. Another 278 people were left homeless and 2,000 residents suffered other losses.

The air-raid warning sirens did not sound initially, and inhabitants gleefully watched the bombardment from their windows as though viewing a fireworks display. The fascination with air power quickly turned to panic, however. A lasting effect was the rancor generated among a populace for whom the Allies had lost credibility. From then on, the day was remembered as "black Thursday." A series of later aerial attacks and one by a submarine against the aircraft factory at La Bocca never erased the memory of that initial storm over Cannes.[43]

Applying their experience with air raids in Berlin, after the failure of alarms during the first bombing the Germans utilized church bells for a general alert. Residents set up shelters in caves, emptied attics of inflammables, and packed sacks of sand onto upper floors to help absorb the impact of explosions. Elderly men and boys too young to leave home put on helmets, mustard-gas masks, and brassards marked "DF" for Defense Passive (or civil defense) and patrolled the streets after dark on the lookout for violations of blackout restrictions, among other infractions. Windows painted blue were covered with draught-proof, reinforced paper to contain shards of glass in case of shattering. Engineers constructed shelters, dug trenches, and destroyed walls likely to crumble during an attack. Safe havens were marked with large black letters painted on an outside wall. The population on the sea side of the tracks in Cannes was instructed to move away from the shoreline during a crisis, using underpasses beneath the railroad to flee toward communities in higher elevations.

Looking ahead to a possible landing from the Mediterranean, the frequency and intensity of carpet bombings by American warplanes increased on the South of France. One Niçois remarked that the citizenry did not seem to mind when the office for compulsory work in Germany was destroyed in one such raid. Another recalled that bombing the Nice harbor did not do much naval damage but the percussions irritated inhabitants by breaking windows.[44]

On May 25, 1944, a squadron of 36 American B-24 Liberators was returning to its base in Italy from a bombing raid on Lyon. Chased by the Luftwaffe, one of the planes was hit by a coastal battery over Cannes about 2.00 p.m. and the pilot killed. Members of the crew began jumping out and were fortunate not to be wounded by rifle and machinegun fire directed at their parachutes floating down. Upon landing they were immediately captured by the Germans to the dismay of gendarmes rushing to the scene to rescue them. Suddenly, a violent explosion erupted in the parasol pines on the 540-foot heights of La Croix-des-Gardes behind the city. Before exiting the plane, the copilot blocked the controls to steer the stricken craft away from the populated area. Today a monument on the precipice remembers his heroism.[45]

For many Niçois, the next day was the worst of the war. Another bombing mission left more than 300 people dead, 480 wounded, and 100 missing in

Nice. Another 5,600 residents suffered in other ways, many left homeless.[46] Thousands more suffered as houses were left without water, gas, or electricity. The attacks came in two waves, targeting the freight depot at Saint-Roch and Establishments Michel beside it, a large repair facility for rolling rail stock. A student engaged in sports with his classmates at a nearby stadium recalled the roar of engines as bombers flew overhead in formations of four at 10.20 a.m.[47] One survivor remembered, "Suddenly, a part of the house collapsed. I did not know what happened to me. Huddled in the middle of the rubble, I hurt everywhere, I suffered but I was conscious. The first rescuers who arrived, after a time which seemed to me very long, made a tourniquet at my thigh, then transported me to the hospital Saint-Roch." She vividly recalled a man getting out of a car, carrying in his arms a child rolled in a bloody burnoose and rushing into the clinic Sainte-Croixe.[48]

The death and destruction were severe for two primary reasons. First, the all-clear alarm sounded after the first attack, and inhabitants were therefore in the open helping victims amidst the rubble when more bombs fell. A member of the Resistance has written that the Germans could have ended the alert prematurely to increase the number of victims as they were reported to have done in other cities including Marseille.[49] In some cases, curious Niçois had chosen to remain outside to watch the planes, contributing to the heavy casualties. Second, the bombers flew in formation 4,000 feet above the ground to avoid anti-aircraft fire, but at the same time making it more difficult to place ordnance preciously on target. One contemporary remembers American bombers being called "ants" as that is how they appeared way up in the sky.[50] A billowing cloud of smoke masked the objectives for the second wave of attackers. Pilots of the ten-man Flying Fortresses misidentified the vélodrome as the train station, extending the scope and severity of the civilian damage. In contrast with Cannois at the outset of air attacks six months earlier, many Niçois could rationalize the catastrophe as the fault of the Germans and forgive the Americans for just trying to liberate France.[51] On the other hand, the pro-Vichy daily *Le Petit Niçois* wrote of "Massacre de la France," denigrating the Americans for causing the deaths.[52]

The National Aid, a Vichy organization created to respond in such emergencies, rushed in to provide food and clothing at a center quickly set up. Within 24 hours it had collected 115,000 francs to clothe residents left with nothing. In addition, the charity served 150,000 meals, 24,000 breakfasts, and 28,500 snacks.[53] Sad to say, but Nice had at last experienced the pain and despair suffered across Europe for five years and more. The following Sunday a huge memorial service on the esplanade of Paillon demonstrated the city's mourning.

The Hunger of Occupation

In response to demonstrations and cries for more food, a year earlier the prefect, mayor, and bishop in Nice had joined in drafting a letter to be read in all churches. Monseigneur Rémond instructed his diocesans, "Give no one a look at our misery, our denouement, our hunger. Share fraternally what we have so that all may live and hold in dignity, in unison, in faithfulness to God and country."[54] By December 1943, epidemics proliferated to such an extent that the French Red Cross in Cannes needed to organize X-ray screenings for an outbreak of tuberculosis. By the first quarter of 1944 the Swedish Red Cross was welcomed in Nice to provide milk, Hungarian stew, cheese, preserves, gingerbread, and other snacks to the department's youngsters. In January, Jules Grec went to Vichy with nine other mayors to plead their common cause. Each hoped that liberation was not far away.

Prefect Jean Chaigneau reported that the 580,000 persons living in the Department of Alpes-Maritimes could not survive for long considering the devastated economy and extreme shortage of foodstuffs in his area. Four months earlier the national government had provided nourishment from wagonloads of meat, vegetables, rice, and pasta taken from the retreating IV Armata, but these provisions were exhausted and the situation had become desperate. The problem of small yield from few farms in an arid area was exacerbated by the occupier levying reparations that included 3,500 to 14,000 pounds of fruits and vegetables from local markets every day and defensive measures taken to plant land mines on agricultural terrain. Orchards were surrounded by barbed wire with signs warning, "Achtung! Minen." Sixteen starving people had been killed by mines and another 17 crippled seeking something to feed their families. By springtime, an infestation of Argentinean ants ravaged crops of oranges, citrus, and strawberries, further slashing available produce.[55]

Chaigneau had taken a firm stand on this deteriorating situation in November. He ordered the police to watch for large shipments of food intended for the black market. "Your suppression will never be severe enough," Chaigneau declared.[56] At the same time, contraband nutriments were being smuggled from Italy across the border patrolled by an insufficient number of German customs agents.

On the positive side, Cannois recalled rutabagas and grapes being available. Harvest from the vines in 1943 was also bountiful. Yet, arrivals of vegetables from other departments, most often turnips and squash, had become rare. Many inhabitants of Alpes-Maritimes were forced to rely solely on dry vegetables, when available, as local authorities further up the rail line helped themselves to foodstuffs which never reached the terminus in Nice. At Ariane and La Trinité, women collected 102 signatures on a petition asking for more bread and fatty substances. In July 1944, however, the ration of bread was cut in half to 50 grams, causing an even bigger uproar when wagons of wheat destined for the coast were rerouted to other departments. Niçois queued to buy cauliflower leaves while the compact white heads went to Germany.[57] At the request of the Fascist-Republican Party, German authorities agreed to trade salt from the South of France for wheat from the Italian Piémont.

At the same time, General Nickelmann told the population that "terrorists," otherwise known as the Resistance, were stealing and eating this wheat and that the German army was fighting to save it for starving civilians. Quite naturally, by the summer of 1944 the extreme shortages had produced a new wave of fraud and price gouging on the black market. At one point, banks were said to be recalling 500-franc notes to suppress illegal trading. Another report had the Resistance fighting to extinguish the black market to free produce for the general public. A youngster on a farm outside Fréjus at the time cited meat, cheese, and cloth as the precious items for which coastal residents brought their jewelry to exchange.[58]

Dying of starvation was no longer unusual. As olive oil had reached the price of 2,000 francs on the black market, the monthly pay of a laborer, women began cooking instead with large amounts of salt. Finally, in August, in the face of further deterioration in nourishment, the Germans became so agitated by complaints that to encourage more edible crops they prohibited cultivation of annual flowers. Some cultures, however, such as certain strains of roses, could be maintained for future promulgation. For how long could this situation continue?

Constriction of the economy was expressed in ways other than food. Repeated bombings incapacitated heavy industry, most notably at the Aciéries du Nord. The giant steel plant lost thousands of man hours reconstructing its own facilities, as well as repairing the railway that brought in raw materials and carried away output. Product measured in carloads or truckloads exported per month dropped from triple digits into the 10–40 range during mid-1944 as air raids and guerrilla attacks increased. On a lesser scale, but representative of small manufacturers and exporters, the union of cooking potters in Vallauris, a historic center for the craft, submitted a plea in July 1944 for removal of restrictions on transporting its products. Railroad cars had been unavailable for over three months, nor were trucks provided. Closing the pottery mills would put artisans out of work, eliminating wages on which they and the community relied.[59] Vallauris would not fully recover until Pablo Picasso discovered the village and began working there after the war.

Prelude to Liberation

Bombs rained down on the Côte d'Azur between the landing in Normandy and the one to take place in Provence. By summertime, inhabitants could distinguish between the drone of a bomber and the roar of other aircraft. The word "chapelet," used to designate a rosary, became slang for a string of bombs falling from the sky. Hopes of liberation rose among inhabitants suffering under the German occupation, while anxiety increased in those who had wagered their futures on victory by the Third Reich. On July 2 "a good Frenchman who is at the same time a good European" wrote an anonymous letter to General Nickelmann with a suggestion for maintaining discipline within the populace: "I am outraged that terrorists have killed German soldiers. To stop it can we not take reprisals, that is, to shoot the arrested terrorists and execute them on the Place Masséna in front of everyone. Perhaps the members of the Resistance will think about that."[60]

Torrin and Grassi: these names are seared into the memories of anyone living in Nice during the summer of 1944. Séraphin Torrin and Angelo Grassi, a French Provençal farmer and an Italian stonemason, were in the village of Gattières on July 3 when an SS battalion appeared with the Gestapo to collect workers to send to Germany in retaliation for a nearby attack on a Wehrmacht sergeant. When everyone was gathered in the square, one man stepped forward and denounced six of his cohabitants, including Torrin and Grassi. Both were communists, and Grassi was an obvious target as he had fought in the International Brigades in Spain and was former president of the local section of the leftist Italian Popular Union. The prisoners were taken to Nice, savagely tortured and condemned to death.

The most notorious spectacle in Nice during the war took place at 3.00 p.m. on July 7, when Torrin and Grassi were hung from lamp fixtures at the arcade on avenue de la Victoire across from Galleries Lafayette and one block from Place Masséna, police blocking the street with their bicycles. Schoolchildren were forced to file past the bodies labeled with the admonition that this was the fate of members of the Resistance. Now mature adults, this remains a traumatic experience in their lives. The bodies remained exposed for almost 20 hours at a corner where plaques now memorialize the grisly execution. The following day a "ballad to the hanged" had been composed, printed, and was being distributed.[61] Bishop Rémond was not far behind in adding vehement protests to the German authorities.

Preparation for battle became increasingly apparent as 1944 progressed. Apartment buildings around the port wore camouflage paint. Pillboxes were painted to resemble cafes or ordinary homes. At the end of February, Mont Boron was transformed into a minefield. From 6.40 to 8.20 a.m. on March 7, traffic stopped in Nice as large-scale military exercises in the streets trained Wehrmacht troops in urban warfare. German maneuvers took place on boulevard Victor Hugo the following week. Dummy entrenchments and mines were installed on Place Carabacel. Again, on the morning of April 6, military exercises stopped the city's trains and trolleys. In May the windows of structures overlooking the port were walled up. July 14 saw the erection of tank traps on Nice's main streets.[62]

The Resistance also became more active, as will be recounted more fully in subsequent chapters. Résistants blew up the transformer of the Aciéries du Nord, its high tension pylon, and the compressor. On July 4, they undertook one of their riskiest ventures, detonating the foundry supporting the Kriegsmarine. Disrupting telephone communications was another objective. "Harass the enemy by all means relying only upon individual support" (meaning not to expect help from the Allies) was the agreement made by underground leaders meeting at this critical point in time. Even if it was not strong enough to combat the enemy face to face, the Resistance sought to disorganize and demoralize it.[63]

German soldiers became wary in the face of danger from an enemy they could not distinguish from ordinary citizens passing on the street. Charles Tillon, head of the FTP, had issued a call to arms, "Let each man get his Boche," an order not forgotten on the eve of the landing.[64] In response, the Wehrmacht concentrated its forces, both to attack maquis targets and to protect small parties of soldiers such as those sent out to repair cables. Rarely did a German truck traveling alone in the countryside reach its destination. The occupiers had lost control of large areas of Southeast France, as well as the respect of their adversaries.

Meanwhile, the Gestapo and Milice began maximizing opportunities to accumulate wealth before it became too late. The English, Russians, and, especially, Italians were favorite targets for theft and degradation. By arresting wealthy members of these nationalities, the political police could harass them and receive bribes to let them go while accomplices burglarized their domiciles, stealing jewelry, other objects of value, and deluxe vehicles. How could the victims complain or seek restitution?

One final act of desperation occurred in Cannes on August 2, when the Germans blew up the equestrian statue of André Capron, a civic leader and benefactor decades earlier. The patrician looked down from his pedestal onto the seat of the Kriegsmarine at the jetty Albert Edouard, taunting German mariners in their imagination. Such was the extent of frustration of the thousand-year Reich as the curtain descended on occupation of the Riviera.

5

∞

The Jewish Experience

In the story of France during the World War II years, no subject is more controversial and emotionally charged than the treatment of Jews. The image of La Belle France cherished by its citizens is that of a democracy, a republic, a country that opens its arms to the politically and economically oppressed from around the world, a special place where the spirit of the Revolution— liberté, égalité, fraternité—remains the national ethos. As many as 350,000 Jews, half foreign-born and seeking asylum in this heralded safe haven, were estimated to be in France at the outset of the war.[1] Yet there are few absolutes in socio-political matters. In 1938–9, pacifism intertwined with xenophobia fueled fears that Jews were driving France into war and produced anti-Semitic demonstrations in Paris and other cities. After defeat and occupation, the provisional government at Vichy cooperated with the Nazis while attempting to protect French nationals; some Frenchmen conspired with the occupiers while others aided the Jews; and much of the Catholic hierarchy seemed to endorse Maréchal Pétain while at the same time many of its clerics and faithful were offering succor to those hunted and oppressed by the regime.

The Jewish experience in the South of France, and Alpes-Maritimes in particular, is as multifaceted as the rest of its wartime history. The importance of the Riviera in this saga is paramount for its proximity to Italy and easy access and egress by sea. During most of the 1930s, only a thousand or so Jews lived in Nice. By 1939 that number was five times greater. More than 50,000 homeless Jews passed through the Riviera during the war years. How and why did this come about and what were the consequences?

As anti-Semitism exploded in Germany and Austria in the 1930s, Jews were lured to France by its beacon of liberalism, most evident during the rule of the Front Populaire, 1936–8. Artists Max Ernst and Marc Chagall and Theodor Wolff, editor of the *Berliner Tageblatt*, were among the thousands of Jews who came to the Côte d'Azur. Baroness Friedlander-Fuld, who controlled one of the largest fortunes in Germany before Hitler's rise to power, escaped to Cannes. For some, especially university professors, the Riviera was considered a way station on the journey to America. The writer Alfred Neumann stopped in Nice long enough to complete his trilogy set in the time of Napoléon III, before accepting an invitation from Warner Brothers to continue on to Hollywood. For those lacking the financial resources or, later, the transport to continue, Alpes-Maritimes represented a refuge from cruelty and repression.[2]

Ironically, another fascist state, Italy, constituted a gateway to freedom for Teutonic Jews. Mussolini's government allowed Jews to enter from the north. One estimate cites 8,000 German and 5,000 Austrian refugees who crossed the frontier and remained in Italy where anti-Semitism and xenophobia were virtually unknown.[3] This is all the more surprising because in the autumn of 1938 in a concession to his Axis partner, Mussolini promulgated a law requiring a yellow "J" to be imprinted on Jewish passports at the border and prohibiting the entrée of anyone who had actively opposed fascism. A loophole, however, permitted admission with a tourist visa. At the same time, Mussolini ordered the deportation of foreign Jews who had arrived since 1919, excepting spouses of Italians and individuals over the age of 65.

It was not unknown for carabinieri to contribute money for the penniless or to identify clandestine routes between Ventimiglia and Menton. Once inside France, hotels and guest houses charged 2,000 to 3,000 lira for a taxi to Nice, visa and *carte d'identité* included. In April 1939 one family made it into France by surreptitious means only to discover that their contact was not waiting as promised. The situation improved when a bus took them to Nice where they registered for accommodations without papers. The next day, the police issued temporary documents. As the son recalled, "It was just paradise returned—especially in Nice which was paradise to begin with. We were like on a permanent vacation. Nobody thought of war."[4]

The authorities in Nice required immigrants to report to a police station periodically and show they had enough money on which to live. The "non-working" permits granted to most Jews required adequate means of self-support. Organized in a Nice synagogue, a bundle of money made the rounds from one family to another, offering assurance to the bureaucracy that the newcomers would not become a drain on the public treasury. It was during 1939 that a committee of assistance for refugees was established by the resident Jewish community. By November, it had spent almost 400,000 francs to document co-religionists from outside France.[5]

With the declaration of war, controls tightened at the French border. Refugees from Germany and Austria often gathered in Milan before continuing on to the coast. One 17-year-old survivor of the flight to freedom from Leipzig described pushing and shoving to board a train from Milan packed with men, women, and children, some fainting, others getting sick. The next likely destination was San Remo, large enough and well positioned to arrange illegal immigration into France. Arriving at the frontier they found the road barred and the way back denied by a local government already overtaxed by outsiders. Some emigrants tried climbing through Alpine passes, often with fatal consequences. Others sought to skirt border controls by water. All manner of craft, many far from seaworthy, sailed from fishing ports on the Italian Riviera for Menton, Monaco, Nice, and as far west as Cannes, plus all the harbors in between. Fishermen demanded jewelry or 400–500 lira per person to undertake a nighttime subterfuge in overloaded boats, some voyages remembered only by the bodies that washed ashore the next morning. Arriving in France, the youngster recalled being confined for a month in a prison where the guards were cruel, food and water in short supply, and roaches everywhere.[6]

There were other reasons to gather at the Mediterranean besides escaping from the Third Reich. One could become invisible in a crowded city the size of Nice or Marseille. Close to Spain, the South of France had earlier seemed an oasis for Republicans fleeing Franco's reign. Upon declaration of war in Europe, the Midi also became attractive to Jews in northeast France, likely to be invaded by the Germans once again. And later, when Paris came under threat of Nazi occupation, Jewish residents and refugees saw good reason to head south. Indeed, the Non-Occupied Zone soon became widely referred to in French military circles as "chez les juifs."[7]

With emigration to the United States difficult due to so many applicants for limited visa quotas, going on to Latin America evolved as a plausible alternative. In February 1939, for example, 69 Germans, nearly all Jewish, boarded an Italian steamship at Cannes destined for Montevideo and Buenos Aires.[8] Another Jewish family of French nationality left Marseille by train the day the Germans entered Paris in June 1940. The father had assisted members of the International Brigade and was therefore persona non grata in Spain, but fortunately the cars continued into Portugal without papers being examined. At Lisbon the émigrés boarded a Japanese freighter for Panama, stopping en route at New York and Baltimore but denied entry. On the sides of the cargo vessel were displayed two huge flags with the rising sun spotlighted at night to avoid being torpedoed by a German U-boat. A Royal Navy cruiser forced the steamer into Bermuda after a U-boat took off two English passengers. Once in Panama City, the refugees could not initially obtain a visa to enter the United States as the French embassy considered them to be traitors.[9]

Remaining in the South of France became less attractive for foreign Jews swept up in the hysteria directed against all outsiders in the wake of the declaration of war with the Third Reich. Overnight, art galleries opened in Nice to market the valuables of resident Jews, as well as immigrants seeking money to flee or go into hiding. The threat of a fifth column caused Vichy to require inhabitants from Germanic states to report to the police. Fort Carré in Antibes was the collecting point in Alpes-Maritimes for male foreign nationals, ages 17 to 50. In September 1939 detainees slept on cold concrete in the garrison's old football stadium, surviving on a minimum ration of food and water before being taken to Les Milles, a former tile and brickworks between Marseille and Aix-en-Provence. Here Jews from Central Europe, the Balkans, and Spain, plus Germany, Austria, and Italy, were joined with their co-religionists from other departments in the Midi. There was no deliberate torture in French assembly areas, but cold, hunger, disease, and parasites were common, as exhibited by dysentery, typhoid, lice, fleas, and bedbugs. A reserve battalion composed largely of farm workers and artisans from the Ardeche served as guards. In April 1940, when the Phoney War seemed just that, Les Milles closed its doors and the confinés returned home.

The next month, after Germany's actual invasion of France, the center reopened and remained operational until converting to a munitions depot two years later. In between, Les Milles served as a transit facility for deportation to Poland and death.[10] This was but one of 93 internment camps in unoccupied France identified by the Nazi commission charged with overseeing compliance with the Armistice.

Charitable organizations—Jewish and Christian, French and foreign—entered Les Milles to offer aid to the detainees. Those interned included not only Jews, but intellectuals, artists, and political leaders opposed to the ruling powers (Nazi and Vichy), some well-known and long-time refugees in France. Rapidly the population exceeded 1,800 prisoners. A visual memory of their incarceration today is the refectory with walls painted by captives, most notably "The Banquet of the Nations" depicting different peoples amicably dining together.

Anti-Semitism under Vichy

The eminent scholar of Vichy France, Robert O. Paxton, cites three tacks taken by that regime in regard to Jewry. The first was to identify and list all Jews in France and, then, to reduce their role and import in the nation's economic and cultural life. Second, Maréchal Pétain insisted on keeping all administrative and police activities in his hands as opposed to the German occupiers. Finally, the Vichy strategy was intended to prevent the migration of foreign Jews to France, especially into the Non-Occupied Zone.[11] The other side of that coin—offering to deport recent Jewish immigrants—changed the polarity from Gentile/Jew to French/foreigner, by no means the worst dichotomy for prosperous, well-established families in France. Recent immigrants quickly became vulnerable and more susceptible to entreaties from communist organizations, the Resistance, and the maquis. Conversely, the heterogeneity of most Jews residing in France—and their dispersion throughout the society—made them more difficult for the Germans to identify and collect. Indeed,

French historian Renée Poznanski cites this trait as the key to the survival of native-born Jews.[12]

Anti-Jewish policies were promulgated by Vichy in a succession of laws from July 1940 to December 1942. How they were implemented in Alpes-Maritimes varied at times from the rest of France, but before looking at specific cases, it is necessary to be familiar with the statutes.

Xenophobia was a pillar of the Vichy regime. Protection of the jobs of indigeneous workers was therefore a central undertaking. An anonymous denunciation of the employment of foreign workers, especially Italians, was enough to launch a police inquiry. The first sector to be affected was local government. The act of July 17, 1940 removed foreign-born employees from local government. On its heels came the statute of July 22, revoking the citizenship of foreigners naturalized after 1927. In the view of many, a Jew symbolized the foreigner par excellence. From this mindset flowed a stream of laws:

- August 27, 1940—abrogating the enactment of April 1939 which suppressed anti-Semitism in the press, thereby unleashing an outburst of hatred against Jews;
- October 3, 1940—the Jewish Statute, exceeding the German definition by applying to anyone with two grandparents who "appeared" to follow the Jewish religion and removing such persons from the civil service and any activity that influenced the national culture;
- October 4, 1940—authorizing prefects to assign foreign Jews to house arrest or confinement camps;
- March 29, 1941—creating the Commissariat General for Jewish Questions;
- June 2, 1941—refining the text of the Jewish Statute to make it more specific and list penalties and sanctions for infractions;
- June 2, 1941—mandating a detailed census of Jews in the Non-Occupied Zone with an inventory of their assets, unknowingly preparing the way for its German occupation. Subsequent administrative provisions restricted Jews' right to sell assets or realize gains from them by, among other measures, authorizing Aryan executors for Jewish property.
- July 22, 1941—loosening the definition of a Jewish enterprise to permit broader application, and placing the Commissariat General for Jewish Questions under the auspices of its German counterpart;
- November 17, 1941—strengthening powers related to Aryanization of the professions, arts, and trades;
- December 11, 1942—requiring identification papers to be stamped with the word "Jew," facilitating subsequent Nazi roundups.

Expressions of anti-Semitism began at once in Alpes-Maritimes, agitated initially by fascist extremists. On July 29, 1940, the first windows of Niçois shopkeepers were broken with stones inscribed with "the Révolution Nationale begins," "the chastisement of Jews," and "PPF will overcome." Two weeks later, seven more commercial establishments were vandalized in conjunction with demonstrations against Jews on Nice's avenue de la Victoire.[13]

Members of the LFC began harassing people on the streets of Nice during that first summer under Vichy. Anyone with features resembling a Jew was subject to attack, the most violent taking place on the Promenade des Anglais. Aryans, officers retired from the French army, holders of the Légion d'honneur—no one was immune from confrontation. Eight aged worshippers were accosted inside the synagogue on rue Deloye and seriously injured; the perpetrators were found guilty and assessed fines of one franc by the court.[14]

Sinking to the baseness of its most susceptible readership, the local press began to parrot the racist theme. First, Le Petit Niçois declared, "In a regenerated France, there should no more be a place for this parasite: the dark-skinned foreigner." Then, days later, it quoted Vichy as declaring, "Very many people, emigrated or expelled from their country, stateless foreigners, Jews or non-Jews, constitute a certain danger for public peace and order."[15] L'Eclaireur de Nice and L'Alerte, the organ of the Révolution Nationale, amplified the xenophobia and anti-Semitism termed "la question juive."

By 1941 the Vichy regime began to take decisive, systematic action against Jews. Large numbers of foreigners in the Department of Alpes-Maritimes caused the prefecture to order their apprehension, some Jews plus many others. Hundreds of natives of the Netherlands, Belgium, Hungary, Bulgaria, Rumania, and Russia joined other nationalities collected and released earlier. Compared with the harsh treatment in the Occupied Zone, these measures must have hardly seemed noteworthy at first to the larger Jewish population. Indeed, in a letter written in October 1940, a Jewish teenager exclaimed that "over there in the Midi, no one appears to take account of what is happening here [in Paris]."[16]

After the short fighting in 1940, the first Commissariat General for Jewish Questions claimed that anti-Semitism merely reflected the views of officials in departments overrun with outsiders. Initially, there appeared to be popular apathy concerning governmental persecution. But as food shortages increased in the summer of 1942, 30 of 42 prefects in the Vichy South commented on the large influx of Jewish refugees from the Occupied Zone. Even greater hostility was directed at foreign or recently naturalized Jews. Finding food was becoming an obsession with everyone, and extra mouths stretched scarce resources even thinner. Nine out of ten black-market cases could be traced to Jews, the prefect of Alpes-Maritimes reported.[17] A cleric at Valdeblore wrote to protest against non-Christians sent to his community, presumably banished to the back country.

Yet, not everyone complained. A French Jew, Philippe Erlanger, observed an unexpected prosperity arising from the arrival of wealthy co-religionists in Cannes, spawning the city's sobriquet as "Kahn." He recalled wealthy widows of the rich and famous happily riding through the streets on bicycles with baskets on the back for dogs or whatever produce could be found. The census of 1941 sought to identify Jews who had immigrated since 1936, but it registered only 128 in Cannes at a time when its mayor estimated at least 4,000 in his municipality.[18]

While the palace hotels of Cannes provided quarters for ostentatious guests from afar, the majority of the Jewish refugees in every community were to be found in shabby hotels. Their preoccupation, like everyone else, was obtaining nourishment, which was increasingly difficult to find, expensive, and often requiring food coupons not officially issued to illegal immigrants. The Jewish assistance committee in Nice responded by opening a soup kitchen serving kosher meals and was soon feeding as many as 250 refugees twice a day. During 1941, it aided a total of nearly 1,000 different people.[19]

French citizens and long-time residents of the Riviera were also feeling the oppression of the Vichy campaign. Employment restrictions were applied to the region's Jews. A survey in the summer of 1941 found that half the Jews were deprived of the means of subsistence.[20] Except in rare cases, it was no longer possible to be a doctor, dentist, lawyer, professor, journalist, or actor. Four lawyers lost their practices in Nice, while two others were retained for outstanding service. Another reason for an exception was an individual's family having resided in France for five generations. The proportion of Jewish students in universities was capped at 3 percent of total enrollment. Seven hundred businesses in Alpes-Maritimes—from boutiques to hotels, real estate firms and agricultural concerns—were listed among the 3,000 Jewish enterprises in the Non-Occupied Zone identified as candidates for Aryan administrators. Five villas belonging to Edouard de Rothschild in Cannes and Beausoleil were confiscated, as was the residence on Cap Martin of the banker Leon Stern, stripped of his French citizenship.[21]

Similar repression was underway in the Var. The 1941 census recorded no more than 1,900 Jews, yet far more avoided registration or filtered in during the succeeding months. The PPF and LFC accused the Jews of profiting from the black market, but a roundup in the spring of 1941 found none among the 18 dealers arrested. Anti-Semitic slogans appeared on walls in Toulon and Hyères and notices pasted on shop windows identified the proprietors as Jewish. In Saint-Tropez it was proposed to limit Jews to staying no more than two months so as not to "contaminate" the seaside resort with their money. Natives of the department were not sympathetic to these extreme views and actions, however, as a study of public opinion in August 1942 concluded that Varois were inclined to feel sorry for the fate of their neighbors and other Jews of modest means.

Controls applied, as well, to other categories of people—homosexuals, communists, Freemasons, gypsies, and former members of the Front Populaire. For example, the adjunct mayor of Nice, Georges Picard, was forced to resign for being both a Jew and a Mason. But applications of the law were uneven and skewed against Jews, as shown by the fact that 96 percent of deportees in the last year of Occupation were Jewish. One researcher noted:

> Finally, during this period it is more a question of anti-Semitic than racist laws: the gypsies for example almost did not suffer because they were especially prevalent in Eastern Europe. Minorities other than Jews, as for example homosexuals, were no longer worried. Persecutions in France and afterwards in Alpes-Maritimes were really directed against the Jews.[22]

While Vichy was striving to keep abreast of and even exceed the constraints applied to Jewish people and interests in the German-occupied part of France, government oppression weighed especially heavily on the targeted individuals without means of support. These measures caused five Austrians in Nice to commit suicide. Another depressed entertainer chose to drown himself in the Baie des Anges. Other desperate acts seemingly went unnoticed.

The Commissariat General for Jewish Questions soon established a branch in Nice to oversee collection of information, maintenance of files, and production of anti-Jewish propaganda, among other activities. Some Aryan Frenchmen felt it necessary to apply to this office for a "certificate of non-belonging to the Jewish race," issued upon appropriate documentation for use when confronted with mistaken discrimination. Yet, despite these many-and-varied anti-Semitic activities, Jews participated in every public demonstration, involved themselves in intelligence gathering and the clandestine press, became members of liberation committees, and joined the urban resistance and the maquis—any of which could lead to death if detected by the authorities.

Repression of Jews by the Vichy regime came to a head during the last days of August 1942. These events had their genesis at the Wannsee Conference in Berlin the preceding January when the Reich decided on the "Final Solution." Its implementation in France was the responsibility of S.S. Captain Theodor Dannecker, chief of the Gestapo's Jewish Office in Paris. Deportation of Jews was to be disguised as labor details, so initially an age restriction of 16–40 years was set for the victims. In July, Dannecker decided to conduct a personal inspection of camps in the South and was disappointed in the paltry numbers he found assembled in places like Les Milles. Continuing on to Nice he learned that his representatives there wanted to be rid of the 8,000 Jews in that city. Numerous Jewish residents of the Principality of Monaco were also brought to Dannecker's attention. Dates were set for a roundup, instructions disseminated, and exemptions for children ages 2–16 suspended, callously justified on heinous "humanitarian grounds" of preserving family unity. The plan for Alpes-Maritimes specified Caserne Auvare housing 3,000 anticipated detainees in rooms of 40–50 each, men separated from women and children.[23]

The operation kicked off at 2.00 a.m. on August 26, and 12 hours later 510 Jews—207 men and 303 women and children—were collected at Auvare. The Nice section of the Union Générale des Israélites de France (UGIF), an umbrella organization created by the Nazis, sent its secretary to the caserne to comfort the detainees and distribute baskets of fruit.[24] As apprehensions continued through Alpes-Maritimes (and, indeed, across the Non-Occupied Zone), accounts were received of suicides to avoid capture. One woman jumped to her death from a window, another swallowed poison. Fear and panic gripped the Jewish community as no one knew how long the raids would continue.

The numbers realized for Nice itself over the next four days were disappointing to the Nazis. Several explanations accounted for the shortfall. The BBC broadcast a warning of the roundup. Information on whereabouts was often inaccurate: respondents had departed France clandestinely, moved away from the area, or simply disappeared by changing domicile. In many instances, municipal officials and police were knowledgeable accomplices to these relocations.[25]

Early on the morning of August 31, a train slowly pulled away from Saint-Roch station. On board were 560 Jews from Nice and the environs. A mother threw her infant out of a window for someone among the onlookers to protect and nurture. The next morning the cars arrived at Drancy, located just outside Paris, the final collection point in France before transfer by convoy to Auschwitz, a "work camp" in the Nazi parlance.[26]

The summer of 1942 represented a turning point in the attitude of many Frenchmen toward Vichy. Jews were no longer the source of a problem; they had become victims. The infamous roundup of Vel d'Hiv in Paris in July and reinstatement of the medieval requirement to wear a yellow star seemed to prove finally that Pétain's government was incapable of standing up to the occupiers. Instead, it had become their partner. The August raids had a numbing effect on residents of the Non-Occupied Zone. Vivid recollections of families being taken out of their homes and children pulled away from their parents were difficult to dispel. Immediate feedback came from the police commissaire of Cannes where raids of fashionable hotels had been delayed until mid-morning on August 26 so as not to disturb the Aryan guests. "'Free the Jews' has been written today in chalk and charcoal on walls and benches, the promenade de la Croisette and near the *hôtel de Ville*. They have not held a great deal of public attention."[27] A prime reason was that French newspapers remained silent on the roundups. The Resistance, Gaullists, and communists in London, as in all of France, condemned the arrests and held the state responsible.

Not that first day of the raids but the day after, the commissaire of the national police in Nice reported to Vichy that the local people were taking pity on the downtrodden. In addition to the Resistance, Catholics and Protestants deemed it their Christian duty to hide Jews. Informal networks of "the Jewish resistance" were composed in many instances of simple people moved by the fate of Jews and ready to help them when the opportunity presented itself.[28] A flyer signed by La Comité du [Communist] Front National, and disseminated September 12–15, issued a stirring call to arms. It began by asserting, "The anti-Jewish measures have raised our indignation!" Occupation troops are pillaging and starving France and murdering French patriots while the government encourages the public to blame Jews and forget the Germans, the tract continued. Niçois were implored to unify, stand up against arrests and deportations, fight against the occupation, refuse to work for Hitler, and oppose anti-Semitism and racism, for "le liberté et l'indépendence de la France."[29]

In October, the Sûreté Nationale collected a tract being placed in Niçois letter boxes. Referring to the "Hitler bandits who demand Jewish children," it exclaimed, "tomorrow, if we do not immediately stop the criminal hand of the murders, to be sure, they will attack our little French children in order to exterminate our people [...] The leaders of the Catholic and Protestant church have risen up in indignation against this tragic and barbarian hunt [...] By not doing anything, by your silence, you are accomplices to the murders."[30] Help was on the way, however, from an unlikely source.

The Italian Respite

The lot of Jews during the Italian interregnum, November 1942–September 1943, is a prime example of differences in the wartime experience on the Riviera from elsewhere in France. Italian occupation markedly reduced the threat of Nazi oppression. Nowhere was this contrast more important than in Alpes-Maritimes with a large Jewish presence that would grow exponentially. Italy's attitude has been attributed to five factors: a desire to demonstrate independence from Germany on humanitarian matters; a will to affirm its sovereignty on a region coveted by Rome; intrigues organized by an influential Jewish Italian banker; American pressures on the Vatican and key Italian personalities; and the absence of a visceral national anti-Semitism.[31] In reality the Jews became a pawn in a German–Italian rivalry. Nonetheless, for the Jews, Italian governance was the quiet between the storms of subjugation directed from Vichy and Berlin.

The good fortune was not necessarily obvious at first. Marie-Louise Villiers wanted to commit suicide on the Croisette at Cannes when she first heard the sound of boots marching in unison on November 11, 1942.[32] But it did not take long for the lighthearted Bersaglieri to disarm apprehensions in the Jewish community. The Italians arrived just in time. Agents of Vichy soon undertook to enforce the law of December 11, 1942 along with a regulation promulgated at the same time to remove consular protection for foreigners who had arrived after 1932 from neutral countries or those hostile to the Axis. The Italian government quickly intervened. Its consul general in Nice and the commander of its army of occupation instructed the prefect neither to apply reference to Judaism on *cartes d'identité* nor to intern foreign Jews or send them to collection points outside Alpes-Maritimes, as directed by Vichy. Italian authorities were to be notified immediately whenever a Jew was arrested for any reason.[33]

Not to be overlooked is that in February 1943 foreign-born Jews in Alpes-Maritimes were spared the mass arrests carried out by French police in German-occupied parts of the southern zone, with the by-product of a sharp increase in the influx of Jewish immigrants into the Italian area. A typical incident occurred at Saint-Martin-Vésubie, where carabinieri took control of three Jews from Languedoc whom Vichy gendarmes were preparing to deport. In Nice, carabinieri were posted at synagogues to use force, if necessary, to prevent local policemen from apprehending illegal immigrants and harassing other worshippers.

Breathing this fresh air, the Jewish community in Nice flourished. From over 13,000 members at the end of 1942 (5,300 French and 7,800 foreign, including 1,500 Poles), the Jewish population grew to 30,000 by September 1943, of whom half were French according to the prefect's information.[34] The S.S. chief in France, Dr. Helmut Knochen, informed Berlin, "Lyon and the Côte d'Azur are flooded with rich and influential Jews. The movement of Jews from the German-occupation zone to the Italian is growing. I have reports that the Italians are passing Jews illegally not only into Switzerland, but also into Italian territory."[35]

Refugees were seen returning to religious practices as one way of calming their fears. Judaic schools, cultural circles, and occupational training centers opened in Nice. The welcome center at the synagogue on boulevard Dubouchage expanded its food service once more. These activities were possible through the generosity of individuals such as Yaakov Doubinski, a wealthy Russian Jew from Odessa who chose to remain in Nice. Erlanger characterized the area as a "micro-Palestine."[36]

Within a few months, leaders of the Reich perceived the extent of the cozy relationship developing between the Riviera's Jews and Italian troops. Alpini officers cultivated friendships with foreigners settled on the coast. Italians lived in Jewish homes. Their hosts invited them out for dinner, frequently paying the bill. Soldiers dated Jewish women. Italian functionaries and military officers alike spoke out publicly against anti-Semitism and continually intervened on behalf of Jews. The Jewish community in Nice collected 3 million francs to give to Italian victims of Allied air raids. Its influence was so pervasive that Italian soldiers were thought by the Nazis to be turning toward communism and pacifism and even becoming pro-American. The occupation forces were also being brainwashed into thinking that Italians had more in common with the French, their Latin brothers, than with Germans, Knochen believed.[37]

Dannecker's successor as S.S. Obersturmfuhrer, Captain Heinz Roethke, went further with a vitriolic diatribe against the freedom permitted Jews. "Come see each day on the Promenade des Anglais or the terraces of the grand hotels, groups of Jews who by the hundreds or thousands wallow, well dressed and well nourished, loud and arrogant, and come see them around deluxe restaurants, places of pleasure and dining, swarming, doing business, going, coming, always insolent, dealing without stop, insulting the French misery: 'the paradise of the Jews'." "This maneuvering is encouraged," he concluded, "by intrigues of the Holy See and especially by the pro-Jewish superior attitude of the French clergy."[38]

In the spring, the Vichy hierarchy unintentionally helped the Jews by recalling Marcel Ribière, a personal friend of Pétain and ardent collaborator, replacing him as prefect with Jean Chaigneau, sympathetic to the Resistance from the outset. Meeting with local Jewish leaders during his first days in office, Chaigneau is said to have offered a heartfelt expression of sympathy and determination to aid them: "I shall not leave to the Italians the noble privilege of being the sole defenders of the tradition of tolerance and humanity, which is really the role of France." Under Chaigneau's direction, a regional police logistician organized a system to manufacture and distribute in Nice's grand skating rink nearly 70,000 *cartes d'identité* to French national and foreign Jews alike, which would complicate execution of the Nazi roundup just over the horizon. But the cards were hardly foolproof. Many signatures were reproduced in identical green ink, easily spotted by fascist authorities.[39]

Italy's intervention to block the Final Solution in southeastern France was raised at meetings held by Mussolini in late winter 1943 with Joachim von Ribbentrop, the Reich's minister of foreign affairs, and Heinrich Müller, commander-in-chief of the Gestapo, but without concrete results. Subsequently, the German ambassador to Rome obtained a small concession from Il Duce, if not full compliance with the Fuhrer's policies as Berlin intended. Mussolini assigned the problem to the Italian civilian police and designated Guido Lospinoso as inspector general of racial police with the rank of general. He was directed to transfer Jews settled on the Côte d'Azur into forced residence in the back country at least 60 miles from the sea. The new chief departed the next day for Nice, where he established his headquarters in the villa Surany at 42, boulevard Cimiez.[40]

The Pope of the Jews

Compassionate treatment of Hebrews on the Riviera at this time was due in large measure to the extraordinary sway of Angelo Mordechai Donati, an Italian Jew. As a successful businessman, he had founded the French-Italian bank in Paris where he served as president of the Italian Chamber of Commerce during the 1930s. When the Germans threatened the capital in 1940, Donati moved his financial affairs to Nice, living at 37 Promenade des Anglais. His importance derived in part from decorations for service as a captain of infantry and Italian liaison with the French army in World War I, earning him the distinction of Grand Officer of the Crown of Italy and the rank of commander in the French Légion d'honneur. As an aviator, Donati set the world altitude record in 1927. He derived greater influence, however, through his friendship with officials in the ministry of foreign affairs in Rome and close personal relations with senior officers in the Italian army.

The Jewish community knew Donati's power. He was a gray eminence exercising influence over the consul general, military chiefs, and Lospinoso who immediately sought him out upon arriving in Nice. Donati's adopted son and daughter recalled officers coming to their home and leaving kepi and leather belt with revolver in the entry hall. A friend visiting his residence in mid-November 1942 described him as "a general on the eve of battle, with the consul general practically under the direction of Donati." In remembrance of this brief moment of Riviera sunshine during the darkness of the Holocaust, it was said that many male babies born to Jewish families were named "Angelo."[41]

Dorothy Chamaide, an Englishwoman, was one of many who sought Donati's help. When her countrymen departed France, she chose to stay behind with her new husband, a Jewish shopkeeper in Nice. After two Italian officers were shot by the Resistance on May 6, 1943, local authorities prepared to take 400 prisoners in retribution. The couple was warned but did not react, and when sirens began to blare at midnight it was too late. Henri was arrested and sent to a holding area in Fréjus. Dorothy went to see Donati who obtained forged papers for the couple. Armed with his backing and some perfumes he advised her to take along, Dorothy went to the headquarters of the Italian police at the Hôtel Regina in Cimiez to beg for her spouse's release. Henri was freed with the understanding that he leave Nice, and the couple fled to Tourrettes-sur-Loup where they went into hiding for the remainder of the fascist occupations.[42]

By working closely with Lospinoso, obtaining contributions at the Dubouchage synagogue, and using his contacts in Rome, Donati gathered the funds to relocate Jewish families from the coast into house arrest in the interior. The Italian government consequently requisitioned hotels in Vence and Saint-Martin-Vesubie, plus accommodations in Mégeve, Barcelonnette, and other communities in the Departments of Haute-Savoie and Basses-Alpes. At their own request, more than 4,000 Jews moved to these locations on transportation provided by the occupiers. Lospinoso liked this initiative because it gave Nazis the idea that Italy was complying at last with their racial policies.[43]

The first impressions of two new "residents" are illuminating. "I arrived at Saint-Martin in the evening, and I saw something I was not accustomed to seeing for a long time: Jews were walking peacefully in the streets, were also seated in the cafes, speaking French, German, some even Yiddish. I also saw some carabinieri who were walking in the streets."[44] An Austrian Jew remembered being one of a small group sent to a military base in Sospel where he was required to report to the commandant twice a day.

> They treated us beautifully well. They gave us food, nothing was rationed. We had clean beds. As a matter of fact, the Italian soldiers made up the beds because the inmates of this camp were all American and British citizens that lived in the Southeast of France in their own big villas and were very rich people, so they treated them like they hoped the Americans and British would treat Italian prisoners of war.[45]

Donati was aided in his efforts by a Capucine priest, Father Marie-Benoît, who was educated in theology at the Vatican and had been organizing Jewish removals from Marseille to Nice and helping maintain escape routes to Spain and Switzerland. Working in tandem, Donati and Marie-Benoît urged Lospinoso to avoid contact with the Germans and confer only with the French. For example, the Nazi intelligence service wanted the names of Jews originally from Germany and Austria in exchange for returning Italian nationals apprehended under various pretexts. The Spanish government also asked for its Jewish citizens to be returned to an uncertain fate.[46] Together the banker and the priest sensitized the Italian hierarchy to the Jews' dangerous situation. As the summer drew on, Mussolini's government fell and the stability of Italy's axis with Germany wavered. The need for an enduring solution to the plight of the Jews became critical to Donati.

Troubled with the threat posed by the Gestapo, Donati's plan was to transport Jews into Italy and then send them on to North Africa. He dispatched Marie-Benoît to confer with Pope Pius XII while Donati traveled to Rome several times to confer with high officials in the administration of Marshal

Badoglio, who had succeeded Mussolini. As a result, the government created a type of passport specifically to permit foreign Jews to enter Italy. Some 5,000 copies were quickly printed. At the end of August, Donati was back in Rome completing arrangements for four ships to carry Jews of all nationalities concentrated on the Riviera to ports in Libya and elsewhere along the south Mediterranean coast. He met on September 8 with the minister of the interior to arrange for ground transportation and to facilitate the formalities of entry into Italy. That same morning, Donati finalized naval protection for the convoy with emissaries of the British and American governments. The operation was set to take place during the second half of September. Fully satisfied, Donati was flying back to Nice when news reached him of an armistice signed by Italy and the United States. The Germans were poised to react while it was too late for Donati's plans to be executed.[47]

The Nazis had been wringing their hands over the situation in the Italian zone almost from its inception. At the turn of the year, Knochen bemoaned, "If the Italians are now taking all Jews of foreign citizenship under their protection, it will make it impossible to continue to carry out the anti-Jewish policy according to our conception. We cannot therefore expect that the French police should in the coming months deliver into our hands the Jews of French nationality for deportation." In February, Adolf Eichmann communicated with Ribbentrop on the situation before his meeting with Mussolini. It was early April when Donati's role finally commanded their attention. Knochen wrote to Eichmann and to the Reich's office of security, "We have meanwhile learned that there is in the Italian zone a powerful financial group of Italian Jews under the leadership of the former Director of the Banque France-Italie, Donati, which protects the Jews." In May, Klaus Barbie reported from Lyon that among the 400 Jews resettled by Italian authorities in Mégeve were 12 reputed to be wanted by the Sureté. The French government is proposing to the Italians to send children away from coastal towns likely to be bombed, Barbie added. Donati and Lospinoso were identified as the masterminds of these relocations.[48]

By early September, Roethke set forth an action plan to deal with the Jewish problem. Their complete evacuation was necessary both in the interests of the Final Solution in France and as "an urgent security need for German troops" sure to be moving into the Italian area soon, given the deteriorating political situation in Italy. Mass deportation should be carried out only after initial shipment to the camp at Drancy of those Jews naturalized after August 10, 1927.[49] Included in the plan was kidnapping Donati. Roethke's after-action report to Berlin stated, however, "It was the intention here to seize Donati in Nice and bring him to Marseille. The agents who were instructed to do this could not get hold of him, because having regard for German–Italian relations at that time they were ordered to proceed with extreme care." The account concluded, "It is believed that Donati will attempt to join the Anglo-American troops. Donati's arrest is of capital importance, since he was the directing brain of the Jews in the Italian zone of influence, and he had quite openly the best connections with the former Italian Government departments in Rome."[50]

Upon hearing the news of the premature revelation of Italy's surrender, Donati diverted his plane to Milan where he sought refuge at the home of a nephew. He remained under cover in northern Italy for the remainder of the war. The man whom the Nazis derisively called "the pope of the Jews" died at the close of 1960.

The German Occupation

The celebration in Nice sparked by news of Italy's surrender did not extend to the Jewish community. Jews were counseled to move into the small area still controlled by the Alpini. The welcome center on boulevard Dubouchage arranged for vehicles to carry immigrants loaded with baggage back to the high country. Heading north was difficult on roads clogged with dislodged Jews lacking food and shelter and heading south and east to be shipped to North Africa. Hotels in Nice were filled to overflowing with Jews awaiting a Moses to lead them to safety. By concentrating in the city, the refugees were falling into a trap that would make roundups all the easier for the Nazis.

The appearance of German troops ignited panic among families on the road and crowded together in hostelries. It was too late to flee as the Wehrmacht quickly took control of rail stations and border posts. The Hôtel Continental, seat of the Italian consulate in Nice, was besieged by a mob of Israelites frantic to obtain documentation that would enable them to enter Italy, as if the Nazis would honor any such authorization.

Arrests began in Cannes that first night of September 8–9, targeting the hotels. The following day, the Feldgendarmerie set up a roadblock at a bridge over the Var, catching five cars filled with Jews from Saint-Martin-Vésubie. The search extended into all the towns and villages along the Côte d'Azur, including the back country. The prey sought shelter in farm buildings, garages, caves, anywhere to avoid detection. A young Jewish man whose family was hiding in Clans, perched high in the valley of Tinée, recounted that the warning to be given upon sighting a vehicle climbing the winding road to the village was simply, "The milk is rising." After repeated false alarm, the fugitives became complacent. The caution was ignored on the morning of October 25. The hunters appeared and loaded 27 men, women, and children onto military vehicles and carried them to Nice. Roundups continued for the remainder of the year and well into 1944. Indeed, on December 23 the dreaded black Citroëns full of Gestapo agents swept into the village of Opio and seized a family hiding in a deep cupboard carved into a wall beside the fireplace. Safety was not assured anywhere.[51]

Farther north at Saint-Martin-Vésubie, which had acquired the nickname, "capital of Niçois Switzerland," the Italian authorities had fled by 10.00 a.m. on September 9. The square became packed with taxis arriving from Nice carrying old folks in their eighties, pregnant women, and parents dragging children by the hand, all taking flight to escape the Gestapo. At that time, Saint-Martin was only two miles from the frontier, and the Jews fled in this direction. For some fugitives the high peaks of the Mercantour constituted a beautiful landscape, but the climb was too much for many persons not in physical condition to hike through the mountains and without proper clothes and shoes for the trek. After the war one child recalled, "We walked a lot; my father carried two suitcases on his back and one in his hand: little by little, he threw the first valise into the ravine, then the second, and he was able to carry me in his arms because I was very tired and he was afraid that I would fall in the ravine." Another survivor insisted, "The road to the border was no less dangerous than the Germans themselves; high mountains, tortuous and narrow trails, high precipices, and for light only a match lit from time to time. Alone in the middle of the threatening nature, we felt lost [...] We were dying of cold and hunger." A third recounted, "Italian soldiers were also on the route with us. Some seemed to be alone without officers and without uniforms. Others loaded part of our luggage on their shoulders or took children in their arms. 'Take long steps but slowly,' they said to us." The survivors compared their experience to "the exodus from Egypt."[52]

Using the passes at Fenestre and Cerise, each almost 8,000 feet above sea level, 1,500 of the heartier refugees succeeded in escaping the purge. The hikers naturally trembled at the thought of running into Germans, and some armed Italian soldiers provided reassurance by accompanying them on the other side of the frontier. Yet after surviving the mountain ordeal, some of the outcasts were subsequently seized by the Gestapo at Cuneo, Italy, or later picked up in mass arrests by Fascists in Florence and Rome. On September 18 the Waffen S.S. reported intercepting 410 Jews and interring them in the German caserne at Borgo San Dalmazzo, Italy.[53]

Arriving in Nice, the Germans began a massive roundup, aided by their collaborators, the Milice, and Italian Fascists. At 3.30 p.m. on September 10, the Nazis barricaded streets and burst into hotels suspected of quartering Jews, such as the Busby and the Windsor across from one another on rue Maréchal Joffre. People were accosted at stations and in the streets. The police even entered hospitals and medical clinics and took away invalids, many hauled out of bed and loaded into trucks shivering in their night clothes. Every circumcised male, man and boy, was treated as a Jew; documentation, valid or counterfeit, had lost its value.[54]

A satisfied Reich official observed, "The city has lost its appearance of a ghetto since the arrival of the German soldiers. The Jews no longer circulate; the synagogues are closed and the Promenade des Anglais offers to Aryan strollers numerous armchairs which, until present, were occupied by the Jews." One eyewitness turned historian, Léon Poliakov, encapsulated what transpired during this torrent:

> For the Nazis, Nice was the place where the crime had been committed. It was at Nice where Angelo Donati lived, the Italian banker who had succeeded to intervene with Italian generals in favor of the Jews. It was at Nice that the most notorious, the richest Jews were sheltered. It is then evidently at Nice that world Jewry, aided by Churchill and by the Vatican, secretly schemed to overthrow Mussolini. The S.S. fanatics thought themselves at the scene of the crime. What they did until then was nothing in comparison with what they were going to do.[55]

The man directing the hunt for Jews in Alpes-Maritimes was S.S. Hauptsturmfuhrer Aloïs Brunner, age 31, an Austrian who at one time had served as Eichmann's personal secretary. He arrived in Nice after having organized roundups in Paris and deportations in Austria and Greece, and had just been assigned to take charge of the camp at Drancy. Brunner was described by someone who could not be considered impartial: "Having an insignificant physique: small in size, poorly figured, puny, with a look without expression, small mean eyes, he spoke in a monotone voice which was rarely raised. Perfidious, unpitying and lying, he was insensitive to behavior worthy of the victims, to their rectitude and to their good faith." Brunner was good at his work; he was considered "outstanding in brutality." Yet even he made mistakes. Edwige Isoart was arrested and threatened with death during a roundup on October 25. Obviously well prepared, Brunner charged her, "You warn the Jews and the terrorist by telephone." Denying everything, Edwige was freed at the end of the day.[56]

Brunner's first stop was the Italian consulate to collect the files on Jews in Alpes-Maritimes. The consul replied that they had already been sent to Rome. Indeed, on the evening of the armistice, trucks commandeered by his staff had been loaded with documents for export. Two days later the consul and his deputy were deported. Across town, Chaigneau destroyed lists of Jews compiled by his predecessor. Among other actions taken to thwart the Nazis, he hid wanted families in the prefecture. The following spring, the Germans arrested Chaigneau at the Hôtel Martinez in Cannes and shipped him to Bergen-Belsen.[57]

Brunner chose for his headquarters the Hôtel Excelsior on avenue Durante, just a few steps from the main train station in Nice. A beautiful Belle Époque structure with sculpted façade, frieze encircling the lobby, and gay chandeliers, the outward appearance gave no clue of what transpired in the 39 rooms on five floors. Upon "checking into" the hotel, *détenus* were relieved of money, jewelry, and other valuables to pay for the food and expenses incurred in the provision of suffering and terror. Four doctors, ten Red Cross nurses, and a Jewish chaplain were on hand to minister to the residents who soon needed succor. The staff included a dozen torturers under Brunner's direct supervision. Seemingly endless questioning proceeded with repeated blows to the face and body and threats with a pistol. One captive recounted his interrogator extinguishing a cigar on his thigh and the odor emitted from multiple cigarette burns. The Gestapo was determined that prisoners reveal the whereabouts of parents, spouses, children, siblings, and friends in the Jewish community. When required, co-religionists were drafted to serve as interpreters.[58]

The communist-founded Union of Jews for Resistance and Mutual Assistance recorded happenings of extraordinary cruelty. More than 40 young children were summarily killed with shots of strychnine. Women and girls were sterilized at the Excelsior and sent to the Reich's eastern front "for the pleasure of the soldiers." A bordel of imprisoned Jewesses serviced the Wehrmacht in Cimiez. Another contemporary source described Gestapo agents taunting a Jewish baby before hurling him against a wall, fracturing his skull. Other examples of sadism were quietly spoken of in sorrowful tones.[59]

For Jewish captives considered of no intelligence value, initial confinement could be a far different experience. A Niçoise who after the war became one of France's most admired and politically influential women, Simone Veil (née Simone Jacob), related a far different ambiance in Brunner's holding area.

> During the week we spent at the Hôtel Excelsior, we did not have to submit to torture. We ate even in a more decent manner than outside. I recall among the S.S. who guarded us an Alsatian showed himself to be compassionate with the detainees. Did he know what awaited us? I doubt it. We could write to friends if we desired it, to bring to us personal things, books and warm clothes. So as extraordinary as that seems, these six days passed in uncertainty and apprehension, but not in the anguish that could have been imagined.[60]

Nazi roundups across France could not have taken place without help from two sources—individuals with a reputation for being able to detect Jews by their facial features (physiognomists) and the country's police. French Jews, especially those whose families had lived there for generations, were often indistinguishable in dress, mannerisms, habits, and views from their neighbors. For many, the best way to avoid detection was to become invisible, to drown oneself in the mass of humanity assembled on the Côte d'Azur. To hide their origins, Jewish women were even known to go to a hairdresser and have their curly hair straightened. In large measure these people held the respect of their fellow citizens. False identification papers issued to illegal immigrants and the absence of a yellow Star of David to spot them on the street made the business of recognition all the more difficult in the Italian zone. "Consequently it is necessary to appoint French anti-Semites to spy out and denounce the Jews who are camouflaged or hidden," Roethke concluded. "Money should be no consideration (propose to pay 100 francs per Jew)."[61]

When they could obtain photos of former prisoners, the Nazis used them to seek out and identify Jews. Otherwise, the Gestapo used physiognomists who were for the most part white Russians. They relied on more tricks than merely pointing to someone with olive skin, dark hair, and a Mediterranean nose. Informers provided leads. Checking the names on letter boxes was a common technique. Nor was it unusual for an informer to spy on a gathering of Jews, at a funeral for instance. Maintenance of religious services was necessary to bolster Jewish morale, as well as providing an opportunity for attendees to glean some news, but public worship could lead to dire consequences. One Niçoise turned in 53 persons in just a few months (and was subsequently executed by the Jewish Resistance). White Russians were known to arrest their quarry, then torture the prisoners to obtain information before delivering them to Hôtel Excelsior. Unscrupulous denouncers called the "fake Gestapo" burst into the residences of rich Jews, stripped off their valuables as presumably a pay-off for not apprehending them, and then turned in the victims for the official reward. As time went by and catches became more difficult, payments grew to as much as 5,000 francs in some cases.[62]

Paxton and others contend that without the compliance of Vichy and the participation of the Milice, national gendarmes and local policemen, the Nazis would have had insufficient manpower to make all these arrests. The Wehrmacht did not join in the Jewish manhunt, only the Nazi S.S. In the wake of the decision to execute the Final Solution, Knochen acknowledged, "To carry out the anti-Jewish orders in the newly-occupied zone we must have the co-operation of the French police." With only 1,000 German police in all of France in 1942 and less than 3,000 at its height, the arrest and deportation of tens of thousands of Jews and other persons considered undesirable would have been impossible without support from the French authorities.[63]

The prefect in Nice made an effort in late February 1944 to obtain clarification from Vichy of orders for French police to aid the S.S. The reply acknowledged that accords with the Reich did not appear to oblige French police to arrest all individuals designated by the Germans, but because of the "close collaboration" advocated by the two powers, information would continue to be passed to law enforcement officers in Nice to enable the apprehension of targeted individuals. A caveat added that in isolated instances an exception could be made, thereby making incumbent a report of the matter.[64]

The secretary-general to the mayor of Cannes, André Chataigner, took a more subtle tack. "Immediately before the arrival of the Germans, we decided of common accord—I speak of the employees in my service—to make all the files of good ration cards with Israelite-sounding names disappear […] During the entire occupation period, we delivered no less than 4,000 false cards for rations and identity." He went on to say that at times Jews would come to the *hôtel de ville* and offer money for these cards. "We gave them the papers," he insisted, "and refused the money."[65]

The viciousness of the German roundups after the peaceful Italian occupation coalesced the general population in support of victims of Nazi persecution. Ordinary citizens befriended Jews of any nationality—sheltering them, safeguarding family valuables, tending to their shops during the worst of times, and simply offering the gift of silence. In his bi-monthly report in November, the prefect observed that residents of Alpes-Maritimes were sickened by the sight of Frenchmen taking part in the arrests, whether in the Milice and PPF or not. The women of Nice were hiding Jews in reaction to what was characterized as "economic anti-Semitism." Their displeasure was shown by the large crowd demonstrating and shouting at the railway station, even wounding German soldiers when the first train of deportees pulled away. On other occasions, a silent stream of women filed through the city streets in protest, babes in arms.[66]

More needed to be done. During the months of the Italian interlude, Jewish charity organizations had become accustomed to operating in broad daylight. The Young Zionists distributed 6,000 *cartes d'identité*, 200 books of food coupons, 1,000 copies of (counterfeit) demobilization papers, and 900,000 francs in various aid. In addition, they evacuated 70 adults and 120 children to Switzerland from Nice and another 600 persons from the interior. The major contribution of the Union of Jews for Resistance and Mutual Assistance was publishing and distributing tracts in Yiddish for immigrants. Now the false sense of security brought about reversals. The fight cost the lives of over 40 Jewish Scouts and 17 other youth trying to stem the deportations. The General Union of Israelites of France, Federation of Jewish Associations of France, Organisation Sociale des Etrangers, Organisation de Sauvetage des Enfants, and committee on boulevard Dubouchage were all forced to close their doors. Their leaders were particularly hounded by the Nazis.[67]

The irregular Jewish Army was more combative. A commando squad from Nice went as far afield as Lyon to destroy files and lists of Jews.[68] Another team targeted a Marseille arms dealer to steal revolvers and ammunition. Bombs were planted in nightclubs and shops known as centers of anti-Jewish activities. Equipped and ready, the Army's soldiers stalked Gestapo agents, French collaborators, and white Russians, looking for opportunities to exact revenge.

A celebrated success in the spring of 1944 involved a Caucasian named Georges Karakaeff who lived in Nice with his mistress, Madeleine Teissier, an artist. "Kara," as he was known, was wanted by the Jewish Resistance as a notorious informer and executioner for the Nazis, but he kept an irregular schedule and was difficult to track. Coming out of a bar one morning, he observed an attractive woman on a bicycle have a minor accident on boulevard Victor-Hugo. She happened to be the underground's best woman agent, and while she did not recognize Kara, his bronze tan, crudeness, and khaki jacket and pants piqued her curiosity. She permitted him to accompany her for some shopping and then agreed to meet again that afternoon at place d'Alsace-Lorraine. Checking at headquarters, Kara's identity was ascertained and a plan conceived. At the appointed time and place, the girl apologized for not being able to spend time with Kara as she had an errand to do for her mother some distance away. Kara took the bait and insisted on accompanying her on the trek up a long, rough path away from the city center. Rounding a bend after a half hour, the couple came upon a young man who hesitated for a moment, then pulled out a revolver and shot Kara three times. When the police arrived ten minutes later, Kara was dead. The curious epilogue is that when the German occupation was over and a search made of the Hôtel Excelsior, a receipt was found for 10,000 francs paid by the Gestapo to Madeleine Teissier for the death of Kara.[69]

Even residents of German nationality in Nice joined in the fight against Nazi fascism. Margarethe Becker, a shorthand-typist employed by the Gestapo, saved lives by passing to the Resistance the names and addresses of Jews who had been denounced. Gerhardt Steinberg and his sister were arrested in August 1944 and convicted by a court-martial for encouraging Polish soldiers to desert. They escaped punishment when the Côte d'Azur was liberated.[70]

The role of the Catholic Church in Southeast France continues to raise questions to this day, as it does elsewhere in the Europe during the dark war years. There were two ways in which clerics tried to protect the Jews. One was to baptize them or at least issue papers to that effect. The second way, of course, was to shelter refugees. Priests and many of their faithful took in Jews hunted by the authorities both before and during the Nazi reign of terror. The curé in Séranon in the high country of western Alpes-Maritimes, for example, sheltered 20 Jewish children in his presbytery. The cloisters at Cimiez were another haven. Other clergy stood out for different reasons. Abbé Pierre Roubaudy, director of College Sasserno in Nice, set up an entire dormitory for Jewish children without asking for any sort of conversion. Abbé Alfred Daumas, director of the Christian labor exchange, joined James Bass of Service

André to form an action group to resist the deportation of Jews. Daumas provided access to the Jesuit fathers, facilitating passage of 3,000 fugitives to Southwest France and from there to safety, before being denounced and arrested himself. Bass, a Jew, had taken the nom de guerre of André and later worked as Father Marie-Benoît's assistant when allied with Donati.

An individual's public words and appearances regarding treatment of the Jews was not always a clear indication of personal feelings and actions. The primate of the French Catholic Church, the archbishop of Toulouse, and bishops and priests in other cities wrote open letters of protest against wholesale arrests and deportations.[71] Why not the Bishop of Nice, Monseigneur Paul Rémond, some historians have asked?[72] Rémond burnished his credentials with the right wing by celebrating Mass during the formation of the LFC at the grand Place Masséna in Nice and at other ceremonies. The bishop had a greater contribution to make to the cause of humanity, liberty, and freedom of religion, however, than anti-fascist pronouncements that might well have led to his forcible removal from office.

Unbeknownst to many, Rémond's credentials as a Germanophobe were well established by his military service in World War I, and consequently he had come under the watchful eye of the Gestapo after the Franco-German Armistice was signed. The prelate had visited foreign Jews confined in internment camps and intervened on numerous occasions on behalf of prisoners. German authorities intercepted at least one letter from an anonymous Niçois identifying the bishop as someone who helped Jews. Indeed, the Gestapo sent a woman dubbed Alice-la-Blonde to Rémond's door at one point with some young Jews in tow, pleading with him to hide them. He resisted the temptation and quite likely saved his life as a result. Nevertheless, it was soon thereafter that pro-Nazi demonstrators appeared outside Notre Dame on avenue de la Victoire shouting, "Down with Rémond," "Rémond to the firing squad," "Gaullist," "Jew [...]"[73]

Monseigneur Rémond was deeply troubled by the threat posed to the growing population of Jews concentrated in Alpes-Maritimes. Under his leadership the priests in his diocese administered the sacraments to members of the Resistance and provided spiritual support for actions by Catholics to befriend Jews and other persecuted individuals. Rémond's concern reached a zenith during a campaign initiated by Brunner to deport the Jewish children of France. The organization dedicated to protecting them, the Organisation de Sauvetage des Enfants, was under pressure across the country and had stopped coordinating with the tainted UGIF, also thrown into confusion. One hundred youths were taken from a secret children's home in Nice as part of the Nazi drive to find and eliminate the next generation of French Jews.[74]

It was providential therefore that Rémond met Moussa Abadi and Odette Rosenstock. Originally from the Middle East, Abadi had been studying at the Sorbonne when war erupted. He was given the nom de guerre "Marcel." Rosenstock was a physician before the war but, like other Jews, had been denied the right by the Vichy regime to continue practicing. Her concern for protecting Jewish children led her to Rémond, where she joined with Abadi to form *Réseau* (Network) Marcel. He was labeled an inspector of independent education, and his partner designated a social worker. The bishop baptized her "Sylvie Delattre," although she was known throughout the diocese as Sister Marie. At the bishopric, Rémond provided an office for Réseau Marcel to create false papers, among other tasks.[75]

With the imprimatur of Bishop Rémond, Sister Marie began searching for hiding places for Jewish children in the back country. She contacted priests for housing in rectories or with parishioners and visited youth holiday camps, orphanages, and boarding schools where young Jews could be integrated into larger groups of children, thereby becoming less visible to the authorities. Ration cards were fabricated to enable their protectors to obtain the necessary provisions. Every Jewish child received a basic wardrobe. Rémond agreed to baptize them and authenticate a certificate as proof. A different story and background had to be invented for each child. Indicating North Africa as place of birth made it impossible for the Nazis to double-check. Children were drilled in using new names and trained not to respond to their real ones, a reflex naturally difficult to explain and justify, especially to the youngest. Reliable records of who the children really were and where they were sent were prepared, one copy placed in hiding and a second sent to the Red Cross in Geneva for safekeeping. It was not unusual, in response to a call for help, for the bishop to appear and verify the communion of a child, thereby preventing apprehension. While this subterfuge was underway, parents were required to make a complete break with no knowledge of where their young ones had been taken. Sister Marie visited the youngsters regularly, though, and occasionally passed along bits of news to their families.[76]

The account of one beneficiary of Réseau Marcel illustrates how the program was carried out. Jeannette Swita, age 13½, initially met Sister Marie at a dispensary in Nice. She proposed to Jeannette's mother to send the girl and her brother to safety in the mountains, and after being refused, Marie provided the address of a pharmacy in Nice where they could be left if the situation changed. When the Nazi roundups commenced, the parents sought out the appointed place. The following morning a man described by Jeannette as tanned with a warm voice came to take the siblings away. It was Monsieur Marcel. The children were separated, as boys and girls were hidden in separate locations. Jeannette was told to forget her name; she was now Jeanne Moreau, born at Marrakech in Morocco. With the Sisters of Saint-Vincent-de-Paul she learned the Lord's Prayer and to say the "Hail Mary." At the end of the month, Sister Marie took her to the Jeanne d'Arc boarding school in Grasse where three other Jewish girls were under cover. Jeannette remembers the bright points in that scholastic year being the numerous occasions when Sister Marie came to visit. Petite, quiet, blonde, always smiling, happy and proud, she was their only tie to the lives left behind. Marie seemed always available to comfort the children and make them laugh.[77]

Only five of more than 500 wards placed by Réseau Marcel were arrested. The seizures occurred during an unexpected visit by medical authorities, and the two adult helpers with them suffered torture before being deported along with their charges.[78] This rate of success compares with about 100 Jewish children who lost their lives across the southern zone out of approximately 5,000 youngsters hidden with non-Jews. Historian Lucien Lazare concludes his treatment of this subject with the observation, "France is in debt to the rescue networks of the Jewish resistance, to their very numerous allies within humanitarian organizations and the Resistance, and finally to the thousands of peasants, workers, teachers, priests, men and women of all walks of life, who took in Jewish children and protected them."[79] In this roster will be found Catholic priests like Paul Rémond and Protestant ministers such as Pierre Gagnier.

Pastor Gagnier provided baptism documents for refugees in Nice after finding names in the old parish register of persons the same age and asking the *hôtel de ville* for extracts of their register of births in order to issue credible-appearing certificates. Pastor Monod did the same in Cannes. A corollary was denying the Gestapo access to church records that might disprove a christening had taken place. Other Protestant clergy were no less determined. Parsons sheltered youngsters, collected money for their welfare, and attempted to secure safe passage to Switzerland. Rectors in Nice and Cannes found themselves the subjects of investigations by the Vichy police for engaging in the illusion of baptism. Lazare Pelleur, minister of the reformed church in Antibes, hid Jews behind a false wall in the basement of his parsonage. A Baptist pastor organized the collection of 10,000–12,000 francs per week to sustain Jewish outcasts.[80] The Lutheran Swedish consul in Nice was equally sympathetic, providing sanctuary for two Jewish boys who climbed over his garden wall before handing them over to Réseau Marcel.

On December 14, 1943, Brunner closed the Hôtel Excelsior and headed to Drancy. By this time the Nazis had concluded that the French police were no longer reliable collaborators in anti-Semitic operations. The changing tide of the war undoubtedly contributed to the shift in attitude. Paxton's collaborative study of the Holocaust in France concluded that "Indifference to the fate of Jews was the predominant attitude" in Vichy France.[81] That complacency was shattered in Alpes-Maritimes by the Nazi barbarity toward Jews following on the heels of the benevolence of the Italians. Having studied the subject extensively, Poliakov concluded, "The 'human hunt' on the Côte d'Azur in the autumn of 1943 surpassed in horror and brutality everything of this kind previously known, at least in Western Europe."[82] Indeed, outside Paris, Alpes-Maritimes was one of the French departments most haunted by Nazi genocide.

On the other hand, Serge Klarsfeld, France's foremost expert on the fate of Jews during the war years, which he personally experienced, has gone so far as to state that the campaign against Jews in Nice was a relative setback for Brunner.[83] Both he and Paxton identified 1,820 prisoners shipped off in 27 convoys by the Gestapo during Brunner's tenure, of whom 1,400 were from the Côte d'Azur (and 1,100 of those from Nice). When considering the overall number which Klarsfeld estimates to be not less than 25,000 Jews along the coast between Menton and Cannes (15,000 being foreigners), this historian considers Brunner's results "mediocre." Another scholar agrees by asserting, "They [résistants] won a special victory, saving the lives of almost ninety percent of the prey whom Brunner's Gestapo wanted to seize." Simone Veil attributes the Gestapo's mixed success to genuine solidarity in the Niçois population against the occupiers and to the French police becoming less willing to reinforce an invader who seemed more and more likely to lose the war as the Allies rolled up a string of triumphs on the battlefield. Erlanger adds his voice "to the honor of the Niçois, the majority of whom, atoning for the Miliciens and other collaborators, soon applied themselves to hiding Jews."[84]

Yet Brunner accomplished his strategic purpose of destroying the principal Jewish sanctuary in Occupied Europe. At the same time, the purge had the unintended effect, Klarsfeld continues, of solidifying against the Nazis the population as a whole, members of the Catholic and Protestant clergy, and even the local government and police. Like Paxton at the national level, Klarsfeld concludes, "The example of Nice is then to show there that the Jews of France could have been saved altogether if Vichy had the courage at the beginning of the summer of 1942 to refuse the assistance of its police to the Germans."[85]

Deportation numbers from Nice fell off sharply after Brunner departed. Large-scale roundups became rare, being replaced by raids targeted at private homes. From January through March 1944, 660 Jews were captured in Nice and sent through Drancy to Poland and extermination. This figure declined sharply in April–July, dropping 80 percent from the preceding three months.[86] In total, 2,949 persons were deported during the Nazi occupation.[87] It was only when the Allies landed in Provence that the Jewish nightmare in the Southeast was over.

The final tally showed 4,200 deportees sent from Alpes-Maritimes to Germany during the war years. Returnees overall numbered 590 individuals, or 14 percent; of the Jews only 3 percent survived, the same tiny proportion as in all of France. Vichy propaganda insisting that by sacrificing foreign Jews, French nationals would be spared was a convenient and incredible rationalization. More than 76,000 of approximately 300,000 Jews resident in France, the largest population in Europe, were deported to die in former Polish territory considered at the time as eastern Germany. One quarter were French citizens, 2,000 under the age of six, and 8,700 over 60 years old. The 25 percent killed of the Jewish population then in France is thought to represent the third lowest mortality rate in Europe. What is not often mentioned is that only 5 percent of the non-naturalized Jews returned from the death camps.[88]

These statistics show no winners. The only bright spots were those many instances when individuals helped other human beings to survive, often at the risk of their own lives, thereby providing expressions of the innate goodness of mankind.

6
𝕰𝕏𝕮𝕭

British Agents in the Midi

Great Britain's interest in liberating Europe from fascist domination did not end with the pell-mell escape from Dunkirk. Cynics might gibe that "England would always fight to the last Frenchman," but that was purely prejudicial. From Maréchal Pétain's armistice with Germany in 1940 through the landings on French shores in 1944, the government in London planned and conducted a campaign to undermine Nazi control of France led by operatives recruited and trained in Britain. The instrument for this subversion was the Special Operations Executive.

The SOE was an independent entity, one of nine British wartime secret services. Sometimes referred to cynically as "The Ministry of Ungentlemanly War," the main business of the SOE was to coordinate subversive and sabotage activity against the enemy. Two groups were concerned with France: SOE's F Section, a stand-alone operation inserting agents into the country, and R/F Section, organizing cells with the French themselves and coordinating with General de Gaulle's staff, with whom relations were always tense. The in-house history of the SOE offered the generalization that "F Section was dependent on bilingual British subjects, on Frenchmen with some English background and a special affection for Britain, and on Frenchmen who combined patriotism with distrust for De Gaulle and had the energy and initiative to act independently of his authority." Conversely, the SOE viewed R/F men as possessing limited educational or administrative experience. While clearly patriotic and well trained as saboteurs and instructors, they lacked the organizational skills to become leaders of the resistance.[1]

The story of the SOE may be bracketed between two oft-repeated statements. Prime Minister Winston Churchill launched the organization on July 16, 1940 by directing the minister in charge, "And now set Europe ablaze!" At the conclusion of the war, General Eisenhower was quoted as saying that the French Resistance (supported for four years by the British) had shortened the war by nine months.[2] Between this baptism and benediction blazed a galaxy of courageous characters, adventures, and trials in SOE operations in the Midi.

The going was slow at first as the Foreign Office wanted to avoid causing disturbances in the area controlled by the Vichy government, which initially seemed worth courting. Still, French patriots who escaped to London after the surrender of their national sovereignty lobbied for British aid. Pierre de Vomécourt recalled after the war that he had met with the chief of the imperial general staff for this purpose. "I impressed on him the vital importance of arming the French resistance as soon as humanly possible, and managed to convince him that the resistance, although only small at the time [1940] really did exist and that it was in Britain's own interests to help us."[3] Creating circuits was naturally easier in the South than in northern France where German counter-espionage was stronger.

Allied Intelligence Services

From its inception the SOE was confronted with de Gaulle's sensitivity to British operations on his home turf. Looking beyond the war to the government that would take office, de Gaulle was insistent that French insurgents be deployed under his direction rather than as agents for London. To Colin Gubbins in charge of SOE training and operations, by January 1942 "it [was] clear that we cannot build up a proper secret army in France under the aegis or flag of de Gaulle; that we must do through our independent French [i.e., F] section, until such time as a combination is practical politics."[4] Consequently, SOE policy was to utilize agents of nationalities other than French to the maximum extent.

Individuals who fancied working for the SOE were informed that they could not apply, rather they were invited to join. Furthermore, it was a band unlike London's other clubs: women could be members. Everyone was an amateur; no one was a professional clandestine agent. Recruits hailed from overseas territories such as Mauritius, the Seychelles, and Indo-China, had parents of mixed nationality but held British passports, or had lived a long time in France. Security required that operatives speak flawlessly with no discernible accent; schoolhouse French was unacceptable despite the zeal of many applicants.

SOE agents were carefully instructed not to take sides in the country's politics, a rule not often violated. French men and women joined together in collective resistance; the British contribution was to furnish the tools wherever possible. Despite the outwardly good intentions of Maurice Buckmaster, director of F section, to run an apolitical operation, after the war France's foremost historian of the Resistance concluded that the English played off their rivals, promising résistants in the Métropole arms and money that it said de Gaulle could not provide.[5] At the same time, the Resistance tied to de Gaulle held distinct political views generally incompatible with communists' intent on controlling postwar France.

De Gaulle set up his own network of operatives, the Bureau Central de Renseignements et d'Actions (BCRA). At the outset, many of the Frenchmen who served as its agents on the Continent did not even know how to distinguish the rank on a German uniform or the caliber of an artillery piece, nor could they convey critical military intelligence when the Italian army occupied the Southeast. But that quickly changed as the BCRA attracted specialists and persons previously employed in sensitive positions key to obtaining this information. At its peak, the BCRA was also engaged in guerrilla warfare, counter-intelligence, escapes, and political and other non-combative activities.

Networks recruited by the BCRA were different from its clandestine counterparts in France. Alliance, for example, was a group originally set up by French dissidents themselves and became affiliated, first, with the SOE and, then, with the BCRA. Its specialty was military intelligence. The members were older than the average spy (over 60 percent at least 50 years old), more bourgeois (62 percent from managers, entrepreneurs, and those in private practice as lawyers, doctors, and accountants), with a greater feminine component (14 percent) and more urban (90 percent city-dwellers). With 3,000 agents, Alliance was also the only resistance circuit headed by a woman, Marie-Madeleine Fourcade, who began intelligence work from her youth center in Vichy. In Alpes-Maritimes the strength in the field comprised 56 percent civil servants of whom 36 percent were connected with the armed forces, 18 percent private managers and practitioners, and 8 percent entrepreneurs. Despite differences in backgrounds, their dedication was the same.

The BCRA in Alpes-Maritimes carried out several dramatic operations. In November 1942 it accomplished a maritime mission at Cagnes to extract six persons requested by General Henri Giraud. In January 1944, a BCRA team sabotaged a petroleum barge in Nice harbor. Other examples were destroying two anti-aircraft guns in a battery outside Cannes and burglarizing a blockhouse in Théole.[6]

Concurrent with the creation of the British and French services, in the autumn of 1940 the Polish headquarters in London organized an intelligence network of its own in France, first, named F and, then, after being decimated by the Nazis, with the designation F2. Having lost their country due to the perfidy of Germany and Russia, Polish Resistance fighters were among the most highly motivated of tyranny's victims. F2 headquarters in the South moved constantly between Marseille and Monaco. Urgent intelligence was transmitted via radio to London by operators in Beaulieu, Vence, Le Bar-sur-Loup, and Mandelieu on the Riviera.

The Alpes-Maritimes operation tried to make contact with the French Resistance, leading to a double agent slipping into the Polish fabric. Despite the Poles' obsession with security because of a painful awareness of the severity of reprisals, in December 1942 the Gestapo arrested 17 of their members, dismantling the Southeast operation. A new chief arrived the following February, reactivating F2 and leading efforts to contact Polish nationals in the Wehrmacht when the Germans arrived as occupation troops. By employing former members of the Polish army, liaisons were established with soldiers and civilians stationed at Nice, La Trinité, Roquebrune-Cap Martin, Antibes, Grasse, and Cannes, preparing the way for defections and sabotage once the Allies arrived on the Côte d'Azur.[7]

SOE Mode of Operation

What traits characterized SOE personnel that might not have been common in other intelligence services? First and foremost, the men and women who served with the SOE exhibited individualism. They tended to make their own decisions, a quality that would not have served them well in conventional military ranks. Technical skills imparted in their earlier training sharpened awareness of what they observed. Another important characteristic was an ability to make quick, instinctive, and accurate assessments of the people they encountered. By misjudging the character of an acquaintance, a former agent emphasized after the war, an operative could put in danger his or her life or that of those who placed trust in the envoy from London.[8]

The employment of women as agents behind the lines was a courageous decision in the early 1940s. Had the use of women as guerrillas leaked out, the government would have been forced to deny it due to strong popular sentiment in opposition. Indeed, a controversy was ignited at the war's end when a few female SOE agents emerged emaciated but alive, if barely, from Nazi concentration camps. It soon became known that the SOE had dispatched 39 women to France, one-third of whom perished. This mortality rate was higher than overall figures for France: of 470 SOE operatives deployed, 117 (25 percent) died.[9] These ratios compare, for example, with 42 percent of the members of the Resistance in Alpes-Maritimes who perished during deportation. Females were no less daring than their male counterparts and had the invaluable facility to move about freely by bicycle or train without drawing undue attention. In town or city it was natural to see women busily shopping in the streets or tending to children or relatives. In the country they could explain that they were collecting eggs, milk, fruit, or vegetables from a farm. Before the war, German women tended to remain in the domestic sphere, so it was not instinctive for the Gestapo to suspect a woman of engaging in espionage. Conversely, as the war progressed, French men were automatically under suspicion for not working for the Wehrmacht or having been deported to labor in German factories.

Candidates for SOE missions underwent weeks of training in physical fitness and marksmanship on the west coast of Scotland, afterwards receiving briefings on the Nazi occupation and how to operate in this domain, the living environment in the region where they would be assigned, and special skills necessary for an agent behind enemy lines—parachuting, map reading, "silent killing," use of a variety of weapons, and/or operation of a wireless. Not only did trainees learn how to apply and detonate volatile devices, in particular plastic explosive and time fuses perfected in England just before the war, but also the vital points of power stations, rail systems, telephone exchanges, factories, reservoirs, and canals. Recruits were instructed in the methods and procedures of the Axis police, ways to blend into the populace, the latest restrictions imposed by the gauleiter, and techniques to survive an interrogation. The Gestapo applied torture over several interrogation sessions. If the subject could hold out before disclosing a name or address, compatriots would have time to learn of his arrest and flee, leaving behind an empty hideout.

While language aptitude, operational skills, and knowledge could be tested to ensure proficiency, perhaps the most important attribute of a recruit, his or her character, was purely a subjective determination by Buckmaster.[10] Despite the interviews, tests, and evaluations, reprobates occasionally slipped through the screenings. Nigel Low was a professional gambler referred to the SOE because of his thorough knowledge of the French language and people, especially on the Riviera. He had a long record of convictions in Britain unbeknownst to the SOE, but had never been arrested by the Sureté. Low successfully underwent months of training until the spring of 1942 when he was sent to France with what Buckmaster characterized as "a largish sum of money." He was never heard of again.[11]

When cross-Channel crossings were cut off by German vigilance early in the war, the British looked to the south coast of France, not yet occupied by the Nazis, for access to the Continent. Transport by water was often the preferred choice. While flyers preferred a full moon to navigate at low altitude, clandestine mariners sought to enter hostile waters with no light at all. Seventeen nautical operations, both landing and embarking personnel, took place on the Côte d'Azur during 1942 alone. Arrivals by submarine in the Var took place from the open sea outside Ramatuelle on the Saint-Tropez peninsula.[12] Unlike today, long stretches of deserted beaches, deep water just off shore, and only a scattering of small towns facilitated disembarking illicit passengers and cargo. The first craft employed was the merchant ship HMS *Fidelity*, a seven-cabin cargo vessel refitted for undercover work involving British evaders and escapers, as well as operatives. It became apparent, however, that an easily visible steamboat was less well suited for clandestine operations than a light, narrow felucca. These small fishing boats used Gibraltar as a home port even though the voyage to the Riviera covered 700 miles each way, consuming nine days or twice that long in bad weather. Agents stepped ashore from rowboats or other open craft, often the two-man, Klepper folding canoe built to withstand heavy seas, launched from a felucca or submarine.

Seawolf, with a new 88-horsepower engine and Polish crew, immediately became the workhorse of the small felucca fleet. With engines and sails both working, the vessel could attain a speed of 8–9 knots. Passing through the Balearics between the islands of Ibiza and Majorca, the captain painted French colors on the hull of his craft and set course for Antibes, steering by the powerful lighthouse on Cap d'Antibes, visible from 15 miles even in bad weather. On a voyage in April 1942, *Seawolf* reached Antibes Bay to land agents on the same night Captain Peter Churchill arrived by submarine. The two vessels spotted one another running without lights and, suspecting the other to be hostile, each took evasion action. For lack of fuel, it was unusual to see even fishermen off the French coast, except small boats no more than a kilometer from shore.[13]

In early June 1942, *Seawolf* sailed on an evacuation mission for French authorities near Cassis in conjunction with another assignment for the SOE to deliver three agents with war matériel and bring three other passengers back to Gibraltar. By this time, lighthouses east of Toulon had been extinguished, and the captain had the tricky task of fixing his position in daylight, as the coastline was extremely varied, but without drawing too close to shore. A group of 82 people had waited three days for *Seawolf*, but dispersed when discovered by a forester. Twenty were subsequently arrested. The coastal craft sailed on to the small bay between Juan-les-Pins and the Iles de Lérins where two agents and their weaponry were taken ashore aboard a dinghy. Next stop was Cap-d'Ail near Monaco to drop a third operative. Returning to another landing site near Marseille, as the Cassis beach may have been compromised, the crew exercised caution in light of the recent penetration of Polish maritime activities. The 62 passengers on the homebound voyage included Henri Frenay, founder of the Combat movement, and three women, a first for the small boat without a toilet. Most of the passengers had to spend the journey on deck, hiding under a tarpaulin when other vessels were sighted.

At the end of June, *Seadog* was launched, a second felucca crewed by Poles. *Seadog*'s first appearance on the Côte d'Azur was at Cap d'Antibes where Major Nicholas Bodington, Buckmaster's deputy at SOE headquarters, Henri Frager, deputy chief of Carte network, and other operatives landed. On September 1 the British Admiralty suspended trips to the French coast from Gibraltar except those connected with intelligence. Ten weeks later, covert maritime activities along the Mediterranean coast stopped altogether with the fascist arrival in the Non-Occupied Zone.[14]

The SOE increasingly inserted agents in a variety of other ways, with parachuting used in 90 percent of the cases. Drops could only be made in moonlight, which restricted them to the period six days before or after a full moon. In the absence of a local cell of résistants, a provocateur was dropped "blind" into an area and expected to make his way alone. As the Resistance matured, reception committees met the arrival. Light aircraft were also used and oftentimes carried agents and others back to London on the return trip. Most often a Lysander was employed, its primary limitation being a capacity for only three passengers.[15] Later in the war, when larger groups were involved, a twin-engine Hudson bomber might be used as it could transport up to ten people or a ton of stores, but extra runway length, heightened security expectations, and competition with other military requirements made this an exceptional means of transport for the SOE. The Douglas Dakota DC-3 came into use in the South in the summer of 1944 strictly for operations in well-secured maquis areas.

Buckmaster conceived of the subterfuge of using seemingly innocuous sentiments on a French broadcast to identify agents, announce acts of sabotage, send matériel, warn of danger, and coordinate operations. Clandestine operators radioed London with requests for personnel with special skills or to pick up an outgoing operative or Resistance chieftain. After receiving approval, the circuit involved began listening to the BBC to learn when an aircraft would appear. A series of "personal messages" with double entendre was broadcast between 7.30 and 9.45 each evening, such as "the cow is sick" or "Aunt Marie sends her love," interspersed among a flood of false communiqué to confuse the enemy. Hearing the operable code words, the cell leader dispatched a team to a pick-up site already scouted locally and often pre-certified by the RAF. As SOE activity in France progressed, indications surfaced that networks had been penetrated by the Abwehr. Newly opened files show that as many as one-third of F Section circuits may have been infiltrated by radio deception alone. Indeed, a booklet printed for an SOE memorial at Valençay in the Loire Valley asserts that 27 agents were captured on landing or very soon thereafter.[16]

Reception of light aircraft soon became rudimentary. Ideally, nine résistants were on hand to illuminate the field. Seven individuals with bicycle lamps were spaced in a line at 150-yard intervals. At the end facing the wind, two other participants stood 50 yards apart. All flashlights were extinguished until the drone of an engine could be heard. The agent at the position farthest downwind flashed a codeword or letter skyward in Morse and, in turn, received a confirming signal from the pilot who turned on his lights. Once contact was established, flashlights were switched on, assuring the pilot the field was safe and indicating the axis of the runway and direction in which he should land.[17] A plane needed to be on the ground for only two to three minutes before being airborne once more. The reception committee quickly carted away any weapons and equipment and dispersed into the countryside before a German reaction team could respond.

While these activities became pro forma farther to the west—specifically, in the departments of the Var, Bouches-du-Rhône, and the Vaucluse—the topography of Alpes-Maritimes was not well suited for such operations, as it was too rocky, forested, and vertical, and consequently only parachute deliveries took place there. The terrain required to receive air deliveries were of varying lengths: reception of matériel from the air required a relatively small area; the recommended landing zone for parachutists was twice their size.

One operative who did not undergo training in England or have to be secretly deployed was Virginia Hall, a 33-year-old Baltimorean living in Lyon. Rumored at the time to have a wooden leg,[18] Hall had served in Poland with the US diplomatic service, been a military coding clerk, and driven an army ambulance before Paris fell. Working undercover as a *New York Post* correspondent while America was still neutral, she could file press reports that would pass through Vichy censors yet contain details of worth to the SOE. Her apartment was a safe haven for Allied airmen from downed planes or servicemen who had escaped prison camps and knew of her address on the escape route. On his initial visit to France in early 1942, Captain Churchill was helped by Hall in contacting two SOE agents in place in Lyon and Marseille.[19] By March 1944, when the United States began taking a real interest in southern France, Hall had redirected her energies to supporting its nascent intelligence activities.

One of the first SOE agents inserted into France, François Basin (nom de guerre "Laurent"), landed from *Fidelity* northeast of Perpignan in September 1941. Born in Grasse, Basin had represented French firms in London for almost 15 years before the war.[20] With his personal background and Cannes's history of welcoming foreigners, especially the British, is it any wonder that Basin established his center of operations in the resort? Immediately upon arrival he was arrested at the Hôtel de Bourgognes by Vichy police as a "suspected person" and taken to Fort Saint-Nicolas in Marseille. Fortunately, his interrogators were anti-German and let him go. Basin then proceeded to set up 30 small cells of résistants from Marseille to Grenoble in an SOE circuit known as Urchin.

The story goes that one day on a street in Cannes, Basin ran into Baron Antoine de *1944 Malval*, a former French naval attaché he had known in London. The aristocrat had retired outside town on the route to Fréjus. His Villa Isabelle became the headquarters for Urchin. London soon sent two radio operators by felucca. Basin billeted a "pianist" (or signals communicator) with a Corsican croupier, one of a group of résistants employed at the Palm Beach casino.[21] Cannes soon became a primary transit point for agents passing through the Non-Occupied Zone on their way to destinations both in the Midi and the Occupied Zone.

Louis of Antibes and Carte

To the east of Cannes sat another community, a commercial center and residence for native French in contrast to the playgrounds of Cannes. The two most memorable figures along the Côte d'Azur in those early days of the war years worked in Antibes, not for the Vichy regime but for the Resistance.

The first was Elie Lévy, a Jewish physician in his late forties, bald, clean-shaven, and portly. The doctor lived with his wife and two teenage daughters who frequently served as messengers. His sterling reputation derived not only from his medical practice but also due to his own military experience. Dr. Lévy served in the Zouaves in World War I and in a light mechanized division in the disappointing 1939–40 campaign. He was conferred the Légion d'honneur and Croix de Guerre for each conflict.[22] Lévy had been recruited by Jacques Vaillant de Guélis, who was a French liaison officer with the British Expeditionary Force. Subsequently, in August 1941 de Guélis returned to France to collect samples of ration cards, scout landing sites in Bouches-du-Rhône, and enlist agents, Lévy being among the best.

Known as "Louis of Antibes," Lévy had contacts with several cells of French dissenters including communists. He did not hesitate to mix provocateurs from different circuits around his excellent table, despite the threat posed to the diners' personal safety by being introduced to individuals from adversarial groups who could identify each other to the authorities. Indeed, it was even suggested that Lévy himself might harbor communist leanings among other political persuasions. Until his capture in 1943, Lévy received and dispatched many of the figures who covertly entered and left the Riviera.[23]

Not far from Lévy in a modest apartment near the Hôtel Royal resided André Girard, an artist in his early forties best known for humorous drawings of Hitler, Mussolini, and Stalin. Ambitious, persuasive, and temperamental, Girard refused to acknowledge de Gaulle as head of Free French forces and set out to make himself chief of the Resistance. First, he began collecting his own circle of devoted friends. Both the network and its leader were known as "Carte." Recruiting was not carefully controlled, however, and individuals of various motivations and backgrounds gained access to the organization, severely compromising its security.

Girard yearned to see France free once more. Consequently, he made contact with like-minded groups all along the Côte d'Azur, as well as in the Occupied Zone, and claimed to have connections with senior leaders in the Armée de l'Armistice who pledged support to an uprising. Girard met with Frenay, Baron Emmanuel d'Astier de la Vigerie,[24] and Colonel Jean Vautrin of the truncated French army, all linchpins of the evolving Resistance movement, and seemingly convinced them of his fiber. It was the mirage of a secret army allegedly numbering 300,000 men that attracted the British to Carte, and yet

100,000 of these "résistants" were wearing the uniform of the Armée de la Armistice and not under Girard's direction.

First, Basin became captivated by Carte's charm. Then, Churchill and Bodington came to meet the flamboyant chieftain. Bodington was completely taken in by Girard and his use of military jargon to convey the impression that he was not just a dreamer. Would arms and money sent by the British at the cost of being applied to other causes be well used or wasted?

The SOE's official historian in the 1960s, M. R. D. Foot, asserts that Carte absorbed an excessive proportion of Britain's resources earmarked for France during 1942.[25] Carte asked for wireless sets to communicate with his clandestine agents. London sent 37 battery-operated radios, even though their employment without a sound cipher system would jeopardize the security of all concerned. Carte then requested a regular broadcast that became known as Radio Patrie, first aired in October 1942 with actor Claude Dauphin from his own cell as an announcer. It was perceived by the Free French as competing with Gaullist transmissions. Pressure from de Gaulle not to divide the Resistance eventually convinced SOE headquarters to cancel the program. Tons of explosives and thousands of small arms would be required to equip the saboteurs envisioned by Carte, not to mention transport needed to deliver them. Carte's allure began to fade when Basin was arrested again in August 1942 and confined in Nice. Girard did not seem able to mount a team to organize an escape. His stock fell further after General Giraud succeeded in reaching Algeria, and Girard could not arrange for the general's long-time aide to join him by boat.[26]

The fatal flaw in the Carte circuit was the practice of drawing up lists of members on forms carefully designed by Girard. A batch of over 200 dossiers with the most important names was being taken by train from Marseille to Paris in November. The courier fell asleep on the way and when he woke up, his briefcase was gone, now in possession of an Abwehr agent. Fortunately, a local police chief warned 40 of the men named in the documents, but arrests of the remainder were only a matter of time.[27]

By early 1943, the fault lines in the Carte organization caused it to shatter. In addition to mass detentions based on the lost rolls, Girard and Frager, a distinguished, retired English artillery officer, had a falling out. First, one, then, the other left for London to plead his case. It was immediately clear to SOE command that Girard was all talk and not a leader or manager, his alleged network overblown, and its security non-existent. It seems almost incredible that the SOE failed earlier to realize that Girard's claims were too good to be true, but the prospect of establishing contact with the Armée de l'Armistice was so enticing as to obscure reality. Girard's family back on the Côte d'Azur went into prison, his wife to a concentration camp, and he soon sailed for the United States to lecture on secret operations, never to return.

Frager went back to pick up the pieces in a smaller, workable SOE operation farther to the north, Circuit Donkeyman.[28]

John Goldsmith

John Goldsmith was a horse trainer who grew up in Paris where his father was a prominent breeder. Initially Goldsmith was another operative sent to southeastern France in October 1942 to advise London on the capability of Carte. When Goldsmith reached Cannes by felucca and paddled a small rubber dinghy ashore, he found no one waiting for him. Suddenly his fears were allayed when four men emerged from the shadows and identified themselves as Girard's reception committee.

Goldsmith was taken to André Bartoli's Villa Caracasa on the coast at nearby Juan-les-Pins. The next day he was transferred to the home of Paulo Leonetti, a former assistant mayor of Antibes. Leonetti was a Corsican who had served in a Marseille infantry regiment before being captured at Verdun in 1917. Now a coiffeur, he could contact a lot of people without causing suspicion. Some of his best information came from the local brothel where he styled the girls' hair.

Goldsmith first went about the business of becoming familiar with the Riviera. His cover story was as a Parisian who had fled to avoid compulsory military service. Acquiring an aluminum bicycle, Goldsmith began giving instruction in explosives at Nice and Juan-les-Pins. This often had the side benefit of not being examined by railway police who assumed a Frenchman in the company of the enemy did not warrant close inspection. In a classroom, Goldsmith passed along the skills he had been taught in Britain in operating and dismantling a Sten, molding plastic explosives, and applying time pencil fuses. Getting to know members of various cells within Carte provided the SOE inspector with insights into its organization and state of readiness. In keeping with SOE theory that the safest place to operate was close to the authorities, training in Nice was conducted opposite the police station. Furthermore, when traveling by rail, Goldsmith made a point of going first class and choosing a compartment with German officers.

The most noteworthy accomplishment of Goldsmith during his sojourn in the Southeast was helping to spirit Giraud out of France to be with General Eisenhower in Gibraltar when the Allies arrived in North Africa. Eisenhower held Giraud in high regard because of the loyalty he commanded among former regular officers. Joined with the Americans, his stature was counted on to prevent French opposition to the landings. The circuit Alliance undertook to coordinate the departure. A British submarine would convey the general across the Mediterranean, and the Resistance felt it needed an English speaker as intermediary. Goldsmith was brought into the operation without being told the identity of the Very Important Passenger. He spent several nights with his co-conspirators on a sandy beach at Cannes waiting for HMS *Seraph* to appear, which eventually it did.[29]

When Carte broke into pieces, Goldsmith moved his base to Toulouse and supervised an area of operations that eventually spread from Lyon and Clermont-Ferrand to Marseille and Nice. Meanwhile, other SOE operatives had begun working assiduously to disrupt the fascist occupation. Notable was Lieutenant Anthony Brooks, who gained the confidence of railway men when inserted in July 1942, coordinating their activities in the Midi right up to the Provençal landing. Another agent, Captain Robert Boiteux, received praise for working effectively with Virginia Hall in Lyon despite repeated harassment from the Germans.[30]

Peter Churchill and Odette Sansom

After the war, the most famous Allied agents to operate in the South of France were Peter Churchill and his courier Odette. The son of a British foreign-service officer, Churchill had grown up abroad. When war erupted, he was 30 years of age, a prematurely graying architect. Odette Brailly was only 19 years old when she married an Englishman in 1930. She left her native France and gave birth to three daughters. When her homeland became weighed down under the oppression of Nazi occupation, Odette felt useless and isolated living with her children in Somerset while her husband served as an officer in the Royal Navy. Placing her girls in a convent, she joined the military and took great pride in, first, wearing the uniform of the First Aid Nursing Yeomanry (FANY) and, then, being selected for training as a spy in France.

During the 1950s, readers in Great Britain were enthralled by this couple's breathtaking adventures as related in three accounts authored by Peter Churchill. If anything, these recollections were eclipsed by his partner's story of active service, imprisonment, and torture at the hands of the Nazis, subsequently portrayed in a book and motion picture entitled, quite naturally, *Odette*. Together, their experiences furnish a colorful account of the perils of resistance in the Midi, if terrifying at the end.

Churchill recalled the instructions on his first mission to France:

> I am to take two million francs in a belt which I shall wear under my clothes and hand this money out to the following people: Laurent [Cannes], 400,000; Charles [Lyon], 300,000; Oliver [Marseille], 300,000. The other million is to go to Colonel Deprez[31] in Marseille for the purpose of bribing lawyers of rather doubtful integrity to get ten French patriots out of the Fort

St. Nicolas prison in that town. I shall have 100,000 francs for my own use [...] My first contact is Louis, whose real name is Dr. Lévi [sic]. He lives at 31, Boulevard Maréchal Foch, Antibes. If I arrive too late in the day, I am to spend the night at the Nouvel Hôtel. When I get into the doctor's consulting-room I am to give the following password, so as to let him know I am a friend from London: *"René de Lyon vous envoit ses amities* [René of Lyon sends you his best wishes]." He will then reply, to show that he has understood: *"Vous voulez dire René la Salle?* [Do you mean to say René la Salle?]"[32]

The agent arrived by submarine at Miramar-de-l'Estérel in January 1942, the first such disembarkation of an SOE agent in this part of the world. He bore French identity papers in the name of Pierre Chauvet, a demobilization card from the French army, a half-used book of Marseille tram tickets, tobacco and ration tickets, and photographs of a man and woman who were supposed to be his parents in South America, where they could not easily be checked. Churchill wore a money belt and carried ten packets of Gauloise cigarettes. His kit consisted of a small suitcase with shirts, pants, sweater, handkerchiefs and pajamas of Continental design bearing French labels, and shaving gear.[33]

Louis of Antibes requested radio sets and operators. Returning to London, Churchill arranged for the assignment of two Englishmen who spoke flawless rapid French. The team flew to Gibraltar to prepare for passage to the Riviera. It was on the dock that Churchill met Alastair Mars, 26-year-old captain of HMS *Unbroken*. Churchill impressed the young skipper. "Of medium build, dark, and with deep, intelligent eyes, he would only be distinguishable in a crowd by his charm and a certain sense of authority. Here was a strong character, I felt, unassuming and quiet, yet capable of decisive violence should the occasion arise."[34]

While waiting, Churchill and his compatriots practiced climbing down from the bridge into a small folding, flat-bottomed canvas boat developed by the SOE and known as a folboat. Navigating it and using the compass were vital to finding a partially submerged vessel when returning from land in pitch-dark night. Then, one evening in April, *Unbroken* slipped into the Mediterranean. When Mars first peered through the periscope at Antibes, he decided not to insert the agents as rain was pouring down, an unidentified boat had appeared (in actuality the Allied felucca *Seawolf*), and the submarine's navigation system had suddenly gone haywire. These problems disappeared by the following night, although a flotilla of fishing boats appeared and illuminated Antibes Bay with acetylene flares to attract their catch. Nevertheless, the crew lowered the folboat and the operatives boarded with suitcases and equipment.[35]

On his first visit to Antibes, Churchill had spotted concrete steps leading from the water to the garden park at the foot of Boulevard Albert 1èr, 300 yards from Lévy's house. Now, before leaving the agents alone on the rocks, Churchill hurried to ensure that the doctor was ready to receive them.[36] Waiting for the submarine was Emmanuel d'Astier. It was 2.00 a.m., and Lévy's wife, Jeannine, "so small and ugly and so very kind" in the mind of d'Astier, had softly awakened him with the words, "You're leaving; they're here."[37] Churchill quietly led the tall, good-looking former naval officer back to the folboat for the first leg on their long journey to London.[38]

When he next landed, this time by parachute near Montpellier on the night of August 27–8, Churchill's mission was to act as liaison officer between London and Carte. A secondary role was to encourage and organize sabotage. He formed a circuit in Cannes (Spindle) to complement Urchin and allow Basin to take a break in Britain. Just before Churchill's arrival, however, Basin was arrested. He discouraged Churchill's determination to rescue him and was released three months later. So, Churchill went about the business of setting up his own network of dissenters by himself.

Spindle's wireless operator was an accomplished Russo-Egyptian code-caller, "Arnaud" (Adolphe Rabinovitch). He began work at Villa Isabelle. The cell was saved from discovery on more than one occasion by de Malval's friendship with Colonel Vautrin who was commander of the military district of Grasse and charged with overseeing the Deuxième Bureau (intelligence) in the Southeast. Vautrin may have also coordinated with Jean Moulin as they both worked in Pierre Cot's office in the Reynaud government before the war.

Churchill's concern with taking precautions led him to move repeatedly from one safe house to another. A second headquarters was established in Cannes at 20 quai St. Pierre, the apartment of the artist Odette des Garets. Roger Renaudi's shop beside the Hôtel Majestic was ideal for a rendezvous because of its dual entrances, one into the Jardin Fleuries and the other onto the street behind. A beauty parlor in the Villa l'Augusta on rue du Canada provided another point of contact.[39]

Churchill was constantly troubled by Girard's lackadaisical approach to security. Upon first visiting the head of Carte, Churchill was proudly intro-duced as a British agent to the painter's wife and four daughters, as well as to their dinner guests. Restricting the number of contacts and compart-mentalizing information were two principal tenets of Churchill's operations, and Girard violated both. Furthermore, Girard composed wordy messages to be relayed to London which increased the risk of the time-consuming transmissions being detected. Churchill was placed in a difficult position.

A contact in the Deuxième Bureau reported that the Germans had deployed 36 radio-detection vans along the coastline to locate enemy spies. The informant was able to supply Churchill with the identification numbers of vehicles assigned to the Cannes–Antibes area. Each had a driver, machine gunner, and sound-detection technician. The units worked in teams and through triangulation could locate a clandestine transmitter within minutes after it began broadcasting. Operators were instructed to limit messages to a single six-minute session per day and to post lookouts to warn of the Gestapo's approach.

In addition to radio communication, Churchill used couriers to send messages to London, especially maps and lengthy communiqués, such as reports that would require so long to transmit in Morse code as to endanger the operator. Three times a week, messengers crossed and recrossed the frontier with Switzerland, as well as the Spanish border in the Southwest. Relays maintained contact among individual cells, officers demobilized by the French army, local officials, and Carte or, later, Churchill.

On November 1, under an evening sky brilliant with stars, the felucca *Dewucca* piloted by a Polish fisherman glided slowly toward the shore near Cassis. When it could safely proceed no further, a dinghy ferried two men and three women to the beach. One of the operatives, Odette Sansom (her husband's family name), now known as Lise, had orders to contact Michel (Churchill's field name) in Cannes. He was to make arrangements for her to cross the demarcation line to her assignment in Auxerre.[40]

Writing in the third person, Michel described Lise upon first meeting her:

about twenty-five [...] her mop of light-brown hair, swept back to reveal a rounded forehead, down to a pair of discerning eyes, there emanated a distinct aura of challenge that was only intensified by the determined set of her chin below a somewhat colourless face. A fearless look suggested that not even the thought of the prisons held any terrors for this girl; so much so that, in the flash of time he gave to his snap judgment of her, it even occurred to [Churchill] that she might not bother to take all the precautions she should to avoid capture [...] But what took and held his gaze above all else were the hands; hands such as he had never seen before in his life. They were long with slim, capable fingers.[41]

It became immediately apparent to Michel that Lise was intelligent, resourceful, and determined, qualities that would make her an excellent addition to his operation. To Lise's astonishment, SOE headquarters agreed to let her remain in Cannes as courier for Spindle. Over the next three months until Carte collapsed and they fled to avoid capture, Michel sent Lise across the South of France on various assignments. Yet Spindle and Carte organized only a single arms airdrop. Weapons delivered earlier by felucca had been efficiently collected, but Carte stored the radio sets, arms, and matériel improperly in containers in the sea at Antibes and in a garage at La Bocca, and they soon became unserviceable.[42] In sum, Churchill maintained the critical liaison expected of him, even if during the autumn of 1942, there was almost no sabotage in the Cannes–Antibes area accomplished by the Resistance resourced from London.

After Italians invaded the Non-Occupied Zone in late 1942, numerous arrests resulted from the compromised list of Carte agents. Vautrin wisely slipped across the Spain frontier. Churchill moved his base of operations away from the Riviera to Savoie in the Alps near Geneva. He and Lise settled into the Hôtel de la Poste, an old, brown, wood and white stucco chalet beside a lake surrounded by snow-clad mountains. A member of the Resistance managed the hostelry. When Churchill took a Lysander back to London to confer at SOE headquarters in March, Odette was left in charge of Spindle. Couriers arrived from Nice, Antibes, Cannes, Marseille, Aix-en-Provence, and other cities, departing with money and explosives, as well as messages.

Churchill could take justifiable pride in his work behind the lines up until this point, but his subsequent capture must have caused him considerable regret. If Churchill was discomfited by their subsequent denouement, Odette surely replayed the events for the rest of her life. Amidst all her activity in Michel's absence, she was approached by a man of average height in his early forties with brown hair and spectacles, plus the gift of being extraordinarily convincing. He introduced himself as Colonel Henri, one of a number of officers in the Abwehr who blamed Hitler for the war and wanted to sue for peace. Henri asked Odette for a transmitting set and code to contact the British War Office. When Buckmaster heard of the proposition his response was unequivocal: break off all contact with the German!

On his fourth and final trip into wartime France, Churchill parachuted onto a field high above Annecy in the wee hours of April 15. His orders were to stay clear of Henri and Odette until she had stopped dealing with the dangerous interloper. Odette was a member of the reception committee, however, and the amorous companions naturally trudged down the slopes together to the hotel. The next evening, Henri arrived to arrest Odette in the lobby and going upstairs had the added good fortune of finding the legendary Michel sound asleep in bed.

In reality, Colonel Henri was Hugo Bleicher, a sergeant in the Abwehr counter-espionage office in Paris. Odette was by no means the only résistant to fall for his line; Frager was arrested by Bleicher the following year, sent to Buchenwald, and executed.[43] Bleicher had been tipped off about a cell in Annecy by a member of Spindle taken into custody. The German agent went to the Alps with a more modest objective in mind than what he accomplished. At considerable personal risk, Arnaud returned to the hotel shortly after the arrest to retrieve a suitcase full of incriminating papers. Yet still among the scraps of paper found on Churchill was the copy of a message addressed to Spindle, "On reaching the coast of France, the agents who have come by felucca will proceed straight to the Baron de Malval, Villa Isabelle, Route de Fréjus." Not surprisingly, Spindle was subsequently broken. De Malval was arrested and attributed his two years in German hands to Churchill's thoughtless violation of routine security procedures. Indeed, de Malval accused the subsequent author of retaining incriminating documents to facilitate writing his memoirs after the war.[44]

Given a choice of being held by the Germans or the Italians, Churchill naturally opted for the latter. Maintaining her wits in the waiting car, Odette pretended to fasten one of her suspenders while cleverly tucking Churchill's wallet out of sight under the seat. The prisoners were taken to Villa Lynwood, where Odette was confined in an upstairs room and Churchill held in the cellar. A week later, he was buoyed to see his old friend Louis of Antibes remain undefeated despite being under arrest, not hesitating to stand up to his captors. Churchill gave no overt sign of recognition so as not to indicate that he and Lévy worked together. After interrogation in Nice, Lévy was quietly transferred to Imperia, Italy, and then deported to Germany. He died while being moved from Auschwitz in advance of Soviet troops in January 1945.[45]

The leadership of Spindle was too valuable a prize to remain long in Italian hands, and Churchill and Odette were soon transported to Fresnes Prison ten miles outside central Paris. She succeeded in convincing the Gestapo that, first, her mate was a close relation to the British prime minister (in actuality, he may have been a 62nd cousin) and thus worth keeping in good health as a potential bargaining chip; second, that they had been secretly married (they hadn't); and, third, that she was the brains of the network, and therefore she alone should suffer the consequences. Odette endured terrible torture inflicted at Gestapo headquarters on Avenue Foch in Paris, branded with a red-hot iron and having her toenails pulled out, before eventually being transported to Ravensbruck concentration camp in Germany.[46] Bleicher coldly dismissed her in his postwar memoirs saying simply, "She remained obstinately silent. She seemed to me less important then and I soon lost sight of her."[47] However, Odette's personal courage and uplifting spirit during two years of captivity served as an inspiration to others with whom she came into contact, German and French alike. American forces liberated both agents in early 1945 and they were married in 1947.

Francis Cammaerts

The same Lysander piloted by Flight Lieutenant Hugh Verity that carried Churchill back to London in March 1943 had returned with the SOE agent later considered the most effective in southeastern France. Before taking off, the pilot remembered Churchill shaking hands with "Roger" and saying, "Welcome, friend [...] There's a car laid on. Good luck!" The incoming arrival's biographer recounts Churchill offering more practical advice: "Be careful you've always got some paper with you when you go to the toilet, they're very short of rolls." The agent was Francis Cammaerts, the son of a Belgian poet. Until his brother was killed, Cammaerts had been a pacifist growing food for the war effort. A Cambridge blue of 27 years, six feet, four inches tall, he was fair like a Nordic with dark eyes and a military mustache. A later comrade described Cammaerts as "a smiling young giant whose coltish appearance was exaggerated by sloping shoulders and an easy resilient poise. These features, to begin with, obscured the contradictory qualities of leadership and modesty with which he subsequently impressed me. It was only later I realized that for him resistance was tantamount to a new religion."[48]

As soon as he set foot on French soil, Cammaerts was troubled by the little attention given to safety measures by the members of the Resistance who warmly greeted him. He was immediately tested when Colonel Henri was referred to him by a member of the underground in German custody. Cammaerts wisely smelled a rat, instinct that proved prescient when he later learned of the apprehension of Churchill and Odette by the same adversary. The arrests prompted Cammaerts to relocate to Cannes where he first occupied a safe house identified by Arnaud and built up a cover story as a schoolmaster, his profession in England before the war. The educator had allegedly come south from Paris to recuperate from jaundice. Once the cell in Cannes was back up and running, Cammaerts handed control over to a former member of Carte and moved westward to continue recruiting and organizing throughout the Midi.

With Carte in shambles, the initial plan was for a tripartite organization with Frager in the North and Cammaerts in the Southeast. Cammaerts undertook to construct a network named Jockey, which eventually comprised eight departments. He soon gained the impression that in southeastern France the Gestapo relied upon the Italians who were rather haphazard about police work. Local inhabitants were generally not too interested in underground activities, he found, although willing to assist in a passive capacity. Students were the most active objectors but often irresponsible as young people can be.[49]

Cammaerts's success as a leader of the Resistance was due to a near fixation with security, causing him to change locations after three or four nights in the same house. He felt it only fair always to tell his hosts he was English, as the penalty for sheltering the enemy was death, but hopefully that realization gave them confidence the Allies were sticking beside France. When arrested, his own deputy could not reveal where he could be found because Cammaerts kept his addresses secret even from his French partner.[50]

Cammaerts constructed a patchwork of many small parts unaware of one another. A team of eight men, of whom two were formerly with the Sureté, was tasked with following prospective recruits and new members. On occasion,

Cammaerts placed himself under surveillance to ensure that his movements were not under watch by the authorities. Elementary training in security was constantly given to sub-groups under his leadership. Located primarily out of towns, arms depots were also kept small and dispersed. Matériel was often hidden on farms, with the owners told exactly what they were asked to conceal. As some of his charges had received sabotage training in the French army, Cammaerts agreed to their working alone as long as the results were satisfactory. It was clearly understood that no member of the organization would be sacked; anyone who violated the rules would be shot.

By early autumn of 1943, Cammaerts had developed 50–60 small independent groups between the Riviera and the left bank of the Rhône. By summer of the following year, he had a force of 10,000 résistants organized and waiting for word to overturn the Nazi occupation. Included were mountaineers and skilled ski instructors, valuable assets in training maquisards to patrol the Alpine high country and, later when it was time, to create avalanches to block roads.

Cammaerts was always on the move, forming new cells, identifying fresh drop zones, and instilling confidence in men and women in communities in the hinterland. Couriers employed "boite aux lettres," literally a "letter box" but oftentimes referring, instead, to a sympathizer of the Resistance who received, held, and passed on clandestine communiqués. Messengers only worked in a single area to compartmentalize operations. Cammaerts instructed women to carry a note on a small piece of paper in one hand where it could quickly be discarded. When possible, communications were oral. Wireless transmissions were also strictly controlled, never lasting more than one minute at a time. Cammaerts insisted that radio operators work in the country and remain in the same locale for no more than three weeks. He personally inspected the safe houses selected as signaling stations beforehand, as well as periodically when in use. One such radio post was in Vence, a hillside retreat preferred by artists in earlier times, although Cammaerts generally found the mountainous Alpes-Maritimes difficult for clear transmissions.[51]

Could Cammaerts achieve anything with his obsession for security? His prime accomplishment was establishing a network all across southeastern France, an area as large as the states of lower New England (Massachusetts, Connecticut, and Rhode Island). Riding an old bicycle or in a car, on foot or by train and bus, Cammaerts met forgotten Resistance leaders and formed groups of *réfractaires* (the term for those who refuse to submit) who had made a conscious decision to rebel. On roads in the Midi where the constant movement of refugees and foragers for food was commonplace, a clandestine SOE operative did not stand out. He exhibited no bias and worked with communist and right-winger, Gaullist and anti-de Gaulle factions. What Cammaerts had to offer was the means to resist—airdrops of weapons and explosives delivered to fields he had personally scouted. Destruction of industrial targets, power stations, or railway stock was not enough. Under his direction, French saboteurs changed the destination labels on German supply trains, poured sand into fuel tanks, and tore up landlines. These overt acts satisfied the smoldering anger of résistants impatient at the seemingly interminable delay before the arrival of Allied forces.

As the occupation dragged on and de Gaulle became accepted by more Frenchmen as the leader of Free French forces and the nation's best hope for restoration, his intelligence arm began to compete with the SOE for partisans, intelligence, arms, and the aircraft to deliver them. The number of Resistance networks increased considerably with the appearance of newcomers tied to the BCRA. The fruits of all their labor would become apparent with the Normandy landing and the rapid success of the Provençal debarkation ten weeks later.

Sir Henry Maitland Wilson, who served as Supreme Allied Commander in the Mediterranean theater, later estimated that these patriots reduced "the fighting efficiency of the Wehrmacht in southern France to forty per cent at the moment of the DRAGOON landing operations" in Provence. The Supreme Headquarters Allied European Forces (SHAEF) was more direct in weighing the accomplishments of the SOE. Its conclusion was that "without the organization, communications, material, training and leadership which SOE supplied [...] resistance would have been of no military value."[52] Although few realized it at the time, the organization of dissidents and the subversion accomplished in the Midi during the troubling times from Armistice to liberation were resourced and masterminded in large measure by the SOE. Perhaps just as important was the role of the British Special Operations Executive in bolstering the spirits of a population struggling under the Nazi boot, nurturing its will to resist.

7
⹓⹏⹒⹐⹑

The Maquis

"Maquis" is a term that originated in Corsica. It refers to bush or thick underbrush. The island's brigands living in isolated elevations were known as maquisards. These words began to be applied to dissident elements geographically separated from French society under the fascist occupation. But it is best to back up a couple years before discussing the role of maquis in the South of France during World War II.

Origins in Metropolitan France

Almost from the announcement of the Armistice with Germany, certain individuals in France felt a need to take to the hills for self-preservation. This feeling was more prevalent in the North and West, of course, the initial areas directly "under the German jackboot," but the departments administered by Vichy also housed persons deemed a threat to good order and therefore subject to arrest. Refugees from the German occupation of Central Europe and veterans of the defeated armies there had migrated to the Midi. In the Southeast, anti-fascist immigrants from Germany, Austria, and Italy were prevalent and wary of apprehension. Primarily in the Southwest, the refugee population included veterans from the losing Republican forces in the Spanish Civil War, many not hiding their intentions to cross the Pyrénées and bring down Franco. From the outset, Vichy was intent on policing its own area, as well as ingratiating itself with its Nazi controllers. Thus, it was not long before foreign Jews, communists, Freemasons and homosexuals, favorite targets of the new regime, quietly disappeared from their homes to escape the gendarmerie. Living alone in the wild appeared less dangerous than remaining in communities under the watchful eye of a hostile state.

As months went by and the ability of Maréchal Pétain to shield France from the horrors of German control was seen as less and less effective, the tide of public opinion turned against the new regime. By 1942, several factors reinforced this dissatisfaction. The first was the Relève which exchanged workers sent to Germany for French prisoners of war. It met with only limited success, being characterized by Vichy critics as "deportation." The real deportation was sending Jewish men, women and children to Nazi concentration camps which did not sit well with many Frenchmen. The final straw was occupation of the South of France by German and Italian forces.

Réfractaires who refused to work in Germany soon joined other exiles in search of refuge in an abandoned farm building, mountain chalet, or deserted forestry camp. The ideal location was isolated, difficult to get to, and easy to guard. There also needed to be several paths for flight. A source of food and water must be available along with occasional employment, if possible. One group found an ideal resting place with a forester north of Grasse. They helped harvest timber, and when the authorities appeared, melted into the woods.

The picture of these fugitives not long after the Armistice was hardly cheerful. Three or four men might camp in a pine forest sleeping on beds made of boughs. They were dirty and smelly, attired in a mixture of clothes, khaki from the German and French armies being common. Footwear was often worn out and unsuited in winter for outdoor living in higher elevations. Food was scarce, perhaps nothing more than bread and butter. Unlike members of the Resistance working at jobs in cities, these dissidents drew no pay. There were probably no weapons of war, and if any were hidden nearby, it was doubtful that refugees or the local peasants knew how to use them. The renegades were of various ages ranging from older Masons and Jews to men of military age who had deserted fascist units or were avoiding exile with the legions of workers exported to the Reich. Boredom weighed heavily on these latter dodgers. They were the next generation. Angry with their lot in a Nazi-dominated society, their youthfulness made them excitable, eager, and energetic. Here was the storied spirit of France, ready to be molded into a force for independence and liberty. But at this point in time, their prime motivation was staying alive as opposed to rising up to smite the fascist oppressors.

Formation

Taking to the hills did not appeal to men in the cities and towns of Provence and the Riviera until February 1943 when the STO, a mandatory work program designed to make up for the shortfall in volunteers to go to Germany and man its war machine, was established. Cynics asserted that the volunteers had nothing better to do anyway. Particular emphasis was placed on obtaining skilled labor for German factories as France had the largest number of industrial workers in occupied Europe.[1] The obligation originally applied only to young men engaged in non-agricultural pursuits, but a few months later was extended to farm workers as well. Many members of the first STO cohort, ages 20–23, disappeared into the hills to avoid this fate, populating the maquis forming there. Some workers were shielded by employers who were desperately short of labor. Others sought medical exemptions from doctors watched closely by Blackshirts and their fascist fellow-travelers to deter preparation of false declaractions.

The battle for the hearts and minds of young men eligible for the STO was as fiercely fought as any conflict during the Italian occupation. The regional director of the German placement office in Marseille wrote to employers at the outset of February, reminding them of the obligation to ensure that none of their workers defected when called to serve. The responsibility for compliance was placed squarely on managers' shoulders. Enforcement of the STO quickly became confrontational with creation of the Milice. To prevent the Resistance from influencing a draftee to defect, it was recommended that he be escorted to the point of departure by the police, Miliciens, or members of the PPF. By the time of the German occupation, gendarmes were also being dispatched to search cafes, hotels, and apartment buildings for STO deserters. In 1944, authorities conducted an average of 1,265 such raids each month. To cite one example, a 21-year-old lad living in a hamlet near Grasse, helping cultivate flowers in the family fields, was seized by the Deutsch Militarpolizei, taken to Cannes, and sent by train to Poland, where he drove trucks loaded with explosives to the eastern front.[2]

Extending the reach of involuntary labor beyond factory workers and other city-dwellers had ancillary significance by causing rural residents to sympathize more readily with the plight of outsiders seeking refuge in the countryside. Farm boys avoiding the STO usually hid close to home, providing a nexus to a nearby community for comrades from urban areas. A tract addressed to the farmers of France and disseminated in March 1943 in Le Bar-sur-Loup, a community in the Alpine foothills, illustrated the evolving situation:

> Yesterday, it was the Alsatians and Lorrains, the farmers of the North and East like their three million Polish comrades, the foreign Jews. Today, it is French workers. Tomorrow it will be your turn, French farmers, to go relieve the German farmers. Tomorrow you will be deported. You will be enslaved [...] For the workers who flee deportation: shelter them! Employ them in your work! Feed their families! In fighting for them, you fight for yourself, you fight for France.[3]

The communist Front National went a step further. Its circular ordered maquis "to set up in each village an aid committee to deal with reception of evaders, assembly of food stocks and collection of funds."[4]

Combat urged wives and mothers to influence their husbands and sons not to go, doctors to sign medical exemptions for as many youth as possible, police not to decimate the ranks of France's youth, and the general populace to do everything possible to defeat the STO. The leaflet disseminated by the Front National in Roquebrune-Cap-Martin urged workers to come together, refuse to leave, and, if necessary, go on strike, which was described as their best weapon: "Against the strike—Vichy, the Gestapo, the OVRA can do nothing."[5]

For the Allies, disrupting the STO was akin to reducing war production in Germany. Furthermore, the STO threatened to remove many of the Frenchmen counted upon to rise up and confront the occupiers when the liberators arrived. Employing radio broadcasts and leaflets to encourage young men to resist labor conscription was not enough; the opponents of fascism had to help the réfractaires survive. Consequently, the French Central Committee of the Resistance created a Comité d'action contre la Déportation to produce false papers—cartes d'identité, work records, certificates of illness, travel permits, and, perhaps most important, ration cards for food. When these counterfeits were unavailable or in short supply, maquisards raided a hôtel de ville where genuine forms were stored and distributed. Sometimes a municipal employee helped by stealing local exemplars or a few ration books. Even then, it was necessary to find a grocer who would honor the coupons, real or false.[6]

At the same time as young men were refusing to enroll in forced labor units, there was an increase in desertions by workers press-ganged into French factories operated by Organization Todt, Hitler's construction arm. These fugitives had been joined in the hills by rétardataires, French prisoners working in war plants in Germany who were granted short periods of home leave but failed to return as promised. The absentee rate quickly reached 50 per cent, threatening cancellation of the privilege. Anyone seeking to avoid compulsory labor might be counseled by a friend to "prendre le maquis" (go to the maquis), new slang heard in the streets of the Midi during the spring of 1943. Indeed, Fritz Sauckel, the Nazi Minister of Labor and initiator of the STO, was soon referred to as the best recruiter for the maquis.

Rural conditions in southeastern France were ideal for maquis, and consequently the Midi was home to a majority of the country's guerrilla camps. Mountains and forests provided fresh water, game, and sunshine. The terrain was rugged and wild and the Germans occupying these areas not numerous, allowing undisturbed freedom for organizing and training. Climbing into the foothills or higher Alpine elevations along narrow, winding paths with rocky escarpments discouraged German patrols. If pursued, those on the run escaped farther into the desolate terrain, as they were in most instances no more than an unarmed handful, no match for the searchers. Their initial acts of defiance were hardly threatening to the pro-fascist regime—misdirecting military convoys, falsifying reports of agricultural production, posting notices at night, or distributing clandestine leaflets.

Various Resistance organizations viewed the maquis differently. Armée Secrète (AS) preferred to keep them in reserve to "wait and see" how the German occupation of France continued to unfold. The Mouvements Unis de Résistance (MUR) visualized them as instruments for direct action. Indeed, young officers in the French army who had not left home in response to de Gaulle's call to arms proved to be good guerrilla leaders. Many were instructors, students, or recent graduates of Saint-Cyr, which had been relocated from the Paris area to Aix-en-Provence. In opposition to attentisme, waiting for the Allies to signal an uprising, the communist-dominated FTP designated their maquis groups as an extension of their militant underground in urban areas. Daily facing the oppression of Nazi occupation, these Frenchmen tended toward immediate action. Long-range planners sheltered in London counseled waiting for an Allied invasion.

Increasing numbers of réfractaires caused the newly formed MUR to create a National Maquis Service to organize, train, and equip these random elements, transforming them into effective guerrilla cells. Spread thin across France, the Service could assist only the largest maquis, trying to ensure they received food, clothing, and medical supplies. At the end of May 1943, a circular declared that all *hommes des maquis* were members of the AS commanded by General de Gaulle. These men were expected to adhere to tough discipline, obey the orders of their leaders, sever ties with family and friends until the war's end, value the lives of non-combatants and their private property, and respect their comrades' beliefs and opinions.[7] The tie to de Gaulle was an indication that socialists were gradually taking control of the MUR at the expense of communists and extending their influence down to departmental liberation committees.

Early in 1943 the FTP formed Camp Faita in the Maures highlands of the Var close to the sea, the first organized maquisard outpost in the region. After engaging in various acts of sabotage, however, pressure from the authorities forced these guerrillas to move into Basses-Alpes in 1944. Fugitives from the STO in Alpes-Maritimes not only faded away into the desolation of the Var or the Alps, but went as far afield as Vaucluse and the Gard, on either side of the River Rhône. Sometimes situated three or four hours' walk from any community, there were few distractions and no news from the family.

Prefects in the North began to complain that they were supplying the vast majority of workers sent to German factories. Pétain's government thus sought to equalize the levy between North and South by stepping up its campaign to ferret out fugitives in the former Non-Occupied Zone. In March 1943 a group of eight unarmed youth hiding from the STO was apprehended in an abandoned sheep shelter on a massif in the northwest corner of Alpes-Maritimes. The next month a similar group living near Tourrettes-sur-Loup was betrayed and traversed a mountain to Touet-sur-Var to avoid capture.

Farther west near Apt, the prefect dispatched police to search prehistoric, beehive-shaped stone huts known as "bories," thought to be the refuge of réfractaires, and claimed to have seized several. Authorities in the Var were cleverer still. They pressured peasants to reveal the locations of springs in order to focus their hunt. A senior Resistance leader in this area, Camille Rayon, remembers water being more precious than food to the maquis, especially in the higher elevations. For some, the lack of tobacco seemed another unbearable hardship.[8]

As the specter of bands of men hiding in the back country became imbedded in the public consciousness, their potency assumed exaggerated proportions. The maquisards were thought to be more numerous, better organized, and heavier armed than was actually the case. Most of the early attacks on rail lines were perpetrated by urban FTP units, but the railway workers responsible readily identified maquisards as the culprits to explain away their own sabotage. Gangs of bandits misrepresented themselves as victims of Vichy oppression to transfer blame for their criminal acts to the maquis. As time went by, the threat posed by outlaws was further exaggerated by Vichy media that inflated the number of thefts and attacks committed by the maquis. An intelligence report prepared by US VI Corps prior to the Provençal landings recognized that "Efforts are also being made by the MAQUIS men to purge their districts of 'terrorists,' i.e., gangsters or réfractaires who have found it possible to live by banditry instead of joining the MAQUIS."[9]

To retain the support of the rural population, the maquis tried to survive without stealing from poorer peasants who could ill afford the loss. Consequently, the outliers took from collective concerns and ambushed German convoys carrying livestock and produce. For clothing, shoes, and equipment, they quickly learned to raid the well-provisioned Chantiers de la Jeunesse. The Chantiers' affinity with the maquis matured that autumn when Vichy attempted to reorient the program toward preparation for entry into the STO. Increasingly instructors and trainees went over to the maquis for, after all, patriotism, morality, discipline, and rugged individualism were characteristic of both groups.

Diversity in the composition of maquis, even those centered on one particular political orientation, sometimes made discipline difficult to enforce. The communists appointed commissars—one for personnel, another for operations, and a third to address all other matters. A maquis organized of recruits with army experience naturally looked to the senior officer as leader. Collections of men on the run gravitated to a chief with charisma, often the group's founder. Instructors who parachuted in to train the guerrillas provided leadership on the basis of their technical knowledge, weapons, and money.

Little of the structure, provisioning, or operations was planned in advance. A maquis consisted of outsiders who appeared without notice, it changed location when sensing a threat, and its members were provisioned by what others provided, intentionally from the air or, perhaps, through nefarious means if unavailable from nearby suppliers. No two maquis were the same. A variety of reasons generated membership, weaponry varied, living conditions changed with each site, and the political orientation reflected their leaders' personal leanings. Indeed, a maquis often derived its name from the leader, for example, Maquis Archiduc, Rayon's nom de guerre. The chief had the difficult job of planning and organizing security, relocating his charges on a moment's notice, maintaining contact with other clandestine figures who could provide information or assistance, finding alternate sources of water and places for shelter, welcoming and screening new arrivals, obtaining false documentation to satisfy police checks, ensuring his men were trained with weapons and explosives, encouraging them to bathe, and, most difficult at times, maintaining morale.

A unique example was Maquis Lorrain. In the high Var a Jewish father and his son and daughter, Jacques and Eva, gathered seven fugitives in October 1943. Coming from the life of, first, a lawyer and, then, a bailiff in Nice, Captain Jean Lippmann encouraged his followers to bring warm clothes, bedding, food, and, unique for these encampments, good shoes with cleats for mountain climbing. The maquis settled near Ubaye for six months over that winter. With a mule as their only transportation, the résistants spent daylight hours seeking food (often bread purchased from farmers), looking for wood (indispensable for warmth and light), and engaging in heated anti-German discussions. At night, pairs of maquisards ascended to guard posts. This maquis was fortunate that the majority of its members knew how to ski, and those who did not used this downtime learning to do so. The training would serve them well.[10]

Although almost never members of maquis, the importance of women to their success was invaluable. With a husband, son, or brother away in the hills, a knock on the door was answered by a woman often caring for the young, requiring her to provide an explanation for the absence of a loved one to the gendarme or Milice.[11] Women served as links with farms and villages for little bands in the high ground. Like their sisters in urban areas, they risked their lives carrying messages by *bicyclette*, hiding contraband, and delivering parcels to the partisans for nourishment or combat. Eva Lippmann went two steps farther, serving as a nurse to her father's maquis and manning a machinegun in combat at Plan-du-Var at one point.

One historian identified three roles contemplated by Allied planners for the underground in the ultimate liberation of France: organizing resisters into an army, igniting a popular uprising beginning in urban areas, and using the maquis to support an Allied landing. Efforts to unify and coordinate maquis activity, however, continually bumped up against the reality of independent clusters of guerrillas. Maquisards in the Midi respected their immediate leaders but were less impressed by directives from sources outside the region seeking to function as higher headquarters. Like resisters elsewhere during the war, the underground also considered international rules of war to be non-applicable to their kind of combat. Hostility to military command lines and impetuosity gave the maquis a colorful, individualistic nature, but it also engendered overall weakness and at times contributed to failure. Adventurers could constitute another danger, less committed personally and politically to the goal of vanquishing the oppressors and thus more likely to talk under interrogation. Conversely, high morale, an aggressive temperament, resourcefulness, and initiative were hallmarks of volunteers of worth who chose to become maquisards.[12]

In November 1943, Francis Cammaerts reported to London his conclusion that the maquis were not strong enough to engage the Germans in open guerrilla warfare. Cammaerts estimated that 22,000 men lived in 4,000 camps under the MUR throughout the South of France, while thousands more maquisards remained in solitary hiding. In his opinion, to ferret them out would require more troops than the Germans were willing to commit to the task. He went on to observe that the "BBC policy of encouraging men to take to the Maquis has given them, at least in their own view, a strong moral claim on us [the British]." Handling the maquis "may have considerable bearing upon Anglo-French relations after the war." That expectation of Allied help was soon tested when German aggression against the maquis grew stronger in the spring.[13]

Trials and Maturation

Old-timers assessed the winter of 1943–4 as one of the most brutal in memory. Ad hoc outdoor accommodation adequate earlier in the year were unlivable in most instances during the extreme cold and snow. Added to the plummeting icy temperatures, inadequate clothing, and scarce food was the gradual realization that, despite the uprising and liberation of Corsica the previous autumn by maquisards supported by the British, the long-awaited Allied rescue of mainland France was still some time off. As living conditions worsened, maquisards were forced to abandon their hideouts and come down to lower elevations for shelter afforded by farmers and hamlets. Almost two-thirds of the 2,844 réfractaires in Alpes Maritimes returned there by the following spring.[14] Many nearby communities came to feel proprietorship of a nearby maquis and took special interest in protecting it. Yet a maquis was a magnet that could attract destruction and violence by the authorities to bystanders as well as dissidents. Tracks in the snow and mud were easy for searchers to follow. A sudden roadblock or identity check created anxiety for innocent and outcast alike. This fear did not necessarily connote hostility by the locals toward the maquis but a realistic apprehension of the severity of possible German or Vichy repression. The death of ten Frenchmen was a steep price for innocent civilians to pay for a maquisard killing a single Wehrmacht soldier. Despite the danger they posed, there were few examples of maquis denounced by local inhabitants.

The discipline and training needed to convert the maquis into true military assets came primarily by three means. The first was from those with military experience. This know-how might be imparted by members of the Organisation de Résistance de l'Armée (ORA), veterans of the defeated French army opposed to Vichy, or in some instances from those who had served against their will in the fascist ranks. A second resource was SOE agents dispatched from London to organize these raw elements and train them in the use of the weapons and munitions supplied increasingly by air. Third were school teachers. The men were often veterans, and some continued as reserve officers. They possessed the military knowledge that young maquisards lacked and held the respect of those réfractaires who had grown up locally and oftentimes been their pupils. Women teachers frequently knew first-aid skills which, when combined with Catholic nuns and Jewish doctors, were critical to the medical underpinning of the maquis. As intelligent and respected members of the community, teachers along with clergy were consistently supportive of résistants hiding in the outback.[15]

Armament also came from multiple sources. British histories of this era rightfully emphasize airdrops and Lysanders landing with agents, arms, and ammunition. Certainly, this was a principal means of supporting the maquis. As France Libre became fully established at a base outside Algiers, it also dispatched matériel by air to maquis associated with the ORA and the AS. In September 1943 maquisards in the southeastern corner of France gathered up whatever they could from the trail of weapons and supplies left behind by Italians soldiers fleeing from the Germans. If they did not pick it up off the ground, they bought it from an Alpini officer as the AS did at Cannes, obtaining a truck loaded with arms for 50,000 francs.[16]

Allied Support

During the formative period of the maquis, the British had occasionally shown reluctance to supply them with arms. In 1943, when the SOE's future looked in doubt, the Air Ministry put off allocating additional aircraft for their mission. With a surge in the number and participation in the maquis, however, came increased attention from both the Allies and the Axis. What was termed a "meeting of ministers" was held in London on January 27, 1944 to acquaint the prime minister with this raw military asset coming to maturity in France. As he became convinced of the guerrilla potential east of the River Rhône, Churchill was said to have exclaimed that "brave and desperate men could cause the most acute embarrassment to the enemy and it was right that we should do all in our power to foster and stimulate so valuable an aid to Allied strategy." Sorties to France grew from 107 in the last trimester of 1943 to 759 the following quarter, and then 1,969 in April–June 1944, excluding air missions directly related to the Normandy landings.[17]

In September 1943, Camille Rayon was named de Gaulle's military delegate with responsibility for autonomous air and maritime operations in the southeastern area designated R-2. At the same time, he headed an independent network with its own teams and radio liaison capability.[18] Its role consisted, first of receiving shipments of arms, ammunition, equipment, and supplies delivered by parachute and light aircraft landing on deserted airstrips. Rayon was to arm the maquis, independent groups of resisters, sedentary members of the FFI, immediate action teams, and commandos dispatched to his region. Sabotage teams would be targeted against railways, factories, and depots.

In total, 403 successful parachute operations took place in Southeast Region 2. Most of the airdrops were made for SOE circuits. Another nine landings took place before the Provençal debarkation when Rayon's team received 25 Dakotas delivering personnel. A total of 186 agents, officers, and political figures arrived and another 72 departed by air. These operations required the employment of 1,785 résistants in September 1943 alone to provide security, carry away matériel, and guide passengers, a figure that climbed to 2,150 in the important month of June 1944.[19]

For the first time, the Americans became significantly involved as well. Cordell Hull was prompted by de Gaulle's assertion that most of his help came from the British, so President Roosevelt and the secretary of state pressured the Army Air Corps to make more planes available for deliveries to the French Resistance. The American commitment eventually reached 11 four-engine Flying Fortresses and Liberators (B-17s and B-24s) and seven dual-engine Mitchell bombers (B-25s), all capable of dropping parachutists and containers, as well as propaganda.[20]

A standard load in a British or American aircraft consisted of 12 containers of Bren and Sten light machineguns, rifles, pistols, grenades, detonators, and field dressings. Ammunition, spare parts, and magazines might also be included. If more payload could be transported, these crates were packed with more explosives, additional rounds, magazines, and first-aid supplies. Heavier weaponry was rare, generally bazookas. The SOE included also sent armbands to serve as the distinctive badges required by the Hague convention to identify combatants and cover them under provisions of that treaty. That tricolore accoutrement, visible in so many photographs after the landings, did wonders to boost maquisard morale.[21]

Obtaining the green light to send more armaments was a big step forward; actually recovering the shipments was equally important. In April 1944 the BBC announced an air delivery on a plateau 20 miles north of Nice at an altitude of 1,600 feet. Fifteen men from Maquis Surcouf, farmers and factory workers, climbed one cold night through fields of thyme, along narrow trails, and over rocky outcroppings to reach the drop zone. Just before midnight, the silence was shattered by the sound of aircraft engines. After circling in the moonlight to ascertain the exact location, the pilot released his parachutes and flew off into the dark. The maquisards scrambled about, recovering 15 containers. The team leader watched the men to ensure they hid the silks in the underbrush instead of taking them home to be made into dresses or draperies and risk discovery by the authorities. An even more difficult task was preventing the scavengers from helping themselves to the food, cigarettes, or shoes of a distinctly Albion style. The load was too large and heavy to carry down the incline by hand in a single trip, so the containers were opened and inventoried, and a portion concealed until the next day. Preparing to depart, the chief took out some British Sten sub-machineguns, still packed in grease, to carry for protection. The Sten was the standard weapon issued to the maquis as it was easily dismantled and hidden, designed to use captured German 9-mm. ammunition, accurate to 30 yards,and mass-produced from a metal mold for 15–30 shillings (less than $10) a copy. One porter could not resist firing a burst of rounds into the air, shattering the peacefulness with his exuberance.[22]

Rayon recalled an incident at Gréolières, north of Grasse, illustrating how an air operation could go awry:

On the night of 7 to 8 January, some of the parachutes, fabricated on an experimental basis of canvas rather than in nylon, twisted like a candle provoking the explosion of containers filled with grenades. Alerted by the detonations, elements of the German garrison of Grasse arrived the next day, discovered the parachutes on the roofs of houses and farms and identified two of my men who were deported.[23]

Nor was the recovery of airborne matériel always according to plan. In January 1944 a load floated down by parachute onto the plain de Cheiron in the middle of Alpes-Maritimes and was intercepted by the Germans; two months later, another delivery onto the Dina plateau was also confiscated. Altogether nearly 60 tons of arms were lost. If the Germans did not threaten collection efforts, other maquis often did. When the FTP reached misdirected cargo first, its maquisards were quick to take possession. Organized into three companies for military purposes, by the end of May FTP maquis announced that two of them were now fully armed.

The competition between maquis was understandable. In the formative months of the maquis, a réfractaire's politics had been unimportant. What was critical was cooperation among disparate refugees seeking nothing more than survival in a world seemingly out of control. As maquisards banded together in small groups and settled upon a leader, his political leanings tended to stamp that encampment as partial to the communists or to France Libre. Looking ahead to postwar France, de Gaulle was wary of arming contingents committed to a political agenda dictated by Moscow. Maquis politically identified with the left wing therefore complained constantly of being ignored in the arming of partisans counted upon to help set France free. One postwar writer, a veteran of the movement Combat, went further: "I had the impression that the British played to the maximum the division of the Resistance."[24]

Representatives of the Allies tell a different story. Cammaerts stated that he worked closely with the pro-communist FTP. He observed that they were ashamed of France's capitulation in 1940 and so anxious to evict the occupiers that they preferred to blow up the infrastructure rather than quietly disabling it. In line with setting aside differences in time of trouble, Cammaerts recalled no anti-British sentiment. He contended that socialists in the countryside were different from their brethren in Marseille who were waiting patiently for a national uprising once the Germans departed.[25] The regional ORA chief, Jacques Lécuyer (nom de guerre, "Sapin"), recalled giving the following instructions to Lippmann when providing him with 400,000 francs: "You can if you judge it useful, give a part of this sum to the FTP to help them, making, however, a remark that this money is not owed to them, that the ORA gives it to them because we have the same goals."[26]

On the other hand, SOE agent John Goldsmith encountered suspicion and hostility for Churchill and the British inbred among French communists. Well after the war he wrote that a leftist maquis chief deep in the mountains agreed to receive guns, bullets, and francs for food, critical for his famished followers, only after being assured that there were no political strings attached. Another SOE operative in the South, H. M. R. Despaigne, insisted that "Vichy meant nothing to us." He was unconcerned with politics in France during or after the war and was only interested in defeating the Nazis.[27]

Effective teamwork seemed to be the trademark of Camille Rayon, the native of Antibes responsible for receiving supplies airdropped from Algiers in the seven departments of Southeast France (Region R-2). When asked how, as chief of the Section d'Atterrissage et de Parachutage (SAP, Section for Landing and Parachuting), he earned and retained the allegiance of Resistance leaders at both ends of the political spectrum, Rayon replied simply that he had the ability to provide them with arms, ammunition, and money, thereby buying their loyalty.[28]

Other résistants strongly disagreed. The socialist Max Juvenal, district MUR president, exclaimed, "I hope that one day it will be explained to us why arms in our region were refused to the patriots, why the smallest radio set was not put at the disposal of the regional leader." A contemporary wrote, "The insufficiency of arms, explosives and money parachuted by the SAP and especially their poor distribution will be very heavily felt by the Resistance [...] The poor functioning of the SAP in Region R-2 will be evoked each time that there will be a question of matériel."[29]

The leader of SAP in Basses-Alpes was René Char, a literatus considered by Albert Camus as "our greatest living poet." Code-named Alexandre and serving as a captain in the AS, Char headed the network Action allied with the FTP. His determination for civilian resistance clashed with de Gaulle's program of military resistance and the two did not get along when meeting face to face, according to Char's wife. With 40 ambushes and a dozen or so air deliveries to his credit, Char compiled *Cahiers d'Hypnos* (Notebooks of Hypnos), published as a tribute to his maquis after the war, just as he had written poetry to memorialize the Spanish Republicans in 1936.[30]

Cooperation between French and Italian Maquis

Six maquis made up of Italians were in place along the eastern frontier. The first formal contact between the French maquis and their Italian counterparts in the Volunteer Corps of Liberty occurred on the crest of an Alpine mountain at midnight on May 11, 1944. This exchange led to two subsequent meetings. Juvenal and Lippmann signed an accord concerning joint participation in the liberation of both countries and went on to specify French administration in the freed areas under direction of Algiers. Apparently at this point in time when fascists still controlled much of their country, the Italian patriots were comfortable with this concession.

The Germans knew of the hostility organized in the valleys of la Bévéra and la Roya through ambushes of their patrols conducted jointly by French and Italian partisans. Revenge came in May when the Wehrmacht requisitioned men, mules, and trucks in Ventimiglia and Menton and then skirted through Italian valleys to surprise their tormentors back in France, pillage the property of local inhabitants, and fill their vehicles with plunder. Lippmann met his demise not long thereafter when surprised by a German coup de main in the middle of a July night at Sapin's headquarters on a farm in Alpes-de-Haute-Provence. He was executed beside three fellow FTP guerrillas at Les

Eaux-Chaudes as part of the short-lived Wehrmacht campaign that month to eliminate maquis in the back country.[31]

As they prepared the groundwork for an invasion in Provence, US special services began to take notice of irregulars on both sides of the border. A summary of resistance activities in mid-June reported that two agents were being inserted to facilitate coordination of the various high-country maquis.[32] These résistants would come under increasing pressure when Axis troops, both German and Italian, moved into the Alps to seal off the right flank of the Wehrmacht defense of Italy from pressure attendant to a future Allied presence in Provence.

Another fascist offensive erupted on July 10 when German troops from Ventimiglia accompanied by a section of Blackshirts adorned with death skulls on their blouses attempted to eradicate the maquis outside Sospel. In addition to the usual barrage from mortars and automatic weapons, this assault was supported by aircraft. Although subjected to a firestorm, the defenders were able to organize themselves and employ weapons supplied by the Allies to inflict casualties sufficient to halt the attack.[33]

The Allied landing in August prompted German units in northern Italy to attack maquis which had liberated the valleys around Cuneo. Fighting lasted a full week and ended with the Rosselli Brigade fleeing through the valleys of the Stura and the Gesso and into France on August 25 to escape decimation. The Italian irregulars subsequently helped in the defense of the Haute-Tinée before being integrated into a battalion of the South Alpine Group organized in the French army with members of the former Resistance. On his transfer out of southeastern France in November, Lieutenant Colonel William Yarborough, commander of the US 509th Parachute Infantry Battalion, commended Carlo Rosselli on the performance of his men: "We are very proud and pleased that you operated in our sector. Your courageous and efficient acts are already known as far as America. We see a victory in the near future and we are sure that the role that you are in the process of playing will notably influence the total defeat of the enemy."[34]

On the Eve of Liberation

When spring arrived in Alpes-Maritimes, blooming flowers in the back country had been accompanied by major increases in the maquis population. Interest in joining was generated not only by the advent of milder weather, but also by rumors of an imminent Allied invasion and heightened police roundups to fill quotas for the STO. Allied successes in North Africa and Italy, combined with the reversals suffered by the Wehrmacht on its eastern front, encouraged this kind of thinking. Four new maquis reported being operational in March, followed by a dozen more over the succeeding two months. In the Var the task of sorting out and training refugees which had taken place near Saint-Tropez during the winter relocated to Camp Robert, higher in the department.[35] When the newly formed Forces Françaises de l'Intérieur (FFI) appointed Sapin as regional chief, he complained about the shortage of disciplined maquisard organizations and proceeded to form two maquis in the vicinities of Beuil and Vence. FTP maquis gathered at five sites and the communist MOI set up a camp at Peille for foreigner laborers threatened with arrest and deportation. FTP companies were also forming in built-up areas—Cannes, Antibes, Vence, and La Roquette-sur-Var being prime examples.

In total, by June 1944 the Department of Alpes-Maritimes was home to 22 established maquis, as compared with six in 1943. Countless smaller clusters of men remained in hiding, separate and apart from the nationalist and communist affiliates and deaf to the crescendo of patriotism and insurrection. An estimated 250 members of the FFI were spread over this area, of whom 80 or so were affiliated with the FTP.[36]

A drama played out during the first fortnight of June aptly illustrates the multiple problems encountered in receiving airdrops from the Allies and conducting operations in the back country. Seeking matériel for Combat groups in Nice, the network François, loyal to General Giraud, asked Algiers to parachute arms and supplies onto Mont Férion, a prominence overlooking the Var valley. The message misidentified the site as four kilometers west of the town of Levens, whereas Férion is the same distance to the east. Lycée students from Old Nice, plus some other young men, were dispatched by the leaders of their cells to climb 13 miles northward and join 20 or so maquisards on the elevation 4,500 feet above sea level. The maquisards were armed with automatic pistols, hunting rifles, some grenades, and a heavy Italian machinegun without carriage or ammunition.[37] The excited reception party immediately gathered three large piles of wood to ignite as a signal to the pilot. Then they waited. The youths suffered from the cold and snow night after night with no cover. At one point, a Niçois descended to find a goat kept by a peasant that the hungry résistants devoured partially cooked for fear that a fire would be visible to the Wehrmacht. They bided their time smoking tobacco stolen from a truck carrying supplies to German outposts and continued waiting. Another group of men arrived, well organized with tricolore brassards marked FTP and FFI. But still no aircraft appeared. Unbeknownst to them, the airplane had overflown the drop zone, come under fire from German batteries, and departed—never to return.

With the Allied landing in Normandy, German troops and the Milice were on heightened alert for members of the Resistance. Meanwhile, 14 more youths had bicycled to the mountain crater. Discouraged when the shipment did not arrive, the maquisards sent the boys from Nice back home. One was stopped at a control point and found to be carrying a pistol. Next the Deutsch Militarpolizei apprehended a group of five students. Five other teenagers were hidden by a priest in the bell tower of a village church, their arms deposited in a beehive. A nearby intersection came under fire from a hyper-energized FTP maquis, and the Germans responded in force. To retaliate, they demanded 11 hostages and collected the youths plus réfractaires from nearby communities. On June 11, soldiers took the prisoners into a field and shot them. That night, the priest and boys in the steeple recovered the victims and carried them into the chapel. Some were found to have been tortured. The bodies were photographed, coffins prepared, and locks of hair cut for their families. The Germans returned the following day and terrorized villagers suspected of aiding the maquis, threatening the abbot with execution. The pictures were sent for identification to the gendarmerie in Nice where a policeman recognized his son as one of the dead.[38]

The structure of the maquis hardened with the Allies' landing in Normandy. Despite the theoretical unification of all maquis within the FFI, the disparity in matériel heightened the natural political rivalry between Gaullists, the AS, and the communist FTP which wanted to retain its autonomy. Consequently, it had integrated into the FFI in name only. As maquisards obtained greater means to conduct offensive operations, pressure increased to take action. Patience and endless preparation grated against the desire to begin freeing France.

One noteworthy effect of the Normandy D-Day landings was a change in the character of dissent in Alpes-Maritimes. Beforehand, a disproportionate share of dissidents remained in urban areas. Activity in towns and cities by the Communist Party and its Front National in distributing tracts accelerated after June 6. Looking ahead to taking political control of municipalities, their leaders also created clandestine liberation committees to be prepared at the appropriate time. They found the populace compliant, intelligence easy to obtain from police and gendarmes, and insecurity growing among the foreign occupiers as excitement grew in anticipation of a second landing in the South.

Now serving as SOE commander for the Southeast, Cammaerts forbade sabotaging factories after D-Day as he considered the damage useless and an avoidable complication in rebuilding the Côte d'Azur. Instead, he focused on interrupting communications to cut off Wehrmacht outposts from their headquarters. Milder expressions of opposition seemed to Cammaerts more far-sighted and less foolhardy than pitched battles in places where Germans could bring artillery and armor into play or even than organizing ambushes in urban areas, a cornerstone of FTP strategy.[39] Soon, the period of isolated coups de main against the military installations and industrial plants important to the occupiers, and destruction of their collaborators' property, would be replaced by direct attacks against the enemy and its henchmen.

On the eve of the landings in Provence, a senior leader disseminated a set of rules to each person stepping forward to join the maquis at the eleventh hour.

French Forces of the Interior of the Department of Alpes-Maritimes
Constitution of the Parachuting and Protection Teams

(to read to each arrival before leading him to the camp which should
receive him)

When you have joined the movements of resistance, you have come there voluntarily, without any constraint; the discipline to which you will be held to submit to will then be freely consented to and as such, you will be more at ease even if during your presence in our camps, the particular conditions of your existence, due to actual circumstances, seem difficult to you […]

You should then execute all the orders and instructions of your immediate leaders like soldiers, that is to say immediately and without question.

1) The most absolute discretion is required of the men and of the leaders over everything which concerns the clandestine activity of our group, its composition, its matériel. Some words spoken through imprudence or boasting risk leading to the death of all your comrades. Every infraction of this kind will be severely sanctioned.

2) Orders prohibit leaving camp under any pretext, even momentarily.

3) The most rigorous censorship will clamp down on correspondence addressed to your families. Your letters should not make mention of the place where you are, of the number nor even cite the name of one of your comrades […] A spy tabulating the daily ration allocated to the horses can thus calculate their number […] To do this, your letters will be sent unsealed to the sector chief.

4) Teams will take part in all works of maintenance, guard duty judged indispensable […]

5) It is prohibited to keep with you parachuted objects and to retain a weapon which has not been given to you by your leaders […]

6) The camp is under the orders of the sector chief assisted by one or several team chiefs. You should obey them without question and in all instances […]

In the case of non-conformance to the directives and instructions above, sanctions will be applied in proportion to the seriousness of the fault. If that has led to grave consequences, the death penalty will be decided upon […]

Be strong, courageous, united

Be proud of the role confided in you

I count on you as you can count on us at the day of the liberation.

24 July 1944

The FFI Leader[40]

8

Resistance in Southeast France

If Maréchal Pétain is credited with coining the word "collaborateur," then General de Gaulle should be recognized for introducing the word "résistance" into the French vocabulary when he spoke from London on June 18, 1940. Frenchmen formed a resistance second in Europe only to the Yugoslavs in size and complexity. By France's liberation in 1944, hundreds of clandestine newspapers with a circulation of two million urged readers to join a quarter-million citizen-soldiers in the fight against fascism. Estimates of the number of *résistants de 32 août* (résistants of 32 August), as they were sometimes called derisively, varied on whether they were part of the "journalistic resistance," concentrating on postwar planning, or real combatants ready to fight the Boche. After the war the veterans' ministry made a rough estimate of 2 percent of the adult population (or 400,000 French men and women) who became actively involved in opposing Hitler. Thus, the notion perpetuated by communists and Gaullists that résistants were as numerous as "fish in water" was patently false according to the secretary for Jean Moulin.[1]

Resistance in the Southeast differed in important respects from other parts of France. Situated in the Non-Occupied Zone, this corner of the country was spared the mass arrests and brutal repression that handicapped opposition where the swastika flew from 1940 to 1942. Consequently, inhabitants only gradually engaged in non-violent acts of dissent with the ruling regime, such as participating in demonstrations and collecting information on occupying forces. The Côte d'Azur was a target-rich environment for intelligence-gathering with military in the German and Italian Armistice commissions, as well as the rail line tying Marseille to Genoa, carrying Mussolini's trains loaded with confiscated French matériel. The jagged coastline along the littoral was well suited for nocturnal landings to insert and remove dissenters. The terrain behind was ideal for seclusion and well suited to guerrilla warfare.

Spared the threat of a fascist police state, resistance in the Southeast tended to attract those motivated to oppose Vichy. Right after the Armistice when underground cells were few, difficult to find, and scarcely resourced, the refusal to submit to authoritarian rule was a matter of conscience, a choice each man made alone. By 1942, organized resistance in the Midi was de-emphasizing political differences in an effort to attract members. In old age, the cynical Emmanuel d'Astier declared, "I think you could only have joined the Resistance if you were maladjusted," perhaps a self-diagnosis.[2] When the Armée de l'Armistice demobilized, however, thousands of seasoned veterans were no longer bound by their oath of allegiance to Pétain and ripe for dissent.

The politics of resistance definitely leaned toward the left. This generalization holds especially true for the Non-Occupied Zone where most rightists supported Pétain in the early years. With police repression not as vigorous as in the North, the southern underground grew slowly in entities and members. Its leaders tended to be rebellious, alienated types as opposed to the old social elites. By the time a national resistance organization was formed in 1943, the South's numbers provided an advantage in representation, and thus an ability to control the federation.

The nature of maquis opposing the ruling regime differed between communist and non-communist. In general, maquisards associated with the ORA or the AS (75 per cent coming from Combat) collected in isolated areas where they were free to practice weaponry and train in military tactics. The ORA consisted of former members of the disbanded Armée de l'Armistice, many seeking to absolve themselves of responsibility for a defeat not due to lack of courage or self-sacrifice on their part but the result of breakdowns in military and political decision-making. They were men of good education and military background but less adept at underground work as they were too conservative to relate well to underlying popular sentiment.[3] Many were Catholic or monarchist and resisted sharing arms with communists, fearing trouble would arise at liberation.

Maquis in the communist-led FTP were often dependent upon raiding police arsenals, civic warehouses, or Wehrmacht stockpiles, so they often camped near cities and towns. The urban resistance tended to be FTP in allegiance, another reason for its maquis to stay close to coastal communities. Résistants in town maintained their daytime jobs to feed themselves and their families while operating at night before reporting to work the next morning. Interestingly, it is thought that 60 percent of FTP maquisards were not Communist Party members, although they supported its agenda for political and social change.[4]

Statistics provide an insightful profile of the Resistance in Alpes-Maritimes. To begin, men furnished 91 percent of the résistants and 98 percent of the martyrs, even though men accounted for only 47 percent of the population in the 1936 census. Alpes-Maritimes was the department with the greatest proportion of foreigners, 22.5 percent. Not surprisingly, Italians were over-represented and Swiss under-represented. Some 15 percent of the foreigners were executed, 12 percent deported without returning, 19 percent wounded, and 14 percent killed in combat. Their sacrifices were twice that of the indigenous population. Proportionately, farmers and laborers in the department, constituting half the populace, were killed less often. Naturally, the communist Front National counted the most laborers on its rolls, 20 percent. Jews were less involved in the Front National, but more numerous in the MUR than in the general population. In 1936, 84 percent of respondents to the census in Alpes-Maritimes lived in built-up areas, producing an urban flavor to Resistance networks. The interesting rural dimension of the Front National is explained by effective mobilization of certain valleys in the back country during the spring of 1944. Finally, a sample of underground leaders in the department, both martyrs and survivors, shows 46 percent leftists, 23 percent in the center, 21 percent on the right, and 10 percent undetermined. Considering their weight in the most recent elections in 1936, rightists furnished fewer dissenters than might have been expected.[5]

Germination of the Seed of Resistance

Some of the first sprouts of a resistance took root among lycée students. In late summer and fall of 1940, ten youngsters in Nice, recognizing their common hostility to Nazism and the power of Vichy, joined forces to compose tracts on a typewriter or by hand and distribute them in hopes of recruiting more objectors. As one schoolgirl said of her schoolmates at that early stage, "We were neither Gaullists nor anything else: we were French."[6] This early propaganda tended to portray Maréchal Pétain as harmless, still regarded as a savior by many Frenchmen and the nation's best hope for dealing with the Boche.

In the winter of 1940–1, 100 Niçois students came together as a collection of rebels. Lycéens in Nice were not content to merely organize and circulate propaganda. With the exuberance of youth they turned to pranks and vandalism to exhibit their opposition to the failed French state. When the cinema Paris-Palace showed Le juif Suss[7] in October 1941, boys mixed ammonia and carbon disulfide to produce an odor like rotten eggs which spread throughout the theater, driving out the patrons. A news kiosk on avenue de la Victoire was burned in protest against its sale of German papers. Then, students threw acid balls through the windows of Nice shops owned by collaborators with Vichy.[8]

Some former members of the French Foreign Legion started meeting in Nice in October 1940. They would later join Combat. In Antibes, a socialist lawyer, Alex Roubert, gathered together persons of note, such as actors René Lefevre and Claude Dauphin. Dr. Lévy began identifying like-minded inhabitants and joined them for meetings with General Cochet at the Hôtel Grand in Cannes.[9] After fighting in World War I, the physician was rumored to have subsequently served as an intelligence agent for the British, and thus quite likely to be the Frenchman in the Midi best known in London. It is hardly coincidental, therefore, that he engaged an engineer to construct a two-way radio set in late 1940, or that the first clandestine shipment of armaments and ammunition from Great Britain to the South of France arrived by sea at Antibes in February 1941 and was carried to Lévy's residence by some youths who happened to share communist leanings. The weapons were hidden in three places—Fort Carré, the domain of a horticulturist in the Croix-Rouge quarter, and an atelier in the port.[10]

Other bands also coalesced, one of former military fliers. A Parisian lawyer taking refuge on the Côte d'Azur formed a group of intellectuals. Railroad workers and radio broadcast technicians soon banded together, and so on. By so doing the groups gradually lost their professional fiber and took on a political character. At the same time, parallel organizations appeared in Cannes led by a former aviation officer, Raoul Attali, while in Antibes young Gaullists and communists began holding demonstrations before the Monument to the War Dead.

Arrests of dissidents began in the fall of 1940 and continued into the following spring, incarcerating the leadership of the French Communist Party in the Non-Occupied Zone. Italian communists taking refuge in France sent one of their own into the Var in 1941 to reconstitute a cell weakened by numerous apprehensions. He left within a year, leaving behind 100 comrades unknown to the authorities. Yet, another wave of 47 arrests occurred in Provence in 1942 due to the betrayal of a courier who traded the identities of his contacts for release from custody.[11]

Although the Catholic Church was initially drawn to Pétain along with many French citizens, there were certainly dissenters within its clergy. Very early, in January 1941, the vicar of Cavalaire in the Var advocated patriotism with a passion that caused him to be denounced as a Gaullist. Another priest teaching history and geography in Toulon was charged with spreading English propaganda, along with two of his students. In 1942, a Jesuit father would take part in the first vestige of the Front National. More spectacular, however, was Abbé Francis Coeuret of Villars-sur-Var, who had served as a tank officer in the 1940 campaign before beginning his own personal resistance by hiding Jews in his village. Soon he formed a maquis and later served until the end of the war in the French army.[12]

Foremost in the minds of residents in Alpes-Maritimes in this early post-Armistice period was the Italian occupation of 13 French communities along its border. Tracts and graffiti in rail stations in Antibes and Nice made references hostile to Italy and favorable to England. A postcard picturing the cathedral in Strasbourg, mailed from Nice in January 1941, carried a message attributed to President Roosevelt: "The Government of the United States will not consider as valid any attempt to infringe by force the independence and territorial integrity of France." To Alsatians, this referred to their department occupied, along with Lorraine, by the Nazis; to Frenchmen on the Côte d'Azur, the commitment applied to Menton and other towns held by Mussolini's Fascists.[13]

During late 1941 and early 1942 in the perched village of Peille, 12 miles northeast of Nice, a communist schoolteacher, Ange-Marie Miniconi, collected a nucleus of sympathizers drawn to news broadcasts via shortwave radio by the overseas service of the BBC. The doyen of resistance historians, Henri Michel, wrote in the first postwar edition of the *Larousse* encyclopedia "that the resistance of the French people was born around a radio set. The loudspeaker became a kind of sacred altar gathering together, at fixed hours, a larger and larger number of families." Among the patriots in Miniconi's circle was the local curé who helped him get in touch with Italian partigiani fighting fascism underground since 1923. Information gathered about Bersaglieri movements was passed along to left-wing contacts in Monte Carlo.[14]

At first, resistance groups were made up of such simple people, often led by companions without formal military training but motivated by a will to serve. Throughout Alpes-Maritimes, dissenters came together sporadically, sometimes only a few men new to the area or disenchanted with the old political parties. Their fresh ideas could stir up public opinion. The important aspect of the early opposition was its personal contacts, worker to worker, enabling these résistants to begin to organize and plant their ideas in factories, worksites, transportation centers, depots, and utilities in urban areas, and to collect fugitives, outcasts, dissidents, and refugees in the countryside. Contacts could be difficult, recruitment tricky, and diverse and often opposing opinions initially brought together in the same group. It was not rare to see a résistant move from one faction to another. Combat lost two groups to Carte, for example, due to the riches in matériel and money Carte received from the SOE. The aura of success originally surrounding its chief, André Girard, was another attraction. It was only later, with occupation of the southern zone and the infusion of instigators and organizations from outside the region, that larger networks came together. One such leader was Jean Moulin who arrived from London to prepare diverse groups to recognize the authority of Charles de Gaulle.

The French Resistance cannot be discussed without Moulin's name coming to the fore. His capture by the Nazis on the outskirts of Lyon in 1943 is often referred to as "the tragedy of Caluire." More than any other man, including de Gaulle, his "steady, relentless pursuit of the serious organization of resistance" welded it into a fairly "coherent and disciplined body."[15] Moulin's subsequent torture by Klaus Barbie, the infamous Gestapo "butcher," and demise from the effects of that ordeal are the somber finale to a life dedicated to his country.

Resistance in October 1941

As reported back to London by Moulin, three broad opposition movements existed in France in the fall of 1941—Liberté, Mouvement de Libération Nationale (MLN), and Libération. Their common objective was freedom from foreign occupation. In Moulin's opinion, resisters needed to adhere to the British cause and to that of de Gaulle to achieve their goal. Moulin summarized their activities as propaganda, direct action, and military action. The first movement published a monthly newspaper called *Liberté*, considerably to the right politically. MLN was led by Frenchmen in trading, industry, and professional pursuits, many reserve officers. Its weekly paper, *Vérités* (*Truths*), and an intermittent publication, *Travailleurs* (*Workers*), were concerned with police matters and the working class, the same target audience for *Libération*, the farther-left publication by the movement of the same name, created by d'Astier. Editions were printed on either side of the demarcation line and totaled 25,000–45,000, although readership far exceeded that when taking into account reproductions and shared copies.

Moulin found that each movement had cadre and cells in almost every department in both the Occupied and Non-Occupied zones. Counter-propaganda and demonstrations appeared to be their notable endeavors at this time. Military activities were modest, consisting of passing along information to the British secret services and hiding equipment abandoned by French troops in arms and munitions dumps. Coordination between the three organizations was in its nascence and outreach to other groups episodic between leaders, although cooperation was common at the grassroots by individuals struggling against Vichy control.

When the French Communist Party added its weight to the Resistance in 1941, Moulin reported, there were side effects not necessarily constructive. Conservative bourgeoisie turned toward Pétain out of fear of the communist bogeymen portrayed by Berlin and Vichy. All demonstrations were not organized by the Reds, but by routinely citing communists as the culprits, fascists were attracting to their ranks citizens with an unfulfilled desire to stand up for France.

Moulin saw the first signs of what would much later become a national purification as brigades of avengers began publishing the names of "bad Frenchmen" and planning to brand notorious traitors with the swastika. Striking a chord that would become the Allies' credo, Moulin insisted that money and arms be used only to intensify propaganda and organize for collective action in the future, not to encourage acts of violence. At this point in time, Moulin saw these activities as logically leading to support of de Gaulle. If nothing else, resistance movements were forced to identify their political positions in relation to that of the general who declared himself head of the Free French. [16]

At the beginning of 1942, another important movement evolved when 2,000 members of Liberté, Libération Sud, and Franc-tireur[17] consolidated into Combat, led by Frenay as chief. It became the most important but least homogeneous of the organizations in the southern zone. Combat's essence was ROP—*recrutement, organisation, et propagande.* Frenay intended that paramilitary units of 30 men be organized in five squads of six members each, limiting each participant's awareness to five other résistants. Information papers would be signed "Général Cochet," the underground chief in Alpes-Maritimes, but as far as Frenay knew at the time, "an unknown, perhaps a pseudonym."[18] Attali took charge in Alpes-Maritimes.

Communist Resistance

As long as Hitler and Stalin were partners in 1940–1, French communists were prohibited by Moscow from participating in underground activities opposing Vichy, although they contested Pétain's political objectives. Of course, there were exceptions. In November 1940, members of the Communist Youth hung a red flag with the hammer and sickle from a footbridge in Nice and were soon apprehended, along with a teacher. They were sent by train to Marseille, interned in Fort Saint-Nicolas, and sentenced to punishment by the military tribunal there. That autumn at the railroad depot of Saint-Roch in Nice, a stronghold of the communist union, a small group of militant workers began soaking connecting rods used in repairing locomotives in a pool of boiling potash to weaken them and accelerate fracturing. Each of the comrades was initially challenged, "Are you against Hitler?"

Resistance in Alpes-Maritimes blossomed when the Nazis invaded Russia. The PCF understood underground methods and organization in cells, was prepared to accept casualties for "the greater good," and willing to adapt political and economic propaganda to suit the immediate situation, realizing that patriotism was not enough and intending to implement its own program once fascism was extinguished. In Nice as early as September 15, 1941, tracts called for "Sabotage Everywhere!!!"[19] It was a year later when the local Front National papered the city with fliers declaring that to work for Hitler was to betray France. In reaction, the state created the illusion of laborers willing to work in the Reich by paying hoodlums 100 francs per day to stand in line before the hiring office or to board a train heading toward Germany to entice Frenchmen to follow suit.

In the Vichy political climate, repression of the re-emergence of the PCF was naturally severe. Multiple arrests followed by jail terms resulted from disseminating tracts during 1941. In May 1942, two leaders of the Italian Communist Party were caught in Cannes and subjected to cruel interrogation. Wearing only shorts, they received blows on their knees with a steel ruler or whip made from the tough nerves of an ox. Admitting nothing, they were imprisoned in Grasse for allegedly presenting false papers. In early 1943, 18 communists from Nice, Cannes, Grasse, and Vence received prison terms and, in two cases, hard labor for life. The arrival of the Italian OVRA brought more detentions and torture, plus multiple executions. By the beginning of summer, most FTP units in Alpes-Maritimes had been dismantled.[20]

In autumn the communists became aggressive, calling for offices of the German work service to be bombed and directing railroaders to refuse to man trains transporting fascist troops, their matériel or food, much of it originating in France. "Unbolt the rails. Blow them up with dynamite."[21] Sections of track were destroyed, barrels of oil set ablaze, and transformers, machines, and locomotives damaged. At the Saint-Roch station, railroaders daily sabotaged nuts, bolts, washers, and pins of locomotives and railcars, as well as applying abrasive grease to axle bearings. Dock workers were ordered to set fire to wharves and fuel depots.[22]

Other communists took a different tack. "Nice workers, demonstrate against the closure of factories. If you are laid off, form your committee of unemployed and demand 30 francs benefit per day and 10 francs per person, depending on the individual. Engage in action everywhere for a 50 percent increase in wages and better food." [23] A periodical of the Confédération générale du travail (CGT) entitled *The Worker's Life* issued a similar call in its inaugural issue in November 1942.

Italian communists in the Southeast took special pride in their efforts to protect France from Mussolini Fascism. Despite internment and expulsion, with 80 party members being handed over to Italian authorities at the frontier between July 1940 and November 1942, long-time communist inhabitants of Alpes-Maritimes prepared themselves for eventual occupation by Axis forces. The Free Italians of Alpes-Maritimes, as they called themselves, went so far as to denigrate their countrymen as a fifth column for working to undermine Pétain's regime for the purpose of annexing Nice to Italy. Pro-France Italians denounced Vichy for exchanging anti-Fascist political prisoners (i.e., communists) for French spies arrested on the peninsula. One constructive undertaking was finding a clandestine passage from Saint-Martin-Vésubie through the Alps to facilitate contact with their counterparts in Italy. Interestingly, the conspirators did not trust the Bersaglieri who were occupying Menton to aid in this endeavor.[24]

The roots of the communist MOI went back to 1932–3, when it was formed in the spirit of international proletarianism. Its members fought in the International Brigades in Spain and served with the French army in the

Phoney War. Yet there was always tension between individuals' allegiances to the party in their homeland and to the French party. After war broke out, the immigrant group changed into a resistance organization, Mouvement Ouvrier International (also, MOI). This MOI submitted to the discipline of the French party which did not call for opposition to the occupiers in June 1940. Lots of the original MOI adherents were ready to fight, however, especially veterans of the Spanish Civil War.

The French party imposed rigorous rules on MOI members, keeping urban guerrillas isolated in cities so they would know few of their comrades and be dependent on the local communist hierarchy. To diverge from the party line was dangerous; executions of dissenters were not uncommon. Leaders of French communism expected the MOI to join with them, but in reality its members did not always toe the party line. Many were part of the European communist elite and their organizers often the most determined militants. Worries about security made the foreigners extremely mobile, passing from one region to another, lessening ties to a particular cell. Nor were all MOI résistants communists. The primary motivation was the promise of socialism in a new world order.[25]

A woman born in Warsaw served as political commissar of the MOI in Alpes-Maritimes. Once the Italian army moved in, MOI adherents robbed 1.3 million francs from a transport in Nice, attacked a convoy of Fascist tanks in Antibes, blew up a rail line, and assassinated the Italian consul. Arrival of the German army did not seem to intimidate the MOI as it continued to set up ambushes inspired by the example of Corsican maquisards credited with liberating their island.[26]

With fascist losses in Russia and Italy and the likelihood of an Allied invasion growing stronger every day, communist cells became ever more brazen. Significant strikes were organized in the metalworking industry in May 1944. Aciéries du Nord in La Bocca, shipyards in Antibes, and Mobil Metal all endured work stoppages. After the landing in Normandy, formation of patriotic Milice units, pro-France militia to counter the fascist Milice, accelerated in these industrial establishments. In addition, FTP Group Jean-Marie headed by Miniconi, now living in Cannes, joined with the local branch of the AS to sabotage railway matériel at La Bocca, as directed by Allied headquarters in Algiers.[27]

Early Gaullism

One of the earliest expressions of support in Nice for the virtually unknown General de Gaulle was printing and distributing propaganda. On November 25, 1940, *L'Eclaireur de Nice* revealed a group doing just that, and 51 dissenters were arrested for, among other crimes, disseminating a tract which concluded, "Vive de Gaulle, Pétain to the toilets." Combat developed a novel ruse by overprinting a likeness of de Gaulle on stamps franked to the addresses of collaborators.[28]

After Allied landings in Morocco and Algeria and the fascist occupation of all of France in late 1942, Moulin's mission became one of unifying Gaullist movements with communists and other dissenters throughout the country in order to strengthen opposition to the Axis and disrupt the export of labor to Germany. A second objective was to rally around the government of de Gaulle in absentia for the liberation of France, an innuendo intended to dampen the attraction of General Giraud in North Africa, at that time Washington's favorite French military leader. In January 1943, thanks to impetus from Moulin, the main non-communist groups in the Vichy zone accepted de Gaulle's leadership and formed the MUR.

As de Gaulle's personal representative, Moulin made numerous visits to the Côte d'Azur to pull disparate factions into the united movement. Moulin met regularly with the chiefs of the three large sub-rosa organizations in the Non-Occupied Zone—Frenay of Combat, d'Astier of Liberation, and Jean-Pierre Lévy of Franc-tireur. Upon unification in the MUR, Frenay was named commissioner of military affairs, d'Astier chosen to head political affairs, and Lévy selected for intelligence and administration.[29]

Moulin's subterfuge in Nice was proprietorship of Galerie Romanin on rue de France containing his personal art collection, a front to enable him to travel around the countryside as a dealer seeking creative works with commercial value. He stayed at the home of Dr. Lévy in Antibes, in the lodging of the actor René Lefebvre, and with other sympathizers. Moulin made contact with Attali at the Café de Paris in Nice and named him regional chief of the MUR. Meeting with departmental leaders of the Front National and Communist Party, he succeeded in bringing them together with other underground elements into the new confederation under de Gaulle.[30] His success at the national level in organizing a Conseil National de Résistance would take place at Paris later in May followed by his death weeks later. A powerful fictionalized portrayal of the multi-facets of the French Resistance, including Moulin's role, is presented in Jean-Pierre Melville's 1970 film, *L'Armée des Ombres* (*The Shadow Army*). Plaques and memorials dot Moulin's path through the Cote d'Azur as in other regions of France.

In the summer of 1943 a national liberation committee formed at Algiers with de Gaulle and Giraud as co-presidents. Counterparts in Metropolitan France were departmental and local liberation committees intended as coordinators of resistance activity and after liberation as regional and municipal councils.[31]

The return from Germany of prisoners of war due to sickness or discharge, as well as by escape, revealed the true state of morale and physical condition of France's sons held captive. Vichy appointed a commissariat for POWs to repatriate the returnees and help families in difficulty. In June 1942, a group of these veterans met in Hautes-Alpes to decide whether to participate in activities advocated by de Gaulle in London. The Mouvement National de Résistance des Prisonniers de Guerre et Deportés evolved from this gathering. Its influence rapidly spread across the Southeast where it was led regionally by Pierre Merli, later mayor of Antibes, and in Alpes-Maritimes by Georges Foata, who would achieve fame in the Resistance by his nom de guerre, "Morgan".

An officer in the merchant marine, Foata had organized a group of Alsatian draft dodgers and foreign nationals into a maquis known by both its Combat affiliation and association with the prisoners' movement. The group engaged in spectacular feats such as destroying a Milice surgical van and sabotaging a worksite of Organization Todt. The Vichy police labeled Foata a "dangerous and armed terrorist." If captured, he was to be thoroughly searched and closely guarded, along with any companions, and the Sureté in Nice notified immediately.[32]

François Mitterand, an escaped prisoner who had returned four-to-five months earlier, attended the seminal meeting in Hautes-Alpes despite his new staff position with Pétain's commissariat. During his early days at Vichy, Mitterand surreptitiously fabricated false identity papers and counterfeit official cachets to help POWs who broke free from captivity. Until his resignation a year later, Mitterand's contacts with the Resistance increased gradually, step by step. Upon leaving Vichy in June 1943 he spent several weeks with his mother in Grasse. Then, heading to Paris as "François Morland," his nom de guerre, he operated a vibrant underground prisoners' movement for the remainder of the conflict. After the war, during his ascendancy to the presidency of France, Mitterand was repeatedly dogged by two symbols of his Vichy past: a photograph in October 1942 of the young man seemingly enraptured with Pétain in his personal office, and the francisque, Vichy's highest civilian decoration. Mitterand had to nominate himself in order to receive number 2203 of only 2,600 awarded. As president, he reportedly sent his official wreath to be laid at Pétain's grave. And, in the final year of his life, he repeatedly revealed indifference toward Vichy's anti-Jewish policies. Mitterand's serpentine path through the war years and his true loyalties at each juncture will never be clearly known.[33]

With the arrival of fascist occupation all across the Vichy zone, the Resistance in the Southeast began sabotaging industrial and military sites. The three largest factories, each employing more than 100 workers for the

Reich, were the Michel enterprise repairing railway cars in Nice, Aciéries du Nord in La Bocca, and SNCASO at Cannes, a prototype airplane designer. These plants were thought too large and well protected for a ground attack and designated for aerial bombardment. Instead, the Resistance focused its energies on mechanical devices such as cranes, cement mixers, compressors, and electrical transformers. The underground also targeted warehouses, especially those containing armaments and foodstuffs, and forests, often in the proximity of German cantonments. The most dramatic explosion occurred on November 1, 1943, when a munitions depot on the road from Menton to Sospel began burning until it blew up.[34]

The Clandestine Press

While still serving as a captain in the Armée de l'Armistice in Marseille, Frenay had started down the road to opposing the German occupation of France:

> At the end of the summer of 1940, what are the needs? First to be informed, then to go get information. Later, to exploit it. If possible, transmit to the English the military intelligence which they alone have the possibility of using. To diffuse as far as possible general information in order to counteract official propaganda actually placed under Nazi control.

What seems incredible in hindsight is that Frenay's intentions were founded on the belief that "Everything indicates the invasion is near."[35] Is it any wonder that the Resistance became querulous as the war dragged on for years without Allied liberation?

While Frenay created the MLN in 1940, there was no hint of political enmity on his part towards Vichy. His *Bulletin d'information et propagande* soon evolved into *Les Petites Ailes* (*The Little Wings*), encountering the same indifference—little reaction in the southern zone due to apathy, a preoccupation with obtaining food, and growing concern for husbands and sons who remained prisoners of war in Germany. By August 1941, however, *Vérités* was now critical of Vichy but without attacking Pétain.

The amalgamation of *Vérités* and *Liberté* later that year produced a Gaullist newspaper called *Combat*, subsequently edited by Albert Camus, after the organization of the same name. Fifty adherents were arrested in Nice in October, 12 being sent to jail. By the end of 1942, *Combat* was printing 80,000 copies each week. Yet another opposition paper first appeared at the same time, *Franc-tireur*, inspired by Jean-Pierre Lévy. Jean Moulin even created a Bureau of Information and the Press in 1942, and soon hundreds of thousands of copies of free newspapers were circulating in the Midi.[36]

A vignette from these times was provided by Raphaël Konopnicki, a Polish Jew who had earlier held various union jobs and political positions with the Front Populaire in the Moselle and the PCF in Marseille.[37] He recounted being asked to undertake a printing operation for the Resistance in Nice after the incumbent escaped to Monaco to avoid arrest. The equipment was in a duplex in a residential neighborhood at 31 avenue Valrose. This operation reproduced the panoply of documents indispensable at that time relating to identity, food, work, baptism, and, when appropriate, demobilization after the Phoney War. Konopnicki was also expected to publish four-page newspapers—*Notre Parole* for the Union Juive pour la Résistance et l'Entraide (United Jews for Resistance and Self-Help), *J'accuse* and *Jeune combat* of the Union of Jewish Youth, *France d'abord* for the FTP, and the communist *Cri des travailleurs*, plus anti-fascist fliers. Tracts were written in Yiddish, Italian, and German for soldiers of the Wehrmacht.

An anonymous intermediary delivered the copy. Everything was composed on a Remington typewriter and reproduced on a manual duplicating machine. Konopnicki's wife Rose obtained the necessary printing supplies from a sympathetic shopkeeper even though they were forbidden to be sold without authorization. Stacks of the finished product were left in a blind "mailbox" for members of the Resistance to distribute. Rose recalled that she "brought some stencils that she put in a bag of food with some greens on top and said on arriving: 'I have brought you some vegetables.' To have on me reams of paper, ink or stencils—without mentioning the tracts!—it was dangerous."[38] One day, the couple learned that the courier had been arrested, and the following day his replacement was also taken into custody just a hundred meters from their house. Under cover of darkness, the frightened résistants dug a hole in the yard and buried the printing equipment and other evidence. As party members they were under orders not to abandon the operation but fled, nevertheless, to a safe house in Monte Carlo.

Returning some weeks later to move the operation to another location, the Konopnickis were informed by a neighbor that two strangers in black raincoats, the uniform of the Gestapo, rang their doorbell on several occasions to the anxiety of nearby inhabitants. But the printing paraphernalia had not been discovered. The original delivery man threw himself out a top-floor window of the Gestapo headquarters at the Hôtel Excelsior after four days and nights of agony without talking. His replacement, a professor of philosophy, was also subjected to torture without revealing any information. Yet publication always resumed.[39]

It was in 1942 that *Le Patriote Niçois* first appeared as a mouthpiece of the Front National in Alpes-Maritimes. The following year, police raided the operation in Nice and the staff barely escaped. As a landing in the South drew near, the national communist movement sought to speak with a new voice on the Côte d'Azur and in early June 1944 sent Pierre Brandon, a veteran of the International Brigades, to improve the public's perception of its cause. As a *ronéotyper* or mimeograph machine was already producing *Vive la France!*, he now turned to the task of enhancing publication of *Le Patriote Niçois*, heralded as "the organ of the fight for the independence of France."

The subsequent contest over legitimacy spoke volumes about dissension within the left wing in Nice. Brandon maintained that any editions by the name of *Le Patriote Niçois* published before his arrival were false, especially numbers 10 through 15 in January to April of that year. Militant communists would not approve of anything contrary to what their party had decided. The CGT must be subordinate to the Front National which, in turn, was the creation of the PCF. Brandon's issue number 9, printed in August 1944, glorified the patriots who were set to free Nice. It also opened the door on the need for purification after liberation. Another article encouraged the patriotic Milice to follow the example set in Paris by rising up and taking control of Nice before the arrival of Allied troops. It was yet another expression of the determination of the urban resistance to act immediately as opposed to waiting for an opportune time dictated by events.[40]

Escaping the Authorities

The Resistance and, indeed, Allied agents and military personnel throughout France during the occupation could not have succeeded without help from ordinary citizens. Two dramatic instances were daring escapes by airmen from Fort-de-la-Révère. Sited on high ground west of the village of La Turbie, this was one of 14 fortresses built in Alpes-Maritimes by General Raymond-Alphonse Séré de Rivières from 1873 to 1884. With thick stone walls it was an imposing edifice used to imprison fliers captured after parachuting onto French soil, occupied or unoccupied. In spring 1942, 13 prisoners squeezed through a hundred-foot-long tunnel fashioned from an air shaft into the surrounding moat empty of water. They immediately scattered, but most were quickly recaptured. Amazingly, the Vichy guards did not block other openings and another group of 60 airmen disappeared through the fort's sewers in August. Like the earlier band, their destinations were Monaco on the seafront, 1,900 feet below the fortress, and Nice, 13 miles to the west via the upper corniche.

Some 30 escapees shared maids' quarters at Monte-Carlo for more than a month before leaving with the help of local policemen and making their way back to Britain. In Nice, other wanted men sought shelter where they could find it. In every case the prisoners were obliged to ask for refuge from total strangers who by aiding them placed in danger their own lives and those of their loved ones. Two doctors, one who would later die in deportation along with his wife, and a Resistance leader known as "Colonel Triangle" were typical of the caregivers. Another woman in Nice was part of the Pat O'Leary escape route set up across France to aid downed airmen seeking to reach Spain and North Africa.[41] After six months, her four American houseguests successfully headed for Gibraltar on their way home, quite possibly part of a contingent of between 25 and 38 fugitives, depending on the source, who embarked aboard the Polish felucca *Seawolf* in September, or another group of 34 who sailed in October.[42]

Hospital Pasteur in Nice became one collecting point for résistants and other captives. At times the runaways were patients in pajamas or night shirts, riding bicycles or running off on foot; in other cases outside help enabled the unauthorized departures. A US squadron leader left Pasteur with an RAF officer when two French sympathizers neutralized a pair of gendarmes with sleeping powder concocted by Dr. Lévy. Indeed, it was not uncommon for pilots to be safeguarded for two weeks in Lévy's household. An American aviator who parachuted from his burning B-17 near Breil was rescued and treated for injuries by the local Resistance. Sent to Nice by train under the guise of a railroad employee, he continued on to safety in the maquis at Puget-Théniers. In Cannes, Group Jean-Marie enabled the escape of 11 of their number being held in the Hôtel de Ville.[43]

Airdrops at Puget-Théniers

From mid-1943 to the following summer, 15 airdrops landed on the plateau of Dina overlooking Puget-Théniers on the upper River Var. Problems endemic to receiving matériel by air were typified by the experiences around this town as recounted in first-hand accounts. In December 1943, Gabriel Mazier ("Capitaine François"), a veteran of the war in 1939–40 and, later, fighting in Tunisia under General Giraud, came to Puget-Théniers in the assumed role of a forester. He convinced some inhabitants to help him identify drop zones for parachute deliveries and, then, to recover and store the largesse. Nonce Casimiri, a militant communist, was one of the first recruits and brought other members of his family to the endeavor. Casimiri's son acted as courier on a bicycle with messages hidden in his jacket lining. The family's dining room ceiling was covered with wiring of an antenna for transmissions concerning air operations.

The François network became active in January. Its original mission was to receive armaments by air. Mazier bought a motorbike that he used to transport batteries in his backpack for three radio transmitters maintaining contact with Algiers. The operators moved constantly to avoid detection by German triangulation interceptors. An airdrop was soon planned for the Dina plateau.

Mazier figured that if it took two hours to climb there in daylight, the journey would consume an extra half-hour at night. A dozen companions took the hike after hearing a coded message on the BBC the evening of January 16: "I adore turkey and a piece of *pogne*."[44] At 11.00 p.m., a Halifax appeared overhead and after a fly-by returned to drop nine containers of arms, munitions, and explosives. The men marveled to hear the canopies slamming open and see the blossoming parachutes floating down to earth. While Mazier took inventory of the canisters, some containing 8-mm. Hotchkiss machineguns made in World War I, his helpers set about hollowing out ditches to bury the ordnance under the smell of sheep in a barn.[45]

One youth wrote, "By day, we work to earn our keep and give the rest to the inhabitants of the village [...] and, at night, it is necessary to participate in the airdrops, to guard the [arms] depots." Insight into maquis training is provided in instructions found later in a cabin in the woods of Gourdon.

> François is a perfectly competent leader. He assembles and disassembles several models of sub-machineguns and rifles, explains how to activate the pieces of plastic explosive, how to introduce detonators and to spark the pencil flames with a pinch of pliers or the tooth, to know the length of ignition according to their color.[46]

As was sometimes the case, a delivery on the night of January 27–8 failed as the plane made only a single pass, perhaps due to bad weather. After a subsequent broadcast, five résistants heard movement as they trudged onto the heights to meet the rescheduled flight. "If it's the Gestapo, everyone for himself," Mazier whispered. In hiding they saw passing down the hill a group of young men fully loaded down with arms from the earlier shipment. The strangers were members of an urban FTP. They were persuaded to return the precious weaponry.

In mid-February at nearby Col Saint-Roch, an airplane delivered 15 containers and 10 packages which typically contained pharmaceuticals, food, cigarettes, and rugged footwear, plus a radio set and 25,000 francs. On another occasion, four agents intending to land by parachute did not make the jump onto terrain considered dangerous. At the same field a month later, three of ten parcels were lost, including a valuable "S Phone" that would have permitted the reception team to communicate with the pilot to coordinate the operation. About the same time, two airdrops from seven SOE aircraft occurred four nights apart. The contents of 15 containers with 100 kilograms of arms in each, the maximum load of a single plane (depending on the model), totaled 12 tons of ordnance, most of which was covertly stocked in a cave just outside the plateau. On the night of the second shipment, Cammaerts was present along with by his departmental chief from Antibes and subordinates from

Nice and Touet-sur-Var wanting to ensure their fair share. The irony is that the Gestapo later discovered and confiscated the shipment, as described below.

The communists did not give up the idea of arming themselves from this stockpile. An FTP company had formed in the vicinity of Puget-Théniers and Entrevaux, and its leader ordered two comrades to bring back weapons intended for the Gaullists. The pair set out for a farm which one résistant knew to be under the protection of gendarmes from Puget-Théniers. With a Colt pistol in his pocket, one guerrilla approached the farmer and introduced himself as coming from Captain François to alert him that the Germans knew of the arms supply and he had been instructed to remove them. The lie permitted the acquisition of 100 Stens with ammunition. Left behind in some bushes were four machineguns too heavy to carry.

Just because weapons were received did not guarantee their safety from the Boche. Maquisards from the valley of the Paillon drove a van to Puget-Théniers and took back a supply of guns which they hid in the tunnel of a canal. A month later, Pétain's quasi-military Groupes Mobiles de Réserve, wearing helmets and carrying rifles, found the cache and deported two résistants to die in a concentration camp. On the night of April 3, six members of the Gestapo arrived in Puget-Théniers and forced a member of the Resistance to lead them onto Dina where another stockpile was seized, several men arrested, and one of the Nazis gravely wounded. Over the following days, German troops commandeered men, mules, and donkeys from nearby villages to carry the arms down the slopes. Members of the Resistance were sickened by the loss of their weapons.[47] The guide would die under torture at Villa Trianon in Nice.

Later that month a stranger arrived stating he wanted some of the hidden weapons for his FTP camp. When told they were all spoken for, he responded, "That's easy. Say that they've been stolen." Visibly unhappy by the lack of cooperation, the stranger departed as suddenly as he had appeared. On May 3, Wehrmacht troops led by the Gestapo invaded Puget-Théniers and began searching for the parachuted arms. François and four of his men were guarding two tons of matériel on a nearby farm when they were surprised by the screeching of tires. As the aggressors entered their hovel, the defenders reacted by hurling grenades, killing two of the officers, while the others fled. In their haste to get away, a grenade exploded accidentally, killing one of the maquis and seriously wounding François.[48]

The reprisal consisted of assembling 67 men between the ages of 18 and 60 in the Puget-Théniers square and lining up eight villagers to be shot. Only the intervention in German by a non-commissioned officer in the gendarmes convinced the aggressors that the culprits were not among the insurgents. Instead, prisoners selected for execution were sent to work for Organization Todt and the STO.[49]

Women in the Azuréenne Resistance

No account of the Resistance in southeastern France would be complete without mention of the contributions by patriotic Frenchwomen. The typical role is thought to have been serving as couriers, carrying papers and weapons, but women contributed in many other ways as well.[50] Caring for the wounded and preparing meals for résistants in hiding were frequently other activities. An unusual example was a pregnant mother in La Trinité, a suburb of Nice, who complained about, first, Italian officers and, then, Germans continually hanging around her little house. Her job was to type the copy for a clandestine newspaper. When the doorbell sounded, she would conceal the stencil she was working on between the mattress and base of her daughter's bed and put the typewriter in the laundry basket.

Women hid résistants, Jews, young men fleeing the STO and other compulsory German work programs, and fugitives pursued by the Gestapo. They supported the maquis by acquiring multiple food coupons, obtaining clothes and shoes of the correct size, and ordering medication. With the cooperation of the Bureau of Food Supply, each week one woman carried provisions to the prison in Nice for detainees without families, thanks to the generosity of certain shopkeepers and even to the black market. After the sudden departure of her husband, the wife of Colonel Vautrin gathered a coterie of women to help the loved ones of those deported or confined in French prisons until she, too, was forced to flee in March 1944.

Other women took part in paramilitary operations. The female founder of Group Surcouf in the valley of Paillon helped receive parachute drops. In Nice, a woman in the underground convinced Polish soldiers stationed in Magnan to desert. An employee of the central telephone exchange in Grasse succeeded in neutralizing a German soldier and capturing five of his compatriots before sabotaging the communications network the day before the town's liberation.

Esther Poggio was an especially active agent, traveling along the coast from Toulon to Menton, for which she eventually paid the ultimate price. A Niçoise photographed blockhouses on the Promenade des Anglais with a miniature camera inlaid in a pendant. A brave résistante checked out and described anti-aircraft sites, munitions depots, and German troop deployments for French intelligence. Yet another female identified the enemy order of battle all along the Mediterranean coast. In fact, the Tartane network in Cannes, which Hélène Vagliano aided at the end of her life, counted 13 women among its 80 agents.

Perhaps the most extraordinary service was performed over several years by Marie-Louise Paiche who worked for the German Armistice Commission, originally situated at the Hôtel Negresco. A direct line had been installed to

Berlin on Easter Sunday in 1941, proof that the Germans were present on the Côte d'Azur well before the formal collapse of the Non-Occupied Zone. Paiche recalled that the office received a great many visitors and letters, most denouncing patriots to curry favor with the presumed victors in the war. She stole information, photographed documents, and, when a camera was not on hand, copied papers in the toilet while a companion kept watch. Paiche was trusted enough to be asked to join the Wehrmacht when it withdrew in 1944 but naturally declined.[51] Other résistantes were not so fortunate. More than 30 women died during deportation, when sentenced to capital punishment, or by summary execution.

Nor was it extraordinary to find an entire family engaged in resistance. A militant in the Italian Communist Party who emigrated to France, Aristodemo Landini distributed newspaper propaganda in the Italian language. His elder son was co-founder of the FTP maquis in the Maures. His daughter met young réfractaires at the train station and led them to the maquisards. The youngest child, Léon, aged 16, fortunately left the Var for a maquis near the Spanish border two months before his father and brother were arrested by the carabinieri.[52]

Preparing for D-Day

Activities during the month of February 1944 reflected the elevated esprit de corps of the Resistance generated by enhanced leadership, training, and matériel. "Manfred," chief of the maquis Fort de France on the Route Napoléon, assisted by Group August of Antibes, captured a German truck transporting 20,000 liters of gasoline. Using his radio post at Puget-Théniers, the ORA leader Sapin undertook to relay messages to Algiers from Toulouse, Montpellier, and Marseille, reporting, for example, that one coup de main destroyed nine locomotives and another foray rendered inoperable a factory producing 100 tons of a light alloy for Germany each month. In turn, Sapin requested bombardment of a rail depot in the Var housing 80–100 locomotives, half always steamed up and ready to go. Sapin explained that the objective was too important and extensive to be targeted by sabotage.

Heightened guerrilla activity and the natural response from the Wehrmacht resulted in numerous maquisards being arrested and some 40 killed in March. At the same time, a camp was set up where forestry pursuits served as the pretext to gather résistants and sort out youth beginning to take an interest in the maquis since the arrival of warm weather. Having on hand too few arms for self-defense and knowing that the AS had received parachute deliveries in the area, guerrilla leaders were determined to demand weapons or, if necessary, steal them.[53]

Miniconi's Group Jean-Marie acquired a mother lode single-handedly. A Polish FTP member who worked for the German work placement office reported a cache of Wehrmacht arms in an empty house in Antibes. The Croix Rouge quarter was on high ground, and the small building sat on a quiet street nestled among market gardens and greenhouses which dotted the landscape during the war years. Breaking in on the night of March 9, the conspirators found wooden shelves stacked with hand grenades, sub-machineguns and 50 long-barreled Mauser pistols. The plunder was hauled off in a gazogène panel truck under sacks of leaf mold and potted plants and then carefully hidden in the grotto of a villa in Cannes.[54]

Another urban commando told a different story about his ability to obtain and share weapons. Nathan Chapochnik, with a nom de guerre "Paul," was sent to Nice in early September 1943 to lead a party of Bulgarians in reactivating the FTP–MOI detachments broken up by the OVRA working with the Gestapo. In the confusion of the Italian army's rout, a wealth of arms was recovered. Afterwards, Paul stated that the AS gave his men weapons hidden in a depot on the outskirts of Nice. Next, he asked an FTP cell from Antibes to supply the pencil detonators and explosives used to blow up a cinema while it was full of German soldiers. By the following March, Paul's cell no longer needed the AS as it was receiving matériel by parachute. The associated maquis at Peille made wooden cases for some of the sub-machineguns, pistols, and grenades marked "Weights and Measures" on the outside. Paul took the shipment to a Nice rail station and on to Marseille where the weapons were employed.[55]

Looking ahead to the Allied landing, "D-Day" in English and "Jour-J" in French, in mid-March 1944 the Resistance in Southeast France was given five objectives to accomplish: (1) develop guerrilla competence to take large rural areas under patriot control, confining the enemy to populated areas and main roads; (2) sabotage rail movement, in particular along the Riviera; (3) harass enemy road movement, especially on east–west coastal routes; (4) interrupt telecommunications and destroy enemy dumps; and (5) reconnoiter, prepare, and defend landing areas for airborne troops and supplies. To perform these tasks, the British estimated there were 30,000 armed sympathizers in the Southeast, many already organized in maquis. In contrast, postwar French numbers of armed men in Alpes-Maritimes on the eve of D-Day did not exceed 200.[56] Specific instructions would be broadcast from London designated by a color code. Plan Green ordered destruction of roads and railways, and Plan Red directed guerrillas to gather at assembly places for broader sabotage of infrastructure of military importance.

Résistants developed the details to execute Plan Green in the Southeast. The region was divided into seven sectors, each with a chief responsible for liaison with departmental leaders of the AS. Teams recruited for the rail system were organized into three sections: Exploitation for information to interrupt traffic; Traction concerned with rolling stock, switches, and machine shops; and Tracks and Buildings focused on fixed matériel, maintenance, and repairs. Disabling engines and boilers, signals, and dispatching capability were preferred to raw destruction. Six-to-eight specialists circulated to workplaces at a time to instruct railroaders in how to cause damage while at the same time protecting themselves. The authors of the plan explained, "We are not in favor of explosives [...] [this is] a delicate undertaking." Explosions were noisy, drawing immediate attention and intensifying armed surveillance. Better results were obtained surreptitiously.

Exceptions and special conditions limited what could be done. Saboteurs in the Southeast were forbidden to destroy bridges, tunnels, and other important engineering structures. Military transports were to be the sole targets on rail lines, not by sabotage of the routes but by explosives or incendiary bombs. The underground preferred to accomplish terrorism on track that had been put out of regular service before the war and was now used only by the Germany military. Nor should the places selected pose extraordinary problems to repair after liberation. Positioning blockages on curves, in defilades, and at entrances to tunnels was considered ideal. Sparing the lives of innocent civilians, another credo, was shared by guerrilla bands elsewhere, as the well-recounted history of maquisards north of Alpes-Maritimes included the same stipulation—"no French lives must be taken."[57] Finally, looking ahead to Jour-J in Provence, Plan Green placed off-limits three 50-ton cranes attached to the rail stations at Nice, Marseille, and Avignon, foreseeing a need for them after liberation.[58]

On the eve of the landings, matériel received by the underground was spread out in multiple hiding places—caves, sewers, barns, warehouses, and more. The contents of packages dropped from aircraft varied as well, now including brassards marked "FFI" to distinguish friend from foe. Tracts were being printed not only in French but also in Polish, Russian, Ukrainian, et al. as psychological tools to undermine the esprit de corps of the Reich's occupying force.

Reaction to June 6

At 8.00 p.m. on June 5, the BBC broadcast two messages sending the French Resistance into action in support of an imminent Allied invasion. "Nous nous roulerons sur le gazon" ("We will roll on the lawn, Plan Green") and "Méfiez-vous du toréador" ("Beware of the bullfighter, Plan Red") sounded loud and clear in Region R-2.[59] The following day, de Gaulle confirmed the notice proclaiming, "For the sons of France, wherever they are, whoever they are, their simple and sacred duty is to fight the enemy by all the means at their disposal. It concerns destroying the enemy which crushes and soils the country, the detested enemy, the dishonorable enemy."[60]

The Resistance in cities burst into action. The PCF and its Front National in Alpes-Maritimes distributed tracts and newspapers at a rate surpassing any prior effort. Ambushes, sabotage, personal attacks—résistants confronted the occupiers with courage and audacity. Urban guerrillas had a head start on rural maquisards by being better organized and more numerous at the outset and also benefiting from the tacit complicity of the population and intelligence provided surreptitiously by local law enforcement. The Germans' distrust of gendarmes was shown by transferring responsibility for guarding prisons to the police. The occupiers were obviously unaware of the extent of cooperation by departmental police with the Resistance, estimated to be close to 90 percent.[61]

General Pierre Koenig had been assigned by de Gaulle to command the FFI in May. He instructed the maquis that when the débarquement took place to engage in disruption to "tie down considerable numbers of the enemy, isolate them, and keep them surrounded until the intervention of Allied forces from outside."[62] The messages on June 5 were understood as the long-awaited green light to unleash retribution against the German oppressors with the understanding that external military support would be forthcoming. The underground's immediate reaction across France initially helped restrain the Wehrmacht from sending all available forces to the English Channel. By June 10, however, Supreme Allied Headquarters realized that the Germans could no longer be deceived about the importance of the Normandy landings. Now, the Americans and British were struggling to break out of their bridgehead. Koenig appreciated that Allied air power was focused almost exclusively on direct support of the toehold on the English Channel, leaving maquisards vulnerable to German reprisals. The Allies could not send men or supplies to the Resistance at this critical juncture. Therefore Koenig issued an urgent order: "Premature start, suspend action, send back non-armed resisters."[63] Maquis were to adopt a "wait and see" role, harassing and sabotaging but not openly confronting Wehrmacht units.

In Alpes-Maritimes, Sapin feared that dismissing volunteers so quickly would not only create a psychological problem but place them at grave risk. Cammaerts shared the same concern. Workers and civil servants at the Toulon arsenal and gendarmes across the region, for example, could not just casually report back to their jobs. Furthermore, spontaneous resistance was beyond the Allies' power to control, and SOE agents focused instead in harnessing the maquis to the general strategic plan of waiting for a landing from the Mediterranean.

Confusion reigned in the maquis in southeastern France as orders and counter-orders were received. The rail between Nice and Monaco was cut thanks to help from résistants in Menton. Interruption of a narrow-gauge line between Sospel and Cuneo was also carried out by maquisards from nearby Breil. On the other hand, Plan Green assigned priority to cutting the railroad running east and west between Nice and Marseille. After accidentally encountering a German patrol, the responsible guerrilla leader concluded that he would not risk his men's lives by trying to strike the key viaduct at Anthéor again since it had already been hit by air. Nor was the track between Nice and Sospel blown up as planned because that local commander considered its destruction of little importance. Another FFI chief decided that since none of the massive parachute deliveries promised for Jour-J had taken place, his maquis would not budge. One camp tried to seize a member of the Milice, only to see him get away. Even his wife escaped, reaching the safety of a German outpost.[64] In sum, it was an inauspicious display of the potential of the maquis in support of military operations in Alpes-Maritimes. This time the Allied landing was over 600 miles away in Normandy; next time would be different.

The ORA in the Southeast also attempted to put Plan Red into effect. As one enthusiastic lieutenant exclaimed, "The only positive attitude was action." The first attempt was to capture the German garrison at Barcelonnette, a little thirteenth-century walled town a dozen miles from the Italian border and the strategic Alpine pass, Col de Larche. Sapin traveled to the settlement and found that the Wehrmacht presence there had been overcome. He also heard that a relief column marching from Gap had stopped to the west. What he did not learn, apparently, was that on June 9, Germans attacked Lauzet in the Ubaye Valley 15 miles away with six armored cars, an antitank gun, and nine mortars, indicative of a sizeable enemy presence close at hand.[65]

Joining Sapin at Barcelonnette were Cammaerts and Colonel Henri Zeller. A career officer, Zeller had served on the staff of the Armée de l'Armistice at Vichy. Now head of the AS in southeastern France and FFI commander for Regions 1 and 2, Zeller observed that Cammaerts could get six times as many men into the field as he could.[66] This was Cammaerts' initial contact with Sapin. He is reported to have remarked, "With him [Zeller] was Capitaine Lécuyer (Sapin), the officer in charge of the R2 region, a young Giraudist who said to me, no one supports de Gaulle, to which all I could say was—I don't think you'd better say that out loud around here. We met after the war and he had the grace to admit he was wrong."[67]

This area was of strategic importance to controlling the principal route into Italy, as well as being on a motorway connecting with national road to the coast. Maquis Lorrain, by then under the command of Jacques Lippmann, had climbed onto an Alpine summit 8,000 feet above sea level to meet partigiani and obtain four Fiat machineguns. Personal weapons in possession of Lorrain maquisards consisted of two revolvers and some barely serviceable carbines with cartridges abandoned by the retreating Italian army.[68] Only 250 of the 600 French partisans were armed at all and on average had only 20 rounds of ammunition per weapon. Delivery of 100 containers of guns and equipment on the night of June 11–12 by RAF aircraft and American B-24 Liberators from Algiers in response to urgent calls from Sapin enabled the maquis to form roadblocks, but it came too late for all the ordnance to be located, retrieved, and distributed. The armored column rushing toward Barcelonnette was too powerful to be stopped, and the maquisards soon scattered into the hills leaving behind 150 defenders killed and many more wounded and captured.[69]

Having witnessed this brave but futile stand, Cammaerts and Zeller made their way to the Vercors where they set up a command post. The Vercors is a high, limestone, central plateau, 10–12 by 30 miles in size, surrounded by saw-toothed ridges just southwest of Grenoble. Some 4,000–5,000 guerrillas gathered there, many unarmed and untrained. Prominent were former Chasseurs Alpins and cavalrymen recruited by the FTP, who although not necessarily communist were strongly anti-militarist and anti-Catholic. In the euphoria following June 6, they declared the area to be the Free Republic of the Vercors. It was natural for the leadership of the underground to gravitate to this stronghold, intended as a reception area for airborne troops who would join with the résistants to back up the Allied landing. In preparation, a British Allied Mission and an American Operation Group dropped onto the plateau.

In the early morning hours of July 7, an SOE operative flew in from Algeria and parachuted onto the Vercors. Landing far from five French engineers on the same flight, it was two days before she found Cammaerts, her new commanding officer. He had requested a replacement for an assistant taken by the Gestapo and now suddenly she appeared, almost out of nowhere, a woman who was already a genuine heroine.[70]

Born Krystyna Skarbek in Warsaw in 1908[71] and twice married, "Christine Granville," as she became known in exploits for British intelligence after 1939, or "Pauline Armand," her nom de guerre, had already worked against the Nazis in her homeland, Hungary, Turkey, and Egypt before being assigned to SOE headquarters in Algiers in 1944.[72] The record of a meeting with a British agent in December 1939 portrayed "Madame G" as "a very smart looking girl, simply dressed and aristocratic. She is a flaming Polish patriot. She made an excellent impression and I really believe we have a PRIZE." Three years later, another interviewer characterized her as having an inferiority complex and being obstinate. Yet he went on to write, "She is a person of quite outstanding courage with exceptional charms and powers of persuasion," which was tested repeatedly throughout the war years.[73]

Fluent in five languages, poised and vivacious, Christine was a slender five-foot-eight with a heart-shaped face, brown hair, almond eyes, and high cheekbones. A comrade in France fondly portrayed her as a wartime personage.

> Not that she in any way resembled the classical conception of a female spy, even though she had the glamourous figure that is conventionally associated with one; this she preferred to camouflage in an austere blouse and skirt which, with her short, carelessly-combed dark hair and the complete absence of make-up on her delicately-featured face, gave her the appearance of an athletic art student.[74]

Cammaerts would later benefit from Christine's wartime experience, skills, and charm. His mission now was to ensure the maquis were properly supplied and trained to use their weapons and explosives. He made repeated requests that heavy artillery and other matériel be flown to the massif, as did local leaders of the Resistance. Thirty-six Liberators from London dropped 800 loads of arms and equipment through their bomb doors on June 25, but many hit the ground with faulty clasps on their containers and the weapons were rendered unusable. At noon on July 14, about 100 aircraft, 72 B-17 Flying Fortresses plus some Halifaxes in squadrons of 12 with fighters circling above, released almost 1,000 parachutes of blue, white and red (to indicate their contents), the largest daylight delivery of the war. This largesse reinforced the partisans' belief that the uprising could count on heavy Allied support. But there were no large-caliber guns or howitzers. In fact, Cammaerts claimed never to have received a single mortar.[75]

The challenge to their authority from a self-proclaimed independent state had made as strong an impression on the German occupiers as on the Allies. Fighter planes and bombers bearing the swastika arrived in time to attack the reception team out in the open loading trucks to carry off the shipment and to strafe Bastille Day celebrations underway. Cammaerts and Christine were certain they were going to die, and it was then that they sealed a personal bond.[76] Thereafter the Luftwaffe continued daily bombing runs, employing incendiaries to destroy villages and farm buildings sheltering Resistance fighters and even demolishing a field hospital, killing 40 doctors, nurses, and patients.

By July 21, two and a half Wehrmacht divisions totaling 20,000 soldiers with mountain artillery began forcing their way through rocky formations and into the highland citadel while planes and gliders landed SS men blazing away with machineguns and flamethrowers. It was the largest operation undertaken by the army of occupation in France. The situation becoming desperate, on the 23rd the plateau's military commander put an end to the carnage by ordering his men to disperse into the rugged landscape. Zeller,

Cammaerts, and Christine departed by car. Left behind were 640 résistants and 200 civilians killed since Bastille Day.[77] Reinforced by the Waffen-SS and their dreaded Mongol legions, the invaders took bloody reprisals against the populace, raping and stealing, pillaging, killing, and hauling off livestock and produce.

The Vercors would be remembered for the heroism of its defenders and inhabitants but also, unfortunately, for the consequences of abandoning hit-and-run tactics, the strong suit of guerrillas, and confronting a battle-ready military force in positional warfare with light weapons not designed to counter aircraft, armor, and heavy artillery. The tragedy of Vercors might well have turned out differently if the timing had coincided with the landing in Provence.

Cammaerts and Christine moved eastward before parting, the Polish operative sent to utilize her linguistic skills to undermine the morale of Eastern Europeans dragooned into the Wehrmacht. Obtaining information about Polish and Ukrainean troops had been specified as one of her principal tasks by Algiers.[78] Upon leaving the Vercors, Christine advised London, "The morale in the German army is bad, they know that the war is lost. Propaganda is almost unnecessary." Perhaps with a bit of national pride, Christine contended, "The Maquis want the Poles (whom they trust) to join them with arms," and headed off to Gap where there were reportedly 250 of her compatriots.[79] There she assisted a 200-man partisan band holding heights between two main roads strategically important as connectors between France and Italy. Continuing on, she convinced hundreds of Russians serving in the Ost Legion of General Wiese's 19th Army to desert and join the local maquis.

On August 14, Christine's next challenge was to climb up a precipitous mountainside to the fortification dominating Col de Larche and persuade 70 Poles in the garrison to come over to the Resistance.[80] As usual, they had been forcibly recruited and joined in many instances to earn a livelihood or to protect wives and families from retaliation. Before ascending the prominence to convince the Poles to desert, Christine requested definitive information on rival Polish governments and authoritative propaganda in the Polish language.[81] When leaving, the conscripts removed breechblocks from the heavy guns and brought them, along with mortars and machineguns, to the partisans. With Polish support, the maquisards fought to keep Larche from being reoccupied and blew large holes in the main road to deny its use to motorized Wehrmacht troops. Christine's narrowest escape, however, came as she was guiding a partigiani to a maquis and was surprised by a frontier patrol. Holding a live grenade in each hand, she threatened to blow them all up, a price her antagonists were unwilling to pay.[82]

Following the flight from Barcelonnette came a period of relative calm in Alpes-Maritimes, providing an opportunity to reorganize and reinforce the maquis. Sapin received orders to establish an extended security zone there in the shape of a quadrilateral, consistent with an operational concept emanating from London "to develop guerrilla activity to such an extent as to take large areas under patriot control, confining the enemy to populated areas and main routes."[83] The stronghold was isolated geographically by high ground to the south and east. Communication with the outside world was minimal.

As German pressure eased, the large shipment of matériel airdropped earlier near Barcelonnette was hand-carried to a new equipment concentration site in the protected zone. A hundred men from numerous camps had gathered at Sapin's headquarters at Beuil on June 6 under Plan Red, and a request went to Algiers for tents to avoid reprisals against civilians who might otherwise shelter the new arrivals. During the interim, many men had drifted back to their former hideouts and homes. Now, the availability of arms encouraged these volunteers to return and attracted new réfractaires, as well as lifting morale. Maquisards received instruction in weaponry from gendarmes drawn to the discipline instilled by the ORA. They brought with them the few weapons which had been permitted by the Germans.

As settlements were few, nourishment came initially from what could be found on the barren slopes. With more men joining the maquis, the heightened demand for provisions required relying upon farmers. When not offered freely, food, tobacco, ration cards, and fuel were taken from small communes in the surrounding countryside. For the first time the French tricolore with the Croix de Lorraine of Free France fluttered in the breeze of Alpes-Maritimes. A liberation committee was formed and persons suspected of aiding the Germans were arrested, a pattern soon to be seen across France. Cammaerts set about engineering artificial avalanches from the snow-covered peaks of the Alps and dynamiting earth slides to block roads important to Wehrmacht traffic, and it is likely he employed these maquisards in this manner.[84]

Organized, armed, and trained with renewed esprit de corps, it was natural for maquisards in Alpes-Maritimes to want to flex their newly toned muscles. Eight miles south of Beuil was a two-span, stone bridge traversing the River Cians and guarded by a squad of ten German soldiers. A guerrilla's account of its destruction on July 7 describes not only the tactics that strategists in London and Algiers considered well suited to the French insurgency, but also suggests the nervousness building in Axis troops confronting the maquis.

It was necessary, before everything, to complete our defense system by blowing up again the bridge of Pra d'Astier on the Cians that I had destroyed a first time in June, but that the Germans had since repaired. They had installed wooden beams by a local team requisitioned for the job, and they watched this bridge day and night from a guard post set up in the only house in the area. I took notice that they fired a mortar on any suspected movement, regularly setting loose avalanches of rocks which rendered the approach to the bridge unusually dangerous.

One night when the moon was in its last quarter, I took six volunteers equipped with light arms, explosives and incendiary grenades, and we headed toward Pra d'Astier, taking off our shoes not to make any noise. Arriving near the bridge, one of my men, Nino, silently approached a sentinel who guarded it and got rid of him for us with the jab of a dagger. I then placed my plastic cartridges against the wooden pillars of the bridge, attaching two delayed detonators, one of 15 minutes, the other for 30 minutes. For effect, I added an incendiary illuminating device. The German guard post was 100 meters below. We withdrew with no more noise than when arriving, reclimbing some hairpin bends up to a point where we could see the bridge, and then we waited. The explosion at the base of the valley was fantastic: debris came falling quite near us; the incendiary exploded immediately, its flash was blinding due to the magnesium of the grenade. The Germans awoke suddenly, exiting on the run, their silhouettes standing out like shadow puppets, but we were too far to reach them with the Stens. We replaced our shoes and, at nine o'clock in the morning, we returned to Beuil. The expedition lasted twelve hours.

At Beuil were hugging and kissing, the pride of success. Everyone feted us as heroes, as each had wanted to participate in the operation.[85]

Local recruitment produced 45 more sympathizers and 55 maquisards from Entrevaux in the Var valley to the southwest. In the mix of new volunteers, however, were two individuals whose attitude aroused suspicion. Under interrogation they admitted being sent by the Milice in Nice to find out where the maquis was located and what attacks were being planned.[86] New guerrilla camps were forming across Alpes-Maritimes in the valleys of the Tinée and Vésubie and other nearby places. This augmentation was consistent with increases across France that quadrupled the size of the maquis after D-Day in Normandy. Some maquisards referred to these additions, joining at the last minute, as "naphtalines" ("mothballs" who just took their uniforms out of four-year storage).[87] The insurgency at Beuil would soon need all these combatants.

Reinforced by the Waffen-SS, Siecherheitsdienst squads, and the Gestapo, the Wehrmacht in the Midi launched a campaign to eradicate the maquis menace and did not slow down when the underground periodically interrupted their operations. Defending against attack, while at the same time receiving air drops, increased the pressure on the maquisards. In the Var, fighting in mid-June left 180 guerrillas and civilians dead. A month later, the villages of Callian and Montauroux were surrounded and searched, resulting in 15 résistants and other hostages being taken away to Grasse. A few days later, Fayence suffered the same treatment.[88]

In Alpes-Maritimes, maquis camps in the back country were held harmless at first for they had accomplished little so far. Indeed, a US intelligence report for June 18–21 remarked that "Alpes Maritimes has been almost 'dead' as far as Resistance Groups are concerned for some considerable time."[89] Meanwhile, on the morning of July 18, a heavy German force was reported at the hamlet of Touet-sur-Var. That evening a two-pronged envelopment kicked off but failed to dislodge the maquisards. As many as 1,500 attackers employed mortars, machineguns, and motorized infantry in an offensive to decimate the high-country Resistance. Over the next four days the Germans conducted multiple forays against the FFI by moving up the valleys of the Var and the Cians to threaten Beuil and Valberg, which were finally evacuated but, surprisingly, not occupied by the enemy.

No sooner had the Wehrmacht accomplished its mission of dislodging the partisans, when its soldiers returned to the coast on July 28. There was interesting speculation as to why the invaders withdrew so quickly. Perhaps biased by his leadership of tactical operations, Sapin wrote that the enemy was afraid of being cut off from behind by the maquis. Historian Joseph Girard concluded that the military force were called back to help defend against an anticipated Allied landing. Saint-Cyrien Lieutenant Pierre Gautier, a subordinate of Sapin, presented the hypothesis that the troops' reassembly was related in some way to the July 20 assassination attempt on Hitler involving numerous Wehrmacht officers directly or indirectly.[90]

Conforming to a pattern across the country in the wake of the Normandy landing, as well as to the heightened threat posed by the Resistance, the German military in the back country now confined itself to small garrisons, notably at Puget-Théniers and an electric plant at Bancairon in the valley of Tinée. At the same time the maquis quickly moved to regain control of the quadrangle by deploying units to the south and east, thereby expanding its dimensions to approximately 19 miles wide and 27 miles long, constituting the northernmost part of Alpes-Maritimes. Additional volunteers, this time 25 naval firemen from Marseille, joined up. Buoyed by growing numbers, small bands of FFI insurgents began a series of ambushes against German convoys, notably along the Tinée. Maquisards cut Wehrmacht communications to the west by destroying two bridges on August 9 and 10, thus isolating the outpost at Puget-Théniers. The enemy garrison at Saint-Martin-Vésubie also became stranded after a series of attacks along its route to the coast.

Looking ahead to a Provençal landing, Algiers was becoming concerned by friction apparent among elements of the Resistance in Region R-2. Coordination was hindered by a dispute between Sapin as leader of the ORA and Robert Rossi, the pro-communist regional FFI chief. After Koenig's instructions to stop guerrilla activity, Rossi had condemned in the strongest terms Sapin's right to order FFI fighters to cease fire in the southeastern region.

A Marseillais and former air force captain, Rossi subscribed to the FTP view that resistance take the form of urban insurrection to help establish leftist control after liberation. On June 16, a dozen youth sympathetic to Rossi's underground were surprised at a nearby farm and shot dead on the spot. Next, a pair of French scouts were taken and killed in the back country.

Matters took a turn for the worse on July 16, when the Milice arrested members of the Basses-Alpes Liberation Committee, and the following day as the Gestapo captured Rossi and his cohorts in Marseille. The roundup was made possible by the treason of Erick Seignon de Possel, a young officer parachuted into the South by the Free French Forces to synchronize speedboats plying between Corsica and La Ciotat. Instead, de Possel offered to sell the local Gestapo chief a list of key names in the Resistance, wiping out much of the leadership in Region R-2. After being tortured at Gestapo headquarters in Marseille, Rossi and 25 other prisoners were led to a secluded hollow near the hamlet of Signes, 15 miles north of Toulon, and summarily executed on July 18.[91] A month later, eight more résistants were shot and buried in shallow graves at the same place after another agent sent from Algeria sold information to the Germans.

Resistance leaders gathered on August 4 to re-establish a command structure broken since Rossi's death. Sapin acknowledged openly criticizing the MUR for sitting by passively at the time of the clashes in Barcelonnette and during the German offensive in July. He was nevertheless appointed chief for the Department of Alpes-Maritimes while retaining his leadership of the ORA in Region R-2.[92] Having served in the rank of captain in the Armée de l'Armistice, Sapin was junior to some of the departmental chiefs in Region R-2. Recognizing his delicate position, he gave his subordinates maximum freedom in organizing, recruiting, identifying parachute drop zones, deploying maquis, and contacting other Resistance organizations.[93]

More efforts at organization and reorganization accompanied the continuing expansion of the maquis. The competence of the Beuil encampment was strengthened by appearance of the Inter-Allied Mission BASSES-ALPES, dispatched from Algiers. Its operational area encompassed Alpes-Maritimes and the Var. French Commandant Christian Sorensen ("Chasuble") was designated head of the Mission. His responsibilities included maintaining liaison between American, British, and French forces and the FFI; collecting information; centralizing supply to the FFI; and organizing paramilitary activities. The orders stated, "You will wear uniform in the field and maintain your proper status as an Allied officer save in exceptional circumstances … All Italian resistance groups in the area come under the direction of the Mission."[94]

Major Havard Gunn, a Scottish reserve officer in the Seaforth Highlanders, was among the new arrivals. His rich background included education at Oxford, accomplishment in five languages, military experience in guerrilla warfare with mountain tribes, liaison with an armored unit and with the French Foreign Legion, and prior political services for the FFI. Tall, thin, quiet and almost always wearing a kilt, he had chosen "Bambus" as his nom de guerre from a clump of bamboos he came across while training with Christine Granville in Algeria.[95] The Scotsman's companions included another Frenchman and two Britons. Captain Jean Fournier was a graduate of Saint-Cyr, a colonial officer, and veteran of the fighting in 1940. The British members, Captain John Halsey and Sergeant-Major Campbell, would be sent to the Col de Larche.

Gunn became Sapin's shadow, while Sorensen was initially immobilized by a leg injured in the parachute landing. On August 8, Sapin moved his headquarters to Valberg, closer to the River Var and Nice. Among the first tasks assigned to Gunn was to use partisans to disseminate the following rumors: (1) The Army Group G commander, Generaloberst Johannes Blaskowitz, was involved in the plot against the Fuhrer; (2) German army conspirators have flooded the Normandy and Brittany fronts with false orders; (3) Himmler has kept back 40 percent of Luftwaffe fighters to quell riots in Germany; and (4) 50,000 German deserters are already in Switzerland and Spain. In exercising his responsibilities, Gunn wrote in his official report, "difficulty of movement, area surrounded by German garrisons; made first recce [reconnaissance] area Barcelonnette–Larche, had to travel as Gendarme, uniform hidden."[96]

About the same time, General Zeller[97] requested approval to fly to Algeria to impress upon Allied headquarters the silent control being exercised by the Resistance outside heavily populated areas and a few small-town garrisons. With the tragedy of Vercors fresh in mind—devastation that could have been lessened by the air support promised but never delivered—Zeller intended to push for more help for the Resistance. The coordinator for air operations in the greater Marseille region, Camille Rayon, succeeded in obtaining Zeller a Lysander flight to Corsica, where he continued on to Algiers and met with de Gaulle on August 5. Impressed by Zeller's impassioned plea, the leader of the Free French informed him of the forthcoming landing in Provence, revealing the Top Secret operation plan. Zeller insisted that the time factors were far too conservative, as the Allies could use the valley of the River Durance to bypass the lower Rhône Valley, catch the 19th German Army from behind, and quickly reach Grenoble due to control of this region already exercised by the Resistance.

De Gaulle sent Zeller on to Seventh Army headquarters which was finalizing the debarkation plan in Napoli. Zeller briefed Major General Alexander Patch and his staff, along with the leadership of General Jean de Lattre de Tassigny's French Army B, all of whom revealed ignorance of the military situation in the intended landing area that surprised and disappointed the outsider. On August 9, Zeller returned to Algiers to provide feedback to de Gaulle. Now fully informed of the pending southern invasion, Zeller was prevented from returning to France before its execution as a security precaution. He had succeeded, however, in having added to the operation order provision for an immediate thrust up the Durance River Valley that would take the form of Task Force Butler.[98]

Festering problems concerning command and control caused Cammaerts to want to confer with de Gaulle's representatives when they arrived by air at Rayon's maquis camp 15 miles from Apt. Cammaerts took Sorensen along as well as another member of his mission, British Major Xan Fielding, who had been reared on the Riviera. They traveled in a Red Cross truck driven by Claude Renoir, youngest son of the painter. On their way back on August 13, the three agents were arrested at Digne when the Gestapo found that serial numbers on Cammaerts' bank notes were idential to those carried by Sorensen and Fielding.[99] So, ironically, Francis Cammaerts, the SOE leader considered by many to be the most effective in the Midi, was in German custody when the Allies finally landed in Provence.

Learning of their capture from Renoir, Christine first put Cammaerts' successor in touch with as many Jockey contacts as possible.[100] Then she cycled the hilly 25 miles to Digne to contact various FFI leaders for help, but they refused on the grounds that it was too dangerous. Next, she found an Alsatian gendarme to act as go-between and began negotiations with a Gestapo agent for release of "Roger," whom she stated was her husband, and his two friends. "From the beginning I openly told him that I was a British parachutist, that I had worked there for two years and I also said I was General Montgomery's niece," the last two falsehoods. Warning of the liberators' imminent arrival in Digne late on August 17 (more disinformation), just hours before their scheduled execution, Christine obtained release of the prisoners and safe conduct for everyone, including the Nazi. His conditions were that he be protected from the vengeance of the populace, not be imprisoned, and recognized by the British government for having rendered the Allies "an important service."[101] Cammaerts placed Christine's courage and initiative in clear perspective, writing, "She took voluntarily one chance in a hundred, and undoubtedly if it had not come off she would have been shot with us."[102]

The Impact of the Resistance

M. R. D. Foot cites figures that he admits are optimistic—75,000 men armed by the SOE's F Sections in 90 circuits and another 50,000 guerrillas supplied with weapons through de Gaulle's network. Foot goes on to recall the testimony of Gerd von Rundstedt in his postwar trial when, Foot admits, he was more interested in defending himself than providing an accurate account of the military situation in the Midi in 1944. The German marshal stated, "From January 1944 the state of affairs in southern France became so dangerous that all commanders reported a general revolt [...] The life of the German troops in southern France was seriously menaced and became a doubtful proposition."[103] The ability of men and women in the organized resistance to prepare themselves and then achieve a series of combat victories away from French, American, and British units had a strong foundation, as Foot asserts—overwhelming popular support.[104]

Von Rundstedt's ulterior motives do not negate the truth that on the eve of the Allied landings along the Provençal coast, the Resistance had become a psychological impediment for the occupiers. Surprise attacks followed by quick withdrawals weighed on the minds of German commanders and soldiers alike. A French lieutenant colonel who was military chief of a Resistance command to the west, André Malraux,[105] mused that the Gestapo might have been curious to see all these mysterious irregulars. Malraux realized, even if the occupiers did not, that the maquis exaggerated their numbers and sometimes struck targets that could easily be repaired because they could do no better. As a jocular aside, he related the story of a member of the Resistance confronted by a jailor who after consulting his roster pronounced the prisoner a "terroriste." Not "terroriste" came the reply, "touriste."[106]

By no means light-hearted, the Wehrmacht had learned to stay protected in their casernes unless moving about in force. An uncertainty, an apprehension, even a fear had infected the hitherto confident invaders, thanks to a disjointed movement of men fighting for their own lives even if not necessarily prepared to die for France. Now disciplined, trained, armed, and outfitted, mainly by sources outside the French Métropole, resisters in the Midi were poised to repay their Allied benefactors for their support once the debarkation in Provence began.

9

Preparations for Landing

An invasion of southern France was mentioned in strategic deliberations among the Allies throughout 1943 and 1944, notably at Quebec and Tehran.[1] The priorities at these conferences, however, were the offensive already underway in Italy and an eventual landing in Europe from England, code-named Overlord. US military leaders envisioned a three-division operation in the South of France either before, during or after Overlord to stretch thin the German defenses in Western Europe. It soon became clear, however, that demand for ground forces and amphibious craft needed to cross the English Channel was so great that the operation against Vichy France, referred to as Anvil, must follow rather than occur simultaneously with the invasion of northern France.

After the Allies' success across North Africa in 1943, however, more divisions were freed up than could be gainfully employed in an offensive up the narrow Italian boot. At the same time the Free French were assembling troop formations in North Africa. Shipping was not available to transport all these elements to staging areas in southern England, nor were port capacity and infrastructure available there to receive and support them. General Eisenhower reasoned that these military assets could become stranded in the Mediterranean if not utilized to complement his initiative in the North. The question therefore became where to launch an invasion in the South. The preference for planners in Washington was the area east of Marseille and Toulon. Yet it might be necessary to provide support over the beach for 30 days after landing, and there was uncertainty about the effects of the mistral—strong, northerly winds that could blow up in that region any time after the end of September.

Churchill registered his strongest objection to the plan after July 2, 1944, when the Combined Chiefs of Staff of America and Britain directed General Wilson to launch a three-division attack complete with airborne landings in southern France by August 15, followed by insertion of the French army. Using troops in this manner would leave southeastern Europe prey to Russian domination after the war, Churchill contended. Undoubtedly with this in mind, Josef Stalin had been a strong proponent of Anvil. Churchill had long pushed for opening a new front up the Adriatic to provide access to Vienna, the Danube, and beyond. The prime minister now advocated switching a second French landing to Brittany where he asserted it would play a direct role in support of Overlord, while at the same time preserving Allied power in the South for his anti-Soviet strategy. But Breton ports would be less accessible than the larger ports of Marseille and Toulon when the Allies marched eastward into the Reich. The Mediterranean harbors also presented the advantage of having no tidal fluctuations. Only with France as a solid base for logistical operations could the Western Allies squeeze Fortress Germany. Consequently, the British were overruled one last time, and on August 11, Wilson received the final order to execute the invasion long under consideration.

Office of Strategic Services

A new player had been introduced in the war in Europe and would be involved in the Provençal operation. The US Office of Strategic Services (OSS) was formally established in June 1942 to gather, coordinate, and analyze intelligence and conduct counter-espionage, sabotage, guerrilla warfare, and psychological paramilitary operations. Until Washington severed diplomatic relations with Vichy and the North Africa landing was accomplished, the OSS played only a minor role in the South of France. Once the US military took an interest in unconventional warfare in France in 1943, the OSS was already two years behind the British. The OSS mandate was more complex than the SOE, consisting of Operations and Intelligence, as well as research and analysis. Just as important was what was excluded from the Intelligence role—developing relations with French guerrillas and serving as interpreters for the vanguard of the Allied forces. These functions would be performed by the Operations section and the SOE.[2]

The first OSS agents parachuting into France were Frenchmen in civilian clothes using assumed names with false papers. In August 1943, a pair of these operatives jumped into the Rhône Valley not far from Lyon. The principal resistance movements had staffs there, as Lyon was the largest city close to the Swiss border, but there would be no American presence in the southeast corner of France until the following year. Allen Dulles, OSS chief of the Berne (Switzerland) branch, joined with General Giraud's staff to drop a former Cagoulard[3] into southeastern France on January 8–9, 1944. His mission was to serve as liaison with two dissident officers in the Abwehr, the chiefs of its Nice and Lyon branches. The SOE office in Algiers sent three radio operators to a villa in Nice where negotiations took place, but it was only after the Allied landing that the pair of Germans finally defected.[4]

As the British had established an SOE base code-named Massingham at a former seaside resort 15 miles west of Algiers, the OSS followed suit. The Intelligence branch was run by Henry Hyde, a 29-year-old New Yorker who had been partially educated in France, enabling him to communicate with its people better than most of his countrymen. Missions of the two clandestine services were flown from an airfield near Blida, 30 miles southwest of Algiers. In its first year in Algeria, the OSS was handicapped by few staffers and a dearth of fluency in French. Furthermore, Operations agents were unfamiliar with the country's various regions. When southern France evolved into a potential area for US military operations in 1944, the headquarters grew to more than 50 personnel. The Americans struggled to deliver agents and matériel with only the three Boeing B-17 Flying Fortresses available for OSS operations. Consequently, they relied primarily on British air assets, which fed 40 OSS operatives into the South of France leading up to the Provençal landing.[5]

The report on OSS operations prepared for the US Joint Chiefs of Staff at the end of the war made some insightful observations about the recruitment and deployment of American agents in Algeria. "The late entry of [Intelligence]/France into the field, in comparison with the British and French intelligence services, meant that the most suitable agents had been preempted."[6] Frenchmen who had worked with Americans in preparing for the North African landing provided the best pool of candidates for France, the report explained. The OSS was inclined to dispatch agents to localities they knew well so they could depend on friends there for help.

Just 100 miles southeast of the Riviera, Corsica became an important forward position for the Allies after its liberation in October 1943. British and French secret services, in addition to the OSS, set up operating stations at Bastia on the island's northeast corner to relay communications from Algiers and dispatch agents to southern France. A squadron of American PT boats and British motor launches and gunboats constituted the Corsican fleet of small craft. Populated with French speakers, Corsica also offered a rich recruiting ground for undercover operatives to place on the mainland.

London was controlling plans and operations preparatory to a Continental invasion from England, so at the end of 1943 Hyde began to concentrate on building networks in the South of France in anticipation of a landing there. His opening agent of note, code-named "Ben," was Bernard Bermond, a 27-year-old Jewish furrier who had fled the Nazis in Marseille to fight alongside the maquis on Corsica. Accompanied initially by a captain in de Gaulle's intelligence arm, the BCRA, Ben was directed to return, first, to Saint-Tropez and, then, take the train to Marseille and establish contact with an agent using the password "Gustave embraces Clo-clo." His mission was to obtain drawings of fortifications between Marseille and Menton, concentrating on the ports at Toulon, Hyères, Saint-Raphaël, Cannes, Nice, and Villefranche. In addition,

Hyde was interested in the exact placements of defensive positions along the valley of the River Durance and between and including Aix-en-Provence and Marseille. The designations of Wehrmacht units stationed on the coast were also important, of course, as were the identities of individuals who might constitute a German fifth column left behind when enemy units pulled out. Ben was cautioned about Saint-Raphaël where roundups by the Gestapo were frequent and the Milice especially active. He was ordered to return to North Africa via Spain no later than the beginning of February.[7]

Ben landed by PT boat from Corsica on December 31 and recruited seven agents, each knowing only the friend who approached him and the person he enlisted in turn. American staff maps were soon discarded in favor of French ones with better detail. Natives were employed to cover specific areas and agents assigned to double-check the work of others. When Ben departed he left behind a network called Yves which included two engineers for the railway between Nice and Saint-Raphaël. His report was the first to list the German order of battle in the South, critical to confirming other intelligence.[8]

In August 1943 the Operations planning section had foreseen two kinds of American covert operations in the South of France: programs not directly connected with any particular invasion plan and those supportive of specific military operations. By the spring of 1944, however, SHAEF had clearer immediate concerns. It set up a separate Special Project Operations Center (SPOC) at a villa across the road from OSS headquarters in Algeria to direct both SOE and Operations activities in the South of France. French officers were not permitted access to this hut even as late as five weeks after the Normandy landing. Hyde defended the exclusion as warranted by "the struggle between the Gaullist and the non-Gaullist, embittered in this case by professional rivalries between the old guard and the rapidly becoming professionals of the BCRA."[9]

The Americans estimated the number of French patriots in the Southeast had grown upwards of 50,000 armed sympathizers, 60 percent of whom were organized in maquis. Based on experience in Corsica, America's strategic planners believed that lightly armed civilians could be an effective mobile force if properly led and supported.[10] As D-Day in Normandy approached, Eisenhower's headquarters refined its expectations for resistance groups in the South of France to delaying movement of enemy forces to the lodgment area, severing enemy lines of communication, and effecting other sabotage.[11] Naturally, more specific tasks would be expected of the French underground once the Allies came ashore from the Mediterranean:

- To hinder enemy reinforcements moving by rail and road to the beach-head from any parts of the AFHQ area or from northern France towards the Mediterranean and to attack tele-communication and other priority targets.

- To create major diversions in the enemy's rear.
- To assist the breakout from the bridgehead area by guerrilla action and by assisting parachute troops to form airheads along the axis of the breakout.[12]

Operational Groups (OG) were the military element of the OSS. Intended to work together as teams instead of as individual operatives, OG members received specialized instruction in enemy organizations, communications, weapons, explosives, and vehicles, as well as unconventional warfare. Most were bilingual. Ordnance included machineguns, bazookas, automatic rifles, mines, and explosives. OG sections were assigned missions considered too difficult for untrained members of the Resistance. In addition, the mere presence of American soldiers in uniform far behind enemy lines was expected to raise the population's spirits. The first OGs for France were dispatched from Washington in February and March 1944.

The OG command for the South of France was Company B, 2671st Special Reconnaissance Battalion, headquartered in Algiers and consisting of 14 combat sections which parachuted into France between June 8 and September 1944. The second unit to deploy, OG Justine, was comprised of two American lieutenants and 13 Frenchmen who were inserted onto the Vercors on June 28, not long before the Germans began attacking in force. The detachment's primary task of training maquis in using Allied weapons was quickly overtaken by events there. Instead, the OG executed two successful ambushes on its own, suffering two casualties.[13]

The component of Company B to operate in the southeastern region was OG Ruth, which dropped into Basses-Alpes on the night of August 3–4. Ruth also consisted of two lieutenants and 13 enlisted men. Landing on a small, rocky plateau suitable for supply drops but not parachutists, two soldiers were injured. Met by "four or five unorganized F.T.P. boys," the next 48 hours were spent carrying gear two kilometers to a place where it could be picked up by maquis trucks. The group set up near the town of Saint-Jurs. One maquisard later painted an unflattering portrait of Ruth's presence: "As the Americans had nothing to do, everything which was worth blowing up having been destroyed long since, they pitched their tents about 500 meters from us, a little vacation camp."[14] The OG then went to work detonating railway and road bridges to tie up German traffic. Once the Allied landing took place, Ruth received orders to concentrate on ambushes, so armed squads lay in wait along highway 96 but encountered no enemy vehicles. Contacting Task Force Butler, the OG was directed to protect its right flank on the Route Napoléon. Only three men went on this mission because the rest of the unit did not have shoes that could hold up for the eight-hour hike required to reach the designated control point.[15]

Next, Ruth's main body went to Seventh Army headquarters at Saint-Tropez where it was ordered to assist the maquis. The German truck given them broke down, the Inter-Allied Mission representative (Major Gunn) failed to meet them as scheduled, and the Americans wasted an entire day at Digne trying to obtain automatic weapons from a maquis without getting any. Finally encountering Commandants Sapin and Chasuble, the OG agreed to send six men with two bazookas to establish a blockade on the road along the River Var near Puget-Théniers. Firefights ensued over several days. Much later, when the area was cleared of enemy, the section leader reported to the 517th Parachute Infantry Regiment headquarters in Grasse and conferred with Captain Geoffrey Jones. Team Ruth retired to Brignoles and soon thereafter to Grenoble, the OG collecting point for departing the theater.

The two group members injured in the initial entry had different experiences. One went with Jones to meet the airborne forces spearheading the invasion. He reported that nearly all of the 50 maquisards sent into the drop zone to clear anti-glider stakes were killed as no one realized the fields were mined. Shelling from German .88s compounded the casualties. The other enlisted man accompanied maquis to the hamlet of Montauroux between Fayence and Grasse, where they found 50 or so American and British paratroopers dropped off course. When a contest ensued with the Wehrmacht over control of Callian, a nearby hilltop village, the OG soldier left with three infantrymen to go to Saint-Raphaël for help.

In his after-action report, Ruth's leader characterized the organization of the local resistance as much better than expected with a well-established chain of command and members who were enthusiastic and cooperative. He criticized the weapons issued his section as only suitable for short range and footwear as inapt for rugged terrain, praising only the mountain sleeping bags as the commandos' most valuable piece of equipment. Like his counterparts leading other sections, the lieutenant emphasized that to be effective his outfit should have been inserted much earlier. As an example, he specified the impossibility of consolidating the FTP in his area during the short time provided. In short, scant benefit was derived from the single OG active in the Var and Alpes-Maritimes.[16]

Multi-National Units

Inter-Allied missions were composed of representatives of the SOE, BCRA, and OSS, or Britain, France, and the United States. As a general rule, these were the first elements with American representation to land in southern France. They were sent out for a specific purpose of short duration. Unaware of the date and details of D-Day, their liability if captured and tortured was considered less serious. These teams were to "act as liaison between the FFI and the Allied High Command. They report on the state of training, equipment and morale of Maquis, and explain their needs to SOE/OSS Operations. In fact they have freedom of action to act as the situation demands as long as they work in agreement with the Chief of the FFI."[17]

Among the first groups inserted was Inter-Allied Mission Michel. It was dispatched in June to organize maquis in the mountains of the Vaucluse, Basses-Alpes, and Alpes-Maritimes for attacks on the enemy's line of communications in conjunction with future landings in Provence. On July 20, however, all three team members were killed at Saint-Tropez, including an American lieutenant, Jean Muthular d'Errecalde. Investigations after liberation found that d'Errecalde had been tortured at the Gestapo headquarters in Marseille. In case of arrest, he had protected the reports of his activities which he planned to take to Algiers. They were found in a letter drop.[18]

British and American intelligence chiefs prepared another type of organization to intensify the disturbances swelling behind enemy lines. As an intermediate between the SOE's long-term agents in place and SAS strike parties, Jedburgh teams were formed to motivate and sustain bands of guerrillas, attacking targets specified or as opportunities arose.[19] The composition of the teams has been misconstrued. Conventional wisdom says each grouping consisted of an American, a Briton, and a Frenchman, but in fact only seven of the teams deployed to France represented all three nationalities. The Americans' inability to come up with their share of French speakers resulted in fewer GIs (83) compared with the requisite number of British (90) and extra Frenchmen (103).[20]

The idea of dispatching small bands behind enemy lines first surfaced in London in the spring of 1943 and, interestingly, was approved for the Americans in late August by Lieutenant General Jacob Devers who would be a key figure in the landing in Provence. Six weeks of basic combat instruction and another 6–10 weeks or more of operational training prepared the "Jeds," as they were commonly referred to, for deployment. Instruction in parachuting was critical and, perhaps, faulty for in too many instances commandos were injured descending from the sky. From a British perspective, Jeds did not always gain a full and clear picture of what they would find in their area of operations and what they should do about it.[21]

On May 2, 15 Jedburgh teams embarked from Glasgow for North Africa aboard the liner *Capetown Castle*. Another ten teams would follow. But concerned about the need for a strong indigenous resistance to support the fragile Normandy foothold, Eisenhower had earlier transferred command of the FFI to French General Marie-Pierre Koenig who now inherited responsibility for the Jeds and other agents already in France. His BCRA staff naturally exercised control, although theoretically the French sections of the SOE and OSS were also involved. The British were not pleased.

A uniformed Jed was fully loaded upon exiting an aircraft high above France. His firearms were a .30 caliber carbine (a light shoulder weapon) and a .45 caliber-Colt M1911, developed for its shock effect to hold off Moros fighting in the Philippine insurrection. Additional ammunition clips, a first-aid kit, and canteen were standard issue. A commando dagger and binoculars were extra, as was a bag of emergency rations. What clearly identified the bearer as an agent behind enemy lines was his cash—100,000 francs in small denominations and 50 US dollars—and a cyanide capsule enclosed in a glass container.

Two Jedburgh teams dropped into the southeastern corner of France on the night of August 13–14, just 24 hours before the landing. Allied chiefs worried that if Jeds were on the ground earlier, an agent might be captured and reveal details of the debarkation under torture. Team Sceptre consisted of two Americans (1st Lieutenant Walter C. Hanna and 1st Sergeant Howard Palmer) and a French officer (Lieutenant Francois Franceschi); Team Cinnamon was composed of a Briton (Captain Robert Harcourt) and two Frenchmen (Captain Henri Lespinasse-Fonsegrive—"Ferandon"—and Sub-Lieutenant Jacques Morineau).

Sceptre's mission was to engage in guerrilla warfare in cooperation with maquis along the Franco-Italian border. Unfortunately, the team floated to earth 70 miles from the area where it was to conduct operations. It never did contact the Resistance leader specified before take-off. Upon landing, 12 miles north of Fayence, Franceschi broke his foot, Palmer sprained his knee, and the radio was slightly damaged. The first two days on the ground were therefore spent obtaining medical care and distributing equipment to the maquis. On August 16, British and American parachutists who had also been dropped off course on the landing day began to gather at the Jeds' campsite. The liberation of Fayence with the aid of Lieutenant Hanna will be discussed later. With his contribution as its sole notable accomplishment, by the beginning of September the team was inactivated, their supplies given away and its members in Grenoble awaiting departure.[22]

Captain Harcourt fractured both legs when Cinnamon landed in a wooded area in the western Var. He and his mates, experienced parachutists, blamed the crew of the American Flying Fortress for going faster than prescribed, navigating inaccurately, and pushing them out of the aircraft at an altitude too high (almost 2,000 feet), causing two of the team to somersault in midair. Met by a reception committee, the Jeds learned that clashes after June 6 had shattered the maquis there, leaving a dozen small guerrilla bands each led by an officer of the AS. A former colonel in the French Colonial Army recommended a safe house in Saint-Maximin, 10 kilometers away, but that was the only town in the vicinity occupied by the Germans. Instead, Harcourt was billeted in another village and eventually treated at an American field hospital.[23]

On the night of August 15–16, Ferandon planned to destroy a bridge over the railway on Route Nationale 7 that had not been hit in the intensive Allied bombing the day before. The demolition team from a local band of résistants failed to show up as agreed when their chief independently decided that the destruction was useless. A second operation to set up an ambush was worthless when the passing vehicles lacked importance. As the Germans withdrew, FFI guarded houses and cleared the woods of Wehrmacht stragglers. Taking off his uniform and traveling about in civilian attire, Ferandon found the résistants to be young men recruited and organized locally but without any military instruction. Some had never even handled a weapon. They were full of goodwill but lived in an impoverished area and were therefore incapable of prolonged physical effort. Ferandon did state that he benefited from information passed along by monks at the monastery of Saint-Maximin who also served as couriers.

Cinnamon accomplished nothing. Like other OSS outfits inserted at the last minute, this team concluded that its arrival was ill-timed for meaningful feats. Ferandon wrote, "We were dropped 5 or 6 weeks too late. For one thing it is difficult to undertake partisan warfare with the maquis, without having had frequent contacts with one's troops beforehand." He went on to question another of the program's basic tenets: "It was quite evident that this work of instruction, coordination, and liaison could not possibly be done by officers in uniform."[24]

Cadre sent by Britain to assist the underground reached similar conclusions. In midsummer 1943, the incomparable Francis Cammaerts met an American officer called Fred who turned out to be with the OSS and announced in a hideous French accent that he had been sent to organize "all the Maquis groups." Another SOE operative, George Millar, found the same mindset in Team Cedric deployed north of Alpes-Maritimes in eastern France. The Jedburgh leader was severely injured as he landed, nevertheless the team was "throbbing with zeal" and the radio operator requested massive arms drops. Millar first asked the soldiers to change into civilian clothes. Millar's indigenous maquisards were already organized and operating well under SOE leadership when the Jeds appeared on the scene.[25]

Opinions on the contribution made by the OSS vary according to the source. De Gaulle's chief of intelligence, "Colonel Passy" (André Dewavrin), was quoted as saying, "The OSS did virtually nothing in France."[26] The SOE chronicler, M. R. D. Foot, summarized the Jedburgh experiment:

> Gallant and important though their work was, it all depended on what had been done already. They normally went into areas where resistance had

already been brought well beyond the seedling stage to that of vigorous young growth. Their task was to bring it to maturity. The most difficult and most dangerous stages were already past. Necessarily, more of this early work had been done by SOE than by the OSS.[27]

A now familiar assessment came from a former member and historian of the SOE who observed that "for the very reason that [the OSS] began its operations much later, its role in Europe could never be more than complementary to that of SOE."[28] It is difficult to argue with this conclusion as regards organizing, training, supplying, and leading members of the French Resistance, tasks which enabled the SOE to build trust for over two years before American agents first set foot in the South of France.

At the opposite end of the spectrum, the intelligence chief on the US Seventh Army staff cited a different and important benefit: "A rough estimate of the proportion of accepted ground Intelligence supplied by the three Allied agencies shows that 50 percent was provided by O.S.S., 30 percent by the S.R. [its French counterpart headed by Passy], and 20 percent by the I.S.L.D. [British]." He therefore concluded, "The intelligence provided for Operation 'DRAGOON' [ANVIL] was probably the fullest and most detailed of any provided by G-2, AFHQ in a series of combined operations commencing with 'TORCH' [Allied invasion of North Africa]."[29]

Commands and Plans

Overall responsibility for planning and preparing for the Provençal landing rested with General Wilson. Reporting to him from the field would be the commander of the US VI Corps. Initially, this was Major General Lucian Truscott, but when Allied troops from the Mediterranean made contact with Overlord, control passed to SHAEF, and Devers, Wilson's deputy, would take over as 6th Army Group commander. Major General (later Lieutenant General) Alexander Patch, a grizzled veteran of Pershing's expedition into Mexico, World War I, and Guadalcanal in the Pacific, became commander of the subordinate Seventh Army.

Working together, Devers and Patch provided strong support for planning to proceed in early 1944 even though the prospect of an invasion in southern France appeared moribund at the time. The task seemed almost impossible at first due to the absence of decisions on the size and composition of the assault force, availability of shipping and amphibious lift, and a specific landing site. Eventually, three American divisions with amphibious experience were identified, all veterans of the fighting in Italy—the 3rd, 36th and 45th

Infantry Divisions. Each had three subordinate regiments composed of three battalions of 800–900 men each. The assault forces would be accompanied by teams of French officers and non-commissioned officers to conduct liaison with the local population.

Five infantry and two armored divisions were assigned to de Lattre's command initially designated French Army B. One of its armored combat commands was initially attached to VI Corps to provide a mobile assault capability. French forces other than the tank unit were not scheduled for landing on the first day as they had little experience in amphibious warfare. It was hoped that Resistance elements in Provence, stronger and better organized than in the North, would rally enthusiastically to French troops under Gallic leadership. Just before the invasion began, the Allies dropped pamphlets along the southern coast, bearing this message: "French forces are participating in this operation, beside their Allied brothers in arms, on the sea, the land and the air. The French Army is once more a reality. It is fighting on its own soil to liberate the Mother country, with all its traditions of victory. Remember 1918!"[30]

Logistics planning called for a seven-day allocation of rations, unit equipment, and petroleum products, including three-day rations and ammunition carried by individual soldiers. An estimated 84,000 troops and 12,000 vehicles were expected to go ashore the first day, with another 33,500 troops and 8,000 vehicles mainly associated with the French army unloading over the following three days. Logistical capabilities at the beach were thought to be unable to support tactical forces farther inland than 20 miles. With the expectation of determined enemy resistance and limited amphibious vessels and cargo space, logisticians packed ammunition at the expense of the vehicles and petroleum products required to haul supplies long distances rapidly. This loading plan would be subject to second-guessing as the offensive unfolded.

The operational concept of Anvil was straightforward—to land in southern France, seize and develop a major port, and drive northward up the Rhône Valley. Allied planners selected the coastline from Toulon east to Cannes for, among other factors, its proximity to Toulon and Marseille and the availability of minor harbors that might supplement over-the-beach supply operations. Coming immediately to mind were Saint-Tropez, Sainte-Maxime, and Saint-Raphaël, all on the Golfe de Saint-Tropez but with inadequate draft and dock facilities for large-scale military purposes. Putting into shore farther west than Cap Nègre would position the invaders in range of heavy German naval artillery in Toulon. Conversely, the series of beaches east of Cap Nègre were within range of Allied close air support aircraft based on Corsica. Upon landing, Seventh Army would have three primary missions—occupy the high ground controlling the landing areas, ensure protection to the east, and prepare to launch attacks to the north and west.

Enemy Strength and Disposition

The Wehrmacht order of battle in the South of France had been seriously depleted by the transfer of units to the Normandy front. Leading up to August 15, the senior German command, Army Group G headquartered in Toulouse, lost four divisions—three infantry and one panzer. Three solid infantry divisions had been replaced by units suffering battle fatigue from the Russian campaign and reserve outfits with old men and boys in their ranks. Much of the armor and artillery capability was stripped away as well—motorized cannon, antitank weapons and anti-aircraft guns. Consequently, German forces in southern France relied upon captured artillery of all types—French, Italian, Russian, and Czech—creating challenging supply problems. Group G figured it could count on only about 30,000 troops in the landing area, although a total of 200,000 uniformed personnel of every description were within a few days' march.[31]

The diminished combat readiness of a number of troops was compounded by a critical reduction in firepower. General der Infanterie Friederich Wiese, commander of the subordinate 19th Army, was left with neither assault gun battalions, mobile mortar companies nor the transportation assets to move troops rapidly to combat zones. Instead, his command was reduced to six static infantry divisions and a panzer division. Furthermore, Wiese regretted the redeployment of what he termed "specialists," personnel with skills in short supply. He also pointed out that he was left with old subordinate commanders unsuitable for assignment to the daunting eastern front, a high percentage of ethnic Germans from occupied countries, and under-strength and poorly equipped Ost battalions also from Eastern Europe with little training or experience.[32]

Responsibility for defenses east of Toulon resided with the 19th Army's LXII Corps commanded by Generalleutnant Ferdinand Neuling. His primary subordinate units were the 242nd Infantry Division under Generalmajor Johannes Baessler, arrayed from Toulon to Anthéor Cove, the sector that would receive the invasion; and General Otto Fretter-Pico's 148th Infantry Division, charged with defending the Riviera coast eastward from Anthéor as far as Italy. Neuling's command was considered a reserve corps as all its components had suffered combat fatigue on the Russian front and were now expected to train and deploy badly manned units of doubtful reliability.[33] The coastline from Toulon west to the Rhône delta was the responsibility of another corps (LXXXV) with only one full division (244th) upon which to rely.

The Wehrmacht leadership was also dissatisfied with defenses along the Mediterranean coast. Von Rundstedt had assigned priority to the Channel and Atlantic coasts for construction materials and labor. Generaloberst Blaskowitz, Army Group G commander, complained that no heavy installations could be erected and he was forced to rely instead upon fortifications left by the Italians. Concrete walls on beaches, barbed wire, and a scattering of mines had been strengthened with pillboxes, bunkers, tank traps, anti-aircraft searchlights, radar stations, and land and sea mines during the German occupation. Still, he characterized these as mere "field fortifications."[34]

In his area of responsibility, Neuling counted 300 pillboxes but only 80 or so armed along a front of over 400 miles. Furthermore, for lack of supplies it was necessary to utilize insecure postal wire communication rather than military landlines or radio.[35] His predecessor had criticized the plan of shattering the enemy landing forces while still in the water at the expense of constructing installations in the rear that would permit a mobile defense or one in depth. A military leader was reduced to being a "strong-point commander" in this application of the outmoded static defense. After the war, German generals complained about the enormous quantities of concrete "squandered" on U-boat pens at Marseille, part of a strategy clung to obstinately by Hitler despite lacking a credible submarine presence in the Mediterranean.[36]

As Alpes-Maritimes possessed no heavy industry or armament works of consequence to give it strategic value in Allied planning, its importance lay in its proximity to the border with Italy where an important campaign was well under way. Therefore, when German and Italian field commanders met near Antibes on August 10, 1944, they agreed that if the Allies intended to execute a Mediterranean landing it would come along the Italian Ligurian coast and, otherwise, a French beachhead in Provence would be for the purpose of moving northward up the Rhône Valley.[37]

Senior German leaders focused on Marseille and Toulon as likely focal points for the landing. The Fascist Army Liguria reckoned on the Gulf of Genoa close to Allied forces gathering on Corsica and around Napoli. Yet that command consisted of two under-strength German divisions and twin Italian divisions of uncertain dependability. There was no intention of reinforcing the defenses in southern France with Wehrmacht units being assembled by Field Marshal Albert Kesselring in northern Italy as a central reserve for his theater. The German commander in Southwest France did foresee such an assessment, however. He stood ready to transfer his reserve with the belief that after landing on the Provençal coast, the enemy would turn toward Italy. Wiese later stated that when bridges over the Rhône and Var were repeatedly attacked by enemy aircraft in early August, he became convinced that the invasion would take place between these two rivers. After the fact, he said that without German air and naval forces to contend with, there was no question of the Allied landing succeeding.[38]

As the 11th Panzer Division was the sole armored element in Army Group G and being held in reserve to confront a debarkation somewhere along the coastline, the perceptions of its leadership hold special interest. Its commander,

Generalmajor Wend von Wietersheim, believed an attack in concentrated formation shortly after the landing would be at the enemy's moment of greatest weakness. Von Wietersheim estimated that under normal conditions his tanks would require two to three days to travel the 250–300 plus miles to the area to be contested.[39] Allied air superiority would lengthen this march to four to six days, and possible destruction of the Rhône bridges add even more time. Receiving orders from Army Group G to move eastward on August 13, his troopers began their trek at night. Aware of the strong maquis presence to the north, the column stayed on a single route of march nearer the sea. Without air coverage, during daylight tankers were required to camouflage their armor with greenery and dash from one covered refuge to the next. The lack of anti-aircraft guns was keenly felt.[40]

After the war, the 19th Army quartermaster provided colorful details of transportation available to respond to the invasion. He began by asserting that supply had been no problem in the battles and retreat in southern France but pointed out that fuel was issued only in small quantities. Horse-drawn vehicles were used in urban areas and railways through the countryside whenever possible. French factories and workers were employed to repair vehicles, but to a certain degree an effort was made to convert them to wood-burning power just as the populace did with gazogène cars. It was difficult to train drivers for these contraptions, however. Numerous vehicles were therefore "hired" (in his terminology, or more likely confiscated), along with French drivers. It proved possible to buy horses and wagons, although the Germans were hoisted on the petard of their earlier scrap-metal confiscations when harnesses and horseshoeing material were found to be in short supply. As the frequency and intensity of air raids increased, use of civilian vehicles converted for military purposes was prohibited during daylight hours. On their way back from the front, conveyances carried gear, ammunition, and fuel from depots likely to be threatened by Allied advances.[41]

As for enemy naval and air presence in the Western Mediterranean, Allied intelligence reported little cause for concern that summer. Surface ships of the Kreigsmarine were limited to a single destroyer, five torpedo boats, eight escort vessels, six fast merchant vessels, and some 30 or more torpedo boats. The last class would prove the most troublesome to the invaders. A small flotilla of patrol boats was positioned outside Antibes to watch that portion of the coastline. Under the sea could roam three German U-boats docked at Toulon and two 200-foot submarines and one supply type in the vicinity of Genoa-La Spezia, but it was uncertain they were all operational. Enemy aircraft in the South of France were thought by the Americans to consist of 175 long-range bombers, 35 fighters, and 30 reconnaissance planes. In April, French intelligence had estimated a potential of as many as 600 enemy aircraft available to oppose Operation Anvil.[42]

The head of the Western Naval Task Force in the Mediterranean was Vice Admiral Henry Kent Hewitt, who wore a second hat as commander of the US Eighth Fleet. From the time all ground and naval echelons embarked for Provence until they landed, Hewitt was in charge. This singularity of American command and control would become relevant during debarkation of the 36th Infantry Division. The Eighth Fleet carefully studied the problem of breaching underwater obstacles such as concrete pyramids, wooden pilings, and mines. As the Mediterranean has no tide, these obstructions remained under water and thus were not visible for bombing or shellfire. Reliance was therefore placed on combat underwater demolition teams and radio-directed drone boats each carrying 8,000 pounds of high explosives. Hewitt allocated 54 of these craft, plus 27 control boats, to the landing.

Final Readiness

Our plans were based upon a thorough knowledge of terrain and beaches in southern France, particularly of the assault area, and on an unusually complete intelligence concerning enemy strength and dispositions. Not even the Normandy invasion had better advance information. Basic intelligence as represented by the British ISIS [detailed geographic analyses] and similar studies was as complete and detailed as for any area in the world. Superior maps were available. Aerial reconnaissance was continuous, and there was no dearth of expert photographic interpreters. And the French underground, the Maquis, in continuous communication, with AFHQ in Algiers, kept us informed of every German movement and change in disposition.[43]

So effused General Truscott about the foundation for planning provided by Allied intelligence. With reception of ULTRA intercepts, decryption of signals enciphered on German ENIGMA machines, the Allied planners had a reasonably accurate picture of the organization and strength of German forces in the Midi. They estimated approximately 100,000 soldiers, sailors, and airmen of the Reich along the Mediterranean between the Rhône delta and the Italian border.[44] From various sources including human intelligence, Seventh Army planners realized that ground formations were not consistently up to strength and well trained.

The assigned Allied naval vessels were docked in the Bay of Napoli and at Sicilia and ports on the heel of Italy. These included battleships, cruisers, destroyers, and merchant ships. Positioned at Malta were a carrier task force and gunfire support group consisting of one American, one French, and four British cruisers, plus various destroyers. At Oran were transports for the French armored division and 2nd Moroccan Infantry and 4th Moroccan

Mountain Divisions, along with supply ships and escorts. As the largest amphibious operation conducted in the Mediterranean, more than 850 hulls were to be employed—543 American, 266 British,[45] 35 French, and seven flying other flags, complemented by a miniature navy of 1,267 small landing craft.[46] Organized into convoys that gathered at an assembly point off Corsica, the warships were to steam up the west Corsican coast as far as possible, as if bound for Genoa, and only head northwest to the assault beaches at the last minute to disguise the final destination.

Leading up to the invasion, Allied aircraft apportioned their bombing among four possible landing areas: the fortified industrial port at Sète, Marseille–Toulon, the Cap Cavalaire–Anthéor Cove coastline, and Genoa. In particular, on August 10, P-47s of US XII Tactical Air Command took off from Corsica to blast gun positions on the Estérel, Ile du Levant, and other coastal targets. Two days later, the strategic air force sent B-17s and B-24s against Sète and fighter bombers to destroy bridges in the Rhône Valley that could be used by the Wehrmacht to send reinforcements to the coast.

As a concluding counter-intelligence ploy, the Mediterranean command changed the name of the offensive. The code word Anvil had undoubtedly been compromised, so on August 1 the invasion of southern France became Operation Dragoon.

10

The American Landing

A campaign targeted against the French Riviera promised important paybacks for American strategists. Invasion from the Mediterranean would engage German troops and deny their redeployment at a time when the Reich's personnel assets were being exhausted on three other major fronts—Russia, Normandy, and Italy. Introduction of sizeable French formations for combat not only in their own country but in the drive to Berlin would be welcome support for the other armies allied against Hitler. Success in Provence might well provide the added dividend of sealing off German forces in Southwest France. A landing on the Mediterranean coast could be a critical factor in winning the war in Europe.

Millions of men and women were anticipating H-Hour of this landing. Combat infantrymen, tankers and artillerists, airborne troopers, pilots, crews on ships and landing barges, and military staffs nervously awaited the unknown. Countless Provençal inhabitants were disappointed when the Allies did not arrive on June 6 and had been expecting an invasion ever since. Perhaps none were more anxious than the patriotic and proud soldiers in French divisions who for four years had looked forward to stepping onto their native soil and freeing countrymen from the chains of totalitarianism.

Shipping 60,000 American combatants across hundreds of miles of water, flying in almost 10,000 paratroopers, and inserting them on relatively confined beaches and landing zones in a short period of time was no mean feat. Admittedly, the enemy's sea and air assets on the Mediterranean were minimal at this point. The strongest impediments to the invasion would be passive defenses in place—mines, coastal artillery, pillboxes, seawalls, and fraise. The troubling unknown was what could be moved to the landing site for a German counterattack. The Allies would be most vulnerable once ashore, and introduction of a strong enemy force complete with armor and artillery could be devastating. The Wehrmacht had contested all previous intrusions onto the Continent, and Allied planners knew that interdiction of enemy movement into the landing area was critical to the success of Operation Dragoon. Deployment of a strong airborne component behind the shore and insertion of commandos to block lateral roadways to the beaches were vital for protection.

Diversionary tactics code-named "Ferdinand" were employed to disguise the exact location of the invasion. General Devers later recalled that documents and other material evidence were carefully positioned to be discovered by German agents operating behind Allied lines and convince them that the expedition would be directed against the port of Genoa.[1] This deception was enhanced by Operation "Rosie," a mock fleet of two British gunships, four PT boats, and a fighter-director vessel with sound equipment to broadcast a recording of naval gunfire, all commanded by Lieutenant Commander Douglas Fairbanks, Jr., a well-known Hollywood actor.[2] His special operations group first appeared outside Genoa and then continued along the coast to Cannes. Radio Berlin proudly announced, "A major Allied force attacked Cannes during the night and was repulsed with heavy losses. Antibes and Nice were bombarded by four or five large battleships," presumably the small deck guns aboard the little squadron. Notional circuits broadcast a stream of false messages on radio nets to further mislead German listeners. The illusion of an airborne assault was created outside Toulon by Allied aircraft dropping 600 dummy paratroopers rigged with explosives, rifle simulators, and other combat noise, complemented by strips of tin foil floating down to confuse enemy radar.[3]

Prelude

In the open sea at the western edge of the landing area outside Hyères stood two islands, Ile du Levant and Port-Cros, thought to shelter artillery pieces with ranges sufficient to reach the Allies' operational area. To isolate the battlefield, the Canadian-American 1st Special Service Force (FSSF) was charged with seizing these batteries and knocking out their coastal guns. This unit had scaled the cliffs at Kiska in the Aleutians and joined in the Anzio landing. They were uniquely qualified for the physical and tactical challenges this mission entailed.

At 11.00 p.m. on August 14, 2,000 rangers of Sitka Force descended into rubber boats from the decks of four-smokestack, World War I destroyers converted for troop transport. The dinghies were preceded by scouts in kayaks to mark the landing sites. The islands' sea faces were particularly foreboding, a rocky ridge with sheer drops on Levant and steep slopes on Port-Cros rising 50–80 feet above the water. It was precisely these features that caused the Sitka Force commander, Colonel Edwin A. Walker, to select the seaward side of these outcroppings which were seemingly insurmountable for entrée so expected to be lightly defended. Before 2.00 a.m. the invaders were safely on the shores of both islands without a shot being fired and poised to neutralize the two small German garrisons by one hour before daybreak, as directed.

Reaching the top of Levant, the Forcemen pushed through chest-high underbrush to reach the coastal batteries shown in aerial reconnaissance photographs. Instead of 6.5-inch artillery as expected, they found ordinary drainpipes set up to resemble gun barrels. What appeared to be sentries turned out to be military scarecrows. Moving toward the other end of the island, the Force found defenders hiding in ruined fortifications and monastic buildings. After exchanging fire all the next day, the rangers subdued the island, killing two Wehrmacht soldiers, and taking 240 prisoners.

The 650 men atop Port-Cros discovered its 60-man garrison holed up in an old fortified château and three small forts dating back to the seventeenth and nineteenth centuries. Infantry assaults and aerial bombardment with 5-inch rockets proved ineffective. The 8-inch shells fired from the heavy cruiser USS *Augusta* bounced off 12-foot-thick concrete tops and walls. Determined to know what was going on after a radio blackout, General Patch sent his aide-de-camp to find out. He was accompanied by James Forrestal, US Secretary of the Navy, one of numerous dignitaries to observe the landing. It was midday on August 17 before the enemy finally capitulated after being pounded by 12 rounds from the 15-inch guns on the British battleship HMS *Ramillies*.[4]

Walker was fit to be tied when he discovered the heavy coastal guns were fakes. Later, he announced that all his objectives had been taken 15 minutes before H-Hour on the landing beaches (an assertion off by 48 hours), and consequently he was left out of Dragoon's historic invasion. Walker even claimed that rehearsals on islands off the Italian coast had been more rugged than the actual climbs up the Ile du Levant and Port-Cros.[5]

The Dragoon Beachhead

Mist and fog obscured the Mediterranean coast at daybreak on August 15. Devout Catholics would know it was Assumption Day. History buffs might remember the date as Napoleon's birthday and, indeed, the Resistance in the Var was using "Napoléon" as its password. The thoughts of assault troops eating a final breakfast of steak and eggs aboard ship, however, were focused on the reception awaiting them on shore. Poor visibility delayed the start of the air attack until 5.50; naval shelling commenced one hour later. In between, the fog began to dissipate about sunrise at 6.38, but vapor and dust from the bombardment covered the shoreline, heightening the obscurity of the drama set to unfold.

The firing stopped after almost 16,000 shells and 774 tons of explosives had softened up enemy defenses. Soldiers loaded with as much as 90 pounds of gear began climbing down rope ladders from transports into smaller landing craft or packed themselves onto self-propelled vessels. One GI recorded being in a group of five boats, each carrying 40 men, heading toward land in V formation. With square prows rising out of the water, the assault troops passed slower rocket-launching craft, amphibious platforms for 105-mm. howitzers, patrol boats, and tiny minesweepers. A mile from shore, Allied missiles began screeching overhead. Great geysers of smoke and earth rose skyward. The din became terrifying 1,000 yards from land when concussions roughing up the water caused the small vessels to lurch from side to side. For a few minutes the destination was hidden behind a murky curtain of smoke, haze, and spray. Then, suddenly, the coast loomed in front and the skipper yelled, "Brace yourself!" as the boat crashed onto the beach.[6]

The landing area was 28 miles straight across including the flanks necessary for security, but the irregularities of the shoreline curving in and out onto 18 separate beaches amounted to more than double that distance. The beachhead was divided into three invasion areas. Alpha beaches to the west consisted of a Red zone at Cape Cavalaire and a Yellow zone six miles to the right at Pampelonne, just south of the port of Saint-Tropez. This long strand of firm golden sand was destined for screen immortality a decade later when Brigitte Bardot waded ashore in *And God Created Woman*. In the center area, Delta was subdivided into four beaches—Red, Green, Yellow, and Blue—east of Sainte-Maxime in Bougnon Bay. On the eastern flank outside Saint-Raphaël were four Camel beaches with the same color designations. Route Nationale 98 passed close by the latter two landing areas. The initial objective of the three infantry divisions was the Blue Line, an arc 10–20 miles inland identified on tactical maps as the beachhead's perimeter. Within that confine were the airborne landing sites which would facilitate the consolidation of incoming units.

Noteworthy in the fleet gathering along the Riviera coast were the USS *Catoctin* and HMS *Kimberly*. The former had been specially outfitted as a flagship complete with communications equipment and antennae. Watching intently while attempting to appear confident and relaxed were Admiral Hewitt, Generals Patch and Truscott, and French Admiral André Lemonnier. "What happiness," wrote Lemonnier, "to return to this coast of Provence, the most lovely and beautiful shore of France!" On the destroyer *Kimberly* was Winston Churchill staring through binoculars to observe the landing with a derby hat and black cigar clenched tight. Also on board were Forrestal, Robert P. Patterson, Undersecretary of War, and General Brehon B. Somervell, commanding general of Army Service Forces. The presence of floating mines caused the ship's captain to hold his vessel 10,000 yards off shore, plunging the prime minister into a dark mood as he could not even hear the sounds of battle. Before long, however, Churchill coaxed the skipper to approach within 7,000 yards.[7]

Alpha was assigned to the 3rd Infantry Division, the corps' one active army command led by Major General John W. ("Iron Mike") O'Daniel, as this location was vulnerable to long-range artillery on the west flank and well positioned for a subsequent advance to the River Rhône, both requiring strong leadership and seasoned soldiers. The division's first objective was to secure the squat Saint-Tropez peninsula with rocky, pine-clad hills, small fields, tiny vineyards and olive groves. The area was defended by an Eastern European battalion of the 242nd Division. To take control, the far-left regiment was to drive inland and occupy the dominant high ground and then hold the intersection of two national roads in order to cut off access to the landing sites. Coming ashore at Alpha Yellow, the right was ordered to seize Saint-Tropez after clearing the peninsula.

Eighteen radio-controlled landing craft with high explosives led the way to blow up the double-rows of concrete tetrahedrons armed with mines lining Cavalaire beach. All but three robots detonated properly. One went out of control and headed back toward the fleet, putting a sub-chaser out of action when it exploded. At the same time, ships equipped with 700 rocket-launching tubes blasted the shoreline.[8] Channels were soon opened through obstacles offshore and at the water's edge. Three of the four amphibious tanks launched from landing craft reached shore safely, but the last one received a direct hit from a naval rocket falling short and sank after striking a mine close to the beach. Two other boats carrying 60 men also went under when hitting explosive charges. Splashing ashore, each man hurried toward the tree line, adhering to the invasion axiom of "Get off the beach fast," although careful to follow in his predecessor's footsteps. Thankfully, armed opposition on the beach was light. The experience at Alpha Yellow was similar to Alpha Red, as fixed explosives rather than enemy fire caused the few casualties suffered. Army engineers immediately began clearing roads through the heavily mined terrain and laying pontoons on a gradient otherwise too shallow for LSTs (landing ship, tank) to discharge their loads.

Staff Sergeant Audie Murphy in the 15th Regiment, later to be awarded the Medal of Honor and become among the most decorated soldiers of the war, led his platoon inland from Yellow beach. Encountering "a group of krauts in a series of foxholes," he killed them with his carbine before running out of ammunition. Seizing a machine gun from a traumatized squad of GIs, Murphy moved forward again but was soon driven to ground by fire from a ridge up ahead. When the Germans waved a handkerchief, Murphy's buddy stood up and was shot instantly. Murphy went berserk, exhibiting the bravery that would earn the Distinguished Service Cross for this firefight.

Stunned, I lie for a moment [...] Instinctively I spin about to find a machine gun being trained upon me from a position a few yards to my right. I leap back into the hole, jerk the pin from a grenade, and throw it. At its blast, I scramble from the pit with my carbine [...] It is in perfect condition. Holding it like a BAR [Browning automatic rifle] for firing from the hip, I start up the hill. I remember the experience as I do a nightmare [...] When I find the gun crew that betrayed Brandon, the men are concentrating on targets downhill. They do not see me, and I have time to take careful aim before pulling the trigger. As the lacerated bodies flop and squirm, I rake them again; and I do not stop firing while there is a quiver left in them.[9]

Is it any wonder that Murphy was quoted later as saying, "I've heard a lot of people say the landings in southern France were soft. That's not true. We had plenty of trouble, and the fighting was tough [...]"[10]

In other instances Wehrmacht soldiers lay down their arms rather than fight. A US infantry officer remembered everyone guarded by his company wearing "a Hitler mustache, the small square and closely cut mustache for which Hitler was famous [...] They looked ridiculous!"[11] The main surprise for the invaders on Alpha Yellow, however, was arriving at Saint-Tropez to find it already in American hands, as related shortly.

The center operational area was designated for the Thunderbird Division from Oklahoma, which included Apache and Cherokee Indians in its ranks. The 45th was led by Major General William W. Eagles, the only West Point graduate of the three division commanders. No offshore obstacles existed to deter a landing, and by and large each of the landing beaches was defended by a single battalion. The main problem was mines. Four tanks struck them on Blue beach and another on Yellow beach. A six-foot-high, four-foot-thick seawall provided another challenge until demolition charges blew a 12-foot hole through the barrier. The sounds of explosions and shells bursting were so terrifying that residents took shelter in a nearby quarry. Once ashore the division's first mission was to capture the town of Sainte-Maxime, which was accomplished in short order.

The 45th Division history printed right after the war summarized their soldiers' mood on August 15. Landing on Delta beaches proved so different from what the soldiers had experienced in Italy that morale soared. A feeling of exhilaration accompanied men quickly overcoming the opposition and racing from one objective to the next.[12] The creator of "Willie and Joe," dogface characters who typified World War II GIs, was a member of the 45th and accompanied it on the landing. Cartoonist Bill Mauldin echoed these sentiments:

The best invasion I ever attended was that of Southern France [...] The weather was swell. The invasion came off much better than we had expected, with only one division—the one which had been hurt so terribly at Salerno [36th

Infantry]—meeting really tough resistance. The aerial and naval support was far greater than any of the divisions had ever had before. Everything went off according to schedule.[13]

Units of the 45th were soon racing for the Blue Line. Beyond the beaches, enemy resistance consisted of occasional roadblocks, sniper fire, and scattered uncoordinated ambushes. Consequently, that evening a patrol from the 45th reconnaissance troop met elements of the 509th Parachute Infantry Battalion outside Le Muy. Division losses on D-Day amounted to just 12 killed and 58 wounded.[14] When Truscott discovered Eagles's ease in accomplishing his objectives, he ordered a regiment to push eastward to assist in protecting Seventh Army's right flank.

That responsibility was assigned primarily to Major General John Dahlquist, Truscott's sole direct subordinate commander with no combat experience, who headed the 36th "Texas" Division. Landings at Camel Blue and Green took place on schedule with no underwater obstacles. Blue was somewhat inconsequential as it could accommodate just two small boats at a time. The first infantrymen to land had to contend with antitank guns challenging the debarkation. Murderous fire opened up from scattered blockhouses, some in the direction of Anthéor viaduct, the vulnerable point on the coastal rail line that had been so tempting a target from the air but extremely difficult to disable before the invasion. Once ashore on Camel Green, antitank, mortar, and artillery batteries opened fire from camouflaged seaside villas, concrete bunkers, and personnel trenches. By midday Germany artillery to the west began targeting logistics operations. Two landing craft were sunk before reaching shore and another burst into flames as it began to unload. Eventually the opposition was neutralized thanks to naval gun support. Enemy defenders pressed into service from Eastern Europe then started surrendering. But as division elements tried to expand their foothold toward the roadway to the north and the Estérel ridge to the east, they encountered new resistance from 148th Division units.

Camel Yellow beach facing the small resort of Agay was in a narrow horseshoe-shaped inlet protected by underwater mine netting. The surrounding high ground was honeycombed with gun emplacements. Consequently, the site was quickly assessed as more heavily defended than it was worth and the direct attack cancelled. By approaching on land from the Green flank, however, soldiers of the 36th cleared the cape separating Yellow from Green beach with extremely light casualties.[15]

The major reverse took place at the fourth beach. Camel Red was located at the head of the Golfe de Fréjus providing direct access to the town, its port and small airfield, the best beaches for discharging troops and cargo, and a road network up the Argens River valley into the interior. Recognizing its importance, the Wehrmacht had embedded a formidable array of coastal defenses—a minefield across the mouth of the gulf, rows of tetrahedrons studded with mines at the shoreline, and on the beach, two strands of barbed wire, a concrete antitank wall seven-feet high and over three-feet thick (painted to resemble a row of bathhouses), a 12-foot-deep antitank ditch outside this barrier, and extensive fields of Teller mines on the roads, paths, and airfield. Gun emplacements consisted of machinegun positions in the antitank wall and pillboxes and other redoubts behind. The beach was in range of German gun emplacements at Saint-Raphaël, some sheltering 88-mm. artillery. The town and its surroundings also housed batteries of 75-mm., 100-mm., and 105-mm. ordnance along with light anti-aircraft guns. Two reinforced companies of grenadiers from the 242nd Division completed the defensive complement. Anticipating the strongest opposition at Camel Red, debarkation was not scheduled until 2.00 p.m.

Attempting to clear the deep-water approaches at 11.00, minesweepers came under a heavy enemy artillery barrage and were forced to retire. Bombardment for 15 minutes by 93 B-24 Liberators failed to prevent more heavy shelling when the minesweepers returned. A battleship, two cruisers, and four destroyers engaged in a 45-minute preparation before landing craft finally headed for shore at H-Hour. Rocket ships fired missiles, but only three of the radio-controlled drones exploded as intended. Incoming rounds became so intense that Rear Admiral Spencer Lewis in command of the naval task force transporting the 36th Division determined that sending the 142nd Regiment into Camel Red would be a fatal mistake. Unable to contact Dahlquist who was already on an adjacent beach, Lewis decided to switch the invasion to Camel Green, which the two leaders had earlier identified as an alternate landing site. Once ashore, the 142nd joined with other division troops in wheeling westward to attack Fréjus. Evidence of the enemy's hasty withdrawal was everywhere—large quantities of supplies and matériel, especially foodstuffs, left behind on the ground.[16] Yet as night fell, firefights with Wehrmacht units left the 36th still three miles outside town. It was the next day before the 142nd and 143rd Regiments could clear Fréjus and San Raphaël, respectively, in lively street combat.

Lewis's judgment in backing off Camel Red led to the only major controversy of the operation even though the move was quickly backed by Dahlquist. Truscott criticized the decision for wasting six or seven hours which delayed securing the beaches, taking Fréjus, capturing the airfield, and moving into the Argens valley, censure not shared subsequently by other officers and historians.[17]

A reporter for *Stars and Stripes*, the US Armed Forces daily, later described what he observed at the landing sites:

- As anti-airborne assault defenses, thousands of tree trunks set up in open fields hundreds of yards back from the beach, many laced with barbed wire
- Mines on beaches, bridges, and wide areas on both sides of coastal roadways but not on the surfaces themselves
- Barbed wire everywhere to include roadblocks
- Other roadblocks with pyramidal concrete antitank defenses
- Squat and camouflaged pillboxes dotting the coast, mostly unmanned and often armed with outmoded, captured French guns
- Heavy coastal artillery identified beforehand in intelligence reports[18]

Radio broadcasts from the beachhead provided snapshots that first day. At noon, Eric Sevareid of CBS reported:

A few minutes ago, I talked with an American woman who had been living here since war began, with her two children. They are all right, but they are thin from lack of food [...]When the bombardment began this morning, she ran with her two children to take cover. The noise, she said was deafening. When she saw people in the village, she came out of hiding to find to her inexpressible joy that they were Americans [...]

Apparently many French Fascists and Vichyites were living here and are here also. One is the Director of one of the worst Pro-Nazi, anti-Semitic French newspapers, which was a great help to the Germans in confusing the French before the war began.

The village and country people have welcomed us most sincerely, but not with a tremendous outburst of enthusiasm [...] There were a few strained tears. And they are people who suffered a long, long time [...] They are a little more shrewd than the Italians, and they are not counting upon the unending flow of manna from the American armies. And we are only the beginning.

Vaughan Thomas, a BBC reporter, saw it differently.

This millionaires' playground is now teeming with guns and jeeps and bulldozers and all the myriad workers of a modern army [...] From the beach, I drove up to the steep pine-clad hills. I saw fires burning here and there among the woods from naval guns. But on the whole, the country looked astonishingly untouched by the devastation of war [...] But inland, the people were out in the roads waiting. Even the children are obviously suffering from malnutrition [...] no one asks you for food. They ask you to use their wine instead [...] There's no doubt about it now—the first phase in our adventure is a major success.

Another commentator surveyed the coast from a seaplane in late afternoon.

> Down in the harbor where we landed was an incredible collection of ships; the big fleet battleships and cruisers lay offshore at anchor and destroyers whipped around them, throwing out screens of smoke, though it did hardly seem necessary. Our big silver barrage balloons were hoisted around the beach and it seemed as if we were already unloading fairly good-sized ships, perhaps Liberties, at the docks.[19]

As a result of naval operations that first day, 60,150 troops, 6,737 vehicles, and an estimated 50,000 tons of stores were safely ashore. Naval losses were one LST sunk, nine LCTs (Landing Crafts, Tank) and eight LCIs (Landing Crafts, Infantry) damaged, and nine ship-carried landing craft sunk or damaged.[20]

Rugby Force

While the combatants plowing ashore were virtually all American, another component of 9,700 airborne troops—a mixture of GIs and British—was being inserted 10–12 miles behind the Camel beaches set for the 36th Division. Rugby Force was assigned the mission of taking control of the Argens Valley which separated the Massif des Maures from the Estérel ridgeline just west of Cannes. Cutting through the higher elevations, the Argens was the obvious path for German troops in the interior to strengthen the coastal defenses. The town of Le Muy where the paratroopers would land was at the crossroads of Route Napoléon and Route Nationale 7 that could be blocked to deny the Wehrmacht access to the beaches on hard-surfaced road. An Allied presence behind the amphibious operations could also prevent enemy soldiers besieged on the shore from escaping up the highway. A secondary task for airborne units was to advance on Fréjus from the rear should the 36th Division need help in taking that objective.

The 1st Airborne Task Force (1st ABTF) was activated on July 15 specifically for this operation. It consisted of infantrymen in the 517th Parachute Infantry Regiment,[21] the 509th and 550th Parachute Infantry Battalions, and the 551st Parachute Infantry Regiment, augmented by two parachute field artillery battalions and a variety of glider units. The latter consisted of infantry and pack-howitzer battalions and chemical mortar and antitank companies. The British 2nd Independent Parachute Brigade completed the order of battle. These outfits would be transported by 535 aircraft and 465 gliders.[22]

The Task Force commander was Robert T. Frederick, a West Pointer already famous for leading "the Devil's Brigade" in Italy, designated as the Canadian-American First Special Service Force. When promoted at age 37,

Frederick became the youngest major general in the US Army. Belied by his dandified black moustache, at the end of the war he would hold the distinction of being wounded eight times, earning the title of being "the most shot-at-and-hit general in American history."

Paratroopers wore silk scarves printed with green, brown, and blue maps of the main road network in Provence and were equipped for any eventuality. Each man was issued an armband with the American flag, compass, escape kit, and first-aid packet with morphine and needles. Soldiers took French francs and cigarettes, as many as they wanted for both personal use and exchange. Faces and hands were camouflaged with green and black paint causing more than one to be mistaken for a Negro by peasants encountering them. Rations for three days and a supply of ammunition and grenades rounded out the load. With helmet, jump boots, Mae West jacket,[23] weapons, and equipment, the average-sized man weighed at least 250 pounds.[24] Many of the British wore leg kitbags as well. Waiting for take-off, a paratrooper in the 551st Parachute Infantry Battalion heard Berlin Sally assure radio listeners that the Germans knew where they were going to jump and would be waiting there.[25]

The weather was cool and clear when 396 transport planes escorted by night fighters and radar jammers left Italy after midnight on August 15, carrying half of the Task Force's infantrymen, artillerymen, and engineers. Not a single anti-aircraft battery opened fire when this first wave crossed over the coast after flying 500 miles. Nor were enemy fighters aloft to challenge the invasion, according to one participant, due to P-51 Mustangs having knocked out radar installations responsible for watching southeastern France.[26] Pilots found fog blanketing the ground up to 800 feet. Preceding the troop carriers were aircraft to insert nine pathfinder teams. With only a thin sliver of moonlight, soon obscured by clouds, the American scouts were all dropped off course. Two of three British teams were delivered properly, however, and set up directional beacons. Consequently, almost two-thirds of the 2nd Brigade landed in the correct drop zones. Indeed, the 1st Independent Parachute Platoon claimed to have been the first Allied troops on the ground although descending to earth a mile from where they needed to be.[27]

Drop zones identified for parachutists were small cultivated farms, many consisting of vineyards and orchards. The fields were not cluttered with large buildings, telephone wires, tall trees, or other formidable obstacles although some anti-airborne poles had been planted. It was amazing that even some battalions wound up in the target area after being pushed out blindly through the clouds, while many others landed far away. About 25 B-24s dropped American and British soldiers near Fayence, 12 miles northeast of Le Muy. Other paratroopers exited planes over Saint-Tropez, 15 miles to the south. Tragically, two "sticks" fell into the sea, one fatally, the other taken aboard naval vessels.[28]

At 4.45, three hours after take-off, the green light came on and Frederick was the first man out the door of his aircraft. That was a mistake, he admitted later. He had told the Air Corps to make the drops over 600 feet in altitude, and with the heavy cloud cover he jumped at about 2,200 feet. Frederick's stick landed far from Le Muy amidst a group of Germans who ran off when confronted. The rest of his staff came down 35 miles to the east. After studying a map, Frederick set off alone when suddenly he saw a silhouette which he mistook for the enemy. Leaping on him, the general only released his hold when the figure let out a curse in a thick English accent. Frederick then resumed hiking to his headquarters at Le Mitan a mile north of Le Muy.[29] The password and countersign that first night were "Lafayette"—"Democracy." (After 24 hours they became "Billy"—"The Kid.")

Soon waves of C-47s[30] pulling gliders passed over the coast at two-minute intervals, their altitude only 1,200 feet above the hills and fields, thereby drawing sporadic fire from German anti-aircraft batteries. When the first flight arrived outside Le Muy at 8.15 the ground was still covered in fog. The US birds circled for a while and eventually landed, but the heavier British Horsa aircraft were quickly sent back to Rome due to their limited fuel capacity. They returned successfully in early evening.[31] One account described some GIs firing at their allies as they emerged, having never seen British airborne troops in camouflaged "smocks" and round steel helmets. A second wave of 71 American gliders set down at 9.30. The tugs released 300-foot tow ropes allowing the gliders to dive at 85 miles per hour toward a place on the field picked out to land. These motorless aircraft would carry either a dozen men or two men sitting in a jeep and perhaps a six-pounder gun, plus pilots. Ideally, once on the ground the vehicle's driver pulled a rope to release the lock holding the nose of the glider secure, and the jeep drove out of the front. After crash landings, wings, tails, fuselages, and equipment were strewn at crazy angles among the anti-glider poles.

Many of the glider pilots were veterans of the Normandy invasion. Yet, in Italy they needed training flights as they were unfamiliar with Waco gliders used by the Americans in Operation Dragoon. For this mission, passengers and crews would be issued escape kits with maps of France and the equivalent of 40 dollars in francs.[32] The pilots examined aerial photographs of the landing zone. These pictures were misleading as they were taken several weeks earlier before the Germans planted stakes 12 feet high and six inches thick into the flat terrain. The defenders had insufficient time, however, to rig the obstructions with barbed wire, electric circuits, or explosive charges as specified in their plans. Some poles were deliberately sunk shallow and loose by impressed French laborers and served to break the speed of incoming aircraft. Others snapped off wings causing ground loops. Late arrivals found the best spots already packed with debris and had to settle for rougher tracts, some a mile away at La Motte. Four of the nine gliders released prematurely made landings in the sea, and the crew and passengers were only saved by prompt action on the part of mariners.[33] In sum, just 50 gliders were salvageable after the operation, which resulted in 16 pilots killed, 37 injured, and 80 paratroopers and 150 other soldiers incapacitated, representing almost 3 percent of Rugby Force. Even then, 90–95 percent of the glider troops reported ready for duty at 19.00 that first evening.[34]

Transporting troops and artillery by air was always a challenge, but Frederick soon learned that delivering ammunition that way was also chancy. Finding that antitank guns assigned to his command would not fit into American gliders, in Italy he had traded two truckloads of cigarettes to the British to carry his field pieces while he carried theirs. Unfortunately, the C-47s dropped American ammunition where the British were and vice versa.[35]

A farm outside Le Mitan was designated the Task Force assembly area. In the early morning light the landscape was sprinkled with hundreds of limp, motionless parachutes of many colors—on the ground, in trees, covering rooftops. Pack howitzers were snagged on branches as well. Villagers soon cut off the parachute silks to fabricate ladies' underwear. Through the valleys, farmland, orchards, vineyards, and thickets men plodded slowly under the weight of heavy loads to join up with their comrades in arms.

Frederick arrived about 7.00. He found that a battalion of the 517th had taken possession of La Motte, but Le Muy remained occupied by the Wehrmacht. The general was astonished because the British parachutists were supposed to go in and take Le Muy. According to the war diary of the 2nd Independent Parachute Brigade, a headquarters was established at Le Mitan at 6.15. This command was led by Brigadier Charles Hilary Vaughan Pritchard, described by Frederick as a "tall, rather good-looking officer," with a moustache he added. When questioned by the senior officer, Pritchard was reported by Frederick to have said, "Well, we jumped!" "Aren't you gonna go in and capture the town?" Frederick responded. "No, there are Germans in there!" came Pritchard's reply. Frederick's account concludes, "So the next day I sent in the 550th Glider Battalion because I needed it. Then I sent the 2nd Independent British Parachute Brigade back to Italy."[36] At the 65th anniversary of the landing when Brigade veterans were questioned about what happened, one answered coyly, "A month later we liberated Athens."[37]

In Le Muy were remnants of Wehrmacht units originally stationed in the area but now fighting in the North. Only two or three companies remained, consisting mainly of Austrian Tyroleans assigned to anti-aircraft units plus some wounded and older veterans. From the steeple of an ancient church in the town center a lookout observed the fields through which traipsed the Allied invaders. One paratrooper recalled a column of German infantry and horse-drawn equipment moving into Le Muy. A battalion commander remembered looking down at Le Muy from the high ground at Le Mitan and seeing "the Germans down there like rats in a trap, trying to go this way and go that way, trying to find their way out."[38]

The untested 550th launched its assault against Le Muy at 2.30 a.m. on August 16. As the airborne unit was issued only nine Jeeps and seven trailers, it crossed a bridge over the River Nartuby from Le Mitan on foot. Suddenly the GIs were caught in the open by illuminating flares and withdrew under antitank, machinegun and mortar fire. When the attack resumed at midday, it was supported by coordinating fire after the airmen were themselves targeted by tanks from the 45th Division just arriving from the landing beaches. A house-by-house search flushed out pockets of defenders. The garrison's surrender completed the tally of 500 prisoners taken and more than 50 Allied captives freed, including several squads from Headquarters Company of the 517th Parachute Infantry Regiment taken prisoner immediately upon setting down. By 4.30 p.m., Le Muy was firmly in friendly hands, and members of the 550th were collecting 38 usable Wehrmacht bicycles.[39]

On a small hill near Le Muy was a church being used as a hospital, with wounded men spread out on the floor. Outside were German prisoners digging shallow two-foot graves, one next to the other. The bodies of GIs arrived on the hoods of jeeps with blood dripping down the fenders. They were stacked like cordwood on parachutes awaiting burial. The chutes were of all colors, some camouflaged green and brown for individual use, but now sickening for their buddies to see with blood running out at the edges.[40]

A short time before the invasion kicked off, SPOC in Algiers had dispatched an operative to the South of France to prepare landing sites for airborne troops. When he was captured by the Gestapo, a second agent was sent as the spymasters could not be certain with whom they were communicating on the radio connection still in operation. The successor was Geoffrey Jones, an American lieutenant in the training section who had spent part of his youth in the Fréjus area and well understood French mentality and culture. Promoted to captain to give him more clout, Jones parachuted in on the night of August 10–11, landing above Fayence. In his jacket was a poison pill to swallow in the event of capture because of his comprehensive knowledge of the planning for Dragoon. "In those days, the Germans already had drugs that would make anyone spill their secrets. I couldn't take that chance—too many lives were at stake."[41]

Posing as a mute French laborer wearing a blue suit with false papers, including an identification card as "Paul Georges Guillot," Jones gathered two local maquis chieftains and seven local gendarmes from different towns and proceeded to Sainte-Roseline, well known for its château, nunnery, and delicious wine, to help set up a headquarters for the 517th Parachute Regimental Combat Team. Then, on August 15, his party continued on to Le

Muy to reorganize the landing fields for the afternoon arrivals. When Jones eventually met Frederick, he asked, "What do you want to know?" confident that between the maquisards, gendarmes, and himself they could brief the general on conditions in his area of responsibility. Thus began a long and profitable association, as will be recounted.[42]

Less than two miles west of the 517th regimental headquarters, Les Arcs straddled a series of crossroads and a rail line. An important road connected La Motte with Wehrmacht headquarters at Draguignan, the prefecture or administrative center of the Department of the Var. Landing in nearby hamlets and vineyards, 40–50 soldiers from 1st Battalion, 517th Parachute Infantry Regiment took possession of high ground commanding the road network at Les Arcs on D-Day but encountered heavy enemy machinegun fire the next morning when elements of the German 244th Division arrived. The paratroopers could barely maintain their toehold. Fortunately, units of the 45th Division began to appear. Lieutenant Colonel Richard J. Seitz, commander of 2nd Battalion, 517th, also received orders to help. Seitz's leadership that day earned him the Silver Star. Selecting an excellent tactical position for an advanced observation post, Seitz personally directed mortar fire and called in P-51s to discharge 500-pound bombs on the enemy, silencing its automatic weapons and relieving his comrades.

In mid-afternoon the weary men of the 3rd Battalion staggered into Sainte-Roseline after a two-day march from the area around Fayence where they had been erroneously scattered. No sooner had they arrived than the paratroopers were ordered to move out to support 2nd Battalion. German combatants were eventually silenced with 700 rounds of white phosphorous delivered by artillerymen using 4.2-inch mortars brought in on gliders the previous day. Still, the paratroopers suffered under renewed machinegun fire before eventually securing the high ground south of the intersections. By obtaining firm control of Les Arcs, Frederick's command was relieved of pressure from that direction.[43]

While still in Italy, a special squad of paratroopers from the 517th Regiment had been fully briefed on Villa Gladys situated six miles to the northwest at the edge of Draguignan. The mansion was headquarters of the Wehrmacht LXII Corps, commanded by General Neuling whom they intended to capture. Descending through a thick cloud generated fear of falling into the sea, but upon landing on solid ground the team set out blindly through the fog. The failure of their raid was shown by a signpost indicating their destination to be 20 miles away, for the squad had been inaccurately dropped. Neuling escaped to the east, but this mission would soon be accomplished by GIs when Task Force Butler advanced into the interior.

A similar prize was taken the next day, however, when the 551st Parachute Infantry Battalion was sent to Draguignan to rescue a band of maquis surrounded by the enemy. Reaching the center of town, the paratroopers came upon the headquarters of Brigadier General Ludwig Bieringer, German military governor of the Var, as well as the staff of LXII Corps. The intruders burst in and captured Bieringer and other officers who were passed up the chain of command to Frederick's headquarters. A proud private first class claimed the huge black-and-red Nazi flag emblazoned with a swastika hanging over the villa's entrance. He later wrote that he and his buddies entered a storage area in the back that contained four or five large burlap sacks full of German and French currency, plus barrels of beer, cognac, and wine. Moving through Draguignan to seize other key buildings, the GIs threw handfuls of money at astonished civilians.[44]

Erroneous wind forecasts and zero visibility had caused 29 C-47s to release troops over and near the Saint-Tropez peninsula. The 250 men in Companies B and C, 509th Parachute Infantry Battalion, plus two full batteries of the 463rd Parachute Field Artillery Battalion, were lucky not to land in the sea. However, the senior officer present, Captain Jess Walls, realized they were in the middle of the target area for an aerial bombardment scheduled to begin momentarily. He had his men spread the orange panels of their parachutes to spell "U S" on open ground, hoping to alert the pilots overhead. But, first, at 5.45 the ground trembled with the sound of explosions from nearby Saint-Tropez.

The town's residents had been instructed to depart in the middle of the night and left lugging mattresses, food, and water for several days. Sixty mines, each with 25 pounds of explosives, had been laid by the Wehrmacht along the mole and docks. Another six mines amounting to a ton of dynamite were set to destroy the 800-foot jetty. Even the main sewage disposal system below sea level some 250 feet offshore had been wired to explode. In addition to this destruction, town records show that 670 buildings were damaged. Only 132 structures escaped unscathed.

Miraculously, the Americans survived without injury the preparatory fires for the imminent invasion. Before long, a member of the underground met up with the GIs and reported that most of the Germans had left Saint-Tropez and the townsfolk were slowly returning. Putting five of their artillery pieces into service, the paratroopers advanced by foot burdened with equipment and ammunition in the August heat. They were too weary to appreciate the warm scent of Provence, a mixture of thyme, laurel, pine, mimosa, and eucalyptus. Along the way, almost without firing a shot, the invaders seized an anti-aircraft gun, two coastal batteries, and 240 prisoners of war. With the aid of the Resistance, troopers seized the high ground at Saint-Tropez, flushed out some machinegun nests, and captured the command post in a hotel. When forward elements of the 3rd Division arrived at 3.00 p.m., the airborne warriors were coaxing the surrender of 67 Germans in the small garrison holed up in a medieval fortress known as the Citadelle.[45]

German Reaction

The 19th Army issued instructions early on August 15 to initiate action in response to the invasion underway. It was understood that a landing under cover of heavy fire was in process outside Saint-Raphaël and Sainte-Maxime involving "a strong armored force." (In fact, none of the three American divisions included tank units although a French armored combat command was included in the landing.) An estimated 1,000 parachute troops were reported to have gone into position in the area of Le Muy and Les Arcs (the total would be ten times that). To counter the threat as it was understood, Combat Command Bruendel was created. The task force's mission consisted of "relieving the 242nd Reconnaissance Battalion surrounded in Le Muy and eliminating the parachute troops in the areas [...]" The operation would employ two infantry battalions, an artillery battalion, and smaller units for signal, engineering, and security.[46]

General Wiese summoned Generalmajor Richard von Schwerin, commander of the 189th Infantry Division, to take charge of the provisional force being assembled. In addition to Colonel Carl Bruendel's task force, the reaction units would include two grenadier battalions and a flak regiment. Wiese directed von Schwerin to assemble his troops in the vicinity of Le Luc, eight miles west of Le Muy. At first, it was assumed that LXII Corps was trapped at Draguignan, but after communication wires to its headquarters were cut, it was useless to try and reach Neuling. Instead, von Schwerin was ordered to counter the airborne troops and turn back whatever Allied units might be pushing up the Argens valley. By nightfall, von Schwerin had gathered no more than the equivalent of a disorganized regiment. At the same time, the Wehrmacht's 148th Infantry Division began moving a force equivalent to an infantry battalion westward from Alpes-Maritimes but was stopped by the Resistance and the British paratroopers mistakenly dropped near Fayence. All told, German efforts to counterattack the invasion on August 15 were stillborn.[47]

Bruendel's command was armed with handheld weapons. Its means of transportation were bicycles to carry machine guns, mortars, and ammunition. The artillery consisted of 105-mm. howitzers hauled behind antiquated Italian tractors with a maximum speed of six miles per hour. His soldiers arrived in a state of exhaustion exacerbated by taking no breaks for food due to their haste. Reaching the 242nd Infantry command post at Brignoles, Bruendel found its commander without any form of intelligence. Soon word came in of the Allied presence at Les Arcs and the arrival of additional airborne troops. Bruendel dispatched soldiers to Les Arcs as they reported in and seemed satisfied that partisans had sustained heavy losses in house-to-house fighting with grenades and bayonets late on the first day. Moving toward Le Muy the next morning, the combat command was ordered to halt the advance and relieve the corps in Draguignan. The understrength German contingent was soon turned around once more to try and prevent the landing of more enemy assets by air. Bruendel recognized the negligence in not closing passes from the sea to the high country to prevent their use by armored vehicles. At 5.00 a.m. on August 17, after burning all maps and papers, the commander climbed into his staff car full of wounded, and the task force departed the combat zone around Le Muy. Thus closed a footnote in the history of Operation Dragoon.[48]

The only serious Allied loss at the coast occurred the first evening of D-Day. About 9.00 p.m., as a fog cover was beginning to conceal warships collected in the Saint-Tropez roadstead, the drone of aircraft engines swept across the water. Powerful searchlights illuminating the big white numbers which identified ships simultaneously snapped off. Minutes later, a wave of five Junker-88 light bombers dropped anti-personnel explosives on the Delta beaches as four Messerschmitts dive-bombed the vessels at anchor. One air-launched missile struck a fully-loaded LST. A destroyer screening the area to the east was just missed by a glider-bomb, pineapple-shaped with hundreds of pieces of shrapnel set to explode on slightest contact. Tracer bullets streaked through the darkened sky from the defenders in response, while 40-mm. shells from Bofors anti-aircraft cannon barked out in unison. One plane was sent spiraling in flames down into the water. Reports of Allied casualties ranged around 40 men.[49]

Further naval episodes ensued. The next morning the British sank two Italian vessels off Marseille-Toulon, fishing out 211 German submariners who were attempting to escape to Genoa. That evening after a senior commanders' conference aboard the *Catoctin*, anti-personnel bombs rained down from above, killing six sailors and wounding 42 others. After midnight on August 18, Kriegsmarine torpedo boats endeavored to penetrate the Rade d'Hyères and four were sunk. USS *Frankford* suffered casualties from enemy torpedoes exploding nearby. Regular nightly attacks by fewer and fewer warplanes represented the Luftwaffe's dying effort on the Riviera coast.[50] By August 22, evacuation of German airfields at Avignon and Lyon terminated the air threat.

Reactions by the German military hierarchy to the landing differed quite naturally. After the war, Devers paraphrased the reaction of his counterpart, General Neuling.

Yes we knew you were planning to move north. We knew when you sailed and followed your convoys at sea. But you were fully expected by the high command to attack at Genoa this morning. In fact I was informed on the 13th and again later yesterday that you would positively attack Genoa today. That is over one hundred miles east of here so my command was not alerted in its defense.[51]

The chief of staff of the 19th Army was in no mood to praise his adversary:

> The strip of coastline selected for the landing was one which the German command did not particularly expect the Americans to use. Thus the theory was applied that success is most likely to be attained at a point where the enemy does not expect an attack. The terrain of Monts des Maures was considered by us to be relatively easy to defend. It was not expected that the enemy would direct their first landing toward this central and highest part of the mountain chain. Thus this strip of coastline would have been more [strongly] defended if the weak 19th Army had had a normal defending force.[52]

As for opinions of their opponents, perhaps not surprisingly, they were far from complimentary. A source at the Wehrmacht headquarters for the defense of France opined, "The American soldier is naively persuaded of victory, but he is undisciplined, materialistic and prefers to avoid violent offenses. For him the victory will be acquired by materiel at his disposal and not by commitment of personnel. The officer corps does not make a good impression on the whole." Concerning French soldiers, their "colored troops possess a weak combative value [...] White soldiers, in particular the officers, think only of taking revenge against all Germans."[53]

GIs had their own prejudices revealed one veteran of the 3rd Infantry: "[Germans] were always referred to, at least in my Division, as 'Krauts,' usually preceded by one or more colorful adjectives which I no longer use. The British called them 'Jerries.' The Germans called us 'Amis' and called the British 'Tommies.' The term 'Amis' should not be confused with the French word for 'friends' [...] 'Amis' was simply short for Americans [...] The Russians we called the 'Ivans' or 'the Russkies.'" The infantryman concluded with opinions on his Gallic Allies. "We liked neither the French Army nor de Gaulle. We used to say that the French haven't won a battle since they exiled Napoleon! [...] The French we called the 'Frogs,' or worse!"[54]

Shifting Gears

The rapid success in Seventh Army achieving its initial objectives led to the next stage in the operation, reorganizing the force to mount an aggressive drive to the west and northwest. Advancing north, the 36th Division relieved the 1st ABTF in the vicinity of Le Muy on August 17. Frederick moved his troops just east of Fréjus to a bivouac site in a wooded garden area where small farms grew tomatoes, onions, green peppers, eggs, melons, and grapes—fresh delicacies many of his soldiers would not enjoy again for a while. According to Allied Forces Headquarters, in the first two days of action alone over 1,000 prisoners were taken by American airborne units and another 350 by the British. There was a price to be paid, however. By August 20 a total of 434 US airborne personnel were listed as killed, captured, or unaccounted for, plus another 292 men hospitalized. The British Parachute Brigade counted 52 of its members killed, 130 injured, and 181 missing in action.[55]

Truscott's numbers on the loss of Allied lives in the first two days included the entire operation but were based on initial reports, always less than fully accurate. Considering the complete and rapid accomplishment of strategic objectives at the beachhead, these figures caused Truscott to judge Operation Dragoon a complete success: over 4,700 prisoners taken (and no way to estimate the number of enemy killed and wounded) at a cost of 300 Americans killed and wounded and another 900 "non-battle casualties." He characterized the total as "light—much lighter than we anticipated."[56]

On August 17, soldiers of the three American divisions that had crossed the beaches of Provence were on their way inland, eventually coming together in the Rhône Valley. The 1st ABTF would soon march eastward across the Riviera in what was euphemistically called the "Champagne Campaign" by those lucky GIs who remembered wine, good food, and enthusiastic women more than firefights with the enemy. Two weeks after landing in France, British glider pilots were loaded onto American landing craft and headed back to Napoli, ending what they termed the "Champagne Invasion." But how about the ally that gave birth to champagne? What became of the major component of the Provençal landings, the seven French divisions?

At dusk on August 15 a launch with the tricolore fluttering from its stern sped up the Golfe de Saint-Tropez carrying a French dignitary and honor guard. As a bugle sounded "Aux Morts" (taps), Lieutenant General Joseph de Monsabert stood stiffly at attention. Then he disembarked to receive a situation report from the Americans. Leaving staff on shore, Monsabert quickly headed back to sea to report to General de Lattre aboard the SS *Batory*. The French would arrive in force the following day.[57]

11

⊰✵⊱

The French Landing

General Eisenhower had made clear his intention to open a large port on the Mediterranean. Whether a second port was necessary or not for the Allied advance on Germany was somewhat irrelevant for French morale, as the first priority was to redeem national self-esteem. As early as December 1943 the Allies were put on notice that unless the Americans and British guaranteed a landing in the South of France, de Gaulle's government-in-exile would not reinforce the French Expeditionary Corps which had begun arriving in Italy in November. At its highest point, 120,000 Frenchmen were engaged there.[1] Thus, as agreed, all available French land, sea, and air forces were allocated to the invasion from the Mediterranean.

The Provençal landing occurred at a propitious time for the Free French. The German front in Normandy had collapsed, Major General Philippe Leclerc's 2nd Armored Division was headed for Paris, and the Resistance across France was poised to rise up against its tormentor. As de Gaulle characterized it, "The Allied battle of France was also the battle of Frenchmen *for* France. The French were fighting 'a united battle for a united country'."[2]

Debarkation

Among the most colorful combatants in the southern invasion were French commandos. To help ensure Operation Dragoon's success, two groups were assigned to capture German strongholds on the flanks of the landing area and hold them to protect the vulnerable Allied beachhead. To the west, Roméo Force consisted in large part of Algerians and Moroccans along with some European volunteers from North Africa commanded by a cadre of veterans of the pre-Armistice French army.

The sunset was brilliant and spirits high as a flotilla of landing craft made its way toward the coastline. Roméo's mission was to neutralize defensive positions atop the rocky height of Cap Nègre west of the Bay of Cavalaire and block the road parallel to the shore to prevent the approach of German reinforcements.[3] Just after midnight on D-Day an electric surf boat was launched carrying a French and an American naval officer to light a lamp on the beach at Rayol to guide the 20 men in the first wave ashore. The scouts became disoriented, however, and landed too far west. Now their beam could not be seen as it was shielded behind a mound of boulders. Two inflatable dinghies soon began making their way slowly along the shoreline looking for the signal. One team landed and crossed the highway heading for high ground. The second pulled in farther left at the base of Cap Nègre. Its leader decided to destroy the gun emplacement on the summit, and the commandos began climbing the perilous 250-foot cliff facing the sea. Up above, the Germans heard noise and dropped grenades among the rocks, mortally wounding the squad leader and putting the team out of action.

Similarly disoriented, the pair of craft in the second wave became separated, one squad landing and moving inland with minimal opposition, and the second beaching at Cap Nègre and tackling the difficult ascent on a different precipice. Twice they were surprised by flares illuminated by the defenders, but clinging to their precarious positions remained undetected. Reaching the top and cutting through rolls of barbed wire, the ten attackers, armed with .45-caliber pistols and Thompson sub-machineguns, surprised and overcame the Germans. By 2.45 the key prominence on Cap Nègre was in Allied hands.[4]

The naval assault group tasked with securing the eastern flank was not so fortunate. Designated Rosie Force, it was counted upon to deny the coast road to German reinforcements coming from Cannes. Silently landing in inflatable boats at Pointe de l'Esquillon south of Théoule and crossing ground pockmarked by explosions, the 67 commandos arrived at a sign announcing "*Achtung! Minen.*" The commanding officer considered the warning to be a ruse as information furnished by the Resistance provided assurance of a safe crossing. Two days before, however, the Germans had seeded the field with landmines. Moving ahead, the commander stepped on an explosive, losing a leg, as two seamen by his side were killed almost simultaneously. In quick succession other mines were detonated, and the Germans, alerted to the invaders, began firing at the desperate mariners. Trying to retrace their steps led to more French deaths. Finally surrounded, the sole surviving officer surrendered the invaders. Thirteen commandos had been killed and 36 wounded. Of the remainder, all taken prisoner, ten were freed by the FFI that afternoon, and the others taken away by the defender. A monument now marks the location of their sacrifice.

The convoy conveying Army B converged from Italy, Corsica, Malta, and North Africa. It consisted of passenger ships carrying the soldiers and commercial cargo vessels bearing matériel. From the deck of the Polish liner SS *Batory*, now serving as a troopship,[5] the landing was watched by "le Roi Jean" (King Jean), its commanding general. General de Lattre had taken a personal interest in training his conscripts, attired in shorts and berets, running and jumping in the pine woods of Algeria. He spoke to them individually, in a sharp but amicable voice, sometimes thumping a soldier's chest with the back of his hand to emphasize a point. There was no doubt that he had a sense of drama and theatrical dimension to his leadership, and he was certainly autocratic, hence his nickname. But his style was effective. De Gaulle found de Lattre to be "emotional, flexible, farsighted and widely curious, influencing the minds around him by the ardor of his spirit and winning loyalty by the exertions of his soul." As the British military historian Liddell Hart found when talking to one soldier about the strain of meeting his exacting standards, "General de Lattre is a terrible man to serve—but I wouldn't care to serve anyone else."[6]

The 1ère Division de Marche d'Infanterie [7] and 3rd Algerian Infantry Divisions coming from Italy were the first to land at Cavalaire and Saint-Tropez, respectively. Simultaneously, the headquarters of the 1st Armored Division, two antitank regiments, and two groups of heavy artillery, all directly from North Africa, came ashore at Saint-Raphaël and Sainte-Maxime. In the days and weeks that followed, they would be joined by another armored division (5th), the 2nd Moroccan Infantry and 4th Moroccan Mountain Divisions, the 9th Colonial Infantry Division, artillery, engineers, and other diverse units with 28,000 men and 3,500 vehicles. For the first time in the French army, included in this mélange of uniformed personnel, were female volunteers who served as secretaries, ambulance drivers, nurses and radio operators, mostly *pied-noir*[8] and constituting 8 percent of the effectives.[9]

The lead elements began disembarking about 6.00 p.m. on August 16. In the gathering mist, the shoreline was barely visible. One member of the 1ère Division de Marche d'Infanterie described the experience: "For a moment all eyes were held toward the north, searching to catch sight of this land of France which some had left several years ago, others under tragic circumstances, and others finally were seeing for the first time, this land of France that for a long time they had lost hope of ever seeing again."[10]

The landing craft passed through a flotilla of ships at anchor. Fifteen balloons could be seen above Saint-Tropez connected to the ground by cables as an anti-aircraft measure, a sign that the port was safely in Allied hands. Everything was quiet except for the occasional roar of cannon far to the west. Suddenly, three German planes appeared high above the fleet, briefly surveying the operation below, and precipitating a barrage of anti-aircraft fire. Then, the first foot soldiers jumped into water up to their chests and began wading ashore or, if fortunate to approach the beach at the right place, stepped onto a hastily erected wharf. A French non-commissioned officer attached to the first American assault waves had prepared a trench bordered with small phosphorescent signs through a minefield. To the left and right were rolls of barbed wire, jagged trees, villas in ruins, and signs with skull and crossbones marked "MINES." Despite ample warnings, an exuberant sailor off to one side or another periodically charged straight ahead, igniting a blast that sent chills through his comrades-in-arms. An ensign remembers coming ashore from a fast whaler and seeing six or seven defenders, whom he thought were Armenians enlisted by force, throw away their rifles and flee in haste. Individual companies moved quickly off the beach into a pine forest or vineyard a couple kilometers away to spend the night before marching to the brigade assembly area the next morning.[11]

Men, vehicles, and supplies arrived all night. Soldiers of European extraction were issued rations for two days; Muslim troops received the porkless variety. The tanks of vehicles were completely filled and gasoline trucks were loaded to 90 percent capacity as Allied warplanes controlling the skies suppressed fear of enemy air attack. Unloading was slow as civilians on shore expected to shoulder the loads had disappeared during the German occupation leaving the too-young and the too-old to do the work.[12] Roadways were clogged with "Ducks"[13] delivering freight and then heading back to their mother boats for more cargo. By 7.30 a.m. the final units arrived.

While the receipt of matériel continued that evening, the French command decided to take advantage of the weak resistance and push right up behind American units heading into the interior.[14] Local inhabitants welcomed the new arrivals, their joy and emotion readily evident, heightening the troops' enthusiasm. Many residents were surprised by the continuous flow of soldiers and equipment as they had not expected liberation to be so grand. One officer remembered some folks thinking the invaders were a bit crazy. Do you really expect to defeat the mighty German army with this motley assortment of pied-noirs, Muslim colonials, and black Africans, they stated in so many words?[15] Other veterans recall being asked for ten francs for water (the Germans supposedly had paid five) or being told by a vineyardist to reimburse him for damage to his crops from the emplacement of anti-aircraft guns.[16] Thankful folks offered flowers and kisses in the classic French manner.

Arriving at his command post in Cogolin, de Lattre learned that the enemy had concentrated its forces between Toulon and Hyères, leaving the port city's northern defenses relatively unmanned. During the morning of August 19, de Lattre went to Latitude 43, the hotel in Saint-Tropez where General Patch had established Seventh Army headquarters, and obtained approval to proceed directly to the investment of Toulon. As explained in the official report of de Lattre's army during the landing phase, "The intention of the general commanding the army is to benefit from the disorganization of the enemy coastal defense in the zone occupied by the Americans to undertake the surprise attack of Toulon at the earliest opportunity with the first elements debarked."[17] Allied plans called for the French to take Toulon at Jour J plus 20. By Jour J plus 45, Marseille was also expected to be in Allied hands.[18]

Colonial Order of Battle

Tirailleurs, Cous Cous
Tirailleurs, Cous Cous
Tirailleurs, Tirailleurs, Tirailleurs,
Cous Cous Tirailleurs

As accustomed as they might have been to the colorful tribes of the African continent, the residents and foreigners sheltered in Provence, nevertheless, must have been excited by the appearance of l'Armée d'Afrique. The scarlet fez, or chéchia, of the Sénégalais, red-and-white Spahis burnoose (a hooded wool cloak) with broad black sash around the waist, the traditional white sarouel (pantaloon) of troops from the Sahara—African troops were easily identifiable from afar when on parade. Tirailleurs from Algeria wore a Turkish-style uniform of light-blue jacket, waistcoat, and baggy pants embroidered in yellow, accompanied by turban and cartridge belt. French officers commanding the goums (Moroccan companies from the high ground) wore the standard, native, sky-blue kepi stamped with crescent and Solomon's seal. These warriors spoke six different languages.

The ways of the goumiers were most unusual. A unit was often a family affair. Members encouraged relatives to join. No contract was signed. Instead, the recruit said to the local French officer simply, "Je vais avec toi" (I am going with you). His tribesmen would follow the commander as long as he led from the front, thereby being seen as superior to his men and often armed with no more than a riding crop or swagger stick.[19] Behind came his troops in brown or coffee-colored turbans instead of helmets, wearing wool robes narrowly striped in somber colors. An American pistol belt completed the uniform.

Goumiers exhibited exceptional valor relying on "Inch Allah" (God willing). They had little awareness of modern weaponry, often resulting in heavy casualties. There were no bands in goum formations as the rank and file found it impossible to march in step. Instead, they loped along for long distances beside their animals, each goum maintaining herds of horses and mules along with flocks of sheep. Self-sufficiency was one of the goums' prime assets. Mules were sometimes used to clear paths through minefields, and sheep served as dinner on the hoof. Goumiers acquired a well-deserved reputation for savagery, as raping and pillaging were considered rewards for military success. The coupe-coupe—the traditional, large, African machete—was employed to cut off ears, organs, or the head of a captive. This was normal practice, a reward without which they would not fight.[20]

Civilians in the combat zone feared for their lives. One Italian eyewitness recounted his community suffering more in 24 hours with the goums than during eight months of Nazi occupation. Well after the Provençal landing, de Lattre recalled that his sailors had objected to transporting mules aboard troop ships. The division commander persisted, however, and finally de Lattre conceded to his staff, "When we speak of 1,000 goumiers, we think of 2,000 and we embark 6,000."[21]

North Africans comprised approximately 50,000 of de Lattre's troops. About two-thirds of soldiers in the colonial infantry divisions were indigenous as compared with just a quarter in the armored commands. Not surprising for that time, only 2 percent of the officers were native Africans.[22] The composition of the forces that would liberate Toulon and Marseille were in sharp contrast to Leclerc's command, as on orders from the Americans it had been purged of native troops to become 100 percent white.[23]

A Marseillais recalled tireurs (riflemen) in the 3rd Algerian Infantry Division having shaved heads under their helmets with a small braid for Allah to pull them to paradise.[24] The 4th Moroccan Mountain Division included ten mule companies each with 231 men and 300 animals, and ordnance comprised of 65-mm. mule-pack mountain guns. The 9th Colonial Infantry Division was composed of soldiers from Sub-Saharan Africa, referred to collectively as Tirailleurs Sénégalais, although these regiments originated in the various French colonies in West Africa. In the ranks were men from Dahomey, Guinea, Ivory Coast, Mali, and Upper Volta, not to mention a few recruits from Mauritania and Niger. The majority of these troops trained for combat in North Africa where they were issued American uniforms and equipment. An estimated 20,000 black Africans landed with de Lattre.[25]

Overall the proportions of French and indigenous troops in Army B were nearly equal. There is now disagreement about how North Africans fared once they crossed the shores of Provence to help liberate France. The 2005 fictional treatment from the Algerian-Moroccan perspective in Days of Glory (Indigenes in the French release) tells of exceptional bravery contrasted with discrimination in the ranks. On the other hand, a non-commissioned, pied-noir veteran of a colonial unit recalled a close bond between officers and enlisted as well as among white and native men in the ranks. Medical support was good, with French doctors and American drugs and bandages. Virtually all the soldiers spoke French. "We all responded to patriotism," he summarized.[26]

What caused black Africans to risk their lives on a continent they had never before seen, defending a country which had enslaved and mistreated their forebears, and taking orders in a language not always understood? Despite it all, inhabitants of overseas territories referred to their homeland as "France" for, indeed, the colonies were considered part of the French Republic. Nancy Ellen Lawler interviewed veterans of World War II in the Ivory Coast for a study, Soldiers of Misfortune. She received answers that were trusting and simple. There was talk of "fighting for the noblest country on earth." "I was glad to go. France—the French—were truly our cousins," one exclaimed. Although many of the *anciens combattants* from 20 years earlier were unhappy to be called up again, one recalled, "We were with the French and if the French didn't like something, neither did we. We were with them." Another observed, "If you're not at war, the French army is not difficult. Life in Africa is harder—much harder." A propaganda campaign by Free France quoted the enemy's leader, as yet unknown to most of the Sub-Saharan natives, as saying in *Mein Kampf* that blacks were "born half-monkeys" and broadcasting German designs on France's African colonies. Some believed in the invincibility of the French army; others were encouraged by the Catholic Church, which worked with the military authorities to make the liberators feel at home in the metropole. All seemed glad to be shipping out with white European comrades in arms, transferred earlier by Vichy from the Armée de l'Armistice to protect French West Africa from the Allies.[27]

De Gaulle himself was a reason for natives fighting in Europe. The general's great height and imposing presence impressed all who saw him in person. One white African recalled him saying, "We are all Jews. We are all Freemasons. We are all Communists. But we are all French." A black legend told of Corporal de Gaulle lying dead in an African village for five years before rising from the grave to lead his nation to victory as General de Gaulle. When the forces of Vichy France first opposed the landing at Casablanca, one old veteran believed that de Gaulle had descended from an airplane to order a ceasefire, and the fighting stopped.[28] Whatever their individual motivations, the colonials stepping onto the beach in Provence dreamed of returning to their villages regarded as men with La Force, the strength attributed to veterans of World War I who commanded respect for fighting beside and against white men, learning their secrets, and, most important, surviving.

> We're the men of Africa
> Come here from afar
> We've come from the colonies
> To save the fatherland
> We've left behind our families and homes
> Our hearts are full of invincible fervor
> For we wish to bear high and proud
> The cherished flag of sweet France
> Should someone try to part us
> We're here to die at her feet
> Drums roll to mark our love
> For our country and land
> We've come from afar to die
> We're the men of Africa.

Battle of Toulon

At one time a penal colony, Toulon was and is today France's most important naval center. The city is situated behind an anchorage considered one of the most secure harbors in the Mediterranean and, in 1944, was surrounded by high hills dotted with more than 30 forts. It was the most heavily defended point on the southern French coast. Admiral Hewitt declared, "Toulon [was] ringed with some of the strongest anti-aircraft defense that I have yet seen."[29] The heart of the naval complex was the shipyard and arsenal that maintained the fleet. In November 1942 the French navy had scuttled the flotilla there rather than allow it to pass into the hands of the Germans who were occupying the formerly free zone. On August 21, 1944, Berlin would order that Toulon and Marseille be defended "to the last man and the last cartridge."[30]

At this point in the disembarkation, de Lattre had available 16,000 combatants, 30 tanks, and 80 medium guns to confront 25,000 men and more than 200 artillery pieces of various calibers guarding the naval base. The Battle of Toulon would be the fiercest and most costly in combat casualties of the encounters between Allied and German forces in southeastern France.

From August 19 to 26 the investment of Toulon was conducted at the small-unit level, as were all the clashes in this region after the initial landing, therefore minimizing the importance of overall figures. It was not 16 versus 25 in personnel terms, but rather a question of how much firepower the attackers could concentrate on any defensive position at a particular point in time. Unavailable to their adversaries, aerial bombardments were an asset important to the French and, when close to the sea, naval gunfire also contributed significantly to the outcome of individual clashes. Aircraft from a single carrier, USS *Tulagi*, flew 68 missions with 276 sorties. At the same time, the 17th Bomb Group encountered the heaviest, most accurate flak it had ever seen, costing eight B-26 Marauder twin-engine bombers lost and damage to 125 other warplanes.[31]

The French order of battle consisted of the 1ère Division de Marche d'Infanterie with three brigades (1st, 2nd, and 4th), the 3rd Algerian Infantry Division, and the 9th Colonial Infantry Division still in the process of unloading. In addition, two armored commands provided support. The 1ère Division was sent by the coast road on a plain that provided the best route of attack to liberate Hyères before proceeding to the final objective; the 3rd swung to the north and west and approached the port from those directions; while Major General Henri de Vernejoul, commanding the 9th, was ordered to take the high ground to Toulon's northeast before advancing on the city. 1st Armored Division units and a regiment of Algerian Spahi cavalry were assigned to cover the northern flank of the assault area. Elements of the 5th Armored Division would arrive in time for the coup de grace.

Proceeding on its right flank on August 20, the second brigade of the 1ère Division de Marche d'Infanterie, commanded by Colonel Pierre Garbay,[32] took control of Mont Redon to the north behind Hyères, a key piece of military terrain, and then held on under a fierce German counterattack. Artillery fire and bursts from automatic weapons continued all night. Finally driving off the Wehrmacht, the ravenous infantrymen were elated to discover a stockpile of provisions—canned food, drinks, and tobacco abandoned by the Germans.[33]

The division's other two brigades had the tougher assignment of moving directly westward toward Toulon. This route was the most heavily defended, primarily by seamen under Vice Admiral Heinrich Ruhfus, the senior naval officer responsible for the southeastern French coastline as well as commander of the port's naval facilities. The coast road ran through Hyères, the southernmost Riviera resort, popularized at the turn of the century by the English upper class who had mostly gone home at the start of the war. In making this approach, French commanders had to be mindful of a battery of 340-mm. naval cannon at Fortress Saint-Mandrier adjacent to the port with a reach of 21 miles, nicknamed "Big Willie" by Allied gunners. Two of its four guns had been sabotaged by workers at the arsenal, however. Eventually, the 20-year-old French battleship *Lorraine* arrived with a main battery of the same size as Willie. In tandem with the battleship USS *Nevada*, the two functioning Willies were eventually put out of action.[34]

Marching along the coast road through coastal pine trees, BM 21 (Infantry Battalion 21) pushed ahead to the cheers of inhabitants, a happy prelude to the deadly contest to come. Progress stalled on the plain of the River Gapeau.[35] Proceeding straight ahead at a fork in the road, BM 24 reached the waterway directly opposite the Hôtel Golf, an immense gray building turned into a fortress by the Germans. Surrounding it was a complex of defensive positions in protected concrete shelters. Two antitank guns and three 88-mm. anti-aircraft pieces covered approaches from the east. Fording the river could only be done under enemy fire from automatic weapons in bunkers. Fortunately, the site was near enough to the sea to permit support from naval gunfire. Still, several assaults were repulsed on August 20. The next day, enemy riflemen suddenly appeared in the woods behind the attackers, delivering a deadly fire. Late in the afternoon, following a French artillery barrage of 1,000 rounds that reduced the hotel to ruins, a determined surge by 100 volunteers finally overpowered the defenders. During a struggle lasting over 40 hours, the attackers captured a total of 240 prisoners. French casualties were categorized as "European" (70) and "indigenous" [African] (108).[36]

At the fork in the road, another element had veered to the left and soon came upon a bridge that was out, causing the invaders to descend a steep bank and wade through water. Mortars and another 88-mm. gun opened fire, projectiles pouring down at irregular intervals. Once through this torment, every house up ahead seemed occupied by defenders whose tracer bullets illuminated the darkness. The attackers replied with automatic weapons and rifle grenades. Fighting continued through the morning of August 21 when the attackers were finally able to infiltrate Hyères. Two tank destroyers reached the railway station where they encountered sharp opposition from defenders armed with machineguns and panzerfausts, a hand-held weapon similar to the bazooka.

As fighting eased, inhabitants emerged from cellars to demonstrate their joy at being liberated. The victors were feted with fruit and wine. Lieutenant General Diego Brosset, 1ère Division de Marche d'Infanterie commander, entered the city center in a jeep to check on his troops and then rushed back to his units still outside the town. "Come on," he exclaimed, "I have already kissed at least two hundred girls!" At the command post established in a villa used for the same purpose by the vanquished occupiers, headquarters staff found documents concerning the defense of Toulon and Organization Todt. The French troops were also surprised to find the men captured to be, in many cases, Armenians from the Wehrmacht's Ost Legion.[37]

At this stage in the debarkation, the 9th Colonial Division consisted of only a single regiment of infantry supported by a detachment from the armored division. Senegalese riflemen freed communes northeast of Toulon but not without fierce fighting. A sergeant recounted what happened:

> It is the assault, the orders in French, in Senegalese: Charge! Yanfe! Yanfe! In the dust, the explosions of grenades, bursts of sub-machineguns, the infantrymen jump on the terrace, overwhelm the Germans, Diara! Diara! The lions! The lions! Victorious cries of war! The wounded and dead are assembled. Two indigenous sergeants are missing. Ousmane Takerou, a former Songhai tracker from the south of Gao, a terrible handler of machetes, has been killed.[38]

A violent counterattack by the Germans succeeded. The final combat took place in the central village. Victorious at the conclusion, the colonials tried to catch their breath and recover while shells from 88-mm. batteries in Toulon continued to land with precision. The blood of officers and enlisted, Europeans and North Africans, ran together on the ground.

Three miles to the southwest of one commune, Solliès-Pont, is Mont Coudon, a fortified rock 2,300 feet high dominating Toulon. There African commandos encountered 120 German seamen who fought fiercely in the afternoon heat. Finally, a French company commander took off his boots and barefooted climbed the 30-foot outer wall of the fort followed by a squad of grenadiers. A lieutenant found a ladder and led his men into place. Surreptitiously they all entered the fortress through a hole blown in the inner wall. Discovering the intrusion, the enemy commander called in artillery, "Fire on us." Projectiles exploded in both ranks, the clash ending in hand-to-hand combat in subterranean galleries. Only six Germans were taken unscathed.

The 9th Division painstakingly liberated other towns, overcoming more pockets of enemy resistance, until on August 21 a tank platoon occupied La Valette just outside Toulon. At this point, its radio stopped working, and the unit realized it was running low on munitions and fuel. Encircled by the enemy, these liberators spent a harrowing 48 hours firmly planted in the village, holding on until finally being rescued.[39]

Meanwhile, the 3rd Division was taking an 80-kilometer circular route around Toulon, cutting it off from reinforcements to the north and, once the Spahi cavalry reached the beach at Bandol, 24 kilometers west of the port, completely isolating the enemy. Guided by FFI partisans, the foot soldiers began making their way back toward Toulon. Coming from the rear, it was not difficult to surprise and overcome the *feldjagers*.

Back in the 1ère Division, BM 21 moved forward bit by bit in the face of an artillery onslaught that knocked out four of its five tank destroyers. Its ultimate objective was the inner ring of forts protecting Toulon from the east. One remaining strongpoint was Fort Carquiranne on the cape, forming the eastern boundary of Toulon. According to one account, the company commander interrogated two prisoners who offered to take a delegation to the stronghold and talk its defenders into surrendering. Bullets whistled overhead as the small party cautiously approached the fort, but neither the German captives walking in front nor the French behind were hit. Commanded by a stern first lieutenant, the Germans at first refused to concede, but after a siege of 24 hours they gave up. In another version, the attackers seized an enemy communications hub which permitted the French company commander to call the garrison and directly negotiate surrender. The installation chief agreed to capitulate on condition that no German would be shot. Somewhere between 120 and 150 men were thus taken prisoner.[40]

The castle atop Mont Touar was a formidable threat. The range of its artillery easily reached the 4th Brigade of the 1ère Division, slowly moving along the coast road in the face of this fire and shells from 88-mm. guns farther west at Fort Sainte-Marguerite. The approach was further contested by incoming rounds from batteries protected under concrete shelters. Eventually, however, the two attacking battalions were stunned at the sound of thunder caused by munitions detonated by the enemy before abandoning its positions.[41] The most remarkable episodes, however, were yet to come.

Another company was approaching Fort Sainte-Marguerite, perched on a steep rock dominating the coast just outside the port. The soldiers rushed forward in increments, many taking shelter in a nearby chapel and large yellow villa. One section, however, was out in the open when it encountered the violent explosions of mortar shells. Local residents had all double-locked their doors, requiring the frenzied attackers to force their way inside for cover. As the company log observed in describing the clash, "Nothing is more demoralizing than to be taken under bombardment in a street and not be able to take shelter in houses carefully barred by friendly hands." The company commander radioed for help which brought gunfire from three destroyers and a cruiser, along with support from field artillery. After allowing time for the barrage to have full effect, the French leader told the senior German officer that it was useless to resist as Toulon had been taken (which was not yet the case), and he had the choice of surrendering or holding on with no hope. "Too many dead, too many wounded, I cannot continue," came the reply. But allow us time until tomorrow to destroy our arms, the German added. Throw your guns into the sea now, the Frenchman responded, and gave him one hour to do so. We do not need them. "I have seen you have weapons," sighed the resigned commander, and complied. The prisoners numbered 21 officers (three of senior rank) and 547 non-commissioned officers and enlisted.[42]

All inner approaches to Toulon were dotted with antitank obstacles, pillboxes, and minefields. Clearly, by subduing the external fortifications protecting the city one by one, the French invaders had produced a demoralizing effect on the remaining defenders, even though they undoubtedly remained superior to their adversaries in numbers of personnel and field ordnance. Yet a decided advantage for the attackers was the availability of Allied warships which fired more than 7,500 shells during the battle.[43] The offensive also benefited from support by four groups of light Marauder bombers, including some Thunderbolt fighter-bombers flown by French air force and navy pilots. The Free French were now poised on all sides of Toulon. It was time to enter and liberate.

Like other communities across the Midi, news of the landing in Provence had invigorated patriotic men and women in Toulon. When the invasion took place, the number of résistants in Toulon was estimated at 140; by the time French troops arrived, the number was thought to be 750 partisans, many armed with weapons taken from the enemy.[44] As was happening throughout France, the occupiers were withdrawing into protected enclosures for security, assembling in the city's forts and arsenals. Leadership of the Comité Local de Libération (CLL) soon announced a general uprising. The FFI undertook sabotage and surprise attacks on defenders pulling back to regroup. German convoys were prevented from crossing the city. Sporadic gunfire began in the suburbs as well as in the town center. On August 22, small groups of uniformed combatants started infiltrating the downtown area, now empty of *feldgrau* uniforms,[45] and engaged in guerrilla activities in support of local résistants now running low on ammunition.

At the same time, a company of sailors climbed the 130-foot sheer northern face of Mont Faron, seemingly inaccessible from that side. The Germans inside signaled by flare to their artillery positions, bringing heavy shelling raining down on invaders and defenders alike. Finally reaching the top, the commandos found the fortress had been abandoned.[46] The FFI quickly occupied Fort Saint-Antoine at its base. Less successful, at first, was a combined assault on La Poudrière, the storage area for gunpowder and munitions, by infantrymen and light tanks supported by artillery. Moving forward, the bataillon de choc[47] fought with grenades, sub-machineguns and flamethrowers in an attempt to overpower the defenders. Finally, a 76.2-mm. gun was used at point-blank range to blast the galleries, igniting ammunition that incinerated its occupants. Inside were 250 bodies, plus the 180 Germans who surrendered. "It was a Dantesque sight and in a flash it brought back to my mind the most tragic memories of Douaumont," wrote de Lattre, referring to the fort at Verdun during World War I, the site of a bloody engagement and, later, repository for the bones of 125,000 French soldiers killed in that drawn-out battle.[48]

August 23 brought the hardest combat in all sectors of the Toulon–Marseille operation.[49] In the morning, a violent Wehrmacht counterattack at La Poudrière was stopped by the bataillon de choc. The Germans showed their frustration by lining up the members of one section they had encircled and shooting them all. By afternoon, two motorized machineguns and a few jeeps had dodged the defenses at the principal crossroads and arrived in place de la Liberté with its monumental fountain, the heart of modern Toulon. It is difficult to appreciate the emotional impact on Toulonais upon seeing the French tricolore flying once again in the square. The population left their homes and streamed into the streets, demonstrating enthusiasm and gratitude. Quietly standing aside were the "compris," collaborators who had compromised themselves in some manner with the occupiers—"a breed that the former Free French Forces did not suspect still existed"—and they soon hid themselves behind locked doors and closed shutters.[50]

The naval arsenal was the next target. The commander was ordered to give up and, when he refused, firing erupted that soon destroyed the blockhouse protecting its primary entrance. Infantrymen dashed for the door but did not reach it before it was barricaded once more. In addition to the arsenal, there were other military installations within Toulon remaining in German hands. The next day, the Senegalese and the FFI captured Forts Sainte-Catherine, Artigues, and Arenes, taking 1,000 prisoners in the process. The first work was especially imposing with its high walls and drawbridges, but it fell easily. Using his driver from Alsace as translator, the battalion commander demanded that the defenders come out with their hands up, and the entire contingent of 65 complied. After a full day of bombardment, a French signal officer contacted the chief of Fort Artigues to deliver an ultimatum: "At 1900 my Senegalese will receive the order to massacre you all!" This was cause for reflection. "To whom will the garrison be prisoners—the Americans, the French or the civilians. What will be its fate?" The proud answer immediately followed: "You have been beaten by the French army; you will be prisoners of the French army and treated as soldiers by soldiers." More than 500 men filed out of the enclosure. [51]

Fighting continued on August 25 at the maritime arsenal before it, too, was finally overpowered. After its ammunition depots were blown up, the dominant fortress at Six-Fours on Cap Sicié, jutting out into the sea to the southwest of the city, surrendered without much difficulty along with a nearby redoubt. But the colonials had to fight hard to occupy the batteries at Pointe Aiguillette, of historical significance as the area where Colonel Napoléon Bonaparte defeated the English in 1793.

The sole remaining stronghold was the cape of Saint-Mandrier. Admiral Ruhfus and his headquarters were entrenched there. Since the outset of the siege, Allied planes and warships had bombarded this small landmass, setting its pine trees ablaze and producing general chaos. For days the thunder of cannons made the fortification a living hell. Waves of B-26s and P-47 fighter-bombers blasted the bastion. Shelling from US and French ships continued for eight successive days.[52] By the evening of August 27 the commanding officer finally agreed to capitulate. The next morning Ruhfus led 40 officers and 1,800 enlisted sailors out of the fortress and down the road to captivity.[53]

De Lattre said that he had Ruhfus brought to him and gave him three hours to deliver a detailed plan of the minefields on the cape. "I warned him unequivocally that, after that interval, he would be shot if in his sector a single one of my men trod upon a German mine." The diagram was delivered on time and no one lost his life as a consequence. In summarizing the cost of taking Toulon, de Lattre wrote that he lost 2,700 troops killed and wounded, of whom 100 were officers. On the German side, casualties were numbered in the untold thousands, plus 17,000 men taken prisoner.[54]

The international dimension of the success was illustrated by a liberation parade three weeks later once the area was completely cleared of the enemy. A company of American sailors and a detachment of the Royal Navy, each led by its own band, joined 800 French seamen in blue blouses, white trousers, and caps adorned with distinctive red pompons, marching to trumpets and drums.

Battle of Marseille

If Toulon was Western Europe's greatest naval port—and it was—Marseille was France's biggest shipping port with an unloading capacity of 10,000 tons, twice that of Toulon. In 1944, Marseille was the second-largest city in France with 600,000 or more inhabitants.[55] It was truly an international crossroads situated beside the delta of the mighty Rhône. In addition to housing a strong North African contingent, since 1932 the city had provided shelter for economic and political refugees fleeing totalitarianism in Germany, Italy, Poland, and other eastern countries. At this time, foreigners from Belgium and Holland, including numerous Jews, were also trying to become invisible here.[56]

It was Marseille's reputation as a den of bandits, terrorists, and refugees that led to massive destruction once the Germans occupied the city. Using the excuse of an FTP–MOI attack at a banquet of the German Armistice Commission on January 3, 1943, the Nazis undertook to destroy the old port quarter of Saint-Jean. Following two days of roundups, early on January 24, 25,000 remaining inhabitants of the old port were awakened by an announcement to leave their domiciles "for 48 hours." Residents packed their most precious possessions in anticipation of the worst. Five thousand persons were permitted to depart freely. The remainder was sent to Fréjus in cattle cars, and from there, youths went into the STO, Jews were sent to camps, and others sought refuge with family or friends. The Germans proceeded to blow up 14 hectares of buildings, leaving the historic center of Marseille in ruins.

Elimination of the surrounding civilian population facilitated strengthening the harbor's defenses. Offshore minefields, boom nets, and submarine detectors were complemented by block ships anchored at strategic places to be sunk on a moment's notice. Onshore protection included heavy coastal batteries and rail spurs built specifically to handle railroad guns with barrels up to 15 inches in diameter.[57]

The city's defense was organized and led by Generalmajor Hans Schaefer, commander of the 244th Infantry Division, who had come back from the Russian front seriously wounded. He was expected to hold onto Marseille without hope of air cover or ground or naval support. His garrison consisted of 20,000 troops, primarily 4,000 to 5,000 seamen who manned the coastal artillery, and 10,000 to 12,000 soldiers in the 244th. The men in Schaefer's division came from every corner of greater Germany, but in particular from the eastern provinces. Furthermore, there was great diversity of age, physical capacity, and experience. Schaefer assessed its morale as good, at least until four infantry and two artillery battalions were sent north to help contain the Allied landing in Normandy. Their loss was not compensated by the addition of coast artillerymen with no training in ground combat.[58] Other outfits were of mixed reliability, consisting in large measure of "Volksdeutsche," men of German heritage from Austria, Czechoslovakia, and Poland, plus numerous Ukrainians, Armenians, and Russians, many press-ganged into the Wehrmacht. The leadership remained German nationals, of course. Some members of the Luftwaffe also remained even though they no longer launched warplanes.[59]

Schaefer later said that he was aware of the various possibilities for an enemy advance on Marseille. He assessed his mission to be holding the city's outer defensive ring in order to prevent penetration into the metropolis.[60] Although its natural defenses were not as formidable as those of Toulon, its military ordnance was impressive. Nearly 200 artillery pieces defended the perimeter, with shells ranging from 65-mm. and 75-mm. up to unique cannon with 240-mm. projectiles. The guns were encased in multiple works, many new and some old like Saint-Jean and Saint-Nicolas[61] which had been strengthened and rearmed. Searchlights and barrage balloons complemented the ordnance. At points along the highway north to Aix-en-Provence crisscrossed concrete pillows and dragon teeth flanked by six-foot-thick antitank walls.

Having just arrived in March, Schaefer had gained no real appreciation of the civil unrest in Marseille after 21 months of German occupation. The populace was stirred up by the Relève and the STO, plus the roundup of Jews and other minorities deported to concentration camps. Worsening economic conditions added to the malaise. Discontent was heightened by the multiplication of clandestine publications now printed in large quantities and advocating specific action. Demonstrations, strikes, and sporadic occupations of factories by workers all increased in number. No longer were just German troops targeted. French collaborators were attacked as well, causing members of the Milice to depart in haste as the tide turned. German intelligence estimated that, in total, the city might contain as many as 80,000 rebels, many secretly armed by Allied agents. Widespread revolt was seen as a distinct possibility.[62]

As soon as the landing took place, spirits lifted among dissidents. At the outset the FFI numbered less than 1,000 men and women.[63] When their leaders inventoried the arms available to attack the Boche, they counted revolvers, hunting rifles, a few Sten sub-machineguns, and some grenades, but no heavy weapons. The leftist cast to the underground assigned it low priority on both the British and French lists for military supplies. Consequently, on August 22, FFI headquarters notified its components to economize on the use of munitions as they were irreplaceable. One dissenter remarked:

> The people were nervous [...] since 16 August a very perceptible tension reigned in the city, the forces charged with maintaining order were suddenly non-existent, the Germans pulling back to their solidly defended positions [...] a certain euphoria set in [...] looting and distribution began of everything that was nourishable [...] people were going to fight to eat [...] the tracts multiplied and insurrection developed [...] In that environment our groups could do good work.[64]

On August 18, political and social organizations in opposition to the occupation passed from passive and guerrilla to openly aggressive and combative. General insurrection was advocated on loudspeakers manned by maquisards driving through the streets in requisitioned trucks adorned with the tricolore. Members of the underground openly wore armbands identifying themselves as FFI or FTP. The MUR and ORA were also represented. These patriots began disarming agents of the police and vulnerable German troopers. Fearing the occupiers' retaliation, many residents were afraid to leave their cellars. One Marseillaise exclaimed, "There is no more water, no more gas, no food, women's faces dignified, almost severe. Little ones cry, the older ones say nothing; not one complaint."[65]

Yet nothing dramatic happened immediately. A general strike paralyzed transportation on August 20. When the prefect of the Bouches du Rhône declared his willingness to hand over power on August 21, he was promptly taken into custody by communist partisans who marched to the prefecture to do so. That evening the FTP summarily executed a member of the Gestapo and a notorious Italian fascist.[66] A proclamation declared the government of Vichy no longer in control; government workers and police must obey new orders; traitors, members of the Milice, and black marketeers were to be arrested; and foodstuffs handed over to the people. The Resistance was active in the streets, throwing up roadblocks, sabotaging warehouses, destroying bridges, capturing isolated German patrols, attacking with pistols and grenades, killing and being killed. There was scant reaction to any of this by the occupying power, which was focused on their enemy gathering strength outside the city.

The following day, the CLL installed itself in the prefecture, but little of the discussion concerned armed insurrection. Instead, the representatives talked about what would happen after liberation—which institutions would be re-established, how to define roles, the positions and functions to fill. Reportedly, a heated argument also took place as to whether de Lattre would, in fact, bypass their city, condemning the résistants to Nazi reprisals, and pursue the Americans northward into Germany, a more glorious calling. The ambiguity would be ended by events taking place outside the city.[67]

His army's drive westward from the landing sites was proceeding so expeditiously that de Lattre agreed that certain elements could advance to the outskirts of Marseille on August 20 while most of his force was simultaneously committed to the capture of Toulon. In his opinion, it was imperative not to allow the enemy a respite, to deny him an opportunity to recover and send reinforcements from Marseille toward Toulon, in short, to maintain the momentum. Two days later, patriots from Marseille crossed the lines and pleaded for immediate help for the FFI, few in number and poorly armed. Almost immediately, a battalion of the 7th Regiment of Algerian Chasseurs (infantrymen) encountered maquis of Camp Atilla—gendarmes, policemen, sailors, and workers in dungarees and shorts confronting a superior force of Germans. Without external help the uprising in Marseille would be ruthlessly crushed. The more the liberators drew the enemy to the periphery, de Lattre reasoned, the more he could avoid street fighting, terribly costly to his warriors and highly destructive for the civilian population.[68]

De Lattre handed the assignment of liberating Marseille to General de Monsabert, commander of the 3rd Algerian Infantry Division which was already positioned between the two cities. The division's tripartite standard reflected its cultural heritage—red, white, red—with three waning crescent moons of blue, white, and red arranged in the center band. The 2nd Moroccan Infantry Division would join in the investment. Both commands were to be supported by the element of the 1st Armored Division which had been released after covering the landing of Seventh Army. Brigadier General Aimé Sudre's 2nd Combat Command consisted of Moroccan goumiers wearing padded leather helmets in Sherman tanks, regiments of Algerian reconnaissance Spahis, and colonial antitank hunters, along with various artillery formations.[69]

The Moroccans had just touched French soil that same day and immediately been sent off to battle. By nightfall, Moroccan Tabors and half-tracks manned by Berber Zouaves were at the gates of Aubagne northeast of Marseille, a key to access from that direction. Tabors were colorful troops not just for the mules that carried supplies, but for their practice of wearing the ears of opponents overcome in combat. The "Berber cavalry" attired in striped *djellabas* marched from the invasion beaches in sandals with boots hanging around their necks. Aubagne was well defended by blockhouses with walls three-to-four meters thick manned by three enemy battalions. Multiple antitank traps and numerous minefields restricted circulation in the vicinity.

The assault began in the stifling heat of August 22. German guns were once again effective, but by mid-morning the tanks had overcome the obstacles and reached the main church. The attackers resorted to the bayonet late in the day when Tabors penetrated the defenses from the north and captured 19 artillery pieces. Schaeffer credited the quick success by French tankers at Aubagne as critical to de Monsabert's rapid occupation of the port city.[70]

Taking note that the Germans were not defending the roadways through the mountains, de Monsabert sent the 7th Regiment of Algerian Chasseurs onto the massif of Etoile to enter the suburbs north of Marseille. At the same time he dispatched a group of Tabors northward to sever the route from Aix-en-Provence, reducing the threat of German reinforcement from that direction. To the south, other Tabor units captured Cassis, the famous wine-producing village on the coast, and proceeded to de-mine the road from there to Aubagne. The succeeding day, various elements occupied other towns as they moved closer and closer to the ultimate objective. The prize trophy was the aqueduct of Roquefavour over the River Arc northwest of Marseille, constructed in the nineteenth century to supply water for industrial needs and household consumption. The commanding general ordered the unit which reached it to remain there and guard this essential structure.

The initial penetration into Marseille came on the morning of August 23 when tanks and infantry from North Africa, guided not by chance by members of the communist FTP, moved down a city thoroughfare from Canebière on the high ground. Crowds gathered, cheered, and offered flowers. Everywhere people greeted their saviors who were singing the marching song of the North Africans, "*C'est nous les Africains qui revenons de loin*" ("It is we the Africans who come back from afar"). Quite naturally, the residents were inclined to respond with "La Marseillaise." The liberators soon came under fire from the big guns at Forts Saint-Jean and Saint-Nicolas, however, and the procession halted. Civilians covered their ears as windows vibrated and houses trembled. Shells whistled and cried in a veritable concert.[71]

De Monsabert and his men eventually succeeded in reaching the prefecture where the French command established itself next door in the headquarters of the French XV military region. About this time, Captain Crosia, an intrepid priest from Lorraine who was the intelligence officer of the 7th Regiment of Algerian Infantrymen, made contact with the CLL and learned that the German consul general was being held hostage at the prefecture. Through this intermediary he arranged a meeting at 6.00 p.m. between de Monsabert and Schaefer. A truce went into effect as the two commanders met in the German lines before Fort Saint-Jean. The French general would not agree to an armistice which he considered a ploy to gain time. Rather than surrender, Schaefer began to harangue the FFI, insisting that the city should be declared a combat zone as armed civilians were conducting themselves like regular soldiers. He asserted that the arrival of the French army was not improving this situation.[72] Negotiations ceased and the guns resumed firing an hour later.

Marseille remained relatively quiet until August 25 when the French endeavored to take control of the hilltop of Notre-Dame de la Garde overlooking the city and port. The basilica there had been denied to worshipers since the landing. From their casemates and the roof of a nearby hospital, the Germans fired with precision at 7th Regiment infantrymen ascending the hill, guided once more by the local Resistance. The bishop's residence became an aid station as the prelate and his assistant cared for the wounded like military paramedics. The tank *Jeanne-d'Arc* was set afire by an 88-mm. round with its crew inside; another tank, *Jourdan*, blew up in the first row of mines. All at once a young German at the end of his nerves activated nine flamethrowers positioned at the base of the church but to no avail. Before it was over and the sanctuary freed, the operation had involved infantry, Sherman tanks, sappers, the FFI, and Moroccan goumiers attired in tin pith helmets, hobnailed boots, and what resembled golf pants.[73]

The bishop related that in the morning several disarmed German soldiers had entered the church to place themselves under his protection as prisoners. "Monseigneur, the French are out there," they exclaimed. The conquerors proceeded to collect 74 prisoners whose captain explained, "If we go downtown, the populace will kill us." When assured they would be safe, he responded in amazement, "You will protect us against [your own] civilian population?" He was assured that "officers will be treated as officers."[74]

Schaefer remembered the situation differently. He recalled that on August 25 the harbor commander's headquarters below Notre-Dame de la Garde was raked with mortar and machinegun fire emanating from the basilica. The commander himself was killed which would lead to serious difficulties later when his map of the port's mines could not be found, a concession specified in surrender negotiations. Schaefer's subordinates requested artillery fire upon the cathedral but he declined. As the situation worsened, however, he informed de Monsabert that he would change his mind if the firing did not stop. The French commander stated that soldiers from his division had not entered the basilica, and the perpetrators could only be members of the Resistance beyond his control. The Germans continued to withhold return fire, Schaefer testified.[75]

One by one, other strongholds fell in turn. In the case of fortifications on the islands of Frioul in front of the harbor, it was necessary to call in several hundred large American bombers from Italy to bring closure. The human reactions were touching. One observer remembered a German soldier asking for a drink, worn out by the heat. "Poor guys! They were so happy to have ended it that they were throwing their packets of cigarettes to passers-by."[76] After a heated exchange in Parc Borély, a resident looked into the faces of the men who had liberated the quarter. "They are great lords, silent and stoic," she said of the North Africans. "I would have wanted to speak to them. They could not understand me. That is not true. There are sentiments which have no need for words."[77]

There remained the final surrender. On August 25 the Spanish consul general offered his good offices to meet with the Wehrmacht high command but got nowhere. Captain Crosia succeeded in securing the garrison commander's agreement for the evacuation of several hundred old men, women, and children taking refuge in a tunnel at Fort Saint-Nicolas. The last fortifications in Marseille began giving way as well, yielding 300 prisoners and the works on Cap Janet. German defensive positions were shrinking in number while de Monsabert now began receiving personnel reinforcements from Toulon. On the evening of August 27, Schaefer finally requested a ceasefire until 8.00 the next morning.

Monday, August 28, glistened under bright blue skies yet the streets were deserted, everyone waiting in anticipation. One hour before the deadline, the capitulation was signed on the hood of a jeep. A last-minute problem had erupted when the German officer carrying the documents stepped on a landmine, destroying himself and the precious papers. Schaeffer turned over 10,000 prisoners along with considerable matériel. First, the deep voice of the bourdon of Notre-Dame de la Garde sounded to mark a momentous occasion, then, church bells began chiming throughout the city to announce the final liberation to anxious inhabitants and to notify the two sides to stop fighting at last.[78]

Marseille surrendered 36 hours after Toulon. An enthusiastic crowd greeted the troops of Army B passing in review while the 3rd Division band played the national anthem. French military losses at Marseille numbered 1,400 killed and wounded, almost half of whom were goumiers, plus 200 civilians. The Germans suffered 5,500 killed, one quarter of their effectives, and another 7,000 taken prisoner. De Lattre sent de Gaulle a telegram summarizing the French success in Operation Dragoon: "Today, J plus 13, in Army B's sector there remains no German not dead or captive."[79]

If French combat losses at Marseille numbered well below those at Toulon, there was far more physical damage to the larger city. Hardly any structure lacked scars from the fighting—roofs taken off like wigs, and the fronts of buildings opened to streets like doll-houses. An estimated 100,000 Marseillais lost their lodging in the conflict. Windows in shops and cafes were blown out. Streets were littered with stones, glass, and electrical wiring. Collections of newspapers, libraries full of books, and archives of irreplaceable documents were destroyed. The port was even worse, if possible. At every 20 meters along the wharves had been planted two barrels with 100 kilograms of explosives at water level, 2,000 mines in total, tearing up the docks. Virtually all the ships and floating equipment were sunk. The harbor was obstructed by 170 wrecks, and the liner *Cap Corse* had been towed into its entrance and sunk to block passage. Only three Swiss vessels and one of 257 marine cranes were spared, and the Wehrmacht and Kriegsmarine had tried to find the latter, *Goliath*, a giant of 150 tons relinquished by Germany as part of the reparations after World War I. A local writer concluded, "I do not believe that Marseille in the course of its history has ever suffered as in these past months."[80]

Minesweeping operations began right away to clear channels into the port. Fortunately, the tourist quay was spared as considered unsuited for heavy transport, and it subsequently became the keystone to the Americans' first logistical operations.[81] The port began offloading equipment and heavy matériel by September 3. To complicate the recovery, the first mistral blew up in mid-September, but that did not prevent a Liberty ship from docking on the 15th. As the month progressed, more supplies were being discharged onto the wharves of Marseille and Toulon than labor-intensive unloading across the sand.[82] When they closed at the end of September, Dragoon beaches had received 380,000 troops, 306,000 tons of cargo, almost 70,000 vehicles, and 18,000 tons of gasoline. While impressive, these numbers paled in comparison with over 4 million tons of matériel and 900,000 combatants that before the war's end landed at Toulon, Marseille, and Port de Bouc to the west, the lion's share coming into Marseille.[83]

How significant was the role of the Resistance in the liberation of Marseille? Urban guerrillas occupied strategic points abandoned by the enemy and created zones of insecurity for their oppressors. The underground was able to guide military patrols to their objectives with little time and few lives lost after already taking note of German gun positions and their fields of fire, as well as the location of pillboxes, minefields, and antitank obstacles. Estimates of civilian militants grew to 4,500 street fighters by liberation day. The foremost authority on the French Resistance cites 14,000 requests for cards verifying participation after the liberation, of which 6,000 were granted. Whatever the total, 106 members of the FFI died in combat in Marseille as compared with 43 in the Battle of Toulon.[84]

What was more significant was the psychological effect on the occupiers of urban combatants perceived as numerous, lethal, and fanatical. The Germans' apprehension was clearly illustrated by withdrawing into fortified installations. In the final days, the Resistance was given free rein in Marseille because tricolore divisions were closing in, but the invisible army was also crucial in complementing and aiding their liberators and drawing the senior French commander into the Battle of Marseille.

Standing back to consider the overall effect of French forces passing through the South, from their landing beaches to Marseille and beyond, one finds that casualty reports vary, even according to figures cited at different times by de Lattre's Army B. They range from 933 to 1,513 combatants killed and from 3,732 to 5,393 wounded. The figures on the other side show approximately 35,000 prisoners, including 700 officers. The numbers of enemy killed and wounded are less well known. Estimates of German dead range around 5,500.[85] What is important is that with the help of the local Resistance, the French army liberated Toulon and Marseille and lots of smaller places in the Var and Bouches du Rhône.

The strategy adopted by the Allies in taking the port cities was commended by the chief of staff of the 19th German Army, Generalleutnant Walther Botsch:

> The American command was correct in not attacking the great ports of Marseille and Toulon frontally, but from the land side. The defense of the ports was planned by the German Navy on the basis of a frontal attack and so almost all the coastal batteries (they were the best batteries) were concentrated in the vicinity of the ports, and others, because they were

behind embrasures, and emplaced in such a way that they could fire only toward the sea and a small sector of the land. Thus it happened that most of the coastal batteries fired not a single shot, either during the landing itself or during the struggle for the harbors of Marseille and Toulon.[86]

The campaign in Provence gave Frenchmen something of which to be proud. When it was over, the French army continued up the Rhône Valley to resume fighting with the Americans and be present at Germany's final surrender. Its soldiers would not be seen again in the Southeast until late in the winter of 1945 when they would conduct the last battle on French soil at Authion. But, more on that later.

12

ഇൽങ

Fighting in the Back Country

Four years after the Allied landing in Provence, General Wiese, the senior German commander in southeastern France, recalled being at his headquarters in Avignon on August 17, 1944 and receiving "the completely surprising order of the Supreme Commander West to withdraw from the OB [headquarters]." He cited the wording, "The Nineteenth Army will withdraw with all Wehrmacht parts assigned there through the Rhône Valley into the area of Chalons-sur-Saone. Each hour is precious. No more orders will be issued." Wiese continued, "The terrain of the Rhône Valley was the worst possible for the ordered withdrawal—mountains on both sides, many defiles, increasing activity of the resistance movement, excellent possibilities for the enemy to block the routes of retreat."[1] How prepared were the Allies to react to this strategic pullback?

Task Force Butler

After the successful debarkation, the primary objectives of the advance northward up the Rhône Valley were to join up with Lieutenant General George Patton's Third Army sweeping across France from Normandy toward Germany and, in the process, capture large numbers of Wehrmacht troops, decimating the Reich's military commands fleeing the South. Allied planners had foreseen the possibility of taking advantage of gaps in the enemy lines when the Germans reacted to the landing. By moving rapidly up the valleys of the Rivers Durance and Rhône toward Lyon, US forces hoped to encircle and destroy ground formations withdrawing from the Midi. The driving force for exploiting American success at the beachhead during this transitional period was a brigade-sized unit under Brigadier General Frederick B. Butler.

General Truscott later wrote that planning for the organization, assembly, and employment of this command had been accomplished during the two weeks prior to sailing from Napoli.[2] The armored task force he drew together included Sherman tanks, motorized infantry, armored field artillery, tank destroyers, and a cavalry reconnaissance squadron, plus support outfits—some

3,000 troops and 1,000 vehicles in all. A light Piper Cub helped with scouting and relaying communication as at times the mountainous terrain interrupted radio signals on the ground. Coordinating with the local Resistance, Butler's mission was to cut off the enemy retreat.

Early on the morning of August 18 the task force rumbled away from the coast. Butler moved his command by leaps and bounds, cavalry squadrons scouting, advancing, and protecting until the slower vehicles and engineer equipment could lumber into the next secure area. This technique economized on fuel and minimized vulnerability to enemy warplanes, as at least one flight of Luftwaffe bombers with fighter escort passed over the column while it, fortunately, had taken cover for the night.[3] Reaching the River Verdon, Butler's main column found the bridge was out as a result of Allied bombing and added demolition by the maquis. But maquisards soon rallied local inhabitants and cleared a ford in the waterway to allow the march to continue.[4]

Advancing along a slightly different route, a separate reconnaissance troop received shots from a grotto near Aups. Returning fire with high-velocity tank shells, the Americans forced German LXII Corps staff into the open with hands held high, along with their commander, General Neuling. His headquarters was one of the elements unable to join the Wehrmacht retreat up the Rhône Valley and pivoted instead toward Italy.[5]

Sapin was checking out possible aircraft landing sites in Alpes-Maritimes, along with Gunn and Fournier. Learning of Butler's thrust inland, Sapin dispatched one of his officers to accompany Fournier in providing assistance to the Americans. These envoys were intended to provide liaison with the maquisards. About the same time, as Butler recalled, he was being introduced to the commander of OG Ruth:

> [A]n American captain [actually, a lieutenant wearing captain's bars]—a paratrooper. He was one of several teams who were dropped in prior to the invasion. With him he had a tough little Frenchman, a sergeant. The Frenchman was in the uniform of a Blue Devil [*Diables Bleus*, nickname of the Chasseurs Alpins], beret and all. And was he a tough bunny—about five feet tall and five feet broad. He was a World War I veteran, but a regiment of his like would wrestle tanks![6]

Butler decided to send detachments to the north and east to subdue the enemy garrisons at Digne and Gap, thereby providing flank protection. Digne was located at the strategic intersection of the Route Napoléon and a road by which the Germans could bring reinforcements from Italy. The arrival of an American armored squadron so soon after the debarkation clearly surprised the Wehrmacht which was thinking in terms of the slow breakout underway in Normandy. The commandant, Generalmajor Hans Schuberth, was found comfortably quartered in the grand Hôtel l'Ermitage. Two tank rounds brought him rushing out to surrender in his underwear. The garrison of 500–600 men, the largest German contingent in the vicinity, gave up that afternoon.[7] When a rescue attempt was made, the FFI blew up two bridges over the Durance to prevent German reinforcements from crossing. Otherwise, the Resistance focused on ousting Vichy officials from positions at the *hôtel de ville* and replacing them with their own candidates.

At dawn on August 19, Fournier and his mate intercepted an American armored column of detachment size led by a jeep carrying officers who appeared to be interpreters for the Americans. They were very likely Captain Jacques Martin (French) and Lieutenant Henry McIntosh (American), members of Jedburgh Team Chloroform. The two officers had just joined up with the vanguard of Butler's command.

When Butler's main body reached Sisteron, an inexplicable encounter occurred. The senior SOE leader in the Southeast as well as General Zeller's representative, Cammaerts, came to Butler's headquarters in uniform along with Christine Granville. Cammaerts offered to brief the general on the number and location of FFI units in the mountains ahead and maintain contact with them by radio and courier. Without taking his eyes off the map in front of him, Butler remarked that he was "not the slightest bit interested in private armies" and dismissed the visitor.[8] A senior staff member quickly apologized outside the general's presence. Butler's pride was seen, as well, in other American commanders who did not respect the intimate knowledge of the terrain or the tactics of the Resistance. The response was the same on a subsequent visit. On the other hand, Butler had confidence in regular military men, writing, "Officers of the old French Army were coming in now, and the assistance of these trained officers was invaluable."[9]

The reception was very different at Seventh Army headquarters. Patch received Cammaerts and Christine with courtesy. He assigned the SOE leader to de Lattre's Army B west of the Rhône. US VI Corps thereby lost the expertise, knowledge of the French people and their language, and inter-personnel skills of the English-speaker most experienced in operating in Southeast France. Christine went in a different direction to help rehabilitate Polish prisoners in Italy, her work for the SOE in France having come to an end.

Butler sent troopers northward on Highway 75 to Grenoble and a platoon of tanks with a reconnaissance element along the Route Napoléon northeast to Gap. The long bridge perched on pilings over the Durance had been destroyed earlier by explosives attached by Team Chloroform to isolate the town from reinforcement. FFI forces and 700 US troops surrounded Gap as tankers fired 40 rounds to demonstrate the strength of the invading force. After first haggling over surrender terms, including the usual demand that the garrison surrender only to Americans and not to guerrillas, in the early evening of August 20 three maquis groups entered Gap and accepted the capitulation of 1,200 Wehrmacht soldiers, mainly administrative, supply, and limited-service personnel, non-combatants all. A particular prize was the capture of two dumps, one full of rations and the other with demolition devices. There followed the customary parading in the streets, punishment of women friendly to the Germans, and execution of three Gestapo agents.[10]

Butler then received orders from Truscott to head west along the River Drome at first light on August 21 and cut off the German retreat up the Rhône at Montélimar. The narrow river gorges traversed to get to the Rhône would surely have been impassable without flank protection provided by the FFI. Their harassment prevented the Germans from detonating explosives to send avalanches of rocks hurtling down onto roadways, potentially holding up the motor column for hours or days. The irregulars also guarded the lines of communication to the rear. In praise of these French patriots, Butler was later to reflect, "A French soldier with confidence is the equal of any soldier in the world. And so was our Maquis."[11]

Three main arteries followed the Rhône from Avignon toward Lyon— Route Nationale 7 and a rail line on the east bank, and Highway 86 on the west. The latter was a winding road past high limestone cliffs and steep quarry faces considered a beehive of maquis activity.[12] The headquarters of Army Group G had identified bridges, railroads, canals, and auto routes sabotaged by partisans on the west side as serious impediments to a road march.

The 3rd Division was ordered to advance from Alpha landing zone toward the lower Rhône, isolating Toulon and Marseille from German reinforcements. At the same time, the 45th Division, first, made contact with American and Canadian airborne troops near Le Muy and, then, headed due north, sending one regiment far to the east astride Highway 85 to Apt. On its way to the Italian border, the 36th Division began relieving Butler's units above Gap until it, too, was ordered to swing west to the Rhône to help seal off the Wehrmacht's escape route.

Before long, progress by the 36th was stymied by shortages of fuel and ammunition. The rapid success at the beach, due in large part to the unexpected weakness of the defenses, allowed the invaders to advance faster and farther than anticipated. Planners had not loaded the first wave of cargo ships with petroleum and delivery trucks sufficient for a rapid thrust over hundreds of miles. Limited over-the-beach capability also slowed logistical operations, demonstrating the need for ports in the South equipped to offload bulk freight. The final straw was when the galloping cavalrymen ran off their army maps.

Sergeant Mauldin offered the infantryman's point of view when describing his 45th Division's march into the interior behind the Riviera.

Even though that campaign was a very fast one for the first few weeks, it was not an easy war. No war is easy for those who fight it.

The guys were tired from constant marching and they were running into stubborn resistance in spots, but it was such a tremendous change from Italy that their morale was a little better. They had expected a tough beachhead, and even tougher mountain fighting. They were very much relieved to find that they could push ahead.

The Maquis and FFI helped a lot, particularly in the mountains. By actually pitching in and helping to chase the krauts out, the French saved many of their towns from destruction. The French were honestly and sincerely glad to see the Americans come, and the farther north we worked the more hospitable the people became. I had a feeling that we were regarded truly as liberators, and not as walking bread baskets. It was a far cry from Italy.[13]

Montélimar

A major confrontation was building north of Montélimar, a road and rail center on the Rhône's east bank. This would be the heaviest fighting in the Southeast emanating from the Allied landing in Provence. Six miles above the town at La Coucourde, the river valley narrows to one mile for a 10-mile stretch so that a ridgeline dominates National 7 and the railway, as well as the parallel road on the west bank. It was here that the Americans would attempt to stem the Wehrmacht exodus consisting not only of units of Wiese's 19th Army, but also those of Army Group G.

IV Luftwaffe Field Corps controlled German elements heading to the Rhône Valley from Southwest France. They included naval and coastal troops, air force ground organizations, and administrative sections with minimal organic transportation. The departure was accomplished by whatever means possible—bicycles and pushcarts if trucks, cars, and buses were unavailable, or else the retreat took place on foot. Mule-drawn wagons carried cases of ammunition, soldiers' knapsacks, and officers' briefcases. Aerial reconnaissance indicated that dismounted units were also using the road network on the west side of the river. Going on foot made it easier to skirt roadblocks manned by the Resistance. Suffering alongside their uniformed comrades were men from Organization Todt, young women who had worked at signal stations, and railroad security personnel, accompanied by vehicles piled with supplies.[14]

German forces were moving through the gorge at La Coucourde when Butler's vanguard arrived late on August 21. He established outposts and began firing on the convoys with an artillery battery, five tanks, and a section of machineguns. Fifty French maquis joined the effort. Running low on ammunition, at one point down to 25 rounds per gun, Butler's attempts to solidify a roadblock proved unsuccessful. Just as serious, in his eyes, was the lack of infantry trained to defend a barricade. At first, the traffic proceeded day and night, but gradually more movement occurred after dark. Indicating yet again the ineffectiveness of guerrillas against regular army formations, Butler called the 36th Division for help. "French [maquis] infantry support absolutely unsatisfactory repeat absolutely unsatisfactory. Request one infantry battalion by motor without delay."[15]

The 11th Panzer Division was Wiese's prime asset, but it took the tankers seven days to come from Toulouse. Forward elements employed a ferryboat to cross the Rhône; later units adapted a large coal lighter for tanks and guns weighing up to 60 tons. Once on the east side of the river, the Division was assigned a variety of tasks. At first, its missions were to repel enemy pursuit while, at the same time, protecting the withdrawal northward. Soon the 11th was fighting at four dispersed points, and rearguard security passed to an infantry division. When higher headquarters became concerned that the Allies might threaten the retreat at the River Drome north of La Coucourde, the armored priority changed to preventing encirclement by American and French forces converging from different directions. Fighting up the Rhône Valley was made more difficult by two days of high water brought about by downpours in the Alps.[16]

To execute their assigned tasks, the 11th Panzer and 198th Infantry Division began infiltrating Butler's lines, slipping through the interspersed American defenses. On August 24 the Germans had a stroke of luck when a copy of the 36th Division operation order fell into their hands. The enemy now knew the thin US troop dispositions providing flank security. Striking against a company of combat engineers 12 miles east of Montélimar, the 11th Division achieved a significant breakthrough for German tankers and infantrymen.[17]

Indecision at one point by Truscott and extreme caution on the part of General Dahlquist delayed the arrival of American infantry and tank reinforcements. Limited resupply of fuel by transport, plus gasoline captured from the Germans at Draguignan, Le Muy, and Digne, finally enabled more US troops to head for Montélimar. Meanwhile Wiese was inserting forces faster than his adversary. He urged combat units forward to facilitate the steady stream of Wehrmacht traffic back toward Germany. Consequently, at midday, August 29, the town was finally clear of German snipers, 48 hours after the vanguard of the 3rd Division arrived to dislodge the enemy.

From August 21 to 31 the two adversaries took turns attacking here and defending there with neither gaining an advantage. Both armies had difficulty concentrating sufficient strength at a critical time and place to decide the contest. Even with benefit of the captured operational order, the Germans were unable to overcome the defenders. At one point on August 25, the 11th Division's commander personally led a column of tanks, armored personnel carriers, and self-propelled guns through the gauntlet at La Coucourde, but it was not enough to keep open the escape route.[18] The 3rd Division bypassed German garrisons in several small towns in their rush to intercept the withdrawal. Yet the Americans' progress was slowed by land mines, destroyed bridges, felled trees, booby traps, and other obstacles emplaced by the foe. Once arriving on the scene, division artillery poured a torrent of 75,000 rounds down onto the roadway, expenditure of ammunition three times the normal daily rate. But with inadequate support from infantry and tanks, the barrage failed to completely interdict the route.[19] Added to FFI guerrilla attacks and bombing and strafing by Allied fighter aircraft based in Corsica, the deluge left vehicles, guns, wagons, and dead horses strewn along the road and wrecked engines and rail cars on the tracks. As the highway became impassable, the Germans took to paths between the main road and the river to maintain the flow.

While the Battle of Montélimar ebbed and flowed, the maquis pressured isolated enemy outposts to surrender, guarded prisoners, and passed information to American commanders. Some of the Wehrmacht soldiers held fast, others tried to join their comrades on back roads, and more than a few just wandered around. Many of the enemy stragglers taken into custody were Polish. Nevertheless, the retreating 19th Army succeeded in maintaining a distance of 12 to 18 miles between its rearguard and advance elements of the 3rd Division.[20]

The Germans frustrated American attempts to stop their withdrawal but at a heavy price. By August 31, when the last Axis soldiers crossed the Drome and the valley widens again, the column moving along the east side of the Rhône had lost 600 killed, 1,500 wounded, and 5,800 captured (including numerous Russians).[21] Countless others were missing, casualties amounting in total to 20 percent of the procession in retreat. Many of these losses came from front-line units, reducing combat strength already dwindling throughout the Wehrmacht. To the human cost were added 2,000 vehicles, 1,000 horses, six railway guns, and hundreds of pieces of artillery destroyed or captured by the Allies.

Nor were the Allies able to entirely stop movement along the highway on the west bank of the river. Nevertheless, the Luftwaffe Field Corps lost another 3,000 members fleeing in disarray. This number compared with a total of 1,575 American casualties at Montélimar or less than 5 percent of US personnel employed.[22]

From the German perspective, the engagement at Montélimar succeeded in preserving the bulk of the five divisions retreating from southern France. However, after the war, one subordinate commander opined that rear echelon units clogging the roadways should have been ordered out of the way to provide freedom of movement for combat troops, thereby conserving more irreplaceable personnel.[23] The chief of staff of 19th Army credited command posts located almost in the midst of the fighting for enabling forces to shift with greater agility than the enemy. Commanders positioned forward could make tactical decisions as the situation evolved, providing a distinct advantage over their adversaries.[24] Only Butler and (eventually) Dahlquist were on the scene of the fighting, while the headquarters of Truscott and Patch remained well to the rear. Allied air superiority, among other factors, limited the Germans' concept of the battlefield. With a clearer understanding of the positioning of opposing forces, Wiese could have taken greater advantage of gaps in the American lines.

On the other side, the FFI gained the satisfaction of supporting the liberators by harassing vulnerable German elements, ferreting out Nazis, providing intelligence to their hunters, and augmenting American combat forces where possible. US combatants could take well-deserved pride in acquitting themselves credibly against a numerically superior adversary attempting to outflank their blocking positions. The Americans may not have achieved victory in the only major engagement emanating from the Riviera landings, but from a strategic perspective they clearly diminished their foe's capacity to contribute to the ultimate defense of the Fatherland.

By August 29, when senior Allied commanders met at Seventh Army headquarters, de Lattre was not content merely to provide flank security for the Americans progressing up the Rhône and eastward into Germany. Consequently, two French divisions advanced along the west bank of the Rhône to participate in the liberation of Lyon. The Wehrmacht stopped there only long enough to collect, rest, feed, and equip 3,000 stragglers who had successfully traversed the killing field outside Montélimar. After the Germans departed, the 1ère Division de Marche d'Infantrie was allowed to be the first to enter France's third largest metropolis.

The cherished remembrances of this extraordinary event by a 12-year-old boy living at Lyon are worth noting. What a thrill for the youngster to see French troops finally entering his city attired in GI combat apparel and driving Sherman tanks. Shortly thereafter, he heard shouts that the Americans were coming and ran into a square to see them, too. They were identically clothed and equipped. "What are you doing wearing French uniforms?" he exclaimed incredulously.[25]

Eisenhower wrote, "There was no development of that period which added more decisively to our advantages or aided us more in accomplishing the final and complete defeat of the German forces than did this secondary attack coming up the Rhône Valley [from the Riviera]."[26] General Monsabert, a French oenophile, jocularly observed that the Americans did not bother to pass by a single vineyard of quality in their march northward.[27]

The Valley of the Vésubie

One historian noted a measured response in the higher elevations to the debarkation on August 15 due to what was commonly considered abandonment by the Allies, including Free France, when the populace there rose up and was crushed following the Normandy landings.[28] Nearer the coast in Alpes-Maritimes, reaction to the Provençal landing was well thought out and made in conjunction with the arrival of external armed forces. In the department of the Var alone more than 100 guerrilla attacks immediately took place after August 15, mainly ambushes outside built-up areas followed by the attackers' swift withdrawal.[29] Nor does the generalization apply to maquisards under the control of Commandant Sapin.

FFI in the back country was trained and ready to support the Allied landing whenever it occurred. Sapin's 1,800 men were lightly armed with Browning machineguns, Sten sub-machineguns, American and English rifles, and various mines and grenades. Uniforms and equipment were non-existent. The résistants dressed like the civilians they were.[30] Yet, many proudly wore tricolore armbands for identification as combatants. When word arrived of the Mediterranean landing, Group Sapin immediately descended to Puget-Théniers on the Var and Bancairon on the River Tinée, where the small German garrisons (30 and 38 men) capitulated on August 16 and 19, respectively. Before the defenders of Bancairon were willing to give up, however, Sapin had to be summoned wearing a makeshift uniform and armed with a magnificent Colt revolver given him by General Frederick, to convince the commander that he was, indeed, a genuine French soldier. "I really am an officer, Saint-Cyrien; I arrived a little more than three years ago, and you will be treated as prisoners of war according to the laws of war."[31] Perhaps as important as the surrender was acquisition of laced regimental boots and high-quality German weapons which were distributed to new companies formed by the FTP, among other maquis.

On August 16 an order was disseminated to local elements of the Resistance to liberate the valley of the Vésubie. One of the first steps was to alert Italian maquis encamped not far to the east. Group Morgan of Combat set up headquarters midway up the valley between Levens and Saint-Martin-Vésubie. It was strengthened by the addition of Group Hochcorn. Success came quickly. Despite the continuing presence of enemy troops on the crater overlooking the terrain, the German garrison at Saint-Martin agreed to surrender its 40 soldiers to Paul Sola, a Socialist *notaire* and local leader in the Resistance. The chief of Group Morgan solemnly pledged that the international Geneva Conventions would be applied and all went well. The FFI was soon reinforced by 150 partigiani.[32]

Over the next ten days, the Resistance consolidated its gains in the valley. Prisoners from the various German garrisons were taken to Beuil for confinement. Wehrmacht squads launched armed forays into one village or another to obtain provisions, but generally the gorge was at peace. Allied forces were heading in their direction, and it was natural for the Resistance in this area to think that conflict was drawing to a close. Then, on August 27, the Germans returned.

From a French perspective, the operation is now remembered as a reprisal to terrorize a populace who had contributed to the fall of the Wehrmacht occupiers. Saint-Martin was undefended since the maquis had departed after the garrison's capitulation. The Germans believed there were as many as 800 partisans present so the invaders came in force, 3,000 men by one estimate.[33] Their arrival was preceded by a short artillery bombardment but without armed opposition. Many residents had long before hidden their precious possessions outside town in isolated houses and barns, but any remaining valuables were systematically confiscated. The blacksmith was drafted as a locksmith to open doors; otherwise, grenades sufficed for keys. The officers chose to spend the night in Sola's villa with a townswoman commandeered as cook. The fascists hauled off their spoils of war the next morning.

The record left by one of the occupying units—4th Battalion, 5th Austrian High Mountain Assault Division—is somewhat different. There is agreement that their arrival was not contested. Preparing to depart the following morning, the Austrians found that most of the mule skinners, probably shanghaied Italians, had disappeared during the night. Reportedly, the muleteers stole the villagers' armoires, filled them with the best clothes, and carried off the booty. Axis troops loaded their trucks and what animals remained with the population's meager store of foodstuffs—potatoes, cereals, wheat, corn, beans, cheese, butter, and bottles of wine. Then, as quickly as they appeared, the invaders returned to their strongholds on the heights. The FFI immediately reoccupied the town and by September 2 the Americans had arrived.[34]

Moving parallel to the coastline and, then, toward the Vésubie marched the 517th Parachute Regimental Combat Team. On August 26, one of its platoons entered Carros, a town high above the River Var already taken by the FFI.[35] Looking down, the platoon leader noticed a bridge with its demolished center span being rebuilt by an impressed French crew. Taking clothes off workmen and placing their weapons in a wheelbarrow, a couple of GIs sauntered across the planks connecting the two ends. When the Wehrmacht sentry on the far bank challenged them, the intruders shot him and another German trying to get away.[36]

Five miles upriver, other paratroopers were stopping at Gilette. There they found the Pont Charles-Albert over a wide, sandy river basin planted with hundreds of anti-airborne poles bearing 150-mm. shells with tension on the fuses set to explode. On the east bank were La Roquette-sur-Var and Levens, to the south and north, respectively. An FFI officer crossed over from the other side under enemy fire to inform the liberators of the situation in the two towns. Situated on the topographical prominence, Levens offered military dominance of the surrounding heights and the confluence of the Var and Vésubie below. As the perched village was occupied by Germans, an extended bombardment of the high ground was requested from Allied warships, which lasted for 12 hours. That midnight the Americans followed an FFI guide across the rocky riverbed and through the water rushing down the middle, climbed a ridge, and entered La Roquette at first light. Seventy-seven defenders surrendered. Germans attempting to flee across an open field were mowed down by rifle and light machinegun fire, leaving 15 dead. Continuing cautiously onward, the paratroopers discovered the enemy had abandoned Levens. Some of the GIs soon headed for Nice, arriving after its liberation but in time for the celebration.[37]

Isolated communities were vulnerable because of the departure of many law enforcement officers. The national police were frustrated by years of being caught between Vichy, Italians, Germans, and the inhabitants with whom they identified. De Lattre considered the majority of the remaining police as "perfectly faithful to a truly national mentality."[38] To avoid a bigger bloodbath, gendarmes often chose not to offer armed opposition when German soldiers or members of the Resistance stole shamelessly from the meager stock of rations accumulated by villagers. With tacit consent from their hierarchy, individual gendarmes had started taking their weapons and gear and drifting away after dark to join the ranks of the résistants.[39]

As the Resistance fanned out through the valleys of the back country, skillful German small-unit tactics and use of artillery on the heights kept the liberators below at a constant disadvantage. On September 2 a strong Wehrmacht detachment attacked the combatants without uniforms by surprise from the mountain village of Isola. Partigiani united with the populace and local maquis in a successful rebuttal. Two days later the Germans sprung another ambush between Isola and Saint-Etienne-de-Tinée. Proceeding was treacherous as roadways through many of these valleys were carved out of steep mountainsides with sheer drops into narrow rapids far below, ideal for ambushes. Furthermore, Austrian soldiers were accustomed to living and operating in such treacherous terrain, while generally the liberators were not.[40]

Conditions did not settle down until the 551st Parachute Infantry Battalion arrived and its members formed long-range patrols. Each consisted of 12 volunteers with skiing experience. After receiving special training in small groups, they were issued skis, snowshoes, and other gear such as reversible parkas for camouflage which were unavailable to the maquis.[41]

The German withdrawal resumed at an orderly pace. In contrast to the Italian army fleeing the advancing Wehrmacht in September 1943, weapons, equipment, and uniforms were not strewn along the roadside by the disciplined feldgrau. Arriving in one town after another, the Americans found their opponents had already departed, thus avoiding combat in built-up places with their uncertain risks and casualties. When enemy soldiers did set up a defense, it was on favorable terrain of their own choosing. Trails were mined and bridges and roads blown up at strategic points, oftentimes on steep slopes difficult to repair. Only the occasional appearance of an armored reconnaissance patrol caused the retreat to hasten. When chance encounters did occur, the size and strength of the opposition were difficult for the GIs to estimate.

Nearing the frontier the Americans began sending out small patrols of seasoned scouts for several days behind enemy lines to disrupt Wehrmacht formations and lines of communication. US cannoneers came to relish enemy troops taking refuge in a tunnel. The concussion caused by firing into such a passageway was terrific, the noise deafening, and shrapnel traveled hundreds of yards, hindering effective return fire.

The pursuers soon learned to position intelligence personnel with forward elements to relay credible information on the enemy's strength and whereabouts. The enemy who held this ground had a greater familiarity with the terrain than the incoming Americans, making reconnaissance all the more important. Civilian reports were plentiful but erroneous and misleading at times. Periodically the pursuers lost contact with the enemy. When fired upon at other times they soon realized that Red Cross markings on the helmets of first-aid personnel served as targets for snipers. But the Americans pushed on and the two sides did not reach a standoff until arriving at the Italian border.

French Forces of the Interior (FFI)

Farther to the northwest, a US reconnaissance platoon and 60 maquis accompanied by Jedburgh Team Chloroform headed toward Barcelonnette to occupy the fort of Tournoux facing Italy. The Germans had retaken control of the entrance of nearby Col de Larche and delivered a persistent fire to deny access to their adversaries, causing nearby inhabitants to flee. Leaving the maquis to run continuous patrols day and night assisted by the Jedburghs, the platoon withdrew the next day. A small American task force arrived on August 30, in accordance with Patch's orders to Frederick to extend the 1st Airborne Task Force area of responsibility to the pass. Their mission was to deny the enemy use of Larche to escape from Alpes-Maritimes, as well as defend against German incursion from the east. Consequently, the maquisards and Team Chloroform soon pulled out, the Jeds reporting to Grenoble.

As the Americans established themselves along the Italian border, the Resistance began consolidating its diverse outfits to provide maximum strength to confront an influx of fresh German troops from Torino, Italy.

Whereas before the Allied landing the Resistance had operated in small cells to harass the enemy, now it became part of larger military operations with the objective of liberating southeastern France. In some instances, Italian maquisards participated in this expanded endeavor. The enlightened policy of Seventh Army toward these collections of irregulars is well expressed in a communiqué from the FSSF, the principal North American outfit engaged in small-unit combat in the upcountry.

> It is most important that all ranks likely to be in contact with Resistance forces should be reminded that they will be dealing with members of the recognized armed forces of an Allied nation. These people have been in constant combat against the invaders of their country; in so doing, they have taken far greater hazards than the usual military forces of a country are expected to do; for more than four years many of them have carried their lives in their hands; their participation in resistance has exposed their families to hostage and revenge by an unscrupulous foe; tens of thousands have been tortured and killed; hundreds of thousands have been robbed, imprisoned and expatriated; the self-sacrifice and patriotic devotion of those who survive and continue the fight should readily ensure them the respect and confidence of the Allied forces of liberation from whom they expect so much and for whose advance they are in a position so ably to pave the way.[42]

The FFI was told to disband in late August by order of General de Gaulle, now president of the provisional French government. Résistants were given three choices: (1) demobilize; (2) join the Republican security forces, a choice attractive to a good number of the patriotic Milice; or (3) sign up for the remainder of the war in the First French Army which appealed primarily to FFI maquisards.[43]

In the two maquis led by Morgan and Hochcorn, 90 percent of the members decided to stay with buddies and follow their chiefs into the ranks en masse. What might have motivated résistants to continue fighting after years of living in danger opposing the fascist occupation? For young men who had hidden in the high country and suffered deprivation for months and years in some cases, the notion of stopping short of the border and not pushing the Germans completely out of France was difficult to accept. Some sought news of friends deported to the Reich and never heard from again. Others were certainly looking to avenge the humiliation of June 1940. From the army's point of view, it was vital to "whiten" their liberating force in the colonial army with citizens from metropolitan France as well as relieve troops from Sub-Saharan colonies, for cold nights were becoming increasingly common in higher elevations.

A career French army officer, Colonel Lanusse, took military command in the Southeast. His orders were "to assure, in liaison with the American troops, the cover of the right flank of the Allied armies on the Alps and the route of the corniche."[44] In turn, Lanusse named Lécuyer his second-in-command with the rank of lieutenant colonel. Sapin described the man who took the position that might rightfully have been considered his as "cold, honest, a little eccentric."[45]

A report dated September 27 listed FFI strength in the Southeast as 3,000 men involved in operations and 5,000 in French army units or in the process of joining. Five battalions were filled with members of the maquis. Sapin counted 500 or so men from his own command who initially signed up at Nice for the duration of the war. As the FFI in Alpes-Maritimes disbanded, it could look back with pride and sorrow at 124 of their comrades in arms who had perished from June to September 1944, 65 in combat and 59 executed by the enemy.[46]

Blending into de Lattre's First Army was not easy for the former guerrillas. Their mentality was very different from the regular army in terms of discipline, formality, and the variety of groups led by a heterogeneous cadre. Pay, medals, uniform, and equipment were just some of the day-to-day problem areas. Certain cliques had regional allegiances, others adhered to particular political orientations, and some just considered themselves part of a new revolutionary French army. An infantry offensive was not the same type of combat engaged in by urban guerrillas or rural maquisards. A few may just have been resentful or jealous of the professional soldiers and longed for personal autonomy. In turn, the army's regulars viewed the self-promoted underground leaders with disdain and their followers as ill-disciplined, untrained, and unreliable under fire. It was a difficult marriage at first.[47]

The composition of these outfits was far from homogeneous French. Corsicans, dockworkers from Marseille, even British nationals joined up. Deserters from Mussolini's army who hid in the back country when the Germans forcibly evicted the Italians from the Riviera were now assigned to protect the border from the French side. The Americans had misgivings about some of these volunteers, suspecting FTP labor unionists from the cities of being communists. To be sure of obtaining accurate information on their activities, company commanders were directed to send along at least one GI on every patrol.

Without a doubt, the most colorful of these new outfits was the 21st Battalion of Foreign Volunteers. It was led by Commandant Michel, the nom de guerre of Miklos Zoldelhyi, a Hungarian who had been organizing foreign resistance in France since 1939. He had previously served as a lieutenant in the Imperial Austro-Hungarian Army of 1914–18, a general in Mexico, and a colonel in the International Brigade in Spain. His command consisted of 20 officers, 61 non-commissioned officers, and 500–600 men, along with others in subordinate units for motor transportation and mules. Veterans of IV Italian Armata comprised a majority of the battalion although 23 nationalities were represented.[48] Italian was the dominant language. Second most populous were Spaniards coming from Marseille, next Poles dragooned into the Wehrmacht, then some Russians. An assortment of veterans of fighting in Ethiopia, Spain, and Libya served as non-commissioned officers. The soldiers were uniformed, fed, paid, and administered the same as other French battalions. Individual weapons were Anglo-American, although many members tried to retain their national arms, Berretas and Bredas in particular. A foreign artillery group was constituted with a mix of nationalities to utilize the variety of captured armament abandoned by the enemy during its withdrawal—a pair of German 150-mm. batteries and an Italian battery of 149-mm. artillery.[49] Stationed initially as a reserve in the valley of la Roya claimed by France, the soldiers engaged in lively discussions over whether the cross of Savoie royalty or the *croix de Lorraine* should be overlaid on their French tricolore.[50] Three French captains were assigned to this command to be the eyes and ears of South Alpine Group.

To the north of Menton, two US battalions were reinforced by a French detachment of 350 men. An American and a French battalion shared responsibility for the river valleys of the Vésubie and Tinée. Coming from a mélange of political parties, occupations, and nationalities, oftentimes with incompatible equipment and weapons (36 types of arms by one count), the glue holding these organizations together was the personalities of their leaders. These disparate bands of résistants were joined in the ideal of freeing the country, but beyond that there was far less unity. As explained in the history of the FSSF, while the zeal and determination of these French patriots were unquestioned, they were ill-prepared for what was now being asked of them.

> Their main limitations were lack of unified training, lack of uniform ordnance, and lacks in warm clothing and proper supply in the mountains. Both discipline and command were good. The lieutenants were mostly graduates of Saint-Cyr, and most of the officers and NCOs [non-commissioned officers] had gone through the invasion of France with regular organizations. Later in September, in line with De Gaulle's policy of putting the FFI on full military footing, Hochscorn [sic] Battalion was withdrawn to Nice for a month to train, equip, and organize.[51]

The military aid agreement between France and the United States provided for equipping and supplying only certain combat units, not new outfits made up of former partisans. Nor would the US Army provide ingredients common to French cuisine such as wine, brandy, and olive oil.[52] It therefore required a combination of second-hand clothing and equipment and local food products to provision the Resistance forces deployed along the defensive line. Lanusse obtained 3,000 helmets from the Passive Defense and invited the population to furnish wool clothing, blankets, and laced boots to help his soldiers survive the cold. When he could, the FSSF quartermaster at Menton thanked volunteers who served as bearers of provisions and munitions to GIs posted in higher elevations by providing them food, clothing, and matériel from unit stocks. Until his death in 2015, one French member of that winter army proudly showed a photo of himself in the Alpine high ground surrounded by four GIs. He shoulders an American rifle and wears a French helmet and uniform with a potato masher hanging from his belt.[53]

By the end of October, de Lattre's command was pleading for FFI veterans. His pool of trained replacements from North Africa had been exhausted. More than 60,000 troops from FFI units across the South constituted the majority of the fillers, but recruiting in metropolitan France had also begun to pick up. Naturally, these young volunteers needed general military training, as well as specific instruction on the use of the surplus American and British weapons and equipment allocated to the French army. The training cadre was enlarged by establishment of a non-commissioned officer academy at Puget-Théniers and a nearby camp that certified Scouts-Skiers.[54]

Sospel and Castillon

Sospel is situated in the back country, 25 miles northeast of Nice on the winding River Bévéra. In autumn 1944 its population was close to 1,500, half the prewar number, consisting mostly of women, children, and the elderly. The town's military importance lay in its location at an opening in the high ground going into the valley of la Roya which led to Italy. The depression along the River Roya was valuable to both the Germans as a possible escape route and Italian Fascists intent on protecting their Piémont. Free France's designs on Northwest Italy, to be addressed in a subsequent chapter, made this critical terrain for political leaders as well.

Two fortifications overlooking Sospel were part of the southern extension of the Maginot Line. Saint-Roch and Agaisen were elaborate structures built largely underground, with tunnels running in various directions to air-ventilated command centers. Gun turrets poked up looking in all directions, many with cannon that could be raised and lowered. The concrete bunkers were impervious to enemy artillery, but the roar of countless shells reverberating inside these complexes, plus other noise and fumes from the guns, demoralized defenders if under siege for weeks. A third citadel, Fort du Barbonnet, had been constructed by General Séré de Rivières with battlements above ground encircled by a moat.

Surrounded by these fortifications, the citizens of Sospel had combatants in their midst continually after 1939—French Chasseurs Alpins, Italian Alpini, and, now, the Boche. The town's caserne had served as an internment camp for as many as 600 prisoners during the Italian and German occupations. It was to this holding area that Nazi henchmen brought 15 French and Italian members of the maquis, barefoot with hands tied behind their backs, on August 4, 1944. During the next eight days, residents shuddered at blood-curdling screams from these prisoners being tortured. They were then seemingly released from custody only to be attacked outside the compound by German shepherds let loose by their captors, after which a firing squad finished off the martyrs. Sospel men who dug the graves and buried them without coffins described the bodies as unrecognizable.[55]

A different threat loomed on the morning of September 2, when violent detonations erupted around Sospel as Germans and Americans along with their allies contested approaches to the town. The impact of bombs exploding caused the ground to tremble and timeless walls to tumble down. Over the following days the refugees noticed that before each bombardment a small observation plane circled slowly overhead oftentimes followed by smoke bombs. Inhabitants retreated into caves deep into the banks of the Bévéra. A candle sitting on a barrel provided the only light at first. Then, the cave dwellers learned to illuminate their refuges using a series of mirrors beginning at the mouth. Sacks of sand half-closed the openings. After dark, entrances were reinforced with blocks of wood, both to deaden the sound of nighttime explosions and from fear generated by reports of rapes committed by fascist soldiers.

After the Americans' initial appearance, the 148th Wehrmacht division concentrated its five batteries on protecting the route from the Col de Braus to Sospel. A heavy engagement soon unfolded. Ground attacks failed to settle the contest, and only two days later did the GIs overrun the road. The two sides then settled into artillery duels. US guns fired 300–500 shells daily, receiving comparable numbers of incoming rounds. German guns on Mt. Agaisen and Mt. Barbonnet chased jeeps up and down the mountain roads. Civilians from Sospel risked their lives by crossing the lines to inform the Americans where German cannon were housed in impregnable fortifications and tunnels. As the 34th Wehrmacht Division began replacing the worn-out 148th, four companies of the 517th Parachute Regimental Combat Team assaulted the guns and mortars on Tête de la Lavina, a large wooded hill overlooking the whole Sospel Valley but were repelled. Three days later, after a violent preparation by naval gunfire and field artillery, including phosphorous shells, the Americans launched an attack that succeeded in capturing the promontory. Repulsing a German counterattack and subsequent fighting over three additional days finally settled the contest on September 21. The fighting had cost 21 American lives, plus 123 wounded and three prisoners, casualties almost equivalent to a rifle company.[56]

After two weeks of hard combat, Frederick ordered a halt to offensive operations around Sospel. By this time the front had stabilized, following in most part the dominant terrain along the border northward from Pont Saint-Louis. The Wehrmacht had established a strong defensive line paralleling the Americans. While most of the terrain in southeastern France remaining under German control was not taken until 1945, a few parcels would be relinquished before year's end, most notably Sospel and Castillon.

Frederick's intelligence officer, Captain Geoffrey Jones, later provided glimpses into the situation confronting the Americans.

> Sospel was kind of no-man's land, but we weren't doing much except praying as we were very outnumbered. I think they thought we were building up and we were hoping they kept thinking it [...] We had skirmishing all the time along the lines, back and forth [...] Later on after Bob Frederick left, I think, we had like 2 days a week the Americans would go in, 2 days a week the Germans were in, and the rest of the time you took your chances [...] As I say, although it was routine, there was always something going on and there was always some excitement. And I say again, because it was a holding operation, there were very few people knew we were even there. But I know there were soldiers being hit every day. We were having casualties all the time—snipers, skirmishing activities.[57]

For example, on October 13 the Germans suddenly appeared at the gendarme caserne in Sospel to recover matériel formerly belonging to the Italian army. They found little as the police had long since handed the bounty over to the maquis.[58]

Due south of Sospel was Castillon, another massive fortification along the Maginot Line. The fortress was held by two companies of German soldiers. Within range of the Allied fleet, Castillon was a tempting target for naval gunfire as light 75-mm. field howitzers were completely ineffective against the fort's masonry. In turn, the defenders employed automatic weapons, grenade launchers, and mortars to good advantage against repeated advances by the FSSF. One intelligence report warned of the Germans employing a "Rollbombe" developed on the Russian front, consisting of 40–50 pounds of concrete, wood, and wire netting encasing explosives ignited by a fuse upon arriving within enemy lines. Indeed, American combat engineers clearing a landing strip at the Nice airfield found a similar device consisting of a Teller antitank mine attached to two wooden hemispheres to roll downhill.[59]

During lulls in the naval barrage, ambulances drove down the road from Sospel and into Castillon. Riding on their axles, the vehicles appeared heavily laden. Upon departing, the same conveyances were obviously lighter. Refugees from Sospel reported that the Germans were using medical transport to haul supplies. The senior American officer[60] opted to warn the citadel commander before opening fire on the ambulances. He lobbed a dozen mortar shells into the fort with messages addressed to the lieutenant in German, demanding that he stop misusing Red Cross vehicles. The traffic continued as before. About the same time, the French Red Cross in Menton undertook to negotiate for removal of the civilians. Mademoiselle Giselle Fraissinet, chief of the office, walked up the mine-strewn road to the fort to speak with its commander, but he would not agree to the release and denied violating the Geneva Convention. It was only days later that the Germans finally freed 70 inhabitants, all elderly, women, and children.[61]

In early October, Mlle. Fraissinet tried to free the residents of Sospel. The situation there was dire as heavy Allied bombardment had killed 687 civilians, 700 homes were destroyed or damaged, the hospital had been hit by a white phosphorous shell on September 11 and burned to the ground, and no food or medical supplies were being received. Rations had shrunk to the starvation level of 1¾ ounces of bread daily with the same pittance of meat on a weekly basis.[62] Again, there was refusal. As weeks passed, only the dwindling garden harvests of July and August sustained the townsfolk huddled in caves. Their anxiety was heightened upon observing the forced relocation of more than 450 residents from the nearby village of Moulinet.[63]

Preceded by a white flag bearing a red cross and guarded by soldiers, a procession of men and women, old people and children from the hamlet moved slowly along the national road through Sospel. Families shared small carts to carry their belongings. One farm girl brought her cow which had to be left along the way. The cortege turned around at Col de Braus when 20 refugees were killed by American aircraft misidentifying the movement as hostile. A week later the evacuees were forced off the roadway once more. The 517th regimental journal for September 29 recorded, "Enemy horse-drawn and motor convoy observed moving from Moulinet to Sospel. Artillery fire placed on road, results unknown." Eventually, reaching Breil, 540 Moulinais were loaded onto a cattle train bound for Cuneo, where they remained until April 1945. Returning home months afterwards, the residents found buildings in ruins, corpses rotting in lofts, and belongings looted by marauding soldiers and the few townsfolk who had hidden in the hills.[64]

Due to the obstinacy of Sospel's town fathers, the Germans reluctantly accepted a group of elderly hostages in lieu of evacuating their village. The Wehrmacht may have been more lenient to the Sospellois, as the Moulinais were correctly suspected of having long supported the maquis with provisions.

Then, on October 27, news passed by word of mouth that the Germans were about to blow up bridges over the Bévéra, one dating from the eleventh century. Explosions after dark left civilians without potable water.[65]

On October 25–6 the Americans detected signs of apparent withdrawal. Outposts reported sounds of heavy motor movement. Scouts made no contact with the enemy the next night. Patrols cautiously entered Castillon the following day, encountered no resistance, and discovered that the fortress was abandoned. The next two days the enemy gave indications of more movement. Fourteen explosions erupted around Fort Barbonnet and another 20 were audible nearer the coast. Sending riflemen cautiously across the one remaining footbridge into Sospel on October 29, the Americans found the town clear of Germans. Engineer troops soon discovered that the enemy had left behind booby traps in redoubts and pillboxes and even on a 88-mm. artillery piece. Equally dangerous were over 100 duds found on paved roads, mostly lying flat although some burrowed into the asphalt.[66]

The liberators were not met by pretty *mesdemoiselles* with kisses, flowers, and wine as stereotyped by the misnomer "Champagne Campaign." With their buildings destroyed and no longer habitable, the survivors of Sospel had little to celebrate and no provisions to do so. The prefecture evacuated three-quarters of the inhabitants to Nice, with the American trucks returning with food for those who insisted on remaining in Sospel.

The hard work of clearing occupiers out of the back country had been accomplished by the complementary forces of Allied airmen and soldiers and Resistance irregulars. This partnership was also evident along the coast during liberation of the Riviera.

13
ဆၣၡ

Liberation of the Riviera

As Seventh Army headed north to chase the Germans out of the Rhône Valley, General Patch directed the 1st ABTF to relieve the 36th Division so it could join the push into Germany. General Frederick's old buddies in the FSSF were added to his command and given this assignment. He also received an order to establish a defensive line from the Estérel coastal ridge east of St. Raphaël to Fayence, 15 miles inland.

The swift breakout from the beachhead fanning out units from Avignon to Grenoble extended the Allied army's exposure to Italy. Even if the Germans did not dispatch forces through the Alpine passes for an attack, they could conceivably conduct ambushes to interrupt Seventh Army's lines of communication. Pushing to the Italian border would permit formation of a credible Alpine defense. Liberating Nice in the process had the political benefit of assuaging anger still deeply felt by Frenchmen in the Southeast over Mussolini's "stab in the back" in 1940. A historian of the US Navy interpreted Patch's intentions as "more psychological than military, although harbor facilities at Nice would no doubt be useful."[1]

The war plan originally assigned responsibility for protecting the right flank to French Army B. After its successes at Toulon and Marseille, however, de Lattre insisted on joining the march toward Germany. The only major uncommitted command was the 1st ABTF. Devers later explained, "We put them over there because Frederick was a commander I could trust, and he took it over, organized it with very little confusion. But there would have been if I hadn't had the right people."[2]

Beyond the slopes of the Estérel, the next natural line of defense to the east was along the River Var, running north and south into the Mediterranean. When the BBC broadcast "Nancy has a stiff neck" signaling execution of Plan Red, once again summoning the Resistance to action, the maquis forced surrender of the few concentrations of German troops remaining in the high country and supported uprisings in Peille, Gourdon, and other perched villages. On August 16, Sapin and Gunn in regimental kilt formed a convoy of two motorcycles and a Citroën and headed for the Americans to convince them to push on to the Var.

They found Frederick camped outside Fréjus and recounted their trip from 50 miles north on the Route Napoléon without seeing one German or firing a single shot. Sapin explained that the entire area north of a line from Fayence through Grasse and Vence to the Var was liberated and that it was possible to advance uncontested to within a few miles of Nice.[3] At first Frederick refused to budge, citing his orders to remain in place. Contending that Frederick's instructions did not take into account the results obtained by the Resistance, Sapin convinced the general to consult with Patch, still billeted on a ship offshore even though his headquarters had moved into Saint-Tropez. Patch was not uncomfortable with the advance on Grasse and Cannes as he had obtained access to the ULTRA decryption of Wehrmacht orders on August 17, directing Army Group G to withdraw from the South of France. Furthermore, there was no indication the enemy would enter France from Italy but rather solidify its defense on the heights along the border.[4] But Patch told Frederick to verify first the information he had received. Consequently, an escort of armored jeeps followed Sapin and Gunn without incident to the confluence of the Rivers Var and Vésubie at Plan-du-Var where the GIs turned around and went back to reassure their commanding general.

Along the coast marched the 509th Parachute Infantry Battalion of the 1st ABTF. On the far left were the 550th Airborne Infantry Battalion and the 551st Parachute Infantry Battalion. In the back country in between maneuvered the 517th Parachute Regimental Combat Team and the main body of the FSSF. An engineer company transported supplies in captured enemy trucks and other vehicles. At times, soldiers relied on mules, carts, and gazogène conveyances. Having transitioned from an airborne to a ground mission, the artillery battalion commander had particular difficulty moving his 75-mm. pack howitzers without adequate transportation. The artillerists soon began using whatever conveyances could be found to displace their guns to positions already occupied by riflemen, and subsequent shuttles brought up ammunition. The foot soldiers eventually covered the 60–70 miles over rugged Riviera terrain.[5]

Fayence

Liberation of the hilltop town of Fayence was a classic example of the adage that success has many parents. American soldiers and the OSS, French maquis and British paratroopers played roles of varying import, and each took credit without always giving recognition to their fellow actors.

The drama began when elements of the 517th and the British 2nd Independent Parachute Brigade floated to earth 12 miles northeast of the intended drop zone. Their landings were spread out across rocky foothills in the Var from Seillans eastward through Fayence to Tourrettes-sur-Loup and Callian. In one unit of 480 men, 35 injured paratroopers stayed behind and 50 others were so scattered they could not join the main body in time when it formed up and headed toward Frederick's designated assembly area. A second group of 60 Americans, including a dozen men hurt landing, along with medics to care for them, gathered around Tourrettes. They were soon joined by 80 British paratroopers under Major J. A. Blackwood, also dropped off-target near Fayence. The maquis reported more injured troops clustered north of the town that stretcher parties carried back to a partisan hospital now under Resistance control.[6]

Starting out toward Le Muy, Blackwood and more than 100 soldiers sighted a convoy of 15 enemy vehicles being held up by 25 Britons and Americans. The parachutists hurried ahead and opened fire on 60–70 Germans with 81-mm. and 60-mm. mortars and a light machinegun. The attack damaged several trucks, caused a dozen casualties, and scattered the opposition. A handful of prisoners were turned over to the maquis.[7]

Another contest was playing out at Callian where maquisards were engaged in a firefight with Wehrmacht troops. After scattered groups of Americans joined in, the enemy gave up and close to 50 men laid down their arms. Led by the maquis, other GIs teamed up with British comrades to blow up bridges and harass the Germans in any way possible. Wounded were cared for at Seillans and the monastery at Montauroux.

German defenses positioned around Fayence had come under command of a Major Turnov who was stranded at Saint-Raphaël by the invasion. He collected 200 men and various 20-mm. anti-aircraft pieces, cleared Allied fighters from the immediate area, and burrowed into the old fortress of La Roche overlooking Fayence. On August 20, advance units of the 517th began arriving south of the town and quickly responded to firing from La Roche with their own artillery. That evening a maquisard reported that the Germans wanted to discuss surrender terms. A couple soldiers from the 517th had made contact with Lieutenant W. C. Hanna of OSS Team Sceptre, who sent a message informing the enemy commander that he would be surrendering to American troops if he came out peacefully. Turnov's representative arrived in the Red Cross vehicle belonging to a woman who was a Resistance leader in Fayence. During a three-hour meeting in a house near the fort, Hanna's report stated that he told the German that Allied paratroopers were massing for an all-out assault. His bluff was reinforced by periodic shellfire. Lieutenant Colonel Seitz remembered sending a message, "Surrender or I'll blast you out of town." The reply declared he couldn't do it "with those peashooters," referring to the Americans' pack 75-mm. artillery. Seitz ended his account by pointing out that when his guns hit the German ammunition dump, surrender took place the next morning. After stacking their weapons outside, 184 defenders emerged with hands held high. The Fayence locale was thereby secured on August 21.[8]

Everywhere the GIs went, people emerged from their homes to welcome the liberators. One rustic outside Grasse recalled encountering a soldier in a jeep who gave him a box of K rations and, with tears in his eyes, the Frenchman concluded his account by remembering that he had had nothing to eat for some time.[9]

Approaching Grasse, the Americans proceeded with caution. The town was headquarters of the 148th Division, with well-stocked supply dumps. Heavily fortified not long before, its artillery had included an 88-mm. anti-aircraft gun. Rumor put the strength of its defense anywhere between two brigades and two divisions, but fresh reports from locals indicated that only about 2,000 troops remained and they were pulling out. A soldier in the 517th remembered his platoon being led through the night toward Grasse by a civilian armed with a .22 caliber pistol. One regiment circled around to attack from the north while another came in from the south. Entering the town without opposition on August 24, the GIs could not help but notice the thick smell of factories making perfume essence from hillsides of flowers growing in the region. The liberators soon learned that a column of German troops had already withdrawn under fire from cannon captured and manned by maquisards on a nearby prominence. Frederick transferred his headquarters to Grasse the day following its liberation, and the town soon became a collecting point for the bodies of American soldiers killed in fighting along the coast.[10]

These were small unit operations at their best, the exact type of combat for which paratroopers were well suited. Yet the trek through the countryside behind the Riviera coast in late August was a grueling experience. The going was slowed by destroyed bridges and roadblocks, at times covered by machinegun and sniper fire. Land mines and booby-trapped blockhouses presented additional hazards.[11] Catching up with the enemy was difficult for invaders with few organic vehicles.

A Canadian newspaperman who accompanied his compatriots in the FSSF expressed awe at their endurance:

> I have seen them start marching with full packs under a broiling sun, trudge all afternoon along a dirty, dusty road, or throughout the forests of Southern France, in order to reach the starting line at nightfall, so they could fight.
>
> I have seen them fight for 60 hours straight to capture a town, then still have enough energy left to help the townspeople celebrate their liberation in an all-day party before they moved forward again at night.[12]

Mougins, between Grasse and Cannes, was found to be clear of enemy combatants, although the hospital was full of their wounded. Valbonne and

Opio behind Antibes were also deserted by the Wehrmacht. At times the GIs found souvenirs of their adversaries, unreadable Russian names left written on signposts by impressed soldiers.[13]

Arriving at Biot three miles north of Antibes late on August 24, the invaders found another town void of Germans. The welcome for the American and Canadian soldiers was in the grand Gallic manner. A delegation consisting of the mayor and prominent citizens wearing frock coats and silk hats stood before the *hôtel de ville*. In this instance, indigenous combatants from the FFI in berets and brassards bearing the croix de Lorraine gathered on one side and a group of FTP fighters with Stens huddled separately. The mayor greeted the commanding officer in French, or perhaps halting English, whereupon the Americans and town dignitaries climbed to an iron balcony overlooking the square so everyone could see and cheer their liberators. A variation of this ritual occurred again and again along the coast.[14]

Cannes

The Cannois realized that something was afoot at 11.00 p.m. on August 14 when the groans of repeated air squadrons sounded overhead, followed by series of explosions. According to the municipal log, bombs first fell on the city in boulevard d'Italie (now rue de la République) shortly after midnight.[15] Detonations persisted throughout the night. Bombers were also striking the Iles de Lérins in the bay in front of Cannes where German batteries were set up and the heights of Croix des Gardes and Mougins, again targeting gun emplacements. The next day, the Allied navy including the French battleship *Lorraine* began firing 340-mm. shells at the blockhouse at the Palm Beach casino on Cap de la Croisette. The inhabitants' joy at the thought of liberation was tempered by fear generated by the inferno erupting all around them. No one moved through the streets, giving the feeling of a deserted city.

The German occupiers of Cannes were quick to learn of the landing outside Saint-Raphaël. Their most visible reaction was to blow up quai Saint Pierre running along the west side of the port. Curious residents had earlier wondered why manhole covers had been added to the harbor's sewer system. They later learned that barrels of explosives had been implanted and connected to a detonation system. In late afternoon of D-Day, more than 20 explosions hurled debris high into the sky, geysers of stones falling everywhere as thick black smoke filled the air. Buildings facing the piers were turned into rubble. Tremors reverberated across a wide area.

A more sinister response would later become known. The Gestapo had been utilizing Villa Montfleury in a residential quarter for interrogation and torture. Anxiety among the agents heightened as the cannonade west of the

Estérel continued throughout August 15. In the afternoon the secret police piled up and burned files. As darkness was falling, guards began assembling the dozen prisoners in a large underground cell. For an unknown reason, one woman was released. Remarkably, another captive saw an opportunity to flee up a staircase, ran through the garden, grabbed a bicycle, and peddled away through a hail of bullets. Gestapo agents then quickly emptied their weapons at the remaining hostages who collapsed on the floor in a pool of blood. Again, by a miracle, two captives survived the executions and provided an account of what transpired. The eight martyrs included one woman and the former mayor of Vallauris, all arrested in neighboring towns as members of the MUR.[16] One of the murderers was arrested in 1945, condemned to death, and executed in Grasse.

By August 16, people began speculating why the liberators had not arrived. German troops seemed to be withdrawing and certainly the Allies could not be far away. Optimism had overcome the initial fright, but now concerns about obtaining food returned as a prime concern.[17] In the days that followed, authorities restricted circulation in the streets. An exception was made for three hours in the morning when residents looking for provisions could move quietly along the walls of buildings, but stopping anywhere was forbidden. Anyone outside during curfew hours would be shot. Detonations multiplied as Allied barrages targeted every military installation. The railway tunnel at La Bocca was hit three times, killing civilians taking refuge there. A pair of cruisers and two other ships passed regularly in front of Cannes conducting reconnaissance and at times emitted artificial smoke to obstruct firing from shore batteries. USS *Nashville* launched shells toward Vallauris and other targets behind the beaches.[18] Naval gunfire hit the popular Forville market one morning, wounding numerous shoppers, 15 mortally. Readily visible from the sea, the *hôtel de ville* suffered extensive damage as did numerous large villas.

Miniconi tried with mixed success to hold the members of his FTP in check, forbidding them to carry arms until ordered to rise up and take action. In preparation, his wife agreed to prepare 650 armbands in blue, white, and red with the croix de Lorraine overprinted to identify the wearers to the Allies and, hopefully, protect them from execution as spies or terrorists if captured. Obtaining colored material was almost impossible without divulging its purpose and so, thanks to a milliner who located some prewar dyes, precious sheets and pillow cases offered by housewives were transformed into brassards.[19]

A communiqué to the Resistance from Free French Headquarters in Algiers, dated July 25, detailed a "Plan of Occupation and Protection to be used in Case of Departure by Occupation Troops." Among other guidance, it specified occupying vital public service installations, such as water, gas, electricity, and railway; keeping watch and protecting food stores, refrigeration plants, gasoline dumps, and banks, by force if necessary; searching premises occupied by the Germans and their collaborators; arresting all fascists who remained, military or civilian; and keeping order in the streets to include shooting looters caught in the act.[20]

The 509th Parachute Infantry Battalion commander recalled looking down at the city of Cannes from a prominence and trying to figure out how to attack it. Herbert Mathews of the *New York Times* joined him and said, "You see that building over there? That's the Hôtel Carlton. It's just not only the best hotel in France, it's the best hotel in the world, and I would be much obliged if you don't do anything to wreck it." The promise was made and when they arrived, the Americans found the building tightly sandbagged but with its full complement of waiters on hand. "We had many and many a happy time thereafter at the Hôtel Carlton," the commander concluded his vignette.[21]

On August 23 the MUR decided to make contact with the approaching Americans. Two popular members of the Resistance, Francis Tonner and Henri Bergia, ventured forth, found some GIs, and began leading them toward Cannes. The party halted at the River Siagne on a plain west of the city. German soldiers, initially unaware of their presence, were clearly visible on the other bank, but the paratroopers' orders were to stop there. After an hour they were spotted by the enemy. A platoon leader recalled:

> Then we took the heaviest casualties I have ever been subject to throughout the war [...] even in the Bulge or in the Elbe River crossing. The Germans really gave us an unbearable shelling with their mortars and their heavy 155 millimeters [...] whatever they had. This lasted for a little over an hour, during which time I lost all of my squad leaders killed, and had about one third of the platoon wounded. We accomplished nothing. We just lay there and took casualties until it was over.[22]

The first shell killed Tonner and Bergia. Tonner had headed the team that recovered and stored ordnance sent from Britain and led numerous sabotage missions and ambushes.

What took place in Cannes that night is the stuff of movies. As FTP leader, Miniconi learned that the Gestapo was abandoning Montfleury. The Wehrmacht had already withdrawn from behind the Gestapo headquarters in the Hôtel Gallia. The Resistance knew that the Germans planned to destroy the *hôtel de ville*, palace of justice, records bureau, post office, and hotels along the Croisette. It would later be discovered that 600 explosives totaling three tons had been planted at various locations. The Hôtel Carlton alone had 50 canisters, each with its own detonator. In desperation, Miniconi sent a message to Colonel Erich Schneider, the garrison commander, asking to meet him at Taverne Royale. Taking a big risk by identifying himself as the notorious local leader of the Resistance, Miniconi gave the German a letter signed "A Group of French Patriots" that asked that this pointless devastation not take place. In return, the Resistance would allow the German troops to withdraw without opposition. The request appealed to honor, referring to the difference between the professional Wehrmacht and the Nazi Gestapo and arguing that the targeted buildings had no military value but were important for ongoing civilian life. In the early morning hours of August 24, Schneider led the Frenchman into the cellar of the Hôtel Splendid and indicated the master control for the detonations. Wehrmacht soldiers marched out of Cannes without incident, and four days later Schneider was executed by a firing squad in Nice for dereliction of duty.[23]

During the night, 350 Poles, Czechs, Rumanians, and even a few Germans gave themselves up to civil authorities. The next morning the lieutenant commanding the Cannes gendarmerie was sent to La Napoule to inform an American colonel there that the Germans were departing, assure him that the city was firmly under control of the Resistance, and settle on a time for the Allies' entry. At 5.00 p.m., the Americans arrived in a triumphant parade through the streets, many riding in jeeps or atop tank destroyers. "I'll never forget that day as long as I live," exclaimed the platoon leader who had taken such heavy losses outside town. "The people were really joyful, tears were running down their faces, the girls were kissing everybody [...] People were throwing flowers at us [...] just the way it's supposed to be."[24]

Antibes

August 24 was also the date Antibes was liberated, not in the manner often envisioned—combat involving Allied troops—but in a fashion repeated along the Côte d'Azur, by the indigenous Resistance. In a locale reduced by this time to 18,000 residents, the Antibois underground consisted of 20 or so branches of larger movements with at most 20 or 30 members each, plus a dozen small cells of protestors. Among the more effective groups were those organized at places of employment—postal workers, railroad men, shipbuilders, mechanics, and police. The leader of the FFI sector in Antibes and chief of its headquarters component was 54-year-old Auguste Vérine whose nom de guerre was "Gustel." The native Antibois recorded his recollections of these times in 1951, providing a seemingly credible history of the liberation upon which much of this narrative is based.[25]

Since the debarkation, Gustel had lost contact with his superior, Commandant Sapin. As days passed and Allied forces drew near on land and sea, pressure naturally mounted to take action. On August 23, Gustel decided to act. This was a risky move. An uprising could well focus the wrath of the

Germans on his community. Gustel figured that he could count at most on 300 patriots in Antibes, plus 60 men from nearby Golfe-Juan and Vallauris and no more than 20 in Biot. Their weapons were even less impressive—15 sub-machineguns, 20 or so revolvers, and some rifles with a scant supply of ammunition and explosives. On the plus side, enemy morale appeared low. The Resistance could count on 20,000 liters of stolen fuel surreptitiously stored in oil drums in a city garage serving as a depot for German vehicles. This was an especially important resource as the main petrol storage area behind the train station was struck that day by an Allied bomber and would continue burning throughout the night.

After dark, Gustel gave instructions to the heads of the various groups. Every means should be employed to prevent destruction of facilities vital to the city. The passive defense program, approved by the occupiers, would be used as the subterfuge to circulate and maintain coordination. Gustel set up his headquarters on the Route de Grasse near the central fire station and the Château Salé where General Napoléon Bonaparte had once housed his family.

The following morning different groups commandeered the main post office, electric plant, rail station, and docks. A neighborhood band of résistants took control of a key intersection in Croix Rouge on the north side of Antibes. German reaction was spotty. The PTT [Postal, Téléphone et Télégraph] office in Juan-les-Pins was destroyed, as were communication lines and the bridge crossing the River Brague to the east. Blockhouses on Cap d'Antibes, in Saramartel, and at Sarrazine near the cemetery on chemin de Saint Claude all remained manned and battle-ready.

Decorated with flags everywhere, the city quickly took on a festive air. At 10.00 a.m., Gustel held what he thought would be a clandestine meeting with principal leaders of the underground at Brasserie Jules on a corner across from the bus station. The intended secrecy was for naught, with a crowd outside the café making a great deal of noise and demanding to take over the *hôtel de ville*. Many of the underground chiefs expressed their support and, even though the armed partisans were occupied elsewhere, Gustel reluctantly agreed. Five hundred brassards, fashioned by three women working all night in Juan-les-Pins, were available for distribution. In addition to the croix de Lorraine, they displayed the letter "A" for Antibes. Singing "La Marseillaise" while marching in a long file, the townsfolk reached the *hôtel de ville* opposite the Provençal market to find it deserted. Only the mayor was seated behind his desk on the first floor. Politely presenting himself to Jules Grec as head of the FFI, Gustel introduced the members of the incoming CLL named by Algiers. A pharmacist took over the duties as mayor. Gustel asked city employees to continue to work for the people of Antibes. Residents came forward to offer their services, many well intentioned and others trying to cloud memories of their sympathies during the occupation.

One after another, German soldiers surrendered and military depots fell into the hands of the Resistance. Other public buildings were occupied. The entire gendarmerie was accepted by the new regime. Arrests proceeded, as needed, with a uniformed policeman accompanying each FFI member. The blockhouses surrendered the next morning after some of their defenders slipped away during the night. Three German non-commissioned officers from the Garoupe d'Antibes were captured on the open sea in a small boat rigged and provisioned to reach the Italian coast.

During the afternoon, Gustel received repeated reports that the fascists were returning to retake Antibes and Biot. A column of regular Wehrmacht troops and Miliciens was advancing along the national road from Cagnes to occupy the Biot station and take control of the River Brague. Immediately Gustel dispatched all available armed men to counter the threat. He also sent a messenger to Cannes asking the FFI commander there for help, if possible in unison with the Americans. Erection of barricades began on major roads leading into Antibes. Soon a van full of Miliciens traveling at high speed nearly entered a minefield opposite the Biot station before making a quick U-turn in front of the FFI defense. Next, a strong German patrol stormed by, going as far as the Restaurant Bonne Auberge where it encountered an ambush and responded with machinegun fire. As the defenders received reinforcements from the FFI and gendarmes, they succeeded in pushing the enemy back at the cost of two dead and four wounded. The enemy squad and another truck loaded with troops withdrew to a small fortification between the Rivers Brague and Loup. The blockhouse eventually surrendered, yielding 11 prisoners and one dead soldier. It was the single serious clash in the liberation of Antibes.[26]

A courier arrived in the early evening to announce the first American soldiers rolling along Route Nationale 7 from Cannes. Once more townsfolk displayed flags that had been hidden when the Germans threatened. Wanting to ensure the city was clear of the enemy, a detachment of a half-dozen jeeps continued up the Route de Grasse looking for high ground to survey the environs. At the intersection with chemin des Terriers, the convoy encountered 12-year-old Bobby Chiapello. Raised by an English mother, the youth could speak the GIs' language and led them to a height since obliterated where the toll booth now stands on the autoroute heading west.[27] Meanwhile, the appearance of Yanks on tanks met with exuberance and celebration well into the night. Nine local men had died that day defending the city, but for most Antibois this was a time for rejoicing.

The following day was memorable for several reasons. In the afternoon, artillery shells began raining down on the town center targeting the FFI headquarters among other places. Then, a general sent by Algiers appeared accompanied by other officers in uniform. They were the first French military seen by the populace in well over a year and were welcomed with special fervor. That night Antibes suffered a more violent artillery attack although, fortunately, from small-caliber guns near Villeneuve-Loubet. The city streets were empty and only material damage resulted. These were the first and last bombardments of Antibes during the war.

On August 25, US Army intelligence reported that the enemy had organized its defensive line along the River Loup with strong points at Villeneuve-Loubet, Cagnes, and Saint-Paul-de-Vence. Approximately 100 men were thought to be at each location. Antitank guns protected by machinegun stands were set up outside Villeneuve-Loubet. The Second Regiment of the FSSF was marching up the road toward the town when a mortar round hit the concrete pavement in the middle of the lead battalion, inflicting 17 casualties. Other regiments were sent to approach the stronghold from the north. One unit was unable to reach the river due to small-arms fire. After an exchange of artillery rounds the Americans tried to attack at dusk but found that the number of defenders had been underestimated. Gunshots continued throughout the night.

One GI remembered fording the river and entering the town early the next morning. As the invaders made their way down the main street, it appeared that the Germans had withdrawn, for residents came out of their houses to see the Americans and relieve their bladders. Suddenly rifle fire erupted from camouflaged foxholes covering the Loup as the defenders turned around to confront the intruders. The Forcemen responded with hand grenades, and by 6.00 a.m. the town had fallen, with 73 Germans captured and 100 more killed or wounded. The town doctor was busy all day, while his wife served wine and brandy to the Americans.[28]

As the perimeter along the Loup was pierced and the FFI began harassing their defenses, the Germans pulled back, first, to the Var. On August 27, the day the Americans finally reached the river, the Wehrmacht crossed to the other side, abandoning Cagnes and Saint-Laurent-du-Var. Allied army headquarters was receiving reports that the coastal guns in the Nice area were being dismantled and faced inland to defend the waterway. The FSSF set up its command post in Saint-Paul at the Colombe d'Or, a small inn now renowned for exhibiting a museum-quality collection of impressionist art by struggling painters who patronized it between the wars. The US commander and staff signed the register immediately below the signatures of Fretter-Pico and his entourage who had checked out hurriedly the previous evening.[29]

Nice

The Calvary for the Resistance in Alpes-Maritimes was truly August 15, when cold-blooded murders in Nice were added to summary executions in Cannes.

News of the Allied landing traveled quickly to Nice, bringing joy to the populace and, according to a report from London, imposition of martial law in Alpes-Maritimes.[30] The realization dawned on Germans that this was the beginning of the end of their occupation. Incarcerated in Nouvelles-Prisons in Nice were 21 inmates, all weak and badly disfigured from malnourishment and repeated torture. These members of the Resistance, ages 17 to 57, included three women—couriers Hélène Vagliano and Esther Poggio, and Marie Reschkonski of the Polish network Marine.

Hélène had been arrested on July 29 and tortured repeatedly at Villa Montfleury in Cannes and Villa Trianon in Nice. Her parents were arrested the same day, as the Nazis tried to make her talk by their presence. At one point Hélène had a chance to whisper to her mother:

> I would never have been arrested without a denunciation. I had burned all my papers immediately after the arrest of R.C. Without that there was no proof against me. I have seen her file; she told everything, even the things that no one knew except she and I. She spoke of two letters that I had given her. It's serious, very serious, as well as the information on clandestine routes to Spain. She provided names. They did not hit her; she talked immediately. I believed she was my friend. I had such confidence in her. Oh! Mama!"[31]

Hélène's final act of heroism was to sign a declaration demanded by her torturers in exchange for the release of her parents. She had informed her mother that she was going to make the Boche run all over France by inventing names and identifying people who had already left the country. Moved once again in Nice to the Nouvelles Prisons, Hélène was locked in her cell on August 15 when she heard an unknown voice outside the jail break the silence, "The Allies have landed at Fréjus." She is said to have exclaimed, "My mission is over. Now nothing, nothing left can hurt me."[32]

Realizing full well the fate that awaited if the extent of their cruelty became known, the Gestapo took immediate action to eliminate their victims. At 3.00 p.m., soldiers pushed the captives into a truck which headed not in the direction of yet another jail, but to Ariane in the city's northern outskirts. Waiting on the bank of the River Paillon was a squad of secret police who lined up the captives facing the water in front of a mass of stone, and sprayed them with sub-machineguns. These murders here and in Cannes followed a Nazi practice exercised in Caen and Rennes, among other French cities, where departing members of the SS massacred their prisoners before the liberators arrived.

Evacuations, deportations, and voluntary departures had reduced the population of Nice to 150,000 inhabitants. Now it was almost isolated, bridges over the Var destroyed and fighting in the back country interrupting receipt of produce. There was no bread in the shops. The prefect asked that Nice be declared an open city, but Fretter-Pico was quick to respond that for military reasons that would never be done. Instead, a curfew went into effect on August 18 from 8.00 p.m. until 6.00 a.m., 9.00–11.00 a.m., and 2.00–6.00 p.m.[33] Public transportation stopped. Pressure mounted to take action against the Boche.

The newly formed Comité Départemental de Libération (CDL) dominated by the Front National had elected a socialist lawyer as president, Alex Roubert of Antibes. Recognizing his own lack of power to exercise leadership over the committee's leftist majority, on the eve of the landing Roubert left Nice to meet with a team of Allied soldiers assembled at Valberg. His successor was a small businessman representing the communists and therefore compliant with the committee's wishes. Radical elements of the Nice Resistance could not wait for de Gaulle's MLN to order an uprising. Instead, the communist CGT occupied the gas works, bus station, rail depot and Establishments Michel at Saint-Roch, and the printing plant of *L'Eclaireur de Nice*. A worker recalled his instructions while on guard duty: "Prevent at any cost the Germans entering the factory to blow it up."[34] On August 20 the CGT called for a general strike. Two days later the Resistance seized arms stored in a depot belonging to the gendarmerie in the Saint-Roch quarter. Résistants took turns approaching workers at the train station, transport depot, and gas works to recruit for the recently activated patriotic Milice.

A small aircraft began appearing over Nice, flying at rooftop level to survey what was going on in the city. The hum of its engine recalled the biplanes of World War I. It quickly acquired the designation "phantom airplane" along with invectives when the pilot dropped small bombs on seemingly random buildings. The pilot's mission was to spot and obliterate violations of the blackout. Twelve civilians were killed and 19 wounded in the process.[35]

Finally, on August 25, the CDL issued a summons for the populace to join other departments across France in driving out the Nazi oppressors. Niçois were told to arm themselves, join the underground, sabotage German communications, seize caches of food, destroy supply depots, and "slaughter" the assassins in the Milice and PPF. German artillery booming from Mont Alban and Mont Vinaigrier just outside the city attracted Allied bombers that ignited forest fires which raged all night, impregnating Nice with the smell of smoke.

On August 27 the leader of the MOI declared that it would launch an insurrection against the fascists the next morning. The Front National and FTP joined in the preparations, while Combat and the National Resistance Movement of Prisoners of War and Deportees, both oriented to the right, initially refused to participate without approval from Algiers. Other FFI groups did not hesitate to take part, realizing abstention would be held against them in politics following liberation.[36] Ten thousand handbills announcing a call to arms were posted everywhere.

Only 50 members of the local FTP and 60 from the Nice MOI could be counted upon, although pleas had been sent to outlying maquis and support was expected from the police. An ordnance inventory disclosed a couple of machineguns, 20 sub-machineguns, and 40 carbines, plus hunting rifles, pistols, revolvers, and some grenades taken from the enemy.[37] Despite the departure of the Gestapo, Miliciens, and non-combative administrative personnel, approximately 1,500 garrison soldiers still remained in Nice. The Resistance would eventually oppose them with 350 or so men, of whom a good number came from the MOI maquis at Peille.

Monday, August 28, began well before daylight at the Renault garage on boulevard Gambetta where the available arms were issued. The supply of weapons grew as the morning progressed. At dawn the FFI set up a control point with three youths and a sub-machinegun in an unfinished blockhouse to control Place Gambetta (now Place de la Libération) at rue Gambetta, rue Cessole, and boulevard Joseph Garnier. Other major intersections were surveyed from makeshift outposts. Barricades went up here and there. A Wehrmacht lieutenant and two non-commissioned officers were killed on the corner of rue de la Buffa and rue Dalpozzo. At first, Resistance fighters discouraged civilians from leaving their homes, then began attacking German vehicles, collecting Mausers and other pistols, grenades, and even a full-sized machinegun. As an insurgent exclaimed, "With sub-machineguns it was still guerrilla warfare, with machineguns it was war."[38] One military truck hauled munitions, others pulled trailers or were half-tracks, and all carried occupants with weapons to be confiscated upon death or surrender.

Soon, police and members of the FTP took control of Hospital Pasteur and other public buildings. Insurgents fired from rooftops, doorways, and behind trees, laying siege to the headquarters of the fascists and the PPF, bunkers, blockhouses, and batteries on nearby hills. Men and women were directed to occupy windows and rooftops and hurl rocks and other objects down on troops passing by. Some Polish soldiers were quick to hand over their arms and, in one instance, offered to fight alongside the Resistance. The Germans attacked the Renault garage, first with grenades and then with a mortar battery set up in front. Defenders replied with machineguns, dispersing the assailants and recovering the short-barreled cannon. As street-fighting progressed into the afternoon, the urban guerrillas fired more judiciously, for their ammunition was running low.[39]

The Wehrmacht stronghold on the Château high above Old Nice opened up with machineguns and mortars, killing more than a dozen persons in just a few hours. Hospital Saint-Roch began filling with casualties. In late morning, Feldkommandant Hellmuth Nickelmann called the prefecture to warn that in order to permit his garrison's orderly withdrawal he would launch fire bombs on the old town and city center if attacks by insurgents did not cease. Receiving no reply, Nickelmann ordered the barrage to intensify, raining more shells down on the buildings below. At one point Polish artillerymen refused to fire upon civilian targets, were immediately replaced, and the cannonade resumed. A successful Wehrmacht counterattack returned control of Saint-Roch depot to the Germans, indicating an intention to use the railway there to redeploy troops to Sospel and the Alps.

At 11.00 that morning the occupiers had received a telephonic dispatch from Fretter-Pico: "In the course of a retreat, all units should take in the city of Nice or in suspicious localities hostages whom they should place on their vehicles to prevent terrorist fire."[40] Not long thereafter the communist militia company from the waterworks captured a Wehrmacht colonel carrying documents which included plans for pulling out of Nice, with maps showing routes and phases of withdrawal. These papers were taken first to the FTP headquarters where they were translated into French and then, according to two departmental leaders, conveyed to the American headquarters in Grasse.[41]

By mid-afternoon, Germans in convoys and on foot could be seen on the upper, middle, and lower corniches heading toward Italy. The order for complete withdrawal was received at 6.30 p.m. Artillerymen left the Château. A column formed consisting of seven trucks and 14 cars each armed with sub-machineguns, plus another vehicle carrying 15 machineguns. Passing the port, the retiring defenders sank four ships and destroyed the lighthouse and 11 marine cranes. The quays, damaged by British bombing days before, were demolished by explosives about 7.00 p.m.[42] Two hours later the Allied fleet began shelling blockhouses along the Promenade des Anglais evacuated earlier in the day. After dark the last German units descended from the heights behind Nice via avenue de la Victoire, firing defensively at the windows of buildings they passed, and departed on the lower corniche.[43] Not to be overlooked is the additional destruction to infrastructure by the departing Germans and by prolonged combat by American soldiers supported by their air force and navy if the uprising in Nice had not accelerated the German retreat. The occupiers lost 25 dead and 105 prisoners, plus four Italian Blackshirts in the Nizza battalion who were executed. The insurgents counted their casualties as 27 killed and 280 wounded. The liberation of Nice resulted from three actions, more or less knowingly coordinated—an urban insurrection, the immediate threat of Allied troops, and nearby successes by competent maquis.

Toward midnight, the Resistance began to appreciate that the occupation had finally ended and that Niçois were masters of their own city once more. The next day, 10,000 résistants were in its streets. FFI patrols began making the first arrests of collaborators and clearing away all signs of the Germans and Vichy, most notably removing swastikas and posters picturing Maréchal

Pétain. The communist commandant sent a messenger to the Var to ask the Americans to take custody of the Wehrmacht prisoners. An envoy from the CGT went to Grasse to inform Frederick of the situation.

Frederick already had a good idea of what was going on. In addition to Geoffrey Jones, the OSS had a second agent in the area who spoke French fluently and was sending daily radio reports from Nice. On August 27 some operatives sent into the city returned bragging about ambushing a Wehrmacht staff car. They brought back the knapsack of one of the dead officers, which upon examination contained a field order with maps and overlays prepared that afternoon. Fretter-Pico warned, "Danger: Terrorists are every where. Do not go singly; only armed and in groups. In case of attack open fire immediately. During the withdrawal all troop units are to skirt the town of Nice in a wide circle, as attacks and ambushes from houses are to be contemplated at all times."[44] Frederick directed Jones to fly the documents to Patch, still headquartered on the coast. "I believe, because of that report, was why General Patch went up the Rhône," Jones later opined. "If Gen. Patch wasn't going up the Rhône, he decided going up much faster than he would've, because he wasn't worried about his right flank."[45]

Jones himself entered Nice before its liberation. Admiral Hewitt had asked for intelligence about the marine facilities there, because he needed repairs done as a result of "minor naval skirmishes" with torpedo boats. FFI sources reported that after dark five enemy torpedo boats took to the sea from the Nice port, returning to take refuge there during daylight while camouflaged under nets.[46] About that same time a courier who had earlier identified himself as a nephew of the officer of the port, crossed the lines eager to help. He was in his early twenties and wouldn't know what Hewitt needed to find out, so Jones accompanied the lad back into the city, first swimming across the Var, 20 feet wide at that point and barely over their heads. The uncle quickly produced maps and other needed information. Taking bicycles back toward the river, Jones suddenly heard a German truck approaching. The riders quickly turned around and pretended to be heading toward Nice. The driver stopped them, said they could not go into the city at night and, instead, drove them to the river. The next morning, Frederick was able to report to Hewitt the exact location of the anti-submarine net and how to operate it, the sentry tower which activated mines, where munitions were stored, water depths, and so on.[47]

GIs manning defenses at the river were not as relaxed. A French account relates that when told so on August 29, the Americans did not believe Nice had been liberated. They insisted on sending two men back with the Resistance fighters to confirm the German withdrawal. The emissaries made it as far as the neighborhood La Madeleine where they encountered the excitement of Niçois seeing Americans at last. Returning later to the river, one scout exclaimed, "Yes, libre, Nice. Good!" and fell down drunk.[48] That night, three other paratroopers slipped out of camp, snuck into the city, and met a German straggler who had enjoyed the good life there and led them to a place where 20–25 GIs had the same idea and were carousing all night long. Other veterans told similar tales of clandestine entry featuring wine, champagne, the American national anthem, "La Marseillaise," and lots of compliant women.[49]

Frederick received permission to take Nice that same day. It made sense to penetrate the Maritime Alps. Although the Germans held the defensive terrain by occupying old fortifications, this advantage was outweighed by the tactical necessity of re-establishing firm contact with the enemy lest they use their freedom of maneuver to amass a serious threat to Allied forces. Leaving a no-man's land 15-to-20 miles wide between the river and the Italian border would have created economic and political chaos. A critical food shortage had already developed, and Frederick could envision rioting, looting, and other civil disturbances on a scale detrimental to American prestige.

On August 30, elements of the 551st Parachute Infantry Battalion moved into the city on foot. The 512th Signal Company of the 1st ABTF carefully drove jeeps across the Var between ribbons of white engineer tape tied to stakes marking the passageway cleared of mines. The convoy proceeded down avenue de la Californie and rue de France, past balconies, windows, and shops adorned with flags. Reaching Place Masséna without firing a single shot, the troops received a tumultuous welcome by citizens pinned with little tricolore cockades, patrols proudly wearing the croix de Lorraine, and seemingly endless celebrations.[50]

While the Americans hesitated, a power struggle had unfolded between the communist and non-communist members of the Resistance and de Gaulle's government in Algeria. A designee of the CDL took the position of mayor. On the morning of August 29, the Front National requested that the acting prefect turn over his office to a leader of the CDL, firmly under communist control. The incumbent bowed and conceded. Only minutes later, Maurice Moyon, designated by de Gaulle to be prefect, arrived and installed himself in that post. A Republican with 30 years of government experience, including serving as prefect of l'Aube in 1936, Moyon had come to Nice earlier in the year to position himself to assume these duties immediately upon liberation. He had his work cut out for him. The CDL set up offices in the prefecture consisting of representatives of the Front National, Communist Party, and CGT; plus the French youth, committee of intellectuals, prisoners movement, women of France, and Socialist Party, all left-leaning; and, finally, the more conservative Gaullist National Liberation Movement, Combat, Catholic Movements of Resistance, Christian Union, and National Committee of Doctors. Up to half the CDL members in the entire Southeast were communist.[51]

Moyon faced an immediate problem in summary arrests and executions being carried out primarily by the FTP. Allied observers reported 1,000 arrests and as many as 100 executions by August 31. Another 1,000 apprehensions would occur before September 15. Half the detainees were women of Italian origin who were thought to have been in the pay of the Gestapo. Members of the Milice and PPF were also deemed guilty of treason with good cause. The new prefect tried mightily to channel punitive acts away from the Front National and into the administrative and judicial system.[52]

Lack of sufficient food was another critical problem. The National Aid had offered its customary free midday soup at several centers, but now stocks had run out. People were literally on the verge of starvation. What little produce could be obtained in that dry region was mainly shut off during the last days of the occupation. The city had only a single day's supply of flour. One resident remembered that it was September 2 before bakeries could distribute bread in the form of insipid white cake which customers devoured nonetheless.[53] Moyon announced that three boats with white four and corned beef were going to arrive at the Nice port, and potatoes would come overland from Basses-Alpes. It required some time, however, to clear the mines and wreckage from the harbor. Once this was done, the population could not understand why transport ships did not immediately sail in loaded with victuals.

Not surprisingly, perhaps, a black market developed between the public and Allied troops with access to seemingly limitless provisions. Each morning trucks stopped in the streets and at Place Masséna to auction food and cigarettes. Other goods lifted from ration dumps were sold privately in hotel rooms. Even medical supplies could be purchased from the Yanks. To try to dent this trafficking, the 1st ABTF published a directive that military rations, gasoline, or other military supplies found in civilian possession were to be confiscated. If the army struck a hard bargain, some shopkeepers kept pace by raising prices for American soldiers.[54]

An investigative team of military officers, two French and two American, appeared on August 31. They reportedly found the city in holiday spirits upon arrival but left that same evening in a more somber mood. The fact-finders reached three conclusions. First, the arrests and executions taking place in Nice were far more serious than reported from any other liberated city. Second, the key to public order was an adequate supply of flour, and at the time a daily ration of only 100 grams was possible in Nice. Third, Moyon impressed them as an excellent administrator. His efforts to bring the communist forces into line with the FFI were thought likely to succeed if second-line French troops replaced the undisciplined underground fighters, armed men standing around the city conveying the feeling that another uprising was about to erupt. Frederick jumped into this situation on September 3 by directing that all possible means be employed to demilitarize and disarm members of the Resistance. The joint delegation recommended that leadership from outside the city mediate differences between political factions. This approach had proven successful in Marseille with a stronger communist element than in Nice.[55]

The designee was Raymond Aubrac, a 30-year-old engineer educated at M.I.T. and Harvard whose Jewish parents perished at Auschwitz. A former leader of the movement Libération-Sud and then the AS and now a prominent figure in the Republic, he immediately arrived from Marseille to arbitrate a deteriorating situation. The resolution reached on September 2 was to replace Moyon with someone acceptable to the CDL. The mayor was also dismissed for having incurred the disfavor of local Resistance leaders by taking down the Soviet flag which was hanging at the prefecture alongside other flags of the United Nations.[56] His successor was a former primary school teacher who had been elected a communist deputy under the Front Populaire and had remained in prison during much of the occupation.

The public demonstration to celebrate liberation took place the next day. Résistants paraded in step to the beat of "La Marseillaise" and the "Internationale." French and Russian flags were prominent, as well as fewer numbers of smaller American and English colors. Two communist dailies, *Le Cri* and *Le Patriote Niçois*, heralded the event.

Putting an end to the pro-Vichy press was an important aim of the liberation. Soon after the debarkation, the CGT began to strike against the two Nice newspapers sanctioned by Vichy. Once the uprising erupted in the city, militant communists supported by editors, printers, and a group from the FTP took over *L'Eclaireur de Nice*. Two days later, formerly clandestine papers began appearing openly. *Le Patriote Niçois*, *Le Cri*, and its successor, *L'Aurore du Sud-Est*, were published on *L'Eclaireur* presses. *Combat* and *L'Etincelle*, the voice of the CGT, were produced at the former *Le Petit Niçois*. Differences of opinion over editorial policy evidenced dissension among the communists. Editors of *L'Aurore du Sud-Est* sought pluralist content to attract a large clientele. Communist Party leaders argued that a doctrinaire publication would circulate better. *Le Patriote Niçois* promoted the themes of unifying disparate political groups and promoting the program of the National Council of the Resistance. As time went on, however, the tone of this paper became more dogmatic.[57]

Before long, the Communist Party was publishing 12,000 exemplars of *Combat* and 8,000 of *L'Aurore du Sud-Est*, while the Front National produced 7,000 exemplars of *Le Patriote Niçois*. This compared with a daily run of 1,600 *L'Espoir de Nice*, the organ of the Socialist Party, which was not permitted to begin printing until September 11, and then only late in the afternoon. The ascendancy of the extreme left was aptly illustrated by posters with a large Vichy postage stamp bearing the image of Maréchal Pétain overprinted "R.F. Nice—28 août 1944—Front National."[58]

Nice was not permitted to proceed with general elections which Frederick was advised the communists awaited with great anticipation. Several regions in France remained under occupation and three million electors, including prisoners of war and deportees, were still away. Transitional leaders in Nice were frequently isolated from the provisional government in Paris, unable to receive instructions and at times out of control. Further impediments to an orderly administration were the shortage of police, a gendarmerie, and an armed force loyal to Paris.[59]

The American Occupation

Fortunately, Frederick was accepted by the various factions as the overall military commander. By September 5 he had set up headquarters at the Villa Alhambra on Cimiez heights, a favorite vantage point for dignitaries from Roman times to Queen Victoria, Leopold, King of the Belgians, and Henri Matisse. Because its security was enhanced by a surrounding wall, Jones occupied the former Afghanistan consulate, a nearby Gothic-style mansion called Belgrano, still standing on Boulevard Edouard VII. In a candid admission decades later, Jones exclaimed that no one seemed to know that he was actually deployed to the European Theater of Operations. "With all due respect to the OSS, which did a good job," he continued, "while all those fellows were running around in London in the ETO [headquarters] with arm holsters and trick guns and everything, we had nothing." Jones was, however, designated de Gaulle's military delegate to Alpes-Maritimes and the Var and the senior OSS officer in the Southeast, as he had earned a stellar reputation as a training officer at Massingham. The emissary did not customarily wear a uniform and, if so, one without insignia. Through camaraderie, not rank, information was gathered, he found.[60]

Frederick soon became involved in addressing the shortage of bread, for every Frenchman needs a baguette each day. He contacted Devers and requested a boatload of flour. Yet it was September 14 before the first Liberty ship arrived in the port of Nice. Frederick remembered that when the vessel carrying American wheat landed, a British naval officer was there taking credit for the delivery. One of Frederick's intelligence officers, however, recalled a different ending. Through police sources he learned that the communists put signs on the building distributing the flour: "You are now enjoying this wheat through the courtesy of the U.S.S.R."[61] Subsequent cargo vessels off-loaded gas, oil, coal, and other essentials, in addition to provisions for a starving populace.

On the other principal problem—retribution for what had occurred over four long years—Frederick tried to stay above the fray, believing that local politics were not his responsibility. But he had made it clear to the departmental prefect on September 3 that "He did not wish to be forced to call in the military to keep order." The new prefect assured him that matters were now under control.[62] That did not prevent streams of Frenchmen from mobbing Frederick's headquarters with accusations against their neighbors as being Nazi sympathizers, communists, or other perceived enemies of the state. The general coped with these pressures, in part, thanks to an unexpected resource.

Isabel Pell was an American woman living near Grasse when she came to the attention of the American army. Of medium height and sturdy build, Pell was described by Frederick as "normally attractive." A distinctive white streak at the fringe of her short, bobbed blonde hair quickly earned her the nickname among the French as "La Dame a la Meche [Strand] Blonde." While an artist living under house arrest in Puget-Théniers during the Italian occupation, she had hidden US soldiers and flyers and worked with the underground in the group François.[63]

Pell aided Frederick with his social calendar, being well informed to advise him who was reputable and who was not. Frederick was careful when he went out, almost always in an official capacity, not to allow himself to be placed in a compromising position involving politics, financial dealings, the black market, or sexual liaisons. Using Pell's contacts, Jones soon assembled a team of reliable agents, as well as a high-caliber staff. At its high point, Jones's operation in Nice utilized two GIs, 120 agents and 10–12 female interpreters each speaking two or three languages. Pell only wanted to wear an American uniform and would not accept pay. The French nationals did not insist on money either, just food, clothing, and a sense of doing something worthwhile. When not helping with intelligence collection, Pell often drove truckloads of canned vegetables, meat, and other army rations into the countryside to distribute to needy families. A photo taken in November 1944 at Puget-Théniers shows Pell wearing a double-breasted army overcoat and service cap at a ceremony naming a town square in her honor.[64]

The French Riviera was an exciting place for a soldier. Infantrymen bragged about bedding down in millionaires' unoccupied mansions. One veteran recalled settling in the drawing room of King Carol of Rumania's villa, complete with two grand pianos and lots of statuary.[65] The Germans had been using it so there seemed no reason not to continue occupancy. A battalion commander in the FSSF proudly occupied Averell Harriman's property just outside Menton. When Wehrmacht artillery shelling periodically severed his electrical service, he would call in civilian workmen and tell them to send the bill to Mackenzie King, the prime minister of Canada.[66] The command post of another battalion was the residence of an American heiress married to an Italian count, quarters that came complete with antiques and a cook who prepared haute cuisine for the GIs.[67]

No place defined the Riviera lifestyle, then or now, more than the Hôtel Negresco, a sumptuous watering hole on the Promenade des Anglais. Not long before, its windows along the seafront had been boarded up by the Germans, but now everything was wide open and the entire staff on duty, ready to serve American soldiers on a three-day pass in return for foodstuffs. Troopers brought in rations, took a bath upstairs, and then entered the dining room lit with crystal chandeliers to be served heated olive-drab cans presented on covered silver platters. On more than one occasion, Frederick observed a parachutist escorting a mademoiselle into the elevator to go up to the GI's room with their hands full of prepared K-rations.[68]

Clearing minefields left by the enemy was a common problem for the liberators up and down the coast. The textbook solution was ordering German prisoners of war to remove the explosives. Learning that the airfield at la Californie, then on the western edge of Nice, had been mined, Frederick was anxious to have it cleared. A Wehrmacht sergeant was identified as having laid the mines, and he was soon leading a squad of his compatriots in removing them. A platoon of US Army engineer troops also working at the airport reported deactivating 1,500 explosive devices, demolishing 13 flak towers and two pillboxes, and removing 3,000 feet of seawall erected as an obstacle to landing. Five GIs accidentally died in the process.[69]

Antibes was not so fortunate. The coastline there was infested with thousands of explosives. The FFI captured some German non-commissioned officers who knew their location. Drawings of the minefields turned up as well. But the information vanished as quickly as it had appeared, for American military authorities dispersed the prisoners and temporarily lost the maps. During a long interval before the diagrams returned, dozens of men were maimed or killed trying to detect and remove the deadly devices.[70]

While their command group and French authorities wrestled with problems in Nice, elements of the 1st ABTF kept driving along the littoral. FFI battalion Hochcorn harassed the retreating enemy when not marching alongside the Americans. On August 29 the FFI clashed with the Germans as they were pulling out of Villefranche and Eze. Two days later the 509th and 551st Parachute Infantry Battalions moved along the upper corniche, the national road built by Napoléon for his soldiers high along the ridgeline, and occupied positions facing La Turbie. Even though backed up by strong FFI detachments, the going was rough. One band of French-Italian partisans was led by a British commando, Major Andrew J. Flyte, who had been inserted to form a maquis cell. Young, cocky, and wearing a red beret, he drew mixed reviews from Americans in the Task Force.[71]

German strong points were backed up by fire from swinging turrets with twin 75-mm. guns on more than a dozen fortifications imbedded in Mont Agel, the highest point on the southeastern coast. The US Army's daily intelligence report identified one four-gun 150-mm. battery with a 360-degree traverse. In addition, five gun positions on Cap Martin covered all the main coastal roads. That complex consisted of 75-mm. and 88-mm. artillery. The batteries were surrounded by anti-personnel mines. The main fort utilized six flamethrowers controlled inside to protect mortars and machineguns. Its arsenal held 20 tons of ammunition.[72]

While supporting American soldiers marching eastward, Allied warships were stalked by the enemy. Small Italian patrol craft and 105-foot German torpedo boats tried to penetrate the flotilla's defensive screen. A threat of particular note was a plywood motor launch akin to the kind fabricated at Port Vauban, Antibes, loaded with 700 pounds of high explosives in the bow. Small detachments of these attack drones were sunk on three different nights.

Moving closer to Italy, the paratroopers needed the fleet's heavy guns against the formidable frontier defenses. The 1st ABTF called for naval gunfire 80 times during a ten-day period, directed at forts and artillery emplacements in the Alpine high ground. On a single day the French destroyer *Le Malin* fired 193 rounds at the heights above Monaco. The following day it was attacked by three one-man submarines launched by the Germans from Menton, but destroyed them and captured the operators. Subsequently, the Allied fleet based several French destroyers and minesweepers along with some British warships at Golfe-Juan.[73]

As positions hardened on both sides of the Italian border, the thrust of Jones's operations shifted from gathering intelligence to psychological warfare. He wanted to keep the Germans thinking that their adversaries were building up to push through and join General Mark Clark's advance up the Italian peninsula. Realizing the Gestapo still maintained contacts in Monaco, Jones knew that the Germans would quickly be advised when something of military significance happened along the coast. Consequently, 1st Airborne Task Force headquarters arranged for a tank battalion to rumble through Nice during the night heading toward Italy, and afterwards swing inland around back to the west and repeat the ruse the following evening to simulate a concentration of armor and confuse the enemy.[74]

At first, Allied defenders thought duty on the mountainous border with Italy wasn't bad, especially when compared with what their buddies were facing as they fought their way toward Germany. "It's like camping in the Adirondacks," said one GI during the mild days and nights of early autumn. Canadians in the FSSF concurred. Wounds and injuries were rare. An enlistee from Ohio pointed out, "Our non-Purple Heart casualties come from Beausoleil," referring to fights in bars just outside Monte Carlo, close enough to reach when off-duty. A common complaint was the high prices at the Can-Can in Nice and other late-night watering holes. "It's tough doing heavy drinking on a GI's pay," growled another dogface.[75] The incongruence of duty on the Riviera was summed up by an archetypal account of a GI who rushed out of a café in Nice exclaiming that he had to get back to his unit to go on patrol. A soldier was never more than an hour away from the time of his life or that same distance from death or disability.

Relations between the US Army and the French populace is a delicate subject as it quickly focuses on the behavior of hard-fighting, hard-partying GIs suddenly experiencing downtime on the French Riviera. During daylight, civilians offered flowers, the one thing they had in abundance in this part of France. After dark, the thanks took other forms. Jones remembered, "From the beginning when they, like everybody else, peppered us with flowers and things like that that they considered us as being the Liberators. I would say it lasted—not that first feeling, honestly, it didn't last more than a few weeks when things began to calm down."[76] As time went by, incidents of theft and disorderliness went beyond high spiritedness, and the residents' patience wore thin.

An objective view could well be that of the socialist editor of *L'Espoir de Nice* who wrote to American military authorities about this problem in early winter, pointing out that initially no foreign soldiers had ever been received so warmly by his community. But the climate had changed when the GIs became undisciplined.

> Because of them, because of their fights, thefts, window panes breaking, their armed attacks, because of the well-known story of the woman who died after having been puffed up and God knows what other stories, the Niçois who adored the Americans now detest and even hate them.
>
> And when, one month ago, the paratroopers left Nice, there was a great sigh of relief all over the town.
>
> [...] these paratroopers, admirable, brave soldiers, but bad "civilians. "[77]

Other common offenses were petty theft and larceny. The doctor and his wife who generously treated the liberators of Villeneuve-Loubet had suddenly turned sullen upon discovering that their home was looted while they patched up and entertained the GIs. The soldiers were subsequently called together and told to return the stolen items immediately or be confronted with an investigation and formal charges. The booty reappeared in this case, but in other instances, the victims were not so fortunate.[78]

In one sense, the GIs were being compared with their German predecessors who were under tighter military control. When Wehrmacht troops were told not to go into town or fraternize with the natives, the order was strictly obeyed. By their nature, the young Americans were more friendly and open, less afraid of the consequences if found out by a sergeant or commanding officer. The misbehavior of the Italian occupiers had been discounted as their entire soldierly demeanor was viewed with distain. Conversely, the tough French troops who succeeded the Americans in 1945 had marched through the North African desert and battled the Reich in the Colmar pocket. Many were from the colonies with buddies who had fought and died for a France they may never before have seen. When assigned to occupation duty, the attitude of the surviving veterans might well have been that these comfortable civilians on the Riviera owed them something. Their destructive behavior and lack of consideration for the residents were apparently far worse than their predecessors. Consequently, for some residents along the Côte d'Azur the presence of their own army became their biggest postwar nightmare.[79]

In many ways, the American soldiers' behavior was no different than young men of any nationality away from home. The easy availability of sexual favors was in sharp contrast to what they had known in the United States. Brothels were open for business in every town. There were sometimes two queues of customers outside, one French and the other American, often including Yanks and Canadians who would not allow "coloreds" in their row. Black African colonial soldiers were readily welcomed in the French file. Both lines led to the same beds. To relate another curiosity, when asked for his chief recollection of French civilians, one veteran of the FSSF responded, "The hair-lined streets." Another observed that "it just seemed odd to see all this hair lying on the streets and walks." They were referring, of course, to the punishment of shaving the heads of French girls who had slept with Germans during the occupation. One offender even had swastikas painted on her naked breasts as she was paraded through town. Bald women and those wearing scarves or wigs were thereafter sought out by some GIs for a little "collaborating."[80]

Problems with the conduct of Allied troops, along with the Resistance in some instances, were acknowledged by the US Army's official history of the ETO.

> The Nice–Cannes area, east of the assault beaches, was an especially troublesome region. Here, at the end of transportation lines, near famine conditions existed for some time, compounded by FFI and Allied troop misconduct such as looting and robbery. The disorderly conditions were largely under control by mid-September, but Nice especially remained a hungry area until well toward the end of September.
>
> Nice was also a center of black market activities, which plagued [Civil Affairs] agencies through the coastal area. American troops were guilty of contributing to black market operations, for even common army supplies (especially rations) as well as Post Exchange items brought high prices.[81]

Shutting Down

Now positioned up against the Italian border, the American army delineated two defensive sectors from Lake Geneva to the Mediterranean with the dividing line at Col de Larche some 60 miles from the coast. Two US combat teams, each organized around an airborne battalion, took initial responsibility for the operational areas. Allied troops soon became exhausted by duty in the Alpine back country, the altitude and cold weather accentuating their fatigue. Snow had fallen on October 4 and resumed regularly throughout the autumn and winter. The war diary of the Canadian Parachute Battalion recorded that even though these same men had endured daily artillery shelling for 99 days at Anzio, they were now demoralized after a month on the Italian frontier with no apparent prospect of relief. Engineers supporting the FSSF strengthened the defenses by, among other projects, stringing 12,000 feet of concertina wire and laying 1,500 square feet of anti-personnel mines around Col de Braus. Far more dangerous were impromptu minefields left unrecorded and unmarked, causing an indefinite danger to friend and foe alike, including civilians.[82]

In his lessons learned on holding operations at the Italian border, Robert D. Burhans, senior intelligence officer (S-2) of the FSSF, observed:

> The Force was on neither offense nor defense. For the first time it was expected to hold a line for an extended period of time. Before, troop morale was buoyed by staying on the move or readying for an attack. Now both sides were content to hold the high ground on either side of the border and maintain contact with combat and reconnaissance patrols [...] The high ground afforded observation and domination of surrounding terrain. If select troops are to maintain an aggressive spirit, however, they should be spared the bad weather and continual harassing fire that causes high personnel attrition and breakdown in morale, characteristic of a static defense in mountainous terrain during cold weather.[83]

Utilization of Italians was tricky for the Allies. The British were not unaware or unconcerned with problems generated by Italian Fascists. London deployed a liaison mission to Nice to work with Italian partigiani in the struggle to counter their German-backed countrymen. Long-range patrols crossed the border on missions, returning by different routes to keep from being intercepted. A major in the British Army even persuaded the US Army Air Force to fly sorties in support of Italian resistance forces operating along the frontier.[84] Some former elements of the FFI strongly opposed permitting Italian volunteers, even their maquis, to join in the Battle of the Alps. The Frenchmen considered their ranks solid enough to be able to liberate that portion of Alpes-Maritimes remaining under Axis control without recourse to foreigners who could not be refused naturalization after fighting for France.

Troops manning the opposing lines were weary as well, relying on land mines and traps in the roads for security. As snow began to cover the ground, explosives became a greater menace than ever. Mule trains found it harder to ascend steep slopes in the slush and ice. It was easier to detect tracks of enemy patrols, however, and men in olive-drab uniforms could be quickly spotted against the white backdrop.

Artillery fire screeched back and forth across the lines but without infantry clashes. In fact, during the second week of November there was absolutely no contact between opposing patrols. From the Wehrmacht point of view, the Americans seemed to realize no constraints in expending munitions, discharging artillery pieces seemingly at will, with constancy if without particular effectiveness. Members of a US mortar platoon sent to aid an outpost under enemy fire on a hilltop complained of being soaked by rain, worried about friendly fire because their buddies did not know they were coming, and nervous about mines and booby traps in the darkness.[85] Meanwhile, a reconstituted FFI battalion eventually moved into Castellar and increasingly took over assignments from the GIs near Sospel.

Elements of the 517th Parachute Combat Team around Sospel began withdrawing to their designated assembly area for redeployment closer to Germany. In late November, the 1st ABTF was inactivated and Frederick reassigned to division command. By the time the last unit left the Côte d'Azur, virtually one-third of Task Force personnel had been either killed or wounded. Casualties since the beginning of September numbered 802, of which 144 died in action. At the same time, approximately 4,000 enemy soldiers had been captured, plus an unknown number killed and wounded.[86] Now, to take the place of the 1st Airborne Task Force, arrived the 100th Infantry Battalion of the 442nd (Nisei) Infantry Regiment composed of Hawaiian Japanese-Americans transferred from the Vosges.

The FSSF was also relieved from duty and readied for inactivation. On December 5 beside the River Loup at Villeneuve-Loubet, site of brisk skirmishing four months earlier, the Force cased its flag, a black dagger on a white shield with red background. American and Canadian soldiers marched off the field behind their respective colors to join new units in Norway and England. The Montreal *Standard* characterized the command's importance: "The significance of this Force is that it was the first joint force of its kind, drawn from two neighbor democracies, and that it was a brilliant success throughout."[87]

After helping to liberate the Riviera, the 1st Airborne Task Force and First Special Service Force closed the door on their final, almost thankless, mission of protecting the Alpine flank. The Allies and the Resistance had ended fascist occupation in four-fifths of Alpes-Maritimes. The liberation of that last parcel of the department would require five more months to accomplish, an account that will follow examination of the the special circumstances distinguishing the experiences of Menton and Monaco throughout the war years.

14

Menton

The word *menton* means chin in French, so it is not surprising that the town of Menton is located in the southeastern corner where it might be imagined to be a chin on the face of France. The Italian frontier is not two miles east of the port, just on the other side of the suburb of Garavan. A picturesque fishing village with a few scattered villas in the nineteenth century, Menton was protected from wind and storms by a high ridge to the west, earning it a reputation as the warmest place in France. Despite living in a heavenly location, the Mentonnais experienced hellacious times unlike residents of any other French town during World War II. They were evacuated four times, suffered more than four years under Italian and German occupation, and endured seven months of artillery shelling *after* being liberated by the Americans. The story of Menton is truly unique.

The ease with which the Kaiser's troops entered France at the outset of World War I led to construction of the Maginot Line along the country's eastern border. In the 1930s, as French military strategists began to envision another invasion from the east, an array of *fortins* or lesser fortifications was built at Menton and to the north to hold the border and on Cap Martin immediately to the west to protect against an amphibious landing. A plan code-named MANDRIN was developed to evacuate the frontier communities if fighting broke out. When German troops attacked Belgium and France in May 1940, Italian troops began massing against the border while Fascists in nearby San Remo and Ventimiglia shouted bellicose slogans and demonstrated to take back Italy's rightful territory in Contea Nizza. The escalating threat caused the general commanding France's XV Corps to order execution of MANDRIN.

On the night of June 3, 200 buses and 130 trucks, along with assorted railway cars, assembled to withdraw Menton's inhabitants. The travelers left behind cherished heirlooms, household furnishings, and kitchen gardens believing that the crisis would be of short duration, as was so often the case at the outset of any hostilities. The departing Mentonnais trusted that municipal police and firefighters remaining in place would ensure order, but these protectors were soon evacuated as well, leaving the town open to soldiers, vagabonds, and looters.

The column of refugees journeyed first to Antibes, Juan-les-Pins, Golfe-Juan, and Cannes. Patients in the Menton hospital were cared for at its counterpart in Antibes. About 90 percent of the displaced persons were soon sent on to Pau in the Pyrénées of Southwest France.[1]

The Battle of Menton

As the German army approached Paris, Mussolini gathered the courage to declare war. Fighting between Italy and France was announced to begin at midnight on June 10. French advance posts had been built to hold a maximum of 30 men serving light arms, automatic rifles, and mortars. The point most forward, Pont Saint-Louis, outside Menton and right up against the border, was manned by only nine soldiers. The vedette was considered a listening post and equipped with telephone and short-wave radio to report intelligence. Not surprisingly, the telephone wire was immediately severed.[2]

Positioned between the six fortins outside Menton were 30-man units of Scouts-Skiers trained and equipped to patrol the rugged terrain along the frontier. The five-mile front extending from the sea was held by 500 combatants with 4,000 more men assigned to the fortresses shielding Nice. The reserve consisted of 900 tirailleurs Sénégalais positioned in La Turbie behind Monaco, along with 20 old Renault tanks. Directly across the frontier were two divisions and three battalions of Blackshirts, numbering 19,000 troops. Facing Menton were 260 Italian cannon.[3]

It was several days before fighting actually began. The French used the time to ready their troops and deliver munitions to the fortification on Cap Martin sufficient for one month. In the early morning hours of June 14, preparatory fire by machineguns and mortars announced the commencement of ground warfare. A team of Blackshirts occupied the customs building at Pont-Saint-Louis and opened up on Cap Martin with automatic weapons. Advance posts were surrounded and came under fierce attack. The Saint-Louis outpost tried unsuccessfully to adjust the elevation of its machinegun to respond through its aperture in the casemate. Meanwhile, the Cap Martin blockhouse covered its partner with fire as best it could.

A memorable digression occurred on the afternoon of June 17 when an Italian officer bearing a white flag accompanied by a dozen soldiers with slung arms approached Saint-Louis and declared, "The war is over!" Maréchal Pétain's announcement that day of his willingness to sign an armistice seemed a welcome reason to the Italians for immediate suspension of hostilities. Considering the junior rank of its leader, the squad was conducted to Cap

Martin, but nothing resulted from this unconventional overture.[4] The only engagements continued to be intermittent attacks on Saint-Louis and periodic bombardment of Cap Martin.

All this changed when Mussolini learned that peace negotiations being concluded by the French and Germans provided that the Italian invaders would occupy only the territory they had captured. Artillery preparation began between 9.30 and 10.30 a.m. on June 22. Cap Martin was a prime target for the Fascists. Armed with a single 75-mm. piece, its response was limited. The French commandant called to Mont Agel for fire support. The fortress answered immediately with over a hundred 75-mm. and 155-mm. rounds. At 10.30, an Italian armored train bearing heavy artillery emerged from its hiding place in a tunnel and discharged 250 rounds at Cap Martin before being put out of commission by shells from Mont Agel.

By June 24 the Scouts-Skiers had been exposed to combat conditions for three days and were at the limit of their physical endurance. Reluctantly a decision was made to withdraw all the defenders from Menton and Garavan that afternoon. At 5.35 p.m., the commanding general of the Cosseria Division broadcast a message to his units, heard by the French as well: "At any price, by order of the Government [of Mussolini], push to the limit and, if necessary, make an assault with the whole Royal Regiment. I repeat that it is necessary to advance at any price without taking account of the sacrifices."[5]

French artillery continued firing to interdict passage across the frontier by infiltrators, while the Italians employed mortars against the advance post at Pont Saint-Louis that blocked access to Menton by road. Inside a hollowed-out cliff with a thick concrete facing remained eight French soldiers commanded by a young lieutenant and manning a machinegun and an antitank gun pointing straight ahead. During the final day before the ceasefire went into effect, the sector commander sent patrols back into Menton to protect against Italian advances onto Cap Martin. As ordered, French artillerists stopped firing "with bitterness." A counterattack by the Senegalese and Scouts-Skiers was abruptly cancelled. At 12.35 a.m. on June 25, silence descended on the border.

The cessation of hostilities did not prevent Italian units from redeploying afterwards. The French complained that the new boundaries were more favorable to its adversary than positions held at midnight. The advance post at Saint-Louis never wavered, however, and it was only at 9.00 the next morning, when two French officers approached with news of the ceasefire, that the nine inhabitants, undaunted, emerged for the first time since June 14. According to their commander, when they left the fire team carried off their weapons, locked the bunker in the face of their adversaries, and took away the key.[6]

Mentone Italiana

Italian occupation of Menton was turned into a propaganda bonanza. Mussolini bragged that the "pearl of France," which rightfully belonged to his country, had been returned to Italy through the brave feats of his soldiers. Walls within the town and French defensive positions that had held their own during the contest were desecrated with graffiti exclaiming patriotic slogans in Italian. The headquarters of IV Armata moved into town complete with a garrison of several thousand soldiers.[7] On July 1, Il Duce himself came to review his troops on parade.

As soon as the Armistice went into effect, residents dispersed across France slowly began returning to Menton. The returnees did not like what they found. Potable water was scarce. One hotel had burned; another was requisitioned as barracks for Fascist soldiers. A restaurant was open, but who could afford to buy a meal? An estimated 2,800 quarters had been damaged or destroyed in the fighting. Most of the residences had been plundered. Contents of shelves and drawers were strewn on the floor when intruders searched for valuables. The occupying army was blamed, as were 2,000 workers brought in each day to turn the town into an Italian showplace. The wagons transporting them back to Imperia in the evening were reportedly laden with furniture, clothing, and kitchen utensils. The Fascist Party subsequently accused a ready target for suspicion, the "Senegalese hordes" in the vicinity during combat.

About the only positive aspect seemed to be that, initially, food was relatively abundant. Otherwise, French culture disappeared from Mentonnais life. Public notices appeared only in Italian. The names of streets and locations changed. Refugees allowed to return to live in Menton were permitted to bring a maximum of 5,000 francs which were exchanged for lira at an artificially low rate. Children of French parents found pupils in school singing a new national anthem, "Salve, O Re Imperator," and encountered taunts for being "dirty French."[8] The Fascist revolution imposed the slogan "Authority, Order, Justice" to replace that of the weak, vanquished regime, "Liberté, Egalité, Fraternité."

The numbers of inhabitants reflected the transformation. The 1936 national census had recorded 21,000 inhabitants. An enumeration in April 1941 identified 4,444 Italians, 1,623 French, 119 foreigners, and 539 other naturalized persons. One-third of the Italians had not resided there before the occupation. Included in this count were Fascist agitators promoting a campaign to join Menton to Savoie, and 1,500 Ligurians relocated to colonize the port for Italy.[9]

Extremists were supported by *Il Nizzardo*, a newspaper initially published in Nice by Ezio Garibaldi, who was a general in the Italian Milice and grandson of the great Italian liberator born in that city. Garibaldi commuted between Rome and Menton to prepare for a march on Nizza to rally support for annexation to Italy.

Violation of the demarcation line by Germany and Italy in November 1942 did not have as devastating an effect on Menton as elsewhere in the Midi due to the thorough Italianization already in place. Resident Fascists greeted soldiers marching westward through town with patriotic slogans posted on walls and distributed food and wine to the Bersaglieri and Alpini. It was not long before the border with metropolitan France was reopened to Mentonnais schoolchildren being educated in Monaco where French was still spoken.

In March 1943 in light of the Allies' success in North Africa, Pascal Molinari, Menton's civil engineer, entered into his diary that an Anglo-American landing in the South of France appeared imminent.[10] Eight months after the Italian occupation of southeastern France, there was cause for hope when news of Mussolini's arrest arrived on July 25. While the French rejoiced, the Germans plotted. Three days later, Marshal von Rundstedt came to Menton to discuss the situation with General Vercellino. The friction was shown by the Italians' initial refusal to allow German divisions to pass through their lines to reinforce Axis defenses on the Italian peninsula. It was only at the end of August that the Armata headquarters finally conceded. A cautious status quo continued until September 8 when word arrived that Italy had surrendered to Allied forces.

The following day, shopkeepers stood guard in front of their businesses watching Italian headquarters staff and civilian functionaries prepare to depart. Soon, thousands of soldiers came streaming along the roads from France heading for Ventimiglia. Pricey front-wheel-drive Citroëns passed by driven by an Italian soldier with an officer and young woman in the back seat and suitcases, rugs, and paintings piled in the trunk. Wehrmacht troops were not far behind, and at nightfall German officers requested lodging at the municipal center. All was quiet, the transformation complete. Menton was part of France once more, although still occupied.

German Occupation

"I spent there the most emotional and the most patriotic minutes of my life," recalled a participant about the arrival of the prefect from Alpes-Maritimes the following afternoon.[11] French Mentonnais crowded into the town square to offer an enthusiastic welcome. The prefect was summoned onto the balcony of the *hôtel de ville* amid cries of "Vive la France" and then serenaded with "La Marseillese" being sung publicly for the first time in three years.

It was in the interest of the new occupiers to restore the legitimate municipal regime. A Frenchman assumed the duties of mayor. Signage once again appeared in French. Telephone connections and a bus service to Nice resumed. The exchange rate for francs and lira was set at an equitable level. The return of Mentonnais refugees was encouraged by the offer of the Department of Alpes-Maritimes to provide free transportation plus an indemnity. Those who came back found that furniture and other cherished possessions had disappeared, as discovered earlier by others. Retailers returned to shops stripped of fixtures as well as merchandise. On the positive side, taxes unpaid during the Italian occupation were cancelled.

A series of evacuations began late in the year. On November 5, the German commander ordered the removal of 150 families living along the coastline in places considered critical to military operations. Two more directives in February 1944 emptied 400 more lodgings. Then, in April, came a policy requiring the departure of pregnant women, mothers with children under five years old, all boys and girls less than 15 years of age, and inhabitants considered dispensable. Others chose to leave voluntarily.[12]

Tension peaked in August. The day of the landing in Provence, the Germans disarmed the gendarmes in Menton. It became evident that the Nazis and their partisans were preparing to leave. As the month progressed, the Blackshirts withdrew to Ventimiglia, San Remo, and Milano. When bombs fell for the first time, residents were puzzled because the occupying troops had already left. As the liberators came closer and closer the situation became chaotic.

In the cauldron of defeat, cohesion was crumbling in the ranks of the occupiers. Prussians, Bavarians, Austrians, Czechs, Poles—the nationalities of the routed German army began challenging one another. A brawl erupted at the Hôtel du Globe. Not long thereafter gunshots rang out, bullets striking two Germans. Fearing reprisals against them, the Poles claimed the rounds were fired from windows in the Casa Isabella. The apartment complex was quickly encircled by the Wehrmacht. Machineguns indiscriminately sprayed buildings with bullets. Soldiers grabbed a religious bookshop owner, his neighbor, and an elderly couple standing nearby. When a sergeant in the Menton police arrived, he was captured as well. The aged twosome were summarily executed in the basement of the building; the other three prisoners were lined up against a wall and shot as well.[13]

On September 6 the FTP of the communist Saint-Just brigade appeared in the port. Several hours later elements of 1st ABTF arrived to liberate Menton. The commander, a French-Canadian, was guided by a Mentonnais who was subsequently killed by shrapnel from a shell fired from a French cruiser.[14]

After Liberation

Compared with the Italian presence in Menton, the German occupation had been relatively short-lived, lasting almost exactly one year. The greeting given to the liberators was less emotional than when freed from Italian subjugation and returned to the French colors. Locals had other matters on their minds.

The ordeal of the occupation was far from over. First, the fascists left souvenirs behind. During their retreat the Germans scattered mines along the way. A team of volunteers from nearby Roquebrune-Cap-Martin set out to disarm them. The greater threat came not from land, but from the sky. The enemy still occupied high ground to the north and east and, initially, fortifications as close as Pont Saint-Louis. German batteries began shelling Menton and Garavan. The bombardment continued day and night. Machineguns barked out sporadically; mortars lobbed rounds indiscriminately. Even the maternity ward of the hospital was hit.[15]

Local authorities ordered an evacuation of Garavan on September 23. Now it became apparent that all residents would be required to leave their homes, with the exception of the 700 people and 70 police dispatched from Nice to administer Menton and safeguard property. It was the third evacuation of the war for Mentonnais. A military reporter described what he found that month:

> Menton is the "ghost city of the Riviera." Just a few kilometers away from the Italian border, the resort town that used to house nice old ladies in vacation days is now emptied of civilians and contains only military personnel [...] Most of the streets are deserted, and the footsteps of the solitary passers-by echo on the leaf-strewn pavements and rebound from the boarded-up shops. Headquarters outfits are in a few of the hotels, but the rest cater only to the shadows. One wall bears a mocking memento of the days after the 1940 French armistice when the Italians occupied this spot. "Vinceremo," [we will win] it says.[16]

US intelligence documented a number of examples of enemy infiltration. A member of a crack German infantry outfit trained in guerrilla warfare was captured at the port of Menton in the early hours of February 15. Under interrogation he revealed that a party of 18 men had set out on foot from the Hôtel Excelsior in San Remo for a pillbox west of Ventimiglia. In the hotel's basement were hidden handguns and machineguns and covered up in its parking lot were stored several small boats, 30 torpedoes, and 15 depth charges. A spy from either Monte Carlo or Menton reportedly gathered information on the defenses protecting their waterfronts and delivered it to the Germans. His identification papers were said to be hidden in his shoe. Two inflatable rubber boats powered by outboard motors set out from the Italian

Riviera with four men in each. Their mission was to overpower the lookouts on the mole at Menton and return with one or two prisoners. One dinghy turned back due to engine trouble. As soon as the other landed, its crew was overpowered by the guard and killed. Such were the threats to Menton as the war drew to a close.[17]

Vanquishing the fascists did not eliminate thievery in Menton. The American paratroopers were relieved by Japanese-American footsoldiers coming south from the Vosges Mountains. Molinari believed that the new troops started right in robbing uninhabited buildings, including the garden shed where his family had hidden. General Frederick's intelligence officer, Geoffrey Jones, also remembered these replacements as sub-standard:

> We had that motley group that showed up, was the remnants of the 442 Japanese that had been chewed up, you know, and the 44 AAA [Anti-Aircraft] brigade was the 7th Regiment with a couple of extra battalions of colored transport troops. And we had this motley group there and I don't think, very frankly, there was one soldier out of ten that were really soldiers—soldiers except for what was left of the Japanese but they had been sent down there for a rest, in effect, although they were on the line.[18]

The Americans were disliked for other reasons. They were thought to be critical, nonchalant, and impotent in the face of the German bombardment. Fearing attack, they planted explosives in the ground to the east, then departed in early 1945 without leaving a plan of the minefield. There was an even greater grievance. After the enemy artillery barrage intensified in January, the American military headquarters ordered complete evacuation of the border communities, including Menton. The reasons given—to protect against infiltration and espionage as well as to safeguard the citizenry—did not convince Mentonnais with sentimental and familial attachments to their houses and land. Nor did the honesty and patriotism of the FFI that remained behind instill confidence. After the bad experience during the Italian occupation, homeowners recoiled against exposing their property and possessions to military garrisons once again. Farmers outside town were sick at the thought of leaving unattended livestock that, once lost, would take years to replace.[19]

The final 700 Mentonnais were removed on February 17–18, leaving no more than eight municipal employees to man the local government. A month later, US units were ordered to the Rhine. The Americans were replaced by the 1ère Division de Marche d'Infantrie which had proved itself in Alsace. Then, on the night of April 23–4 came a final heavy barrage of more than 200 shells as the Germans began withdrawing from their border redoubts. When an element of the 1ère Division occupied Ventimiglia on

April 25, the shelling of Menton finally stopped for good, 228 days after it commenced the previous September.

Slowly the population returned, the first convoy arriving on May 11. It was estimated that one-tenth of the dwellings were inhabitable and half had no windows. By June there were 5,000 inhabitants in Menton, a figure that doubled by October. Feeding the populace was the immediate problem. Between June and August, a French charity took charge, serving free meals during one four-day period. Representatives of the American Relief for France visited in August and committed to sending 46 crates of milk and food for the town's severely undernourished children. Housewives became irate at the distribution of foodstuffs and at one point ransacked a warehouse containing staples.[20]

A longer-term problem was the hodgepodge of mines left by Italians, Germans, Americans, and French. Some maps were recovered from the Germans and Americans but none from the French. German prisoners of war were mainly utilized to uncover and disarm the explosives, but Frenchmen were also employed. Here again, neighboring landowners decried the destruction of their trees, fruit, lemons, grapevines, and other crops caused by demining.[21]

Menton's experience was hardly tragic compared with the suffering across Europe and Asia during the war. The community counted 17 members of the armed forces and 34 civilians as its wartime losses. The 3,375 quarters destroyed or damaged placed Menton first on the Côte d'Azur, but the devastation was insignificant when considered in the light of so many places in the direct path of warring armies. It would be 1962 before the prewar level of inhabitants was restored.[22] In sum, Menton's special niche in the annals of the war years was not due to the magnitude of its suffering or the intensity of the conflict that periodically encompassed it, but concerned the political, economic, and social consequences in this forgotten corner of France.

15
⍟

Monaco

Monaco: A sovereign state of 372 acres during World War II, the size of Central Park in New York City, and the second smallest sovereign territory in Europe (after Vatican City). The royal palace and old town perch atop a promontory at the water's edge and four other districts that comprise the monarchy cling to precipices under a rocky cupola known as la Tête de Chien. The most renowned of these cantons is Monte Carlo. At the outset of World War II as today, the population of the principality consisted overwhelmingly of non-Monégasques. The 1938 census recorded 22,195 of the 23,956 inhabitants as outsiders.[1]

In 1870 the most renowned Prince of Monaco in modern times, Albert I, the oceanographer and naturalist, fathered a son named Louis, who was born in Baden-Baden and raised by his German mother in her home country and in Austria. Albert did not care much for his heir. The boy was educated at schools far from Monaco culminating with the French military academy at Saint-Cyr. Upon graduation he joined the French Foreign Legion, serving in Algeria among other places, until 1898 when as hereditary prince Louis was recalled to Monaco.

After World War I, with Albert's consent, Louis identified a 20-year-old woman he proclaimed as his heir. Her name was Charlotte, and she was not selected at random but rather the product of an illicit relationship in Algeria with a laundress. Three days after the formal adoption, Charlotte was married to a French count, a union that produced a girl, Antoinette, in 1920, and a boy, Rainier, in 1923, and then the couple divorced. Albert died in 1922, and Louis ascended the throne to which Charlotte renounced any claim, positioning Rainier to eventually succeed his grandfather.[2]

The outbreak of war in 1939 brought about the mobilization of 800 Monégasque residents with their French regiments at the same time 300 French soldiers entered the principality to defend it. The casino closed its doors. Two weeks later, however, the state of emergency ceased when Mussolini declared Italy a non-belligerent and the Riviera entered into the twilight of the Phoney War. By mid-November, roulette wheels were spinning once more and the gambling den was raking in more money than ever as the only casino open on the coast.

Italy's declaration of war against France in June 1940 caused alarm in Monaco. Monte Carlo closed its sporting house once more. The government rounded up a hundred known Mussolini sympathizers and interned them at various sites in the Midi including Fort Carré and Les Milles.[3] When France and Germany signed an armistice, the principality faced a new threat.

Living with Vichy

The ability of Monaco to maintain its independence since the late thirteenth century, when it was acquired by the Grimaldi clan of Genoa, has been due to its wiles in playing off powers competing to take over the vulnerable principality. In early 1940 the ruler of Monaco was confronted with Germany which had defeated and occupied most of the Continental countries to its west, and Italy whose Duce aimed not only to reclaim Nice, Savoie and Corsica, but to take over Monaco as well. The sole protector Louis could turn to was France, a defeated nation but one bound by treaty to guarantee the sovereignty of the principality. In return for this protection confirmed in the pact of 1918, Monaco agreed that France would designate the minister of state, the senior functionary of the pocket state. During the war years that position was held by Emile Roblot, an appointee of the Front Populaire. The confidence in which he was held by the ruler gave Roblot enormous freedom of action. Another principal actor was Victor Jeannequin, consul general of France, whose objectivity and loyalty to his homeland made his observations credible at home but worrisome to Louis.

Roblot and Louis, often at the minister's instigation, repeatedly asserted that Monaco was neutral and free to promulgate its own policies. But when threatened, they were just as quick to play the French card. In mid-August Monaco did not bother to ask permission to reopen its casinos to attract waves of affluent refugees strung out along the Riviera coast. While Vichy France evoked the virtues of "Work, Family, and Country," Monte Carlo promoted luxurious living rather than its antonym. It was not uncommon to see Louis's heavy figure at the Hôtel de Paris with his gray hair in a brush cut and a bleak look piercing the thick lenses of his spectacles.

The prince had reason to be satisfied, avoiding occupation through his realm's association with France's Non-Occupied Zone yet recognized as an independent state. When Italian military authorities wanted to obtain control of the principality's small war production facilities, Roblot could assert that as a neutral entity his government had not been a party to the Armistice. There was one other angle that Louis could and did employ to keep the Italians at bay. The Third Reich was interested in financial access to the outside world. It needed a front to interface with international investors and investments.

Monaco seemed ideal for this purpose, and so Berlin sent a representative to the Riviera to explore the possibility. Pleased by the reception given his overtures by Monaco's ruler, the emissary recommended to the Fuhrer that the principality be maintained in the New Europe as an independent entity.

New financial opportunities opened for the Germans. American and French stocks held by the Reich were blocked in the Occupied Zone but could be transferred to Monaco. Companies controlled by the Nazis were registered in Monaco for the purpose of effecting commerce, conducting industrial operations, and investing capital on behalf of Germany. The exchange rate for marks into francs was set at a favorable 1.20 as an inducement for Monégasques to sell their shares in German companies. Most important to the prince, undoubtedly, was the stake that the Reich now took in maintaining the neutrality of Monaco vis-à-vis Italian intentions.

To accomplish their aspirations in Monaco, the Fuhrer's henchmen considered establishing a bank there. It would permit them to protect personal wealth, shelter the private holdings they had seized or requisitioned, many from Jews, and import and export gold and other currencies, both for themselves and for the central banks of the occupied countries. There was also the motive of investing part of the huge indemnity being paid by France to Germany, amounting to 220 million francs a day, in Monaco. As the United States remained neutral during 1941, Nazi financiers were anxious to do business with sympathetic Americans through an intermediary in Monaco. Officially non-aligned, Spain was another potential trading partner for Germany, hiding behind Monaco.

Other investment projects were under discussion. The Germans were interested in creating a radio station and a film studio to disseminate their propaganda. In anticipation of these undertakings, the Reich started transferring money from its Swiss accounts and began liquidating the estate of Daniel Dreyfus, a Jewish Resistance leader in Marseille. Another use of its Monaco front was to purchase and import munitions and armaments unobtainable for an Axis power on the open market. The Kriegsmarine, Luftwaffe, and SS all made use of this subterfuge. Concurrently, agents for the Reich began buying vehicles of all description, especially trucks, for use by the Wehrmacht. As many as 15,000 carriers were purchased allegedly for the tiny principality, although many never crossed the border into Monaco, going directly to the Russian front. Thought was given to making the principality the headquarters of a European steel cartel. An agent began purchasing precious furniture, fine wines, and costly food delicacies on behalf of the nephew of Marshal Hermann Goering. The opportunities were limited only by the imagination.[4]

In so many ways, Monaco was and remains a paradox. At a time of food rationing and shortages throughout occupied Europe, especially in barren

Alpes-Maritimes, there was plenty of nourishment for select residents of the principality. Many of the recent immigrants brought family wealth and other nouveau riche having acquired fortunes through war profiting now sought the tax shelter offered by Monaco. They were all living in an unreal world with the illusionary protection of a neutrality far from the tragedies produced by armed conflict.

It is too simple to contrast Monte Carlo with the other districts of Monaco, but certainly the image of the former was well grounded. The best films, foreign and domestic, played at its cinema, and the dance troupe formerly known as the Russian ballet continued to perform. Indeed, in this time of trouble the government encouraged dancing to attract the idle rich to the casino. Maurice Chevalier would reserve a table for his friends at a luxury hotel on New Year's Eve, enjoying multiple courses with champagne and fine wines as usual. It was not extraordinary to spend 2,000 francs for a meal, twice the average monthly salary. Beautiful, well-stocked boutiques, the elegantly attired promenading past, sleek autos cruising about with seemingly no concern for petrol—Monte Carlo personified affluence. Nor was it uncommon for the French police to stop suppliers carrying hams, eggs, and butter far distances to take advantage of the prices these scarce staples commanded at the watering holes of Monaco.

But every Monégasque could not afford to survive by resorting to the black market. On the other side of the principality were the vast majority of inhabitants possessing ration cards but nonetheless faced with prices for milk, fruit, and vegetables four times higher than before the war. Refugees might not even possess the coupons required for many purchases or services like having shoes resoled. Some hearty souls rode bicycles to peasants' plots in the Var to bring back food. Others kept rabbits and hens for eggs on their balconies.[5] Thankfully, some food arrived from the United States by sea. Priority was assigned to children from two to six years of age, pregnant women, and those who were breast-feeding. Boys and girls were nourished in school by milk from the International Red Cross. As head of the Monégasque Red Cross, Charlotte was more accessible to Monaco's subjects than other members of the royal family.[6]

Early in 1942, Roblot initiated a dialogue with the Swiss Confederation concerning matters of mutual interest. Surrounded by fascist states, the Swiss were worried about receiving foodstuffs overland. Similarly, the hierarchy of Monaco was concerned about goods transported across France, occupied and unoccupied. The Italian Armistice Commission controlled Monaco's port and had become increasingly assertive after Il Duce went to war against Greece. Consequently, a meeting was held by representatives of the Confederation with the prince to discuss the possibility "to establish a free port in neutral Monaco." "At first, it was a talk about even more audacious plans such as

Monaco could become the 26th canton of Switzerland—so to speak an enclave on the Mediterranean Sea," recalled a Swiss participant in a fictionalized account of the actual meeting written a decade later.[7] Nothing came of the discussions, however.

Another unexpected opportunity to protect the mini-state's sovereignty presented itself on October 31. The Monégasque minister of foreign affairs learned that the United States was finally willing to accede to a request of many years standing and extend diplomatic representation to Monaco rather than continuing to rely upon its consulate in Nice as the interface. In reality, the Americans were looking ahead to the imminent landings in North Africa and shifting its diplomatic foothold on the Mediterranean coast away from Vichy. Receiving a quick affirmation, the State Department immediately appointed Walter W. Orebaugh as its consul. The Italian legate promptly denounced the move as a provocation.[8]

Scarcely a week later, the Allies landed in French Morocco and Algeria. Any euphoria generated in Monaco was short lived. The French legate went to Roblot to protest official recognition of an envoy for a score of Americans in the principality at the very moment Vichy had severed relations with Washington. Roblot fell back on his prince's patented retort: Monaco is independent and neutral. Rushing to meet with the minister of state on November 11, Orebaugh could not help but notice balconies flying the Italian flag and passers-by rendering the fascist salute. Cries of "*Vive Mussolini*," "*Vive l'Italie*," "*Monaco italienne*," and "*Dehors* [out with] *les Grimaldi*" echoed throughout the old city.[9] Louis's worst fear was being realized: the Italians were invading Monaco.

Italian Occupation

At 2.00 p.m. the same day, motorized Italian troops crossed the boundary separating France and Monaco as they headed west to Nice. The procession continued for three days, with only small units initially posted in the principality to guard the railway. Low-ranking soldiers often wore civilian clothes to blend in with the inhabitants as many locals spoke Italian. Helpless with no armed force and only a few policemen, Louis could only think to appeal for papal intercession, to no avail, and to the Germans for preservation of the autonomy of its Mediterranean window onto international finance and commerce. Fully occupied with its own problems related to both German and Italian invasions of the Non-Occupied Zone, Pétain's government was noticeable by its silence concerning the little principality.

The first target of the new masters of Monaco was the Hôtel Metropole in Monte Carlo, seat of the new American consulate. Orebaugh and his staff were herded to the hotel annex while their offices were searched. Two weeks later he was deported to Italy for confinement.[10] There followed a series of arrests of those identified as anti-fascists who were sent to Sospel for internment. Sought out in particular were male Anglo-Saxons under the age of 60, and by the end of the year the entire known population of 29 English and 13 American men had been rounded up and expelled.[11]

As 1942 rolled over into 1943, the casino was never busier, the baccarat table alive until 8.00 a.m. on New Year's Day. The prior year's profits totaled 28 million francs compared with a loss of over 5 million two years earlier.[12] Gamblers ate meat and sipped café au lait. Croupiers and waiters reveled in generous gratuities. On January 25, while spirits continued to flow freely in Monte Carlo, wine for the general population became subject to rationing. The enigma that was Monaco was no closer to resolution and threatening to destabilize it.

Tension heightened between Italian Fascists and anti-fascists as the new year progressed. Military authorities resumed rounding up opponents of Mussolini among their fellow countrymen, Monégasques, and French, dispatching them to the Sospel camp. As reports came in of Allied victories in North Africa and then landings in Italy, repression in the city-state took the form of interrupting black market activities and punishing foreigners. Consulates were closed with the exception of those of Italy, Germany, and Spain.[13]

The fortunes of war were changing for the Axis on the Italian peninsula and in Russia. Monégasques opposed to fascism began carefully following movements on the battlefront. Everyone had some sort of map. One young boy used a string anchored by a lead weight to mark these shifts on the map on his wall. Listening to foreign radio broadcasts was permitted in the early years of the conflict. Interestingly, no mention was made at school of the hostilities; teachers did not touch the delicate subject of war. Another youngster asserted that the pupils were not even instructed as to how to behave before foreign troops present in the city-state.[14]

In July, Mussolini was arrested, then, as soon as the Italian army signed an armistice with the Allies, the Bersaglieri abandoned Monaco followed closely by the most radical Fascists. Seeing the despised Italians in disarray, the Monégasques expressed the rancor that had built up over the past ten months. In the Italian quarter of Moneghetti as elsewhere in Monaco, demonstrators threw rocks, broke windows, and pillaged shops while police looked on. It was not long before the succeeding military power presented itself. When one armored vehicle rolled up, the German soldiers inside seemed ready to throw hand grenades at the rioters. "It's okay," the Monégasques were assured, "it's the Italians we're after."[15]

German Influence and Occupation

An infantry division set up headquarters in Monte Carlo, succeeded a month later by a motorized division. Next, reserve units consisting largely of Poles and Austrians occupied the principality. The Nazis were quick to take charge. Many persons singled out for harsh treatment by the Italians were released from captivity to be replaced by individuals targeted by the Gestapo. The shoreline was prohibited to non-residents. Italians were targets of special abuse for abandoning the fight. Maintaining civilian order was left to the Monaco police. The STO was not seriously implemented, however, and on occasion young men were enrolled in the police to prevent impressment.[16]

Prince Louis could not have been more hospitable. Retaining his personal realm depended upon pleasing the reigning power. Louis reverted to his German roots. He signed his name *"Ludwig Furst von Monaco* [Prince Louis of Monaco]." He welcomed the new German consul in perfect Deutsche, referring to his formative years in Baden-Baden and declaring himself a friend of Germany. Louis hosted a dinner in honor of the new legate, toasting a bright future for the Reich. What was even more amazing was his choice as Monégasque consular general in Berlin, a lieutenant colonel in the German army. On the other side of the ledger, Louis wrote to Maréchal Pétain to insist that Jeannequin be recalled to Vichy. The change taking place in the balance of military power in Europe somehow escaped the attention of the 73-year-old ruler, or perhaps he could not or did not want to believe it.[17]

For reasons all too obvious, the Reich reciprocated this cordiality. On September 24 it informed the German consul that the principality would be treated as a friendly country like Franco's Spain and Perón's Argentina. Furthermore, Monaco would be the exception in Europe, an occupied state not required to pay the costs of the German presence. Hitler's lieutenants had big plans for the city-state. The first was to carry through on their earlier intention to establish a bank there, presumably to hedge their bets in case Berlin did not win the war. A monetary emissary arrived in November and requested a license to open a financial institution with 100 million francs, omitting reference to the German clientele and the Reichsbank underwriting the new venture. Names such as Goering and Ribbentrop were kept in the background. Secrecy was paramount for, after all, the purpose of the bank was circumventing the American economic embargo in order to gain access to pro-German, American industrial might and other international sources of supply.[18]

The project dragged on until the summer of 1944. When the bank was finally registered in Monaco, the straw men listed as founders were a Swiss, Frenchman, German-American, and American. That fourth investor was Florence Gould who deposited five million francs through a German aeronautical engineer who was a very close companion. For two million francs she also obtained permission to settle in Monaco with her sister and invalid husband if ever necessary to escape the ravages of war.[19] In a single stroke the Nazi hierarchy established an international institution for the purpose of transferring German money, public and private, to the United States via neutral Monaco.

At a time when the spirits of many Monégasques were uplifted by rumors of an imminent debarkation in southern France, Louis blithely continued doing business with the Reich. Up to and during the German occupation Monaco engaged in registering companies at a rate never before imagined. Firms incorporated in Monaco with local agents as surrogates. The real owners were never seen or even known in many instances. All accountability was lost. Companies trafficked in wines, electrical appliances, textiles, and a variety of contraband. One enterprise undertook to manage construction of the Wall of the Atlantic and the Wall of the Mediterranean. Creation of fraudulent businesses became a national industry.

The Germans imposed themselves physically as well as financially. Monaco soon became the home port for tankers, mine sweepers, and patrol boats. As the Allies fought their way through Italy, the Germans became more concerned with defending the coastline than the Vichyites or Italians had been. A small explosion targeting an artillery piece and its munitions on the end of a dike in November demonstrated the defenders' vulnerability. At first, the prohibited zone stopped at the port where the sporting gentry at Monte Carlo engaged in pigeon shooting and the working class tried to cultivate vegetables. Soon, however, barbed wire, mine fields, and blockhouses took the place of recreation and growing food.

When Allied bombers destroyed two sections of the Anthéor rail viaduct, reception of food supplies in Monaco by train was interrupted for the remainder of the war. Malnutrition slowly began making an appearance in youth. Women were unhappy that bi-weekly distribution of cigarettes was restricted to male residents, bringing Monaco into line with tobacco rationing in Germany. In mid-February, Roblot published a notice directing persons with second homes outside the principality to retire to them to ease the worsening shortages. Only those working in government or economic activities within the principality were intended to remain. As always, wealth had its privileges and the government's policy was implemented unevenly.

As summer continued, there was tension in the air as everyone— Monégasques, foreign refugees, and German defenders alike—waited for an invasion somewhere along the Mediterranean coast. Yet Monte Carlo remained a hotbed of provocateurs and agents from all the countries with a stake in the war—spying, collecting information, and radioing their headquarters. And the Gestapo went about its bloody business of ferreting out members of the Resistance taking advantage of the sanctuary afforded by Monaco's official neutrality.

The highest-placed résistant was René Borghini, secretary to the president of the national council. He was also chief of the Monaco Combat unit which collected intelligence for the Allies. At dawn on July 3, agents of the Gestapo accompanied by a Monégasque gendarme burst into Borghini's home, seized him, and conducted a thorough search. At his office they reported finding incriminating documents, a revolver, and a false carte d'identité, whereupon they took him away. Next the Gestapo arrested anti-fascist policemen whose names were discovered in Borghini's records. The following day they apprehended his accomplice, Esther Poggio, who served as courier. Both were shot.[20] After the liberation, Roblot rationalized that had his government not assisted the Nazis, the Gestapo would have acted by itself. In the opinion of a noted historian of Monaco during this era, Roblot was frantic to please the German police because the Reich had threatened to sever its cozy relationship with the principality. An Allied spy at work on the national council was more than Roblot could endure.[21]

As German defenders became more and more anxious about an impending invasion, private telephone service was terminated in the Midi with the exception of Monaco. Next, automobile traffic was prohibited, again excluding Monaco. Allied bombardment along the Côte d'Azur deprived Monégasques, first, of water for a short time, then of bread for a longer period. Construction of the blockhouse sited to protect the port was not completed yet it served as a reference point and later a target for pilots flying in from the sea. On August 6 the first bombs fell on the principality itself. The tunnel that served as an air-raid shelter under the palace remained full, although few of the occupants slept at night. Even German soldiers sought refuge there. War had finally reached the princedom that pretended to be neutral but wasn't.[22]

Food and drink were commercially unobtainable after August 15 although some residents were quick to recover dead fish from the sea. The government acknowledged its responsibility to provide nourishment. Wine merchants distributed water according to the established ration. Residents queued for soup served by public canteens at various hotels depending on where one lived. The crafty supplicant soon learned not to arrive too early, however, as the potage was thin on top.[23]

Fighting drew nearer. Aircraft bombed Monaco on August 27. The next morning the Allied fleet began shelling heights above the principality. Nice was liberated. The German army evacuated Monaco on the night of September 2–3. A Wehrmacht officer commanding Russian troops was observed confiscating a Red Cross truck carrying chloroform to move it out of reach of the invaders.[24] As they prepared to leave, soldiers dynamited strategic military works to protect their retreat toward the Italian border although, according to

Roblot, the port was spared destruction due to intervention by the German consul. The rear guard did not withdraw quickly enough, however, to prevent some members being captured.[25]

Liberation and Aftermath

Dawn arose on September 3 to an eerie silence in the principality. As if by magic, the first flags of Monaco divided in horizontal white and red halves and the tricolore of France began appearing at windows. Excited Monégasques fretted over how many stars and stripes to place on homemade American flags. By midday, patriots had painted the Allied colors at points along the pavement to welcome the liberators—American and British banners, the French ensign with the Croix de Lorraine, and the Canadian flag in recognition of its representation in the ground forces.

From Beausoleil and Cap d'Ail, members of company Cyrano of the Saint-Just brigade were first to appear, ahead of Captain Jess Walls's parachute company. "*Ils sont la*" ("They are here") rang out the joyous announcement. A Monégasque remembers seeing his first Americans in a jeep outside the casino at about 1.00 p.m., one white soldier and one black, surrounded by young women who ran up to kiss them. This scene would be repeated again and again over the next few days. Candy, chewing gum, cigarettes, and chocolate were the tokens of goodwill. For other residents, tears of joy flowed on September 25 when French troops marched into the realm, the first seen there in many years.[26]

That same day, General Frederick made his first appearance in the principality, heading for Roblot's residence in a small convoy with two jeeps full of military police. Greeted by a servant, Frederick waited patiently at the front door while the minister of state escaped out the back.[27] Uncertain of how much Frederick knew about his actions over the past five years, the senior functionary was unprepared to face difficult questions so quickly posed by the latest in a series of conquering military powers.

If he didn't know already, Frederick soon learned a great deal about Monaco, its principals, and wartime dealings. On September 9, Frederick received a full briefing from Captain Geoffrey Jones, now working full time for the OSS. He would be a major figure in US–Monégasque relations over the next several months. Jones's operatives found Gestapo agents hiding out in Monaco to receive and forward information of military value to the Reich.[28] A formal intelligence assessment, translated by Jones into English, addressed the general situation, focusing on the minister of state, as did a confidential report provided by a local national. The catalogue of Roblot's nefarious acts and decisions during the war years was summarized. When the Germans departed,

Frederick learned, Roblot and the commandant of Monaco's carabinieri had each given orders to close all shutters during the entry of Allied troops, not to display flags, and to remain indoors, instructions that had been largely disregarded.

At present, Roblot was known to be sheltering the former secretary of state for propaganda in Vichy at a villa guarded by the prince's special police. In recent days, Jones asserted, Roblot had released two Italian Fascists who profited immensely from buying and selling vehicles sent to Germany. The minister of state was forever inventing plots, Frederick was told, the current one being that "a group of Monégasque and French people in the pay of local financiers are preparing a revolution through which S.A.S. [His Serene Highness] Prince Louis II would lose his throne." At the same time, Roblot offered money to the National Liberation Committee and gave the FFI in Monaco one million francs in a valise to buy its loyalty.[29]

Prince Rainier attended the briefing. He was excused of any wrongdoings by being enrolled in the University of Montpellier during the occupation years.[30] The hereditary prince was an interesting figure during this time of transition. A week earlier, he had left the palace announcing he would not return until Roblot and his subordinates had been dismissed. Rainier brought his sister to Nice with him to complain to the American general about the minister of state. Rainier had become of concern to Louis as he was surrounding himself with a coterie of friends exhibiting all the idealism of youth. The Comité National Monégasque (CNM) also rallied around the young man, further unnerving the ruling monarch who feared for his throne. Then, on September 21, Rainer addressed a letter to his grandfather's subjects offering the only public acknowledgement of the collaboration that had taken place. "During these last five years of war, I have been witness with you to the misdemeanors of political risk by politicians who have succeeded in obtaining the benevolent confidence of His Serene Highness the sovereign prince, my grandfather," he wrote. "I have attended powerless the evolution of events without ever associating myself and without ever the ability to fight them."[31] As a consequence, Rainier announced he had decided to follow his conscience and join the French army. For the final months of the war, Rainier served in the Algerian tireurs, rising from the grade of private to second lieutenant by the time he returned home. This brief service caused his popularity to soar among his countrymen.[32]

Frederick deduced that Louis was an overwhelmed old man who had lost control as Monaco's post-liberation politics swirled about erratically.[33] The Resistance occupying the principality without formal authorization initially enabled French communists to take charge. Their domination of the CDL generated fears of a leftist coup. One day the FFI went to the home of a schoolteacher who had been a member of a collaboration group and killed him in a gunfight. Major Gunn informed Frederick that the FFI contained other elements that had worked with the Germans, including the leader of the Saint-Just contingent who was reported to have embezzled considerable amounts of money. The FFI adamantly opposed an American occupation that would loosen their hold. Countering the FFI was the conservative CNM, with some former pro-German members now calling themselves Gaullists. The casino supported this movement and was said to be using its riches to secretly arm a private guard with 600 rifles. A search of the premises by yet another force, a militia organized by two hotels, uncovered nothing. Gunn concluded that serious trouble, including street fighting between the FFI and the CNM, might soon erupt, a fear shared by other knowledgeable insiders.[34]

Louis and Roblot did what they knew best: they requested help from the prevailing military power. The latter wrote to Frederick explaining that the principality's security could not be guaranteed by the presence of the FFI and asking that he station American troops there to maintain order. Careful to respect the realm's neutrality, Frederick requested written authorization before his soldiers entered, which Roblot immediately provided. The GIs only remained in that unsettled situation for a week before being withdrawn. The commanding general then ordered signs to be posted at entrances into Monaco declaring it off limits to American military personnel.[35] During this period, Frederick paid a visit to the government's offices where Roblot raised the subject of annexing Monaco to the United States. The prince went a step further. Louis called Frederick and asked his assistance in making Monaco an American state, a conversation recounted by Frederick's civil affairs officer, Captain Joseph Welsh, among others. Like the Swiss had earlier, the Americans did not take the idea seriously.[36]

The bifurcated lifestyle of the city-state rapidly returned. Restaurants were closed to ordinary diners, but meals using ingredients acquired on the black market were served in the private rooms of Monte Carlo's grand hotels for the customary steep price. Although good-timers were prohibited for a while from entering the neutral state from outside, a few gambling tables continued in play for well-heeled guests in residence.

Otherwise, Monaco was reportedly famished. The resupply of foodstuffs had completely stopped by September 13. A civil affairs press release on October 8 stated:

> This former playground is like a house of mourning, shuttered and hungry. Producing nothing itself and with railroad connections virtually suspended, it has been living on the community soup kitchens and the black market. The latter is under sharp fire, and penalties for those engaging in black market activities are severe, but it flourishes nevertheless. An idea of the prices may be gained from the fact that a kilo of chicken is 1200 francs, a

kilo of mutton is 1300 francs. Most things, no matter what the price offered are unobtainable.[37]

Frederick became personally involved in addressing the problem, inquiring whether a fair allocation was being made to the principality from produce available to Alpes-Maritimes. First, he found there were only 2,000 true Monégasques presently in the realm, as compared with 8,000 or more Frenchmen and other nationalities, including Germans and other fascists. Then, his civil affairs officer found that food was being obtained from Marseille and Paris and channeled through the Monte Carlo casino to the fantastically high-priced black market managed by the same people who controlled it during the German occupation. Unable to afford these prices, the vast majority of Monaco residents were virtually starving. It was further reported that medical supplies were being purchased from American soldiers.[38]

Pressure was building for Roblot's departure when on September 23 a company of Zouaves replaced the remaining FFI elements. The French army took full control. Within a week, Roblot left for Paris with a military escort to account for his behavior. Having lost his right-hand man, Louis reached out to de Gaulle for the first and only time. Beginning his correspondence by taking credit for his grandson's enlistment in the army of France, the writer summarized the travail he and his subjects had suffered over many long years. He assured the recipient that "for a long time [he] had been proud to be on your side." The letter was signed, "Louis Prince de Monaco, Général de Division," the honorary rank conferred by France.[39]

The excesses of the CDL led to its reconstitution as the liberation committee of the French community. As such, it undertook the four missions common across France: providing staples, re-establishing a free press, cleansing the society of collaborators, and reforming the economy.

Meanwhile, Captain Jones was busy using Monaco as a base of operations for gathering intelligence in Italy. He based two Chriscrafts and four fishing boats in Monte Carlo, complemented by PT boats in Corsica and an aircraft used to insert and recover agents. They even captured one of the low-slung Italian torpedo boats. Following in the footsteps of information-gatherers throughout the war, Jones utilized the international give-and-take in the salons of Monte Carlo to his advantage, but he had to be careful as some of his counter-intelligence personnel became ensnared in what he termed "the fleshpots of Monaco."[40]

The business of cleaning up the little state took a long time. It seemingly required forever to remove rolls of barbed wire, de-mine the seafront, and demolish blockhouses. Until Germany finally surrendered, nothing could be taken for granted. The following March, Sénégalais tirailleurs captured two German soldiers plus a couple of fascist Milice landing at the principality. The next month a torpedo guided by a Wehrmacht commando exploded against the city's commercial quay. Inhabitants also claimed to have been struck by a shell fired by the Germans holding Mont Authion. Indeed, it was not until July 2, 1945, when a naval vessel struck a German mine at the wharf, that Monaco was shaken by the war for the last time.

The basic question repeatedly coming to mind in considering the principality then or now, when looking at an oasis of high-rise buildings on a coastline otherwise developed to human proportions, is why France has permitted this enclave to exist in her socialist state. Having received a report concerning the excessive control exercised by members of the Resistance shortly after liberation from the French legate to Monaco, a minister in the new government in Paris proposed its annexation to de Gaulle. He responded, "If you had annexed Monaco, I would have officially and publicly blamed you, but personally approved. But you ask my permission. I cannot give it to you."[41] At a time when de Gaulle was actively plotting to acquire Italian territory along the border, France did not have the political will to absorb this parcel and try to charm the snakes living in its rocks.

At some point, one must ask whether in fact Monaco was neutral at all. The 1918 treaty with France left matters of defense and foreign affairs to the major signatory, while recognizing the independence and neutrality of the minor. The civil court in Nice addressed this question in 1946:

> According to the administration and record supporting [...] the Principality, having not conducted a belligerent act at the side of France, is a neutral nation [...] Tied by reason of the relations of the Principality with the French government, German and Italian troops entered its territory and found the means to identify persons and damage their belongings; that in September 1944, French troops liberated Monégasque territory in the same way as French territory; that Prince Louis II of Monaco is Général de Division in the French Army; recognizing that the legal nature of relations existing between the two states, their actual cooperation, places the Principality of Monaco in a state of liaison at least as close as concerns a nation tied by an explicit treaty of alliance.[42]

Two years later, however, the King's Bench in England took notice that "there was some doubt as to whether Monaco was, strictly speaking, 'enemy-occupied' territory in 1944," the year of the German military presence there.[43] It is not difficult to defend that proposition.

To paraphrase F. Scott Fitzgerald's overused characterization of the rich, "Monaco is not like the rest of the Riviera. It's different." Or, to recall an observation by W. Somerset Maugham, Monaco is "a sunny place for shady people."

16

Authion: The Final Battle

Less than 20 miles due north from Monaco, one last battle remained to be fought on French soil only a few weeks before Berlin surrendered. In January 1945, General de Gaulle was asked by a journalist about "the forgotten front," referring to the confrontation still taking place on the Atlantic coast around Bordeaux. The term could, instead, have been used to refer to the stalemate in the Alps where the Germans persisted in occupying a stronghold in French territory up against the Italian border.[1] Eight border communes remained occupied by the enemy in addition to five others under artillery fire—Menton, Castellar, Castillon, Sospel, and Moulinet. Focused on prosecuting the war inside the German homeland, the American army had largely overlooked this provocation. The political importance to de Gaulle's provisional government in Paris of evicting the invaders from the last kilometers of French soil and pushing the postwar border eastward into Italy would lead to one last fight in Alpes-Maritimes.

When they landed in Provence, the Americans had been wary of their right flank, but that threat seemed lessened by more important military engagements now underway. The 148th German Division, which initially resisted the Allied debarkation, had withdrawn largely intact into the Alpine foothills where it joined another Wehrmacht command, the 157th Reserve Division, two Italian divisions, and smaller but aggressive units of Fascist Blackshirts. After the Germans pulled back to the frontier at the end of October, the skeletal American presence at the border declined to leave their dug-in positions and move forward into outposts abandoned by the enemy that would be exposed to fire from the east. Combatants stared at one another from their respective heights across sparsely populated terrain, exchanging artillery fire but nothing more. During a mild spell in the fading autumn light, the picturesque peaks, sharp slopes into virgin valleys, and total silence evinced a heavenly presence for small teams of scouts seemingly alone. Then, suddenly, roared the sounds of shells ricocheting back and forth between the hills like gargantuan billiard balls.

On its side, the German high command wanted to protect against an Allied incursion threatening Torino and the plain of the Po as the Wehrmacht contested the peninsula with General Mark Clark's liberators. After the war the commanding general of the 157th explained, "From the very beginning, it could be supposed that the American forces would attempt an advance into Italy from southern France over the Alpine passes. It was very tempting, indeed, highly possible and promising." His undermanned division could deploy only a single company, however, to each mountain gap in its area of responsibility.[2]

Defensive lines were not exactly along a border that was, after all, strictly a political demarcation drawn when the future king of Italy, Victor Emmanuel II, ceded the Duché de Savoie and Comté de Nice to France as payment for helping expel the Austrians the previous year. In many places the frontier was indefensible. Hence, the Wehrmacht initially occupied forts built by General Sére de Rivières to protect against an invasion from Italy or by the unified German states after the Franco-Prussian War of 1870–1. Often protected by a moat, these casemates might include an open courtyard as they were designed to protect against the less-lethal weapons of that era. They are still found above Monaco (la Tête de Chien), west of Sainte-Agnès (Mont Ours), and on Mont Authion (Milles Fourches and La Forca).

The better-known defensive positions were erected in the 1930s according to a plan devised by André Maginot, the French minister of war. In Alpes-Maritimes these fortifications were often near their antecedents as Sére de Rivières had sited his strongholds on strategic terrain. The twentieth-century emplacements were covered with four or five meters of earth as protection against aerial bombardment, had the capability of elevating heavy artillery to fire through protected embrasures, contained a magazine for munitions and a communication center, and included barracks, kitchen, hospital, and other facilities sufficient to house hundreds of men under ground or dug into a rocky hillside. The stone-and-concrete strong points of the Maginot Line may still be seen (and visited in many cases) on Cap Martin and Mont Sainte-Agnès Agel and at Roquebrune-sur-Martin, Sainte-Agnès, Castillon, Barbonnet, Saint-Roch, and elsewhere.

The Germans were quick to occupy the existing forts. Almost 100 structures were in the Mercantour Range with those on Mont Authion the most imposing.[3] Defensive positions by Séré de Rivières and Maginot were oriented toward the east where France had anticipated an attack, and the Germans were now defending to the west. Conversely, forts on the Italian side of the border faced in the right direction for Wehrmacht purposes, and they, too, were manned by the enemy. The Reich could afford to assign a maximum of 100 troops to these fortresses with as few as 15 soldiers allocated to the redoubts which served as advance posts. To strengthen the forces along the frontier, the German High Command dismantled coastal artillery positions along the Ligurian shore and redeployed naval personnel to the border defenses. Poorly armed with rifles and machine pistols, these reinforcements had no ground combat training or experience.[4]

The 148th Division was soon replaced by the 34th Infantry Division. The new outfit had an impressive war record, but only 550 of its men were actual veterans of earlier campaigns in Russia and France. Furthermore, at any one time a quarter of its strength was unfit for duty. The sparse manning was reflected in its depleted organization of two battalions per regiment and companies comprised of 100 soldiers filling 180 authorized slots. Late in the war, replacements tended to be older men, many unfit for combat, the average age being 35. On the positive side, most of the 34th recruits were Rhinelanders bearing a grudge for their region being occupied by the Allies, their homes destroyed and families displaced. Consequently, they were thought to be strongly pro-Hitler.[5]

The high rate of desertion among troops impressed in Eastern Europe resulted in few of these soldiers being placed on the front line where they could cross over to the French. Until mid-December, a German officer, four non-commissioned officers, and an interpreter were attached to each company in the Italian divisions. Even so, Italian soldiers attempted to defect and, when this became too risky, sought to join their country's partisans. After reassignment of the dwindling German cadre, the increased frequency of abandonment precluded stationing Italian troops up front as well. Therefore, the perimeter itself was almost all-German. They relied on conscripts and the last remnants of the Italian army, however, for manpower to resupply and support them.

The German defense drew upon a more reliable ally in the Italian Blackshirts. These men, numbering about 3,500, were trained and commanded by German staff and used at first to repress partigiani. The Italian Milice was centered initially on the coast in the vicinity of Imperia and San Remo. Once the French Milice fled their homeland, the Germans employed mixed detachments of fascists from both countries to help protect the border.[6] As 1944 drew to a close, the fascist front was manned by defenders who held on, dreaming of the introduction of innovative weaponry promised by Hitler to turn the tide of war in the new year.

Winter 1944–5

In winter the weather protects the Alps, observed Field Marshal Albert Kesselring.[7] The winter of 1944–5 in the Southern Alps was one of the coldest in the twentieth century. On January 5 it even snowed at the seaside. Harsh conditions, inadequate clothing, and scant rations combined to erode troop morale on both sides of the line. German soldiers were faced with new regulations promulgated by Hitler imposing severe penalties, including death, for a variety of acts considered treasonable. The political officer of the 34th Division justified holding northern Italy to the rank and file as vital to feeding the Fatherland. But German reversals in the Ardennes after the initial success of the December offensive and the advance of Soviet hordes from the east demoralized Wehrmacht defenders. Mail censors attempted to intercept bad news, especially troubles at home, but never with complete success. The unintended consequence was the generation of unfounded rumors compounding the unrest.

As the cold intensified, more and more defenders fell sick or suffered frostbitten hands and feet. German positions at altitudes over 6,000 feet were accessible only by narrow trails. Provisions had to be carried to the defenders by mule or on the backs of men. Snowfall in the passes soon made it impossible to transport food or munitions to the highest outposts, causing them to be abandoned. The threat of avalanche was enhanced by artillery fire and movement along trails all but invisible in the snow. Burrowed in well behind the military crest, Wehrmacht defenders relied more and more on minefields to alert them of an enemy advance and to channel attackers into pockets of concentrated fire. Direct fire support would be provided by German mortars emplaced and pre-registered on the counter-slopes.[8]

French soldiers were scarcely better off. Each man was issued one uniform, a pair of shoes, often with holes pervious to water, and three pairs of socks. Frostbitten hands stuck to icy gun barrels for want of gloves. Some soldiers even lacked helmets. Commanders complained bitterly about inappropriate gear. As the newest additions to the French army, FFI veterans were poorly provisioned in almost every case. Men were sent on patrol without warm white coats, skis, or snowshoes. It was truly a ragtag force that fortunately was forced to only take part in an occasional firefight during that bitter season.[9] Not surprisingly, this army also experienced desertions by volunteers who had lost faith in their leadership or, for former members of the FFI, were mixed in with soldiers espousing different political views.

Before 1st Airborne Task Force left in December, the combined Allied force was thought to number about 9,500. The following month, however, French XV Corps had only 6,100 soldiers on its rolls, 40 percent armed but many with antiquated weaponry. Conversely, one estimate of the strength of the German–Italian force in January counted between 10,000 and 12,000 men, of whom 60 percent were combatants.[10] It would require the Alpes-Maritimes front to become a priority for both US 6th Army Group and the provisional government in Paris before the French army deployed in the Southeast could expect to receive the personnel, clothing, arms, equipment, and munitions needed to engage in combat.

During the brutal winter both sides engaged in psychological warfare. Tracts intended for American servicemen harped on the gutters of Wall Street and unfaithful wives cavorting with draft dodgers. French soldiers were presented with the treachery of English financiers and communist traitors undermining their country. The minds of Italians who sided with the Allies were confused by stories of their countrywomen being raped by African troops serving with the French army. In their turn, US aircraft dropped tons of leaflets behind the lines guaranteeing safe conduct to defectors and promising humane treatment in accordance with the Geneva Conventions. Handbills printed in Nice for dissemination in Italy named specific persons characterized as turncoats and fascist agents. Undoubtedly, most effective was the repeated question, "Why die for a lost cause?"[11]

The constant military presence was difficult for inhabitants on both sides of the border. In France, soldiers and sailors of the Free French Army engaged in thievery and fighting with locals soon overshadowed the initial euphoria at being occupied by their fellow countrymen. To the east, the Germans dragooned French and Italian civilians for jobs especially dangerous or difficult, such as laying mines or emplacing barbed wire. These workers were continually exposed to the remaining American artillery batteries still deployed along the frontier. Some impressed laborers tried to escape into France but when caught were accused of espionage and deported to Germany. Italian families fleeing the German occupation risked the same punishment and in some cases perished in the cold and snow while trying to cross over to safety. Upon reaching France, refugees faced internment in special camps. The prefectorate asked that the military give preferential treatment to Italian partisans passing through the lines, but this policy generated complaints from French nationals shivering and undernourished themselves.[12]

As winter progressed, the Italian resistance became better organized and bolder. It was not uncommon for partigiani to ambush Wehrmacht trucks making the 30-mile journey from its supply center at Cuneo. One Sunday at the end of February, the Germans observed a squadron of B-25s discharge hundreds of containers of supplies by parachute onto a snowy massif. The occupiers arrived before the irregulars and recovered machineguns, sub-machineguns, rifles, mortars, ammunition, and explosives. The next morning another squadron delivered 100 crates of foodstuffs. Over three weeks, 100 Axis bearers shouldered 2,000 loads and climbed five hours to deliver them to the front lines before descending another four hours under close guard by well-armed German soldiers.[13]

For Frenchmen guarding the mountain perimeter, the contrast between their austerity and the life envisioned along the coast was difficult to accept. Many of their former comrades in the Resistance, now civilians, were sleeping in warm beds in Nice, Juan-les-Pins, Cannes, and other coastal towns. French servicemen off-duty joined their Allied counterparts in buying on the black market, enjoying rich American tobacco, and chasing mesdemoiselles. As in the old days, lights twinkled brightly all night. The hedonistic ways of the Riviera had quickly returned apart from, and seemingly unaware of, the suffering in mountains merely 30 miles away.

Looking ahead to spring, the Germans strengthened their defenses at the mountain passes. The most important of these led to the gorge of the River Roya which entered the narrow Tende to cut through the mountains at the top of the valley. As the direct way from Nice onto the plains of Piémont and the industrial might of Torino, this conduit was therefore the access of greatest strategic significance to the German defenders. It was also the most reliable resupply route for the Axis when snow closed the higher Alpine passes. For this reason, 34th Division engineers reconstructed bridges over the Roya that had been destroyed during the German withdrawal the previous autumn. Farther to the north, the fascists had to be concerned with invaders using the gap through the mountains at Larche for direct access to Conde and the Piémont plateau. To defend against Allied entry into Italy from the sea, the Germans massed more than 40 batteries of heavy artillery between Ventimiglia and Fontan.[14]

Over four exceptionally frigid months, the US Army suffered 43 killed and 136 other casualties and the French military eight dead and 32 wounded.[15] German–Italian losses were unspecified but negligible. The principal victims during the winter confrontation in the Alps were French and Italian border inhabitants. The bloody conclusion to this somber drama awaited the advent of warm weather.

Spring 1945

Over the winter, the order of battle of the Allied forces in Alpes-Maritimes changed. In November the 100th Infantry Battalion from Hawaii was redeployed from northern France where the cold, wet weather, as well as combat, had cut its strength in half. Shortly thereafter, the 65th Infantry, a separate regiment from Puerto Rico, was transferred to the sunny South. North African tirailleurs were replaced by volunteers from metropolitan France, former maquisards, and young men who had received basic military instruction at Vichy youth camps.

Important in reordering the composition of Allied forces was transfer of responsibility for the Alpine sector from American commanders itching to join the final drive to Berlin. The French 27th Alpine Division was assigned to the northern part of the frontier. The 1ère Division de Marche d'Infanterie relieved hybrid American units deployed in southeastern France. Both divisions reported to the new Détachement de l'Armée des Alpes led by Lieutenant General Paul Doyen, a subordinate command of General de Lattre's First

French Army. The 1ère Division commander, Brigadier General Pierre Garbay, established his headquarters at Beaulieu.

Units of the 1st French Colonial Division occupied Sospel and Moulinet in mid-March, bringing an upsurge in enemy bombardments which, fortunately, caused few civilian casualties. In Sospel were 1,460 inhabitants who excitedly welcomed the arrival of French combat troops. After the autumn evacuation of Moulinet, only 20 residents remained behind. The Germans had sacked the town, house by house. Plats of property, books, and other records in the archives and library were scattered on the floor where anyone could step on documents or carry them away. When asked why the streets and houses had not been cleaned up, a young man replied that no one did so for fear of being suspected of having pillaged the properties. Entr'Aide Française (French Self-Help) sent two vans of clothing to the inhabitants, but the survivors asked, as well, for a ton of potatoes, 45 pounds of wheat, and seed and fertilizer to grow vegetables with a mule to plow the fields.[16]

On March 24 the renewed French presence on the Côte d'Azur was heralded in a parade which included an ambulance convoy named "The City of Nice." A sparse array of onlookers lined the Promenade des Anglais. A far larger crowd, estimated at 60,000 patriotic Niçois, gathered on April 9 at Place Masséna to greet de Gaulle. Caught up in the excitement, the local press quoted the national hero as exclaiming, "After Paris, it is in your city that I have received the most enthusiastic welcome." Reminiscent of his phrasing at Paris's liberation, the head of state proclaimed to "Free Nice, Proud Nice, Glorious Nice" that the "wind of Victory," which passes across Europe, "blows now on the Alps, on our Alps."[17]

What did he mean? For Niçois the humiliation of the Franco-Italian armistice and the resulting enemy occupation of French territory along the eastern border remained a festering sore. As the end of World War II grew near, it was high time for the victorious French to acquire a slice of Italy, specifically that portion of the high country including Tende and La Brigue that had been detached from the former Kingdom of Savoie in 1860 when Comté de Nice was ceded to France. This would also constitute a payback for Fascist Italy holding onto French soil from 1940 until 1943. It could be rationalized that a state of war still existed with its neighbor since France had not been a party to the armistice signed by Italy and the United States in September 1943. Radicals called for accession of the entire Italian Riviera, but de Gaulle expressed an interest only in those communities whose inhabitants were French.

De Gaulle had succeeded in obtaining military responsibility for the Franco-Italian frontier from the Allied command. Yet, to advance eastward through the fascist defenses and claim land for France required more troops and logistical support than available in Alpes-Maritimes that winter. A letter to General Eisenhower requesting reassignment of three divisions of the First French Army to liberate territory remaining in German hands elicited a tripartite response. First, military operations must be concluded by April 1 to free units for the final push through Germany. Second, French forces would remain under operational control of 6th Army Group. Third, only two divisions could be redeployed to the Alps.[18] To Eisenhower's provisos, Devers added his own—French troops must not cross the frontier into Italy.

The 1ère Division de Marche d'Infanterie had a nucleus of proud combat veterans from campaigns in the Middle East, Africa, and Italy. It arrived exhausted from hard fighting in Alsace over the winter. The command was missing over one-third of its authorized strength of 15,400 men, as well as a good portion of its prescribed supplies and ammunition. Its equipment consisted of outdated American hand-me-downs. In place of tanks, the division inherited 80 horses and 731 mules left by the departed Yanks. At least 600 wranglers would be tied up caring for and utilizing animals which would soon prove valuable hauling munitions up treacherous Alpine slopes.[19]

To mask the true intention of de Gaulle's offensive—to push the border into Italy—Operation Canard (Duck) had as its ostensible mission taking possession of the massif of Authion and liberation of three French communities in the valley of la Roya still held by the Germans—Fontan, Saorge, and Breil.[20] The Americans were surprised by the large quantity of ammunition requested to recover the lost territory. Instead, the French initially received only the stocks left when the 44th Anti-Aircraft Brigade departed. Doyen's request for an additional 18,000 artillery rounds was denied. In April, however, Devers did allocate 25,000 gallons of fuel to exploit a breakthrough in the German defenses if the attack succeeded.

When spring arrived, Allied thinking had changed since Eisenhower's reply in February. Indeed, Eisenhower signed a subsequent message to 6th Army Group recognizing the difficulty of defining "an exact limit to these operations without depriving the local commander of the initiative necessary for the successful execution of his mission."[21] Consequently, Devers modified his earlier guidance to permit the French initiative to cross the border but not advance beyond Cuneo. The Allies liked the idea of pressure being applied on the Alpine border as their offensive renewed up the Italian peninsula and into Germany.

The French assault was scheduled to kick off on April 9. The senior US liaison officer to the Détachement de l'Armée des Alpes reported the challenges facing French troops on the eve of the assault. Outposts are located on top of rugged mountains, he advised, some over 10,000 feet high and accessible by only one or two narrow passes easily defended. Targets are too small to expect artillery support to be effective. Only 105- and 155-mm. howitzers are effective, as 75-mm. pieces make no impact on the sheer rock, ice and snow. Warfare of this type requires a large expenditure of ammunition to stop traffic through passes, which entails moving batteries over great distances. Munitions must be hauled up steep roads. Trucks cannot be filled to full capacity and must travel long distances in low gear, causing abnormally high consumption of fuel. In the writer's opinion, success would rest on the proper amount of supplies, "as the moral[e] and efficiency of the troops is in my opinion exceptionally high."[22]

The Battle of Authion

De Gaulle's desire to occupy Italian territory extending as far as Torino was intended to present the Allies with a fait accompli when permanent boundaries were fixed after the war.[23] This could be achieved most easily by proceeding up one of two routes from the coast into the narrow passages which opened onto the broader valley formed by the River Roya. The immediate task was to take the German stronghold on Authion which at an altitude of over 7,000 feet controlled the line of craters west of the valley of la Roya.[24] The offensive would have the advantage of being close enough to the coast to receive air and naval support. A diversionary action, Operation Laure, was planned at Col de Larche to occupy German troops manning supporting positions. An advance eastward along the coast to Ventimiglia would distract the enemy from the primary military objective.

The strategic importance of Authion was recognized at least as far back as 1793, when the Sardinians and their Austrian allies manned the mountain ridge. When a direct assault failed, French troops bypassed the stronghold leading to its abandonment. After Italy's unification in 1870, relations deteriorated to the point where the French military established camps on the massif and erected twin stone forts of modest size on the spurs of La Forca and Mille Fourches to defend against an assault from the south. Each structure was protected by high grillwork, a deep moat, and five meters of earth over a concrete capstone, the latter being a derivation from the standard model of Séré de Rivières.

Additional construction followed. A third fortification was built at the end of the nineteenth century on the Pointe des Trois Communes on the northern side of Authion. Two teams worked uninterrupted in consecutive eight-hour shifts for 176 hours to fabricate concrete reinforced with 4,550 steel bars. An imposing silhouette, cut stone, and vertical-lift bridges over its moat gave this redoubt a distinctive character. At the outbreak of World War II a fourth work was nearing completion as part of the Maginot Line, Plan Caval built into the east slope with very little showing above ground. Supporting military structures included a cable station and a cantonment, Cabanes Vieilles, consisting of an assortment of stone barracks and wooden huts.

Wehrmacht soldiers manning these positions were well armed with automatic weapons and benefited from knowledge of the terrain acquired over the winter months. Impact areas for their mortars, set 600 meters to the rear, had been carefully selected and registered. The three points on which they were concentrated coincided with where the French assaults would take place. A complex network of trenches, extensive barbed wire, and five types of land mines tied together the forts. What meager reinforcements could be gathered were redeployed to the Authion battlefield, including decimated infantry regiments of 80 and 253 men and a field battalion of the Luftwaffe. In their detailed organization for field combat, the Alpine defenders were adhering to the doctrine that Marshal Kesselring had proven successful in weakening the aggressive spirit of the numerically superior Allies in Italy.[25] What the German defense lacked was the ready support of heavy artillery with sufficient ordnance.

An assault on the mountain fortifications of Authion would be the first such operation for the 14,400 men of the 1ère Division. In reserve was the 13th Demi-Brigade of the French Foreign Legion hailing originally from the mouth of the Rhône Valley and consequently known as "La Marseillaise." Its two battalions initially set up camp between Saint-Laurent-du-Var and Antibes before moving closer to Authion at Levens, Ariane, Eze, La Turbie, and Laghet in the back country.[26]

A doctor and 20 stretcher-bearers were assigned to each battalion and a field surgical station established at nearby Saint-Etienne-de-Tinée. Six civilian hospitals prepared to receive the wounded at Nice, Antibes, and Cannes. In addition, the Red Cross put an ambulance at the disposition of the Alpine troops driven by two pretty mesdemoiselles certain to lift the spirits of the casualties being transported. On the other hand, the attending physician admitted his drugs were not the most modern or particularly effective.[27]

Brigadier General Garbay could rely upon naval gunfire against German communication lines along the coast, which he employed to simulate the preparation for a debarkation. Most of Flank Force Mediterranean was French, commanded by a *contre-amiral* (rear admiral). The cruisers *Gloire* and *Duguay-Trouin* targeted the bridges of Ventimiglia and Bordighera rendering them useless to tanks and artillery. The destroyer USS *Kendrick* was also engaged, firing five missions at or near Ventimiglia.[28] As Luftwaffe aircraft were non-factors by this time, Garbay planned to employ French aviation to isolate the battlefield by interrupting his opponent's supply lines. In this endeavor, he drew upon the Jeanne d'Arc squadron of 24 P-39 Aero-Cobras and a squadron of US P-47 Thunderbolts. Both units were based at the airfield at Californie, site of the present-day Nice International Airport.[29]

The frontal attack was assigned to 4th Brigade of the 1ère Division. To prepare, one battalion underwent firing exercises and training marches in the mountainous terrain. Companies conducted visual reconnaissance of Authion as well. Patrols gave a stark report of "very difficult terrain, impassable often even for mules, absolutely stripped bare."[30] Battalion and company commanders were summoned to Beaulieu to study a mock-up of Authion's fortifications fabricated by division engineers.[31] DeGaulle himself made a special visit to the division headquarters on April 7 to confer with Garbay on the imminent operation. "Gentlemen, I am aware of the sacrifices that I ask of you. The campaign which opens will be hard, I know it. It will open the doors of the Piémont and you will drive to the Tyrol." Then, he added the clincher. "Anything you can do is useful and gives me arguments to raise in the name of France. We want to retake the natural frontier of our country."[32]

American dive-bombers flew 16 sorties for battlefield preparation early on April 9 but achieved minimal effect when their explosives failed to penetrate fortifications buried underground. The attack scheduled to commence the same day was postponed for 24 hours to permit one last battery to reach the combat zone.[33] That night, infantry moved into place to launch an assault at 9.00 the next morning following more aerial bombardment.

The first company advancing toward the fort of La Forca was soon halted by mortar fire. The German defenders were so well camouflaged that French observers could not spot them. Nor was French artillery, using American 57-mm. antitank cannon, able to destroy defensive concentrations on the rear slope. Crossfire from trenches, casements, and machinegun nests caused frightful losses for the attackers. After a direct strike by a French fighter aircraft, one company finally reached the casements at 5.00 p.m., but not long thereafter a vigorous German counterattack forced the invaders to surrender their hard-won terrain. The assault cost 66 casualties, representing half of the unit's effectives.[34]

Another company had Cabanes Vieilles as its objective. The infantrymen were to follow behind a platoon of light M-5 Stuart tanks which only entered action in late morning because their engines had difficulty going upward in the thin air at that altitude. The attackers employed smoke to obscure visibility from nearby Mille Fourches which they bypassed along with La Forca, already fully engaged. The advance halted suddenly in front of a 15-meter cut in the trail made by the defenders. The riflemen resumed the move forward but were now separated from their armored support. Firing from the valley of la Roya, German 88-mm. artillery unleashed a brief but torrid bombardment. The infantrymen were frozen in place by fear and the deaths of several leaders. Gaping holes blown in the road behind the lead tanks prevented their withdrawal. Once the torrent abated, division engineers used a bulldozer to begin repairing the surface while still under constant fire. It was after dark before the first two armored vehicles could catch up with the foot soldiers. About 10.00 p.m. the tanks were permanently put out of action by mines only

500 yards from the objective. Reinforcements finally arrived with the support of accurate shelling by French artillerists.[35]

To the south a third company approached the cable station, but its progress was slowed by numerous mines and entangled barbed wire. The climb toward the summit was made more difficult by the hazardous incline and intermittent small-arms fire. In the early afternoon, a violent bombardment on three Wehrmacht batteries by a dozen P-47s permitted the top of nearby Bosc peak to be approached, but a fierce counterattack forced the French to fall back with heavy losses. The summit was retaken, although heavy mortar fire all around brought additional losses. Reinforcements finally carried the day for the attackers but at grave cost.[36]

To sum up, the French swarmed all around the objective on the first day of fighting but proved unable to subdue the stubborn defenses on Authion. Of the 12,000 rounds allocated to the offensive, half were fired on April 10. More than 50 attackers were killed or missing in action, 150 wounded, and two of six tanks destroyed. Losses were heavy with minimal gain. The Germans had proven adept in the defense, requiring the aggressors to rethink their tactics.[37]

Garbay decided to launch an offensive against Mille Fourches using an assault group specially configured to overcome fortified emplacements. Its members had trained for this kind of mission in March by besieging a mountainous salient at Roquebrune-sur-Martin and maneuvering on Mont Agel. The commander of the unit code-named "Z" was Lieutenant Colonel André Lichwitz, a physician and veteran of El Alamein and wounded several times. He had recently determined tactics for assaults making heavy use of bazookas, flamethrowers, and phosphorous grenades. The outfit was composed of four sections of infantry. Three consisted of six men equipped with flamethrowers, six bazooka firers, and six sub-machinegunners. There was also a fourth section of automatic riflemen and some engineers. Specialized equipment included light mortars, smoke and phosphorus grenades, and long ladders to scale hardened sites.[38]

Lichwitz later recalled that the operation began at 1.00 a.m. on April 11 to avoid enemy observation. The men climbed the slope of Authion in silence for some time when suddenly a flare exploded overhead, and then another and another. The attackers flattened themselves against the roadbed but nothing followed. Resuming the ascent at 4.00, they entered a minefield resulting in several casualties. It was necessary to wait until first light of day to figure their way out of the trap. Farther ahead, Lichwitz called for artillery preparation. The fire of 155-mm. guns showered rocks down on his own troops. Soon afterwards, French mortars blanketed Mille Fourches in smoke. Still, there was no sign of the enemy.

Suddenly as Lichwitz's men reached the top, firing erupted from behind at La Forca which had spotted the advance. Again, everyone scrambled for cover while the bastion ahead became illuminated by flames darting out of its apertures from incoming shells. Despite mounting personnel losses, Group Z moved close enough for flamethrowers and bazookas to engage the fort. Artillery rounds blew a breach in the grill protecting the moat. Hastily four ladders were erected in the ditch for the aggressors to climb onto the fortress roof. The coup de grace was dropping phosphorous grenades into the ventilation ducts. The garrison of 30 officers and men quickly emerged, coughing fiercely with hands held high.[39]

Not far away at Cabanes Vieilles the attackers finally achieved their objective. After a short artillery preparation, tanks and infantry moved to within 100 meters of the fortified barracks. Under this relentless pressure the Wehrmacht defenders begrudgingly evacuated their emplacements and pulled back. After 36 hours of combat the French foot soldiers were exhausted and permitted to rest in place. Pursuit of the Germans by the light tanks was prevented by more fire from 88-mm. artillery.[40]

Stretcher-bearers required as long as 20 hours to descend from the heights and deliver casualties to medical facilities. Periodically it was necessary to dispatch a nurse to Nice to buy more medicine and bandages for continuing medical operations.[41] The division hospital company received 271 casualties from the first 48 hours of fighting, a record number in its long history. A fire fueled by the amputated arms and legs of soldiers who had challenged Authion and lost burned late into the night in the courtyard of the caserne serving as a field hospital.[42]

Overnight on April 11–12 the weather deteriorated. The mercury dropped to five degrees Fahrenheit. Men suffered terribly and climbing became more treacherous after another blanket of snow. Morning light revealed a low cloud cover which delayed air operations until late afternoon. The weary attackers of La Forca halted short of their objective due once more to mortar fire from the reverse side of the mountain. At noon, however, Group Z arrived from Mille Fourches and a combined assault carried the day, flamethrowers and grenades being employed to good advantage. Ladders permitted the Frenchmen to mount the structure, but their presence alerted defenders to flee the dreaded phosphorous. Fifteen prisoners were taken.[43]

Plan Caval was the Wehrmacht's last major stronghold. An attack at 3.00 p.m. precipitously stopped when German bazookas forced the armored vehicles to retire. After successes with phosphorous at Mille Fourches and La Forca, the field commander sent in French fighter aircraft guided by an observation plane to drop chemical bombs inside the structure, forcing the Germans to evacuate.[44] Consequently, the subterranean fortress survived the battle virtually undamaged.

Now, only the redoubt at Trois Communes remained in Wehrmacht hands. Sensing the defenders' confusion at the successive fall of other bastions, at 6.00 p.m. the French opened fire with two 75-mm. antitank pieces captured in Alsace to try to disable the structure's hydrolifts. Through apertures in the walls, exploding shells and surging flames were clearly visible to the attackers. Within three hours the disheartened defenders surrendered, 38 in all including two officers disgusted at being defeated by German guns.[45]

The soldiers, Légionnaires, and sailors of France paid a heavy price for the conquest of Authion. The human cost to French units was 408 killed, 1,234 wounded (including well over 600 maimed), and 286 lost as prisoners. In sharp contrast, German and Italian defenders lost 126 dead, 498 wounded, and 397 taken prisoner.[46]

The assault on Authion resulted in a tactical victory for French forces but with significant casualties. The Wehrmacht held out for 72 hours at one-to-five odds and then withdrew in good order, retaining the means to fight another day. Their morale was remarkable considering the enemy's superior numbers and firepower. On the other side, the French fought tenaciously but were inexperienced in mountain warfare and initially misused their superiority in tanks and aviation. Once the attackers concentrated their fire, however, the enemy was unable to remain in place. Wehrmacht prisoners taken on Authion acknowledged their astonishment when suddenly faced by tanks, even the light models employed by the French. Their surprise eventually turned to despair and, then, to defeat.[47]

The End Game

General Doyen was sobered by the extensive consumption of munitions scarce to his command. Assessing the men of 1ère Division to be exhausted by their efforts over three days in severe terrain and climatic conditions, Doyen ordered a halt. The 13th Demi-Brigade was brought forward in relief to plaintive objections from the Division's proud officers. The French won the battle, but the Germans had retired to another strong defensive line along the frontier. Critics contended that nothing had really changed.[48]

The Légionnaires who took over the fighting were an odd-looking bunch. African colonials who filled the ranks earlier in the war had been left by the sea due to the extreme cold at these elevations. In their place, among others, were hundreds of Alsatians fluent in German which would prove useful. An American reporter found a collection of men who typified the French soldiers in this campaign. "They were dressed in a weird un-Pattonlike mixture of ODs [Olive Drab combat attire], fatigues and khakis, plus parts of British battle dress. They wore French overseas caps of various bright colors, sprinkled with a few American and British helmets. Several had brown berets—these were the only distinguishing marks of the French Foreign Légionnaires."[49]

Over a ten-day period, engagements involving Légionnaires and other small formations of French troops exhibited specific characteristics. Armed confrontations were local in nature as opposed to the coordinated assault on Authion. The French maneuvered under cover of darkness. Fascist defenders consistently threw up stiff resistance. The silence of the forest was shattered by artillery shells whistling overhead and the rat-tat-tat of machineguns and stutter of other automatic-weapons fire. When supported by an artillery preparation or a few light tanks, a French attack could overwhelm a fortified point. Sometimes this led to a strong counterattack which often prevailed. When the pressure became too intense, the Germans abandoned their defenses after dark, leaving behind anti-personnel mines. They then took up successive positions farther back, delaying the advance once more.

The nadir in this series of small-unit contests took place at the pass of Cerise on the border directly north of Saint-Martin-Vésubie. This French offensive could readily serve as a textbook example of how *not* to conduct an assault. During the night of April 17–18, trucks used their bright headlights when transporting troops into position. The next morning, the soldiers waited to advance in the open, readily visible to enemy observers. The attackers departed late, well after the cover of night as intended. The firebase assigned to support the offensive was so spread out in the pass that many of the guns were outside range of the combat zone. No coordination between the two teams, assault and support, was possible for lack of radios and flares. Consequently, the mortars did not fire a single round. The attack itself was disastrous, with incompetent field leadership and poorly trained troops. At the conclusion of this abortion, the French side reported five killed and 32 men taken prisoners, including three officers. They had been defeated by 12 Italian soldiers, one of whom was wounded, commanded by a captain detested by his men as a "fanatical Fascist."[50] But he must have been the archetype of a combat commander.

The last stand by Axis mariners in the Mediterranean was spectacular, if largely ineffective. On the night of April 17 the German commander sent out a one-man canoe filled with explosives against a French destroyer on patrol off Ventimiglia. Lacking radar, there was no warning of the explosion which killed 20 sailors and wounded 12 others, sending the vessel limping back to Toulon for repairs and creating a sensation there and in Fascist Italy.[51] Consequently, a flotilla of craft embarked after dark on April 23 but failed to achieve similar success. The attackers consisted of 17 torpedo vessels, 23 suicide canoes, and a pocket submarine. A German version of the underwater torpedo craft was piloted by a single man while the Italian model, older in design, was guided by two men breathing from diving tanks.[52] The first wave headed for Monaco and Villefranche, others continued farther west.

With knowledge of the previous attack and the assistance of observation planes, Allied warships were alert to the threat. Three canoes went down at

Cap Martin; two more were sunk off Cap d'Antibes by submarine hunters. An American torpedo boat blew up two mini-craft. A pair of canoes was abandoned, one off Beaulieu and the other at Monaco. Others were ditched when the fascist mariners realized they were being targeted by their prey. Two boats exploded on the jetty at the port of Antibes, and a couple more were found floating at large in the harbor. The crew of the pocket submarine scuttled it rather than be captured. In sum, 23 boats were destroyed and 18 others scuttled or abandoned.[53]

France's success at sea seemed finally to be replicated on land. At an altitude of 7,000 feet above the valley of Chastillon, not far from the present-day ski slopes at Isola 2000, the Légionnaires achieved a strategically important victory. By stealth at night, a company of men approached a garrison manned by Italians. Knives were used to silence the two sentinels after which 70 Alpini were captured, many while still in their beds. Inadequately clothed and wearing light shoes, the infantrymen awaited the enemy response. It came the following day in a counterattack by 80 fascists, including ten Germans, supported by a 149-mm. Italian artillery piece. Now the treacherous terrain was an advantage and the French line held. Doyen's men were finally beginning to penetrate the Alpine wall.[54]

It had become evident that neither of the two principal entry points to Italy could be cleared in time to advance into the Piémont as far as de Gaulle envisioned to gain a political bargaining chip. German demolition interrupted the road beside the River Roya, the preferred route. In fact, French forces were finding that they could hold on to the Roya only by erecting roadblocks to prevent fascist infiltration back into the valley. The second choice, Col de Larche, had been closed by massive rock obstructions left behind by the withdrawing Wehrmacht. Defenses at less-accessible passes, such as Cerise, had proven too difficult to overcome. Consequently, French tacticians focused attention on the Col de la Lombarde at over 7,000 feet, located almost midway between Larche to the northwest and Authion to the southeast. To conceal his intention of entering Italy this way, Doyen directed his troops to the north to engage in further diversionary operations and ordered French warships to shell the shoreline repeatedly to simulate a pending landing along the Ligurian coast.

Taking control of Castillon Valley provided the Légionnaires access to Lombarde pass which they entered during a storm on the night of April 25–6. Soon animals carrying munitions and supplies were stopped by two meters of fresh snow requiring combat engineers to clear. Once accomplished, the advance resumed. By April 28 the column had descended from the Alpine elevations onto the plateau of Piémont with Cuneo just ahead along the River Sturca. The Germans had already passed through Cuneo where its advance guard made a deal with the partigiani, to wit, they would pay for food and forage for their horses if the partisans left them alone. At this stage, everything had its price for the Italians. An airdrop resupplied the French vanguard with rations, and its spearhead leaned forward for the final push to Torino.

The Légionnaires' march from Alpine heights down slopes through forests of pine, oak, and chestnut trees and onto the broad plain below—the first, well suited for partisan ambushes; the second, ideal for armored engagement—had been uneventful due to the absence of enemy resistance. Foreseeing an end of hostilities, the Wehrmacht elected to preserve its few remaining forces by pulling back to the Fatherland. Generaloberst Heinrich von Vietighoff who had succeeded Kesselring ordered a withdrawal on April 20 despite the Fuhrer's insistence on holding positions at all costs. On April 23, General Hans Schlemmer, commanding LXXV Army Corps, directed the retreat of all elements of the 34th Division, which was completed the following night. When Italian soldiers heard that an American force coming from the northwest was closing in on Milano, they threw down their arms, deserted, and returned to their villages. The French advance made no contact with any element of its opponent's rear guard as enemy pioneers repeatedly destroyed tunnels and bridges while withdrawing. Thus the entry into Italy hardly constituted a military victory for the French but rather a concession by the enemy.[55]

Fanning out in several directions, French troops encountered civilians driven from their homes by the Wehrmacht. A youngster sitting dreamily on the grass pacified by the sun's warm rays was suddenly shaken from his reverie by soldiers' boots. The wearers were not German, but French. Happily leading the fellow countrymen to his parents, an air of suspicion was only too evident. Are you enemy agents, the liberators barked accusatorily? Refugees from Sospel, they pleaded, and were soon taken to Nice by truck.[56]

There had been several indications of a change in strategy. On April 23–4 the enemy abandoned the towns of Saorge and Fontan in the valley of la Roya after first sacking them. In a grande finale to seven months of daily bombardment, that same night the Germans fired more than 700 shells at Sospel, Castellar, Breil, and Menton to cover their retreat.[57] The next day Wehrmacht engineers began destroying bridges, tunnels, and viaducts in the valley, cutting their own lines of communication but denying adversaries the ability to pursue. On April 26, without fascist opposition, advance patrols entered the vertical village of Tende, hanging onto the side of a cliff, and remote La Brigue, dwarfed by snow-capped mountains. The tricolore was quickly hoisted over these prize communities which were historically part of Comté de Nice.

Doyen's response to the pullback was to order execution of Operation Pingouin (Penguin)[58] to pursue his retreating adversaries, again a cover-up for the greater political objective. To the south the advance included entering coastal towns across the border in Italy as far as Imperia. When French troops arrived in Ventimiglia they found 90 percent of the buildings had been destroyed during naval and artillery bombardments over the preceding eight months. The 700 remaining inhabitants were discovered cowering in nearby caves. Yet the greeting accorded the victory parade was friendly, including crude placards hastily drawn up to welcome the invaders and praise General de Gaulle. At nearby Vallecrosia and Bordighera, the reception was the same. Among the conquering heroes was the 18th Regiment of Tirailleurs Senegalais, as colonial troops remained a component in the French order of battle. Only in San Remo was there a different state of affairs, for the triumphal entry was preceded by naval shelling under the mistaken impression that the town was still occupied by Fascists. Italian partisans intervened with the Allies to bring the firing to a close.[59]

France would thereby seem to have achieved its strategic objective along the Italian border, yet there was one more serious confrontation ahead. As the Allies closed in on Berlin, the Supreme Allied Command in the Mediterranean came to the conclusion that pressure from French troops in Northwest Italy was no longer necessary to support the main offensive. On April 28, just when the Légionnaires and 1ère Division were poised to strike out for Torino, Devers ordered Doyen to halt his advance and prepare to return to the border. Doyen declined to pull back until so instructed by his government. Although 1ère Division units were only 50 miles from Torino, de Gaulle directed Doyen to consolidate his command at Borgo San Dalmazzo, which he did on May 1, and then remain in place. The following day, a truce stopped fighting across Italy.[60]

Cooperation between Paris and the Allies had already begun to fray. A similar confrontation had just taken place at Stuttgart where, on instructions from the French provisional president, General de Lattre refused to turn over the city to American control. In another episode, de Gaulle prevented British and American agents from crossing the Franco-Italian border out of concern that they might poison public opinion against the French intruders. Meanwhile, the prefect of Alpes-Maritimes went so far as to take a military detachment to Tende on April 30 and to a nearby hamlet two weeks later to preside over referenda that, not surprisingly, voted in favor of annexation to France. In one commune, 976 voters expressed a desire to be attached to France while 49 others abstained; in another precinct, 893 votes were in favor, plus 37 blank ballots.[61]

During the month of May, relations between French occupiers and Italian inhabitants also deteriorated as local authorities became increasingly aware of de Gaulle's intention of acquiring their territory. Partigiani refused to provide mules to the French army, declaring they were waiting to be liberated by the Americans. The situation worsened when a colonial infantryman was murdered by Italian irregulars.[62]

On May 30, Doyen wrote to his superior protesting Allied attempts to establish a military government in the province of Cuneo which he had been ordered to occupy and administer. Doyen asserted that he would be forced to oppose it due to the plan's "definite anti-friendly character, indeed even hostile, and might have severe consequences." What these "consequences" might be became clearer on June 2 when Doyen wrote once more that de Gaulle had instructed him to make absolutely clear that he was to prevent establishment of an Allied military government in areas occupied by French forces "by all necessary means without exception." The thought of Frenchmen taking up arms against their American liberators was too much for President Harry Truman. He cabled de Gaulle on June 6 expressing alarm and asking him to reconsider. Truman added that he was suspending supply of military equipment and munitions to France until the matter was resolved.[63]

De Gaulle responded that "of course, it had never been the intention neither in the orders of the French government nor in those of General Doyen to oppose by force the presence of American troops in the Alpine zone," and an agreement would be reached. Consequently, French troops retired progressively to the frontier of 1939. In accordance with instructions from his government in Paris, on June 21 the commanding general of the 27ème Division d'Infantrie Alpine directed "French troops stationed in Italy will be relieved by American and South-African elements."[64] Towns in the Sturca valley were handed back to Italian control and communities along the Ligurian littoral were abandoned. On July 10 even those two sanctuaries of French culture, Tende and La Brigue, were surrendered by French troops. While the return of Alsace and Lorraine was being celebrated, the Niçois press opined that the five border localities being administered by France were not turned over because of fierce opposition by former Fascists in Italy. The withdrawal appeared a personal humiliation for de Gaulle. France had obtained an occupation zone in Germany but was unable to acquire what was considered its rightful possessions just across the Italian border. In combination with other disagreements with the Allies over Algeria, Syria, and Indochina, the dispute over a French entitlement in Italy was a factor in excluding de Gaulle from sitting alongside Truman, Churchill, and Stalin at the decisive conference in Potsdam.

The conquest of Authion generated political capital in Menton as its inhabitants, many cast out from their homes for five years, were now free to return without fear of enemy occupation or artillery bombardment from that mountain top. The scene at the central Nice railway station was far different, however, as trainloads of injured soldiers arrived, some mortally wounded. Considering the lack of any real gain from fighting on Authion and afterwards to the east, a native of Alpes-Maritimes in 1945 had good reason to assess the material costs and loss of French lives on "the forgotten front" to have all been for naught.

17

Rebuilding the Riviera

Winning battles is not the conclusion of a military campaign. Restoring order to a society disrupted by war is sometimes harder and often a longer undertaking. Now it was time in France for the transition from occupation to democracy. General de Gaulle intended that the Gouvernement Provisoire de la République Française which he headed would determine the nation's destiny. De Gaulle had made it clear at the outset of planning for the liberation of France that he would decide who succeeded the puppet prefects, mayors, and bureaucrats appointed by Vichy, not Churchill or Roosevelt. The prefect of the Var and the mayor of Toulon had already been selected, for example. Nor was it coincidental that on the third day of the debarkation, Raymond Aubrac, de Gaulle's personal choice for high commissioner in the Midi, came ashore with French and American soldiers. On behalf of de Gaulle, General de Lattre and General Cochet, commander of the FFI in the South of France, approved the French liaison officers who would accompany US and French divisions in order to oversee the transformation of civil governments as cities and towns were liberated. These envoys had responsibility for resolving local political issues and installing officials designated by Algiers.[1]

The Supreme Allied Command's sole interest was defeating the Third Reich and could not countenance the nightmare of civil clashes erupting in France before conclusion of the war. Expediency called for relying upon de Gaulle. Allied Forces Headquarters published the following directive to Seventh Army: "Military government will not be established in liberated France. Civil administration in all areas will normally be conducted and controlled by the French authorities."[2] That left the US Army's civil affairs officers to serve as coordinators at key locations and perform liaison and intelligence functions only indirectly engaged in civilian administration.[3] The headquarters for the South of France was established at Marseille with one of its field offices responsible for Nice, Cannes, and Grasse. Consequently, General Devers recorded that at least 100 officers were released from the Allied Military Government of Occupied Territories as, in his words, "the French were taking hold in great shape and would, with help from us in getting food into the larger cities, be able to carry their own load; that all we would need would be liaison officers to keep both the American and French operatives informed."[4]

A side effect of the rapid advancement by Allied invasion forces was that military commanders, American and French, had little time to set up responsible governments in every jurisdiction that fell into their hands. To their pleasant surprise the liberators found the FFI well organized and knowledgeable in installing people who knew how to run the railway, post office, and police. Resistance groups performed criminal justice functions to include collecting and incarcerating collaborationists, for just before the landings the Germans had been neutering law enforcement by moving gendarmes from smaller to larger communities and in many towns stripping police officers of their vehicles and firearms.[5]

As throughout the Midi, CLLs were installed across Alpes-Maritimes, beginning in Vence on August 27. Their composition was more homogeneous in the back country where the leftist Front National was often in the majority. The littoral was pluralistic with various factions more balanced. Thus the two principal Resistance confederations, the Front National and MUR, coexisted with the Socialist and Communist parties, the prisoners' movement, organizations of women and youth, and other groups of dissenters. The CLL helped form post-occupation governments in 128 of the department's 161 communes, supervising committees organized to provide food and cleanse all traces of Vichy and fascism. In some locales, like Saint-Laurent-du-Var and Saint-Paul-de-Vence, the CLL was challenged by elements of the Resistance.[6]

Priorities and Problems of Reconstruction

Underlying the rebuilding of the Riviera, at least in the initial months, was an inherent conflict between France's natural desire to restore the fabric of its society and America's determination to end the war. One of the primary reasons for the debarkation in Provence was to establish logistics bases important to demolishing Fortress Germany. Consequently, priority at Mediterranean ports went to unloading US troops, weapons, equipment, supplies, and matériel. Southern France received between one-fourth and one-third of the military tonnage discharged at Continental ports during the last three months of 1944. Civilian provisions came second. Creating military installations and housing troops produced additional tension as school buildings and gendarme casernes sought by the liberators were the same facilities needed to resume education and shelter citizens whose homes had been destroyed, along with housing displaced persons and refugees. By November a general policy had been promulgated in Alpes-Maritimes that municipal property, including schools, sports fields, and playgrounds, would not be requisitioned for military use.[7]

At the same time, the Allied armed services moved ahead to create rest and recreation areas on the Riviera to accommodate 100,000 military men and women, taking priority over the civilian holiday trade that innkeepers and restaurateurs were anxious to restore. Tens of thousands of displaced persons and prisoners of war also had to be received, fed, and lodged in the Midi. Eighty luxury hotels were identified by the US Army for requisition in Nice and Cannes alone, not to mention various villas and apartments. Acquisitions in Nice soon became so numerous that General Frederick began consulting the prefect before agreeing to any more.[8]

In town after town the major problem was shortage of food. Individual communes often had no more than one or two days of provisions on hand. In the Var, small stocks were uncovered in captured German dumps and caches secretly set aside during the occupation by the supply centers at Draguignan and Sainte-Maxime. While there were no apparent overall health or sanitation problems, children were underfed in Digne, Sisteron, and other localities entered by the liberators. Milk supplies were inadequate everywhere, leading Seventh Army to release 100,000 cans of condensed milk and 3,450 pounds of dried milk from its stocks in early September to help meet the need.[9]

Aubrac considered Nice's shortages the worst in the southern region, exacerbated by the destruction of bridges over the River Var cutting off wholesale resupply from the west. When the situation became dire, the prefect of Alpes-Maritimes wrote to the minister of supplies in Paris to inform him: "The department produces practically nothing. Everything must reach it from outside," reiterating an old truth and emphasizing that his residents were not receiving their fair share of victuals.[10]

Charities again filled the gaps. The National Plate served an average of 3,145 meals per month over the year following liberation of the Riviera. The Municipal Restaurant of Self-Aid in Nice and FFI soup kitchens fed the families of soldiers still engaged in fighting. The Swiss came forward once more, distributing 48,000 boxes of condensed milk and 9,000 kilos of powdered milk, and the Swedish Red Cross offered 2,000 daily snacks, 2,000 tons of almonds, and 5,500 tons of figs. The American War Relief Service contributed boxes of gelatin, chicken bouillon, vegetables, breakfast cereals, and more.[11]

Even today, old-timers who were in Nice immediately after liberation refer to the city being short-changed on food by other municipalities, especially Marseille where most overseas shipments arrived. Cities up the rail line sometimes helped themselves first before sending provisions on to Nice. The inequality involving Marseille was caused at one point by Aubrac "freezing" foodstuffs intended for other departments by the National Ministry of Agriculture. When Aubrac ignored Nice's desperate situation and refused to change his priorities, the government in Paris stepped in and countermanded his restrictions on distribution.[12]

Limited production was reduced by mines sewn in farmers' fields. Relief in agricultural revenue resulted from lifting the government ban on the cultivation or sale of fresh flowers in Alpes-Maritimes in December, as the climate permitted them to be grown out of doors year round. The revenue derived could be used to purchase foodstuffs. American authorities initially prohibited fishing in the rich waters off Golfe-Juan and La Napoule. Yet seafood was of great importance to the Riviera economy, and eventually some daytime activity was allowed. Night fishing continued to be forbidden because lights disclosed the presence of Allied ships, increasing their vulnerability to enemy attack.[13] Morale suffered accordingly. It was only in mid-1945 that the availability of meat, fruits, and vegetables really improved. Despite all this, one Niçoise remembers heavy bread or, perhaps worse, rice bread continuing well into 1945. Another resident still recalls having nothing to eat at the city seminary for two weeks in 1947.[14]

A real problem in feeding the Southeast was obtaining transportation to the famished coastal area. Transport did not return to normal any faster than other distortions brought about by five years of privation. During the occupation, clever technicians in some areas had dismantled trucks and hidden their major components—wheels, engines, and bodies—in separate locations, but now they needed to be reassembled. The shortage of mechanics posed a problem as most competent workmen were German prisoners of war, had been rounded up as forced labor, or joined the Resistance. Tools were scrounged from army ordnance shops. Trucks remained powered by gazogène but, fortunately, charcoal was abundant in the Var.[15]

Typically the local Resistance had one or two trucks and a few more were available for government use depending on a town's size. A boat arrived at Saint-Tropez on August 25 with flour, sugar, and other staples in the hold. The first Liberty ship did not anchor there until September 2. It was difficult to unload the 4,000 tons by small craft. Once ashore, the cargo was vulnerable to theft as hired guards were undisciplined and unreliable.[16] By early September, 40 wood-burning conveyances were reported operating between warehouses in Saint-Tropez and Nice. Other departments were holding food for Alpes-Maritimes until sufficient transport could be mustered. A few vans drove as far as the Vaucluse looking for fruits and vegetables. Civilian traffic over the Var was halted to give priority to vehicles carrying food into Nice and beyond.

The municipal government's chief of supplies acknowledged to the US civil affairs liaison office in Nice that his people would be starving without importation of American flour. A meager 175 grams of flour were being distributed per person in Nice at the end of August, a month in which just 75 grams of meat had been given out. Numerous US citizens, many wives of Frenchmen, expected to receive extra rations and were disappointed. In a throwback to the somber days of fascist occupation, at the end of September, 2,000 people demonstrated for more food before the prefecture in Nice.

An American civil affairs officer acknowledged on October 5, "It is a well-established fact that the people ate better under the Nazi occupation, though the black market was running rampant, but we are now employing all facilities to halt the black market and they no longer can rely on this source of food."[17] Police operations concentrated on illicit traders and courts followed up with strict sentences. The media publicized the campaign stressing the harm done to the economy. An estimated 1.5 million francs had been seized and perpetrators jailed, deported, and fined by mid-October.

At mid-month, criticism of the Americans' failure to deliver sufficient food to the civilian population appeared in newspapers in Nice and Cannes, communist and non-communist alike. Finally, by the end of October, the regular arrival of supply ships enabled the bread ration to attain 300 grams a day. Local markets began displaying some produce at reasonable prices, although meat, sugar, and fats continued in short supply. Improvement was not quick or easy.[18]

The next month the government reported that there were 1,100 tons of potatoes earmarked for Nice at the port of Sète; however, the minister for merchant marine ordered the intended cargo vessel to carry coal instead. Flour remained a problem. Some stocks brought into Toulon were moldy, others smelled of diesel oil. Fifteen tons stored at the quartermaster dump in Saint-Raphaël included broken bags spilling loose flour onto the floor. Dirty and wet and therefore considered unfit for American soldiers, it was sifted and cleaned for civilian consumption, taking special care that it not be diverted to the black market. A train transporting 240 head of cattle arrived in December, but fats and fuel were still scarce.[19]

Épuration (Purification)

It did not require liberation to begin dealing with persons friendly to the occupiers and thereby considered enemies of the French state. As early as 1943 the Resistance started attacking collaborators with the fascist police. Before the summer of 1944, 57 persons were shot down across Alpes-Maritimes. After the Allies' arrival, summary executions continued, totaling 73 in just 18 communes before Courts of Justice began hearing cases in September. Even then, another eight outright murders were perpetrated as punishment for crimes committed by Frenchmen against Frenchmen under the umbrellas of Italian and German control. By Christmas, total assassinations after the Allies landed reached 120, the highest number for a department outside Southwest France. Killings were often committed by "résistants of the 25th hour" settling personal scores.[20]

The Milice had killed partisans in 1943–4, and it was not uncommon for the Resistance to get even as soon as the occupiers were vanquished. Returnees from concentrations camps did not always know who had betrayed them and were at first too weak to retaliate, but their families might well take vengeance against the real or suspected culprits. The instances are too numerous to relate in full, but two examples convey the atmosphere. A boy who had worked with the Italians and, later, with the Germans was taken by the FTP and shot by the roadside in front of his mother who was then dispatched in the same manner. A zealous young member of the Nice underground had taken a German soldier prisoner in August 1944 when a restaurateur came to the captive's assistance. The rescuer was summarily executed.[21]

Extra-judicial justice of all types in Alpes-Maritimes constituted 61 percent of the comparable number in the Department of Bouches-du-Rhône, which included Marseille where three times as many unofficial verdicts of capital punishment were pronounced and carried out. This was part of a pattern throughout France that counted 10,000 victims, explained an eminent European scholar. "It is hatred and a passion for hasty vengeance which swelled the inevitable wave of summary executions in the weeks that preceded and followed the Liberation."[22]

Orderly handling of accusations of collaboration had to await sorting out governmental structures and leadership. The Front National and its sister organizations demanded representation on the CLLs and their big brothers, the CDLs, where they obtained 46 percent of the presidencies and 34 percent of the delegate seats in Alpes-Maritimes. In 53 departmental communes the same person functioned as president of the CLL and provisional mayor. This was the case in Antibes where a member of the Front National was elected by acclamation. His town council conformed to the composition of its underground by including seven communists, four socialists, four members of the MUR, and one representative each from the Femmes de France and the United Force of Patriotic Youth, an FTP front.[23] The 18 members of the CLL were a cross-section of the local working class—two painters and a pair of primary school teachers, accountants, carpenters, a lemonade maker, a gardener, a grain merchant, a ship designer, the ubiquitous attorney, and a coiffeur who led a Resistance group in Juan-les-Pins.[24]

Meanwhile, an unprecedented wave of apprehensions was taking place across Alpes-Maritimes from the end of August through September. The communist-dominated FTP had structure and discipline, a large number of members, and a sufficient supply of weapons to remake governance to its satisfaction. In some places the FFI had taken over the functions of city government and police. Disorganization among these various networks resulted in 2,532 arrests, far beyond the capacity of the holding areas—hotels and casernes in Nice, prisons in Nice and Grasse, Fort Carré at Antibes, and the notorious former Gestapo address in Cannes, Villa Montfleury. Lack of hygiene and thin straw mattresses contributed to suicides and attempts to escape. More troubling were payoffs, extortion of funds, lost files, and wholesale arrests, including the former mayor of Grasse who was beaten by his captors and left paralyzed. Worse yet was that too often subalterns were taken into custody while the principal chiefs and torturers in the Milice and the rightist PPF escaped justice by following the Gestapo back to the Reich or into Italy. The excesses in Alpes-Maritimes caused Aubrac to send a warning to its mayors and CLL presidents on September 28 related to this intemperance. Clearly the number of detentions in the department was disproportionate to its counterparts along the Mediterranean coast and its rate of release far below the median.

Aubrac hardly had clean hands, however, as he had formed a private "security force" in Marseille (Forces républicaines de sécurité), a pool of mainly pro-communist fugitives who engaged in widespread rape, torture, and murder. The protracted violence finally led to Aubrac's dismissal the following January. De Gaulle directed his successor "to reestablish a republican order and reattach a region to France which is completely out of control."[25]

After years of repression of the media, southern France saw an outbreak of newspapers in late 1944, all providing extensive coverage of épuration. Before long, ten dailies replaced the two in Nice during the war. Every political nuance was expressed. The Socialist *L'Espoir de Nice* argued that the sacrifices of the Resistance would be rendered meaningless if traitors were allowed to walk away with impunity. Communists championed the need for vengeance against trusts (many having confiscated the wealth of Jews), businessmen, black marketeers and their collaborators, as these actions harmed the local economy. Other leftist papers used the codeword "justice" to denote punishment. Positioned in the political center, the Gaullist *Combat* denounced false résistants who with "a tricolore brassard on their arms are going to steal, pillage, extort in the name of the Resistance." A month later, it referred to a couple of defendants as "a monster of nastiness" and "a harmful beast," and, in the case of one woman, "a little shrew, aggressive and exhausted." The right emphasized the need for speedy trials, just and in accordance with the rules of law. Moderates generally spoke of indulgence with the possibilities of amnesty and rehabilitation, to which opponents replied that amnesty first required condemnation.[26]

One thing the press agreed upon was culprits. *Combat* blamed the Italians, as did the Christian-Democrat *Liberté*. *L'Aurore de Nice et du Sud-Est* and its partners in the Front National publishing *Le Patriote* preferred to focus on businessmen and leaders in Vichy. Newly enfranchised once more, the United Forces of Patriotic Youth was not satisfied with just the purification commission. "Form vigilance committees in each quarter!" Its newspaper, *Nos Lendemains* (Our Future), insisted on immediate retribution:

> We call for an exemplary and merciless justice against all the Milice, the PPF and other Cagoulards who associated themselves of their own free will with Nazi atrocities against the French who have not hesitated to sell and to torture their brothers. There can be no pity for these sadistic traitors. We demand immediate judgments and immediate gunfire.[27]

Le Cri des Travailleurs, the voice of the French Communist Party in Alpes-Maritimes, agreed.

> PPF, Milice, collaborators, appointees who for five years pretended to possess the monopoly on devotion to the public cause and their partners ran away in a rush fifteen days before the popular insurrection with weapons and baggage [...] Those who remain [...] will present us tomorrow a red shirt they have dyed in the blood of suspects tortured in the villa Lynwood. We will not be fooled, Niçois!"[28]

As in all of France where only 40 percent of the persons arrested ever went to court, the number tried was far less than the total incarcerations even though four judicial bodies heard cases in Alpes-Maritimes. An FFI military tribunal met in Nice during five weeks in September and October and sentenced to prison four of the eight men appearing before it. Three others were fined and one shot. Judging more serious matters dealing with providing intelligence to the enemy, bearing arms against France, complicity in murder, and so on, the three Courts of Justice seated in Nice and Grasse considered 1,167 cases. Of the 481 foreigners involved in these matters, 421 (or 36 percent of the total) were Italian. Nine were executed primarily for informing and helping the Gestapo, the last one in April 1947. Twenty-four others were condemned to capital punishment but their sentences commuted to forced labor, along with another 223 non-Italian defendants. There were 674 penalties of solitary confinement. Finally, 237 persons (or 20 percent) were acquitted. The last man punished for collaboration was freed in 1964.[29]

Quite likely the most sensational execution was that of César Fiorucci, the taxi driver convicted of involvement in the arrests of Torin and Grassi in Gattières and their subsequent torture and hanging in Place Masséna. An FFI military tribunal headed by Commandant Chasuble judged the Gestapo driver guilty and condemned him to death. A 12-man firing squad performed a public execution at Nice's quai des Etats-Unis[30] in September 1944.[31]

Initially, as the Republic's commissioner, Aubrac had the thankless task of deciding on appeals for clemency from defendants sentenced to death. He was provided with dossiers to study along with impartial legal advice, but in the final analysis the decision was his alone. A half-century afterwards he was said to have explained, "Well, if I thought a pardon would lead to more disorder, I rejected it. It is scandalous, indefensible, appalling, but that's what I did."[32] A decade later, he was quoted as agonizing, "I signed at the right, the fellow was shot the next day at 6:00. At the left, he was sent to prison. It was terrifying." Finally, to Aubrac's relief, in November 1944 de Gaulle assumed the authority. Aubrac had reprieved half of the verdicts.[33]

Other defendants received prison terms for political choices as well as for activities during the occupation. A former judge at a tribunal de commerce was sentenced to three years in jail and a fine for joining the PPF. A taxi driver for the Germans and a naturalized Italian who publicly rejoiced at the failure of the Dieppe landing[34] were each found guilty. On the other hand, when a man who volunteered to work in Germany to obtain the release of a prisoner of war and subsequently returned to take an active part in the liberation of Nice was acquitted, spectators in the Court of Justice broke out in applause for the first time.[35]

Civil courts in Nice and Grasse considered lesser offenses leading to loss of legal rights, exclusion from public office and the professions, and the like. The small city of Grasse was especially vigorous, pronouncing over 300 guilty verdicts against citizens who assisted the occupiers.[36] In sum, 753 defendants appeared in civil court in Alpes-Maritimes, and 64 percent were found guilty and penalized.

Less well remembered were impositions of administrative sanctions. Ten detectives and commissars of police, eight teachers, and 12 persons in the Chamber of Commerce found their permits revoked. Nine doctors were prohibited from practicing medicine, while another 15 retired to avoid prosecution. Heavy monetary sanctions were levied against entrepreneurs who realized illicit gains while participating in construction of the Wall of the Mediterranean. More than 20 firms had 59 million francs confiscated and another 55 million francs collected in fines. A dozen bosses spent weeks in preventive detention, one of them implicated in demolition of the Casino de la Jetée on Nice's waterfront and sentenced to 20 years of forced labor. Sanctions were also applied by the local committee of the Syndicat National des Journalistes which issued the *carte de presse* without which a writer could not be employed. Its subjectivity was shown by the credential given the editor-in-chief of *L'Aurore de Nice et du Sud-Est* who previously served on the staff of *L'Eclaireur de Nice,* and not to one of several reporters for *L'Espoir de Nice* and *Combat,* all professional journalists well qualified for that prestigious position. At the same time some employers' syndicates proceeded with their own épuration.[37]

Some individuals had their holdings sequestered—for example, Emmanuel Martinez, whose hotel in Cannes was headquarters for the German garrison; and the owners of *L'Eclaireur de Nice* and *Le Petit Niçois,* for being apologists for Pétain. The Goulds' Hôtel Provençal in Juan-les-Pins was closed. Hôtel Belles Rives across the road was shut, its Jewish owners in hiding. On Cap d'Antibes, the proprietor of Hôtel du Cap and an Italian friend of Mussolini who received fascists throughout the war caused its proprietor to be confined for three months in Fort Carré on charges of collaboration.[38]

The treatment of females who had engaged in "collaboration horizontale" is more complex than first apparent. Numerous considerations influenced liaisons between French women and German men. Wives of prisoners and others separated from their husbands for years on end naturally felt lonely. In some cases want of material favors or desperation for necessities for family or self led to this behavior. Then, there was always the desire for adventure or a perceived need for protection. A genuine affection between lovers was immaterial.

Scholarly studies have focused on this phenomenon, most notably by Fabrice Virgili, a French historian. Shaving the heads of women thought to have slept with the enemy had begun during the occupation, usually after dark by armed, masked men who were members of the underground. This penalty went back at least to Biblical times and was carried out in Belgium and the Rhineland after World War I and by Nazis on German women for sexual relations with foreign workers. By the time of liberation, cutting off hair was not uncommon and thus could hardly have taken the subjects by surprise. After the national trauma accompanying the sudden defeat in May–June 1940 and the dark years that followed, freedom from fascism provided an opportunity to reestablish a proud new identity. Shaving heads was not an act of violence or punishment but rather a symbol of someone's disloyalty to France in which common folk could express themselves. It might be performed in prison. Being found guilty in court, a defendant could also lose her citizenship and the right to vote just afforded French women. If townspeople deemed sentences inadequate, shearing women's hair in the street or square in front of the *hôtel de ville* provided a patina of legitimacy, especially when administered in the presence of uniformed police acting as escorts or guards, making the arrests, or even doing the cutting. It is estimated that 20,000 women were so treated throughout France, especially in rural departments. More than 30 women were shorn in Nice, although the practice had stopped there by the war's end unlike other parts of France. A practical consequence of the clipping was a run on wigs that exceeded stocks in boutiques, as well as the sudden fashion of wearing turbans.[39]

Eric Sevareid, later to become an American television oracle, was naturally troubled as a young reporter in southern France by what appeared to be mistreatment of the fairer sex. He spoke with a French lieutenant in temporary charge of a town who provided a different perspective. "We've got to let them. We can't suppress all this—we can only let them blow off steam and try to keep it under control. You don't know how these people feel [...] Some of those girls probably would have been murdered if they hadn't paid the price this way." The alternative, Sevareid reasoned, would have been civil war and chaos while the fight to eradicate Nazism in Germany was still being waged.[40]

Italophobia

In mid-November, General Frederick received a particularly disturbing staff paper. The subject was the disrepute into which Italians had fallen, a sentiment seemingly unique to Southeast France. The discussion began, "The population is unanimous on the subject of the Italian 'épuration'." The memory of thousands of French soldiers who died in Italy in 1915 to help save that nation from defeat was still vivid for veterans of World War I. Refugees machinegunned by Mussolini's aircraft on the roadways of France during the panic attendant to the 1940 capitulation were also not forgotten. Prominent in the minds of many, although unstated, was the unprovoked attack that same year by Italy, still thought of as a "knife in the back," the annexation of Menton, and the proposed march on Nice to execute Mussolini's stated intention of returning Contea Nizza to Italia. "To a majority of French people the Italian appears with 'a dagger in his right hand and a crucifix in the left one'," the author of the staff paper asserted. The memo concluded that French residents postulated that the majority of Italians on the Riviera had taken a position against France and her Allies. Large numbers of non-naturalized Italians in the area contributed to this severe judgment. Matters did not improve when these border-crossers used branches of Casa d'Italia, local Fascist headquarters during the Italian occupation, to obtain food, tobacco coupons, and other scarcities. The analysis ended with reference to a decree from de Gaulle, dated September 3, 1944, ordering that all Italian males, ages 18 to 60, be sent to internment camps if they did not enlist in the Foreign Legion. Their property was to be sequestrated and bank accounts frozen. Reportedly, Niçois public opinion demanded that the directive be promptly executed.[41]

About the same time, the Italian Committee of Liberation was reporting to the minister of foreign affairs in Rome that "a campaign of Italian phobia has started in the [southeast] region" and "very many Italians [have been] arrested

[...] a certain number whose only crime is to be Italians." One of the first places dynamited in Nice was a butcher shop on the avenue de la Républic whose Italian owner was accused of "making sausage with the blood of Frenchmen." Liberation was having unintended consequences in Alpes-Maritimes.[42]

An extreme example occurred at Antibes on September 23 when ten Italians were summarily executed. The episode began the previous evening when one of 40 young members of the Antibes FTP, Jean Demicheli, entered a villa in Juan-les-Pins to confront an Italian Fascist. His comrades said they heard Demicheli cry out and rushed to the house where they found an old man, his daughter, and a family friend all dead, along with their compatriot. Speculation arose as to whether Demicheli had been accidentally killed during the gunfire involving the rescuers. One of the casualties was a French intelligence agent during the war, and before dying he related how the attackers outside had fired blindly through the shutters. The confrontation was clouded by different versions set forth by other key players.

During the occupation, the Antibes FTP cell planned and executed acts of violence, and now the volatile dissidents sought to exact revenge against Italian Fascists. The commander of Fort Carré, where 676 persons suspected of being collaborators were being held, refused to turn over anyone without proper authorization. Louis Piétri, an FTP battalion commander at this time, met with Mayor Olivier to discuss the matter. Olivier later alleged there was a misunderstanding between the two on resolution of the Demicheli killing, dismissing the matter by saying that neither he nor Piétri were culpable in his mind. The fort's commandant and Piétri subsequently agreed that ten members of the Italian Milice who had been condemned to death by a military tribunal would be executed as a reprisal. According to Piétri, the unfortunate prisoners were selected with the mayor's acquiescence. Piétri assembled 12 volunteers as a firing squad. He marched the condemned men into the moat facing the sea where the vigilantes fired two rounds, killing the ten. In Piétri's view, the execution was a military act.[43] The occupations of the male victims are worthy of note: director of a medical clinic, baker, deliveryman, watchmaker, sharecropper, tax collector, mattress maker, and photographer. The doctor was the head of the Milice. Two women, ages 19 and 49, were also shot, allegedly for being Gestapo informants.[44]

Piétri was tried twice, acquitted by the military tribunal in Nice and, then, found guilty by other army authorities who cashiered him. After being sent to a combat unit on the front line in the Alps, he eventually returned to civilian life. The causes underlying the tragedy at Fort Carré were not unique to that community. The Côte d'Azur was elated to be free, inhabitants were worked up to punish the traitors among them, and the combatants involved in this incident were immature and anxious to avenge the sadism of Axis agents over several years. The hatred between Italians loyal to Mussolini and fascism and their fellow countrymen who were socialists and communists was particularly strong. As *Libération*, the official organ of the Antibes Liberation Committee, cried out in its eighth edition, "Is the blood of traitors purer than that of our heroes?"[45]

The press contributed to the Italophobia. "We demand then that French nationality should be withdrawn from all Frenchmen convicted of having collaborated with the enemy, that the benefits of naturalization should be taken away from fascist foreigners or collaborators," *Combat* urged. Then, it went further: "Nice does not need naturalized suspects owning real estate agencies, nor fascists selling women's hats [...] Leave in France the fortunes that they earned here [during the war and occupation]."[46] Over a four-month period beginning on October 10, 1944, *L'Ergot* published the names of 168 Italian nationals who had registered for the Fascist March on Nice, commenting that these individuals were traitors to French hospitality. Specific individuals were denounced for having been agent provocateurs and aiding the OVRA. Tracts appeared demanding "La France for the French," and posters shouted, "Our country is in danger!"[47]

When antagonism against Italians reached the point where stores and homes were being blown up after dark, the police and courts became heavily involved in trying to restore order. They seemed to turn a blind eye, however, to a dozen personal attacks in Cannes, Le Cannet, and Nice against Italians who had been released from custody after what was considered by extremists to be insufficient punishment.

Cross-border tensions simmered as a consequence of French occupation of Italian territory with the intention of annexing it. OSS reports from Nice in May 1945 specified that the French had set up provisional governmental entities in occupied territory and were disarming the *partigiani*. One Italian maquis leader refused to do so, stating that his weapons were British and American and berating the French for behaving like conquerors rather than allies. Inhabitants along the Ligurian coast displayed British, American, and Russian flags in protest to hundreds of French Moroccan troops camped at Ventimiglia, Bordighera, and San Remo.[48]

While the war was still underway, the OSS had established a presence in Menton to serve as intermediary between the French and Italians. Former members of the FFI were reportedly cooperative, but a basic hatred of the French for Italians, and vice-versa, made the relationship highly inflammable in the eyes of the third party. Fortunately, receipt and distribution of nearly ten tons of heavy equipment in the region over the next nine months helped ingratiate the Americans on both sides of the border.[49]

Relaxing After Fighting

As the war drew to a close, the famous French Riviera became a locus for rest and relaxation for foreign troops who had come to liberate Continental Europe. The Americans opened the United States Riviera Recreational Area which welcomed officers in Cannes and sergeants and enlisted men in Nice. Nurses and WAC (Women's Army Corps) officers stayed in Juan-les-Pins and Antibes. By May 1945, 150 enlisted WACs were also arriving at Nice each week for seven days at the Alhambra, Frederick's former headquarters. That surely produced lively times. By the end of that year, it was estimated that 350,000 GIs had been hosted on the Côte d'Azur.[50]

A French woman, 21 years old at the time, who was trained in piano, ballet, drama, and comedy, given classical concerts and appeared in nightclubs in the early 1940s, remembered many Americans in the audience at the Palais de Méditerranée in Nice after liberation. Next to the Palais was a military post exchange where Miss Red Cross made an appearance that summer. Inside the PX were the imported drinks craved by Americans but unobtainable at that time on the Riviera— beer, Coca Cola, and fruit juice. Also available to the GIs was a snack bar and post office to send perfume and other French delicacies back to the States. While uniquely open to US service members, the commercial activities were staffed by French personnel. The Red Cross held afternoon dances for the GIs, checking the mesdemoiselles who attended to ensure none were prostitutes. It was, the impressionable young woman assessed, two hours of tea, "lousy doughnuts," and dancing to an army band. Not long thereafter an outbreak of marriages between soldiers and French girls led a Nice newspaper to print an advice column entitled "All the 'Sammies' are not millionaires."[51]

Opinions about relations between the local populace and their American liberators differed depending upon the source. On the one hand, the talented Niçoise referred to above described paratroopers of the 82nd Airborne Division as the worst of a rowdy lot, falling dead drunk on the streets, provoking fist fights, breaking the showcases of high-priced shops and stealing fine merchandise. Proprietors soon made the downtown area look abandoned by boarding up store windows, she remembered. On the other hand, in November US military intelligence told Frederick, "The fact that Americans came to fight for an idea at thousands of miles from their own country, is highly appreciated and the majority of Frenchmen do their best to entertain 'Sammies' to whom they try to give a feeling of home."[52]

Only a few unscrupulous shopkeepers could not resist the temptation of raising prices for American customers presumed to be rich. In the opinion of Frederick's staff, these were isolated cases just as the lawlessness of a few soldiers did not represent the conduct of most troops enjoying a week of relaxation on the French Riviera. American military police developed a warm rapport with the Niçois. Their methods were described as pleasantly different from those of the Gestapo. MPs were polite and helpful to the citizenry and handled their comrades in arms firmly but correctly, especially in comparison with the treatment afforded drunk doughboys in 1917–18. GIs also received credit in the Nice press for giving out candies to children and cigarettes to the old.[53]

The daily intelligence bulletin of the Nice police, dated December 15, related a different story: "The relations of the population with the troops and particularly with detachments of paratroopers, without being bad, are less confident than at the outset; in fact, some of the military have engaged in numerous acts of violence (thefts, breaking store windows) under the effect of alcohol." The prefect reported the same thing, notifying the minister of interior in Paris that after finally being relieved from duty, drunken members of the 1st ABTF had during 48 hours broken shop windows, fired their weapons, and engaged in brawls. Perhaps the most outrageous incident occurred in Beausoleil where combat troops took the gendarmerie into custody and locked them up in their own jail. After Frederick was reassigned, Nice was declared off-limits to paratroopers, and disturbances by American soldiers subsequently exhibited a marked decline.[54]

The authorities in Nice had reason for concern about the explosion of prostitution attendant to the arrival of tens of thousands of combat veterans. Right behind them came whores from Paris, Bordeaux, Toulouse, Marseille, and Toulon. The number of registered street walkers jumped from 105 in 1944 to 508 when the military recreation area opened the next year. Another 1,136 women were thought to be clandestine "professionals." Hospitalization of prostitutes increased accordingly, rising 3.5 times in 1945 over the prior year. Gonorrhea and syphilis consultations grew correspondingly. Military authorities were worried as well. On July 3, 1945, American MPs raided a night club and arrested 16 prostitutes, 15 of whom tested positive for contamination. Obviously the women's requirement to be examined three times a week was no guarantee of cleanliness. While taking a firm stand against the epidemic of venereal disease, the regional communist newspaper could not resist addressing the outbreak in a political context, denigrating the surge in "the poorly paid social profession. It is a consequence of the conception of capitalism which exploits female workers."[55]

Perhaps the worst aspect of this phenomenon was the involvement of minors, constituting the black market of the trade. It was not uncommon for parents to push their young daughters onto the street where they could earn 5,000 to 10,000 francs a night, at a time when the father's monthly pay did not exceed 3,500 francs. There even existed a bordel called the "*pension* [guesthouse] bourgeoise" which specialized in under-age sex workers. Most of the clients were reported to be Americans. The press ran a campaign in

June 1945 urging protection of the city's youth.[56] One heart-rending case personified the tragedy in the public's mind. A 12-year-old was treated at the Nice anti-venereal center the day before her church communion. When it was discovered that she was also pregnant, the girl entered a ward of 13- to 16-year-olds in the same condition at Saint-Roch hospital.

As soon as firing subsided along the coastline, communities began holding events to remember bravery exhibited over the preceding five years. Plaques honoring Torrin and Grassi were installed where they had been executed at Place Masséna. Fighter pilots of the Nice air group with 73 confirmed "kills" at the war's end were honored before a crowd of fellow citizens. At Théoule the 13 sailors who died in the aborted landing by the naval assault group were remembered as well. Streets, squares, and parks were renamed, one Niçois esplanade naturally christened De Gaulle on June 18. And, on August 28 various movements of the Nice Resistance gathered to commemorate that city's liberation, an observance that still continues there and in Antibes, Cannes, and other communities along the Riviera to remember their liberation days.

The presence of US soldiers, sailors, and airmen on leave attracted dignitaries such as General Omar Bradley and stars like Sonja Henie to a gala organized by the military recreation area. A grand July Fourth commemoration took place featuring a floating dance floor opened at the deep-water naval harbor of Villefranche. Jean Gabin came back from Hollywood and swam in the Baie des Anges at Nice. Soon the aristocracy returned, the Aga Khan once again inhabiting his villa at Cannes. The Duke and Duchess of Windsor reoccupied their residence on Cap d'Antibes, but only after a "priority order" had been sent to American civil affairs officers to check on the condition of their properties spread from Toulouse to Grenoble, including "furniture, *objects d'art* and souvenirs."[57]

After it was all over, leaders from the three western Allied powers sought out the Riviera for respite from the weight of war. In late summer, Winston Churchill checked into the Hôtel de Paris in Monte Carlo under an assumed name to recover from his defeat at the polls in Britain's general election. He returned to spend two weeks on Cap Martin and in Cannes during the autumn of 1945, while British ambassador Duff Cooper and de Lattre made shorter visits. General Eisenhower came to the Riviera twice in 1945. One day in June, he awoke in London, lunched in Leipzig, Germany, and dined that evening at the Hôtel du Cap with some West Point classmates. Especially intriguing to the locals was a conference that took place at Nice and Cap d'Antibes in September involving Eisenhower, General Mark Clark, Brigadier General John Deane, US chief of mission in the Soviet Union, and Averell Harriman, American ambassador to Moscow. And, after the wedding of his daughter, de Gaulle spent a holiday in January 1946 at a villa on Cap d'Antibes, reading and walking in the pine groves nearby.[58]

Also appearing on the coast was a singer already becoming a legend. The highest paid entertainer in France, at 600 dollars per appearance, Edith Piaf agreed to perform gratis for the US Army's Special Services in a show including Yves Montand. "The Little Sparrow" was thus described in *Stars and Stripes*:

> She walks forward to the footlights, so that they make her seem taller than she is. She seems to plant her feet on the stage, and sets her body much in the manner of an athlete who is about to perform a strong and difficult feat [...] With her voice, with her songs of unrequited love, of prostitutes, of dead soldiers, she may set the listener aflame [...] Only the nod of her head comes in response to the audience's adulation.[59]

Obviously, American entertainers were not the only ones to enthrall GIs.

Removing the Vestiges of War

Restoring and modernizing the Mediterranean coast consumed scarce resources and time. Only 83 passengers passed through the port of Nice in 1945 but cargo increased exponentially. The Nice airport at Californie, restricted to military use during the conflict, inaugurated scheduled flights to Paris and Bastia, Corsica, after US Army engineers extended the temporary runway to 4,500 feet. Engineers of the 1ère Division de Marche d'Infantrie re-established communications in the back country over the summer. Rail lines and viaducts needed repair. Hospitals, schools, and water, gas, and power lines were reopened and reconnected.

Residents welcomed work projects to clear up the streets of Nice and construction along the Promenade of Anglais protecting the so-called "fortress of the Mediterranean." Blockhouses, pillboxes, tank traps—all were targeted for demolition, oftentimes by teams of German prisoners. What irony that those who constructed the casements were in many instances the same ones who destroyed them. Grass had to be removed from flower beds before they could burst forth in color the following spring. Those left homeless by German civil destruction and Allied bombardment, however, pressed for houses to be rebuilt before beginning beautification.

Inhabitants just outside Menton were upset at landmines planted in their fields when Americans evacuated the town in September 1944. The following year de-mining entailed burning foliage in the affected areas to locate the devices, a practice that destroyed fruit trees, vineyards, and, most regrettably, the celebrated lemon crop. Cannois credited GIs with assisting to rebuild their port with jackhammers and bulldozers. Much longer was required to complete the task of detecting and removing mines underwater in the harbor. In the 12 months after liberation, a total of 178 civilians and 67 de-miners (16 French and 51 Germans) lost their lives from explosives along the shore. Children were naturally attracted to something strange-looking and lethal, paying a heavy price as well for their curiosity.[60]

The liberation and épuration did not automatically halt activities by Pétainists and collaborationists, certainly not while pro-German and Italian fascists continued to resist. A wave of nocturnal attacks served to put residents on edge all along the Riviera. A grenade exploded in October 1944 wounding the former leader of a Resistance cell. More noticeable, perhaps, were flyers contending that the liberation of France had not come about due to the Anglo-Saxons. Anonymous leaflets screamed, "Amnesty, Amnesty, Amnesty," "Down with Gaullists," "Down with communists," and "Vive Pétain!" US Army intelligence was concerned that a fifth column was at work to divide public opinion by questioning a lull in military operations and circulating rumors that the lack of food was due to the Allied forces and the transportation shortage they caused. The Americans' conclusion was that too many police inspectors and agents who served as "Pétain's valet" hunting down STO dodgers were still in service and could not be counted upon to offer protection against a small, pro-Nazi, Italian minority.[61]

SOE leader Francis Cammaerts summarized the situation he had observed in the Midi when debriefed in January 1945:

> There are without doubt a great many Milice left in France who are trying to increase the present political difficulties. It is more than likely that there are a number of Germans lying low, who are being supplied with arms and food, and are being helped by the Milice. There is still a strong fifth column in France, who will continue to do everything in their power to sabotage the effort being made to reorganize the country.[62]

At the same time, the Americans were aware that stay-behind agents might well have been left by the retreating Wehrmacht. For example, the civil affairs detachment in Nice cited a press report that the guard post at the Anthéor viaduct had been attacked, supposedly by traitorous Frenchmen.[63] A woman assigned to a team to ferret out such operatives and plant double agents described her technique:

> We had at least a dozen people. They said, "We have German agents along southern France and we'd like you to find them." We would move into a town such as Nice and then we would contact the post office and find anyone that had recently moved into the area in the past five years or so. We would go to the police and see if they had information about anyone that was a

new arrival. Typically, the Germans wouldn't recruit people that had been there all their lives. Usually they would insert people. We would also look for anyone that didn't have a French profile—Tunisians, Algerians, people who would generally have a beef with the French. Many of the agents were Algerians.[64]

For the Americans, communism was a particular worry. Frederick was informed that three-quarters of the members of the Cannes CLL were communists. The staff was affiliated with the party, he was briefed, and prisoners were guarded by the FTP. Furthermore, Army intelligence discerned that after liberation resisters in the FTP had their friends enlist in the patriotic Milice to use these disproportionate numbers to outweigh the FFI and create a sort of people's army.[65]

The return of former residents of the Midi added more demands. Devastation during the occupations and pillage of abandoned homes by Germans, Italians, and Americans meant that former inhabitants often found almost no necessities of life remaining. For example, the few English people who came back to Vence discovered to their dismay that their homes had been looted and damaged. French Mutual Aid asked for donations of clothes, shoes, underwear, and blankets. Beds, cooking utensils, and housekeeping items were needed as well. Prisoners of war, deportees, and refugees also required these necessities. The prefect went the extra mile by requisitioning the essentials for Azuréens who had fled France or volunteered to work in Germany. In November the Département du Service des Réfugiés estimated that in Nice were 2,000–3,000 pre-liberation refugees, another 7,000 persons displaced from combat zones like Sospel and Menton, and 50,000 homeless.[66]

One Niçoise recounted the scene at the Nice station in the evenings when trains bringing home French prisoners of war were scheduled. She was a brave woman who had participated in the Resistance, spending time in prison as a consequence. Now she was standing anxiously with a crowd waiting for their loved ones. A full buffet stood by, but she remembered the men who arrived rarely took time to eat or drink. Reunions were extraordinarily emotional, especially with children. Many of the returnees were changed, haggard, and seemed almost to be sleepwalking. But when her own husband appeared, she did not think of any of that.[67] It was not unusual to see Monseigneur Rémond welcoming the former prisoners and returning deportees and helping them assimilate back into French society.

A repatriation center opened in Villefranche. Situated up against the border, Alpes-Maritimes was a first stop for French nationals originally from all over the country. Almost 8,000 repatriates from across France passed through the welcoming station from April 15, 1945 until the end of that year. Prisoners of war from the Russian campaign, Italian collaborators, and others were received and processed. The 569 people intercepted by military security included some of the 22,000 French who took refuge in the Reich when threatened for being collaborators in their home towns.[68] Of course, all returnees did not pass through that portal or immediately return to the Côte d'Azur, some stopping en route with family across France and others entering convalescent facilities to regain their strength.[69]

Political Rebirth

Elections held in late April and mid-May 1945 were historic. These were not only the first ballots cast since 1937, but also the first time women were eligible to vote. The campaign was complicated in Nice by the plethora of candidates and lists, reflecting the multifaceted character of the Resistance that had contributed so importantly to the return of democracy to the Midi. The CDL, Socialist Party, Combat, MLN, PCF, Front National, and other leftist organizations all fielded candidates. In the French manner, after the first round, separate groups agreed on consolidated lists to attract more votes and obtain seats in the second ballot.[70]

Not only was the voter confronted with this fluid situation, he or she also had to weigh other considerations, such as whether a candidate who left Nice before the war deserved to attain political leadership upon returning after the occupation. All those standing for office had explanations for their actions over the prior six years, but were they credible? Was confinement in Germany more worthy of reward than living and fighting under sparse conditions in a maquis or risking the welfare of family members by actively participating in the urban Resistance? Old animosity was not forgotten, especially concerning the controversial Front Populaire, Maréchal Pétain, and the Vichy regime. Even one's status as a Gaullist was subject to criticism as well as praise in a region containing as strong a communist presence as Southeast France.

Noticeable by his absence was Jean Médecin, the popular mayor descending from one of the oldest families of Comté de Nice, who had worked to protect residents from the excesses imposed by Vichy and the subsequent foreign presence. Considered compromised by having served under Pétain, he was not permitted to put forth his name for mayor in 1945. (Médecin was subsequently allowed to run for office in October and elected to the Assemblée nationale.) Instead, Jacques Cotta, a Socialist lawyer and member of the Popular Republican Movement closely associated with the CDL, became the first mayor of Nice in the Fourth Republic.[71] He would only serve until 1947 when Médecin and his cohorts were permitted to contest the next election. Still, the political process in mid-1945 evidenced the victory that had been achieved. The freedom of citizens in opposition to the government to speak out and criticize, form parties, be elected, and replace incumbents was at the heart of the long and perilous struggle against fascism during the war.

Another matter of civil rights concerned publication of a Christian newspaper. The Niçois press after the liberation reflected communism, socialism, and Gaullism, but not Christian resistance. Monseigneur Rémond requested permission in September 1944 to begin a morning daily baptized *La Liberté*. It was denied at the regional level, and Rémond then requested Abbé Alfred Daumas, a former leader in the Catholic Movements of Resistance, to intervene with the national Ministry of Information which gave its approval. But the communists and socialists would not share their printing equipment and *Combat* feared this competitor would eat into its readership of moderates. Again, there were delays until Rémond purchased an ancient rotary press and the first edition appeared on April 6, 1945. Production was tortuous and more arbitration was required to print *La Liberté* in limited numbers on presses after *L'Eclaireur* was produced each night. By July, 40,000 copies were being sold after *Combat* was rebaptized *Nice Matin*, by which it continues to be known. *La Liberté* rejoiced in the restoration of liberties and return of morality. It advocated protection of the family and augmentation of payments to the aged. The excesses of the épuration were naturally reproved as the editors cautioned against arbitrary incarcerations and severe sentences.[72]

One more triumph was to come. The unsuccessful, 11th-hour drive into Italy in the spring of 1945 to take territory considered rightfully French finally attained its objective by diplomatic means in the Treaty of Paris of February 1947. The frontier was redrawn similar to that in 1796 when the King of Sardinia ceded Comté de Nice, Breil, and Tende to France. Of the 694 square kilometers transferred, 560 with 5,526 inhabitants joined Alpes-Maritimes, including those in the upper valley of the Roya where residents voted unanimously to align with France in the 1860 plebiscite. The House of Savoie no longer sat on the Italian throne, and so after 87 years, the Republic of France reunited its lands west of the Alps.[73]

Epilogue

World War II in France was not a replica of what occurred in World War I. Nor were the 1940s on the Riviera a microcosm of the occupation and liberation of France as a whole, for these were multi-textured times and places. The French people and their liberators were not always the good guys, nor the invaders and occupiers all bad. The populace was hardly of one mind—résistants held various opinions on what to do both during the occupation and later once France was freed, military leaders disagreed on strategy and tactics to overcome the Axis and defeat its forces, and politicians, national and local, had different plans for after the war.

What must never be forgotten in evaluating the choices made immediately after the fall of France is the apparent certainty of the Reich's victory in Western Europe. Only Britain remained hostile to Germany, and its preparation for war was still underway. After the Armistice with Berlin, Frenchmen in the South lacked the incentive to oppose the new regime led by Maréchal Pétain, for the full weight of German occupation was yet to be felt there as it was increasingly being revealed in the rest of the country. At this point in time, the wounds inflicted on the Riviera were economic, social, and political, but not yet those of domineering fascism.

Elsewhere, residents of northeastern France had lived through the fighting of World War I and were experiencing déjà vu as the hated Germans returned to devastate their homes. But in the Southeast, inhabitants had not suffered under foreign troops in that first conflict. Initially men and women struggled to know how to give their families the best chance of survival under the new right-wing Vichy regime. Should they hide family treasures, leave valuables behind, or carry them off if evicted from their homes for military or political reasons? Folks worried about loved ones captured and held as prisoners in Germany. As in every war, people thought, or rather hoped, the conflict would be of short duration, and now Frenchmen hoped that Germany would lose and any occupation be curtailed.

As time passed and Pétain's inability to shield France from fascism became clearer, popular attitudes changed and obedience to Vichy declined. Whereas initially the limited opposition to Vichy had been nationalistic, as time wore on the disadvantaged and persecuted came together to act against the regime. Communists, socialists, political parties on the far right, and even Catholics and war veterans found some common ground to band together. Resisters formed cells in cities and retreated to camps in isolated areas.

At the same time, thousands of Jews who had gravitated to Alpes-Maritimes to escape persecution elsewhere created a quandary for inhabitants once the Germans took complete control and began arresting and deporting them to concentration camps. Motivated by religious beliefs, shocked by extreme acts of injustice and brutality, and stirred by a personal sense of morality and dignity, numerous political and religious leaders and courageous individuals risked their lives and welfare to help Jews avoid capture and death. Thankfully, the persecution and economic suffering drew to a close with the arrival of the Allied forces.

Once ashore, American troops progressed farther and faster than projected. In addition to enemy resistance being far less than expected, other factors explained the rapid progress of US soldiers from the beachhead: it was a force superbly trained, equipped, and led; tactical surprise was achieved as the enemy did not know where to position its forces; and the timing was perfect, coming in the wake of the Normandy invasion. Furthermore, the American corps and division commanders and their staffs were experienced in amphibious landings from earlier combat in the Mediterranean and North Africa.

It must not be forgotten, however, that these were not solely American military successes. In November 1943, de Lattre had asserted that "the French are not prepared to accept their liberation as a gift from their Allies."[74] Seven of the ten divisions crossing the beach in August 1944 were French. These troops liberated Toulon and Marseille in two weeks, an objective expected to take 45 days to accomplish. As contrasted with Normandy where only 177 French soldiers came ashore on D-Day, over 100,000 Frenchmen landed in Provence. French combatants could once again hold their heads high as their national army joined in the defeat of fascism. It was even said that news of the debarkation in the South was one of the factors that unleashed the popular uprising in Paris days later.

The Resistance stood up and ambushed the enemy behind their lines and in populated areas. In many cases the guerrillas had been instructed, armed, and provisioned by British agents during the occupation. Ships of the Royal Navy supported combat ashore with heavy artillery, adding to the British contribution to ending German dominance on the Rivera.

The Provençal landing must be considered a complete success in traditional military terms. It led to a rapid advance, taking 57,000 enemy prisoners and opening harbor facilities capable of handling well over a half-million tons of supplies per month, including provisions for 900,000 Allied soldiers. Added to these achievements were 42,000 prisoners the FFI reported capturing.[75] The

2,700 American and 4,000 French casualties suffered in the entire Operation Dragoon paled in comparison with an estimated 6,600 American and 3,700 British and Canadian casualties incurred in Normandy on June 6 alone. These numbers should not obscure the strategic importance of the victory on the Riviera that positioned a friendly force on the Allies' southern flank rather than leaving a hostile German presence.

Even after liberation, Alpes-Maritimes had to contend with food shortages, political discord, and repeated disruptions caused by American and French soldiers given a break from military duties and causing trouble in Nice. Artillery barrages persisted later along the Italian frontier in Alpes-Maritimes than in any other part of France, continuing almost until Berlin's surrender. But as bad as these times were for those who lived through them in the Southeast, the total cost was nowhere as severe as in some other parts of Europe.

Tourists on the Riviera today may be disappointed not to find battlefields laid out and explained for visitors as is the case in other areas of France. The conflicts here were numerous but small in size. Nonetheless, the heroism displayed is preserved on statues, steles, plaques, monuments, and other memorials, numbering in the hundreds.

These various forms of remembrance of World War II on the Riviera recognize a variety of people, activities, and organizations. One subject is a courageous senator who was one of the few to vote against granting full powers to Pétain at the outset of Vichy. A plaque remembers Louis Aragon who composed "Witness of the Martyrs" in Nice which was read on the BBC in 1942. Among the tributes are multiple markers recognizing international figures—Charles de Gaulle, Winston Churchill, and Franklin Roosevelt; French generals accorded the rank of Maréchal—de Lattre de Tassigny, Alphonse Juin, Koenig, and Leclerc; Jean Moulin, the national leader of the Resistance; Antoine de Saint-Exupéry, the celebrated author and pilot who perished in the war; and the editor of Nice's *L'Eclaireur*, who was arrested by the Nazis and died in a concentration camp.

Acknowledgment of those who perished during the war include combatants in the brief campaign against Italy, 8,700 prisoners from Alpes-Maritimes sent to Germany after fighting in 1940, and casualties of the closing clash on Mont Authion. Civilian victims of bombardments in Nice, Cannes, St. Laurent du Var, Sospel, Isola, and Menton are not forgotten. Plaques recall the fate of Jews in Southeast France by citing the massive roundup in 1943, deportations, and the train station in Nice where the few survivors returned.

Public appreciation is also given to the common man who fell during the war years, notably SNCF railroad workers, police officers, and firefighters. Countless students in lycées died opposing the occupiers and are recognized. Gratitude to the liberators cites pilots and airborne forces, as well as the French and American armies as a whole and in individual cases, such as Captain Jess Walls.

Specific heroes in the Resistance were not always known. Commemorations treat their sacrifices and achievements collectively but, where possible, identify individuals who died on special missions as well as in combat. Not forgotten are many executed on the Riviera and others who perished in concentration camps, such as the beloved Dr. Elie Lévy.

Nor are special monuments the only remembrances of these heroes of another era. Site markers, place and street names, and building designations keep alive their memory. The Croix de Lorraine, the symbol of Free France, the Resistance, and Gaullist opposition movements, is still found across the region.

This corner of France, often forgotten and under-provisioned, was a difficult place in which to subsist and work under Vichy control, Italian and German occupation, American liberation, and military conflict that continued after the Allied combatants left but trying times remained. Six years were required for the vistas of the French Riviera to escape from this hell and reclaim the heavenly aura for which the region is renowned.

ຂ໐ຕ

Notes

Preface

1 One veteran confirmed the human inclination to want to have it both ways: 'The thing which amazes me most when I talk to people who I know very well supported Pétain is [...] they all tell me how they did their share for the Resistance. They've all done one thing or another, there's always something they can think of [...] Sometimes it's quite incredible [...] I have to listen to these fairy tales without wincing.' Marcel Ophuls, *The Sorrow and the Pity* (New York: Berkley Windhover Books, 1975), xvi, 109.

Prologue

1 Sylvia Plath, *Journals of Sylvia Plath*, ed. Frances McCullough (New York: Dial Press, 1982), 94–5.

Chapter 1: The Phoney War

1 Henri Michel, *The Second World War*, trans. Douglas Parmée (New York: Praeger Publishers, 1975), 89.
2 The succeeding eight months were known in French as *la drole de guerre* (the funny war) and in German as *der Sitzkrieg* (the sitting war), comparable to the English sobriquet, "phoney war," to refer to this period of non-action on the Western front.
3 Jean-Louis Panicacci (ed.), *Les Alpes-Maritimes de 1939 à 1945* (Nice: Centre Régional de Documentation Pédagogique de Nice, 1977), 81.
4 Walter Hasenclever, *Côte d'Azur 1940: Impossible asile*, trans. Jean Ruffet (La Tour d'Aigues: Editions de l'aube, 1998), 12–16.
5 Didier Digiuni, *Cannes 1939–1945* (Nice: Alandis Editions, 2002), 21; Panicacci, *Les Alpes-Maritimes de 1939 à 1945: Un département dans la tourmente*, 36, 48–50; Gérard Helion, "Antibes pendant la Deuxième Guerre Mondiale (1939–1945)," Maitrise d'Histoire, Faculté des Lettres de Nice, 1972.
6 Maureen Emerson, *Escape to Provence: The story of Elisabeth Starr and Winifred Fortescue and the making of the Colline des Anglais* (Sussex: Chapter and Verse, 2008), 128; Jean-Louis Panacacci, *Les Alpes-Maritimes de 1939 à 1945: Un département dans la tourmente* (Nice: Editions Serre, 1989), 39–40.
7 Digiuni, *Cannes 1939–1945*, 25–6.

8   Michel Braun, Jean-Pierre Garacio and Jean-Louis Panicacci (eds), *1939–1945: La guerre dans les Alpes Maritimes* (Breil-sur-Roya: Editions du Cabri, 1994), 16.

9   Gérard Helion, "Antibes de juin 1944 à juin 1945," Actes du Colloque de Nice, June 22, 1974, Centre de la Méditerranée Moderne et Contemporaine," *Cahiers de la Méditerranée* (June 12, 1976): 27–8.

10 Alex Baussy, *La Mémoire d'une Ville: Une évocation de la vie à Cannes et sur la Côte d'Azur durant les sombres années de guerres et à la Libération* (Spéracèdes: TAC Motifs, 1994), 12, 21; *Le Littoral*, February 1, 1940.

11 Panicacci, *Les Alpes-Maritimes de 1939 à 1945: Un département dans la tourmente*, 40.

12 Helion, "Antibes de juin 1944 à juin 1945," 24.

13 Digiuni, *Cannes 1939–1945*, 22–4.

14 *Le Progrès Provençal de Grasse*, November 11, 1939.

15 *Le Petit Niçois*, April 21, 1940; *Le Message de Cannes*, October 25, 1939; *Le Progrès d'Antibes*, February 24, 1940.

16 Other monikers were "Fritz," "Schlok," "Stol," "Chleuh," and some earthier references.

17 *Le Progrès d'Antibes*, May 11, 1940; *L'Eclaireur de Nice*, May 14, 15, 21, 1940; *Le Progrès Provençal de Grasse*, May 18, 1940.

18 Panicacci, *Les Alpes-Maritimes de 1939 à 1945: Un département dans la tourmente*, 56; Helion, "Antibes de juin 1944 à juin 1945," 35.

19 Hugh Gibson (ed.), *The Ciano Diaries, 1939–1943: The Complete, Unabridged Diaries of Count Galeazzo Ciano, Italian Minister for Foreign Affairs, 1936–1943* (New York: Doubleday & Company, 1946), 263.

20 Len Deighton, *Blitzkrieg: From the Rise of Hitler to the Fall of Dunkirk* (Edison, NJ: Castle Books, 2000), 267.

21 Franklin D. Roosevelt, *The Public Papers and Addresses of Franklin D. Roosevelt: War and Aid to the Democracies*, ed. Samuel I. Rosemann (New York: MacMillan Company, 1941), 259–64.

22 Charles Glass, *Americans in Paris: Life and Death under Nazi Occupation* (New York: Penguin Press, 2010), 15; *New York Times*, June 11, 1940, 6.

23 The next day *L'Eclaireur de Nice* entitled its front-page article, "Le poignard dans le dos" (The dagger in the back) and went on to say, "Mussolini, in forcing the point in the back of the wounded France has committed not only a horrible forfeit, but also an act of supreme cowardice;" *Le Petit Niçois* announced, "Le coup de poignard" (The stab), June 11, 1940.

24 *New York Times*, June 11, 1940, 4.

25 Giorgio Rochat, "La campagne italienne de juin 1940 dans les Alpes occidentales," *La Revue historique des armées* 250 (2008): 80.

26 Romain H. Rainero (ed.), *La Commission italienne d'armistice avec la France: Les rapports entre la France de Vichy et l'Italie du Mussolini, 10 juin 1940–8 septembre 1943* (Paris: Service historique d l'armée de terre, 1995), 12–13.

27 Hyacinthe Chiavassa, "Juin 1940: la bataille de Menton," *Annales Monégasques: Revue d'Histoire de Monaco* 8 (1984): 16; Panicacci, *Les Alpes-Maritimes de 1939 à 1945: Un département dans la tourmente*, 59, 86.

28 Margaret Turner and Rosemary Teychenné, in discussions with the author, June 4 and 13, 2005, respectively.

29 Jean-Louis Panicacci, "10–25 juin 1940: la 'guerre oubliée'." *Les Cahiers du Musée de la Résistance Azuréenne* 64 (May 2010): 14–16.

30 Rochat, "La campagne italienne de juin 1940," 78–83.

31 Jean-Louis Panicacci, *L'Occupation italienne: Sud-Est de la France, juin 1940–septembre 1943* (Rennes: Presses Universitaires de Rennes, 2010), 22.

32 *New York Times*, June 17, 1940, 14.

33 Richard Carrier, "Réflexions sur l'efficacité militaire de l'armée des Alpes, 10-25 juin 1940," *La Revue historique des armées* 250 (2008): 85–93.

34 Jean-Louis Panicacci, *En territoire occupé: Italiens et Allemands à Nice, 1943–1944* (Paris: Vendémaire, 2012), 19.

Chapter 2: The Vichy Regime

1 Charles Williams, *Pétain* (London: Little, Brown, 2005), 330.

2 Mark M. Boatner III, *Biographical Dictionary of World War II* (Novato, CA: Presidio Press, 1996), 421.

3 French newsreel in Marcel Ophuls, *Sorrow and the Pity* (New York: Berkley Windhover Books, 1975), 20.

4 Literally, tri-colored, the French flag with three wide vertical stripes of blue, white, and red.

5 Wags soon quipped, "Veni, Vidi, Vichy."

6 For an accurate and poignant description of the panic ensuing from the entrance of the Germans into Paris and the attendant occupation of northern France, see Irène Némirovsky, *Suite Française* (New York: Vintage International, 2007). Others recorded their observations and memories as well. Georgette Guillot, for example, typed 77 pages entitled "Three weeks of exodus," *Le Monde*, July 21, 2010, 14–15.

7 In addition to specific references noted throughout the narrative, discussions of Rayon's experiences during the war are based upon four personal interviews with Camille Rayon—October 25 and November 24, 2005, and March 30 and June 9, 2006—plus Rayon's military personnel records.

8 Philippe Burrin, *France under the Germans: Collaboration and Compromise*, trans. Janet Lloyd (New York: New Press, 1996), 186.

9 Alix Bergmann, in discussion with the author, May 9, 2005.

10 Now designated Alpes de Haute-Provence.

11 Registre des délibérations du conseil municipal, 99:159, AMN.

12 Romain H. Rainero (ed.), *La Commission italienne d'armistice avec la France: Les rapports entre la France de Vichy et l'Italie du Mussolini, 10 juin 1940–8 septembre 1943* (Paris: Service historique d l'armée de terre, 1995), 135–6.

13 Varian Fry, *Surrender on Demand* (New York: Random House, 1945), 160–3.

14 *Le Progrès Provençal de Grasse, Le Progrès d'Antibes*, May 25, 1940.

15 Jean-Louis Panicacci, "Le traumatisme de la défaite de juin 1940: perceptions et réactions de l'opinion Azuréenne de l'été à l'automne 1940," *Cahiers de la Méditerranée* 74 (June 2007): 276n; ibid., *Les Alpes-Maritimes de 1939 à 1945: Un département dans la tourmente* (Nice: Editions Serre, 1989), 86.

16 Panicacci, "Le traumatisme de la défaite de juin 1940," 301–2; Gérard Helion, "Antibes pendant la Deuxième Guerre Mondiale (1939–1945)," Maitrise d'Histoire, Faculté des Lettres de Nice, 1972, 48, 49, US.

17 *L'Eclaireur de Nice*, July 20–1, 1940.

18 *Le Progrès Provençal de Grasse*, June 29, October 19, 1940.

19 Panicacci, "Le traumatisme de la défaite de juin 1940," 279.

20 Ibid., *Les Alpes-Maritimes de 1939 à 1945: Un département dans la tourmente*, 99–100.

21 Robert Mencherini, *Vichy en Provence* (Paris: Editions Syllepse, 2009), 87; Jean-Louis Panicacci (ed.), *Les Alpes-Maritimes de 1939 à 1945* (Nice: Centre Régional de Documentation Pédagogique de Nice, 1977), 42.

22 Didier Digiuni, *Cannes 1939–1945* (Nice: Alandis Editions, 2002), 45–7; Panicacci, *Les Alpes-Maritimes de 1939 à 1945: Un département dans la tourmente*, 58–62.

23 Raymond Gatti, in discussion with the author, September 6, 2008.

24 Ophuls, *Sorrow and the Pity*, 50.

25 "L'impact de l'appel du 18 juin 1940 dans les Alpes-Maritimes," 3, MRA.

26 Williams, *Pétain*, 213.

27 Panicacci, *Les Alpes-Maritimes de 1939 à 1945: Un département dans la tourmente*, 148–9.

28 *L'Eclaireur de Nice*, May 12, 1941.

29 Jean-Louis Panicacci, *En Territoire Occupé: Italiens et Allemands à Nice, 1943–1944* (Paris: Vendémaire, 2012), 82–3.

30 Peter Schjeldahl, "Art as Life: The Matisse We Never Knew," *New Yorker*, August 29, 2005, 82; Françoise Gilot, *Matisse and Picasso: A Friendship in Art* (New York: Anchor Books, 1992), 235–6, 241–2.

31 Philippe Erlanger, *La France sans étoile: Souvenirs de l'avant-guerre et du temps de l'occupation* (Saint-Amand: Librairie Plon, 1974), 201–2; Ted Jones, *The French Riviera: A Literary Guide for Travellers* (London: Tauris Parke Paperbacks, 2004), 78, 84–5; Alan Riding, *And the Show Went On: Cultural Life in Nazi-Occupied Paris* (New York: Alfred A. Knopf, 2010), 179, 200.

32 Frederic Spotts, *The Shameful Peace: How French Artists and Intellectuals Survived the Nazi Occupation* (New Haven, CT: Yale University Press, 2008), 78.

33 Panicacci, *Les Alpes-Maritimes de 1939 à 1945: Un département dans la tourmente*, 165–6.

34 Conseulo de Saint-Exupéry, *Oppède* (New York: Brentano's, 1945), 20.

35 Gilbert Borelly, in discussion with the author, December 15, 2005.

36 Panicacci, *Les Alpes-Maritimes de 1939 à 1945: Un département dans la tourmente*, 157–8; Florence E. Pinglier, "Reminiscences, 1939–45," *Holy Trinity Church Newsletter* 8 (Spring 1995): 4–5; Borelly, discussion; Louis Martin, a native Niçois, in discussion with the author, March 11, 2005; Digiuni, *Cannes 1939–1945*, 45–7.

37 Alda Giraud, in discussion with the author, April 21, 2005.

38 Panicacci, *Les Alpes-Maritimes de 1939 à 1945: Un département dans la tourmente*, 161.

39 Antonin Blanchi, a native Niçois, in discussion with the author, March 14, 2008.

40 Jean-Louis Panicacci, "Les Alpes-Maritimes," *Les Cahiers de l'IHTP* 32–3 (May 1996): 201, 209.

41 *Le Petit Niçois*, August 13, 1940; Erlanger, *La France sans étoile*, 187–8, 192.

42 Darnand had been running a small trucking concern in Nice between the wars. Immediately after the German invasion of Nice in September 1943, Darnand's transport company was the target for a bomb set by the Resistance.

43 *L'Eclaireur de Nice*, October 6, 7, 1940. This oath is similar to the one taken by members of the Armistice Army.

44 Robert O. Paxton, *Vichy France: Old Guard and New Order, 1940–1944* (New York: Columbia University Press, 1972), 74; Jean-Louis Panicacci, "La Légion française des combattants dans les Alpes-Maritimes (octobre 1940–août 1944)," *Nice Historique* 105 (October–December 2002): 189–90.

45 Panicacci, *Les Alpes-Maritimes de 1939 à 1945: Un département dans la tourmente*, 134.

46 Ibid., "La Légion française des combattants," 194.

47 Jérome Gautheret and Thomas Wieder, "De la haine dans l'air," *Le Monde*, July 27, 2010.

48 *L'Eclaireur de Nice*, June 23, 26, 1940.

49 By 1943 these ceremonies attracted only 500 inhabitants.

50 Panicacci, "La Légion française des combattants," 200–1.

51 Surprising in retrospect, as prime minister Laval had been named *Time* magazine's Man of the Year in 1931.

52 A fascist party created in the 1930s and believed to have 30,000 adherents nationwide in 1941.

53 H. R. Kedward, *Resistance in Vichy France: A Study of Ideas and Motivation in the Southern Zone, 1940–1942* (Oxford: Oxford University Press, 1978), 88.

54 "L'impact de l'appel du 18 juin 1940," 6.

55 Ibid., 3.

56 Erlanger, *La France sans étoile*, 204.

57 *L'Eclaireur de Nice*, June 24, 1940.

58 Ibid., October 31, 1941.

59 Ibid., June 20, 1940.

60 Junior high or middle school in the United States.

61 Borelly, discussion.

62 Henri Aiglon, in discussion with the author, June 15, 2007; see, also, Burrin, *France under the Germans*, 182.

63 Jean-Marie Guillon, "Catholiques varois et résistance," *Provence historique* 42 (January–June 1992): 421–8.

64 Panicacci, *Les Alpes-Maritimes de 1939 à 1945: Un département dans la tourmente*, 166–7.

65 Ibid. (ed.), *Les Alpes-Maritimes de 1939 à 1945*, 75.

66 Edward L. Homze, *Foreign Labor in Nazi Germany* (Princeton, NJ: Princeton University Press, 1967), 148, 195; Paxton, *Vichy France*, xv; Burrin, *France under the Germans*, 282–6.

Chapter 3: *The Italian Occupation*

1 Philippe Erlanger, *La France sans étoile: Souvenirs de l'avant-guerre et du temps de l'occupation* (Saint-Amand: Librairie Plon, 1974), 245.

2 "Rapports entre le Gouvernement français et le Commandement italien," 6, CARAN; Robert O. Paxton, *Vichy France: Old Guard and New Order, 1940–1944* (New York: Columbia University Press, 1972), 317–18.

3 *L'Eclaireur de Nice*, November 12, 1942.

4 Préfet des Alpes-Maritimes à Monsieur le Sous-Préfet, "1942–1943, Troupes d'opérations italiennes," AMC.

5 *L'Eclaireur de Nice*, November 12, 1942.

6 Hugh Gibson (ed.), *The Ciano Diaries, 1939–1943: The Complete, Unabridged Diaries of Count Galeazzo Ciano, Italian Minister for Foreign Affairs, 1936–1943* (New York: Doubleday & Company, 1946), 263, 543.

7 Erlanger, *La France sans étoile*, 247; Pierre Nicot de Villemain, "Les armées à Nice 1942–1945," *Nice Historique* 4 (October–December 2002): 221–2; Didier Digiuni, *Cannes, 1939–1945* (Nice: Alandis Editions, 2002), 85.

8 Joseph Aquilino in Grégoire Georges-Picot, *L'innocence et la ruse: Des étrangers dans la Résistance en Provence, 1940–1944* (Paris: Editions Tirésias, 2000), 113–15. Aquilino was later arrested,

tortured at Villa La Cigale in Cagnes, condemned to death, imprisoned in the Italian Piémont, and finally deported to Mauthausen, Austria, where he alone among his comrades survived the war.

9   Jean-Louis Panicacci, "La Légion française des combattants dans les Alpes-Maritimes (octobre 1940–août 1944)," *Nice Historique* 105 (October–December 2002): 214; Florence E. Pinglier, "Reminiscences, 1939–45," *Holy Trinity Church Newsletter* 8 (Spring 1995): 6.

10   Alda Giraud, Aimée Chabert and Henri Aiglon in discussions with the author, April 21, 2005, June 8, 2007 and June 15, 2007, respectively.

11   Association Montagne et Traditions, *Pays Vésubien* (Saint-Martin-Vésubie: Musée des Traditions Vésubiennes, 2005), 70–1.

12   Michel Braun, Jean-Pierre Garacio and Jean-Louis Panicacci (eds), *1939–1945: La guerre dans les Alpes Maritimes* (Breil-sur-Roya: Editions du Cabri, 1994), 81.

13   Gérard Helion, "Antibes pendant la Deuxième Guerre Mondiale (1939–1945)," Maitrise d'Histoire, Faculté des Lettres de Nice, 1972, 71, US; Jean-Louis Panicacci, "Nice 1939–1942," *Recherches Régionales: Côte d'Azur et Contrée Limitrophes* 4 (1968): 8.

14   "Les Femmes dans la Résistance Azuréenne," Documents, Témoignages, Recherches No. 22, 9; Marcel Guizard, *Mémoires de Simon, 1941–1945: Marseille Nice Lyon Paris Chronique de la Résistance et de l'Occupation par le Responsable Interrégional du Front National Zone Sud* (Marseille: n.p., 1989), 97; Max Burlando (ed.), *Le parti communiste et ses militants dans la Résistance des Alpes-Maritimes par 120 combattants et témoins* (La Trinité: La Societé Nouvelle Imprimerie de la Victoire, 1974), 71.

15   "Let's go sons of Italy, the day of flight has arrived," a take-off on the opening lines of the French national anthem. Panicacci, "La Légion française des combattants dans les Alpes-Maritimes," 216.

16   Alain Roullier, "Tende et La Brigue: Les oubliées du Rattachement de 1860," *Lou Sourgentin* 116 (March–April 1995): 34.

17   Erlanger, *La France sans étoile*, 247–8.

18   Giraud, discussion.

19   Digiuni, *Cannes, 1939–1945*, 95–6, 99–100; Emmanuel Volpi, "Les Italiens et l'Économie Varoise," *Notre Musée* 198 (March 2011): 16.

20   Jean-Louis Panicacci, "La vie quotidienne des Niçois de 1939 à 1945," *Nice Historique* 2 (April–June 2004):78; Helion, "Antibes pendant la Deuxième Guerre Mondiale," 75, US.

21   *Le Petit Niçois*, June 24, 1943.

22   Colette Poisson, a youngster in occupied Nice, in discussion with the author, October 1, 2009.

23   Helion, "Antibes pendant la Deuxième Guerre Mondiale," 74–7, US; Jean-Louis Panicacci, *Les Alpes-Maritimes de 1939 à 1945: Un département dans la tourmente* (Nice: Editions Serre, 1989), 222–4.

24   Burlando, *Le parti communiste*, 74.

25   Préfet des Alpes-Maritimes à Monsieur le Sous-Préfet de Grasse et à Messieurs les Maires du Département, November 13, 1942, "1942–1943, Troupes d'opérations italiennes," dossier 4 H 31, AMC; "Plages 1943," dossier 4 H 31, AMC; Panicacci, *Les Alpes-Maritimes de 1939 à 1945: Un Département dans la Tourmente*, 188; Erlanger, *La France sans étoile*, 265.

26   Henri Michel, "Les relations franco-italiennes de l'armistice de juin 1940 à l'armistice de septembre 1943," in Comité de la 2e guerre mondiale, *La Guerre en Méditerranée, 1939–1945*, 485–511.

27   Jean-Louis Panicacci, "L'occupation italienne (novembre 1942–septembre 1943)," *Les Cahiers du Musée de la Résistance Azuréenne* 55 (July 2008): 5.

28 Le colonel Chomel de Jarnieu à le Directeur des Services de l'Armistice, CARAN.

29 Charles Williams, *Pétain* (London: Little, Brown, 2005), 442–3.

30 Panicacci, *Les Alpes-Maritimes, de 1939 à 1945: Un Département dans la Tourmente*, 134; Paul Isoart, "11 novembre 1942: l'armée italienne occupe le comté de Nice," *Nice Historique* 4 (October–December 2002): 215; Cabinet, rapports au Préfet, May 15 and 31, 1942, ADAM.

31 Isoart, "11 novembre 1942," 213–15.

32 Jean-Louis Panicacci (ed.), *Les Alpes-Maritimes de 1939 à 1945* (Nice: Centre Régional de Documentation Pédagogique de Nice, 1977), 60–1; Délibérations au Conseil Général, 1945, ADAM.

33 Paolo Veziano, "L'échec du renouveau idéologique et matériel du fascisme dans les terres irrédentes (Menton et Nice, 1940–1943)," *Nice Historique* 2 (April–June 2004): 123–4.

34 Georges-Picot, *L'innocence et la ruse*, 116–17.

35 Panicacci, *Les Alpes-Maritimes, de 1939 à 1945: Un département dans la tourmente*, 62.

36 Pierre Fugain, *Ici l'Ombre: un réseau dans la guerre de libération 40–44* (Grenoble: C.R.D.R., 1992), 162–3.

37 Jean-Louis Panicacci, "Les communistes italiens dans les Alpes-Maritimes (1939–1945)," *Annali della Fondazione Giangiacomo* 24 (1985): 162; Burlando, *Le parti communiste*, 75; Panicacci, *Les Alpes-Maritimes de 1939 à 1945: Un département dans la tourmente*, 346.

38 Panicacci, "Nice 1939–1942," 8.

39 Headquarters, 3rd Infantry Division, "Economic and Political Conditions in France," MHI.

40 *Le Cri des Travailleurs*, December 1942.

41 *Le Petit Niçois*, March 13, August 1, 1943 in Panicacci (ed.), *Les Alpes-Maritimes de 1939 à 1945*, 66, 67.

42 Panicacci, *Les Alpes-Maritimes de 1939 à 1945: Un département dans la tourmente*, 190.

43 *L'Eclairieur de Nice*, March 1, 1943.

44 Panicacci, *Les Alpes-Maritimes de 1939 à 1945: Un département dans la tourmente*, 179–81; Paxton, *Vichy France*, 297–8; Helion, "Antibes Pendant la deuxième guerre mondiale," 79, US.

45 Ralph Schor (ed.), *Nice et les Alpes-Maritimes de 1914 à 1945: Documents d'Histoire* (Nice: Centre Régional de Documentation Pédagogique de Nice, 1991), 126.

46 Pinglier, "Reminiscences 1939–45," 7; Guy Perrier, *Le Colonel Passy et les Services Secrets de la France Libre* (Paris: Hachette Littératures, 1999), 204.

47 At the time of the Armistice, France agreed to pay Germany 10 million marks a day in francs plus 5 million in gold and foreign exchange. After the total occupation in November 1942, the cost rose to 25 million marks a day, causing the highest rate of inflation of the Western-occupied countries. Paxton, *Vichy France*, 362.

48 Girard, "La Résistance dans les Alpes-Maritimes," 1:219, US.

49 Panicacci, "L'occupation italienne," 7; Jean-Louis Panicacci, *L'Occupation italienne: Sud-Est de la France, juin 1940–septembre 1943* (Rennes: Presses Universitaires de Rennes, 2010), 231–3.

50 Georges-Picot, *L'innocence et la ruse*, 72–3.

51 Much of the description of Antibes during the Italian occupation came from Piétri, an Antibois, discussion with the author, March 5, 2010.

52 Louis Piétri, "Les centres d'internement de Sospel et d'Embrun sous l'occupation italienne," *Les compagnies de travail et les camps d'internement en France (zone Sud): 1940–1944* (Nice: Association Nationale des Anciens Combattants de la Résistance, n.d.), 9–10.

53 Panicacci, *L'Occupation italienne*, 234–36; "Les Souvenirs de Deux Internés Politiques Azuréens," *Notre Musée* 198 (March 2011): 19.

54 Registre des délibérations du conseil municipal du 30 décembre 1942 au 17 juin 1943, AMN.

55 Panicacci, *Les Alpes-Maritimes de 1939 à 1945: Un département dans la tourmente*, 186; ibid., "L'occupation italienne," 7; Burlando, *Le parti communiste*, 75–6.

56 Intendance de police de la région de Nice, 0166w000.2–3, ADAM; Jean-Louis Panicacci, *En territoire occupé: Italiens et Allemands à Nice, 1943–1944* (Paris: Vendémaire, 2012), 70.

57 Charles Graves, *The Riviera Revisited* (London: Evans Brothers Ltd, 1948), 100.

58 Digiuni, *Cannes, 1939–1945*, 108–9.

59 Braun, Garacio and Panicacci (eds), *1939–1945*, 81; Michel, "Les relations franco-italiennes de l'armistice de juin 1940," 509.

60 Joseph Girard, "La Résistance dans les Alpes-Maritimes," Vol. 1, Thèse, Université de Nice, 1973, 231–4, US.

61 Meanwhile, in New York City, French expatriates danced in the streets under lampposts festooned with American and French flags. A song proclaimed, "There was a France—There is a France—There will always be a France—ALWAYS." Marlene Dietrich and Jean Gabin were among those who took part in festivities. *New York Times*, July 15, 1943, 13.

62 Léone Gueron, "Les Femmes dans la Résistance: Hébergement et Ravitaillement, IV Partie," *Les Cahiers du Musée de la Résistance Azuréenne* 52 (December 2007): 14–15; Peter FitzSimons, *Nancy Wake: A Biography of Our Greatest War Heroine* (Sydney: HarperCollins, 2001), 152, 215.

63 Digiuni, *Cannes, 1939–1945*, 106.

64 Henri Michel, *Pétain, Laval, Darlan, Trois Politiques?* (Tours: Flammarion, 1972), 109.

65 Erlanger, *La France sans étoile*, 248–9, 338.

66 Braun, Garacio and Panicacci (eds), *1939–1945*, 84.

67 Erlanger, *La France sans étoile*, 278; Braun, Garacio and Panicacci (eds), *1939–1945*, 82; Panicacci, *L'Occupation italienne*, 258–9.

68 Ob.kdo, von Sodenstern, NARA.

69 General der Infanterie Georg von Sodenstern, "To the History of the Times Preceding the Invasion Engagements in France with Special Regard to the South-French Zone," December 13, 1950, 24, NARA.

Chapter 4: The German Occupation

1   Michel Braun, Jean-Pierre Garacio and Jean-Louis Panicacci (eds), *1939–1945: La guerre dans les Alpes Maritimes* (Breil-sur-Roya: Editions du Cabri, 1994), 82; Association Montagne et Traditions, *Pays Vésubien* (Saint-Martin-Vésubie: Musée des Traditions Vésubiennes, 2005), 72.

2   Max Burlando (ed.), *Le parti communiste et ses militants dans la Résistance des Alpes-Maritimes par 120 combattants et témoins* (La Trinité: La Societé Nouvelle Imprimerie de la Victoire, 1974), 79.

3   Braun, Garacio and Panicacci (eds), *1939–1945*, 85.

4   Didier Digiuni, *Cannes, 1939–1945* (Nice: Alandis Editions, 2002), 113.

5   Jean-Louis Panicacci (ed.), *La Résistance Azuréenne* (Nice: Editions Serre, 2003), 41.

6   AOK 19, "Tatigkeitsbericht . . ," n.d., T-312/978/9170877–78, RG 549, NARA.

7   General der Infanterie Georg Von Sodenstern, "To the History of the Times Preceding the Invasion Engagements in France with Special Regard to the South-French Zone," 13 December 1950, MS B-276, RG 549, 26–7.

8   Francis Cammaerts interview by Capt. Howard, 14, Cammaerts, FCA, NA; Robert Chiapello, a youngster in occupied Antibes, discussion with the author, September 10, 2009.

9   Von Sodenstern, "To the History of the Times," 28; General der Infanterie Friederich Wiese, "The 19th Army in Southern France (1 July to 15 September 1944)," April 11, 1948, MS B-787, RG 549, 2, NARA; Generalleutnant Walther Botsch, "Critique of the American Seventh Army," William W. Quinn Papers (Military History Institute), Box 19, HTL.

10 Irène Némirovsky, *Suite Française* (New York: Vintage International, 2007). Another fictionalized account on the same subject quickly became a classic in occupied France and to this day, *Le Silence de la Mer* by Vercors, the nom de plume of Jean Marcel Bruller.

11 Rémi-Nuna Stevelberg, *La Gendarmerie dans les Alpes-Maritimes de 1942 à 1945* (Nice: Serre Editeur, 2004), 71.

12 Jean-Louis Panicacci, "La repression allemande dans les Alpes-Maritimes," *Les Cahiers du Musée de la Résistance Azuréenne* 58 (March 2009): 13, 17; Cammaerts, interview, 12, NA.

13 Pierre Nicot de Villemain, "Les armées à Nice 1942–1945," *Nice Historique* 4 (October–December 2002): 224. Parisian prostitutes in Montmartre shared the same opinion that German soldiers were more "correct" and "disciplined" than GIs. Mary Louise Roberts, *What Soldiers Do: Sex and the American GI in World War II France* (Chicago: University of Chicago Press, 2014), 146.

14 Jean-Louis Panicacci, *Les Alpes-Maritimes de 1939 à 1945: Un département dans la tourmente* (Nice: Editions Serre, 1989), 201–2.

15 *L'Espoir de Nice*, January 4, 1945.

16 Louis Seneca, teenager in occupied Antibes, discussion with the author, May 11, 2005; Chiapello, discussion.

17 Henri Aiglon, teenager in occupied Antibes, discussion with the author, June 15, 2007.

18 Digiuni, *Cannes*, 115–18.

19 Paul D. Adams, Oral History, Section 2, Side 1, Tape 2, Session 1–5 May 1975, MHI.

20 "Plan d'action contre les transports et communications ferroviaires allemands Région Sud-Est," March 8, 1944, Interrogation Reports, Entry 427, RG 407, NARA.

21 Frederic Spotts, *The Shameful Peace: How French Artists and Intellectuals Survived the Nazi Occupation* (New Haven, CT: Yale University Press, 2008), 163; Braun, Garacio and Panicacci (eds), *1939–1945*, 127.

22 Jean-Louis Panicacci (ed.), *Les Alpes-Maritimes de 1939 à 1945* (Nice: Centre Régional de Documentation Pédagogique de Nice, 1977), 78.

23 Délibérations, séance du 21 février 1944, AMA.

24 Panicacci, *Les Alpes-Maritimes de 1939 à 1945: Un département dans la tourmente*, 226–7.

25 Alain d'Ille, discussion with the author, May 23, 2006; Digiuni, 133–35.

26 *La Résistance en Provence*, Vol. I: *Les Français dans la Résistance* (Geneva: Editions Famot, 1974), 47; Philippe Burrin, *France under the Germans: Collaboration and Compromise*, trans. Janet Lloyd (New York: New Press, 1996), 4.

27 For a complete account of Florence Gould's literary salon in Paris during the war, her friends and lovers there, both German and French, and her financial manipulations, see Alan Riding, *And the Show Went On: Cultural Life in Nazi-Occupied Paris* (New York: Alfred A. Knopf, 2010), 118, 255–68.

28 Panicacci, *Les Alpes-Maritimes: Un département dans la tourmente*, 201.

29 Louis Martin, discussion with the author, March 1, 2005. Probably an alias, as Martin is one of the most common surnames in France.

30 Schutzstaffel, a paramilitary protection command within the Nazi Party.

31 Jean-Louis Panicacci, "Janvier–février 1943: Création de la Milice et du STO," *Les Cahiers du Musée de la Résistance Azuréenne* 68 (February 2011): 13.

32 Freemasons were considered a threat to the Nazi regime because they were thought to be heavily influenced by Anglo-Saxon values, were defenders of parliamentary democracy, and opposed any totalitarian regime.

33 Georges Sentis, "Le Service B des F.T.P. et les Alpes Maritimes" (Association Azuréenne du Musée de la Résistance Nationale, 1990), 27; Cammaerts, interview, 12.

34 Roger Maccario, teenager in Monaco during the war, discussion with the author, March 21, 2009. A more sinister practice was known to take place in Bretagne where miliciens dressed in Allied uniforms would knock on the doors of farmhouses and identify themselves as English or French. If help were offered, the men were shot, women beaten and, houses burned. André Hue and Ewen Southby-Tailyour, *The Next Full Moon: The Remarkable True Story of a British Agent Behind the Lines in Wartime France* (London: Penguin Books, 2004), 159.

35 Camille Rayon, discussion with the author, March 30, 2006.

36 Jean-Louis Panicacci, "Enquête sur la Collaboration dans les Alpes-Maritimes," *Comité de Histoire de la 2e Guerre Mondiale* 230 (March/April 1978): 29–30.

37 Jean-Marie Guillon, "La Place de la Résistance dans la Libération," *Provence historique* 36 (April–June 1986): 206.

38 Panicacci (ed.), *Les Alpes-Maritimes de 1939 à 1945*, 80; "Les Ouvriers dans la Résistance Azuréenne," Documents, Témoignages, Recherches No. 29, MRA, 9; Grégoire Georges-Picot, *L'innocence et la ruse: Des étrangers dans la Résistance en Provence, 1940–1944* (Paris: Editions Tirésias, 2000), 236.

39 Panicacci, *Les Alpes-Maritimes: Un département dans la tourmente*, 214–17.

40 Gérard Helion, "Antibes pendant la Deuxième Guerre Mondiale (1939–1945)," Maitrise d'Histoire, Faculté des Lettres de Nice, 1972, 84–6, US; Burlando (ed.), *Le parti communiste*, 79.

41 *Le Petit Niçois*, May 31, 1944.

42 Braun, Garacio and Panicacci (eds), *1939–1945*, 113.

43 "Le bombardement meurtrier de la gare de triage," *L'Express*, July 14–20, 2010, vi; Digiuni, *Cannes*, 118–22.

44 D'Ille, discussion, and Aimée Chabert, teenager in occupied Nice, discussion with the author, June 8, 2007.

45 "La légende du Liberator de la Croix-des-Gardes," *L'Express*, July 14–20, 2010, xx.

46 Secours national, "Hébergement de 800 sinistrés dans les hôtels de la ville," May 28, 1944, boite 168 W 1, ADAM.

47 Jean-Louis Garac, "26 mai 1944, le bombardement de Nice," *Lou Sourgentin* 112 (June 1994): 12; "Note sur l'action du Secours National à la suite du bombardement aérien du 26 mai 1944 à Nice," boite 168 W 1, ADAM.

48 Louis Fiori, "Souvenirs du Bombardement de Nice," *Les Cahiers du Musée de la Résistance Azuréenne* 59 (May 2009): 16–17.

49 After similar massive bombardment the day before in Marseille, residents there were incensed by what they understood to be the American practice of bombing from a height of 6,000 meters (more than 10,000 feet) with little concern for civilians. Hilary Footitt, *War and Liberation in France: Living with the Liberators* (New York: Palgrave Macmillan, 2004), 101.

50 *De l'Occupation à la Libération*, Fabrizio, *OSS: La guerre secrète en France, 1942–1945* (Paris: Hachette, 1990), 47.

51 Colette Poisson, teenager in occupied Nice, discussion with the author, October 1, 2009. This sentiment was expressed in Paris and Biarritz, among other places, in reaction to Allied air raids. Alice-Leone Moats, *No Passport for Paris* (New York: G. P. Putnam's Sons, 1945), 237.

52 *Le Petit Niçois*, May 27, 1944.

53 Secours national, "La Libération de Nice"; Panicacci, *Les Alpes-Maritimes: Un département dans la tourmente*, 209, 224.

54 *Le Petit Niçois*, December 5–6, 1942.

55 Panicacci, *Les Alpes-Maritimes: Un département dans la tourmente*, 221–2.

56 *L'Ergot*, October 20, 1945.

57 Léone Gueron, "Les Femmes dans la Résistance: Hébergement et Ravitaillement, IV Partie," *Les Cahiers du Musée de la Résistance Azuréenne* 52 (December 2007): 13; Florence E. Pinglier, "Reminiscences 1939–45," *Holy Trinity Church Newsletter* 8 (Spring 1995): 10.

58 Alda Giraud and Paul Marcel, discussions with the author, April 21, 2005 and April 3, 2008, respectively.

59 Panicacci (ed.), *Les Alpes-Maritimes de 1939 à 1945*, 73–4.

60 Poisson, discussion; Panicacci, *Les Alpes-Maritimes: Un département dans la tourmente*, 353.

61 Jean-Louis Panicacci, "La libération de Nice," *Lou Sourgentin* 112 (June 1994): 11; Gilbert Borelly, in discussion with the author, December 15, 2005, and Monseigneur Antonin Blanchi, teenager in occupied Nice, discussion with the author, March 14, 2008; Burlando (ed.), *Le parti communiste*, 128–9; Panicacci (ed.), *Les Alpes-Maritimes de 1939 à 1945*, 81.

62 Braun, Garacio and Panicacci (eds), *1939–1945*, 127.

63 Digiuni, *Cannes*, 141–4.

64 Henri Michel, *Shadow War: European Resistance 1939–1945*, trans. Richard Barry (New York: Harper & Row, 1972), 218.

Chapter 5: The Jewish Experience

1 Foreign Jews coming to France in the belief that it was a refuge for all, regardless of religion, were seemingly unaware of anti-Semitism rampant at the end of the nineteenth century that reinforced explanations of the causes of national crises including an economic depression, financial fraudulence undermining the Panama Canal project, and, most famously, the Dreyfus affair.

2 Jacques Grandjonc and Theresia Grundtner (eds), *Zones d'ombres, 1933–1944: Exil et internement d'Allemands et d'Autrichiens dans le sud-est de la France* (Aix-en-Provence: Editions Alinea, 1990), 108–9; Jean-Louis Panicacci (ed.), *Les Alpes-Maritimes de 1939 à 1945* (Nice: Centre Régional de Documentation Pédagogique de Nice, 1977), 185.

3 Grandjonc and Grundtner, *Zones d'ombres*, 94.

4 Harry Burger, "A Holocaust Survivor: Memoir of the War—1938–1945." Survivor Testimonies, RG 02, 5, HMMA.

5 Ibid., 4–6; Agnes Faraldo, "L'Application des lois racistes et antisémites à Nice pendant l'occupation," Mémoire de Licence de Droit—Libertés Publiques, Université de Nice, 15, US.

6 Alexander, Harry, interviewed by Sandy Bradley, Larchmont, New York, February 11, 1992, HMMA.

7 Robert O. Paxton, *Parades and Politics at Vichy: The French Officer Corps Under Marshal Pétain* (Princeton, NJ: Princeton University Press, 1966), 177.

8 Panicacci (ed.), *Les Alpes-Maritimes de 1939 à 1945*, 82.

9 When they finally reached New York after Gaullists overthrew Vichyites at the Panamanian embassy, the family's clothing was taken by the US government, which was looking for authentic

garments and labels for secret agents to wear in Occupied France. Isaac "Ike" Ergas, 15 years old when he left France, in discussion with the author, April 4, 2005.

10 Grandjonc and Grundtner, *Zones d'ombres*, 228–30.

11 Richard J. Golsan (ed.), *Memory, the Holocaust, and French Justice: the Bousquet and Touvier affairs*, trans. Lucy B. Golsan (Hanover, NH: University Press of New England, 1996), 82–3.

12 Renée Poznanski, *Les Juifs en France pendant la Seconde Guerre mondiale* (Paris: Hachette, 1997), 581.

13 Jean-Louis Panicacci, *Les Alpes-Maritimes de 1939 à 1945: Un département dans la tourmente* (Nice: Editions Serre, 1989), 109.

14 Faraldo, "L'Application des lois racistes et antisémites à Nice pendant l'occupation," 10–11.

15 *Le Petit Niçois*, August 30, September 11, 1940.

16 Jérome Gautheret and Thomas Wieder, "De la haine dans l'air," *Le Monde*, July 27, 2010.

17 Michael R. Marrus and Robert O. Paxton, *Vichy France and the Jews* (New York: Basic Books, 1981), 181–3.

18 Philippe Erlanger, *La France sans étoile: Souvenirs de l'avant-guerre et du temps de l'occupation* (Saint-Amand: Librairie Plon, 1974), 184–8; André Kaspi, *Les Juifs pendant l'Occupation* (Paris: Editions du Seuil, 1991), 159.

19 Sophie Urso, "L'Application des Lois Racistes et Antisémites à Nice pendant l'Occupation," Licence en Droit—Libertés Publiques, Université de Nice-Sophia Antipolis, 1995–6, 14, US; Grandjonc and Grundtner, *Zones d'ombres*, 98; Erlanger, *La France sans étoile*, 185.

20 Grégoire Georges-Picot, *L'innocence et la ruse: Des étrangers dans la Résistance en Provence, 1940–1944* (Paris: Editions Tirésias, 2000), 143.

21 Urso, "L'Application des Lois Racistes et Antisémites à Nice," 21.

22 Ibid., 2.

23 Serge Klarsfeld, *Les Transferts de Juifs de la Région de Nice vers le Camp de Drancy en vue de leur Déportation 31 août 1942–30 juillet 1944* (Paris: Les Fils et Filles des Déportés Juifs de France, 1993), 2, 8; Marrus and Paxton, *Vichy France and the Jews*, 256.

24 Representation by a Jewish Council vis-à-vis the occupying power set an unfortunate example of cooperation with the enemy. It was obligatory for every Jew to become a member of this organization whose unstated purpose was preparing for their segregation and deportation.

25 Kaspi, *Les Juifs pendant l'Occupation*, 240–1.

26 Klarsfeld, *Les Transferts de Juifs de la Région de Nice*, 24.

27 "Premier rapport des Renseignements généraux sur une opération du 26 août: celui du commissaire principal de Cannes," August 27, 1942, Klarsfeld, *Les Transferts de Juifs de la Région de Nice*, 11.

28 Georges-Picot, *L'innocence et la ruse*, 145–7.

29 Klarsfeld, *Les Transferts de Juifs de la Région de Nice*, 18.

30 "Sûreté Nationale—Inspecteur Cauvin-R.G.—Tract trouvé dans une boite à lettres," Klarsfeld, *Les Transferts de Juifs de la Région de Nice*, 36–7.

31 Jean-Louis Panicacci, *L'Occupation italienne: Sud-Est de la France, juin 1940–septembre 1943* (Rennes: Presses Universitaires de Rennes, 2010), 197.

32 Urso, "L'Application des Lois Racistes et Antisémites à Nice," 7.

33 "Rapports entre le Gouvernement français et le Commandement italien pendant le stationnement des troupes italiennes en France du 11 novembre 1942 au 9 septembre 1943," dossier 50, AJ 41 1182, 41–2, CARAN.

34 Klarsfeld, *Les Transferts de Juifs de la Région de* Nice, 50.

35 Knochen to S. S. Gruppenfuehrer Mueller, "Subject: Final solution of the Jewish question in France," Telegram 9675, February 22, 1943, Léon Poliakov and Jacques Sabille, *Jews under the Italian Occupation* (Paris: Editions du Centre, 1955), 64–6.

36 Erlanger, *La France sans étoile*, 256.

37 Knochen to Mueller, 60–3.

38 "Extraits de la Note sur les Effets de la Protection accordée par l'Italie aux Juifs de Nice," June 1, 1943, Klarsfeld, *Les Transferts de Juifs de la Région de Nice*, 46–8.

39 Poliakov and Sabille, *Jews under the Italian Occupation*, 30; Simone Veil, *Une Vie* (Versailles: Editions Feryane, 2008), 51.

40 Klarsfeld, *Les Transferts de Juifs de la Région de Nice*, 41–3.

41 Madeleine Kahn, *De l'oasis italienne au lieu du crime des allemands* (Nice: Editions Bénévent, 2003), 102–3; Erlanger, *La France sans étoile*, 246, 267; Kaspi, *Les Juifs pendant l'Occupation*, 294.

42 Dorothy Chamaide, in discussion with the author, June 2, 2005.

43 Lucien Lazare, *Rescue as Resistance: How Jewish Organizations Fought the Holocaust in France* (New York: Columbia University Press, 1996), 228; Jean-Louis Panicacci, *En territoire occupé: Italiens et Allemands à Nice, 1943–1944* (Paris: Vendémaire, 2012), 42–4.

44 Kahn, *De l'oasis italienne au lieu du crime des allemands*, 45.

45 Burger, "A Holocaust Survivor," 7, HMMA.

46 Kahn, *De l'oasis italienne au lieu du crime des allemands*, 60, 63.

47 Erlanger, *La France sans étoile*, 273–4; Klarsfeld, *Les Transferts de Juifs de la Région de Nice*, 52.

48 Poliakov and Sabille, *Jews under the Italian Occupation*, 50, 67, 75, 81, 91, 106.

49 Roethke to S.S. Strumbannfuehrer Hagen, September 4, 1943, Klarsfeld, *Les Transferts de Juifs de la Région de Nice*, 119–22.

50 Roethke to the Reich Security Head Office, Berlin IV B4, "Subject: In particular, the Jew of Italian nationality, Donati," September 26, 1943, Poliakov and Sabille, *Jews under the Italian Occupation*, 126.

51 Kaspi, *Les Juifs pendant l'Occupation*, 298–9; Henry Bily, *Destin à Part: Seul rescapé de la rafle de Clans du 25 octobre 1943* (Paris: Éditions L'Harmattan, 1995), 41–5; Maureen Emerson, *Escape to Provence: The story of Elisabeth Starr and Winifred Fortescue and the making of the Colline des Anglais* (Sussex: Chapter and Verse, 2008), 187.

52 Panicacci, *L'Occupation italienne*, 301–4.

53 Lazare, *Rescue as Resistance*, 231.

54 Serge Klarsfeld, *Nice Hôtel Excelsior: Les rafles des Juifs par la Gestapo à partir du 8 septembre 1943: les transferts de Juifs de la région préfectorale de Nice (Alpes-Maritimes et Basses-Alpes) et de la principauté de Monaco vers le camp de Drancy en vue de leur déportation, 8 septembre 1943–30 juillet 1944* (Nice: Les Fils et Filles de Déportés Juifs de France, 1998), 54, 56, 67.

55 Kahn, *De l'oasis italienne au lieu du crime des allemands*, 72.

56 Urso, "L'Application des Lois Racistes et Antisémites à Nice," 31; Mary Felstiner, "Commandant of Drancy: Alois Brunner and the Jews of France," *Holocaust and Genocide Studies* 2 (1987): 26; Jean-Louis Panicacci, "Les Femmes dans la Résistance Azuréenne," 74.

57 Urso, "L'Application des Lois Racistes et Antisémites à Nice," 41; Panicacci, *Les Alpes-Maritimes de 1939–1945: Un département dans la tourmente*, 200.

58 Klarsfeld, *Nice Hôtel Excelsior*, 55–6; Bily, *Destin à Part*, 49.

59 Urso, "L'Application des Lois Racistes et Antisémites à Nice," 34.

60 Veil, *Une Vie*, 52–53.

61 Roethke to Hagen, September 4, 1943, Poliakov and Sabille, *Jews under the Italian Occupation*, 121.

62 Faraldo, "L'Application des lois racistes et antisémites à Nice pendant l'occupation," 29–30; Klarsfeld, *Nice Hôtel Excelsior*, 56.

63 Golsan (ed.), *Memory, the Holocaust, and French Justice*, 54, 82; Knochen to Mueller, 63.

64 Le secretaire general au maintien de l'ordre à le préfet régional de Nice, April 12, 1944, "accords OBERG définissant les conditions de coopération entre les services de police française et de police allemande, 1943–1944," ADAM.

65 Urso, "L'Application des Lois Racistes et Antisémites à Nice," 42; Klarsfeld, *Nice Hôtel Excelsior*, 63.

66 Urso, "L'Application des Lois Racistes et Antisémites à Nice," 5–36.

67 Faraldo, "L'Application des lois racistes et antisémites à Nice pendant l'occupation," 35–6; Lazare, *Rescue as Resistance*, 193, 209; Urso, "L'Application des Lois Racistes et Antisémites à Nice," 31, 40; Klarsfeld, *Nice Hôtel Excelsior*, 62.

68 Lazare, *Rescue as Resistance*, 208, 279.

69 David Knout, *Contribution à l'histoire de la Résistance Juive en France 1940–1944* (Paris: Editions du Centre, 1947), 159–62.

70 Panicacci (ed.), *Les Alpes-Maritimes de 1939 à 1945*, 89.

71 Faraldo, "L'Application des lois racistes et antisémites à Nice pendant l'occupation," 37–9.

72 See, for example, the differences of opinion expressed by Jean-Louis Panicacci and Ralph Schor, both professors at the University of Nice. Schor points out that Rémond defended himself against such charges by recalling that he had condemned fascism even before fighting began. Ralph Schor, *Un évêque dans le siècle: Monseigneur Paul Rémond (1873–1963)* (Nice: Editions Serre, 1984), 126–7.

73 Schor, *Un évêque dans le siècle*, 115, 117, 121, 124.

74 Felstiner, "Commandant of Drancy," 33.

75 Lazare, *Rescue as Resistance*, 193.

76 A superb film account is presented in the program *Le Réseau Marcel*, written and directed by Maria Landau and Jacqueline Sigaar and produced by France 3 Méditerranée in 2003. See, also, Faraldo, "L'Application des lois racistes et antisémites à Nice pendant l'occupation," 38.

77 Jeannette Wolgust, "Témoignage de Jeannette Wolgust, l'une des 527 enfants Abadi," *Les Cahiers du Musée de la Résistance Azuréenne* 53 (February 2008): 17–18.

78 Schor, *Un évêque dans le siècle*, 121–2.

79 Lazare, *Rescue as Resistance*, 204–7, 214–15.

80 Klarsfeld, *Nice Hôtel Excelsior*, 59–60; Faraldo, "L'Application des lois racistes et antisémites à Nice pendant l'occupation," 40.

81 Marrus and Paxton, *Vichy France and the Jews*, 346.

82 Poliakov and Sabille, *Jews under the Italian Occupation*, 43.

83 Klarsfeld's own father, Arno, a member of Combat, was arrested in the Nice roundups and deported to Auschwitz where he died in October 1943.

84 Klarsfeld, *Nice Hôtel Excelsior*, 65; Lazare, *Rescue as Resistance*, 235; Veil, *Une Vie*, 49; Erlanger, *La France sans étoile*, 292.

85 Klarsfeld, *Nice Hôtel Excelsior*, 63, 65.

86 Lazare, *Rescue as Resistance*, 278–9.

87 Jean-Louis Panicacci, "Nice sous l'Occupation," *L'Express*, June 7, 2011, ii.

88 Paxton, *Vichy France*, 183; Marrus and Paxton, *Vichy France and the Jews*, 343–5, 356; Poznanski, *Les Juifs en France pendant la Seconde Guerre mondiale*, 566; Felstiner, "Commandant of Drancy," 37.

Chapter 6: British Agents in the Midi

1   The first comprehensive history of the SOE, compiled from official records immediately after the war but kept secret for over 50 years, W. J. M. Mackenzie, *The Secret History of SOE: The Special Operations Executive, 1940–1945* (London: St. Ermin's Press, 2000), 257–8.

2   Maurice Buckmaster, *They Fought Alone: The Story of British Agents in France* (London: The Popular Book Club, 1958), 18, 216; M. R. D. Foot, *SOE in France: An Account of the Work of the British Special Operations Executive in France 1940–1944* (London: Her Majesty's Stationery Office, 1966), 11.

3   Marcel Ruby, *F Section, SOE: The Buckmaster Networks* (London: Leo Cooper, 1988), 31.

4   Foot, *SOE in France*, 231.

5   Henri Michel, *Histoire de la Résistance en France (1940–1944)*, 10th edn (Paris: Presses Universitaires de France, 1987), 42.

6   "Les Réseaux de Résistance dans les Alpes-Maritimes," Document, Témoignages, Recherches No. 20, 2, 4, MRA.

7   M. R. D. Foot, *Resistance: An Analysis of European Resistance to Nazism 1940–1945* (New York: McGraw-Hill, 1977), 251; Joseph Girard, "La Résistance dans les Alpes-Maritimes," Vol. 1, thesis, University of Nice, 1973, 149–51, US.

8   Patrick Howarth, *Undercover: The Men and Women of the Special Operations Executive* (London; Routledge & Kegan Paul, 1980), 229.

9   Foot, *SOE in France*, 59–60. Mackenzie's numbers compiled right after the war differ from Foot's. At one point Mackenzie cites 390 F Section agents in the field, at another he writes of 500 highly trained men dispatched to France. Mackenzie, *The Secret History of SOE*, 574, 624.

10 Buckmaster, *They Fought Alone*, 27.

11 Ibid., 43–6.

12 "Sous-Marins et felouques au large d'Antibes: L'opération du 27 avril 1942," Documents, Témoignages, Recherches No. 14, 11, MRA; Boris de Gueyer, *L'Organisation de Résistance de l'Armée dans la Région R2: Provence–Alpes–Côte d'Azur*, 2nd edn (Paris: n.p., 2004), 59.

13 Peter Churchill, *Duel of Wits* (London: Hodder and Stoughton, 1953), 240; Brooks Richards, *Secret Flotillas: The Clandestine Sea Lines to France and French North Africa, 1940–1944* (London: Her Majesty's Stationery Office, 1996), 444–68.

14 Richards, *Secret Flotillas*, 480–99.

15 Howarth, *Undercover*, 223; Mackenzie, *The Secret History of SOE*, 239.

16 Penny Starns, *Odette: World War Two's Darling Spy* (Stroud: History Press, 2009), 134–6; Sarah Helm, *A Life in Secrets: The Story of Vera Atkins and the Lost Agents of SOE* (London: Abacus, 2006), 297–8, 363, 434.

17 Peter Churchill, *Of Their Own Choice* (London: Hodder and Stoughton, 1952), 122.

18 An authoritative secondary source identifies the prosthesis as a brass foot. Mackenzie, *The Secret History of SOE*, 252n. After meeting her, Churchill recalled she said, "It's actually made of aluminum, and there's an opening where it fits round the heel." They agreed that the indentation was a perfect hiding place for secret information. Churchill, *Of Their Own Choice*, 114, 133.

19 Churchill, *Of Their Own Choice*, 115 passim.

20 Foot, *SOE in France*, 173.

21 E. H. Cookridge, *Inside SOE: The Story of Special Operations in Western Europe 1940–45* (London: Arthur Barker Ltd, 1966), 149–52, 356–7.

22 Churchill, *Of Their Own Choice,* 93, 99; "Sous-Marins et felouques au large d'Antibes," 4, MRA.

23 Foot, *SOE in France*, 170, 204; "L'Organisation *Carte* dans les Alpes-Maritimes," Documents, Témoignages, Recherches No. 25, 5, MRA.

24 There were two other d'Astier de la Vigerie brothers: François, an air force general, and Henri, a monarchist who helped prepare Algiers for the North African landings and was suspected of complicity in the assassination of Admiral Darlan.

25 Foot, *SOE in France*, 205.

26 Ruby, *F Section, SOE*, 128; Girard, "La Résistance dans les Alpes-Maritimes," 1:158, US.

27 John Goldsmith, *Accidental Agent* (New York: Charles Scribner's Sons, 1971), 76.

28 Foot, *SOE in France*, 250–1; Elizabeth Nicholas, *Death be not Proud* (London: White Lion Publishers, 1958), 17; Ray Jenkins, *A Pacifist at War* (London: Arrow Books, 2010), 68, 72.

29 Goldsmith, *Accidental Agent*, 48–50; Mark W. Clark, *Calculated Risk* (New York: Harper & Brothers, 1950), 95–7.

30 Mackenzie, *The Secret History of SOE*, 255, 256, 581.

31 A man of influence in Marseille and veteran of World War I who had been decorated by the British and was now recruiting for the *Légion des volontaires français contre le Bolchévisme* to be trained by the Germans and sent to fight in Russia.

32 Churchill, *Of Their Own Choice*, 36.

33 Ibid., 39–40.

34 Alastair Mars, *Unbroken: The Story of a Submarine* (Barnsley: Pen & Sword Books, 2006), 41.

35 Ibid., 51–60.

36 The house at the corner of Boulevard Maréchal Foch and Avenue des Frères Roustan was torn down early in the twenty-first century.

37 Emmanuel de la Vigerie D'Astier, *Seven Times Seven Days*, trans. Humphrey Hare (London: MacGibbon & Kee, 1958), 63.

38 Once in London, D'Astier met with General de Gaulle, who reacted sharply upon learning of his return from France by submarine, "Kidnapped by those British." Churchill, *Duel of Wits*, 31–2, 47.

39 Ibid., 102–13 passim.

40 Odette's incredible wartime experiences were first related in full in a biography by a major in the War Office's public relations department, drawing on interviews with Odette and Churchill embellished with literary license. At times the narrative seems to lapse into contrasting British efficiency and heroism with what is portrayed as French incompetence. Jerrard Tickell, *Odette: The Story of a British Agent* (London: Pan Books, 1955). Recent scholarly treatments offer more credible accounts based in large measure on oral history interviews with Odette in 1985 archived at the Imperial War Museum and the SOE personnel files of Odette and Churchill opened to the public in 1985. Starns, *Odette*, and Clare Mulley, *The Spy Who Loved: The Secrets and Lives of Christine Granville* (London: Macmillan, 2012).

41 Churchill, *Duel of Wits*, 155.

42 Foot, *SOE in France*, 210; also, "Interview of Roger" [Cammaerts's nom de guerre], November 21, 1943, P1018565, Francis Cammaerts FCA, HS 9/285, NA.

43 Hugh Verity, *We Landed by Moonlight: The Secret RAF Landings in France, 1940–1944*, rev. edn (Manchester: Crécy Publishing, 2000), 74.

44 Foot, *SOE in France*, 251–2; Jean Overton Fuller, *The German Penetration of SOE: France 1941–1944* (London: William Kimber, 1975), 37.

45 Hugo Bleicher, *Colonel Henri's Story: The War Memoirs of Hugo Bleicher, Former German Secret Agent* by Ian Colvin (London: William Kimber, 1954), 99; Churchill, *Duel of Wits*, 315; Peter

Churchill, *Spirit in the Cage* (London: Hodder and Stoughton, 1954), 28–9; "Sous-Marins et felouques au large d'Antibes," 5, 10, MRA.

46 Churchill, *Spirit in the Cage*, 25–6, 105; Tickell, *Odette*, 222–4, Starns, *Odette*, 88–95.

47 Bleicher, *Colonel Henri's Story*, 101.

48 Verity, *We Landed by Moonlight*, 71, 72; Jenkins, *A Pacifist at War*, 4, 80; Xan Fielding, *Hide and Seek* (London: Secker & Warburg, 1954), 234.

49 Mackenzie, *The Secret History of SOE*, 568–9; Cammaerts, interview, 2–3, Cammaerts, FCA, NA.

50 Jenkins, *A Pacifist at War*, 79; Foot, *SOE in France*, 253–4, 376.

51 Cammaerts, interview, 4–7, Cammaerts FCA, NA; E. H. Cookridge, *They Came from the Sky* (New York: Thomas Y. Crowell Company, 1967), 95.

52 Foot, *SOE in France*, 442.

Chapter 7: The Maquis

1 Edward L. Homze, *Foreign Labor in Nazi Germany* (Princeton, NJ: Princeton University Press, 1967), 178, 186–8.

2 Jean-Louis Panicacci (ed.), *Les Alpes-Maritimes de 1939 à 1945* (Nice: Centre Régional de Documentation Pédagogique de Nice, 1977), 65, 76; Raymond Gatti, *Taxi de guerre, Taxi de paix* (Cannes: S.E.D.A.IN., 1957), 15–16.

3 Intendance de police de la région de Nice, 0166w001.3, ADAM.

4 Henri Michel, *The Shadow War: European Resistance 1939–1945*, trans. Richard Barry (New York: Harper & Row, 1972), 271.

5 Panicacci (ed.), *Les Alpes-Maritimes de 1939 à 1945*, 57, 69.

6 Henri Michel, *Histoire de la Résistance en France (1940–1944)*, 10th edn (Paris: Presses Universitaires de France, 1987), 92–5.

7 M. R. D. Foot, *SOE in France: An Account of the Work of the British Special Operations Executive in France 1940–1944* (London: Her Majesty's Stationery Office, 1966), 353; H. R. Kedward, *In Search of the Maquis: Rural Resistance in Southern France, 1942–1944* (Oxford: Clarendon Press, 1993), 34–5.

8 Jean-Louis Panicacci (ed.), *La Résistance Azuréenne* (Nice: Editions Serre, 2003), 106; Kedward, *In Search of the Maquis*, 45; Camille Rayon, discussion with the author, October 25, 2005.

9 Headquarters, VI Corps, G-2 Notes, "The Maquis of France," July 28, 1944, Box 7, John W. O'Daniel Papers, MHI.

10 Claude Lippmann, "Jean Lippmann et le maquis 'Lorrain' au Laverq et en Ubaye, août 1943–juin 1944," Documents, Témoignages, Recherches No. 5, 2–4, 8–9, MRA.

11 After the war Francis Cammaerts stated that he never heard of a single person put in danger by a child's indiscretion. Kedward, *In Search of the Maquis*, 278.

12 Michel, *Shadow War*, 7, 271.

13 "Interview of Roger," FCA, NA; "The Maquis," NA.

14 Julian Jackson, *France: the Dark Years 1940–1944* (New York: Oxford University Press, 2001), 484.

15 Kedward, *In Search of the Maquis*, 102, 110.

16 Panicacci (ed.), *La Résistance Azuréenne*, 108.

17 Foot, *SOE in France*, 354–5.

18 Boris de Gueyer, *L'Organisation de Résistance de l'Armée dans la Région R2: Provence–Alpes–Côte d'Azur*, 2nd edn (Paris: n.p., 2004), 13.

19 Joseph Girard, "La Résistance dans les Alpes-Maritimes," Vol. 1, thesis, University of Nice, 1973, 206, US.

20 Arthur Layton Funk, *Hidden Ally: The French Resistance, Special Operations, and the Landings in Southern France, 1944* (New York: Greenwood Press, 1992), 34–5.

21 Foot, *SOE in France*, 475–7.

22 Sapin et al., *Méfiez vous du Toréador* (Toulon: Association Générale de Prévoyance Militaire, 1987), 327–9.

23 "Les Réseaux de Résistance dans les Alpes-Maritimes," Document, Témoignages, Recherches No. 20, 7, MRA.

24 "Sous-Marins et felouques au large d'Antibes: L'opération du 27 avril 1942," Documents, Témoignages, Recherches No. 14, 8, MRA.

25 Kedward, *In Search of the Maquis*, 276.

26 Gueyer, *L'Organisation de Résistance de l'Armée dans la Région R2*, 29.

27 John Goldsmith, *Accidental Agent* (New York: Charles Scribner's Sons, 1971), 141–2; Kedward, *In Search of the Maquis*, 275.

28 Rayon, discussion, October 25, 2005.

29 Girard, "La Résistance dans les Alpes-Maritimes," 1:201, US.

30 *De l'Occupation à la Libération*, Fabrizio, *OSS: La guerre secrète en France, 1942–1945* (Paris: Hachette, 1990), 20–1, 68.

31 "La liberté descend des montagnes," Documents, Témoignages, Recherches No. 17, 9–10, MRA; Panicacci (ed.), *La Résistance Azuréenne*, 118–19.

32 Special Force Staff Headquarters, Force 163, "Summary of French Resistance Activities No. 3," June 9–11, 1944, Entry 158, Folder 42, Box 3, RG 226, NARA.

33 "Le Maquis franco-italien de l'Albarea et le drame de Sospel," Documents, Témoignages, Recherches No. 12, 2–3, MRA.

34 Michel Braun, Jean-Pierre Garacio and Jean-Louis Panicacci (eds), *1939–1945: La guerre dans les Alpes Maritimes* (Breil-sur-Roya: Editions du Cabri, 1994), 109; Panicacci (ed.), *La Résistance Azuréenne*, 83.

35 Panicacci (ed.), *La Résistance Azuréenne*, 56.

36 Ibid., 108–9.

37 Sapin et al., *Méfiez vous du Toréador*, 311.

38 "Le drame du maquis du Férion (1–12 juin 1944)," Documents, Témoignages, Recherches No. 2, MRA.

39 Lieut-Col. F. Cammaerts interviewed by Capt. Howard, 19, Cammaerts, FCA, NA.

40 Panicacci (ed.), *La Résistance Azuréenne*, 46–7.

Chapter 8: Resistance in Southeast France

1 Gordon Wright, "Reflections on the French Resistance (1940–1944)," *Political Science Quarterly* 77 (September 1962): 337–9; Daniel Cordier, *De l'Histoire à l'histoire* (Paris: Editions Gallimard, 2013), 147.

2 Marcel Ophuls, *The Sorrow and the Pity* (New York: Berkley Windhover Books, 1975), 118.

3 W. J. M. Mackenzie, *The Secret History of SOE: The Special Operations Executive, 1940–1945* (London: St. Ermin's Press, 2000), 266.

4 H. R. Kedward, *In Search of the Maquis: Rural Resistance in Southern France, 1942–1944* (Oxford: Clarendon Press, 1993), 197, 206.

5 Jean-Louis Panicacci, "Sociologie de la Résistance dans les Alpes-Maritimes," *Provence historique* 44 (octobre-décembre 1994): 480–6.

6 "Les Débuts de la Résistance Gaulliste dans les Alpes-Maritimes (1940–1943)," Documents, Témoignages, Recherches No. 8, 2nd edn, 2000, MRA.

7 *Le juif Suss* was a vitriolic, anti-Semitic, German book and film portraying the worst imaginable Jewish man.

8 "Les Jeunes dans la Résistance Azuréenne," Documents, Témoignages, Recherches No. 24, 3–4, MRA.

9 Joseph Girard, "La Résistance dans les Alpes-Maritimes," Vol. 1, thesis, University of Nice, 1973, 31–2, 35, US.

10 Louis Piétri, a young Antibois with communist leanings, in discussion with the author, March 5, 2010; Louis Piétri, "Souvenirs d'un ancien résistant: Les jeunes Antibois dans la Résistance," *Les Cahiers du Musée de la Résistance Azuréenne* 69 (April 2011): 17.

11 Grégoire Georges-Picot, *L'innocence et la ruse: Des étrangers dans la Résistance en Provence, 1940–1944* (Paris: Editions Tirésias, 2000), 28, 30; *De l'Occupation à la Libération*, Fabrizio, *OSS: La guerre secrète en France, 1942–1945* (Paris: Hachette, 1990), 30.

12 Jean-Marie Guillon, "Catholiques varois et résistance," *Provence historique* 42 (January–June 1992): 423; Sapin et al., *Méfiez vous du Toréador* (Toulon: Association Générale de Prévoyance Militaire, 1987), 124.

13 *New York Times*, June 16, 1940, 22; Girard, "La Résistance dans les Alpes-Maritimes," 1:35, US.

14 Girard, "La Résistance dans les Alpes-Maritimes," 1:57–59.

15 M. R. D. Foot, *SOE in France: An Account of the Work of the British Special Operations Executive in France 1940–1944* (London: Her Majesty's Stationery Office, 1966), 182.

16 Ibid., 489–98.

17 While consisting of radical socialists, Franc-Tireur (literally "free shooter") should not be confused with Francs-Tireurs et Partisans, the military arm of the Communist Party.

18 *La Résistance en Provence*, Vol. I: *Les Français dans la Résistance* (Genève: Editions Famot, 1974), 42–3.

19 "Les Ouvriers dans la Résistance Azuréenne," Documents, Témoignages, Recherches No. 29, 6, MRA.

20 See, especially, Jean-Louis Panicacci (ed.), *La Résistance Azuréenne* (Nice: Editions Serre, 2003), 86–7, passim; Georges-Picot, *L'innocence et la ruse*, 233.

21 "Les Ouvriers dans la Résistance Azuréenne," 8.

22 Panicacci (ed.), *La Résistance Azuréenne*, 42.

23 "Les Ouvriers dans la Résistance Azuréenne," 7.

24 Jean-Louis Panicacci, "Les communistes italiens dans les Alpes-Maritimes (1939–1945)," *Annali della Fondazione Giangiacomo* 24 (1985): 158–61.

25 Georges-Picot, *L'innocence et la ruse*, 13–21.

26 André Odru, "Les F.T.P., la M.O.I., les Milices Patriotiques dans les Alpes-Maritimes," 2005, 6–7, MRA.

27 "Les Ouvriers dans la Résistance Azuréenne," 2–8; Panicacci (ed.), *La Résistance Azuréenne*, 41; Peter Leslie, *The Liberation of the Riviera: The Resistance to the Nazis in the South of France and the Story of Its Heroic Leader, Ange-Marie Miniconi* (New York: Wyndham Books, 1980), 159–64.

28 "Les Ouvriers dans la Résistance Azuréenne," 3; Panicacci (ed.), *La Résistance Azuréenne*, 31.

29 Colonel [André Dewavrin] Passy, *Souvenirs du B. C. R. A.*, Vol. I, *Deuxième Bureau-Londres (juin 1940–décembre 1941)* (Paris: Raoul Solar, 19472), 64.

30 Laure Moulin, *Jean Moulin* (Paris: France Loisirs, 1982), 289–91; "L'action de Jean Moulin à Nice et dans les Alpes-Maritimes (1941–1943)," Documents, Témoignages, Recherches No. 3, 3rd edn, Sept. 2000, 3–4, MRA; "Essai sur les Origines du Gaullisme à Nice et Cannes," Documents, Témoignages, Recherches No. 8, 10, MRA.

31 M. R. D. Foot, *Resistance: An Analysis of European Resistance to Nazism 1940-1945* (New York: McGraw-Hill, 1977), 238.

32 Panicacci (ed.), *La Résistance Azuréenne*, 97, 100; Jean-Louis Panicacci, "Georges Foata-Morgan, François," *Les Cahiers du Musée de la Résistance Azuréenne* 49 (May 2007): 13.

33 At the close of his life, Mitterand's right-wing inclinations before the war and his indifference to anti-Semitism in Vichy, as shown by the government's support for the deportation of Jews, became a matter of national controversy upon publication of an exposé by journalist Pierre Péan. Still president of France at the time, Mitterand is quoted as telling the author, "I was not thinking of anti-Semitism of Vichy. I knew that there were unfortunately anti-Semites who had assumed an important role next to the Maréchal, but I was not following the legislation at the time and the measures taken. We were on the fringe." Pierre Péan, *Une jeunesse française: François Mitterrand, 1934–1947* (Paris: Librairie Arthème Fayard, 1994), 17, 210; Ronald Tiersky, *Mitterrand: The Last French President* (New York: St. Martin's Press, 2000), 59–69, 348–9; Walter Laqueur (ed.), *The Holocaust Encyclopedia* (New Haven, CT: Yale University Press, 2001), 221; Julian Jackson, *France: the Dark Years 1940–1944* (New York: Oxford University Press, 2001), 621–3.

34 Girard, "La Résistance dans les Alpes-Maritimes," 1:237, US.

35 *La Résistance en Provence*, 1:38, 42.

36 Jean-Luc Fournier, "La presse clandestine durant l'occupation," *Le Déporté* 563 (1er trimestre 2010): 10.

37 Max Burlando (ed.), *Le parti communiste et ses militants dans la Résistance des Alpes-Maritimes par 120 combattants et témoins* (La Trinité: La Societé Nouvelle Imprimerie de la Victoire, 1974), 80–3.

38 "Les Femmes dans la Résistance Azuréenne," Documents, Témoignages, Recherches No. 22, Musée de la Résistance Azuréenne, 2.

39 Raphaël Konopnicki, "L'imprimerie Valrose de Nice (1943–1944) pendant l'occupation allemande," Les *Cahiers du Musée de la Résistance Azuréenne* 53 (February 2008): 12–16; Georges-Picot, *L'innocence et la ruse*, 171–4.

40 Panicacci (ed.), *La Résistance Azuréenne*, 165–8.

41 Albert Guérisse, a Belgian doctor with the nom de guerre "Pat O'Leary" ran one of the most successful British escape lines.

42 Jean-Louis Panicacci (ed.), *La Résistance Azuréenne* (Nice: Editions Serre, 2003), 70–1; Léone Gueron, "Les Femmes dans la Résistance Azuréenne: III Partie," *Les Cahiers du Musée de la Résistance Azuréenne* 51 (October 2007): 16, and "Les Femmes dans la Résistance: Hébergement et Ravitaillement: IV Partie," *Les Cahiers du Musée de la Résistance Azuréenne* 52 (December 2007): 14–15; *Nice Matin*, July 11, 1972; Brooks Richards, *Secret Flotillas: The Clandestine Sea Lines to France and French North Africa, 1940–1944* (London: Her Majesty's Stationery Office, 1996), 545–6.

43 "Les Réseaux de Résistance dans les Alpes-Maritimes," Document, Témoignages, Recherches No. 20, 7, MRA; Panicacci (ed.), *La Résistance Azuréenne*, 35–7.

44 Unique to the Southeast, a large, round bread weighing as much as a kilogram and enriched with olives and other additives.

45 Gabriel Mazier, *Un Officier d'occasion dans le haut pays niçois: Mémoires du "Capitaine François" sur la libération du Haut-Pays Niçois*, ed. Gaston Bernard (Nice: n.p., 1992), 35–8.

46 Sapin, *Méfiez vous du Toréador*, 331.

47 Mazier, *Un Officier d'occasion dans le haut pays niçois*, 48–9.

48 "Parachutages et Répression à Puget-Théniers," Documents, Témoignages, Recherches No. 7, 2–6, 10–14, MRA.

49 Jean-Louis Panicacci, *Les Alpes-Maritimes de 1939 à 1945: Un département dans la tourmente* (Nice: Editions Serre, 1989), 213–14.

50 This treatment is based primarily on Panicacci (ed.), *La Résistance Azuréenne*, 69–74; and "Les Femmes dans la Résistance Azuréenne," MRA.

51 Burlando (ed.), *Le parti communiste et ses militants*, 91–2.

52 Georges-Picot, *L'innocence et la ruse*, 72–3, 262–5.

53 "Parachutages et Répression à Puget-Théniers," 7–10, 13.

54 Leslie, *Liberation of the Riviera*, 131–8.

55 Nathan Chapochnik in Georges-Picot, *L'innocence et la ruse*, 235–6.

56 "Resistance in South-East France," March 22, 1944, Entry 190, Folder 12, Box 329, RG 226, NARA and NA; Boris de Gueyer, *L'Organisation de Résistance de l'Armée dans la Région R2: Provence–Alpes–Côte d'Azur*, 2nd edn (Paris: n.p., 2004), 41.

57 George Millar, *Road to Resistance: An Autobiography* (London: Bodley Head, 1979), 354.

58 "Plan d'action contre les transports et communications ferroviaires allemands Région Sud-Est," March 8 1944, Interrogation Reports, Entry 427, RG 407, NARA.

59 Sapin, *Méfiez vous du Toréador*, 44.

60 *Les Voix de la Liberté: Ici Londres 1940–1944*, Vol. 5: *Le Bataille de France: 9 mai 1944–31 août 1944* (Vichy: Imprimerie Wallon, 1976), 47.

61 Joseph Girard, *La Résistance et la Libération de Nice: La fin d'une légende?* (Nice: Serre Editeur, 2006), 62–3.

62 Kedward, *In Search of the Maquis*, 64.

63 Sapin, *Méfiez vous du Toréador*, 58.

64 Panicacci (ed.), *La Résistance Azuréenne*, 110–11; Girard, *La Résistance et la Libération de Nice*, 68.

65 Special Force Staff Headquarters, Force 163, "Summary of French Resistance Activities No. 3," June 9–11, 1944, Entry 158, Folder 42, Box 3, RG 226, NARA.

66 Hugh Verity, *We Landed by Moonlight: The Secret RAF Landings in France, 1940–1944*, rev. edn (Manchester: Crécy Publishing, 2000), 175.

67 Ray Jenkins, *A Pacifist at War* (London: Arrow Books, 2010), 142.

68 Claude Lippmann, "Jean Lippmann et le maquis 'Lorrain' au Laverq et en Ubaye, août 1943–juin 1944," Documents, Témoignages, Recherches No. 5, 8, 11, MRA.

69 E. H. Cookridge, *They Came from the Sky* (New York: Thomas Y. Crowell Company, 1967), 112–15.

70 In 2012, a biography, assiduously researched, sharpens the facts and adds atmosphere to Christine's life story. Clare Mulley, *The Spy Who Loved: The Secrets and Lives of Christine Granville* (London: Macmillan, 2012). Official papers are found in her dossier, Granville, Christine, FCA, HS 9/612, NA.

71 Another biographer cites 1915 as Christine's birth year, but Mulley provides details to support an arrival in 1908. Mulley, *The Spy Who Loved*, 1–2.

72 Among the most memorable vignettes of Christine concern a time when she dropped out of sight of London, and an SOE operative was dispatched to Budapest to find her. Upon meeting Christine, he fell madly in love, a reaction common to men when first meeting her. When his

feelings were unreciprocated, he attempted suicide by jumping off a bridge into the Danube. Fortunately or unfortunately, he forgot the river was frozen and merely broke his arm. Marchand, D/H Madame, March 11, 1940, P1019770, NA. ("Madame Marchand" was Christine's nom de guerre while operating in Eastern Europe at the war's outset.)

73 "Fryday," "Notes on Madame G," December 7, 1939, 1019996, and R. T., "Gizycka and Kowerski," December 16, 1942, P1019945–46, Granville, FCA, NA. Gizycka was Christine's married name and Kowerski was her close companion on and off for the remainder of her life.

74 Xan Fielding, *Hide and Seek* (London: Secker & Warburg, 1954), 234.

75 Madeleine Masson, *Christine: SOE Agent & Churchill's Favourite Spy* (London: Virago Press, 2005), 191–2; Arthur Layton Funk, *Hidden Ally: The French Resistance, Special Operations, and the Landings in Southern France, 1944* (New York: Greenwood Press, 1992), 53.

76 Jenkins, *Pacifist at War*, 172.

77 Kedward, *In Search of the Maquis*, 176–80; Michael Pearson, *Tears of Glory: The Betrayal of Vercors 1944* (London: Pan Books, 1978), 241; *1944: La victoire du Débarquement à la Libération* (Malesherbes: Editions Tallandier Historia, 1994), 131–40.

78 Howarth, Patrick, to Col. Dodd-Parker, "Discussions during my recent visit to Algiers," July 6, 1944, Folder 844, E190, Box 140, RG 226, NARA.

79 "To Brooks from Pauline," 27 July 1944, P1019912, Granville, FCA, HS 9/612, NA.

80 F. C. Bovensohen to Sir Robert Knox, "Krystina Gizycka (alias Christine Granville)," January 22, 1945, P1019850–52, Granville, FCA, HS 9/612, NA.

81 F. B. Richards to Howarth, "Subversion of Satellite Troops," August 5, 1945, Folder 844, E190, Box 140, RG 226, NARA.

82 Masson, *Christine*, 207–9; Funk, *Hidden Ally*, 184.

83 "Resistance in South-East France," NARA and NA.

84 Cookridge, *They Came from the Sky*, 108–9.

85 Mazier, *Un Officier d'occasion dans le haut pays niçois*, 66.

86 Sapin, *Méfiez vous du Toréador*, 61.

87 Millar, *Road to Resistance*, 377.

88 Gueyer, *L'Organisation de Résistance de l'Armée dans la Région R2*, 29; Panicacci (ed.), *La Résistance Azuréenne*, 54.

89 Special Force Staff Headquarters, Force 163, "Summary of French Resistance Activities No. 3," NARA.

90 Sapin, *Méfiez vous du Toréador*, 62, 129; Panicacci (ed.), *La Résistance Azuréenne*, 114.

91 Baudouin, "La Marine dans la Résistance à Toulon," 180; *De l'Occupation à la Libération*, 30; Funk, *Hidden Ally*, 66; Gueyer, *L'Organisation de Résistance de l'Armée dans la Région R2*, 17.

92 Sapin, *Méfiez vous du Toréador*, 67.

93 Gueyer, *L'Organisation de Résistance de l'Armée dans la Région R2*, 56–7.

94 P1018214, P1018222, Massingham Inter-Allied Mission Reports, NA.

95 G-3, SPOC, to Gunn, Operation Orders, P10182233, Massingham Inter-Allied Mission Reports, NA.

96 P1018199, Massingham Inter-Allied Mission Reports, NA; Funk, *Hidden Ally*, 90.

97 Zeller had just been promoted to the rank of brigadier general in July after serving in the rank of colonel for most of the war. *Résistance et Libération de la Provence: Témoignages et récits* (Genève: Editions de Crémille, 1994), 180.

98 The account rendered by Zeller himself after liberation is, of course, the most authoritative. Sapin, *Méfiez vous du Toréador*, 351–3. See also Funk, *Hidden Ally*, 69–70, 72.

99 Francis Cammaerts, interview by Capt. Howard, January,16–18, 1945, 13, Cammaerts FCA, NA.

100 "Short resume of Pauline's activities," Folder 844, E190, Box 140, RG 226, NARA.

101 "Statement of Miss Christine Granville," November 1, 1944, P1019905, Granville, FCA, HS 9/612, NA.

102 Lt.-Col. Roger, Officier de Liaison Britannique FFI-R.1–R.2, "Report on Christine Granville, known as Pauline," October 22, 1944, P1019757, Granville, FCA, HS 9/612, NA.

103 Foot, *SOE in France*, 356.

104 Ibid., 443.

105 Malraux was a renowned writer and the national minister of culture during de Gaulle's tenure as president of France. Earlier Malraux had taken political positions close to the communists and, according to one account, at this point in the war worked mainly with the FTP. Mackenzie, *Secret History of SOE*, 585.

106 André Malraux, *Le Miroir des Limbes: Antimémoires* (Paris: Gallimard, 1972), 181–2, 195. See also André Malraux, *Fallen Oaks: Conversation with De Gaulle* (London: Hamish Hamilton, 1972), 5.

Chapter 9: Preparations for Landing

1   A comprehensive overview of the lead-up to Operation Anvil/Dragoon is found in the volume on Seventh Army and VI Corps in the series on the US Army in the European Theater of Operations. Jeffrey J. Clarke and Robert Ross Smith, *Riviera to the Rhine* (Washington, D.C.: U. S. Army Center of Military History, 1993), 3–92. The narrative continues with the landing and invasion.

2   Arthur L. Funk, "American Contacts with the Resistance in France, 1940–1943," *Military Affairs* 34 (February 1970): 15; Arthur Layton Funk, *Hidden Ally: The French Resistance, Special Operations, and the Landings in Southern France, 1944* (New York: Greenwood Press, 1992), 30.

3   A member of the right-wing Cagoule before the war.

4   George C. Chalou (ed.), *The Secrets War: The Office of Strategic Services in World War II* (Washington, D.C., National Archives and Records Administration, 1992), 259.

5   US War Department Strategic Services, *War Report of the OSS (Office of Strategic Services)*, Vol. 2, *The Overseas Targets* (New York: Walker Publishing Company, 1976), 169; Funk, "American Contacts with the Resistance in France," 18.

6   US War Department Strategic Services, 2:188.

7   "Mission 'Tomate'," Entry 97, Folder 620, Box 35, RG 226, NARA.

8   Fabrizio Calvi, *OSS: La guerre secrète en France, 1942–1945* (Paris: Hachette, 1990), 381–3.

9   Maj. Robert R. Dodderidge to Capt. Paul Van der Stricht, August 28, 1943, "SO Program for Southern France," Entry 190, Box 329, Folder 12, RG 226, NARA; SPOC, subject: SPOC, July 12, 1944, Entry 190, Folder 266, Box 349, RG 226, NARA; Henry Hyde, "Relations with Other Intelligence Services," Entry 97, Folder 575, Box 33, RG 226, NARA.

10 "Resistance in South-East France," March 22, 1944, Entry 190, Folder 12, Box 329, RG 226, NARA. The SOE's own internal history cites 100,000 resisters with arms in France. The maquis were thought to have 35,000–40,000 "well armed" men. To these were added 350,000 unarmed men of the AS, plus 500,000 railway men and 300,000 trade unionists. W. J. M. Mackenzie, *The Secret History of SOE: The Special Operations Executive, 1940–1945* (London: St. Ermin's Press, 2000), 602.

11 Lt. Gen. W. B. Smith to Gen. Sir Henry Maitland Wilson, May 21, 1944, "Role of resistance groups in the South of France," Folder 12, Entry 190, Box 329, RG 226, NARA.

12 "History of OSS Aid to French Resistance in World War II," Entry 190, Folder 1464, Box 740, RG 226, 63–4, NARA.

13 Somewhat at odds, descriptions of OG JUSTINE may be found in the company commander's report and Michael Pearson, *Tears of Glory: The Betrayal of Vercors 1944* (London: Pan Books, 1978), 130.

14 Funk, *Hidden Ally*, 77.

15 This was not an isolated incident of OSS operatives not being able to keep up with maquisards. Lieutenant Henry McIntosh of Jedburgh Team Chloroform found his leg muscles and lungs were not conditioned for hiking in the mountains despite the rigorous OSS training program. Will Irwin, *The Jedburghs: The Secret History of the Allied Special Forces, France 1944* (New York: Public Affairs, 2005), 185; "Operation Name-'RUTH'," 3, "Operational Report: Company 'B' 2671st Special Reconnaissance Battalion Separate (Prov.)," September 20, 1944, Entry 99, Box 35A, RG 226, NARA; Funk, *Hidden Ally*, 123–5.

16 "Operation Name-'RUTH," 12–13, "Operational Report: Company 'B'," 5, NARA.

17 SPOC, August 1, 1944, Entry 190, Folder 266, Box 329, RG 226, NARA.

18 Jean Muthular D'Errecalde, "Recommendation for Award," (draft), March 29, 1945, Citation file, Seventh Army, RG 226, NARA; Capt. G. de Piolenc to X-2 Caserta and X-2, August 20, 1944, Seventh Army, RG 226, NARA.

19 The name's origin is often ascribed to a small Scottish border town known for tough fighters or to the proximity of that place to the Jedburgh training area.

20 Roger Ford, *Steel from the Sky: The Jedburgh Raiders, France 1944* (London: Weidenfeld & Nicolson, 2004), 8; US War Department Strategic Services, 2:199.

21 Mackenzie, *The Secret History of SOE*, 605.

22 "Jedburgh Team SCEPTRE," 190/6/15/4, Entry 101, Folder 39/40, Box 1, RG 226, NARA; "Team SCEPTRE," Serial No. 22, HS 6/557, NA.

23 Capt. Robert Harcourt, "Report on Jedburgh team CINNAMON," Serial No. 27, HS 6/496, NA.

24 Capt. Ferandon, "CINNAMON," Serial No. 26, HS 6/496, NA.

25 Ray Jenkins, *A Pacifist at War* (London: Arrow Books, 2010), 90; George Millar, *Road to Resistance: An Autobiography* (London: Bodley Head, 1979), 379–81.

26 Chalou (ed.), *The Secrets War*, 248.

27 Ibid., 295.

28 Patrick Howarth, *Undercover: The Men and Women of the Special Operations Executive* (London; Routledge & Kegan Paul, 1980), 231.

29 US War Department Strategic Services, 2:239.

30 Hilary Footitt, *War and Liberation in France: Living with the Liberators* (New York: Palgrave Macmillan, 2004), 95.

31 Anthony Tucker-Jones, *Operation Dragoon: The Liberation of Southern France 1944* (Barnsley: Pen & Sword Books, 2009), 76–7.

32 General der Infanterie Friederich Wiese, "The 19th Army in Southern France (1 July to 15 September 1944)," April 11, 1948, MS B-787, RG 549, 2–3, NARA.

33 Clarke and Smith, *Riviera to the Rhine*, 67–8.

34 Generaloberst Johannes Blaskowitz, "German Reaction to the Invasion of Southern France," MS A-868, RG 549, 2, NARA.

35 Wiese, "The 19th Army in Southern France," 4.

36 General der Infanterie Georg von Sodenstern, "To the History of the Times Preceding the Invasion Engagements in France with Special Regard to the South-French Zone," December 13, 1950, MS B-276, RG 549, 30–1, NARA.

37 Pierre-Emmanuel Klingbeil, *Le front oublié des Alpes-Maritimes (15 août 1944–2 mai 1945)* (Nice: Serre Editeur, 2005), 16–17.

38 Wiese, "The 19th Army in Southern France," 10–11, 13; Clarke and Smith, *Riviera to the Rhine*, 64; "German (OB Southwest) Estimate of Situation Prior to Allied Invasion of Southern France," MS B-421, RG 549, 4, NARA.

39 Interestingly, the senior receiving commander estimated the cross-country route to the Rhône to be only 300 kilometers. Wiese, "The 19th Army in Southern France," 11.

40 Generalmajor Wend von Wietersheim, "Report of the former Commander of the 11th Panzer Division," 10, 10, June 4, 1946, MS A-880, RG 549, NARA.

41 Generalleutnant Otto Witek, "The Department of the Oberquartiermeister of the 19th Army," June 4, 1946, MS 1–950, RG 549, NARA.

42 Admiral H. Kent Hewitt, "Executing Operation Anvil-Dragoon," *U.S. Naval Institute Proceedings* 80 (August 1954): 901, 903; Lt. Col. de Chassey, Mémorandum, "Renseignements sur les forces allemandes dans le sud de la France," April 4, 1944, Débarquement et bataille de Provences, January–August 1944, dossier 2, 2ième Bureau, dossier 10P 186, SHAT.

43 Lucian K. Truscott, Jr., *Command Missions: A Personal Story* (New York: E. P. Dutton and Company, 1954), 391.

44 The foremost French historian of the war cites a figure of 250,000 men under command of the German 19th Army. Many were ex-casualties or of non-German origin, such as Armenians, Croats, and Georgians, so their reliability was inconsistent. Henri Michel, *The Second World War*, trans. Douglas Parmée (New York: Praeger, 1975), 641.

45 Built in American shipyards, many of the British hulls were courtesy of Roosevelt's Lend-Lease program.

46 Hewitt, "Executing Operation Anvil-Dragoon," 897–9, 901.

Chapter 10: The American Landing

1 Jacob L. Devers, "Southern France: Invasion of …" [speech by Devers], Southern France, Box 15, 24–5, HTL.

2 Samuel Eliot Morison, *History of United States Naval Operations in World War II: The Invasion of France and Germany, 1944–1945*, Vol. 11 (Boston: Little, Brown and Company, 1975), 250.

3 William B. Breuer, *Operation Dragoon: The Allied Invasion of the South of France* (Novato, CA: Presidio Press, 1987), 179; Jeffrey J. Clarke and Robert Ross Smith, *Riviera to the Rhine* (Washington, D.C.: U. S. Army Center of Military History, 1993), 104; Allied Forces Headquarters, "Report on Airborne Operations in Dragoon," October 25, 1944, RG 226, 9, NARA. Indeed, during the spring a French general staff officer had foreseen the need for diversionary actions to weaken the enemy response at the actual landing sites, emphasizing avoidance of heavy bombing in inhabited areas to minimize the loss of civilian lives. Col. R. E. Serre, French G.S., to Col. William W. Quinn, Asst. Chief of Staff, Seventh Army G.S., Mémorandum , April 8, 1944, 8–11, dossier 2, 2ième Bureau, 10P 186, SHAT.

4 Robert D. Burhans, *The First Special Service Force: A War History of the North Americans, 1942–1944* (Washington, D.C.: Infantry Journal Press, 1947), 257–70; Jacques Robichon, *The Second D-Day*, trans. Barbara Shuey (New York: Walker and Company, 1962), 253–4, 257–8.

5   Clarke and Smith, *Riviera to the Rhine*, 91.

6   Office of the Theater Historian, European Theater of Operations, "Invasion of Southern France," 35; *Five years—Five Countries, Five Campaigns: An Account of the One-Hundred-Forty-First Infantry in World War II* (Munich: 141st Infantry Regiment Association, 1945), 57–8.

7   Samuel Eliot Morison, *History of United States Naval Operations in World War II*, 255; Glenn E. Rathbun, "H-Hr D-Day 3rd Inf Division," Breuer Collection, MHI; Winston S. Churchill, *Triumph and Tragedy* (Boston: Houghton Mifflin, 1953), 94–5.

8   John Frayn Turner and Robert Jackson, *Destination Berchtesgaden: The Story of the United States Seventh Army in World War II* (New York: Charles Scribner's Sons, 1975), 39.

9   Audie Murphy, *To Hell and Back* (New York: Henry Holt and Company, 1949), 174–7.

10 Harry Yeide and Mark Stout, *First to the Rhine: The 6th Army Group in World War II* (St. Paul, MN: Zenith Press, 2007), 39.

11 Russell W. Cloer, "Infantry Replacement: The Story of My Three Years as an Infantry Officer in World War II," World War II Veterans Survey, 3rd Infantry Division, MHI.

12 Leo V. Bishop, Frank J. Glasgow and George A. Fisher (eds), *The Fighting Forty-Fifth: The Combat Report of an Infantry Division* (Baton Rouge, LA: 45th Infantry Division, 1946), 96–7.

13 Bill Mauldin, *Up Front* (New York: Henry Holt and Company, 1945), 198–201.

14 Turner and Jackson, *Destination Berchtesgaden*, 46.

15 *A Pictorial History of the 36th "Texas" Infantry Division* (Austin, TX: Turner Publishing Company reprint, 36th Division Association, 1995).

16 143rd Infantry After-Action Reports, "Operations in France, August 1944," World War II, 1943–1945, Headquarters, 36th Division, MHI.

17 Clarke and Smith, *Riviera to the Rhine*, 122–3; Lucian K. Truscott, Jr., *Command Missions: A Personal Story* (New York: E. P. Dutton and Company, 1954), 414–15.

18 Stan Swinton, *Stars and Stripes* (Marseilles edition), August 24, 1944.

19 Columbia Broadcasting System, *From D-Day through Victory in Europe* (New York: CBS, 1945), 103, 105, 106.

20 Admiral H. Kent Hewitt, "Executing Operation Anvil-Dragoon," *U.S. Naval Institute Proceedings* 80 (August 1954): 905–6.

21 At various places in different sources, the 517th is referred to as 517th Airborne Infantry, Combat Team, Parachute Combat Team, or Parachute Regimental Combat Team. It was commanded by Col. Rupert D. Graves.

22 Turner and Jackson, *Destination Berchtesgaden*, 37.

23 An inflatable yellow or orange life jacket for emergency use in water, named for the buxom American actress.

24 "Local Paratrooper Gives Vivid South France Invasion Account," *Nashville Banner*, September 1944.

25 Joe M. Cicchinelli, Reminiscences, Breuer Collection, 1, MHI.

26 Capt. Geoffrey M. T. Jones, interview by Robert H. Adleman, March 19, 1967, Box 11, 49, HI.

27 Ron Kent, *First in! The Parachute Pathfinder Company: A History of the 21st Independent Parachute Company, the Original Pathfinders of the British Airborne Forces, 1942–1946* (London: B. T. Batsford, 1979), 89.

28 A "stick" was a group of 20 or fewer parachutists who jumped together from the same aircraft. Allied Forces Headquarters, 9, MHI.

29 Maj. Gen. Robert T. Frederick, interview by Robert H. Adleman and George Walton, November 1966, Box 11, 6, HI.

30 The Douglas C-47 was known as the Skytrain in the United States and the Dakota in Britain.

31 For an in-depth account of the British paratrooper and glider operations, see Michael R. King, "Jedburgh Operations: Support to the French Resistance in Central France," M.A. thesis, US Army Command and General Staff College, Fort Leavenworth, KS, 1991, 97–111. Also found at the Imperial War Museum, London, under both Marshall and Crawshay.

32 Justin P. Buckeridge, *550th Infantry Airborne Battalion* (Nashville, TN: Battery Press, 1978), 28.

33 Allied Forces Headquarters, 11, MHI.

34 Clarke and Smith, *Riviera to the Rhine*, 101–3; Headquarters, 1st Airborne Task Force, "Ground Operations of 1st ABTF in 'Dragoon'," November 20, 1944, 1st Airborne Task Force, Box 8, 5, HI.

35 Frederick, interview, 601, HI.

36 Ibid., 602, 608, HI. Lt. Gen. Jacob Devers related the same incident. "From there visited General Frederick's headquarters. He told us that his paratroopers were giving him some trouble; that the American contingent had performed very well but that he had trouble in getting the British contingent to fight; that they had stated they were equipped for a defensive holding role and could not attack. This, of course, is a fallacy." Jacob Devers, Diary, No. 2, August 19, 1944, Box 52, HTL. The 1st Special Service Force relieved the 2nd Brigade, and a request for orders went out to send it back to Napoli immediately. AFHQCITEFHGCT, August 24, 1944, WO 204/7819, NA.

37 Veterans of the 2nd Independent Parachute Brigade, in discussions with the author at Le Muy, August 14, 2009.

38 William P. Yarborough, Oral history (section 1), March 28, 1975, 68, MHI.

39 Maj. Thomas R. Cross, "Record of Events, 517th Regimental Headquarters Company," Breuer Collection, MHI; *Paratroopers' Odyssey: A History of the 517th Parachute Combat Team* (Hudson, FL: 517th Parachute Regimental Combat Team Association, 1985), 254–5; Buckeridge, *550th Infantry Airborne Battalion*, 38–40.

40 Maj. Thomas R. Cross, Manuscript of Executive Officer, 2nd Battalion, 517th Infantry, 1984, Breuer Collection, chapter 7, 7–8, MHI.

41 Royce Slippin, "Geoffrey Jones '42 Recovers World War II False Identity," *Princeton Alumni Weekly* 97 (May 7, 1997): 45.

42 Robert H. Adleman and George Walton, *The Champagne Campaign* (Boston: Little Brown and Company, 1969), 133.

43 Richard J. Seitz, Autobiography, "Chronology of Important Events in Life of Richard Joe Seitz," 2002, oral history, 54–5, MHI; Rupert D. Graves, "Combat Team," *Blue Book* (December 1947): 58; Breuer, *Operation Dragoon*, 215–18.

44 Breuer, *Operation Dragoon*, 225–7; Cicchinelli, reminiscences, 4–5, MHI; Headquarters, 1st Airborne Task Force, 7, HI.

45 Robichon, *The Second D-Day*, 153–5, 212–14, 247–8; Clarke and Smith, *Riviera to the Rhine*, 111–12; Yeide and Stout, *First to the Rhine*, 44; Turner and Jackson, *Destination Berchtesgaden*, 38.

46 Oberst Carl Bruendel, "Report of Combat Command Bruendel," Battle of Toulon, August 1944, in Oberstleutnant Hasso Grundmann et al., "The Landings of the American Seventh Army in Southern France, Aug 1944," 1952, MS C-086, RG 549, NARA; Generalmajor Richard von Schwarin, "Battle of Toulon, August 1944, Chapter 4: Report of Combat Command Bruendel," M1035, MS C-086, RG 549, NARA.

47 Clarke and Smith, *Riviera to the Rhine*, 106–7.

48 Bruendel, "Report of Combat Command Bruendel," 60–71.

49 Morison, *History of United States Naval Operations in World War II*, 270; Robichon, *The Second D-Day*, 271.

50 Hewitt, "Executing Operation Anvil-Dragoon," 907–8.

NOTES

51 Devers, "Operation Dragoon," 7.

52 Generalleutnant Walther Botsch, "Critique of the American Seventh Army," William W. Quinn Papers (Military History Institute), Box 19, 3–4, HTL.

53 Paul Gaujac, *Août 1944: Le Débarquement de Provence, Anvil-Dragoon* (Paris: Histoire & Collections, 2004), 62.

54 Cloer, "Infantry Replacement," MHI.

55 Allied Forces Headquarters, 13–14. These numbers of casualties suffered and prisoners taken by airborne personnel vary considerably from Frederick's final report which shows 3,800 Germans captured at a cost of 350 men killed, wounded, or missing. Headquarters, 1st Airborne Task Force, 8, HI.

56 Truscott, *Command Missions*, 415, 419.

57 Robichon, *The Second D-Day*, 271.

Chapter 11: The French Landing

1 Charles de Gaulle, *The Complete War Memoirs of Charles de Gaulle* (New York: Simon and Schuster, 1967), 599, 608.

2 Ibid., 627.

3 Col. John S. Guthrie to Commanding Officer, Romeo Force, July 27, 1944, "Comments on Proposed Outline Plan Operation Romeo," author's collection; Lt. Col. Bouvet to AC of S, G-3, Headquarters Seventh Army, "Plan Schématique Romeo: Exécution des prescriptions et commentaries du 27 juillet 1944," August 1, 1944, MHI.

4 Paul Gaujac, *Août 1944: Le Débarquement de Provence, Anvil-Dragoon* (Paris: Histoire & Collections, 2004), 78–83; Raymond Muelle, *Le Débarquement de Provence: La libération de la France de Toulon à Grenoble* (Paris: Trésor du Patrimoine, 2004), 41.

5 This was the same vessel that had carried Peter Churchill to Gibraltar in December 1941, the first leg of his initial insertion into southern France. Peter Churchill, *Of Their Own Choice* (London: Hodder and Stoughton, 1952), 44–7.

6 Harold Nicolson, "Marginal Comment," *The Spectator*, January 18, 1952, 75; De Gaulle, *The Complete War Memoirs*, 603; B. H. Liddell Hart, "Marshal de Lattre de Tassigny," *The Times* (London), January 16, 1952, 61.

7 An English historian explains, "[General] Koenig's 1ère Division Française Libre had to become the 1ère Division d'Infanterie Motorisée (DIM), on joining l'Armée d'Afrique, and later to avoid confusion with the Moroccans, the 1ère Division de Marche d'Infanterie. The Division continued to use its old 1ère DFL title to the end and the Cross of Lorraine on its vehicles." Anthony Clayton, *France, Soldiers and Africa* (Washington, D.C.: Brassey's, 1988), 141.

8 French colonial born in Algeria.

9 These females in uniform were called "merlinettes," named after a French general who created a women's organization in Algers in 1943 to support the French Expeditionary Corps. Before the war's end more than 50 merlinettes would lose their lives.

10 "Récit des Opérations de la 3ème Compagnie en Provence du 16 au 24 août 1944," 4ème Brigade, 1e Division France Libre, 15H153–46, 1, CHETOM.

11 *De l'Occupation à la Libération*, Fabrizio, *OSS: La guerre secrète en France, 1942–1945* (Paris: Hachette, 1990), 52; "Journal des Marches et Opérations, 6ème Compagnie, Bataillon de Marche 11, 8 août 1942 au 21 septembre 1944 (1e partie)," 15H153, August 17, 1944, CHETOM;

"Journal de Marche, 4ème Brigade," 1ère Division France Libre, 16H189, August 16, 1944, CHETOM.

12 Paul W. Turner, "The Logistical Support of the French First Army, August 1944–May 1945," M.A. thesis, University of Georgia, 1991, 32, 38, US.

13 Military slang for an amphibious motor vehicle used to carry and discharge cargo.

14 "Journal de Marche, 4ème Brigade," August 17, 1944.

15 Paul Bentolila, a medic landing with the French army, in discussion with the author, December 12, 2005.

16 *Le Point*, "1966," May 20, 2010, 54.

17 1ère Armée Française, 3ème Bureau, "Rapport sur les Opérations de l'Armée Française, Période du 15 au 28 août 1944: La Bataille de Provence," September 14, 1944, dossier 10P 187, 10, SHAT.

18 Jour J is the French equivalent of D Day or debarkation ashore. Marshal Jean de Lattre de Tassigny, *History of the French First Army*, trans. Malcolm Barnes (London: George Allen and Unwin, 1952), 58.

19 Clayton, *France, Soldiers and Africa*, 292–3.

20 Ibid., 300–2.

21 Ibid., 302–3.

22 Harry Yeide and Mark Stout, *First to the Rhine: The 6th Army Group in World War II* (St. Paul, MN: Zenith Press, 2007), 22–3.

23 John Lichfield, "Liberation of Paris: The Hidden Truth," *Independent* (London), January 31, 2007.

24 Alain d'Ille, in discussion with the author, May 22, 2006.

25 Myron J. Echenberg, "'Morts pour la France': The African Soldier in France during the Second World War," *Journal of African History* 26 (1985): 364.

26 Robert Desnares, a veteran of 64ème régiment d'artillerie d'afrique, 4ème division marocaine de montagne, in discussion with the author, June 19, 2007.

27 Nancy Ellen Lawler, *Soldiers of Misfortune: Ivoirien Tirailleurs of World War II* (Athens, OH: Ohio University Press, 1992), 24–31, 65–8.

28 Ibid., 149–51.

29 Henry K. Hewitt, Transcript of Narrative, "World War II Action and Operational Reports," Box 1728, RG 38, 16, NARA.

30 Generalmajor Hans Schaefer, "244th Infantry Division, Marseille, 19–28 Aug 1944," MS A-884, RG 549, 9, NARA.

31 Anthony Tucker-Jones, *Operation Dragoon: The Liberation of Southern France 1944* (Barnsley: Pen & Sword Books, 2009), 119–21.

32 Garbay would reappear in the Southeast in the spring of 1945 to play a key role in the final battle in France, as recounted in Chapter 16.

33 "Journal des Marches et Opérations, 6ème Compagnie," August 21, 1944.

34 Jean-Marie Guillon and Antoine Tramoni, *Premières Victoires en Provence, août 1944* (n.p.: Conseil Général du Var, July 1994), 5; Samuel Eliot Morison, *History of United States Naval Operations in World War II: The Invasion of France and Germany, 1944–1945*, Vol. 11 (Boston: Little, Brown and Company, 1975), 287–8.

35 Boris de Gueyer, *L'Organisation de Résistance de l'Armée dans la Région R2: Provence–Alpes–Côte d'Azur*, 2nd edn (Paris: n.p., 2004), 61.

36 "Journal de Marche, 4ème Brigade," August 19–21, 1944; Office of the Theater Historian, European Theater of Operations, "Invasion of Southern France,"146, CMH.

37 De Lattre de Tassigny, *History of the French First Army*, 85; "Récit des Opérations de la 3ème Compagnie en Provence," August 20–1, 1945, CHETOM.

38 Guillon and Tramoni, *Premières Victoires en Provence*, 17.

39 Muelle, *Le Débarquement de Provence*, 65.

40 Ibid., "Journal de Marche, 4ème Brigade," August 24, 1944.

41 *La 1ère D. F. L., Epopée d'une Reconquête juin 1940–mai 1954* (Paris: Arts et Métiers Graphiques, 1946), 126.

42 "Récit des Opérations de la 3ème Compagnie en Provence," August 24, 1944, CHETOM.

43 Guillon and Tramoni, *Premières Victoires en Provence*, 14.

44 Gueyer, *L'Organisation de Résistance de l'Armée dans la Région R2*, 60.

45 Literally "field gray" in German, denoting the gray-green color of Wehrmacht uniforms and referring at times to German soldiers.

46 Office of the Theater Historian, "Invasion of Southern France," 151.

47 Special shock battalions were trained to lead assaults.

48 De Lattre de Tassigny, *History of the French First Army*, 88–90. The official record of this engagement reported 250 survivors from a garrison of 700 men. 1ère Armée Française, 3ème Bureau, 25.

49 1ère Armée Française, 3ème Bureau, 23.

50 *La 1ère D. F. L.*, 127.

51 Guillon and Tramoni, *Premières Victoires en Provence*, 21; De Lattre de Tassigny, *History of the French First Army*, 93.

52 Office of the Theater Historian, "Invasion of Southern France," 157–8.

53 Guillon and Tramoni, *Premières Victoires en Provence*, 10–12.

54 De Lattre de Tassigny, *History of the French First Army*, 94–5.

55 The large number of outsiders taking refuge in Marseille at this time makes any exact figure unreliable. One contemporary account by a couple residing in the city cited a wartime population of 660,000 inhabitants, including 200,000 foreigners, down from 914,000 Marseillais recorded in the 1936 census. Pierre Massenet and Marthe Massenet, *Journal d'une longue nuit: Carnet de route de deux Français moyens 1939–1944* (Paris: Librairie Artheme Fayard, 1971), 221. A current historian agrees, placing the total at between 650,000 and 700,000. Robert Mencherini, *Vichy en Provence* (Paris: Editions Syllepse, 2009), 72–3.

56 The discussion of Marseille before its liberation is based in large part on Marcel-Pierre Bernard's concise analysis, "A Propos de la Situation à Marseille à la Veille de la Libération," *Provence historique* 36 (April–June 1986): 183–90.

57 Office of the Theater Historian, "Invasion of Southern France," 164.

58 Schaefer, "244th Infantry Division, Marseille," 10–12.

59 Pierre Guiral, *Libération de Marseille* (Paris: Hachette Littérature, 1974), 81; Laurent Moënard, *Le débarquement en Provence: Opération Dragoon, 15 août 1944* (Rennes: Editions Ouest-France, 2011), 104.

60 Schaefer, "244th Infantry Division, Marseille," 12–13.

61 These two fortresses had been built during the reign of Louis XIV with their guns pointed at rebellious Marseille to keep the inhabitants in line.

62 Schaefer, "244th Infantry Division, Marseille," 14.

63 Moënard, *Le débarquement en Provence*, 106–7.

64 Bernard, "A Propos de la Situation à Marseille," 190.

65 Massenet, *Journal d'une longue nuit*, 280.

66 "Communiqué du Quartier Général de l'Etat Major F.T.P.F.," *La Marseillaise*, August 25, 1944, in Charles Jansana, *Marseille: La liberté retrouvée: 1943–1944* (Nimes: C. Lacour, 1992), 48.

67 Guiral, *Libération de Marseille*, 88–90.

68 De Lattre de Tassigny, *History of the French First Army*, 96, 99–100.

69 Ibid., 54, 56, 73.

70 Schaefer, "244th Infantry Division, Marseille," 38–40.

71 Massenet, *Journal d'une longue nuit*, 283–4, 287.

72 Guiral, *Libération de Marseille*, 92.

73 Ibid., 94–5; Gaujac, *Août 1944*, 179; Muelle, *Le Débarquement de Provence*, 78–9.

74 Guiral, *Libération de Marseille*, 95–6.

75 Schaefer, "244th Infantry Division, Marseille," 32–3, 36.

76 Guiral, *Libération de Marseille*, 94.

77 Massenet, *Journal d'une longue nuit*, 285.

78 Guiral, *Libération de Marseille*, 98–9; 1ère Armée Française, 3ème Bureau, 31; Massenet, *Journal d'une longue nuit*, 286.

79 Gaujac, *Août 1944*, 179; Guiral, *Libération de Marseille*, 100; De Lattre de Tassigny, *History of the French First Army*, 115.

80 Jean Ballard, "Journées d'août 44," *Cahiers du Sud* 268 (October–November–December 1944): 216.

81 Office of the Theater Historian, "Invasion of Southern France," 173; Guiral, *Libération de Marseille*, 102–3; RF Section, "Situation Report," Third Quarter Missions and Sabotage, Entry 190, Folder 1465, Box 740, RG 226, NARA.

82 Hewitt, Transcript of Narrative, 18.

83 Morison, *History of United States Naval Operations in World War II*, 11: 291.

84 Henri Michel, "Sur le régime de Vichy," *Revue d'histoire de la deuxième guerre mondiale* 93 (January 1974): 118; RF Section, "Situation Report," NARA; Guiral, *Libération de Marseille*, 107.

85 1ère Armée Française, 3ème Bureau, 32; Jean-Louis Panicacci, "Le Débarquement en Provence," *Notre Musée* 191 (July 2009): 12.

86 Generalleutnant Walther Botsch, "Critique of the American Seventh Army," William W. Quinn Papers (Military History Institute), Box 19, 5, HTL.

Chapter 12: Fighting in the Back Country

1 General der Infanterie Friederich Wiese, "The 19th Army in Southern France (1 July to 15 September 1944)," April 11, 1948, MS B-787, RG 549, 16, 18, NARA.

2 Lucian K. Truscott, Jr., *Command Missions: A Personal Story* (New York: E. P. Dutton and Company, 1954), 407, 551.

3 Frederic B. Butler, "Task Force Butler, Part II," *Armored Cavalry Journal* 57 (March–April 1948): 30.

4 Arthur Layton Funk, *Hidden Ally: The French Resistance, Special Operations, and the Landings in Southern France, 1944* (New York: Greenwood Press, 1992), 114–15.

5 OKW War Diary, manuscript B-034, M1035, RG549, NARA.

6 Butler, "Task Force Butler, Part I," *Armored Cavalry Journal* 57 (January–February 1948): 17.

7 Sapin et al., *Méfiez-vous du Toréador* (Toulon: Association Générale de Prévoyance Militaire, 1987), 72, 353–6.

8 Distaste for "private armies" was not uncommon in service hierarchies during the war, notably the British, and was specifically expressed about its Special Air Service regiment, among other irregular

commands. This bias is elaborated upon by Max Hastings in *Das Reich: The March of the 2nd SS Panzer Division through France, June 1944* (Minneapolis, MN: Zenith Press, 2013), 187–8.

9   This incident has been related more than once. The most authoritative source is, of course, Cammaerts himself. Also credible, presumably, are the foremost American historian of the Resistance in the South of France, Arthur L. Funk, and a former OSS man who became director of the Central Intelligence Agency, William Casey, but others have cited this lost opportunity as well. Funk, *Hidden Ally*, 127; William Casey, *The Secret War against Hitler* (Washington, D.C.: Regnery Gateway, 1988), 139–40; E. H. Cookridge, *They Came from the Sky* (New York: Thomas Y. Crowell Company, 1967), 149–52; Ray Jenkins, *A Pacifist at War* (London: Arrow Books, 2010), 204–5; Madeleine Masson, *Christine: SOE Agent & Churchill's Favourite Spy* (London: Virago Press, 2005), 221; Clare Mulley, *The Spy Who Loved: The Secrets and Lives of Christine Granville* (London: Macmillan, 2012), 254.

10 "Jedburgh Team CHLOROFORM," Records of the Jedburgh Teams, 190/6/15/4, Entry 101, Folder 39/40, Box 1, RG 226, NARA; Butler, "Task Force Butler, Part II," 32–3; Funk, *Hidden Ally*, 123–9.

11 Butler, "Task Force Butler, Part I," 15.

12 Headquarters, Seventh Army, G-2 Report, August 23, 1944, 107–2.1, RG 226, NARA.

13 Bill Mauldin, *Up Front* (New York: Henry Holt and Company, 1945), 201–4.

14 Wiese, "The 19th Army in Southern France," 16, 18; Headquarters, Seventh Army, G-2 Report, August 24, 1944, 107–2.1, RG 226, NARA; Generalmajor Wend von Wietersheim, "Report of the former Commander of the 11th Panzer Division," June 4, 1946, MS A-880, RG 549, 10, NARA.

15 Headquarters, 753rd Tank Battalion, "Historical Report for the Month of August," September 8, 1944, ARBN-753-0.3 (16986), OPN Rpt, RG 331, NARA; Harry Yeide and Mark Stout, *First to the Rhine: The 6th Army Group in World War II* (St. Paul, MN: Zenith Press, 2007), 78; Headquarters, 753rd Tank Battalion, After-Action Report, RG 331, NARA; Butler, "Task Force Butler, Part II," 36; Task Force Butler, Combined G-2 and G-3 Journal, RG 331, NARA.

16 Von Wietersheim, "Report of the former Commander of the 11th Panzer Division," 5; Generaloberst Johannes Blaskowitz, "German Reaction to the Invasion of Southern France," MS A-868, RG 549, 3, NARA.

17 Office of the Theater Historian, European Theater of Operations, "Invasion of Southern France," Appendix B, v–vi, CMH.

18 Wiese, "The 19th Army in Southern France," 22; Von Wietersheim, "Report of the former Commander of the 11th Panzer Division," 9.

19 *Pictorial History of the 36th "Texas" Infantry Division* (Austin, TX: Turner Publishing Company reprint, 36th Division Association, 1995); Michael E. Bigelow, "General Truscott and the Campaign in Southern France," *Military Review* 74 (August 1994): 75; Jeffrey J. Clarke and Robert Ross Smith, *Riviera to the Rhine* (Washington, D.C.: U. S. Army Center of Military History, 1993), 169.

20 Office of the Theater Historian, "Invasion of Southern France," xii.

21 Headquarters, First Special Service Force, "French Resistance," August 5, 1944, Appendix 12 to Annex 2 to Field Order 29, Seventh Army, G-2, French Resistance Activities, March–August 1944, 107-2.0, RG 407, NARA.

22 Georg Grossjohann, *Five Years, Four Fronts: A German Officer's World War II Combat Memoir* (New York: Ballantine Books, 2005), 141; Donald G. Taggart (ed.), *The History of the Third Infantry Division in World War II* (Nashville, TN: Battery Press, 1987), 220–2; Clarke and Smith, *Riviera to the Rhine*, 167–8.

23 Grossjohann, *Five Years, Four Fronts*, 144.

24 Generalleutnant Walther Botsch, "Critique of the American Seventh Army," William W. Quinn Papers (Military History Institute), Box 19, 9, HTL. Positioning command posts close to the fighting has been cited as one dimension of German battlefield doctrine that brought rapid success in their invasion of France in May–June 1940. See, for example, Julian Jackson, *The Fall of France: The Nazi Invasion of 1940* (Oxford: Oxford University Press, 2003), 221–2.

25 Olaf Paul, then a youngster living in Lyon, in discussion with the author, March 13, 2005.

26 Dwight D. Eisenhower, *Crusade in Europe* (Baltimore, MD: Johns Hopkins University Press, 1997), 294.

27 Don Kladstrup and Petie Kladstrup, *Wine & War: The French, the Nazis, and the Battle for France's Greatest Treasure* (New York: Broadway Books, 2001), 184.

28 Jean-Marie Guillon, "La Place de la Résistance dans la Libération," *Provence historique* 36 (April–June 1986): 203; *De l'Occupation à la Libération*, Fabrizio. *OSS: La guerre secrète en France, 1942–1945* (Paris: Hachette, 1990), 22.

29 Henri Michel, *The Second World War*, trans. Douglas Parmée (New York: Praeger, 1975), 644.

30 Jean-Louis Panicacci (ed.), *La Résistance Azuréenne* (Nice: Editions Serre, 2003), 116–17.

31 Sapin et al., *Méfiez-vous du Toréador*, 74.

32 Paul Sola, "Mémoires de guerre," typewritten manuscript, 26–30, MRA.

33 Rémi-Nuna Stevelberg, *La Gendarmerie dans les Alpes-Maritimes de 1942 à 1945* (Nice: Serre Editeur, 2004), 132.

34 Association Montagne et Traditions, *Pays Vésubien* (Saint-Martin-Vésubie: Musée des Traditions Vésubiennes, 2005), 47–56, 220.

35 A local teenager soon appeared, full of enthusiasm and asking only for shoes and a gun to fight the Boche. His name was Louis Fiori, and he had already served in the underground in Carros. Fiori continues to this day educating Niçois about the successes and sacrifices made by his fellow patriots during the war. "La liberté descend des montagnes," Documents, Témoignages, Recherches No. 17, 13, MRA; Louis Fiori, in discussion with the author, March 1, 2007.

36 *Paratroopers' Odyssey: A History of the 517th Parachute Combat Team* (Hudson, FL: 517th Parachute Regimental Combat Team Association, 1985), 265–6.

37 Rupert D. Graves, "Combat Team," *Blue Book* magazine (January 1948): 58; Sapin et al., *Méfiez-vous du Toréador*, 75, 133–4; Jean-Louis Panicacci, *Les Alpes-Maritimes de 1939 à 1945: Un département dans la tourmente* (Nice: Editions Serre, 1989), 236; Boris de Gueyer, *L'Organisation de Résistance de l'Armée dans la Région R2: Provence–Alpes–Côte d'Azur*, 2nd edn (Paris: n.p., 2004), 47.

38 "Extracts from the Conversation of General de Lattre de Tassigny with Ambassador Winant, 19 November 1943," Biographical-French, Box 13, 8, York.

39 Stevelberg, *La Gendarmerie dans les Alpes-Maritimes*, 132–6.

40 Michel Braun, Jean Pierre Garacio and Jean-Louis Panicacci (eds), *1939–1945: La guerre dans les Alpes Maritimes* (Breil-sur-Roya: Editions du Cabri, 1994), 109.

41 Michel de Trez, *First Airborne Task Force: Pictorial History of the Allied Paratroopers in the Invasion of Southern France* (Wezembeek: Belgium Publishing, 1998), 387, 405.

42 Headquarters, First Special Service Force, "French Resistance."

43 Jean-Louis Panicacci, "L'intégration des FFI Azuréens dans le Groupement Alpin Sud," *Notre Musée* 194 (March 2010): 9.

44 Joseph Girard, *La Résistance et la Libération de Nice: La fin d'une légende?* (Nice: Serre Editeur, 2006), 121.

45 Sapin et al., *Méfiez-vous du Toréador*, 80. Lécuyer had the last laugh, retiring from the French army in 1972 as a major general.

46 "Strength report, FFI in Alpes-Maritimes, Var, Basses-Alpes," P1018204–5, Massingham Inter-Allied Mission Reports, HS 3/34, NA; Pierre-Emmanuel Klingbeil, *Le front oublié des Alpes-Maritimes (15 août 1944–2 mai 1945)* (Nice: Serre Editeur, 2005), 48–50; Jean-Louis Panacacci, "Le Débarquement en Provence," *Notre Musée* 191 (July 2009): 13; Jean-Louis Panicacci, "Des Chasseurs à la Résistance: les FFI Azuréennes," *Lou Sourgentin* 103 (October 1992): 14.

47 Anthony Clayton, *Three Marshals of France: Leadership After Trauma* (Washington, D.C.: Brassey's, 1992), 107.

48 "Les Etrangers dans la Résistance Azuréenne," Documents, Témoignages, Recherches No. 19, 10, MRA.

49 "Le récit de Roger Monteux," Documents, Témoignages, Recherches No. 13, 2, MRA.

50 Sapin et al., *Méfiez-vous du Toréador*, 80, 365–6.

51 Robert D. Burhans, *The First Special Service Force: A War History of the North Americans, 1942–1944* (Washington, D.C.: Infantry Journal Press, 1947), 282–3.

52 Lt. Col. Wendell E. Little, "The 6th Army Group, France and Germany, 1944–45, with Special Attention to Logistical Problems," Historical Report, E242A, Box 162, RG 331, NARA.

53 Panicacci, "L'intégration des FFI Azuréens dans le Groupement Alpin Sud," 9; Frédéric Brega, "La Brigade du Diable: La 1st Special Service Force sur la frontière italienne, septembre-octobre 1944," *Militaria Magazine* 214 (August 2005): 22– 4; Roger Maccario, in discussion with the author, March 21, 2009.

54 Clarke and Smith, *Riviera to the Rhine*, 355–7; Klingbeil, *Le front oublié des Alpes Maritimes*, 49.

55 "Le Maquis franco-italien de l'Albarea et le drame de Sospel," Documents, Témoignages, Recherches No. 12, 9–11, MRA.

56 Richard J. Seitz, Autobiography, "Chronology of Important Events in Life of Richard Joe Seitz," 2002, oral history, 54–6, MHI; *Paratroopers' Odyssey*, 269–76; Klingbeil, *Le front oublié des Alpes-Maritimes*, 62–3.

57 Capt. Geoffrey M. T. Jones, interview by Robert H. Adleman, March 19, 1967, Box 11, 8, 62, HI.

58 Stevelberg, *La Gendarmerie dans les Alpes-Maritimes*, 74.

59 First Special Service Force, Intelligence Annex, September 23–4, 1944, E427, Box 23277, RG 407, NARA; *Paratroopers' Odyssey*, 267.

60 Col. Edwin A. Walker, the leader of Sitka Force during the American invasion.

61 Burhans, *The First Special Service Force*, 290–1.

62 *Paratroopers' Odyssey*, 284.

63 400 inhabitants of Breil, 400 from Fontan, and 350 of Saorge were also evacuated to Cuneo, among 2,207 Azuréens in all. Raoul Nathiez, "Les Breillois dans la tourmente," *Lou Sourgentin* 116 (April–May 1995): 18.

64 *Paratroopers' Odyssey*, 281; Rosa Trucchi and Jacqueline Antoniotti, Moulinaises in the convoy, in discussion with the author, September 18, 2009.

65 Association Montagne et Traditions, *Pays Vésubien*, 75–8.

66 Burhans, *The First Special Service Force*, 292; J. M. Moses to William B. Breuer, August 3, 1985, Breuer Collection, MHI.

NOTES

Chapter 13: Liberation of the Riviera

1 Samuel Eliot Morison, *History of United States Naval Operations in World War II: The Invasion of France and Germany, 1944–1945*, Vol. 11 (Boston: Little, Brown and Company, 1975), 276.

2 Robert H. Adleman and George Walton, *The Champagne Campaign* (Boston: Little Brown and Company, 1969), 167.

3 Sapin et al., *Méfiez-vous du Toréador* (Toulon: Association Générale de Prévoyance Militaire, 1987), 70–2; Arthur Layton Funk, *Hidden Ally: The French Resistance, Special Operations, and the Landings in Southern France, 1944* (New York: Greenwood Press, 1992), 199–200.

4 OKW War Diary, manuscript B-034, M1035, RG549, NARA; James L. Gilbert and John P. Finnegan, *U.S. Army Signals Intelligence in World War II* (Washington, D.C.: U. S. Army Center of Military History, 1993), 153–4.

5 *Paratroopers' Odyssey: A History of the 517th Parachute Combat Team* (Hudson, FL: 517th Parachute Regimental Combat Team Association, 1985), 262; Headquarters, 517th Parachute Infantry Combat Team, "Compilation of Lessons Learned for Period 15 August 1944 to Date," November 2, 1944, 1–2, Rupert D. Graves Papers, MHI.

6 *Paratroopers' Odyssey*, 245–8.

7 2nd Independent Brigade's War Diary, WO 228, NA.

8 Headquarters, 517th Parachute Infantry Combat Team, 1–2; *Paratroopers' Odyssey*, 263–4; "Jedburgh Team SCEPTRE," 190/6/15/4, Entry 101, Folder 39/40, Box 1, RG 226, 2–3, NARA; Richard J. Seitz, Autobiography, "Chronology of Important Events in Life of Richard Joe Seitz," 2002, oral history, 55, MHI.

9 Raymond Gatti, in discussion with the author, September 6, 2008.

10 Capt. Geoffrey M. T. Jones, interview by Robert H. Adleman, Box 11, March 19, 1967, 41–2, HI; Paul Gonnet, *Histoire de Grasse et sa région* (Roanne: Editions Horvath, 1984), 111–13.

11 Headquarters, First Special Service Force, S-2 Periodic Report, August 23, 1944, Box 23277, RG 407, NARA.

12 Robert H. Adleman and George Walton, *The Devil's Brigade* (Annapolis, MD: Naval Institute Press, 1966), 237.

13 *Stars and Stripes*, August 28, 1944.

14 Robert D. Burhans, *The First Special Service Force: A War History of the North Americans, 1942–1944* (Washington, D.C.: Infantry Journal Press, 1947), 273–4.

15 "Le rapport de la Libération heure par heure" in Alex Baussy, *La Mémoire d'une Ville: Une évocation de la vie à Cannes et sur la Côte d'Azur Durant les sombres années de guerres et à la Libération* (Spéracèdes: TAC Motifs, 1994), 54.

16 Didier Digiuni, *Cannes 1939–1945* (Nice: Alandis Editions, 2002), 153–6.

17 "Les Réactions des Cannois au Débarquement du 15 août 1944," August 17, 1944, Rapport 2796 des Renseignements Généraux de Cannes, boite 169 W 13, ADAM.

18 Digiuni, *Cannes 1939–1945*, 57–9.

19 Peter Leslie, *The Liberation of the Riviera: The Resistance to the Nazis in the South of France and the Story of Its Heroic Leader, Ange-Marie Miniconi* (New York: Wyndham Books, 1980), 200.

20 Ibid., 209–10; Jean-Louis Panicacci (ed.), *La Résistance Azuréenne* (Nice: Editions Serre, 2003), 226, 228.

21 Adleman and Walton, *The Champagne Campaign*, 171–2.

22 Ibid., 170.

23 Leslie, *The Liberation of the Riviera*, 218–19, 230–2; Digiuni, *Cannes 1939–1945*, 161–2.

24 Adleman and Walton, *The Champagne Campaign*, 171.

25 Auguste Vérine, "Historique de la Libération d'Antibes," MAC.

26 Gérard Helion, "Antibes de juin 1944 à juin 1945, Actes du Colloque de Nice, 22 juin 1974, Centre de la Méditerranée Moderne et Contemporaine," *Cahiers de la Méditerranée* (June 12, 1976): 38; Joseph Girard, "La Résistance dans les Alpes-Maritimes," Vol. 1, thesis, University of Nice, 1973, 330, US.

27 Robert Chiapello, in discussion with the author, September 10, 2009.

28 First Special Service Force, Intelligence Annex, September 23–4, 1944, E427, Box 23277, RG 407, NARA; Burhans, *The First Special Service Force*, 276–8; Adleman and Walton, *The Devil's Brigade*, 233–4.

29 Headquarters, Seventh Army, G-2 Report, August 29, 1944, 107–2.1, RG 226, NARA; Burhans, *The First Special Service Force*, 279.

30 *Stars and Stripes*, August 18, 1944.

31 Robert Girod, *Résistance: Les fusillés de l'Ariane* (Villefranche-sur-Mer: ARTEPHIS, 1994), 50.

32 Ibid., 52.

33 "La libération de Nice vue par les Autorités Allemandes," Documents, Témoignages, Recherches No. 26, 5, MRA.

34 "Les Ouvriers dans la Résistance Azuréenne," Documents, Témoignages, Recherches No. 29, 10.

35 Christian Colombard, "63ème Anniversaire de la Libération du 15 au 28 août 1944 à Nice," *Les Cahiers du Musée de la Résistance Azuréenne* 50 (July 2007): 10; Jean-Louis Panicacci, *En territoire occupé: Italiens et Allemands à Nice, 1943–1944* (Paris: Vendémaire, 2012), 133–4.

36 *Le Victorieux*, September 25, 1944, translated by Frederick's staff, Box 4, 3, HI.

37 André Odru, "Les F.T.P., la M.O.I., les Milices Patriotiques dans les Alpes-Maritimes," 2005, 20, MRA.

38 Panicacci, *En territoire occupé*, 191, 193.

39 "Les Ouvriers dans la Résistance Azuréenne," 10.

40 "La Libération de Nice vue par les Autorités Allemandes," 12, MRA.

41 "Nice, 28 août 1944: L'insurrection racontée par les insurgés," Documents, Témoignages, Recherches No. 9, 12–13, MRA.

42 The port was soon restored to receive food and matériel but proved of little value to warships. It was December 10, 1944 before the first naval vessel docked in Nice. Association Montagne et Traditions, *Pays Vésubien* (Saint-Martin-Vésubie: Musée des Traditions Vésubiennes, 2005), 167.

43 Panicacci, *En territoire occupé*, 196–7.

44 Earlier in the order, Fretter-Pico characterized the city as "the terrorist infested town of Nice." 148th Reserve Division, Order, August 27, 1944 (translation dated August 29, 1944), Seventh Army, "Captured Documents," 107–2.9, RG 226, NARA.

45 Jones, interview, 45–9.

46 Headquarters, Seventh Army, G-2 Report, August 29, 1944, NARA.

47 Jones, interview, 53–6.

48 Girard, *La Résistance et la Libération de Nice*, 117.

49 Michel de Trez, *First Airborne Task Force: Pictorial History of the Allied Paratroopers in the Invasion of Southern France* (Wezembeek: Belgium Publishing, 1998), 369–70.

50 Girard, *La Résistance et la Libération de Nice*, 116–17; Adleman and Walton, *The Champagne Campaign*, 174–5.

51 Julian Jackson, *France: The Dark Years 1940–1944* (New York: Oxford University Press, 2001), 575.

52 Headquarters, Seventh Army, "Report on the Political Situation in Nice," September 1, 1944, Box 4, HI.

53 Secours national, "La Libération de Nice, " Rapport d'activités du Secours National du 26 mai au 30 août 1944, dossier 168 W 1–4, ADAM; Colombard, "63ème Anniversaire de la Libération," 11.

54 *Le Victorieux*, September 25, 1944, 7–8, HI.

55 Headquarters, Seventh Army, "Report on the Political Situation in Nice;" 1st Lt. Joseph W. Welsh to Asst. Chief of Staff, G-5, Seventh Army, "Conference between Maj. Gen. Frederick and Monsieur Escande, Prefect of the Dept. of the Alpes-Maritimes," September 3, 1944, 1st Airborne Task Force, Box 8, HI.

56 Panicacci (ed.), *La Résistance Azuréenne*, 238.

57 Ibid., 167–8.

58 Girard, *La Résistance et la Libération de Nice*, 119–20; *Le Victorieux*, September 25, 1944, 6, HI.

59 Frederick, "'Notes' for," September 18, 1944, Box 12, HI.

60 Jones, interview, 5, 22, 43, 56, 79.

61 Maj. Gen. Robert T. Frederick, interview by Robert H. Adleman and George Walton, November 1966, Box 11, 14, HI; Adleman and Walton, *The Champagne Campaign*, 190.

62 Welsh to Asst. Chief of Staff, G-5, Seventh Army, HI.

63 "Les Etrangers dans la Résistance Azuréenne," Documents, Témoignages, Recherches No. 19, 7, MRA. Pell is still well remembered by inhabitants who were children during the war years and recall her giving them candy and trinkets. Gilbert Perdigon, then a youngster in Puget-Théniers, in discussion with the author, June 9, 2011.

64 Frederick, interview, 10–11, HI; Jones, interview, 4, 6–7, 67–8, 71–2; Adleman and Walton, *The Champagne Campaign*, 202.

65 Adleman and Walton, *The Champagne Campaign*, 223.

66 The story concludes after the war when an inspector general arrived with a sheaf of these bills and an order from King that the officer face court-martial. Told that he had subsequently been killed, the inspector breathed a sigh of relief and so annotated his file. Dr. John Simms, interview by Robert H. Aldeman, September 28, 1963, Ottawa, Interviews (misc.), Box 12, HI.

67 Paul Green, "Fancy Menton Boasts Classy Villa for CP," *Stars and Stripes*, December 4, 1944.

68 Adleman and Walton, *The Champagne Campaign*, 229–30; Frederick, interview, 14, HI.

69 Frederick, interview, 16, HI; *Paratroopers' Odyssey*, 283.

70 Vérine, "Historique de la Libération d'Antibes," 37–8, MAC.

71 William P. Yarborough, Oral history (section 1), March 28, 1975, 71, MHI.

72 Girard, *La Résistance et la Libération de Nice*, 121–2; Seventh Army—Enemy Order of Battle (BIGOT), Aquitanian Report No. 6, 1944, Appendix I, "Table of French Defenses on the Italian Frontier," 107–2.7, RG 407, NARA; Headquarters, First Special Service Force, S-2 Periodic Report, September 2, 1944; Headquarters, First Special Service Force, F.F.I. Report, September 3, 1944, Box 23277, RG 407, NARA.

73 Morison, *History of United States Naval Operations in World War II*, 11: 277–8, 311.

74 Jones, interview, 8.

75 Paul Green, "SSF on Franco-Italian Border," *Stars and Stripes*, November 30, 1944.

76 Jones, interview, 74.

77 Adleman and Walton, *The Champagne Campaign*, 226.

78 Ibid., 234.

79 Jones, interview, 9–10.

80 Adleman and Walton, *The Devil's Brigade*, 233, 237.

81 Jeffrey J. Clarke and Robert Ross Smith, *Riviera to the Rhine* (Washington, D.C.: U. S. Army Center of Military History, 1993), 218.

82 *Paratroopers' Odyssey*, 284.

83 First Special Service Force, "Lessons Learned," 1, 11, NARA.

84 Major A. F. Radley, 03/20/1, IWM.

85 Michel Braun, Jean-Pierre Garacio and Jean-Louis Panicacci (eds), *1939–1945: La guerre dans les Alpes Maritimes* (Breil-sur-Roya: Editions du Cabri, 1994), 198; Paul Green, "Melting Snows Harry GIs in Maritime Alps," *Stars and Stripes* (Marseilles edition), November 29, 1944.

86 "A Brief History of the 1st Airborne Task Force," Manuscript, 1st Airborne Task Force, Box 8, HI; see also Robert Ross Smith, "France-Italian Border: Protecting the Southeast Flank," Draft of an unpublished chapter in Clark and Smith, *Riviera to the Rhine*, 34, US.

87 Burhans, *The First Special Service Force*, 296–300.

Chapter 14: Menton

1 "Exécutez Mandrin, Le 3 juin 1940: l'Evacuation de Menton," *Bulletin de la Société d'Art et d'Histoire du Mentonnais* 55 (September 1990): 21–3; Louis Hebras, "Le Départ," *Le Petit Niçois*, June 5, 1940; *L'Eclaireur de Nice et du Sud-Est*, July 21, 1940.

2 Jean-Louis Panicacci, *Menton dans la Tourmente, 1939–1945*, 3rd. edn (Menton: Annales de la Société d'Art et d'Histoire du Mentonnais, 2004), 29.

3 Hyacinthe Chiavassa, "Juin 1940: la bataille de Menton," *Annales Monégasques: Revue d'Histoire de Monaco* 8 (1984): 15; Armand Pilon, "A l'Armée des Alpes," *Bulletin de la Société d'Art et d'Histoire du Mentonnais* 18 (June 1981): 8–9; Alain Venturini, "La Défense du Mentonnais en juin 1940," *Bulletin de la Société d'Art et d'Histoire du Mentonnais* 18 (June 1981): 7.

4 Panicacci, *Menton dans la Tourmente*, 35.

5 Chiavassa, "Juin 1940: la bataille de Menton," 27.

6 Ibid., 28–32; Panicacci, *Menton dans la Tourmente*, 133.

7 Jean-Louis Panicacci, "Menton et les Mentonnais de 1939 à 1945," *Recherches Régionales: Côte d'Azur et Contrées Limitrophes* 21 (January–March 1981): 19.

8 Nicole Venturini, "Le 'Parcours du Combattant' d'une Ecolière," *Bulletin de la Société d'Art et d'Histoire du Mentonnais* 18 (June 1981): 11.

9 Panicacci, "Menton et les Mentonnais," 15; Jean-Louis Panicacci, "Menton: Vitrine de l'Impérialisme Fasciste," *Notre Musée* 198 (March 2011): 8.

10 Pascal Molinari, *Journal de Guerre* (Menton: Annales de la Société d'Art et d'Histoire du Mentonnais, 2004), 274.

11 Panicacci, *Menton dans la Tourmente*, 81.

12 Molinari, *Journal de Guerre*, 283–9.

13 *L'Ergot*, December 29, 1944, February 17, 1946.

14 Suzanne Poumellec-Cavelleri, "Un résistant mentonnais: André Poumellec (1925–1944)," *Bulletin de la Société d'Art et d'Histoire du Mentonnais* 71 (September 1994): 5.

15 *Combat*, September 23, 1944.

16 *Stars and Stripes* (Marseilles edn), December 4, 1944.

17 44th AAA Brigade, IPW Report, February 17, 1945, Box 17512, RG 407, NARA.

18 Capt. Geoffrey M. T. Jones, interview by Robert H. Adleman, March 19, 1967, Box 11, 9, HI.

19 Michel Braun, Jean-Pierre Garacio and Jean-Louis Panicacci (eds), *1939–1945: La guerre dans les Alpes Maritimes* (Breil-sur-Roya: Editions du Cabri, 1994), 154.

20 Panicacci, *Menton dans la Tourmente*, 109–11; Jean-Louis Panicacci (ed.), *Les Alpes-Maritimes de 1939 à 1945* (Nice: Centre Régional de Documentation Pédagogique de Nice, 1977), 86.

21 Panicacci, *Menton dans la Tourmente*, 111, 176.

22 Ibid., 115–16.

Chapter 15: Monaco

1 Alain Ruggiero, *La Population du Comté de Nice de 1693 à 1939* (Nice: Editions Serre, 2002), 121.

2 Pierre Abramovici, *Un rocher bien occupé: Monaco pendant la Guerre 1939–1945* (Paris: Editions du Seuil, 2001), 12, 17–21.

3 Ibid., 45–6.

4 Ibid., 98–103.

5 Robert Pérès, a Monagasque teenager during the war years, in discussion with the author, March 5, 2006.

6 Roger Maccario, a teenager in Monaco during the war, in discussion with the author, March 21, 2009.

7 Gottlieb Duttweiler, *Gottlieb Duttweiler und die Maritime Suisse: Ein Roman aus der Wirklichkeit* (Zurich: Ed. Limmat, 1953), 40–1.

8 Walter W. Orebaugh, *The Consul* (Cape Canaveral, FL: Blue Note Publications, 1994), 1.

9 Abramovici, *Un rocher bien occupé*, 158.

10 Orebaugh, *The Consul*, 2–9.

11 Abramovici, *Un rocher bien occupé*, 156–70.

12 Xan Fielding, *The Money Spinner: Monte Carlo and Its Fabled Casino* (Boston: Little, Brown and Company, 1977), 130.

13 Abramovici, *Un rocher bien occupé*, 191–2.

14 Pérès and Maccario, discussions.

15 Pérès, discussion.

16 Maccario, discussion.

17 Abramovici, *Un rocher bien occupé*, 197–202.

18 Ibid., 209–13.

19 Ibid., 255–8; Denis Torel, *Monaco sous les Barbelés* (Vesoul: imb Imprimeur, 1996), 151.

20 Torel, *Monaco sur les Barbelés*, 69; Robert Girod, *Résistance: Les fusillés de l'Ariane* (Villefranche-sur-Mer: ARTEPHIS, 1994), 16–17, 42–3.

21 Abramovici, *Un rocher bien occupé*, 251–4.

22 Ibid., 244–5; Pérès, discussion; Christian Burle, archivist for the principality, in discussion with the author, February 10, 2006.

23 Pérès, discussion.

24 Alix Bergmann, periodic resident of Monaco during the war years, in discussion with the author, May 9, 2005.

25 Torel, *Monaco sous les Barbelés*, 88; Denis Torel, "La Seconde Guerre Mondiale en Principauté de Monaco," *Bulletin de la Société d'Art et d'Histoire du Mentonnais* 22 (June 1982): 16–17.

26 *De l'Occupation à la Libération*, Fabrizio, *OSS: La guerre secrète en France, 1942–1945* (Paris: Hachette, 1990), 45; Pérès, discussion.

27 Gen. Robert Frederick interview by Robert H. Adleman and George Walton, November 1966, Box 11, 13, HI.

28 Capt. Geoffrey Jones interview by Robert H. Adleman, March 19, 1967, Box 11, 8, HI.

29 "Report about the Principality of Monaco, Actual General Situation, the Minister of State Roblot," September 9, 1944, Box 4, HI.

30 Julian Hale, *The French Riviera: A Cultural History* (New York: Oxford University Press, 2009), 49.

31 Abramovici, *Un rocher bien occupé*, 273–4.

32 "Brief report Mission 'Talbot' through Thu. Oct. 5," Box 4, HI.

33 Jones, interview, 13, HI.

34 "Information concerning the Principality of Monaco," undated, signed R. M. des Fontenelle, Box 4, HI; Emile Roblot to Frederick, September 6, 1944, Correspondence, Box 4, HI; "Notes on Monsieur Emile Roblot, Minister of State of the Principality of Monaco," September 9, 1944, Box 4, HI; "Position of affairs in the Principality of Monaco on September 10th, 1944," Box 4, HI.

35 When he came to the Riviera at the war's end, General Eisenhower respected this prohibition and stayed at the Hôtel Eden Roc on Cap d'Antibes. On the other hand, the chief of staff of Devers's Sixth Army Group went to the gambling casino at Monte Carlo on a trip to the coast in the autumn of 1944, leading to a later visit by his boss. Frederick, interview, 17, HI.

36 Roblot to Frederick, HI; Harry L. Coles and Albert K. Weinberg, *Civil Affairs: Soldiers Become Governors* (Washington, D.C.: U. S. Army Center of Military History, 1992), 764; Abramovici, *Un rocher bien occupé*, 276.

37 Coles and Weinberg, *Civil Affairs*, 764.

38 Robert H. Adleman and George Walton, *The Champagne Campaign* (Boston: Little Brown and Company, 1969), 246–8.

39 Abramovici, *Un rocher bien occupé*, 288–9.

40 Jones, interview, 5, 60, HI.

41 Raymond Aubrac quoted from a personal interview by Abramovici, *Un rocher bien occupé*, 294.

42 Torel, "La Seconde Guerre Mondiale en Principauté de Monaco," 17.

43 William W. Bishop, Jr. (ed.), "Judicial Decisions," *American Journal of International Law* 42 (October 1948): 955.

Chapter 16: Authion: The Final Battle

1 Charles de Gaulle, *Discours et messages: Pendant la guerre, juin 1940–janvier 1946*, Vol. I (Paris: Libraire Plon, 1970), 512; a staff reporter for *Stars and Stripes* used the same term on November 5, 1944 to characterize the Alpine stand-off when 1st Airborne Task Force manned the defenses.

2 Generalleutnant Karl Pflaum, "Activities of the 157th Reserve Division in Southern France," MS B-237, RG 549, NARA.

3 Seventh Army—Enemy Order of Battle (BIGOT), Aquitanian Report No. 6, 1944, NARA.

4 First Special Service Force, IPW Report, September 9–10, 1944, E427, Box 23277, RG 407, NARA.

5 Pierre-Emmanuel Klingbeil, *Le front oublié des Alpes-Maritimes (15 août 1944–2 mai 1945)* (Nice: Serre Editeur, 2005), 306.

6 Ibid., 76–7.

7 Albert Kesselring, *Memoirs of Field-Marshal Kesselring* (Novato, CA: Presidio Press, 1989), 212.

8 Klingbeil, *Le front oublié des Alpes-Maritimes*, 182–4.

9   Daniel Damase, "La prise de la redoute des Trois Communes," *Lou Sourgentin* 116 (March–April 1995): 30; Klingbeil, *Le front oublié des Alpes-Maritimes*, 162–5.

10 "Effective Allied Forces on the Alpine Front, September 1944–May 1945," 6th Army Group, E242A, Box 162, RG 331, NARA; Klingbeil, *Le front oublié des Alpes-Maritimes*, 149.

11 Klingbeil, *Le front oublié des Alpes-Maritimes*, 214–16.

12 Ibid., 218, 226.

13 Michel Braun, Jean-Pierre Garacio and Jean-Louis Panicacci (eds), *1939–1945: La guerre dans les Alpes Maritimes* (Breil-sur-Roya: Editions du Cabri, 1994), 199–200.

14 Klingbeil, *Le front oublié des Alpes-Maritimes*, 309.

15 44 Bde of D.C.A., "Report, 21 Nov 44 to 21 Mar 45," April 23, 1945, E240D, Box 11, RG 331, NARA.

16 Lt. Gen. Victor-Nicolas Goudot (Ret.), le délègue départemental, Entr'Aide Française, au Préfet des Alpes-Maritimes, March 17, 1945, boite 168 W 1, ADAM.

17 *Le Patriote de Nice et du Sud-Est*, April 11, 1945; *L'Espoir de Nice*, April 9, 1945.

18 Dwight D. Eisenhower to Charles de Gaulle, February 19, 1945, 240D, Folder 37, Box 9, RG 331, NARA.

19 Klingbeil, *Le front oublié des Alpes-Maritimes*, 291–2.

20 "Ordre d'opérations No. 1, Exercice 'Canard'," CHETOM.

21 Dwight D. Eisenhower to AFHQ, 6th Army Group, 6 Apr 45, G-3 Section, No. 25, Box 9, RG 331, NARA.

22 Lt. Col. John W. Huffer to Commanding General, 6th Army Group, April 6, 1945, G-3 Section, No. 29, Box 9, RG 331, NARA; 1ère Division Française Libre, 2ème Bureau, "Etude de Terrain Préliminaire à l'Opération 'Canard,'" dossier "Opération 'Canard,'" dossier 11P 10, SHAT.

23 There was even talk of taking control of the Brenner Pass in order to reach Hitler's Eagles Nest at Berschtesgaden.

24 Association Montagne et Traditions, *Pays Vésubien* (Saint-Martin-Vésubie: Musée des Traditions Vésubiennes, 2005), 137–8.

25 Braun, Garacio and Panicacci (eds), *1939–1945*, 200; Maj. Gen. Hans Bessel, "Organization of Positions in Italy: Construction of Field Fortifications," D-214, RG 549, 30–1, 33, NARA.

26 "Ordre d'opérations No. 1, Exercice 'Canard'," April 4, 1945, Forces Françaises Libres, 1ère Division, 15H153, CHETOM; Paul Gaujac, "L'Authion: La bataille oubliée: 2e partie-avril 1945, le dernier sacrifice," *Militaria Magazine* (July 2005): 58–9.

27 Damase, "La prise de la redoute des Trois Communes," 29–30.

28 Samuel Eliot Morison, *History of United States Naval Operations in World War II: The Invasion of France and Germany, 1944–1945*, Vol. 11 (Boston: Little, Brown and Company, 1975), 312–13.

29 Klingbeil, *Le front oublié des Alpes-Maritimes*, 303–4.

30 4ème Bde JMO du BM 11, 1ère DFL, March 25–30, 1945, 15H153, CHETOM.

31 Gaujac, "L'Authion," 60.

32 Henri Beraud, *Bataille des Alpes, Album mémorial, Juin 1940–1944/1945* (Bayeux: Editions Heimdal, 1987), 330.

33 Doyen to Devers, April 7, 1945, E240D, folder 46, Box 10, RG 331, NARA.

34 Klingbeil, *Le front oublié des Alpes-Maritimes*, 313–14.

35 Rene Duval, "La Bataille Oubliée de l'Authion (avril 1945)," 27, doc. B69/3, CHETOM; Klingbeil, *Le front oublié des Alpes-Maritimes*, 315–16; Lieutenant-Colonel Jean Perrin, "Les Combats de l'Authion, 10 avril–28 avril 1945," Documents, Témoignages Recherches No. 117, MRA.

36 Gaujac, "L'Authion," 61.

37 Klingbeil, *Le front oublié des Alpes-Maritimes*, 320–1.

38 Ibid., 305; Lt. Col. André Lichwitz, "Schéma d'Attaque de la Forca par une section d'Assaut," April 7, 1945, 1ère division française libre, dossier 11P 13, SHAT.

39 André Lichwitz, "Le groupe d'assaut de la 1ère D.F.L. sur le front des Alpes," *Revue de la France Libre* (June 1955): 60–2; Braun, Garacio and Panicacci (eds), *1939–1945*, 164; Perrin, "Les Combats de l'Authion," 7–8, 11–12, MRA.

40 Klingbeil, *Le front oublié des Alpes-Maritimes*, 309, 323–7.

41 "Cahier Journalier de Suzanne Balzan, avril 1945," Documents, Témoignages Recherches No. 13, 9, MRA.

42 Klingbeil, *Le front oublié des Alpes-Maritimes*, 321.

43 "Histoire de la 4ème Brigade, 1ère Division Française Libre, création et résumé des opérations, juin 1943–mai 1945" (manuscript), 15H153 D4a, CHETOM.

44 Duval, "La Bataille Oubliée de l'Authion," 30, CHETOM.

45 "Histoire de la 4ème Brigade."

46 Jean-Louis Panicacci, "70ᵉ anniversaire des combats de l'Authion," *Les Cahiers du Musée de la Résistance Azuréenne* 89 (May 2015): 14; Jean-Louis Panicacci, *Les Alpes-Maritimes dans la Guerre (1939–1945)* (Paris: De Borée, 2013), 350.

47 "Histoire de la 4ème Brigade."

48 Klingbeil, *Le front oublié des Alpes-Maritimes*, 332–8.

49 Paul Green, "War in the Clouds," *Stars and Stripes*, April 17, 1945.

50 One month later, he was shot by Italian partigiani. Klingbeil, *Le front oublié des Alpes-Maritimes*, 358–9.

51 Morison, *History of United States Naval Operations in World War II*, 11: 312.

52 Christian Burle and André Z. Labarrere, "14 décembre 1943: le torpillage du Netztender 44 dans le port de Monaco," *Annales Monégasques: Revue d'Histoire de Monaco* 34 (2010): 74.

53 Klingbeil, *Le front oublié des Alpes-Maritimes*, 366–7.

54 Ibid., 351–2.

55 Ibid., 207; Braun, Garacio and Panicacci (eds), *1939–1945*, 200–1.

56 Raoul Nathiez, "Les Breillois dans la tourmente," *Lou Sourgentin* 116 (April–May 1995): 17.

57 Klingbeil, *Le front oublié des Alpes-Maritimes*, 364.

58 Forces Françaises Libres, 1ère Division, Ordre préparatoire, April 24, 1945, 15H153, CHETOM.

59 Klingbeil, *Le front oublié des Alpes-Maritimes*, 374.

60 Ibid., 377.

61 Jean-Louis Panicacci, *Les Alpes-Maritimes de 1939 à 1945: Un département dans la tourmente* (Nice: Editions Serre, 1989), 281.

62 Klingbeil, *Le front oublié des Alpes-Maritimes*, 378.

63 Doyen to Maj. Gen. Willis D. Maj. Gen. Willis D. Crittenberger, May 30, 1945 (Fifth Army translation), "French-Italian Border Problem, June 1945," Records of US Army Operational, Tactical, and Support Organizations (World War II and Thereafter), Fifth US Army Correspondence, File 56–8–12–R, Box 1, RG 331, NARA; Marcel Vigneras, *Rearming the French* (Washington, D.C.: US Army Center of Military History, 1989), 368.

64 Charles de Gaulle, *Le Salut*, Vol. III, *Mémoires de Guerre, 1944–1946* (Paris: Libraire Plon, 1959), 196; "Historique Sommaire de la 27ème Division d'Infanterie Alpine," dossier 11P 174, 57, SHAT.

NOTES

Chapter 17: Rebuilding the Riviera

1 Allied Force Headquarters to Général de Division (Air) Cochet, "Command and Operational Employment of the French Forces of the Interior," July 27, 1944, Box 139, E190, Folder 835, RG 226, NARA.

2 Allied Force Headquarters, "Interim Directive for Civil Affairs in Southern France," July 5, 1944, Southern France: Civil Affairs, Box 15, HTL.

3 There was virtually no participation or assumption of responsibility by the British. F. S. V. Donnison, *Civil Affairs and Military Government, North-West Europe, 1944–1946* (London: Her Majesty's Stationery Office, 1961), 93–4.

4 Jacob Devers, Diary, No. 2, August 28, 1944, Box 52, HTL.

5 Harry L. Coles and Albert K. Weinberg, *Civil Affairs: Soldiers Become Governors* (Washington, D.C.: U. S. Army Center of Military History, 1992), 756–8.

6 Jean-Louis Panicacci (ed.), *La Résistance Azuréenne* (Nice: Editions Serre, 2003), 145–6.

7 Roland G. Ruppenthal, *Logistical Support of the Armies: September 1944–May 1945*, Vol. 2 (Washington, D.C.: Office of the Chief of Military History, 1959), 124; Regional Liaison Detachment "B," "Area Report," November 30, 1944, Regional Liaison, Civil Affairs, Nice, Box 12, HI.

8 Hilary Footitt, *War and Liberation in France: Living with the Liberators* (New York: Palgrave Macmillan, 2004), 116; 1st Lt. Joseph W. Welsh to Asst. Chief of Staff, G-5, Seventh Army, "Conference between Maj. Gen. Frederick and Monsieur Escande, Prefect of the Dept. of the Alpes-Maritimes," September 3, 1944, 1st Airborne Task Force, Box 8, HI.

9 Jeffrey J. Clarke and Robert Ross Smith, *Riviera to the Rhine* (Washington, D.C.: U. S. Army Center of Military History, 1993), 218.

10 *De l'Occupation à la Libération*, Fabrizio, *OSS: La guerre secrète en France, 1942–1945* (Paris: Hachette, 1990), 64; Jean-Louis Panicacci (ed.), *Les Alpes-Maritimes de 1939 à 1945* (Nice: Centre Régional de Documentation Pédagogique de Nice, 1977), 85.

11 Panicacci (ed.), *Les Alpes-Maritimes de 1939 à 1945*, 85.

12 Coles and Weinberg, *Civil Affairs*, 774.

13 Regional Liaison Detachment "B," "Area Report," November 30, December 16, 1944, Regional Liaison, Civil Affairs, Nice, HI.

14 Colette Poisson and Monseigneur Antonin Blanchi in discussions with the author, October 1, 2009, and March 14, 2008, respectively.

15 Coles and Weinberg, *Civil Affairs*, 775.

16 Welsh to Asst. Chief of Staff, G-5, Seventh Army, HI; Footitt, *War and Liberation in France*, 110–11.

17 Coles and Weinberg, *Civil Affairs*, 782.

18 Ibid., 776 passim.

19 Regional Liaison Detachment "B," "Area Report," November 17, 30, December 16, 1944, Regional Liaison, Civil Affairs, Nice, HI.

20 "L'épuration dans les Alpes-Maritimes (1942–1947)," Documents, Témoignages, Recherches No. 28, 2–3, MRA; *De l'Occupation à la Libération*, 63.

21 Louis Fiori, a teenager member of the Resistance in Alpes-Maritimes, in discussion with the author, March 1, 2007.

22 Jean-Louis Panicacci, *Les Alpes-Maritimes, 1939–1945: Un département dans la tourmente* (Nice: Editions Serre, 1989), 368; Marcel Ophuls, *The Sorrow and the Pity* (New York: Berkley Windhover Books, 1975), xix.

23 Gérard Helion, "Antibes de juin 1944 à juin 1945," Actes du Colloque de Nice, 22 juin 1974, Centre de la Méditerranée Moderne et Contemporaine," *Cahiers de la Méditerranée* (June 12, 1976): 40.

24 Délibérations, séance du 15 décembre 1944, AMA.

25 Patrick Marnham, *Resistance and Betrayal: The Death and Life of the Greatest Hero of the French Resistance* (New York: Random House, 2000), 209–15.

26 *Combat*, October 14, November 8, 1944; Panicacci (ed.), *La Résistance Azuréenne*, 173–6.

27 Paul Aubanel, "Épuration," *Nos Lendemains*, October 12, 1944.

28 *Le Cri des Travailleurs*, September 13, 1944.

29 Panicacci, *Les Alpes-Maritimes, 1939–1945: Un département dans la tourmente*, 249; "L'épuration dans les Alpes-Maritimes," 8–9, MRA; Panicacci (ed.), *Les Alpes-Maritimes de 1939 à 1945*, 94.

30 Quay of the United States, named in thanks for America's crucial role in bringing World War I to an end.

31 "L'épuration dans les Alpes-Maritimes," 8–9, MRA.

32 Marnham, *Resistance and Betrayal*, 216.

33 *De l'Occupation à la Libération*, 65.

34 A raid on the northern coast of France by primarily Canadian troops in February 1942 that was immediately repulsed by the Germans.

35 Regional Liaison Detachment "B," "Area Report," December 16, 1944, Regional Liaison, Civil Affairs, Nice, HI.

36 Paul Gonnet, *Histoire de Grasse et sa région* (Roanne: Editions Horvath, 1984), 113.

37 Regional Liaison Detachment "B," "Newspaper Survey, Nice, France," November 8, 1944, Civil Affairs, Nice, Box 12, HI; "L'épuration dans les Alpes-Maritimes," 11, MRA; Panicacci, *Les Alpes-Maritimes, 1939–1945: Un département dans la tourmente*, 251; Mission Jaune, "Political Activity," November 16, 1944, Alpes-Maritimes, Box 6, HI.

38 Camille Rayon, in discussions with the author, October 25 and November 24, 2005.

39 Fabrice Virgili, *Shorn Women: Gender and Punishment in Liberation France*, trans. John Flower (New York: Oxford University Press, 2002), 181–2, 219; Philippe Burrin, *France under the Germans: Collaboration and Compromise*, trans. Janet Lloyd (New York: New Press, 1996), 205–7; Panicacci, *Les Alpes-Maritimes, 1939–1945: Un département dans la tourmente*, 248.

40 Eric Sevareid, *Not So Wild a Dream* (New York: Antheneum, 1976), 437.

41 Mission Jaune, "General Information: Civil Security," November 15, 1944, Box 4, 3–5, HI.

42 Mario Longhi, Italian Committee of Liberation, Alpes-Maritimes, to the Minister of Foreign Affairs, Rome, October 28, 1944, Box 4, HI; Alain Roullier, "Tende et La Brigue: Les oubliées du Rattachement de 1860," *Lou Sourgentin* 116 (March–April 1995): 34.

43 Louis Piétri, in discussion with the author, March 5, 2010.

44 *Nice Matin*, November 28 , December 10, 11, 2007, September 20, 2009.

45 Pierre Tosan, "La Tragédie du Fort-Carré," (manuscript), 1998, PRO, 080, 94, TOS, MAC.

46 *Combat*, October 3, 1944.

47 Panicacci, *Les Alpes-Maritimes, 1939–1945: Un département dans la tourmente*, 279–80.

48 "France/Italy: Political: Border Tensions Following French Occupation," May 4, 1945, Entry 190, Folder 266, Box 349, RG 226, NARA.

49 "Story of Detachment 'F' in France," October 17, 1945, Entry 99, Box 35A, RG 226, 27–9, NARA.

50 Panicacci, *Les Alpes-Maritimes, 1939–1945: Un département dans la tourmente*, 283.

51 Aimée Chabert, in discussion with the author, June 8, 2007; Raoul Nathiez, "Lou journal de Madama Pansa," *Lou Sourgentin* 116 (March–April 1995): 39; *Le Patriote de Nice et du Sud-Est*, June 3–4, 1945.

52 Chabert, discussion; Military Intelligence, "Public Opinion and the American Army," November 1, 1944, Box 4, HI.

53 Military Intelligence, "Public Opinion and the American Army;" Mary Louise Roberts, *What Soldiers Do: Sex and the American GI in World War II France* (Chicago: University of Chicago Press, 2014), 242.

54 Panicacci, *Les Alpes-Maritimes, 1939–1945: Un département dans la tourmente*, 256; Regional Liaison Detachment "B," "Area Report," November 30, 1944, Regional Liaison, Civil Affairs, Nice, HI; Regional Liaison Detachment "B", "Area Report," December 16, 1944, Regional Liaison, Civil Affairs, Nice, HI.

55 Panicacci, *Les Alpes-Maritimes, 1939–1945: Un département dans la tourmente*, 284–5; Nathiez, "Lou journal de Madama Pansa," 38–9; *L'Aurore de Nice et du Sud-Est*, June 13, 17–18, 1945.

56 *Le Patriote Niçois*, June 3, 1945; *L'Espoir de Nice*, June 13, 1945; *La Liberté de Nice et du Sud-Est*, June 14, 1945; *L'Aurore de Nice et du Sud-Est*, June 17, 1945.

57 Coles and Weinberg, *Civil Affairs*, 786.

58 *Le Patriote de Nice et du Sud-Est*, June 5, 1945; Antony Beevor and Artemis Cooper, *Paris: After the Liberation, 1944–1949* (London: Penguin Books, 2007), 214, 361.

59 *Stars and Stripes* (Marseilles edition), December 4, 1944, 3.

60 Panicacci, *Les Alpes-Maritimes, 1939–1945: Un département dans la tourmente*, 297.

61 Ibid., 253–4; Mission Jaune, "General Information," 2.

62 Francis Cammaerts, interview by Capt. Howard, January 16–18, 1945, 19, Cammaerts, FCA, HS 6/568, NA.

63 Regional Liaison Detachment "B," "Area Report," December 16, 1944, Regional Liaison, Civil Affairs, Nice, HI.

64 Patrick K. O'Donnell, *Operatives, Spies, and Saboteurs: The Unknown Story of the Men and Women of World War II's OSS* (New York: Free Press, 2004), 202.

65 Mission Jaune, "General Information," 1.

66 Jean Coussmaker, "Alice Shaw and Nesta Comber: The Tale of Two Ladies of St. Hugh's, Vence," Holy Trinity Church, *Newsletter* 48 (Autumn 2009): 20; Panicacci, *Les Alpes-Maritimes, 1939–1945: Un département dans la tourmente*, 270; Regional Liaison Detachment "B," "Area Report," November 17, 1944, Regional Liaison, Civil Affairs, Nice, HI.

67 Georges Tabaraud, "Prisonniers et déportés, le retour," *Lou Sourgentin* 116 (March–April 1995): 14.

68 Panicacci, *Les Alpes-Maritimes, 1939–1945: Un département dans la tourmente*, 271; Burrin, *France under the Germans*, 282–6.

69 A less-publicized problem were the 200,000 babies of French mothers and German soldiers and the corresponding 50,000 offspring of German mothers and French fathers, both prisoners of war and members of the Allied forces. Social aid for the distressed mothers and, in some cases, the orphans did not come easily in these difficult times. *De l'Occupation à la Libération*, 70.

70 Jean-Louis Panicacci, "Les élections municipales d'avril–mai 1945 à Nice," *Lou Sourgentin* 116 (March–April 1995): 19–21.

71 Panicacci (ed.), *La Résistance Azuréenne*, 164.

72 Ibid., 169–72.

73 Association Montagne et Traditions, *Pays Vésubien* (Saint-Martin-Vésubie: Musée des Traditions Vésubiennes, 2005), 215; Roullier, "Tende et La Brigue," 36.

74 "Extracts from the Conversation of General de Lattre de Tassigny with Ambassador Winant, 19 November 1943," Biographical-French, Box 13, 3, HTL.

75 W. J. M. Mackenzie, *The Secret History of SOE: The Special Operations Executive, 1940–1945* (London: St. Ermin's Press, 2000), 621.

❧❧❧

Bibliography

Unpublished Sources

Faraldo, Agnes. "L'Application des lois racistes et antisémites à Nice pendant l'occupation." Mémoire de Licence de Droit—Libertés Publiques, Université de Nice.

Girard, Joseph. "La Résistance dans les Alpes-Maritimes." Vol. 1. Thèse, Université de Nice, 1973.

Helion, Gérard. "Antibes pendant la Deuxième Guerre Mondiale (1939–1945)." Maitrise d'Histoire, Faculté des Lettres de Nice, 1972.

King, Michael R. "Jedburgh Operations: Support to the French Resistance in Central France." M.A. thesis, US Army Command and General Staff College, Fort Leavenworth, Kansas, 1991.

Turner, Paul W. "The Logistical Support of the French First Army, August 1944–May 1945." M.A. thesis, University of Georgia, 1991.

Urso, Sophie. "L'Application des Lois Racistes et Antisémites à Nice pendant l'Occupation." Licence en Droit—Libertés Publiques, Université de Nice-Sophia Antipolis, 1995–6.

Documents

Abbreviations

ADAM	Archives départementales des Alpes-Maritimes, Nice.
AMA	Archives municipales d'Antibes.
AMC	Archives municipales de Cannes.
AMN	Archives municipales de Nice.
CARAN	Centre d'Accueil et de Recherche des Archives Nationales, Paris.
CHETOM	Centre d'Histoire et d'Etudes des Troupes d'Outre-Mer, Fréjus.
CMH	Center of Military History, Washington, D.C.
HI	Hoover Institution, Stanford, CA.
HMMA	Holocaust Memorial Museum Archives, Washington, D.C.
HTL	Heritage Trust Library/Archives, York, PA.
IWM	Imperial War Museum, London.
MAC	Médiathèque Albert Camus, Antibes.
MHI	Military History Institute, Carlyle, PA.
MRA	Musée de la Résistance Azuréenne, Nice.
NA	National Archives, London.
NARA	National Archives and Records Administration, College Park, MD.
SHAT	Service Historique de l'Armée de Terre, Paris.
US	unpublished sources.

BIBLIOGRAPHY

Antibes, France

Archives municipales

Comité de Libération, Réunion Extraordinaire séance publique, 1 September 1944.
Délibérations, séances des 21 February, 15 December 1944.

Médiathèque Albert Camus

Tosan, Pierre. "La Tragédie du Fort-Carré" (manuscript), 1998, PRO, 080,94, TOS.
Vérine, Auguste. "Historique de la Libération d'Antibes." Manuscript duplicated by Union des Anciens de la Résistance Antibes, January 1951.

Cannes, France

Archives municipales

"Plages 1943," dossier 4 H 31.
Préfet des Alpes-Maritimes à Monsieur le Sous-Préfet de Grasse et à Messieurs les Maires du Département, 13 November 1942, "1942–1943, Troupes d'opérations italiennes," dossier 4 H 31.

Carlisle, Pennsylvania

Military History Institute

143rd Infantry After-Action Reports. "Operations in France, August 1944," World War II, 1943–5, Headquarters, 36th Division.
Adams, Paul D. Oral History, Section 2, Side 1, Tape 2, Session 1–5 May 1975.
Bouvet, Lt. Col. to AC of S, G-3, Headquarters Seventh Army. "Plan Schématique Romeo: Exécution des prescriptions et commentaries du 27 juillet 1944," 1 August 1944.
Cicchinelli, Joe M. Reminiscences, Breuer Collection.
Cloer, Russell W. "Infantry Replacement: The Story of My Three Years as an Infantry Officer in World War II." World War II Veterans Survey, 3rd Infantry Division.
Cross, Maj. Thomas R. Manuscript of Executive Officer, 2nd Battalion, 517th Infantry, 1984, Breuer Collection.
———. "Record of Events, 517th Regimental Headquarters Company," Breuer Collection.
Headquarters, 3rd Infantry Division. "Economic and Political Conditions in France," Appendix No. 4 to Annex No. 2 to No. 12, BIGOT-ANVIL, 25 July 1944, Box 7, John W. O'Daniel Papers.
Headquarters, VI Corps. G-2 Notes, "The Maquis of France," 28 July 1944, Box 7, John W. O'Daniel Papers.
Headquarters, 517th Parachute Infantry Combat Team. "Compilation of Lessons Learned for Period 15 August 1944 to Date," 2 November 1944, 1–2, Rupert D. Graves Papers.
Moses, J. M. to William B. Breuer, August 3, 1985, Breuer Collection.
Rathbun, Glenn E. "H-Hr D-Day 3rd Inf Division," Breuer Collection.
Seitz, Richard J. Autobiography, "Chronology of Important Events in Life of Richard Joe Seitz," 2002, 54–55, oral history.
Yarborough, William P. Oral history (section 1), March 28, 1975.

BIBLIOGRAPHY

College Park, Maryland

National Archives and Records Administration

44th AAA Brigade. IPW Report, February 17, 1945, Box 17512, RG 407.

44 Bde of D.C.A. "Report, 21 Nov 44 to 21 Mar 45," April 23, 1945, E240D, Box 11, RG 331.

148th Reserve Division, Order, August 27, 1944 (translation dated August 29, 1944), Seventh Army, "Captured Documents," 107-2.9, RG 226.

Allied Forces Headquarters. "Report on Airborne Operations in Dragoon," October 25, 1944. RG 226.

Allied Force Headquarters to Général de Division (Air) Cochet. "Command and Operational Employment of the French Forces of the Interior," July 27, 1944, Box 139, E190, Folder 835, RG 226.

AOK 19. "Tatigkeitsbericht …," n.d., T-312/978/9170877-78, RG 549.

Bessel, Maj. Gen. Hans. "Organization of Positions in Italy: Construction of Field Fortifications," D-214, RG 549.

Blaskowitz, Generaloberst Johannes. "German Reaction to the Invasion of Southern France," MS A-868, RG 549.

Bruendel, Oberst Carl. "Report of Combat Command Bruendel," Battle of Toulon, August 1944, in Oberstleutnant Hasso Grundmann et al., "The Landings of the American Seventh Army in Southern France, Aug 1944," 1952, MS C-086, RG 549.

D'Errecalde, Jean Muthular. "Recommendation for Award," (draft), March 29, 1945, Citation file, Seventh Army, RG 226.

De Piolenc, Capt. G. to X-2 Caserta and X-2, August 20, 1944, Seventh Army, RG 226.

Dodderidge, Maj. Robert R. to Capt. Paul Van der Stricht, August 28, 1943. "SO Program for Southern France," Entry 190, Box 329, Folder 12, RG 226.

Doyen to Crittenberger, Maj. Gen. Willis D., May 30, 1945 (Fifth Army translation). "French-Italian Border Problem, June 1945," Records of US Army Operational, Tactical, and Support Organizations (World War II and Thereafter), Fifth US Army Correspondence, File 56-8-12-R, Box 1, RG 331.

Doyen to Devers, April 7, 1945, E240D, folder 46, Box 10, RG 331.

"Effective Allied Forces on the Alpine Front, September 1944–May 1945," 6th Army Group, E242A, Box 162, RG 331.

Eisenhower, Dwight D. to AFHQ, 6th Army Group, April 6, 45, G-3 Section, No. 25, Box 9, RG 331.

———. to Charles de Gaulle, February 19, 1945, 240D, Folder 37, Box 9, RG 331.

First Special Service Force, Intelligence Annex. September 23–4, 1944, E427, Box 23277, RG 407.

———. IPW Report, September 9–10, 1944, E427, Box 23277, RG 407.

———. "Lessons Learned from the French Campaign since 15 August 1944," November 2, 1944, Box 23276, RG 407.

"France/Italy: Political: Border Tensions Following French Occupation," May 4, 1945, Entry 190, Folder 266, Box 349, RG 226.

"German (OB Southwest) Estimate of Situation Prior to Allied Invasion of Southern France," MS B-421, RG 549.

Headquarters, 753rd Tank Battalion. After-Action Report, RG 331.

———. "Historical Report for the Month of August," September 8, 1944, ARBN-753-0.3 (16986), OPN Rpt, RG 331.

Headquarters, First Special Service Force. F.F.I. Report, September 3, 1944, Box 23277, RG 407.

———. "French Resistance," August 5, 1944, Appendix 12 to Annex 2 to Field Order 29, Seventh Army, G-2, French Resistance Activities, March–August 1944, 107-2.0, RG 407.

———. S-2 Periodic Report, August 23, September 2, 3, 1944, Box 23277, RG 407.

Headquarters, Seventh Army. G-2 Reports, 23, 24, 29 August 1944, 107-2.1, RG 226.

Hewitt, Adm. Henry K. Transcript of Narrative, "World War II Action and Operational Reports," Box 1728, RG 38.

"History of OSS Aid to French Resistance in World War II," Entry 190, Folder 1464, Box 740, RG 226.

Howarth, Patrick to Col. Dodd-Parker. "Discussions during my recent visit to Algiers," July 6, 1944, Folder 844, E190, Box 140, RG 226.

Huffer, Lt. Col. John W. to Commanding General, 6th Army Group. April 6, 1945, G-3 Section, No. 29, Box 9, RG 331.

Hyde, Henry. "Relations with Other Intelligence Services," Entry 97, Folder 575, Box 33, RG 226.

"Jedburgh Team CHLOROFORM." Records of the Jedburgh Teams, 190/6/15/4, Entry 101, Folder 39/40, Box 1, RG 226.

"Jedburgh Team SCEPTRE," 190/6/15/4, Entry 101, Folder 39/40, Box 1, RG 226.

Little, Lt. Col. Wendell E. "The 6th Army Group, France and Germany, 1944–45, with Special Attention to Logistical Problems," Historical Report, E242A, Box 162, RG 331.

"Mission 'Tomate'," Entry 97, Folder 620, Box 35, RG 226.

Ob.kdo. von Sodenstern, 394/43 g.Kdos.Chefs., 20.8.43, T-312/977/9168361, RG 549.

OKW War Diary, manuscript B-034, M1035, RG549.

"Operational Report: Company 'B' 2671st Special Reconnaissance Battalion Separate (Prov.)," September 20, 1944, Entry 99, Box 35A, RG 226.

Pflaum, Generalleutnant Karl. "Activities of the 157th Reserve Division in Southern France," MS B-237, RG 549.

"Plan d'action contre les transports et communications ferroviaires allemands Région Sud-Est," March 8, 1944, Interrogation Reports, Entry 427, RG 407.

"Resistance in South-East France," March 22, 1944, Entry 190, Folder 12, Box 329, RG 226.

Richards, F. B., to Howarth. "Subversion of Satellite Troops," August 5, 1945, Folder 844, E190, Box 140, RG 226.

RF Section. "Situation Report," Third Quarter Missions and Sabotage, Entry 190, Folder 1465, Box 740, RG 226.

Schaefer, Generalmajor Hans. "244th Infantry Division, Marseille, 19–28 Aug 1944," MS A-884, RG 549.

Seventh Army. Enemy Order of Battle (BIGOT), Aquitanian Report No. 6, 1944, Appendix I, "Table of French Defenses on the Italian Frontier," 107-2.7, RG 407.

"Short resume of Pauline's activities," Folder 844, E190, Box 140, RG 226.

Smith, Lt. Gen. W. B. to Gen. Sir Henry Maitland Wilson. May 21, 1944, "Role of resistance groups in the South of France," Folder 12, Entry 190, Box 329, RG 226.

Special Force Staff Headquarters, Force 163. "Summary of French Resistance Activities No. 3," June 9–11, 1944, Entry 158, Folder 42, Box 3, RG 226.

SPOC. August 1, 1944, Entry 190, Folder 266, Box 329, RG 226.

———. July 12, 1944, Entry 190, Folder 266, Box 349, RG 226.

"Story of Detachment 'F' in France," October 17, 1945, Entry 99, Box 35A, RG 226.

Task Force Butler. Combined G-2 and G-3 Journal, RG 331.

"Tomato" [report of Henry Hyde], Entry 97, Folder 575, Box 33, RG 226.

Von Schwarin, Generalmajor Richard. "Battle of Toulon, August 1944, Chapter 4: Report of Combat Command Bruendel," M1035, MS C-086, RG 549.

Von Sodenstern, General der Infanterie Georg. "To the History of the Times Preceding the Invasion Engagements in France with Special Regard to the South-French Zone," December 13, 1950, MS B-276, RG 549.

Von Wietersheim, Generalmajor Wend. "Report of the former Commander of the 11th Panzer Division," 10, June 4, 1946, MS A-880, RG 549.

Wiese, General der Infanterie Friederich. "The 19th Army in Southern France (1 July to 15 September 1944)," April 11, 1948, MS B-787, RG 549.

Witek, Generalleutnant Otto. "The Department of the Oberquartiermeister of the 19th Army," June 4, 1946, MS 1–950, RG 549.

Fréjus

Centre d'Histoire et d'Etudes des troupes d'Outre-Mer, Musée des Troupes de Marine

4ème Bde JMO du BM 11, 1st DFL, March 25–30, 1945, 15H153.

Duval, Rene. "La Bataille Oubliée de l'Authion (avril 1945)," 27, doc. B69/3.

Forces Françaises Libres, 1ère Division, Ordre préparatoire, April 24, 1945, 15H153.

"Histoire de la 4ème Brigade, 1ère Division Française Libre, création et résumé des opérations, juin 1943–mai 1945" (manuscript), 15H153 D4a.

"Journal de Marche, 4ème Brigade," 1ère Division France Libre, 16H189.

"Journal des Marches et Opérations, 6ème Compagnie, Bataillon de Marche 11, 8 août 1942 au 21 septembre 1944 (1e partie)," 15H153.

"Ordre d'opérations No. 1, Exercice 'Canard'," April 4, 1945, Forces Françaises Libres, 1ère Division, 15H153, BM21.

"Récit des Opérations de la 3ème Compagnie en Provence du 16 au 24 août 1944," 4ème Brigade, 1e Division France Libre, 15H153-46.

London

Imperial War Museum

Radley, Major A. F. 03/20/1.

National Archives

2nd Independent Brigade's War Diary, WO 228.

AFHQCITEFHGCT. August 24, 1944, WO 204/7819.

Cammaerts, Francis. FCA, HS 6/568.

Capt. Ferandon. "CINNAMON," Serial No. 26, HS 6/496.

Granville, Christine. FCA, HS 9/612.

Harcourt, Capt. Robert. "Report on Jedburgh team CINNAMON," Serial No. 27, HS 6/496.

"Interview of Roger" [Cammaerts's nom de guerre], November 21, 1943, P1018565, Francis Cammaerts FCA, HS 9/285.

"The Maquis." November 2, 1943, HS 6/568.

Marchand, D/H Madame. March 11, 1940, P1019770.

Massingham Inter-Allied Mission Reports. HS 3/34.

"Resistance in South-East France." March 22, 1944, HS 6/330.

BIBLIOGRAPHY

"Strength report, FFI in Alpes-Maritimes, Var, Basses-Alpes," P1018204-5, Massingham Inter-Allied Mission Reports, HS 3/34.

"Team SCEPTRE," Serial No. 22, HS 6/557.

Nice

Archives départemental des Alpes-Maritimes

Cabinet, rapports au Préfet, May 15 and 31, 1942.

Délibérations au Conseil Général, 1945, 2:738.

Goudot, Lt. Gen. Victor-Nicolas (Ret.). Le délègue départemental, Entr'Aide Française, au Préfet des Alpes-Maritimes, March 17, 1945, boite 168 W 1.

Intendance de police de la région de Nice, 0166w001.9; 0166w000.2-3; 0166w001.3, série M.

Le secretaire general au maintien de l'ordre à le préfet régional de Nice, April 12, 1944, "accords OBERG définissant les conditions de coopération entre les services de police française et de police allemande, 1943–1944," boite 166 W 5.

"Les Réactions des Cannois au Débarquement du 15 août 1944," August 17, 1944, Rapport 2796 des Renseignements Généraux de Cannes, boite 169 W 13.

"Note sur l'action du Secours National à la suite du bombardement aérien du 26 mai 1944 à Nice," boite 168 W 1.

Registre des délibérations du conseil municipal, December 30, 1942 to June 17, 1943, 105:92.

Secours national. "Hébergement de 800 sinistrés dans les hôtels de la ville," May 28, 1944, boite 168 W 1.

———. "La Libération de Nice," Rapport d'activités du Secours National, May 26 to August 30, 1944, dossier 168 W 1–4.

Archives municipales

Registre des délibérations du conseil municipal, June 20, 1940 to October 17, 1940, 99: 159.

Holy Trinity Anglican Church

Coussmaker, Jean. "Alice Shaw and Nesta Comber: The Tale of Two Ladies of St. Hugh's, Vence." *Holy Trinity Church Newsletter* 48 (Autumn 2009): 20–1.

Pinglier, Florence E., "Reminiscences, 1939–45," *Holy Trinity Church Newsletter* 8 (Spring 1995): 1–19.

Musée de la Résistance Azuréenne

"Cahier Journalier de Suzanne Balzan, avril 1945," Documents, Témoignages Recherches No. 13.

"Essai sur les Origines du Gaullisme à Nice et Cannes," Documents, Témoignages, Recherches No. 8.

"L'action de Jean Moulin à Nice et dans les Alpes-Maritimes (1941–1943)," Documents, Témoignages, Recherches No. 3, 3rd edn, September 2000.

"La Libération de Nice vue par les Autorités Allemandes," Documents, Témoignages, Recherches No. 26.

"La liberté descend des montagnes," Documents, Témoignages, Recherches No. 17.

"Le drame du maquis du Férion (1–12 juin 1944)," Documents, Témoignages, Recherches No. 2.

"Le Maquis franco-italien de l'Albarea et le drame de Sospel," Documents, Témoignages, Recherches No. 12.

"L'épuration dans les Alpes-Maritimes (1942–1947)," Documents, Témoignages, Recherches No. 28.

"Le récit de Roger Monteux," Documents, Témoignages, Recherches No. 13.

"Les Débuts de la Résistance Gaulliste dans les Alpes-Maritimes (1940–1943)," Documents, Témoignages, Recherches No. 8, 2nd edn, 2000.

"Les Etrangers dans la Résistance Azuréenne," Documents, Témoignages, Recherches No. 19.

"Les Femmes dans la Résistance Azuréenne," Documents, Témoignages, Recherches No. 22.

"Les Jeunes dans la Résistance Azuréenne," Documents, Témoignages, Recherches No. 24.

"Les Ouvriers dans la Résistance Azuréenne," Documents, Témoignages, Recherches No. 29.

"Les Réseaux de Résistance dans les Alpes-Maritimes," Documents, Témoignages, Recherches No. 20.

"L'impact de l'appel du 18 juin 1940 dans les Alpes-Maritimes," Documents, Témoignages, Recherches No. 30.

Lippmann, Claude. "Jean Lippmann et le maquis 'Lorrain' au Laverq et en Ubaye, août 1943–juin 1944," Documents, Témoignages, Recherches No. 5.

"L'Organisation *Carte* dans les Alpes-Maritimes," Documents, Témoignages, Recherches No. 25.

"Nice, 28 août 1944: L'insurrection racontée par les insurgés," Documents, Témoignages, Recherches No. 9.

Odru, André. "Les F.T.P. la M.O.I., les Milices Patriotiques dans les Alpes-Maritimes," 2005.

"Parachutages et Répression à Puget-Théniers, janvier–mai 1944," Documents, Témoignages, Recherches No. 7.

Perrin, Lieutenant-Colonel Jean. "Les Combats de l'Authion, 10 avril–28 avril 1945," Documents, Témoignages Recherches No. 11.

Sentis, Georges. "Le Service B des F.T.P. et les Alpes Maritimes," Association Azuréenne du Musée de la Résistance Nationale, 1990.

Sola, Paul. "Mémoires de guerre," typewritten manuscript.

"Sous-Marins et felouques au large d'Antibes: L'opération du 27 avril 1942," Documents, Témoignages, Recherches No. 14.

Paris

Centre d'Accueil et de Recherche des Archives Nationales

Le colonel Chomel de Jarnieu à le Directeur des Services de l'Armistice, October 28, 1944, dossier 50, AJ41 1182.

"Rapports entre le Gouvernement français et le Commandement italien pendant le stationnement des troupes italiennes en France du 11 novembre 1942 au 9 septembre 1943," dossier 50, AJ 41 1182.

Service Historique de l'Armée de Terre

1ère Armée Française, 3ème Bureau. "Rapport sur les Opérations de l'Armée Française, Période du 15 au 28 août 1944: La Bataille de Provence," September 14, 1944, dossier 10P 187.

1ère Division Française Libre, 2ème Bureau. "Etude de Terrain Préliminaire à l'Opération "Canard," dossier "Opération 'Canard,'" dossier 11P 10.

De Chassey, Lt. Col. Mémorandum, "Renseignements sur les forces allemandes dans le sud de la France," April 4, 1944, Débarquement et bataille de Provences, January–August 1944, dossier 2, 2ième Bureau, dossier 10P 186.

"Historique Sommaire de la 27ème Division d'Infanterie Alpine," dossier 11P 174.

Lichwitz, Lt. Col. André. "Schéma d'Attaque de la Forca par une section d'Assaut," April 7, 1945, 1ère division française libre, dossier 11P 13.

Serre, Col. R. E., French G.S. to Col. William W. Quinn, Asst. Chief of Staff, Seventh Army G.S. Mémorandum, April 8, 1944, 8–11, dossier 2, 2ième Bureau, 10P 186.

BIBLIOGRAPHY

Stanford, California

Hoover Institution

Robert H. Adleman Papers

"A Brief History of the 1st Airborne Task Force," Manuscript, 1st Airborne Task Force, Box 8.

Frederick, Maj. Gen. Robert T. Interview, November 1966, Box 11.

———. "'Notes' for," September 18, 1944, Box 12.

Headquarters, 1st Airborne Task Force. "Ground Operations of 1st ABTF in 'Dragoon'," November 20, 1944, 1st Airborne Task Force, Box 8.

Jones, Capt. Geoffrey M. T. Interview by Robert H. Adleman, March 19, 1967, Box 11.

Mission Jaune. "Political Activity," November 16, 1944, Alpes-Maritimes, Box 6.

Regional Liaison Detachment "B." "Area Report," November 17, 30 and December 16, 1944, Regional Liaison, Civil Affairs, Nice, Box 12.

———. "Newspaper Survey, Nice, France," November 8, 1944, Civil Affairs, Nice, Box 12.

Simms, Dr. John. Interview by Robert H. Adleman, September 28, 1963, Ottawa, Canada, Interviews (misc.), Box 12.

Welsh, 1st Lt. Joseph W. to Asst. Chief of Staff, G-5, Seventh Army. "Conference between Maj. Gen. Frederick and Monsieur Escande, Prefect of the Dept. of the Alpes-Maritimes," September 3, 1944, 1st Airborne Task Force, Box 8.

Robert T. Frederick Papers

"Brief report Mission 'Talbot' through Thu. Oct. 5," Box 4.

Headquarters, Seventh Army. "Report on the Political Situation in Nice," September 1, 1944, Box 4.

"Information concerning the Principality of Monaco," [undated], signed R. M. des Fontenelle, Box 4.

Le Victorieux, September 25, October 17, 1944, as translated by Frederick's staff, Box 4.

Longhi, Mario, Italian Committee of Liberation, Alpes-Maritimes, to the Minister of Foreign Affairs, Rome, October 28, 1944, Box 4.

Military Intelligence. "Public Opinion and the American Army," November 1, 1944, Box 4.

Mission Jaune. "General Information: Civil Security," November 15, 1944, Box 4.

"Notes on Monsieur Emile Roblot, Minister of State of the Principality of Monaco," September 9, 1944, Box 4.

"Position of affairs in the Principality of Monaco on September 10th, 1944," Box 4.

"Report about the Principality of Monaco, Actual General Situation, the Minister of State Roblot," September 9, 1944, Box 4.

Roblot, Emile to Frederick, September 6, 1944, Correspondence, Box 4.

Washington, D.C.

Center of Military History, Department of the Army

Office of the Theater Historian, European Theater of Operations. "Invasion of Southern France."

Smith, Robert Ross. "The France-Italian Border: Protecting the Southeast Flank." Draft of an unpublished chapter in Clark and Smith, Riviera to the Rhine.

Holocaust Memorial Museum Archives

Alexander, Harry. Interviewed by Sandy Bradley, Larchmont, New York, February 11, 1992.

Burger, Harry. "A Holocaust Survivor: Memoir of the War—1938–1945." Survivor Testimonies, RG 02.

BIBLIOGRAPHY

York, Pennsylvania

York Heritage Trust Library/Archives

Jacob L. Devers Papers

Allied Force Headquarters. "Interim Directive for Civil Affairs in Southern France," July 5, 1944, Southern France: Civil Affairs, Box 15.

Botsch, Generalleutnant Walther. "Critique of the American Seventh Army," William W. Quinn Papers [at the Military History Institute], Box 19.

Devers, Jacob. Diary, No. 2, August 19, 1944, Box 52.

———. "Southern France: Invasion of __" [speech by Devers], Southern France, Box 15.

Devers to Eisenhower, Message, September 20, 1944, Correspondence, September 16–23, 1944, Box 21.

"Extracts from the Conversation of General de Lattre de Tassigny with Ambassador Winant, 19 November 1943," Biographical–French, Box 13.

Published Sources

Primary

Books

Baussy, Alex. *La Mémoire d'une Ville: Une évocation de la vie à Cannes et sur la Côte d'Azur durant les sombres années de guerres et à la Libération*. Spéracèdes: TAC Motifs, 1994.

Bily, Henry. *Destin à Part: Seul rescapé de la rafle de Clans du 25 octobre 1943*. Paris: Éditions L'Harmattan, 1995.

Bishop, Leo V., Frank J. Glasgow, and George A. Fisher, eds. *The Fighting Forty-Fifth: The Combat Report of an Infantry Division*. Baton Rouge, LA: 45th Infantry Division, 1946.

Bleicher, Hugo. *Colonel Henri's Story: The War Memoirs of Hugo Bleicher, Former German Secret Agent* by Ian Colvin. London: William Kimber, 1954.

Buckmaster, Maurice. *They Fought Alone: The Story of British Agents in France*. London: Popular Book Club, 1958.

Casey, William. *The Secret War against Hitler*. Washington, D.C.: Regnery Gateway, 1988.

Churchill, Peter. *Of Their Own Choice*. London: Hodder and Stoughton, 1952.

———. *Duel of Wits*. London: Hodder and Stoughton, 1953.

———. *Spirit in the Cage*. London: Hodder and Stoughton, 1954.

Churchill, Winston S. *Triumph and Tragedy*. Boston: Houghton Mifflin, 1953.

Clark, Mark W. *Calculated Risk*. New York: Harper & Brothers, 1950.

Columbia Broadcasting System. *From D-Day through Victory in Europe*. New York: 1945.

Cookridge, E. H. *Inside SOE: The Story of Special Operations in Western Europe 1940–45*. London: Arthur Barker Ltd., 1966.

———. *They Came from the Sky*. New York: Thomas Y. Crowell Company, 1967.

Cordier, Daniel. *De l'Histoire à l'histoire*. Paris: Editions Gallimard, 2013.

D'Astier, Emmanuel de la Vigerie. *Seven Times Seven Days*. Trans. Humphrey Hare. London: MacGibbon & Kee, 1958.

De Gaulle, Charles. *Le Salut*. Vol. III: *Mémoires de Guerre, 1944–1946*. Paris: Libraire Plon, 1959.

———. *The Complete War Memoirs of Charles de Gaulle*. New York: Simon and Schuster, 1967.

———. *Discours et messages: Pendant la guerre, juin 1940–janvier 1946*. Vol. I. Paris: Libraire Plon, 1970.

De Lattre de Tassigny, Marshal Jean. *The History of the French First Army*. Trans. Malcolm Barnes. London: George Allen and Unwin, 1952.

Duttweiler, Gottlieb. *Gottlieb Duttweiler und die Maritime Suisse: Ein Roman aus der Wirklichkeit*. Zurich: Ed. Limmat, 1953.

Eisenhower, Dwight D. *Crusade in Europe*. Baltimore, MD: Johns Hopkins University Press, 1997.

Erlanger, Philippe. *La France sans étoile: Souvenirs de l'avant-guerre et du temps de l'occupation*. Saint-Amand: Librairie Plon, 1974.

Fielding, Xan. *Hide and Seek*. London: Secker & Warburg, 1954.

———. *The Money Spinner: Monte Carlo and Its Fabled Casino*. Boston: Little, Brown and Company, 1977.

Five Years—Five Countries—Five Campaigns: An Account of the One-Hundred-Forty-First Infantry in World War II. Munich: 141st Infantry Regiment Association, 1945.

Fry, Varian. *Surrender on Demand*. New York: Random House, 1945.

Gatti, Raymond. *Taxi de guerre, Taxi de paix*. Cannes: S.E.D.A.IN., 1957.

Gibson, Hugh, ed. *The Ciano Diaries, 1939–1943: The Complete, Unabridged Diaries of Count Galeazzo Ciano, Italian Minister for Foreign Affairs, 1936–1943*. New York: Doubleday & Company, 1946.

Gilot, Françoise. *Matisse and Picasso: A Friendship in Art*. New York: Anchor Books, 1992.

Giraud, Général Henri. *Mes Evasions*. Paris: René Julliard, 1946.

Goldsmith, John. *Accidental Agent*. New York: Charles Scribner's Sons, 1971.

Graves, Charles. *The Riviera Revisited*. London: Evans Brothers Ltd., 1948.

Grossjohann, Georg. *Five Years, Four Fronts: A German Officer's World War II Combat Memoir*. New York: Ballantine Books, 2005.

Guizard, Marcel. *Mémoires de Simon, 1941–1945: Marseille Nice Lyon Paris Chronique de la Résistance et de l'Occupation par le Responsable Interrégional du Front National Zone Sud*. Marseille: n.p., 1989.

Hasenclever, Walter. *Côte d'Azur 1940: Impossible asile*. Trans. Jean Ruffet. La Tour d'Aigues: Editions de l'aube, 1998.

Howarth, Patrick. *Undercover: The Men and Women of the Special Operations Executive*. London; Routledge & Kegan Paul, 1980.

Hue, André and Ewen Southby-Tailyour. *The Next Full Moon: The Remarkable True Story of a British Aagent Behind the Lines in Wartime France*. London: Penguin Books, 2004.

Jefferson, Thomas. *The Writings of Thomas Jefferson*. Vol. I: *Autobiography*. New York: John C. Riker, Taylor & Maury, 1854.

Kesselring, Albert. *Memoirs of Field-Marshal Kesselring*. Novato, CA: Presidio Press, 1989.

La Résistance en Provence. Vol. I: *Les Français dans la Résistance*. Geneva: Editions Famot, 1974.

Les Voix de la Liberté: Ici Londres 1940–1944. Vol. 5: *Le Bataille de France: 9 mai 1944–31 août 1944*. Vichy: Imprimerie Wallon, 1976.

Malraux, André. *Fallen Oaks: Conversation with De Gaulle*. London: Hamish Hamilton, 1972.

———. *Le Miroir des Limbes: Antimémoires*. Paris: Gallimard, 1972.

Mars, Alastair. *Unbroken: The Story of a Submarine*. Barnsley: Pen & Sword Books, 2006.

Massenet, Pierre and Marthe Massenet. *Journal d'une longue nuit: Carnet de route de deux Français moyens 1939–1944*. Paris: Librairie Artheme Fayard, 1971.

Mauldin, Bill. *Up Front*. New York: Henry Holt and Company, 1945.

Mazier, Gabriel. *Un Officier d'occasion dans le haut pays niçois: Mémoires du "Capitaine François" sur la libération du Haut-Pays Niçois*. Ed. Gaston Bernard. Nice: n.p., 1992.

Millar, George. *Road to Resistance: An Autobiography*. London: Bodley Head, 1979.

Moats, Alice-Leone. *No Passport for Paris*. New York: G. P. Putnam's Sons, 1945.

Molinari, Pascal. *Journal de Guerre*. Menton: Annales de la Société d'Art et d'Histoire du Mentonnais, 2004.

Moulin, Laure. *Jean Moulin*. Paris: France Loisirs, 1982.

Murphy, Audie. *To Hell and Back*. New York: Henry Holt and Company, 1949.

Némirovsky, Irène. *Suite Française*. New York: Vintage International, 2007.

Orebaugh, Walter W. *The Consul*. Cape Canaveral, FL: Blue Note Publications, 1994.

Paratroopers' Odyssey: A History of the 517th Parachute Combat Team. Hudson, FL: 517th Parachute Regimental Combat Team Association, 1985.

Passy, Colonel [André Dewavrin]. *Souvenirs du B. C. R. A*. Vol. I: *Deuxième Bureau-Londres (juin 1940–décembre 1941)*. Paris: Raoul Solar, 1947.

A Pictorial History of the 36th "Texas" Infantry Division. 1995. Austin, TX: 36th Division Association, Turner Publishing Company reprint, 1995.

Plath, Sylvia. *The Journals of Sylvia Plath*. Ed. Frances McCullough. New York: Dial Press, 1982.

Rainero, Romain H., ed. *La Commission italienne d'armistice avec la France: Les rapports entre la France de Vichy et l'Italie du Mussolini, 10 juin 1940–8 septembre 1943*. Paris: Service historique d l'armée de terre, 1995.

Résistance et Libération de la Provence: Témoignages et récits. Geneva: Editions de Crémille, 1994.

Roosevelt, Franklin D. *The Public Papers and Addresses of Franklin D. Roosevelt: War and Aid to the Democracies*. Ed. Samuel I. Rosemann. New York: MacMillan Company, 1941.

Ruby, Marcel. *F Section, SOE: The Buckmaster Networks*. London: Leo Cooper, 1988.

Ruggiero, Alain. *La Population du Comté de Nice de 1693 à 1939*. Nice: Editions Serre, 2002.

Saint-Exupéry, Conseulo de. *Oppède*. New York: Brentano's, 1945.

Sapin et al. *Méfiez vous du Toréador*. Toulon: Association Générale de Prévoyance Militaire, 1987.

Schor, Ralph, ed. *Nice et les Alpes-Maritimes de 1914 à 1945: Documents d'Histoire*. Nice: Centre Régional de Documentation Pédagogique de Nice, 1991.

Sevareid, Eric. *Not So Wild a Dream*. New York: Antheneum, 1976.

Shirer, William L. *The Collapse of the Third Republic: An Inquiry into the Fall of France in 1940*. New York: Simon and Schuster, 1969.

Slowikowski, M. Z. Rygor. *In the Secret Service: The Lighting of the Torch*. London: Windrush Press, 1988.

Taggart, Donald G., ed. *The History of the Third Infantry Division in World War II*. Nashville, TN: Battery Press, 1987.

Truscott, Lucian K., Jr. *Command Missions: A Personal Story*. New York: E. P. Dutton and Company, 1954.

US War Department Strategic Services. *War Report of the OSS (Office of Strategic Services)*. Vol. 2: *The Overseas Targets*. New York: Walker Publishing Company, 1976.

Veil, Simone. *Une Vie*. Versailles: Editions Feryane, 2008.

Verity, Hugh. *We Landed by Moonlight: The Secret RAF Landings in France, 1940–1944*. Rev. edn. Manchester: Crécy Publishing, 2000.

Articles

Ballard, Jean. "Journées d'août 44." *Cahiers du Sud* 268 (October–November–December 1944): 214–16.

Butler, Frederic B. "Task Force Butler, Part I." *Armored Cavalry Journal* 57 (January–February 1948): 12–18.

———. "Task Force Butler, Part II." *Armored Cavalry Journal* 57 (March–April 1948): 30–8.

Devers, Jacob L. "Operation Dragoon: The Invasion of Southern France." *Military Affairs* 10 (Summer 1946): 2–41.

Garac, Jean-Louis. "26 mai 1944, le bombardement de Nice." *Lou Sourgentin* 112 (June 1994): 12–13.

Graves, Rupert D. "Combat Team." *Blue Book* (December 1947): 52–60.

———. "Combat Team." *Blue Book* (January 1948): 58–65.

Hewitt, Admiral H. Kent. "Executing Operation Anvil-Dragoon." *U.S. Naval Institute Proceedings* 80 (August 1954): 896–925.

"Les Souvenirs de Deux Internés Politiques Azuréens." *Notre Musée* 198 (March 2011): 18–19.

Lichwitz, André. "Le groupe d'assaut de la 1ère D.F.L. sur le front des Alpes." *Revue de la France Libre* (June 1955): 60–5.

Piétri, Louis. "Souvenirs d'un ancien résistant: Les jeunes Antibois dans la Résistance." *Les Cahiers du Musée de la Résistance Azuréenne* 69 (April 2011): 16–17.

———. "Les centres d'internement de Sospel et d'Embrun sous l'occupation italienne." *Les compagnies de travail et les camps d'internement en France (zone Sud): 1940–1944*. Nice: Association Nationale des Anciens Combattants de la Résistance, n.d.: 9–10.

Wolgust, Jeannette. "Témoignage de Jeannette Wolgust, l'une des 527 enfants Abadi." *Les Cahiers du Musée de la Résistance Azuréenne* 53 (February 2008): 17–18.

Secondary

Books

1944: La victoire du Débarquement à la Libération. Malesherbes: Editions Tallandier Historia, 1994.

Abramovici, Pierre. *Un rocher bien occupé: Monaco pendant la Guerre 1939–1945*. Paris: Editions du Seuil, 2001.

Adleman, Robert H. and George Walton. *The Devil's Brigade*. Annapolis, MD: Naval Institute Press, 1966.

———. *The Champagne Campaign*. Boston: Little Brown and Company, 1969.

Association Montagne et Traditions. *Pays Vésubien*. Saint-Martin-Vésubie: Musée des Traditions Vésubiennes, 2005.

Atkinson, Rick. *An Army at Dawn: The War in North Africa, 1942–1943*. New York: Henry Holt and Company, 2002.

Baussy, Alex. *La Mémoire d'une Ville: Une évocation de la vie à Cannes et sur la Côte d'Azur Durant les sombres années de guerres et à la Libération*. Spéracèdes: TAC Motifs, 1994.

Beevor, Antony and Artemis Cooper. *Paris: After the Liberation, 1944–1949*. London: Penguin Books, 2007.

Beraud, Henri. *Bataille des Alpes, Album mémorial, Juin 1940–1944/1945*. Bayeux: Editions Heimdal, 1987.

Boatner, Mark M. III. *Biographical Dictionary of World War II*. Novato, CA: Presidio Press, 1996.

Braun, Michel, Jean-Pierre Garacio, and Jean-Louis Panicacci, eds. *1939–1945: La guerre dans les Alpes Maritimes*. Breil-sur-Roya: Editions du Cabri, 1994.

Breuer, William B. *Operation Dragoon: The Allied Invasion of the South of France*. Novato, CA: Presidio Press, 1987.

Buckeridge, Justin P. *550th Infantry Airborne Battalion*. Nashville, TN: Battery Press, 1978.

Burhans, Robert D. *The First Special Service Force: A War History of the North Americans, 1942–1944*. Washington, D.C.: Infantry Journal Press, 1947.

Burlando, Max, ed. *Le parti communiste et ses militants dans la Résistance des Alpes-Maritimes par 120 combattants et témoins*. La Trinité: La Societé Nouvelle Imprimerie de la Victoire, 1974.

Burrin, Philippe. *France under the Germans: Collaboration and Compromise*. Trans. Janet Lloyd. New York: New Press, 1996.

Chalou, George C., ed. *The Secrets War: The Office of Strategic Services in World War II*. Washington, D.C.: National Archives and Records Administration, 1992.

Clarke, Jeffrey J. and Robert Ross Smith. *Riviera to the Rhine*. Washington, D.C.: US Army Center of Military History, 1993.

Clayton, Anthony. *France, Soldiers and Africa*. Washington, D.C.: Brassey's, 1988.

———. *Three Marshals of France: Leadership After Trauma*. Washington, D.C.: Brassey's, 1992.

Coles, Harry L. and Albert K. Weinberg. *Civil Affairs: Soldiers Become Governors*. Washington, D.C.: US Army Center of Military History, 1992.

Deighton, Len. *Blitzkrieg: From the Rise of Hitler to the Fall of Dunkirk*. Edison, NJ: Castle Books, 2000.

De l'Occupation à la Libération, Fabrizio. *OSS: La guerre secrète en France, 1942–1945*. Paris: Hachette, 1990.

De l'Occupation à la Libération: Provence années 40. Nice: SAPO Nice-Matin, 2010.

Digiuni, Didier. *Cannes 1939–1945*. Nice: Alandis Editions, 2002.

Donnison, F. S. V. *Civil Affairs and Military Government, North-West Europe, 1944–1946*. London: HMSO, 1961.

Doughty, Robert Allan. *The Breaking Point: Sedan and the Fall of France*. Hamden, CT: 1990.

Emerson, Maureen. *Escape to Provence: The Story of Elisabeth Starr and Winifred Fortescue and the Making of the Colline des Anglais*. Cambridge: Chapter and Verse, 2008.

FitzSimons, Peter. *Nancy Wake: A Biography of Our Greatest War Heroine*. Sydney: HarperCollins, 2001.

Foot, M. R. D. *SOE in France: An Account of the Work of the British Special Operations Executive in France 1940–1944*. London: HMSO, 1966.

Footitt, Hilary. *War and Liberation in France: Living with the Liberators*. New York: Palgrave Macmillan, 2004.

Ford, Roger. *Steel from the Sky: The Jedburgh Raiders, France 1944*. London: Weidenfeld & Nicolson, 2004.

Fugain, Pierre. *Ici l'Ombre: un réseau dans la guerre de libération 40–44*. Grenoble: C.R.D.R., 1992.

Fuller, Jean Overton. *The German Penetration of SOE: France 1941–1944*. London: William Kimber, 1975.

Funk, Arthur Layton. *Hidden Ally: The French Resistance, Special Operations, and the Landings in Southern France, 1944*. New York: Greenwood Press, 1992.

Gaujac, Paul. *Août 1944: Le Débarquement de Provence, Anvil-Dragoon*. Paris: Histoire & Collections, 2004.

Georges-Picot, Grégoire. *L'innocence et la ruse: Des étrangers dans la Résistance en Provence, 1940–1944*. Paris: Editions Tirésias, 2000.

Gilbert, James L. and John P. Finnegan. *U.S. Army Signals Intelligence in World War II*. Washington, D.C.: U. S. Army Center of Military History, 1993.

Girard, Joseph. *La Résistance et la Libération de Nice: La fin d'une légende?* Nice: Serre Editeur, 2006.

Girod, Robert. *Résistance: Les fusillés de l'Ariane*. Villefranche-sur-Mer: ARTEPHIS, 1994.

Glass, Charles. *Americans in Paris: Life and Death under Nazi Occupation*. New York: Penguin Press, 2010.

Golsan, Richard J., ed. *Memory, the Holocaust, and French Justice: The Bousquet and Touvier affairs*. Trans. Lucy B. Golsan. Hanover, NH: University Press of New England, 1996.

Gonnet, Paul. *Histoire de Grasse et sa région*. Roanne: Editions Horvath, 1984.

Goubert, Pierre. *The Course of French History*. Trans. Maarten Ultee. New York: Franklin Watts, 1988.

Gueyer, Boris de. *L'Organisation de Résistance de l'Armée dans la Région R2: Provence—Alpes— Côte d'Azur.* 2nd edn. Paris: n.p., 2004.

Guillon, Jean-Marie and Antoine Tramoni. *Premières Victoires en Provence, août 1944.* n.p.: Conseil Général du Var, 1994.

Guiral, Pierre. *Libération de Marseille.* Paris: Hachette Littérature, 1974.

Hale, Julian. *The French Riviera: A Cultural History.* New York: Oxford University Press, 2009.

Hastings, Max. *Das Reich: The March of the 2nd SS Panzer Division through France, June 1944.* Minneapolis: Zenith Press, 2013.

Helm, Sarah. *A Life in Secrets: The Story of Vera Atkins and the Lost Agents of SOE.* London: Abacus, 2006.

Homze, Edward L. *Foreign Labor in Nazi Germany.* Princeton, NJ: Princeton University Press, 1967.

Irwin, Will. *The Jedburghs: The Secret History of the Allied Special Forces, France 1944.* New York: Public Affairs, 2005.

Jackson, Julian. *France: the Dark Years 1940–1944.* New York: Oxford University Press, 2001.

———. *The Fall of France: The Nazi Invasion of 1940.* Oxford: Oxford University Press, 2003.

Jansana, Charles. *Marseille: La liberté retrouvée, 1943–1944.* Nimes: C. Lacour, 1992.

Jenkins, Ray. *A Pacifist at War.* London: Arrow Books, 2010.

Jones, Ted. *The French Riviera: A Literary Guide for Travellers.* London: Tauris Parke Paperbacks, 2004.

Kahn, Madeleine. *De l'oasis italienne au lieu du crime des allemands.* Nice: Editions Bénévent, 2003.

Kaspi, André. *Les Juifs pendant l'Occupation.* Paris: Editions du Seuil, 1991.

Kedward, H. R. *Resistance in Vichy France: A Study of Ideas and Motivation in the Southern Zone, 1940–1942.* Oxford: Oxford University Press, 1978.

———. *In Search of the Maquis: Rural Resistance in Southern France, 1942–1944.* Oxford: Clarendon Press, 1993.

Kent, Ron. *First in! The Parachute Pathfinder Company: A History of the 21st Independent Parachute Company, the Original Ppathfinders of the British Airborne Forces, 1942–1946.* London: B. T. Batsford, 1979.

Kladstrup, Don and Petie Kladstrup. *Wine & War: The French, the Nazis, and the Battle for France's Greatest Treasure.* New York: Broadway Books, 2001.

Klarsfeld, Serge. *Les Transferts de Juifs de la Région de Nice vers le Camp de Drancy en vue de leur Déportation 31 août 1942–30 juillet 1944.* Paris: Les Fils et Filles des Déportés Juifs de France, 1993.

———. *Nice Hôtel Excelsior: Les rafles des Juifs par la Gestapo à partir du 8 septembre 1943: les transferts de Juifs de la région préfectorale de Nice (Alpes-Maritimes et Basses-Alpes) et de la principauté de Monaco vers le camp de Drancy en vue de leur déportation, 8 septembre 1943–30 juillet 1944.* Nice: Les Fils et Filles de Déportés Juifs de France, 1998.

Klingbeil, Pierre-Emmanuel. *Le front oublié des Alpes-Maritimes (15 août 1944–2 mai 1945).* Nice: Serre Editeur, 2005.

Knout, David. *Contribution à l'histoire de la Résistance Juive en France 1940–1944.* Paris: Editions du Centre, 1947.

La 1ère D. F. L., Epopée d'une Reconquête juin 1940–mai 1954. Paris: Arts et Métiers Graphiques, 1946.

Laqueur, Walter, ed. *The Holocaust Encyclopedia.* New Haven, CT: Yale University Press, 2001.

Lawler, Nancy Ellen. *Soldiers of Misfortune: Ivoirien Tirailleurs of World War II.* Athens: Ohio University Press, 1992.

Lazare, Lucien. *Rescue as Resistance: How Jewish Organizations Fought the Holocaust in France.* New York: Columbia University Press, 1996.

Leslie, Peter. *The Liberation of the Riviera: The Resistance to the Nazis in the South of France and the Story of Its Heroic Leader, Ange-Marie Miniconi*. New York: Wyndham Books, 1980.

Mackenzie, W. J. M. *The Secret History of SOE: The Special Operations Executive, 1940–1945*. London: St. Ermin's Press, 2000.

Marnham, Patrick. *Resistance and Betrayal: The Death and Life of the Greatest Hero of the French Resistance*. New York: Random House, 2000.

Marrus, Michael R. and Robert O. Paxton. *Vichy France and the Jews*. New York: Basic Books, 1981.

Masson, Madeleine. *Christine: SOE Agent & Churchill's Favourite Spy*. London; Virago Press, 2005.

May, Ernest R. *Strange Victory: Hitler's Conquest of France*. New York: Hill and Wang, 2000.

Mencherini, Robert. *Vichy en Provence*. Paris: Editions Syllepse, 2009.

Michel, Henri. *Pétain, Laval, Darlan, Trois Politiques?* Tours: Flammarion, 1972.

———. *The Shadow War: European Resistance 1939–1945*. Trans. Richard Barry. New York: Harper & Row, 1972.

———. *The Second World War*. Trans. Douglas Parmée. New York: Praeger Publishers, 1975.

———. *Histoire de la Résistance en France (1940–1944)*. 10th edn. Paris: Presses Universitaires de France, 1987.

Moënard, Laurent. *Le débarquement en Provence: Opération Dragoon, 15 août 1944*. Rennes: Editions Ouest-France, 2011.

Morison, Samuel Eliot. *History of United States Naval Operations in World War II: The Invasion of France and Germany, 1944–1945*. Vol. 11. Boston: Little, Brown and Company, 1975.

Muelle, Raymond. *Le Débarquement de Provence: La libération de la France de Toulon à Grenoble*. Paris: Trésor du Patrimoine, 2004.

Mulley, Clare. *The Spy Who Loved: The Secrets and Lives of Christine Granville*. London: Macmillan, 2012.

Nicholas, Elizabeth. *Death be not Proud*. London: White Lion, 1958.

Nord, Philip. *France 1940: Defending the Republic*. London: Yale University Press, 2015.

O'Donnell, Patrick K. *Operatives, Spies, and Saboteurs: The Unknown Story of the Men and Women of World War II's OSS*. New York: Free Press, 2004.

Ophuls, Marcel. *The Sorrow and the Pity*. New York: Berkley Windhover Books, 1975.

Panicacci, Jean-Louis. *Les Alpes-Maritimes de 1939 à 1945: Un département dans la tourmente*. Nice: Editions Serre, 1989.

———. *Menton dans la Tourmente, 1939–1945*. 3rd edn. Menton: Annales de la Société d'Art et d'Histoire du Mentonnais, 2004.

———. *L'Occupation italienne: Sud-Est de la France, juin 1940–septembre 1943*. Rennes: Presses Universitaires de Rennes, 2010.

———. *En territoire occupé: Italiens et Allemands à Nice, 1943–1944*. Paris: Vendémaire, 2012.

———. *Les Alpes-Maritimes dans la Guerre (1939–1945)*. Paris: De Borée, 2013.

Panicacci, Jean-Louis, ed. *La Résistance Azuréenne*. Nice: Editions Serre, 2003.

———. *Les Alpes-Maritimes de 1939 à 1945*. Nice: Centre Régional de Documentation Pédagogique de Nice, 1977.

Paxton, Robert O. *Parades and Politics at Vichy: The French Officer Corps Under Marshal Pétain*. Princeton, NJ: Princeton University Press, 1966.

———. *Vichy France: Old Guard and New Order, 1940–1944*. New York: Columbia University Press, 1972.

Péan, Pierre. *Une jeunesse française: François Mitterrand, 1934–1947*. Paris: Librairie Arthème Fayard, 1994.

Pearson, Michael. *Tears of Glory: The Betrayal of Vercors 1944*. London: Pan Books, 1978.

Perrier, Guy. *Le Colonel Passy et les Services Secrets de la France Libre*. Paris: Hachette Littératures, 1999.

Poliakov, Léon and Jacques Sabille. *Jews under the Italian Occupation*. Paris: Editions du Centre, 1955.

Poznanski, Renée. *Les Juifs en France pendant la Seconde Guerre mondiale*. Paris: Hachette, 1997.

Richards, Brooks. *Secret Flotillas: The Clandestine Sea Lines to France and French North Africa, 1940–1944*. London: HMSO, 1996.

Riding, Alan. *And the Show Went On: Cultural Life in Nazi-Occupied Paris*. New York: Alfred A. Knopf, 2010.

Roberts, Mary Louise. *What Soldiers Do: Sex and the American GI in World War II France*. Chicago: University of Chicago Press, 2014.

Robichon, Jacques. *The Second D-Day*. Trans. Barbara Shuey. New York: Walker and Company, 1962.

Ruppenthal, Roland G. *Logistical Support of the Armies: September 1944–May 1945*. Vol. 2. Washington, D.C.: Office of the Chief of Military History, 1959.

Schor, Ralph. *Un évêque dans le siècle: Monseigneur Paul Rémond (1873–1963)*. Nice: Editions Serre, 1984.

Seymour-Jones, Carole. *A Dangerous Liaison: Simone de Beauvoir and Jean-Paul Sartre*. London: Arrow Books, 2009.

Silver, Kenneth E. *Making Paradise: Art, Modernity and the Myth of the French Riviera*. Cambridge, MA: MIT Press, 2001.

Spotts, Frederic. *The Shameful Peace: How French Artists and Intellectuals Survived the Nazi Occupation*. New Haven, CT: Yale University Press, 2008.

Starns, Penny. *Odette: World War Two's Darling Spy*. Stroud: History Press, 2009.

Stevelberg, Rémi-Nuna. *La Gendarmerie dans les Alpes-Maritimes de 1942 à 1945*. Nice: Serre Editeur, 2004.

Tickell, Jerrard. *Odette: The Story of a British Agent*. London: Pan Books, 1955.

Tiersky, Ronald. *Mitterrand: The Last French President*. New York: St. Martin's Press, 2000.

Torel, Denis. *Monaco sous les Barbelés*. Vesoul: imb Imprimeur, 1996.

Trez, Michel de. *First Airborne Task Force: Pictorial History of the Allied Paratroopers in the Invasion of Southern France*. Wezembeek: Belgium Publishing, 1998.

Tucker-Jones, Anthony. *Operation Dragoon: The Liberation of Southern France 1944*. Barnsley: Pen & Sword Books, 2009.

Turner, John Frayn and Robert Jackson. *Destination Berchtesgaden: The Story of the United States Seventh Army in World War II*. New York: Charles Scribner's Sons, 1975.

Vigneras, Marcel. *Rearming the French*. Washington, D.C.: US Army Center of Military History, 1989.

Virgili, Fabrice. *Shorn Women: Gender and Punishment in Liberation France*. Trans. John Flower. New York: Oxford University Press, 2002.

Williams, Charles. *Pétain*. London: Little, Brown, 2005.

Williams, John. *The Ides of May: Defeat of France, 1940*. New York: Alfred A. Knopf, 1968.

Yeide, Harry and Mark Stout. *First to the Rhine: The 6th Army Group in World War II*. St. Paul, MN: Zenith Press, 2007.

Articles and parts of books

Bernard, Marcel-Pierre. "A Propos de la Situation à Marseille à la Veille de la Libération." *Provence historique* 36 (April–June 1986): 183–90.

Bigelow, Michael E. "General Truscott and the Campaign in Southern France." *Military Review* 74 (August 1994): 72–6.

Bishop, William W., Jr., ed. "Judicial Decisions." *American Journal of International Law* 42 (October 1948): 927–57.

Brega, Frédéric. "La Brigade du Diable: La 1st Special Service Force sur la frontière italienne, septembre–octobre 1944." *Militaria Magazine* 214 (August 2005): 22–30.

Burle, Christian and André Z. Labarrere. "14 décembre 1943: le torpillage du Netztender 44 dans le port de Monaco." *Annales Monégasques: Revue d'Histoire de Monaco* 34 (2010): 73–94.

Carrier, Richard. "Réflexions sur l'efficacité militaire de l'armée des Alpes, 10–25 juin 1940." *La Revue historique des armées* 250 (2008): 85–93.

Chiavassa, Hyacinthe. "Juin 1940: la bataille de Menton." *Annales Monégasques: Revue d'Histoire de Monaco* 8 (1984): 7–36.

Colombard, Christian. "63ème Anniversaire de la Libération du 15 au 28 août 1944 à Nice." *Les Cahiers du Musée de la Résistance Azuréenne* 50 (July 2007): 10–11.

Damase, Daniel. "La prise de la redoute des Trois Communes." *Lou Sourgentin* 116 (March–April 1995): 28–32.

Echenberg, Myron J. "'Morts pour la France': The African Soldier in France during the Second World War." *Journal of African History* 26 (1985): 363–80.

"Exécutez Mandrin, Le 3 juin 1940: l'Evacuation de Menton." *Bulletin de la Société d'Art et d'Histoire du Mentonnais* 55 (September 1990): 18–27.

Felstiner, Mary. "Commandant of Drancy: Alois Brunner and the Jews of France." *Holocaust and Genocide Studies* 2 (1987): 21–47.

Fiori, Louis. "Souvenirs du Bombardement de Nice." *Les Cahiers du Musée de la Résistance Azuréenne* 59 (May 2009): 16–17.

Fournier, Jean-Luc. "La presse clandestine durant l'occupation." *Le Déporté* 563 (1st quarter, 2010): 8–10.

Funk, Arthur L. "American Contacts with the Resistance in France, 1940–1943." *Military Affairs* 34 (February 1970): 15–21.

Gaujac, Paul. "L'Authion: La bataille oubliée: 2e partie–April 1945, le dernier sacrifice." *Militaria Magazine* (July 2005): 56–64.

Grandjonc, Jacques and Theresia Grundtner, eds. *Zones d'ombres, 1933–1944: Exil et internement d'Allemands et d'Autrichiens dans le sud-est de la France.* Aix-en-Provence: Editions Alinea, 1990.

Gué, Christophe. "Anvil-Dragoon ne s'est pas déroulé sans tensions entre Alliés," *L'Express* 3276, April 16–22, 2014, x–xi.

Gueron, Léone. "Les Femmes dans la Résistance: III Partie." *Les Cahiers du Musée de la Résistance Azuréenne* 51 (October 2007): 14–18.

———. "Les Femmes dans la Résistance: Hébergement et Ravitaillement, IV Partie." *Les Cahiers du Musée de la Résistance Azuréenne* 52 (December 2007): 14–18.

Guillon, Jean-Marie. "La Place de la Résistance dans la Libération." *Provence historique* 36 (April–June 1986): 197–208.

———. "Catholiques varois et résistance." *Provence historique* 42 (January–June 1992): 421–32.

Helion, Gérard. "'Antibes de juin 1944 à juin 1945,' Actes du Colloque de Nice, 22 June 1974, Centre de la Méditerranée Moderne et Contemporaine." *Cahiers de la Méditerranée* (June 12, 1976): 37–45.

Isoart, Paul. "11 novembre 1942: l'armée italienne occupe le comté de Nice." *Nice Historique* 4 (October–December 2002): 207–19.

Konopnicki, Raphaël. "L'imprimerie Valrose de Nice (1943–1944) pendant l'occupation allemande." *Les Cahiers du Musée de la Résistance Azuréenne* 53 (February 2008): 12–16.

"La légende du Liberator de la Croix-des-Gardes." *L'Express: Cannes sous l'Occupation* 3080 (July 14–20, 2010): xx.

"Le bombardement meurtrier de la gare de triage." *L'Express: Cannes sous l'Occupation* 3080 (July 14–20, 2010): vi.

Michel, Henri. "Sur le régime de Vichy. " *Revue d'histoire de la deuxième guerre mondiale* 93 (January 1974): 112–17.

———. "Les relations franco-italiennes de l'armistice de juin 1940 à l'armistice de septembre 1943." Comité de la 2e guerre mondiale, *La Guerre en Méditerranée, 1939–1945*, n.p.: n.p., n.d., 485–511.

Nathiez, Raoul. "Lou journal de Madama Pansa." *Lou Sourgentin* 116 (March–April 1995): 37–9.

———. "Les Breillois dans la tourmente." *Lou Sourgentin* 116 (April–May 1995): 16–18.

Panicacci, Jean-Louis. "Nice 1939–1942." *Recherches Régionales: Côte d'Azur et Contrée Limitrophes* 4 (1968): 1–9.

———. "Enquête sur la Collaboration dans les Alpes-Maritimes." *Comité de Histoire de la 2e Guerre Mondiale* 230 (March/April 1978): 25–33.

———. "Menton et les Mentonnais de 1939 à 1945." *Recherches Régionales: Côte d'Azur et Contrées Limitrophes* 21 (January–March 1981): 1–43.

———. "Les communistes italiens dans les Alpes-Maritimes (1939–1945)." *Annali della Fondazione Giangiacomo* 24 (1985): 155–67.

———. "La Libération de Nice: 28 août 1944 (Soulèvement patriotique ou journée révolutionnaire?)." *Provence historique* 36 (April–June 1986): 213–23.

———. "Des Chasseurs à la Résistance: les FFI Azuréennes." *Lou Sourgentin* 103 (October 1992): 14–16.

———. "La libération de Nice." *Lou Sourgentin* 112 (June 1994): 4–11.

———. "Sociologie de la Résistance dans les Alpes-Maritimes." *Provence historique* 44 (October–December 1994): 477–88.

———. "Les élections municipales d'April–mai 1945 à Nice." *Lou Sourgentin* 116 (March–April 1995): 19–21.

———. "Les Alpes-Maritimes." *Les Cahiers de l'IHTP* 32–33 (May 1996): 195–212.

———. "La Légion française des combattants dans les Alpes-Maritimes (October 1940–août 1944)." *Nice Historique* 105 (October–December 2002): 187–203.

———. "La vie quotidienne des Niçois de 1939 à 1945." *Nice Historique* 2 (April–June 2004): 75–88.

———. "La Contestation de l'Insurrection Niçoise." *Les Cahiers du Musée de la Résistance Azuréenne* 48 (March 2007): 2–3.

———. "Georges Foata-Morgan, *François*." *Les Cahiers du Musée de la Résistance Azuréenne* 49 (May 2007): 13.

———. "Le traumatisme de la défaite de juin 1940: perceptions et réactions de l'opinion Azuréenne de l'été à l'automne 1940." *Cahiers de la Méditerranée* 74 (June 2007): 275–303.

———. "L'occupation italienne (novembre 1942–septembre 1943)." *Les Cahiers du Musée de la Résistance Azuréenne* 55 (July 2008): 4–9.

———. "La repression allemande dans les Alpes-Maritimes." *Les Cahiers du Musée de la Résistance Azuréenne* 58 (March 2009): 13–17.

———. "Le Débarquement en Provence." *Notre Musée* 191 (July 2009): 10–14.

———. "L'intégration des FFI Azuréens dans le Groupement Alpin Sud." *Notre Musée* 194 (March 2010): 9.

———. "10–25 juin 1940: la 'guerre oubliée'." *Les Cahiers du Musée de la Résistance Azuréenne* 64 (May 2010): 13–17.

———. "Janvier–février 1943: Création de la Milice et du STO." *Les Cahiers du Musée de la Résistance Azuréenne* 68 (February 2011): 13–15.

———. "Menton: Vitrine de l'Impérialisme Fasciste." *Notre Musée* 198 (March 2011): 8–10.

———. *L'Express: Nice sous l'Occupation* 3126 (June 7, 2011), ii–iii.

———. "70e anniversaire des combats de l'Authion." *Les Cahiers du Musée de la Résistance Azuréenne* 89 (May 2015): 14.

Pilon, Armand. "A l'Armée des Alpes." *Bulletin de la Société d'Art et d'Histoire du Mentonnais* 18 (June 1981): 8–9.

Poumellec-Cavelleri, Suzanne. "Un résistant mentonnais: André Poumellec (1925–1944)." *Bulletin de la Société d'Art et d'Histoire du Mentonnais* 71 (September 1994): 5.

Rochat, Giorgio. "La campagne italienne de juin 1940 dans les Alpes occidentales." *La Revue historique des armées* 250 (2008): 77–84.

Roullier, Alain. "Tende et La Brigue: Les oubliées du Rattachement de 1860." *Lou Sourgentin* 116 (March–April 1995): 34–6.

Schjeldahl, Peter. "Art as Life: The Matisse We Never Knew." *New Yorker*, August 29, 2005, 78–83.

Slippin, Royce. "Geoffrey Jones '42 Recovers World War II False Identity." *Princeton Alumni Weekly* 97 (May 7, 1997): 45.

Tabaraud, Georges. "Prisonniers et déportés, le retour." *Lou Sourgentin* 116 (March–April 1995): 12–14.

Torel, Denis. "La Seconde Guerre Mondiale en Principauté de Monaco." *Bulletin de la Société d'Art et d'Histoire du Mentonnais* 22 (June 1982): 14–19.

Venturini, Alain. "La Défense du Mentonnais en juin 1940." *Bulletin de la Société d'Art et d'Histoire du Mentonnais* 18 (June 1981): 5–9.

Venturini, Nicole. "Le 'Parcours du Combattant' d'une Ecolière." *Bulletin de la Société d'Art et d'Histoire du Mentonnais* 18 (June 1981): 10–12.

Veziano, Paolo. "L'échec du renouveau idéologique et matériel du fascisme dans les terres irrédentes (Menton et Nice, 1940–1943)." *Nice Historique* 2 (April–June 2004): 119–25.

Villemain, Pierre Nicot de. "Les armées à Nice 1942–1945." *Nice Historique* 4 (October–December 2002): 221–39.

Volpi, Emmanuel. "Les Italiens et l'Economie Varoise." *Notre Musée* 198 (March 2011): 15–16.

Wright, Gordon. "Reflections on the French Resistance (1940–1944)." *Political Science Quarterly* 77 (September 1962): 336–49.

Index